Color
Class
Identity

Color Class Identity

The New Politics of Race

edited by

John Arthur
Amy Shapiro

WestviewPress
A Division of HarperCollins*Publishers*

Published in 1996 in the United States of America by Westview Press, 5500 Central Avenue, Boulder,
Colorado 80301-2877, and in the United Kingdom by Westview Press, 12 Hid's Copse Road, Cumnor
Hill, Oxford OX2 9JJ

Library of Congress Cataloging-in-Publication Data
Color • class • identity : the new politics of race / edited by John
   Arthur and Amy Shapiro.
     p. cm.
   ISBN 0-8133-3114-5 (hardcover).—ISBN 0-8133-3115-3 (pbk.)
     1. United States—Race relations.   2. Afro-Americans—Economic
conditions.   3. Urban poor—United States.   4. Pluralism (Social
sciences)—United States.   I. Arthur, John, 1946–   .   II. Shapiro,
Amy, 1952–   .
E185.615.C645   1996
305.8′00973—dc20   96-14391
                                                                             CIP

10   9   8   7   6   5   4   3   2   1

Contents

Preface

The O. J. Simpson verdict and the beating of Rodney King by white police have forced racial differences once again onto the national agenda as whites and blacks realize how differently they sometimes see the world. In combination with increasingly strident political argument over welfare and affirmative action, these events further underline the differing perspectives and conflicts that some had felt were dissipating. At the same time, we have seen heightened disagreements over multiculturalism in school curricula and the recognition of non-European traditions and cultures as well as growth of interest in issues of assimilation and the importance of group membership (e.g., what it means to be African-American, Jewish, Hispanic, Native American, and so forth).

In this book, we have attempted to bring together the most important and thoughtful writers on these subjects. The book is organized around three themes. Part One focuses on the differences in racial perceptions that have been in evidence in recent political events like the Simpson not-guilty verdict, the Million Man March, and the nomination of black conservative Clarence Thomas to the U.S. Supreme Court. What lessons can be learned about our racial and ethnic divisions from these experiences? Part Two addresses an increasingly explosive topic: the black underclass. Authors consider the nature of the problem, weigh its causes, and evaluate possible solutions. Then, in Part Three, we look at questions of group and individual identity. Here the focus is on the nature of race itself, the importance of ethnicity and race in establishing one's identity, and the political consequences of what some see as a growing "tribalism" but others see as a belated recognition of the realities of America's oft-ignored multicultural past as well as its inevitably more diverse and potentially difficult future.

We have sought to achieve a reasonable balance in viewpoints, representing not just one political perspective but including instead a wide array of voices. Authors range from Clarence Thomas, Shelby Steele, and Arthur M. Schlesinger, Jr., to Cornel West, Derrick Bell, Henry Louis Gates, Jr., Patricia J. Williams, and Ronald T. Takaki. Many of the writers are well known, having already made important contributions to these topics; others were chosen because although not as familiar, they also make substantial and unique additions to these discussions. We wish, finally, to thank Spencer Carr for his enthusiasm and good judgment, and the students at the State University of New York at Binghamton who make teaching fun as well as rewarding.

John Arthur
Amy Shapiro

Introduction

JOHN ARTHUR

AMY SHAPIRO

Two important events in 1995, the O.J. Simpson murder trial and the Million Man March, galvanized Americans' attention once again toward questions of race. Many blacks, focusing on sloppy police work and testimony showing racism on the part of an investigating detective, were elated that a biracial jury did not convict one of the most prominent and successful African-Americans in the country. In contrast, a majority of whites were shocked that somebody they believed to be guilty of murder could be set free, apparently in the face of overwhelmingly incriminating evidence. Reactions to the Simpson not-guilty verdict seemed to raise serious questions about how blacks and whites could hope to understand each other while seeing the world so differently.

Within weeks of the trial, hundreds of thousands of black men and boys marched on Washington in the Million Man March, a historic event lauded by some for its emphasis on pride, responsibility, and self-reliance but distrusted by others for excluding women and for the racially charged rhetoric of a prime organizer, Louis Farrakhan. These events of 1995 recalled others in which differing reactions had suggested a deep and growing racial gulf: the beating of Rodney King by white Los Angeles police officers, the harassment charges brought by Anita Hill against Supreme Court nominee Clarence Thomas, and the increasingly divisive arguments about affirmative action and reverse discrimination.

Into this mix must be added explosions of crime, welfare dependency, illegitimacy, and drugs within a significant segment of the African-American population, problems that seem to have grown to gigantic proportions. The statistics are striking: At any given time, about two out of five young black males are either in prison, on probation, or sought by the police; half of all black children live in poverty; and more than two-thirds of black children are being raised by only one parent.[1] Concerns about crime have become pervasive—a prominent black leader recently reported that one of the saddest moments of his life was when he heard footsteps one night, and then felt relieved to discover that the man coming up behind him was white. "Fear of blacks," wrote Norman Podhoretz in 1993, "has become the dirty little secret of our political culture." At the same time, he continued, "relations between blacks and whites have deteriorated. Gone on the whole are the interracial friendships and the interracial political alliances that were very widespread thirty years ago. In their place we have the nearly impassable gulfs of suspicion and hostility that are epitomized by the typical college dining hall of today where black students insist on sitting at tables of their own and whites are either happy to accept this segregated arrangement or feel hurt at being repulsed."[2]

In addition to the gulf in attitudes and perceptions of blacks and whites and the intractable social and economic problems faced by many African-Americans, there has been a growing emphasis on group identity both on campuses and by the public at large. For some Americans, group identity comes from immigrant ancestors or from shared religious belief. For African-Americans, the defining factor has been physical appearance, more particularly skin color; a source of irony given that the category of black or Negro "race" was developed in the United States as a legal classification to identify persons subject first to slavery and then to segregation, political disenfranchisement, and other legal disabilities under the Jim Crow laws in the South. For most of U.S. history, a defining feature of the black scholar or field hand, minister or criminal was the same: race. Race was not just about appearance; it was about "taint." Knowledge that an unborn child had a "black" grandparent determined the child's race regardless of skin color, facial features, or hair.

Because the category of race identified those subject to legal discrimination, it also unified those working to fight segregation during the era of the civil rights movement in the 1950s and 1960s. The end of legally mandated segregation, however, raised an array of difficult questions. How important are racial, ethnic, and other categories to any individual's identity? Does "race" unify all African-Americans—indeed all Africans and all members of the African diaspora—in a common and unique mission to humanity, as W.E.B. Du Bois argued? Or should the category of a black or Negro race, which from the start obscured the differing cultural heritages of African peoples, be jettisoned along with the slave codes and Jim Crow laws of which it was the intellectual underpinning? In that case, what unity or identity is there in the historical fact that African-Americans share the experience of being victims of racial prejudice? Or is the key unifying factor the disproportionately African-American makeup of America's growing underclass and its prison population?

We have divided this book into three parts, reflecting the three different but related sets of issues that are at the heart of American discussions of race: color, class, and identity. By color, we mean physical appearance, the historic category of organizing Americans by race. How do people of different races perceive themselves and each other? Do they view public events such as the Simpson trial and the Million Man March differently? If so, why?

The second issue is class. Amidst America's vast wealth and great power exists an urban underclass that is increasingly desperate and disproportionately African-American. How are we to understand its causes and cures? How helpful are those who emphasize personal responsibility and values? Is welfare policy partly responsible? What role does racism play?

The third issue is identity. If color refers to the way others view a person, identity addresses questions of how people view themselves. What, exactly, is "race" and how important is it as a category? What is its relationship to culture and ethnicity? To personal ambitions, goals, and values? Clearly, these are difficult and deeply controversial questions.

Part One: Thinking Race

Besides offering fascinating accounts from widely different perspectives of recent events, these five selections are an excellent introduction to the discussions of identity and class that follow. First, in "Thirteen Ways of Looking at a Black Man," Henry Louis Gates, Jr., discusses the different reactions by black cultural and political leaders to the O.J. Simpson verdict and the Million Man March—reactions that shed important light on racial politics, gender, and the different perceptions of blacks and whites.

In "I'm Black, You're White, Who's Innocent?" Shelby Steele discusses the attitudes of whites and blacks toward each other and themselves. He focuses on what he calls "race-holding," a self-description a person uses to justify or hide fears, inadequacies, and insecurities. Whites, Steele notes, feel shame and guilt over slavery and segregation; the responses of blacks to America's historic racism include both feelings of innocence and fears of inferiority.

Two sociologists, Paul M. Sniderman and Thomas Piazza, consider the changes in racial attitudes that have taken place in recent decades, focusing especially on whether racism has moved from an overt to a more covert form. Using recent sociological studies, they show that although prejudice has not disappeared, it is nonetheless a much less important factor in current political debate than is often thought. Exploring the "laid-off worker," "equal opportunity," and "mere mention" of affirmative action experiments, the authors consider whether racial attitudes or policy differences are most important in explaining disagreements about welfare, educational policies aimed at improving opportunities, and affirmative action. In addition to these issues, the authors look at whether conservatives and individualists tend more often than liberals to be prejudiced, the role of "authoritarian" personality traits, and the connections between antiblack and antisemitic attitudes.

Orlando Patterson's "The Paradox of Integration: Why Blacks and Whites Seem So Divided" locates the differing attitudes of whites and blacks toward the Simpson verdict and the Million Man March in the larger context of racial attitudes and social and economic change. Beginning with a description of little-noted but remarkable improvements in the lives of many blacks, along with the worsened situation of others, Patterson discusses the "strange tendency to more loudly lament the black predicament the better it gets." In his view, racial integration, economic success, and different life experiences all play an important role in understanding racial attitudes and tensions.

Having attended the Million Man March, Glenn Loury describes the evolution of his attitudes from early condemnation of the march based on the antisemitism of Farrakhan, to feelings of pride and dignity, to calmer reflections on the "call of the tribe." Why, Loury asks, should such a great moment be led by a "demagogic" leader? And if the "racial essentialism" of Farrakhan is not the real solution to the problems of poverty, family breakdown, and crime, what is?

Part Two: The Black Underclass

Essays in Part Two move from discussions of the Simpson verdict, the Million Man March, and the racial attitudes they uncovered to consider what many believe is simply the most important problem facing the United States: the emergence of a significant black underclass facing overwhelming problems of poverty, crime, illegitimate children, and drugs. As the authors show, there are deep disagreements about the nature and causes of the problem as well as its cure: Some argue that culture and "values" must change; others emphasize economic dislocation and unemployment; still others focus on white racism or segregation of blacks into urban ghettos.

Part Two begins with a recent speech by Clarence Thomas, associate justice of the U.S. Supreme Court, in which he discusses the importance of personal responsibility, the failure of society to provide heroes rather than just victims, and the social and economic costs of what he terms "victim ideology."

The next selection, "Clarence X," is taken from Patricia Williams's recent book *The Rooster's Egg.* She compares Clarence Thomas, General Colin Powell, Malcolm X, and others to explore the importance of role models and symbols, focusing in particular on Justice Thomas's individualistic, self-help vision of politics and the role of government. Lawyer and writer Debra Dickerson then offers a firsthand account of a senseless attack on her nephew and her feelings toward the "brother" whose shots left him paralyzed.

"The Chronicle of the Slave Scrolls," by legal scholar Derrick Bell, is an allegorical account of what he posits to be a negative reaction of whites toward a dramatic transition in black thinking, conduct, and economic success that has made blacks fully competitive with whites.

In an influential study of the "truly disadvantaged," sociologist William Julius Wilson looks at the economic and social dislocations that, he argues, created the urban black underclass, whereas Asian and European immigrants enjoyed relative economic success. He describes the importance of a variety of factors in understanding poverty, including the removal of high-income families from the cities, unemployment, and family breakdown. He concludes with a discussion of the effectiveness of "race-specific" policies and the war on poverty and suggests policy alternatives including economic reform, job training, welfare, and child support. He particularly attacks the idea that race-based affirmative action benefits the truly disadvantaged.

William Tucker's essay, "All in the Family: Illegitimacy and Welfare Dependence," focuses on the role of welfare policies in the creation of the underclass. Disruption of the process of family formation and the decline of marriage, Tucker argues, is a major cause of social disintegration. According to the U.S.

Census Bureau, 68 percent of African-American children are born to unwed women and girls, compared with less than 6 percent of Chinese-American children. Studies also show, Tucker reports, that children from two-parent families not only fare better economically but commit far fewer crimes, produce far fewer illegitimate children, and score higher on intelligence tests. Beginning with a discussion of anthropological studies of the traditional African practice of polygamy, he goes on to explain that welfare has disrupted family formation by allowing unmarried women with children to avoid having to either impose on parents or find a husband: now they can go on welfare. Though these effects are acute among African-Americans, he argues, similar trends are emerging among poorly educated whites. Tucker then offers a brief critique of both liberal and conservative approaches to welfare reform and proposes a third option that, he argues, would reduce illegitimacy and "produce the building blocks for a middle-class society" by breaking the cycle of poverty and welfare dependence.

Peter Shaw proposes in "Counting Asians" the dismantling of all race-based affirmative action in higher education. As a starting point, he discusses recent estimates indicating that if affirmative action were abandoned at the University of California at Berkeley there would be fewer black and Hispanic students, slightly more whites, and significantly more students of Asian descent. Though an Asian-dominated University of California at Berkeley would lose prestige (just as City College of New York did when it was predominantly Jewish), Shaw argues that in the long run, the replacement of race by economic status as the basis for affirmative action would help all students, including blacks and Hispanics. Such a reform would avoid stigmatization and allow all students to get a better education by directing them to institutions where they could succeed academically.

In "American Apartheid: The Perpetuation of the Underclass," sociologists Douglas S. Massey and Nancy A. Denton weigh the importance of the individual, the family, and larger social structures in the development of the black underclass. One of the most important structural variables, they argue, is geographic—where people live has a profound impact on their life chances. Racial segregation, especially in housing, is therefore fundamental. Comparing the experiences of blacks with Jews and other immigrants, the authors also discuss connections between segregation and other factors, including levels of political influence, ghetto isolation and its attendant alienation, black English, cultural values like self-reliance and hard work, educational achievement, and community attitudes toward women. They conclude with a brief discussion of the importance of eliminating residential segregation.

Part Three: Assimilation and Identity in a Multicultural Society

In this section we turn from the black underclass to look in detail at questions of racial identity and culture along with some of the important political implications confronting a multiracial, multicultural America.

We begin with a much-discussed classic of American social thought: W.E.B. Du Bois's 1903 work, "The Souls of Black Folk," in which he describes American blacks as possessed of a "double consciousness" and a "sense of always looking at one's self through the eyes of others." In this essay, Du Bois foreshadows current discussions of assimilation and identity.

The next selection, from Cornel West's well-known book *Race Matters,* contrasts Du Bois's work with that of Malcolm X. West begins by discussing Malcolm X's articulation of black rage and his emphasis on the importance of "psychic conversion" as an alternative to agreeing with Du Bois that black people experience "double consciousness" and inevitably view themselves through "white lenses." Though West, like Malcolm X, rejects the idea that blacks view themselves as whites do, he questions Malcolm X's support of black nationalist ideology. West concludes with a discussion of the debate within the black community over the nomination of Clarence Thomas to the Supreme Court. West sees a "disturbingly low level of political discussion in Black America." By claiming "racial authenticity" and successfully using the story of his personal struggle, argues West, Thomas was able to forestall criticism by black leaders. The leaders succumbed to a vulgar form of racial reasoning: Black authenticity requires closing ranks, which in turn justifies black male subordination of black women (such as Thomas's critic, Anita Hill) in the face of racial hostility. West rejects "racial reasoning" and "close-the-ranks" thinking and advocates a "prophetic" mentality that encourages coalitions with all those committed to opposing racism—a mentality that would have freed black leaders from racial guilt for opposing a black nominee to the U.S. Supreme Court.

Jews were traditional allies of blacks in the civil rights era, but many think relations have deteriorated in recent years. One question sometimes asked is: "Who has suffered the most?" In "Group Autonomy and Narrative Identity," Laurence Mordekhai Thomas argues that although seeking an answer to such a question seems despicable, there is an important sense in which slavery was worse for blacks than the Holocaust was for Jews. Thomas asserts that unlike blacks, Jews never lost "group autonomy," which he regards as an indisputable moral good. Such autonomy is not achieved by economic success but depends instead on the existence of a group narrative with which a group is able to define its own shared identity and thereby to promote self-confidence and pride. Neither Christianity nor Western culture provides such narrative autonomy for blacks, argues Thomas, and without it a people cannot flourish in a hostile society. The Holocaust, however, never extinguished the narrative of the Jewish people—a fact that explains some of the tensions between blacks and Jews as well as Jewish success in the face of American anti-Semitism.

Laurie Shrage pursues issues of race and ethnic identity in "Ethnic Transgressions." Raised in a non-Jewish part of Northern California, she describes early experiences of being thought "Jewish" by others without being certain herself what that meant. Neither assimilation nor its alternative are easy for "partially assimilated" people, she writes. Reviewing works on mixed race, Shrage considers various solutions to the dilemma of assimilation versus separation, including "mixing" categories, rejecting all racial and some ethnic identifications, and claiming more than one identity. She rejects multiple designations, however, because they fail to challenge the supposed inevitability of such classifications. Shrage next looks at work on sexual identity and gender and the possibility of "crossing" such boundaries rather than accepting them. Incorporating the "other" into ourselves, she concludes, is not necessarily to betray or destroy a "pure self" but might instead help reduce racism and oppression.

The next essay, "The Disuniting of America: Reflections on a Multicultural Society," by noted historian Arthur Schlesinger, Jr., begins with a discussion of the formation of the American nation and the search for a unity sufficient to become "one people." The answer, which he traces to Tocqueville, is an American creed that emphasizes the equality and dignity of all along with respect for basic rights to freedom, justice, and opportunity. Schlesinger then traces this ideal, including its failures and successes, from the racist exclusion of Indians and Africans, to the attacks on immigrants and xenophobia of the 1920s, to the struggle against Hitler in World War II and the recent "ethnic upsurge" with its insistence that everybody be assigned an ethnic category. He looks in particular at "Afrocentricity" and self-imposed segregation by blacks. He then considers the role European ideas, cultural values, and colonialism have played in history, concluding with a historian's assessment of recent efforts to reject assimilation and hope that the United States return to common ground and shared traditions.

We conclude with a different historical perspective from Ronald T. Takaki's important book *A Different Mirror: A History of Multicultural America*. By 2056, according to some projections, white Americans will become a minority; Takaki believes that this increasing demographic diversity raises fundamental questions about American identity and culture. By sharing their knowledge about the truth of America's immigrant history, all Americans—African, Chicano, Chinese, Indian, Irish—can use their different experiences to forge a new understanding of each other as well as our collective "self." Rather than ignore the contributions of some and exaggerate the importance or virtue of others, Takaki emphasizes, we must treat fairly the contributions and failures of all groups. Telling stories liberates, he writes: "Through their narratives about their lives and circumstances, the people of America's diverse groups are able to see themselves and each other in our common past. . . . By sharing their stories, they invite us to see ourselves in a different mirror."

NOTES

1. U.S. Department of Commerce, Bureau of the Census, *Statistical Abstract of the United States* (1995), pp. 66, 480; Carrell Peterson Horton and Jessie Carney Smith, eds., *Statistical Record of Black America,* 2nd ed. (Detroit: Gale Research Inc., 1993), p. 348; *New York Times,* October 8, 1995, p. 26.

2. Norman Podhoretz, "My Negro Problem—and Ours; Postscript (1993)" in *Blacks and Jews: Alliances and Arguments,* ed. Paul Berman (New York: Bantam Doubleday Dell, 1994), p. 95.

Part One

Thinking Race

1

Thirteen Ways of Looking at a Black Man

HENRY LOUIS GATES, JR.

"Every day, in every way, we are getting meta and meta," the philosopher John Wisdom used to say, venturing a cultural counterpart to Émile Coué's famous mantra of self-improvement. So it makes sense that in the aftermath of the Simpson trial the focus of attention has been swiftly displaced from the verdict to the reaction to the verdict, and then to the reaction to the reaction to the verdict, and, finally, to the reaction to the reaction to the reaction to the verdict—which is to say, black indignation at white anger at black jubilation at Simpson's acquittal. It's a spiral made possible by the relay circuit of race. Only in America.

An American historian I know registers a widespread sense of bathos when he says, "Who would have imagined that the Simpson trial would be like the Kennedy assassination—that you'd remember where you were when the verdict was announced?" But everyone does, of course. The eminent sociologist William Julius Wilson was in the red-carpet lounge of a United Airlines terminal, the only black in a crowd of white travellers, and found himself as stunned and disturbed as they were. Wynton Marsalis, on tour with his band in California, recalls that "everybody was acting like they were above watching it, but then when it got to be ten o'clock—zoom, we said, 'Put the verdict on!'" Spike Lee was with Jackie Robinson's widow, Rachel, rummaging through a trunk filled with her husband's belongings, in preparation for a bio-pic he's making on the athlete. Jamaica Kincaid was sitting in her car in the parking lot of her local grocery store in Vermont, listening to the proceedings on National Public Radio, and she didn't pull out until after they were over. I was teaching a literature seminar at Harvard from twelve to two, and watched the verdict with the class on a television set in the seminar room. That's where I first saw the sort of racialized response that it-self would fill television screens for the next few days: the white students looked aghast, and the black students cheered. "Maybe you should remind the students that this is a case about two people who were brutally slain, and not an occasion to celebrate," my teaching assistant, a white woman, whispered to me.

The two weeks spanning the O. J. Simpson verdict and Louis Farrakhan's Million Man March on Washington were a good time for connoisseurs of racial paranoia. As blacks exulted at Simpson's acquittal, horrified whites had a fleeting sense that this race thing was knottier than they'd ever supposed—that, when all the pieties were cleared away, blacks really *were* strangers in their midst. (The unspoken sentiment: *And I thought I knew these people.*) There was the faintest tincture of the Southern slave-owner's disquiet in the aftermath of the bloody slave revolt led by Nat Turner—when the gentleman farmer was left to wonder which of his smiling, servile retainers would have slit *his* throat if the rebellion had spread as was intended, like fire on parched thatch. In the day or so following the verdict, young urban professionals took note of a slight *froideur* between themselves and their nannies and babysitters—the awkwardness of an unbroached subject. Rita Dove, who recently completed a term as the United States Poet Laureate, and who believes that Simpson was guilty, found it "appalling that white people were so outraged—more appalling than the decision as to whether he was guilty or not." Of course, it's possible to overstate the tensions. Marsalis invokes the example of team sports, saying, "You want your side to win, whatever the side is going to be. And the thing is, we're still at a point in our national history where we look at each other as sides."

The matter of side-taking cuts deep. An old cartoon depicts a woman who has taken her errant daughter to see a child psychiatrist. "And when we were watching 'The Wizard of Oz,'" the distraught mother is explaining, "she was rooting for the wicked witch!" What many whites experienced was the bewildering sense that an entire population had been rooting for the wrong side. "This case is a classic example of what I call interstitial spaces," says Judge A. Leon Higginbotham, who recently retired from the federal Court of Appeals, and who last month received the Presidential Medal of Freedom. "The jury system is predicated on the idea that different people can view the same evidence and reach diametrically opposed conclusions." But the observation brings little solace. If we disagree about something so basic, how can we find agreement about far thornier matters? For white observers, what's even scarier than the idea that black Americans were plumping for the villain, which is a misprision of value, is the idea that black Americans didn't recognize him *as* the villain, which is a misprision of fact. How can conversation begin when we disagree about reality? To put it at its harshest, for many whites a sincere belief in Simpson's innocence looks less like the culture of protest than like the culture of psychosis.

Perhaps you didn't know that Liz Claiborne appeared on "Oprah" not long ago and said that she didn't design her clothes for black women—that their hips were too wide. Perhaps you didn't know that the soft drink Tropical Fantasy is manufactured by the Ku Klux Klan and contains a special ingredient designed to sterilize black men. (A warning flyer distributed in Harlem a few years ago claimed that these findings were vouchsafed on the television program "20/20.") Perhaps you didn't know that the Ku Klux Klan has a similar arrangement with Church's Fried Chicken—or is it Popeye's?

Perhaps you didn't know these things, but a good many black Americans think they do, and will discuss them with the same intentness they bring to speculations about the "shadowy figure" in a Brentwood driveway. Never mind that Liz Claiborne has never appeared on "Oprah," that the beleaguered Brooklyn company that makes Tropical Fantasy has gone as far as to make available an F.D.A. assay of its ingredients, and that those fried-chicken franchises pose a threat mainly to black folks' arteries. The folklorist Patricia A. Turner, who has collected dozens of such tales in an invaluable 1993 study of rumor in African-American culture, "I Heard It Through the Grapevine," points out the patterns to be found here: that these stories encode regnant anxieties, that they take root under particular conditions and play particular social roles, that the currency of rumor flourishes where "official" news has proved untrustworthy.

Certainly the Fuhrman tapes might have been scripted to confirm the old saw that paranoids, too, have enemies. If you wonder why blacks seem particularly susceptible to rumors and conspiracy theories, you might look at a history in which the official story was a poor guide to anything that mattered much, and in which rumor sometimes verged on the truth. Heard the one about the L.A. cop who hated interracial couples, fantasized about making a bonfire of black bodies, and boasted of planting evidence? How about the one about the federal government's forty-year study of how untreated syphilis affects black men? For that matter, have you ever read through some of the F.B.I.'s COINTELPRO files? ("There is but one way out for you," an F.B.I. scribe wrote to Martin Luther King, Jr., in 1964, thoughtfully urging on him the advantages of suicide. "You better take it before your filthy, abnormal, fraudulent self is bared to the nation.")

People arrive at an understanding of themselves and the world through narratives—narratives purveyed by schoolteachers, newscasters, "authorities," and all the other authors of our common sense. Counternarratives are, in turn, the means by which groups contest that dominant reality and the fretwork of assumptions that supports it. Sometimes delusion lies that way; sometimes not. There's a sense in which much of black history is simply counternarrative that has been documented and legitimized, by slow, hard-won scholarship. The "shadowy figures" of American history have long been our own ancestors, both free and enslaved. In any case, fealty to counternarratives is an index to alienation, not to skin color: witness Representative Helen Chenoweth, of Idaho, and her devoted constituents. With all the appositeness of allegory, the copies of "The Protocols of the Elders of Zion" sold by black venders in New York—who are supplied with them by Lushena Books, a black-nationalist book wholesaler—were published by the white supremacist Angriff Press, in Hollywood. Paranoia knows no color or coast.

Finally, though, it's misleading to view counternarrative as another pathology of disenfranchisement. If the M.I.A. myth, say, is rooted among a largely working-

class constituency, there are many myths—one of them known as Reaganism—
that hold considerable appeal among the privileged classes. "So many white
brothers and sisters are living in a state of denial in terms of how deep white supremacy is seated in their culture and society," the scholar and social critic Cornel
West says. "Now we recognize that in a fundamental sense we really do live in different worlds." In that respect, the reaction to the Simpson verdict has been something of an education. The novelist Ishmael Reed talks of "wealthy white male
commentators who live in a world where the police don't lie, don't plant evidence—and drug dealers give you unlimited credit." He adds, "Nicole, you know,
also dated Mafia hit men."

"I think he's innocent, I really do," West says. "I do think it was linked to some
drug subculture of violence. It looks as if both O.J. and Nicole had some connection to drug activity. And the killings themselves were classic examples of that
drug culture of violence. It could have to do with money owed—it could have to
do with a number of things. And I think that O.J. was quite aware of and fearful of
this." On this theory, Simpson may have appeared at the crime scene as a witness.
"I think that he had a sense that it was coming down, both on him and on her,
and Brother Ron Goldman just happened to be there," West conjectures. "But
there's a possibility also that O.J. could have been there, gone over and tried to see
what was going on, saw that he couldn't help, split, and just ran away. He might
have said, 'I can't stop this thing, and they are coming at me to do the same thing.'
He may have actually run for his life."

To believe that Simpson is innocent is to believe that a terrible injustice has
been averted, and this is precisely what many black Americans, including many
prominent ones, do believe. Thus the soprano Jessye Norman is angry over what
she sees as the decision of the media to prejudge Simpson rather than "educate
the public as to how we could possibly look at things a bit differently." She says she
wishes that the real culprit "would stand up and say, 'I did this and I am sorry I
caused so much trouble.'" And while she is sensitive to the issue of spousal abuse,
she is skeptical about the way it was enlisted by the prosecution: "You have to stop
getting into how they were at home, because there are not a lot of relationships
that could be put on television that we would think, O.K., that's a good one. I
mean, just stop pretending that this is the case." Then, too, she asks, "Isn't it interesting to you that this Faye Resnick person was staying with Nicole Brown
Simpson and that she happened to have left on the eighth of June? Does that tell
you that maybe there's some awful coincidence here?" The widespread theory
about murderous drug dealers Norman finds "perfectly plausible, knowing what
drugs do," and she adds, "People are punished for being bad."

There's a sense in which all such accounts can be considered counternarratives,
or fragments of them—subaltern knowledge, if you like. They dispute the tenets
of official culture; they do not receive the imprimatur of editorialists or of network broadcasters; they are not seriously entertained on "MacNeil/Lehrer." And
when they do surface they are given consideration primarily for their ethnographic value. An official culture treats their claims as it does those of millenarian

cultists in Texas, or Marxist deconstructionists in the academy: as things to be diagnosed, deciphered, given meaning—that is, *another* meaning. Black folk say they believe Simpson is innocent, and then the white gatekeepers of a media culture cajolingly explain what black folk really mean when they say it, offering the explanation from the highest of motives: because the alternative is a population that, by their lights, is not merely counternormative but crazy. Black folk may mean anything at all; just not what they say they mean.

Yet you need nothing so grand as an epistemic rupture to explain why different people weigh the evidence of authority differently. In the words of the cunning Republican campaign slogan, "Who do you trust?" It's a commonplace that white folks trust the police and black folks don't. Whites recognize this in the abstract, but they're continually surprised at the *depth* of black wariness. They shouldn't be. Norman Podhoretz's soul-searching 1963 essay, "My Negro Problem, and Ours"—one of the frankest accounts we have of liberalism and race resentment—tells of a Brooklyn boyhood spent under the shadow of carefree, cruel Negro assailants, and of the author's residual unease when he passes groups of blacks in his Upper West Side neighborhood. And yet, he notes in a crucial passage, "I know now, as I did not know when I was a child, that power is on my side, that the police are working for me and not for them." That ordinary, unremarkable comfort—the feeling that "the police are working for me"—continues to elude blacks, even many successful blacks. Thelma Golden, the curator of the Whitney's "Black Male" show, points out that on the very day the verdict was announced a black man in Harlem was killed by the police under disputed circumstances. As older blacks like to repeat, "When white folks say 'justice,' they mean 'just us.'"

Blacks—in particular, black men—swap their experiences of police encounters like war stories, and there are few who don't have more than one story to tell. "These stories have a ring of cliché about them," Erroll McDonald, Pantheon's executive editor and one of the few prominent blacks in publishing, says, "but, as we all know about clichés, they're almost always true." McDonald tells of renting a Jaguar in New Orleans and being stopped by the police—simply "to show cause why I shouldn't be deemed a problematic Negro in a possibly stolen car." Wynton Marsalis says, "Shit, the police slapped me upside the head when I was in high school. I wasn't Wynton Marsalis then. I was just another nigger standing out somewhere on the street whose head could be slapped and did get slapped." The crime novelist Walter Mosley recalls, "When I was a kid in Los Angeles, they used to stop me all the time, beat on me, follow me around, tell me that I was stealing things." Nor does William Julius Wilson—who has a son-in-law on the Chicago police force ("You couldn't find a nicer, more dedicated guy")—wonder why he was stopped near a small New England town by a policeman who wanted to know what he was doing in those parts. There's a moving violation that many African-Americans know as D.W.B.: Driving While Black.

So we all have our stories. In 1968, when I was eighteen, a man who knew me was elected major of my West Virginia county, in an upset victory. A few weeks into his term, he passed on something he thought I should know: the county po-

lice had made a list of people to be arrested in the event of a serious civil disturbance, and my name was on it. Years of conditioning will tell. Wynton Marsalis
says, "My worst fear is to have to go before the criminal-justice system." Absurdly
enough, it's mine, too.

Another barrier to interracial comprehension is talk of the "race card"—a
phrase that itself infuriates many blacks. Judge Higginbotham, who pronounces
himself "not uncomfortable at all" with the verdict, is uncomfortable indeed with
charges that Johnnie Cochran played the race card. "This whole point is one hundred per cent inaccurate," Higginbotham says. "If you knew that the most important witness had a history of racism and hostility against black people, that should
have been a relevant factor of inquiry even if the jury had been all white. If the defendant had been Jewish and the police officer had a long history of expressed
anti-Semitism and having planted evidence against innocent persons who were
Jewish, I can't believe that anyone would have been saying that defense counsel
was playing the anti-Semitism card." Angela Davis finds the very metaphor to be a
problem. "Race is not a card," she says firmly. "The whole case was pervaded with
issues of race."

Those who share her view were especially outraged at Robert Shapiro's famous
post-trial rebuke to Cochran—for not only playing the race card but dealing it
"from the bottom of the deck." Ishmael Reed, who is writing a book about the
case, regards Shapiro's remarks as sheer opportunism: "He wants to keep his
Beverly Hills clients—a perfectly commercial reason." In Judge Higginbotham's
view, "Johnnie Cochran established that he was as effective as any lawyer in
America, and though whites can tolerate black excellence in singing, dancing, and
dunking, there's always been a certain level of discomfort among many whites
when you have a one-on-one challenge in terms of intellectual competition. If
Edward Bennett Williams, who was one of the most able lawyers in the country,
had raised the same issues, half of the complaints would not exist."

By the same token, the display of black prowess in the courtroom was hearten-
ing for many black viewers. Cornel West says, "I think part of the problem is that
Shapiro—and this is true of certain white brothers—has a profound fear of black-
male charisma. And this is true not only in the law but across the professional
world. You see, you have so many talented white brothers who deserve to be in the
limelight. But one of the reasons they are not in the limelight is that they are not
charismatic. And here comes a black person who's highly talented but also charismatic and therefore able to command center stage. So you get a very real visceral
kind of jealousy that has to do with sexual competition as well as professional
competition."

Erroll McDonald touches upon another aspect of sexual tension when he says,
"The so-called race card has always been the joker. And the joker is the history of
sexual racial politics in this country. People forget the singularity of this issue—
people forget that less than a century ago black men were routinely lynched for
merely glancing at white women or for having been *thought* to have glanced at a

white woman." He adds, with mordant irony, "Now we've come to a point in our history where a black man could, potentially, have murdered a white woman and thrown in a white man to boot—and got off. So the country has become far more complex in its discussion of race." This is, as he appreciates, a less than perfectly consoling thought.

"But he's coming for me," a woman muses in Toni Morrison's 1994 novel, "Jazz," shortly before she is murdered by a jealous ex-lover. "Maybe tomorrow he'll find me. Maybe tonight." Morrison, it happens, is less interested in the grand passions of love and requital than she is in the curious texture of communal amnesty. In the event, the woman's death goes unavenged; the man who killed her is forgiven even by her friends and relatives. Neighbors feel that the man fell victim to her wiles, that he didn't understand "how she liked to push people, men." Or, as one of them says of her, "live the life; pay the price." Even the woman—who refuses to name the culprit as she bleeds to death—seems to accede to the view that she brought it on herself.

It's an odd and disturbing theme, and one with something of a history in black popular culture. An R. & B. hit from 1960, "There's Something on Your Mind," relates the anguish of a man who is driven to kill by his lover's infidelity. The chorus alternates with spoken narrative, which informs us that his first victim is the friend with whom she was unfaithful. But then:

> Just as you make it up in your mind to forgive her, here come another one of your best friends through the door. This really makes you blow your top, and you go right ahead and shoot her. And realizing what you've done, you say: "Baby, please, speak to me. Forgive me. I'm sorry."

"We are a *forgiving* people," Anita Hill tells me, and she laughs, a little uneasily. We're talking about the support for O. J. Simpson in the black community; at least, I think we are.

A black woman told the *Times* last week, "He has been punished enough." But forgiveness is not all. There is also an element in this of outlaw culture: the tendency—which unites our lumpenproles with our postmodern ironists—to celebrate transgression for its own sake. Spike Lee, who was surprised but "wasn't happy" at the verdict ("I would have bet money that he was going to the slammer"), reached a similar conclusion: "A lot of black folks said, 'Man, O.J. is *bad*, you know. This is the first brother in the history of the world who got away with the murder of white folks, and a blond, blue-eyed woman at that.'"

But then there is the folk wisdom on the question of why Nicole Brown Simpson had to die—the theodicy of the streets. For nothing could be further from the outlaw ethic than the simple and widely shared certainty that, as Jessye Norman says, people are punished for doing wrong. And compounding the sentiment is Morrison's subject—the culturally vexed status of the so-called crime of passion, or what some took to be one, anyway. You play, you pay: it's an attitude that exists on the streets, but not only on the streets, and one that somehow attaches to Nicole, rather than to her ex-husband. Many counter-narratives revolve around her putative misbehavior. The black feminist Bell Hooks notes with dismay that what many people took to be a "narrative of a crime of passion" had as its victim "a woman that many people, white and black, felt was like a whore. Precisely by being a sexually promiscuous woman, by being a woman who used drugs, by being a white woman with a black man, she had already fallen from grace in many people's eyes—there was no way to redeem her." Ishmael Reed, for one, has no interest in redeeming her. "To paint O.J. Simpson as a beast, they had to depict her as a saint," he complains. "Apparently, she had a violent temper. She slapped her Jamaican maid. I'm wondering, the feminists who are giving Simpson such a hard time—do they approve of white women slapping maids?"

Of course, the popular trial of Nicole Brown Simpson—one conducted off camera, in whispers—has further occluded anything recognizable as sexual politics. When Anita Hill heard that O.J. Simpson was going to be part of the Million Man March on Washington, she felt it was entirely in keeping with the occasion: a trial in which she believed that matters of gender had been "bracketed" was going to be succeeded by a march from which women were excluded. And, while Minister Louis Farrakhan had told black men that October 16th was to serve as a "day of atonement" for their sins, the murder of Nicole Brown Simpson and Ronald Goldman was obviously not among the sins he had in mind. Bell Hooks argues, "Both O.J.'s case and the Million Man March confirm that, while white men are trying to be sensitive and pretending they're the new man, black men are saying that patriarchy must be upheld at all costs, even if women must die." She sees the march as a congenial arena for Simpson in symbolic terms: "I think he'd like to strut his stuff, as the patriarch. He is the dick that stayed hard longer." ("The surprising thing is that you won't see Clarence Thomas going on that march," Anita Hill remarks of another icon of patriarchy.) Farrakhan himself prefers metaphors of military mobilization, but the exclusionary politics of the event has clearly distracted from its ostensible message of solidarity. "First of all, I wouldn't go to no war and leave half the army home," says Amiri Baraka, the radical poet and playwright who achieved international renown in the sixties as the leading spokesman for the Black Arts movement. "Logistically, that doesn't make sense." He notes that Martin Luther King's 1963 March on Washington was "much more inclusive," and sees Farrakhan's regression as "an absolute duplication of what's happening in the country," from Robert Bly on: the sacralization of masculinity.

Something like that dynamic is what many white feminists saw on display in the Simpson verdict; but it's among women that the racial divide is especially salient. The black legal scholar and activist Patricia Williams says she was "stunned by the intensely personal resentment of some of my white women friends in particular." Stunned but, on reflection, not mystified. "This is Greek drama," she declares. "Two of the most hotly contended aspects of our lives are violence among human beings who happen to be police officers and violence among human beings who happen to be husbands, spouses, lovers." Meanwhile, our attention has been fixated on the rhetorical violence between human beings who happen to disagree about the outcome of the O. J. Simpson trial.

It's a cliché to speak of the Simpson trial as a soap opera—as entertainment, as theatre—but it's also true, and in ways that are worth exploring further. For one thing, the trial provides a fitting rejoinder to those who claim that we live in an utterly fragmented culture, bereft of the common narratives that bind a people together. True, Parson Weems has given way to Dan Rather, but public narrative persists. Nor has it escaped notice that the biggest televised legal contests of the last half decade have involved race matters: Anita Hill and Rodney King. So there you have it: the Simpson trial—black entertainment television at its finest. Ralph Ellison's hopeful insistence on the Negro's centrality to American culture finds, at last, a certain tawdry confirmation.

"The media generated in people a feeling of being spectators at a show," the novelist John Edgar Wideman says. "And at the end of a show you applaud. You are happy for the good guy. There is that sense of primal identification and closure." Yet it's a fallacy of "cultural literacy" to equate shared narratives with shared meanings. The fact that American TV shows are rebroadcast across the globe causes many people to wring their hands over the menace of cultural imperialism; seldom do they bother to inquire about the meanings that different people bring to and draw from these shows. When they do make inquiries, the results are often surprising. One researcher talked to Israeli Arabs who had just watched an episode of "Dallas"—an episode in which Sue Ellen takes her baby, leaves her husband, J.R., and moves in with her ex-lover and his father. The Arab viewers placed their own construction on the episode: they were all convinced that Sue Ellen had moved in with her *own* father—something that by their mores at least made sense.

A similar thing happened in America this year: the communal experience afforded by a public narrative (and what narrative more public?) was splintered by the politics of interpretation. As far as the writer Maya Angelou is concerned, the Simpson trial was an exercise in minstrelsy. "Minstrel shows caricatured every aspect of the black man's life, beginning with his sexuality," she says. "They portrayed the black man as devoid of all sensibilities and sensitivities. They minimized and diminished the possibility of familial love. And that is what the trial is about. Not just the prosecution but everybody seemed to want to show him as other than a normal human being. Nobody let us just see a man." But there is, of course, little consensus about what genre would best accommodate the material. Walter Mosley says, "The story plays to large themes, so I'm sure somebody will write about it. But I don't think it's a mystery. I think it's much more like a novel by Zola." What a writer might make of the material is one thing; what the audience has made of it is another.

"Simpson is a B-movie star and people were watching this like a B movie," Patricia Williams says. "And this is *not* the American B-movie ending." Or was it?

"From my perspective as an attorney, this trial was much more like a movie than a trial," Kathleen Cleaver, who was once the Black Panthers' Minister for Communication and is now a professor of law at Emory, says. "It had the budget of a movie, it had the casting of a movie, it had the tension of a movie, and the happy ending of a movie." Spike Lee, speaking professionally, is dubious about the trial's cinematic possibilities: "I don't care who makes this movie, it is never going to equal what people have seen in their living rooms and houses for eight or nine months." Or is it grand opera? Jessye Norman considers: "Well, it certainly has all the ingredients. I mean, somebody meets somebody and somebody gets angry with somebody and somebody dies." She laughs. "It sounds like the 'Ring' cycle of Wagner—it really does."

"This story has been told any number of times," Angelou says. "The first thing I thought about was Eugene O'Neill's 'All God's Chillun.'" Then she considers how the event might be retrieved by an African-American literary tradition. "I think a great writer would have to approach it," she tells me pensively. "James Baldwin could have done it. And Toni Morrison could do it."

"Maya Angelou could do it," I say.

"I don't like that kind of stuff," she replies.

There are some for whom the question of adaptation is not entirely abstract. The performance artist and playwright Anna Deavere Smith has already worked on the 911 tape and F. Lee Bailey's cross-examination of Mark Fuhrman in the drama classes she teaches at Stanford. Now, with a dramaturge's eye, she identifies what she takes to be the climactic moment: "Just after the verdict was read I will always remember two sounds and one image. I heard Johnnie Cochran go 'Ugh,' and then I heard the weeping of Kim Goldman. And then I saw the image of O. J.'s son, with one hand going upward on one eye and one hand pointed down, shaking and sobbing. I couldn't do the words right now; if I could find a collaborator, I would do something else. I feel that a choreographer ought to do that thing. Part of the tragedy was the fact of that 'Ugh' and that crying. Because that 'Ugh' wasn't even a full sound of victory, really." In "Thirteen Ways of Looking at a Blackbird" Wallace Stevens famously said he didn't know whether he preferred "The beauty of inflections / Or the beauty of innuendoes,/ The blackbird whistling / Or just after." American culture has spoken as with one voice: we like it just after.

Just after is when our choices and allegiances are made starkly apparent. Just after is when interpretation can be detached from the thing interpreted. Anita Hill, who saw her own presence at the Clarence Thomas hearings endlessly analyzed and allegorized, finds plenty of significance in the trial's reception, but says the trial itself had none. Naturally, the notion that the trial was sui generis is alien to most commentators. Yet it did not arrive in the world already costumed as a racial drama; it had to be racialized. And those critics—angry whites, indignant blacks—who like to couple this verdict with the Rodney King verdict should consider an elementary circumstance: Rodney King was an unknown and undistinguished black man who was brutalized by the police; the only thing exceptional about that episode was the presence of a video camera. But, as Bell Hooks asks, "in what other case have we ever had a wealthy black man being tried for murder?" Rodney King was a black man to his captors before he was anything else; O. J. Simpson was, first and foremost, O. J. Simpson. Kathleen Cleaver observes, "A black superhero millionaire is not someone for whom mistreatment is an issue." And Spike Lee acknowledges that the police "don't really bother black people once they are a personality." On this point, I'm reminded of something that Roland Gift, the lead singer of the pop group Fine Young Cannibals, once told a reporter: "I'm not black, I'm famous."

Simpson, too, was famous rather than black; that is, until the African-American community took its lead from the cover of *Time* and, well, blackened him. Some intellectuals are reluctant to go along with the conceit. Angela Davis, whose early-seventies career as a fugitive and a political prisoner provides one model of how to be famous *and* black, speaks of the need to question the way "O. J. Simpson serves as the generic black man," given that "he did not identify himself as black before then." More bluntly, Baraka says, "To see him get all of this God-damned support from people he has historically and steadfastly eschewed just pissed me off. He eschewed black people all his life and then, like Clarence Thomas, the minute he gets jammed up he comes talking about 'Hey, I'm black.' " And the matter of spousal abuse should remind us of another role-reversal entailed by Simpson's iconic status in a culture of celebrity: Nicole Brown Simpson would have known that her famous-not-black husband commanded a certain deference from the L.A.P.D. which she, who was white but not yet famous, did not.

"It's just amazing that we in the black community have bought into it," Anita Hill says, with some asperity, and she sees the manufacture of black-male heroes as part of the syndrome. "We continue to create a superclass of individuals who are above the rules." It bewilders her that Simpson "was being honored as someone who was being persecuted for his politics, when he had none," she says. "Not only do we forget about the abuse of his wife but we also forget about the abuse of the community, his walking away from the community." And so Simpson's connection to a smitten black America can be construed as yet another romance, another troubled relationship, another case study in mutual exploitation.

Yet to accept the racial reduction ("WHITES V. BLACKS," as last week's *Newsweek* headline had it) is to miss the fact that the black community itself is riven, and in ways invisible to most whites. I myself was convinced of Simpson's guilt, so convinced that in the middle of the night before the verdict was to be announced I found myself worrying about his prospective sojourn in prison: would he be brutalized, raped, assaulted? Yes, on sober reflection, such worries over a man's condign punishment seemed senseless, a study in misplaced compassion; but there it was. When the verdict was announced, I was stunned—but, then again, wasn't my own outrage mingled with an unaccountable sense of relief? Anna Deavere Smith says, "I am seeing more than that white people are pissed off and black people are ecstatic. I am seeing the difficulty of that; I am seeing people having difficulty talking about it." And many are weary of what Ishmael Reed calls "zebra journalism, where everything is seen in black-and-white." Davis says, "I have the feeling that the media are in part responsible for the creation of this so-called racial divide—putting all the white people on one side and all the black people on the other side."

Many blacks as well as whites saw the trial's outcome as a grim enactment of Richard Pryor's comic rejoinder "Who are you going to believe—me, or your lying eyes?" "I think if he were innocent he wouldn't have behaved that way," Jamaica Kincaid says of Simpson, taking note of his refusal to testify on his own behalf. "If you are innocent," she believes, "you might want to admit you have done every possible thing in the world—had sex with ten donkeys, twenty mules—but did not do this particular thing." William Julius Wilson says mournfully, "There's something wrong with a system where it's better to be guilty and rich and have good lawyers than to be innocent and poor and have bad ones."

The Simpson verdict was "the ultimate in affirmative action," Amiri Baraka says. "I *know* the son of a bitch did it." For his part, Baraka essentially agrees with Shapiro's rebuke of Cochran: "Cochran is belittling folks. What he's saying is 'Well, the niggers can't understand the question of perjury in the first place. The only thing they can understand is, 'He called you a nigger.'" He alludes to *Ebony's* fixation on "black firsts"—the magazine's spotlight coverage of the first black to do this or that—and fantasizes the appropriate *Ebony* accolade. "They can feature him on the cover as 'The first Negro to kill a white woman and get away with it,'" he offers acidly. Then he imagines Farrakhan introducing him with just that tribute at the Million Man March. Baraka has been writing a play called "Othello, Jr.," so such themes have been on his mind. The play is still in progress, but he *has* just finished a short poem:

> *Free Mumia!*
> *O.J. did it*
> *And you know it.*

"Trials don't establish absolute truth; that's a theological enterprise," Patricia Williams says. So perhaps it is appropriate that a religious leader, Louis Farrakhan, convened a day of atonement; indeed, some worry that it is all too appropriate, coming at a time when the resurgent right has offered us a long list of sins for which black men must atone. But the crisis of race in America is real enough. And with respect to that crisis a mass mobilization is surely a better fit than a criminal trial. These days, the assignment of blame for black woes increasingly looks like an exercise in scholasticism; and calls for interracial union increasingly look like an exercise in inanity. ("Sorry for the Middle Passage, old chap. I don't know *what* we were thinking." "Hey, man, forget it—and here's your wallet back. No, really, I want you to have it.") The black economist Glenn Loury says, "If I could get a million black men together, I wouldn't march them to Washington, I'd march them into the ghettos."

But because the meanings of the march are so ambiguous, it has become itself a racial Rorschach—a vast ambulatory allegory waiting to happen. The actor and director Sidney Poitier says, "If we go on such a march to say to ourselves and to the rest of America that we want to be counted among America's people, we would like our family structure to be nurtured and strengthened by ourselves and by the society, that's a good point to make." He sees the march as an occasion for the community to say, "Look, we are adrift. Not only is the nation adrift on the question of race—we, too, are adrift. We need to have a sense of purpose and a sense of direction." Maya Angelou, who agreed to address the assembled men, views the event not as a display of male self-affirmation but as a ceremony of penitence: "It's a chance for African-American males to say to African-American females, 'I'm sorry. I am sorry for what I did, and I am sorry for what happened to both of us.'" But different observers will have different interpretations. Mass mobilizations launch a thousand narratives—especially among subscribers to what might be called the "great event" school of history. And yet Farrakhan's recurrent calls for individual accountability consort oddly with the absolution, both juridical and populist, accorded O. J. Simpson. Simpson has been seen as a symbol for many things, but he is not yet a symbol for taking responsibility for one's actions.

All the same, the task for black America is not to get its symbols in shape: symbolism is one of the few commodities we have in abundance. Meanwhile, Du Bois's century-old question "How does it feel to be a problem?" grows in trenchancy with every new bulletin about crime and poverty. And the Simpson trial spurs us to question everything except the way that the discourse of crime and punishment has enveloped, and suffocated, the analysis of race and poverty in this country. For the debate over the rights and wrongs of the Simpson verdict has meshed all too well with the manner in which we have long talked about race and social justice. The defendant may be free, but we remain captive to a binary discourse of accusation and counter-accusation, of grievance and counter-grievance, of victims and victimizers. It is a discourse in which O. J. Simpson is a suitable remedy for Rodney King, and reductions in Medicaid are entertained as a suitable remedy for O. J. Simpson: a discourse in which everyone speaks of payback and nobody is paid. The result is that race politics becomes a court of the imagination wherein blacks seek to punish whites for their misdeeds and whites seek to punish blacks for theirs, and an infinite regress of score-settling ensues—yet another way in which we are daily becoming meta and meta. And so an empty vessel like O. J. Simpson becomes filled with meaning, and more meaning—more meaning than any of us can bear. No doubt it is a far easier thing to assign blame than to render justice. But if the imagery of the court continues to confine the conversation about race, it really will be a crime.

2

I'm Black, You're White, Who's Innocent?

SHELBY STEELE

Race and Power in an Era of Blame

It is a warm, windless California evening, and the dying light that covers the red-brick patio is tinted pale orange by the day's smog. Eight of us, not close friends, sit in lawn chairs sipping chardonnay. A black engineer and I (we had never met before) integrate the group. A psychologist is also among us, and her presence encourages a surprising openness. But not until well after the lovely twilight dinner has been served, when the sky has turned to deep black and the drinks have long since changed to scotch, does the subject of race spring awkwardly upon us. Out of nowhere the engineer announces, with a coloring of accusation in his voice, that it bothers him to send his daughter to a school where she is one of only three black children. "I didn't realize my ambition to get ahead would pull me into a world where my daughter would lose touch with her blackness," he says.

Over the course of the evening we have talked about money, past and present addictions, child abuse, even politics. Intimacies have been revealed, fears named. But this subject, race, sinks us into one of those shaming silences where eye contact terrorizes. Our host looks for something in the bottom of his glass. Two women stare into the black sky as if to locate the Big Dipper and point it out to us. Finally, the psychologist seems to gather herself for a challenge, but it is too late. "Oh, I'm sure she'll be just fine," says our hostess, rising from her chair. When she excuses herself to get the coffee, the psychologist and two sky gazers offer to help.

With four of us now gone, I am surprised to see the engineer still silently holding his ground. There is a willfulness in his eyes, an inner pride. He knows he has said something awkward, but he is determined not to give a damn. His unwavering eyes intimidate even me. At last the host's head snaps erect. He has an idea. "The hell with coffee," he says. "How about some of the smoothest brandy you've ever tasted?" An idea made exciting by the escape it offers. Gratefully, we follow him back into the house, quickly drink his brandy, and say our good-byes.

An autopsy of this party might read: death induced by an abrupt and lethal injection of the American race issue. An accurate if superficial assessment. Since it has been my fate to live a rather integrated life, I have often witnessed sudden deaths like this. The threat of them, if not the reality, is a part of the texture of integration. In the late 1960s, when I was just out of college, I took a delinquent's delight in playing the engineer's role, and actually developed a small reputation for playing it well. Those were the days of flagellatory white guilt; it was such great fun to pinion some professor or housewife or, best of all, a large group of remorseful whites, with the knowledge of both their racism and their denial of it. The adolescent impulse to sneer at convention, to startle the middle-aged with doubt, could be indulged under the guise of racial indignation. And how could I lose? My victims—earnest liberals for the most part—could no more crawl out from under my accusations than Joseph K. in Kafka's *Trial* could escape the amorphous charges brought against him. At this odd moment in history the world was aligned to facilitate my immaturity.

About a year of this was enough: the guilt that follows most cheap thrills caught up to me, and I put myself in check. But the impulse to do it faded more slowly. It was one of those petty talents that is tied to vanity, and when there were ebbs in my self-esteem the impulse to use it would come alive again. In integrated situations I can still feel the faint itch. But then there are many youthful impulses that still itch, and now, just inside the door of midlife, this one is least precious to me.

In the literature classes I teach I often see how the presence of whites all but seduces some black students into provocation. When we come to a novel by a black writer, say Toni Morrison, the white students can easily discuss the human motivations of the black characters. But, inevitably, a black student, as if by reflex, will begin to set in relief the various racial problems that are the background of these characters' lives. This student's tone will carry a reprimand: the class is afraid to confront the reality of racism. Classes cannot be allowed to die like dinner parties, however. My latest strategy is to thank that student for his or her moral vigilance and then appoint the young man or woman as the class's official racism monitor. But even if I get a laugh—I usually do, but sometimes the student is particularly indignant, and it gets uncomfortable—the strategy never quite works. Our racial division is suddenly drawn in neon. Overcaution spreads like spilled paint. And, in fact, the black student who started it all does become a kind of monitor. The very presence of this student imposes a new accountability on the class.

I think those who provoke this sort of awkwardness are operating out of a black identity that obliges them to badger white people about race almost on principle. Content hardly matters. (For example, it made little sense for the engineer to expect white people to anguish terribly much over his decision to send his daughter to school with *white* children.) Race indeed remains a source of white shame; the goal of these provocations is to put whites, no matter how indirectly, in touch with this collective guilt. In other words, these provocations I speak of are *power* moves, little shows of power that try to freeze the "enemy" in self-consciousness. They gratify and inflate the provocateur. They are the underdog's bite. And whites, far more secure in their power, respond with a self-contained and tolerant silence that is itself a show of power. What greater power than that of nonresponse, the power to let a small enemy sizzle in his own juices, to even feel a little sad at his frustration just as one is also complimented by it. Black anger always, in a way, flatters white power. In America, to know that one is not black is to feel an extra grace, a little boost of impunity.

I think the real trouble between the races in America is that the races are not just races but competing power groups—a fact that is easily minimized, perhaps because it is so obvious. What is not so obvious is that this is true quite apart from the issue of class. Even the well-situated middle-class (or wealthy) black is never completely immune to that peculiar contest of power that his skin color subjects him to. Race is a separate reality in American society, an entity that carries its own potential for power, a mark of fate that class can soften considerably but not eradicate.

The distinction of race has always been used in American life to sanction each race's pursuit of power in relation to the other. The allure of race as a human delineation is the very shallowness of the delineation it makes. Onto this shallowness— mere skin and hair—men can project a false depth, a system of dismal attributions, a series of malevolent or ignoble stereotypes that skin and hair lack the substance to contradict. These dark projections then rationalize the pursuit of power. Your difference from me makes you bad, and your badness justifies, even demands, my pursuit of power over you—the oldest formula for aggression known to man. Whenever much importance is given to race, power is the primary motive.

But the human animal almost never pursues power without first convincing himself that he is *entitled* to it. And this feeling of entitlement has its own precondition: to be entitled one must first believe in one's innocence, at least in the area where one wishes to be entitled. By innocence I mean a feeling of essential goodness in relation to others and, therefore, superiority to others. Our innocence always inflates us and deflates those we seek power over. Once inflated we are entitled; we are in fact licensed to go after the power our innocence tells us we deserve. In this sense, *innocence is power.* Of course, innocence need not be genuine or real in any objective sense, as the Nazis demonstrated not long ago. Its only test is whether or not we can convince ourselves of it.

I think the racial struggle in America has always been primarily a struggle for innocence. White racism from the beginning has been a claim of white innocence and therefore of white entitlement to subjugate blacks. And in the sixties, as went innocence so went power. Blacks used the innocence that grew out of their long subjugation to seize more power, while whites lost some of their innocence and so lost a degree of power over blacks. Both races instinctively understand that to lose innocence is to lose power (in relation to each other). To be innocent someone else must be guilty, a natural law that leads the races to forge their innocence on each other's backs. The inferiority of the black always makes the white man superior; the evil might of whites makes blacks good. This pattern means that both races have a hidden investment in racism and racial disharmony despite their good intentions to the contrary. Power defines their relations, and power requires innocence, which, in turn, requires racism and racial division.

I believe it was his hidden investment that the engineer was protecting when he made his remark—the white "evil" he saw in a white school "depriving" his daughter of her black heritage confirmed his innocence. Only the logic of power explained his emphasis—he bent reality to show that he was once again a victim of the white world and, as a victim, innocent. His determined eyes insisted on this. And the whites, in their silence, no doubt protected their innocence by seeing him as an ungracious troublemaker, his bad behavior underscoring their goodness. What none of us saw was the underlying game of power and innocence we were trapped in, or how much we needed a racial impasse to play that game. . . .

Black Americans have had to find a way to handle white society's presumption of racial innocence whenever they have sought to enter the American mainstream. Louis Armstrong's exaggerated smile honored the presumed innocence of white society—*I will not bring you your racial guilt if you will let me play my music.* Ralph Ellison calls this "masking"; I call it bargaining. But whatever it's called, it points to the power of white society to enforce its innocence. I believe this power is greatly diminished today. Society has reformed and transformed—Miles Davis never smiles. Nevertheless, this power has not faded altogether and blacks must still contend with it.

Historically, blacks have handled white society's presumption of innocence in two ways: they have bargained with it, granting white society its innocence in exchange for entry into the mainstream, or they have challenged it, holding that innocence hostage until their demand for entry (or other concessions) was met. A bargainer says, *I already believe you are innocent (good, fair-minded) and have faith that you will prove it.* A challenger says, *If you are innocent, then prove it.* Bargainers *give* in hope of receiving; challengers *withhold* until they receive. Of course, there is risk in both approaches, but in each case the black is negotiating his own self-interest against the presumed racial innocence of the larger society.

Clearly, the most visible black bargainer on the American scene today is Bill Cosby. His television show has been a perfect formula for black bargaining in the eighties. The remarkable Huxtable family—with its doctor/lawyer parent combination, its drug-free, college-bound children, and its wise yet youthful grandparents—is a blackface version of the American dream. Cosby is a subscriber to the American identity, and his subscription confirms his belief in its fair-mindedness. His vast audience knows this, knows that Cosby will never assault their innocence with racial guilt. Racial controversy is all but banished from the show. The Huxtable family never discusses affirmative action.

The bargain Cosby offers his white viewers—*I will confirm your racial innocence if you accept me*—is a good deal for all concerned. Not only does it allow whites to enjoy Cosby's humor with no loss of innocence, but it actually enhances their innocence by implying that race is not the serious problem for blacks that it once was. If anything, the success of this handsome, affluent black family points to the fair-mindedness of whites who, out of their essential goodness, changed society so that black families like the Huxtables could succeed. Whites can watch "The Cosby Show" and feel complimented on a job well done.

The power that black bargainers wield is the power of absolution. On Thursday nights, Cosby, like a priest, absolves his white viewers, forgives and forgets the sins of the past. And for this he is rewarded with an almost sacrosanct status. . . .

Now the other side of America's racial impasse: How do blacks lay claim to their racial innocence?

The most obvious and unarguable source of black innocence is the victimization that blacks endured for centuries at the hands of a race that insisted on black inferiority as a means to its own innocence and power. Like all victims, what blacks lost in power they gained in innocence—innocence that, in turn, entitled them to pursue power. This was the innocence that fueled the civil rights movement of the sixties and that gave blacks their first real power in American life—victimization metamorphosed into power via innocence. But this formula carries a drawback that I believe is virtually as devastating to blacks today as victimization once was. It is a formula that binds the victim to his victimization by linking his power to his status as a victim. And this, I'm convinced, is the tragedy of black power in America today. It is primarily a victim's power, grounded too deeply in the entitlement derived from past injustice and in the innocence that Western/Christian tradition has always associated with poverty.

Whatever gains this power brings in the short run through political action, it undermines in the long run. Social victims may be collectively entitled, but they are all too often individually demoralized. Since the social victim has been oppressed by society, he comes to feel that his individual life will be improved more by changes in society than by his own initiative. Without realizing it, he makes society rather than himself the agent of change. The power he finds in his victimization may lead him to collective action against society, but it also encourages passivity within the sphere of his personal life.

Not long ago, I saw a television documentary that examined life in Detroit's inner city on the twentieth anniversary of the riots there in which forty-three people were killed. A comparison of the inner city then and now showed a decline in the quality of life. Residents feel less safe, drug trafficking is far worse, crimes by blacks against blacks are more frequent, housing remains substandard, and the teenage pregnancy rate has skyrocketed. Twenty years of decline and demoralization, even as opportunities for blacks to better themselves have increased. This paradox is not peculiar to Detroit. By many measures, the majority of blacks—those not yet in the middle class—are further behind whites today than before the victories of the civil rights movement. But there is a reluctance among blacks to examine this paradox, I think, because it suggests that racial victimization is not our real problem. If conditions have worsened for most of us as racism had receded, then much of the problem must be of our own making. To admit this fully would cause us to lose the innocence we derive from our victimization. And we would jeopardize the entitlement we've always had to challenge society. We are in the odd and self-defeating position in which taking responsibility for bettering ourselves feels like a surrender to white power.

So we have a hidden investment in victimization and poverty. These distressing conditions have been the source of our only real power, and there is an unconscious sort of gravitation toward them, a complaining celebration of them. One sees evidence of this in the near happiness with which certain black leaders recount the horror of Howard Beach, Bensonhurst, and other recent instances of racial tension. As one is saddened by these tragic events, one is also repelled at the way some black leaders—agitated to near hysteria by the scent of victim power inherent in them—leap forward to exploit them as evidence of black innocence and white guilt. It is as though they sense the decline of black victimization as a loss of standing and dive into the middle of these incidents as if they were reservoirs of pure black innocence swollen with potential power.

Seeing for innocence pressures blacks to focus on racism and to neglect the individual initiative that would deliver them from poverty—the only thing that finally delivers *anyone* from poverty. With our eyes on innocence we see racism everywhere and miss opportunity even as we stumble over it. About 70 percent of black students at my university drop out before graduation—a flight from opportunity that racism cannot explain. It is an injustice that whites can see for innocence with more impunity than blacks can. The price whites pay is a certain blindness to themselves. Moreover, for whites seeing for innocence continues to engender the bad faith of a long-disgruntled minority. But the price blacks pay is an ever-escalating poverty that threatens to make the worst off a permanent underclass. Not fair, but real.

Challenging works best for the collective, while bargaining is more the individual's suit. From this point on, the race's advancement will come from the efforts of its individuals. True, some challenging will be necessary for a long time to come. But bargaining is now—today—a way for the black individual to *join* the larger society, to make a place for himself or herself.

"Innocence is ignorance," Kierkegaard says, and if this is so, the claim of innocence amounts to an insistence on ignorance, a refusal to know. In their assertions of innocence both races carve out very functional areas of ignorance for themselves—territories of blindness that license a misguided pursuit of power. Whites gain superiority by not knowing blacks; blacks gain entitlement by not seeing their own responsibility for bettering themselves. The power each race seeks in relation to the other is grounded in a double-edged ignorance of the self as well as of the other.

The original sin that brought us to an impasse at the dinner party I mentioned occurred centuries ago, when it was first decided to exploit racial difference as a means to power. It was a determinism that flowed karmically from this sin that dropped over us like a net that night. What bothered me most was our helplessness. Even the engineer did not know how to go forward. His challenge hadn't worked, and he'd lost the option to bargain. The marriage of race and power depersonalized us, changed us from eight people to six whites and two blacks. The easiest thing was to let silence blanket our situation, our impasse.

I think the civil rights movement in its early and middle years offered the best way out of America's racial impasse: in this society, race must not be a source of advantage or disadvantage for anyone. This is fundamentally a *moral* position, one that seeks to breach the corrupt union of race and power with principles of fairness and human equality: if all men are created equal, then racial difference cannot sanction power. The civil rights movement was conceived for no other reason than to redress that corrupt union, and its guiding insight was that only a moral power based on enduring principles of justice, equality, and freedom could offset the lower impulse in man to exploit race as a means to power. Three hundred years of suffering had driven the point home, and in Montgomery, Little Rock, and Selma, racial power was the enemy and moral power the weapon.

An important difference between genuine and presumed innocence, I believe, is that the former must be earned through sacrifice while the latter is unearned and only veils the quest for privilege. And there was much sacrifice in the early civil rights movement. The Gandhian principle of nonviolent resistance that gave the movement a spiritual center as well as a method of protest demanded sacrifice, a passive offering of the self in the name of justice. A price was paid in terror and lost life, and from this sacrifice came a hard-earned innocence and a credible moral power.

Nonviolent passive resistance is a bargainer's strategy. It assumes the power that is the object of the protest has the genuine innocence to respond morally, and puts the protesters at the mercy of that innocence. I think this movement won so many concessions precisely because of its belief in the capacity of whites to be moral. It did not so much demand that whites change as offer them relentlessly the opportunity to live by their own morality—to attain a true innocence based on the sacrifice of their racial privilege, rather than a false innocence based on presumed racial superiority. Blacks always bargain with or challenge the larger society; but I believe that in the early civil rights years, these forms of negotiation achieved a degree of integrity and genuineness never seen before or since.

In the mid-sixties all this changed. Suddenly a sharp *racial* consciousness emerged to compete with the moral consciousness that had defined the movement up to that point. Whites were no longer welcome in the movement, and a vocal "black power" minority gained dramatic visibility. Increasingly, the movement began to seek racial as well as moral power, and thus it fell into the fundamental contradiction that plagues it to this day. Moral power precludes racial power by denouncing race as a means to power. Now suddenly the movement itself was using race as a means to power and thereby affirming the very union of race and power it was born to redress. In the end, black power can claim no higher moral standing than white power.

It makes no sense to say this shouldn't have happened. The sacrifices that moral power demands are difficult to sustain, and it was inevitable that blacks would tire of these sacrifices and seek a more earthly power. Nevertheless, a loss of genuine innocence and moral power followed. The movement, splintered by a burst of racial militancy in the late sixties, lost its hold on the American conscience and descended more and more to the level of secular interest-group politics. Bargaining and challenging once again became racial rather than moral negotiations.

You hear it asked, why are there no Martin Luther Kings around today? I think one reason is that there are no black leaders willing to resist the seductions of racial power, or to make the sacrifices moral power requires. King understood that racial power subverts moral power, and he pushed the principles of fairness and equality rather than black power because he believed those principles would bring blacks their most complete liberation. He sacrificed race for morality, and his innocence was made genuine by that sacrifice. What made King the most powerful and extraordinary black leader of this century was not his race but his morality.

Black power is a challenge. It grants whites no innocence; it denies their moral capacity and then demands that they be moral. No power can long insist on itself without evoking an opposing power. Doesn't an insistence on black power call up white power? (And could this have something to do with what many are now calling a resurgence of white racism?) I believe that what divided the races at the dinner party I attended, and what divides them in the nation, can only be bridged by an adherence to those moral principles that disallow race as a source of power, privilege, status, or entitlement of any kind. In our age, principles like fairness and equality are ill-defined and all but drowned in relativity. But this is the fault of people, not principles. We keep them muddied because they are the greatest threat to our presumed innocence and our selective ignorance. Moral principles, even when somewhat ambiguous, have the power to assign responsibility and therefore to provide us with knowledge. At the dinner party we were afraid of so severe an accountability.

What both black and white Americans fear are the sacrifices and risks that true racial harmony demands. This fear is the measure of our racial chasm. And though fear always seeks a thousand justifications, none is ever good enough, and the problems we run from only remain to haunt us. It would be right to suggest courage as an antidote to fear, but the glory of the word might only intimidate us into more fear. I prefer the word effort—relentless effort, moral effort. What I like most about this word are its connotations of everydayness, earnestness, and practical sacrifice. No matter how badly it might have gone for us that warm summer night, we should have talked. We should have made the effort.

Race-Holding

I am a fortyish, middle-class, black American male with a teaching position at a large state university in California. I have owned my own home for more than ten years, as well as the two cars that are the minimal requirement for life in California. And I will confess to a moderate strain of yuppie hedonism. Year after year my two children are the sole representatives of their race in their classrooms, a fact they sometimes have difficulty remembering. We are the only black family in our suburban neighborhood, and even this claim to specialness is diminished by the fact that my wife is white. I think we are called an "integrated" family, though no one has ever used the term with me. For me to be among large numbers of blacks requires conscientiousness and a long car ride, and in truth, I have not been very conscientious lately. Though I was raised in an all-black community just south of Chicago, I only occasionally feel nostalgia for such places. Trips to the barbershop now and then usually satisfy this need, though recently, in the interest of convenience, I've taken to letting my wife cut my hair.

I see in people's eyes from time to time, and hear often in the media, what amounts to a judgment of people like myself: You have moved into the great amorphous middle class and lost your connection to your people and your cultural roots. You have become a genuine invisible man. This is judgment with many obvious dimensions, many arrows of guilt. But, in essence, it charges me with selfishness and inauthenticity.

At one point I romanticized my situation, thought of myself as a marginal man. The seductive imagery of alienation supported me in this. But in America today racial marginality is hard to sell as the stuff of tragedy. The position brings with it an ugly note of self-insistence that annoys people in a society that is, at least officially, desegregated.

For better or worse, I'm not very marginal. In my middle-American world I see people like myself everywhere. We nod coolly at stoplights, our eyes connect for an awkward instant in shopping malls, we hear about one another from our white friends. "Have you met the new doctor at the hospital . . . the engineer at IBM . . . the new professor in history?" The black middle class is growing. We are often said to be sneaking or slipping or creeping unnoticed into the middle class, as though images of stealth best characterized our movement. I picture a kind of underground railroad, delivering us in the dead of night from the inner city to the suburbs.

But even if we aren't very marginal, we are very shy with one another, at least until we've had a chance to meet privately and take our readings. When we first meet, we experience a trapped feeling, as if we had walked into a cage of racial expectations that would rob us of our individuality by reducing us to an exclusively racial dimension. We are a threat, at first, to one another's uniqueness. I have seen the same well-dressed black woman in the supermarket for more than a year now. We do not speak, and we usually pretend not to see each other. But, when we turn a corner suddenly and find ourselves staring squarely into each other's eyes, her face freezes and she moves on. I believe she is insisting that both of us be more than black—that we interact only when we have a reason other than the mere fact of our race. Her chilliness enforces a priority I agree with—individuality over group identity.

But I believe I see something else in this woman that I also see in myself and in many other middle-class blacks. It is a kind of race fatigue, a deep weariness with things racial, which comes from the fact that our lives are more integrated than they have ever been before. Race does not determine our fates as powerfully as it once did, which means it is not the vital personal concern it once was. Before the sixties, race set the boundaries of black life. Now, especially for middle-class blacks, it is far less a factor, though we don't always like to admit it. Blacks still suffer from racism, so we must be concerned, but this need to be concerned with what is not so personally urgent makes for race fatigue.

I have a friend who did poorly in the insurance business for years. "People won't buy insurance from a black man," he always said. Two years ago another black man and a black woman joined his office. Almost immediately both did twice the business my friend was doing, with the same largely white client base.

Integration shock is essentially the shock of being suddenly accountable on strictly personal terms. It occurs in situations that disallow race as an excuse for personal shortcomings and it therefore exposes vulnerabilities that previously were hidden. One response to such shock is to face up to the self-confrontation it brings and then to act on the basis of what we learn about ourselves. After some struggle, my friend was able to do this. He completely revised his sales technique, asked himself some hard questions about his motivation, and resolved to work harder.

But when one lacks the courage to face oneself fully, a fear of hidden vulnerabilities triggers a fright-flight response to integration shock. Instead of admitting that racism has declined, we argue all the harder that it is still alive and more insidious than ever. We hold race up to shield us from what we do not want to see in ourselves. My friend did this at first, saying that the two blacks in this office were doing better than he was because they knew how to "kiss white ass." Here he was *race-holding,* using race to keep from looking at himself.

Recently I read an article in the local paper that explored the question of whether blacks could feel comfortable living in the largely white Silicon Valley. The article focused on a black family that had been living for more than a decade in Saratoga, a very well-to-do white community. Their neighborhood, their children's schools, their places of employment, their shopping areas and parks—their entire physical environment—were populated by affluent whites. Yet during the interview the wife said they had made two firm rules for their children: that they go to all-black colleges back east and that they do "no dating outside the race, period."

I have pushed enough black history and culture on my own children to be able to identify with the impulse behind the first of these rules. Black children in largely white situations must understand and appreciate their cultural background. But the rigidity of these rules, not to mention the rules themselves, points to more than a concern with transmitting heritage or gaining experience with other blacks. Rigidity arises from fear and self-doubt. These people, I believe, were afraid of something.

What was striking to me about their rules, especially the one prohibiting interracial dating, was their tone of rejection. The black parents seemed as determined to reject the white world as to embrace the black one. Why? I would say because of integration shock. Their integrated lives have opened up vulnerabilities they do not wish to face. But what vulnerabilities? In this case, I think, a particularly embarrassing one. On some level, I suspect, they doubt whether they are as good as the white people who live around them. You cannot be raised in a culture that was for centuries committed to the notion of your inferiority and not have some doubt in this regard—doubt that is likely to be aggravated most in integrated situations. So the rejecting tone of their rules is self-protective: *I will reject you before you have a chance to reject me.* But all of this is covered over by race. The high value of racial pride is invoked to shield them from a doubt that they are afraid to acknowledge. Unacknowledged, this doubt gains a negative power inside the personality that expresses itself in the rigidity and absolutism of their rules. Repressed fears tend always to escalate their campaign for our attention by pushing us further and further into irrationality and rigidity.

The refusal to see something unflattering in ourselves always triggers the snap from race fatigue to race-holding. And once that happens, we are caught, like this family, in a jumble of racial ironies. The parents in Saratoga, who have chosen to live integrated lives, impose a kind of segregation on their children. Rules that would be racist in the mouth of any white person are created and enforced with pride. Their unexamined self-doubt also leaves them unable to exploit fully the freedom they have attained. Race fatigue makes them run to a place like Saratoga, but integration shock makes them hold race protectively. They end up clinging to what they've run from.

• • •

Once race-holding is triggered by fear, it ensnares us in a web of self-defeating attitudes that end up circumventing the new freedoms we've won over the past several decades. I have seen its corrosive effects in my own life and in the lives of virtually every black person I've known. Some are only mildly touched by it, while others seem incapacitated by it. But race-holding is as unavoidable as defensiveness itself, and I am convinced that it is one of the most debilitating, yet unrecognized, forces in black life today.

I define a *holding* as any self-description that serves to justify or camouflage a person's fears, weaknesses, and inadequacies. Holdings are the little and big exaggerations, distortions, and lies about ourselves that prop us up and let us move along the compromised paths we follow. They develop to defend against threats to our self-esteem, threats that make us feel vulnerable and that plant a seed of fear. This fear can work like wind on a brushfire, spreading self-doubt far beyond what the initial threat would warrant, so that we become even more weakened and more needy of holdings. Since holdings justify our reticence and cowardice, they are usually expressed in the form of high belief or earthy wisdom. A man whose business fails from his own indifference holds an image of himself as a man too honest to be a good businessman—a self-description that draws a veil over his weakness.

For some years I have noticed that I can walk into any of my classes on the first day of the semester, identify the black students, and be sadly confident that on the last day of the semester a disproportionate number of them will be at the bottom of the class, far behind any number of white students of equal or even lesser native ability. More to the point, they will have performed far beneath their own native ability. Self-fulfilling prophesy theory says that their schools have always expected them to do poorly, and that they have internalized this message and *done* poorly. But this deterministic theory sees blacks only as victims, without any margin of choice. It cannot fully explain the poor performances of these black students because it identifies only the forces that *pressure* them to do poorly. By overlooking the margin of choice open to them, this theory fails to recognize the degree to which they are responsible for their own poor showing. (The irony of this oversight is that it takes the power for positive change away from the students and puts it in the hands of the very institutions that failed them in the first place.)

The theory of race-holding is based on the assumption that a margin of choice is always open to blacks (even slaves had some choice). And it tries to make clear the mechanisms by which we relinquish that choice in the name of race. With the decline in racism the margin of black choice has greatly expanded, which is probably why race-holding is so much more visible today than ever before. But anything that prevents us from exploiting our new freedom to the fullest is now as serious a barrier to us as racism once was.

The self-fulfilling prophesy theory is no doubt correct that black students, like the ones I regularly see, internalize a message of inferiority that they receive from school and the larger society around them. But the relevant question in the 1990s is why they *choose* to internalize this view of themselves. Why do they voluntarily perceive themselves as inferior? We can talk about the weakened black family and countless other scars of oppression and poverty. And certainly these things have much to do with the image these students have of themselves. But they do not fully explain this self-image because none of them entirely eliminates the margin of choice that remains open. Choice lives in even the most blighted circumstances, and it certainly lives in the lives of these black college students.

I think they *choose* to believe in their inferiority, not to fulfill society's prophesy about them, but for the comforts and rationalizations their racial "inferiority" affords them. They hold their race to evade individual responsibility. Their margin of choice scares them, as it does all people. They are naturally intimidated by that eternal tussle between the freedom to act and the responsibility we must take for our actions. To some extent all of us balk in the face of this. The difference is that these students use their race to conceal the fact that they are balking. Their "inferiority" shields them from having to see that they are afraid of all-out competition with white students. And it isn't even an honest inferiority. I don't think they really believe it. It is a false inferiority, *chosen* over an honest and productive confrontation with white students and with their real fears—a strategy that allows them to stay comfortably on the sidelines in a university environment that all but showers them with opportunity.

"I'm doing okay for a black student," a student once told me. "I'm doing well considering where I came from," I have told myself. Race allows us both to hide from the real question, which is, "Am I doing what I can, considering my talents and energies?"

I see all of this as pretty much a subconscious process, fear working on a subterranean level to let us reduce our margin of choice in the name of race. Consciously, we tell ourselves that we are only identifying with our race, but fear bloats our racial identity to an unnatural size and then uses it as cover for its subversive work. The more severe the integration shock, the more fear cover is needed.

Doesn't race enhance individuality? I think it does, but only when individuality is nurtured and developed apart from race. The race-holder, inside the bubble of his separate self, feels inadequate or insecure and then seeks reassurance through race. When, instead, a sense of self arises from individual achievement and self-realization. When self-esteem is established apart from race, then racial identity can only enhance because it is no longer needed for any other purpose.

The word *individualism* began to connote selfishness and even betrayal for many blacks during the sixties. Individualism was seen as a threat to the solidarity blacks needed during those years of social confrontation. Despite the decline in racism, these connotations have lingered. Race-holding keeps them alive because they serve the race-holder's need to exaggerate the importance of race as well as to justify a fear of individual responsibility. Race-holding makes fluid the boundary between race and self, group and individual identity, so that race can swing over at a moment's notice and fill in where fears leave a vacuum.

This is a worse problem than is at first apparent because the individual is the seat of all energy, creativity, motivation, and power. We are most strongly motivated when we want something for ourselves. When our personal wants are best achieved through group action, as in the civil rights movement, we lend our energy to the group, and it becomes as strong as the sum of our energies. When the need for group action recedes, more energy is available to us as individuals. But race-holding intercedes here by affixing the race-holder too tightly to this racial identity and by causing him to see the locus of power in race rather than in himself. In this way race-holding corrupts the greatest source of power and strength available to blacks—the energy latent in our personal desires.

One of my favorite passages in Ralph Ellison's *Invisible Man* is his description of the problem of blacks as

> not actually one of creating the uncreated conscience of [our] race, but of creating the *uncreated features of [our] face.* Our task is that of making ourselves individuals. . . . We create the race by creating ourselves and then to our great astonishment we will have created something far more important: we will have created a culture.

These lines hold up well, more than thirty years after they were written. They seem to suggest a kind of Adam Smith vision of culture: When the individual makes himself, he makes culture. An "invisible hand" uses individual effort to define and broaden culture. In the 1990s we blacks are more than ever in a position where our common good will best be served by the determined pursuit of our most personal aspirations.

I think the means to this, and the answer to race-holding generally, is personal responsibility, a source of great power that race-holding does its best to conceal. . . .

White Guilt

I don't remember hearing the phrase "white guilt" very much before the mid-sixties. Growing up black in the fifties, I never had the impression that whites were much disturbed by guilt when it came to blacks. When I would stray into the wrong restaurant in pursuit of a hamburger, it didn't occur to me that the waitress was unduly troubled by guilt when she asked me to leave. I can see now that possibly she was, but then all I saw was her irritability at having to carry out so unpleasant a task. If there was guilt, it was mine for having made an imposition of myself. Frankly, I can remember feeling a certain sympathy for such people, as if *I* was victimizing *them* by drawing them out of an innocent anonymity into the unasked-for role of racial policemen. Occasionally, they came right out and asked me to feel sorry for them. A caddy master at a country club told my brother and me that he was doing us a favor by not letting us caddy at this white club, and that we should try to understand his position, "put yourselves in my shoes." Our color had brought this man anguish and, if a part of that anguish was guilt, it was not as immediate to me as my own guilt. I smiled at the man to let him know he shouldn't feel bad and then began the long walk home. Certainly, I also judged him a coward, but in that era his cowardice was something I had to absorb.

In the sixties, particularly the black-is-beautiful late sixties, this sort of absorption was no longer necessary. The lines of moral power, like plates in the earth, had shifted. White guilt became so palpable you could see it on people. At the time, what it looked like to my eyes was a remarkable loss of authority. And what whites lost in authority, blacks gained. You cannot feel guilty toward anyone without giving away power to them. So, suddenly, this huge vulnerability opened up in whites and, as a black, you had the power to step right into it. In fact, black power all but demanded that you do so. What shocked me in the late sixties, after the helplessness I had felt in the fifties, was that guilt had changed the nature of the white man's burden from the administration of inferiors to the uplift of equals, from the obligations of dominance to the urgencies of repentance.

I think what made the difference between the fifties and sixties, as far as white guilt was concerned, was that whites in the sixties underwent an archetypal Fall. Because of the immense turmoil of the civil rights movement, and later the black power movement, whites were confronted for more than a decade with their willingness to participate in or comply with the oppression of blacks, their indifference to human suffering and denigration, their capacity to abide evil for their own benefit, and in defiance of their own sacred principles. The 1964 Civil Rights Act that bestowed equality under the law on blacks was also, in a certain sense, an admission of white guilt. Had white society not been wrong, there would have been no need for such an act. In this act, the nation acknowledged its fallen state, its lack of racial innocence, and confronted the incriminating self-knowledge that it had rationalized flagrant injustice. Denial is a common way of handling guilt, but in the sixties there was little will left for denial except in the most recalcitrant whites. And with this defense lost, there was really only one road back to innocence—through actions and policies that would bring redemption.

I believe that in the sixties the need for white redemption from racial guilt became the most powerful, yet unspoken, element in America's social-policy-making process, first giving rise to the Great Society and then to a series of programs, policies, and laws that sought to make black equality and restitution a national mission. Once America could no longer deny guilt, it went after redemption, or at least the look of redemption, with a vengeance. Yet today, some twenty years later, study after study tells us that, by many measures, the gap between blacks and whites is widening rather than narrowing. A University of Chicago study indicates that segregation is more entrenched in American cities today than ever imagined. A National Research Council study says the "status of blacks relative to whites (in housing and education) has stagnated or regressed since the early seventies." A follow-up to the famous Kerner Commission Report says we are as much at risk today of becoming a "nation within a nation" as we were twenty years ago when the original report was made.

I think the white need for redemption has contributed to this tragic situation by shaping our policies regarding blacks in ways that might deliver the look of innocence to society and its institutions, but that do very little to actually uplift blacks. Specifically, the effect of this hidden need has been to bend social policy more toward reparation for black oppression than toward the much harder and more mundane work of black uplift and development. Rather than facilitate the development of blacks to parity with whites, these programs and policies—affirmative action is a good example—have tended to give blacks special entitlements that in many cases are of no use because we lack the development that would put us in a position to take advantage of them. I think the reason there has been more entitlement than development is (along with black power) the unacknowledged white need for redemption—not true redemption, which would have focused policy on black development, but the appearance of redemption which requires only that society, in the name of development, seem to be paying back its former victims with preferences. One of the effects of entitlements, I believe, has been to encourage in blacks a dependency both on the entitlements and on the white guilt that generates them. Even when it serves ideal justice, bounty from another man's guilt weakens. This is not the only factor in black "stagnation" and "regression," but I do believe it is one factor.

• • •

It is easy enough to say that white guilt too often has the effect of bending social policies in the wrong direction. But what exactly is this guilt, and how does it work in American life?

I think that white guilt, in its broad sense, springs from a *knowledge* of ill-gotten advantage. More precisely, it comes from the juxtaposition of this knowledge with the inevitable gratitude one feels for being white rather than black in America. Given the moral instincts of human beings, it is all but impossible to enjoy an ill-gotten advantage, much less to feel at least secretly grateful for it, without consciously or unconsciously experiencing guilt. If, as Kierkegaard says, "innocence is ignorance," then guilt must always involve knowledge. White Americans *know* that their historical advantage comes from the subjugation of an entire people. So, even for whites today for whom racism is anathema, there is no escape from the knowledge that makes for guilt. Racial guilt simply accompanies the condition of being white in America.

I do not believe that this guilt is a crushing anguish for most whites, but I do believe it constitutes an ongoing racial vulnerability, an openness to racial culpability, that is a thread in white life, sometimes felt, sometimes not, but ever present as a potential feeling. In the late sixties almost any black could charge this thread with enough current for a white to feel it. I had a friend who developed this activity into a sort of specialty. I don't think he meant to be mean, though certainly he was mean. I think he was, in that hyperbolic era, exhilarated by the discovery that his race, which had long been a liability, now gave him a certain edge—that white guilt was black power. To feel this power he would sometimes set up what he called "race experiments." Once I watched him stop a white businessman in a large hotel men's room and convince him to increase his tip to the black attendant from one to twenty dollars.

My friend's tact in this was very simple, even corny. Out of the attendant's earshot he asked the man to simply look at the attendant, a frail, elderly, and very dark man in a starched white smock that made the skin on his neck and face look as leathery as a turtle's. He sat listlessly, pathetically, on a straight-backed chair next to a small table on which sat a stack of hand towels and a silver plate for tips. Since he offered no service beyond the handing out of towels, one could only conclude the hotel management offered his lowly presence as flattery to their patrons, as an opportunity for that easy noblesse oblige that could reassure even the harried, wrung-out traveling salesman of his superior station. My friend was quick to make this point to the businessman and to say that no white man would do in this job. But when the businessman put the single back in his wallet and took out a five, my friend only sneered. Did he understand the tragedy of a life spent this way, of what it must be like to earn one's paltry living as a symbol of inferiority?

And did he realize that his privilege as an affluent white businessman (ironically, he had just spent the day trying to sell a printing press to the Black Muslims for their newspaper *Muhammad Speaks*) was connected to the deprivation of this man and others like him?

But then my friend made a mistake that ended the game. In the heat of argument, which until then had only been playfully challenging, he inadvertently mentioned his father. This stopped him cold and his eyes turned inward. "What about your father?" the businessman asked. "He had a hard life, that's all." "How did he have a hard life?" Now my friend was on the defensive. I knew he did not get along with his father, a bitter man who worked nights in a factory and demanded that the house be dark and silent all day. My friend blamed his father's bitterness on racism, but I knew he had not meant to exploit his own pain in this silly "experiment." Things had gotten too close to home, but he didn't know how to get out of the situation without losing face. Now, caught in his own trap, he did what he least wanted to do. He gave forth the rage he truly felt to a white stranger in a public men's room. "My father never had a chance," he said with the kind of anger that could easily turn to tears. "He never had a fuckin' chance. Your father had all the goddamn chances, and you know he did. You sell printing presses to black people and make thousands and your father probably lives down in Fat City, Florida, somewhere, all because you're white." On and on he went in this vein, using—against all that was honorable in him—his own profound racial pain to extract a flash of guilt from a white man he didn't even know.

He got more than a flash. The businessman was touched. His eyes became mournful and finally he simply said, "You're right. Your people got a raw deal." He took a twenty-dollar bill from his wallet, then walked over and dropped it in the old man's tip plate. When he was gone my friend and I could not look at the old man, nor could we look at each other.

It is obvious that this was a rather shameful encounter for all concerned—my friend and I as his silent accomplice—trading on our racial pain, tampering with a stranger for no reason, and the stranger then buying his way out of the situation for twenty dollars, a sum that was generous by one count and cheap by another. It was not an encounter of people but of historical grudges and guilts. Yet, when I think about it now, twenty years later, I see that it had all the elements of a paradigm that I believe has been very much at the heart of racial policy-making in America since the sixties.

My friend did two things that made this businessman vulnerable to his guilt, that brought his guilt into the situation as a force. First, he put this man in touch with his own *knowledge* of his ill-gotten advantage as a white. The effect of this was to disallow the man any pretense of racial innocence, to let him know that even if he was not the sort of white who used the word *nigger* around the dinner table, he still had reason to feel racial guilt. But as disarming as this might have been, it was too abstract to do much more than crack open his vulnerability, to expose him to the logic of white guilt. This was the five-dollar intellectual sort of guilt. The twenty dollars required something more visceral. In achieving this, the second thing my friend did was something that he had not intended to do, something that ultimately brought him as much shame as he was passing out. He made a display of his own racial pain and anger. (What brought him shame was not the pain and anger but his trading on them for what turned out to be a mere twenty bucks.) The effect of this display was to reinforce the man's knowledge of ill-gotten advantage, to give credibility and solidity to it by putting a face on it. Here was human testimony, a young black beside himself at the thought of his father's racially constricted life. The pain of one man evidenced the knowledge of the other. When the businessman listened to my friend's pain, his racial guilt—normally one guilt lying dormant among others—was called out like a neglected debt he would finally have to settle. An ill-gotten advantage is not hard to bear—it can be marked up to fate—until it touches the human pain it brought into the world. This is the pain that hardens guilty knowledge.

Such knowledge is a powerful pressure when it becomes conscious. And what makes it so powerful is the element of fear that guilt always carries, fear of what the guilty knowledge says about us. Guilt makes us afraid for ourselves and so generates as much self-preoccupation as concern for others. The nature of this preoccupation is always the redemption of innocence, the reestablishment of good feeling about oneself.

In this sense, the fear for the self that is buried in all guilt is a pressure toward selfishness. It can lead us to put our own need for innocence above our concern for the problem that made us feel guilt in the first place. But this fear for the self not only inspires selfishness; it also becomes a pressure to *escape* the guilt-inducing situation. When selfishness and escapism are at work, we are no longer interested in the source of our guilt and, therefore, no longer concerned with an authentic redemption from it. Now we only want the *look* of redemption, the gesture of concern that will give us the appearance of innocence and escape from the situation. Obviously, the businessman did not put twenty dollars in the tip plate because he thought it would go to the uplift of black Americans. He did it selfishly for the appearance of concern and for the escape it afforded him.

This is not to say that guilt is never the right motive for doing good works or showing concern, only that it is a very dangerous one because of its tendency to draw us into self-preoccupation and escapism. Guilt is a civilizing emotion when the fear for the self it carries is contained—a containment that allows guilt to be more selfless and that makes genuine concern possible. I think this was the kind of guilt that, along with other forces, made the 1964 Civil Rights Act possible. But, since then, I believe too many of our social policies related to race have been shaped by the fearful underside of guilt.

Black power evoked white guilt and made it a force in American institutions, just as my friend brought it to life in the businessman. Not many volunteer for guilt. Usually, it is others that make us feel it. It was the expression of black anger and pain that hardened the guilty knowledge of white ill-gotten advantage. And black power—whether from militant fringe groups, the civil rights establishment, or big city political campaigns—knew exactly the kind of white guilt it was after. It wanted to trigger the kind of white guilt in which whites fear for their own decency and innocence; it wanted the guilt of white self-preoccupation and escapism. Always at the heart of black power, in whatever form, there has been a profound anger at what was done to blacks and an equally profound feeling that there should be reparations. But a sober white guilt in which fear for the self is contained is only good for strict fairness—the 1964 Civil Rights Act that guaranteed equality under the law. It is of little value when one is after more than fairness. So black power made it its mission to have whites fear for their innocence, to feel a visceral guilt from which they would have to seek a more profound redemption. In such redemption was the possibility of black reparation. Black power upped the ante on white guilt.

With black power, all the elements of the hidden paradigm that shapes America's race-related social policy were in place. Knowledge of ill-gotten advantage could now be evidenced and deepened by black power into the sort of guilt from which institutions could redeem themselves only by offering more than fairness—by offering forms of reparation and compensation for past injustice. I believe this was the paradigm that bent our policies toward racial entitlements at the expense of racial development. In 1964, one of the assurances that Senator Hubert Humphrey and other politicians had to give Congress in order to get the landmark Civil Rights Bill passed was that the bill would not in any way require employers to use racial preferences to rectify racial imbalances. But this was before the explosion of black power in the late sixties, before the hidden paradigm was set in motion. After black power, racial preferences became the order of the day.

If this paradigm brought blacks entitlements, it also brought us the continuation of our most profound problem in American society: our invisibility as a people. The white guilt that this paradigm elicits is the kind of guilt that preoccupies whites with their own innocence and pressures them toward escapism—twenty dollars in the plate and out the door. With this guilt, as opposed to the contained guilt of genuine concern, whites tend to see only their own need for quick redemption. Blacks, then, become a means to this redemption and, as such, they must be seen as generally "less than" others. Their needs are "special," "unique," "different." They are seen exclusively along the dimension of their victimization, so they become "different" people with whom whites can negotiate entitlements, but never fully see as people like themselves. Guilt that preoccupies people with their own innocence blinds them to those who make them feel guilty. This, of course, is not racism, and yet it has the same effect as racism since it makes blacks something of a separate species for whom normal standards and values do not automatically apply.

Nowhere is this more evident today than in American universities. At some of America's most elite universities, administrators have granted concessions in response to black student demands (black power) that all but sanction racial separatism on campus—black "theme" dorms, black students unions, black year-books, homecoming dances, and so on. I don't believe administrators sincerely believe in these separatist concessions. Most of them are liberals who see racial separatism as wrong. But black student demands pull them into the paradigm of self-preoccupied white guilt whereby they seek a quick redemption by offering special entitlements that go beyond fairness. In this black students become invisible to them. Though blacks have the lowest grade point average of any group in American universities, administrators never sit down with them and "demand" in kind that they bring their grades up to par. The paradigm of white guilt makes the real problems of black students secondary to the need for white redemption. It also cuts these administrators off from their own values, which would most certainly discourage racial separatism and encourage higher black performance. Lastly, it makes for escapist policies; there is little difference between giving black students a separate graduation ceremony or student lounge and leaving twenty dollars in the tip plate on the way out the door. . . .

3

The Scar of Race

PAUL M. SNIDERMAN

THOMAS PIAZZA

1. Introduction

The deepest obstacle to understanding the new politics of race—to recognizing what the conflicts over race are now about—is the universal, if unspoken, assumption that we already understand the place of race in contemporary America. But what we understand is the way the world was a generation ago, a world brilliantly described in the 1940s by Gunnar Myrdal in his classic work *An American Dilemma*. Its message has come to serve as the central, if customarily silent, premise of over a quarter-century of social analysis, public policy, and judicial decision. The dilemma of race, in Myrdal's view, was indeed a "problem in the heart of the American." As he wrote in a much-quoted passage:

> It is there that the interracial tension has its focus. It is there that the decisive struggle goes on. Though our study includes economic, social, and political race relations, at bottom our problem is the moral dilemma of the American—the conflict between the moral valuations on various levels of consciousness and generality. The "American Dilemma" is the ever-raging conflict between, on the one hand, the valuations preserved on the general plane which we shall call the "American Creed," where the American thinks, talks, and acts under the influence of high national and Christian precepts, and, on the other hand, the valuations on specific planes of individual and group living, where personal and local interests; economic, social, and sexual jealousies; considerations of community prestige and conformity; group prejudice against particular persons or types of people; and all sorts of miscellaneous wants, impulses, and habits dominate his outlook.

For Myrdal, the deepest-lying dynamics of race are not political, economic, social, but moral. Race excites conflict, but conflict of a specific kind: not one American against another American, not even one group of Americans against another group, but each American against himself. On one side of the struggle are liberty, equality, fair play—general valuations "which refer to man as such and not to any

44

particular group or temporary situation"; on the other side are specific valuations "which refer to various smaller groups of mankind or to particular occasions commonly referred to as 'irrational' or 'prejudiced.'" Specific valuations may have the backing of custom or self-interest, but the general valuations have the backing of the American Creed itself. The fundamental principles of the Creed—liberty and equality, the dignity of the individual, the consent of the governed—have become identified with the very idea of America. As Myrdal writes, when the American "worships the Constitution, it is an act of American nationalism, and in this the American Creed is inextricably blended. The liberal Creed, even in its dynamic formulation by Jefferson, is adhered to by every American." Can there be any doubt, then, that in the event of conflict, it is the specific valuations and not the larger Creed that will give way?

Myrdal was alive to the complexity of the conflict between the Creed and race prejudice; indeed, he called attention precisely to the common effort to avoid awareness of conflict between the two, emphasizing that "the whole issue is enveloped in opportune ignorance and unconcernedness on the part of whites." Yet, having acknowledged this, he exploded the idea that white Americans' devotion to the Creed is a matter merely of hypocrisy, that they pay only lip service to the values of liberty and equality, pointing out that

> the true hypocrite sins in secret. The American, on the contrary, is strongly and sincerely "against sin," even, and not least, his own sins. He investigates his faults, shouts them from the housetops. If all the world is well informed about the political corruption, organized crime, and faltering system of justice in America, it is primarily not due to its malice but to American publicity about its own imperfections. America's handling of the Negro problem has been criticized most emphatically by white Americans since long before the Revolution, and the criticism has steadily gone on and will not stop until America has completely reformed itself.

For Myrdal, the triumph of the Creed over prejudice was assured over the long run.

Myrdal's conception of an American dilemma brought the politics of race a generation ago into focus, becoming part of the American intellectual heritage. But every inheritance, while conferring a possession, exacts a cost. Most observers today continue to view the problem of race through the lens of Myrdal's argument, seeing the clash over race as a conflict between liberty and equality on the one side and prejudice and self-interest on the other. It remains partly that, but only partly. As we will demonstrate in the chapters that follow, there now is not one issue of race but a number of issues, and the terms of their debate, the swirl of sentiments moving people toward support or opposition, differ significantly from one issue to the next.

In Myrdal's America it was sensible to speak of *the* issue of race. It presented itself, to be sure, in a variety of specific ways. Should blacks be free to compete for the same jobs, on the same terms, as whites? Ought blacks to have the right to live wherever they can afford, just the same as whites? Should black and white children be allowed to go to the same school? But underlying these specific issues, and shaping peoples' reactions to them, was one fundamental question: Should black Americans enjoy the same rights as white Americans, or should they be segregated and oppressed by force of law? In contrast, as we will show, the key to the contemporary politics of race is that there is no longer *one* issue of race but a number of distinct issues, and the politics of these issues differ in telling ways: in the line-up of proponents and opponents; in the forces moving people in one direction or the other; and not least, in the ease or difficulty with which white Americans can be persuaded to change the positions they have taken. A quarter-century ago, what counted was who a policy would benefit, blacks or whites; now, what counts as much, or more, is what the policy aims to accomplish and how it proposes to go about accomplishing it.

To say that racial policies set the terms for arguments over race now is also to say that race *per se* matters less. Prejudice has not disappeared, and in particular circumstances and segments of the society it still has a major impact. But race prejudice no longer organizes and dominates the reactions of whites; it no longer leads large numbers of them to oppose public policies to assist blacks across-the-board. It is, as we shall show, simply wrong to suppose that the primary factor driving the contemporary arguments over the politics of race is white racism.

In saying this, we are not at all crossing swords with thoughtful observers who hear the suspicion, anger, and resentment on all sides of the racial divide nowadays. On the contrary, we shall make a considerable effort to establish the continuing prevalence of stigmatizing images of blacks. For example, strikingly large numbers of whites—and blacks—perceive blacks to be failing to make a genuine effort to deal with their problems, and they are perfectly willing to say it publicly. But the arguments over race now cut at new angles. To treat the politics of race as though it is only about race and not about politics misrepresents the nature of contemporary disagreements over issues of race. This study accordingly represents an effort, above all, to make clear *what* Americans are disagreeing over now—not a generation ago—and *why*.

. . . A generation ago, one basic line of division ran through the American public, separating opponents and proponents of public policies intended to assist blacks—regardless of what the particular policies aimed to accomplish or how they proposed to accomplish it. Now, different lines of cleavage run across different issues. Arguments over government spending are not the same as arguments over affirmative action, and neither are interchangeable with arguments over fair housing. Yet the language in which we talk about race has remained the same. And just because the words and habits of thought are so familiar, we fail to recognize we are intermixing different problems, confusing different arguments, in the end leading more than a few to conclude that disagreements over race represent not principled differences but bad faith.

No aspect of the problem of race in American life is more often discussed, or less well understood, than the standing of blacks in the popular culture. It has become nearly a cliché to talk about how white racism is now subtle, and how whites are now reluctant to publicly express negative views of blacks, all by way of trying to establish that a problem of racism still persists; it has just gone underground. But if you want to understand how whites feel about blacks, you must listen to what they actually say. Contrary to fashionable opinion, whites are not reticent about commenting negatively about blacks. Large numbers of them—on occasion a majority even in an especially affluent and uncommonly liberal part of the country—will express frankly negative evaluations of blacks, even to a total stranger.

What is behind this? Some contemporary observers have broken away from the liberal consensus that has shaped the discussion of race since Myrdal. Turning him on his head, they contend that a new racism has entered mainstream America, a racism whose wellsprings are the very values on which Americans pride themselves: hard work, individual initiative, self-reliance—in a word, individualism. Much scholarly effort has gone into this work on the new racism, and still more concern for the well-being of blacks, but . . . the view that mainstream American values foster racism confuses two kinds of traditional values. The traditional American value of individualism does not foster either antipathy to blacks or opposition to public policies intended to help them; on the other hand, traditional authoritarian values like obedience and conformity promote both.

To talk candidly about the problem of prejudice has become difficult. For both straightforward and subtle reasons, many feel the need to insist that the contemporary conflict over racial policies is still being driven by bigotry, both openly expressed and covert; that white racism remains a dominating force in our culture; that opposition to any policy intended to assist blacks is, in itself, proof of race prejudice. All this is wrong; and we shall demonstrate it to be wrong. It has, however, had a corrupting effect. On the one hand, the attribution of the term "racist" has become indiscriminate. At public meetings, it has become routine for opponents to silence those questioning a racial policy—for example, speech codes at universities or hearings on minority set-asides in municipal contracts—by labeling them racist. For that matter, it is not uncommon even for scholars to charge, in a blanket indictment, that opposition to affirmative action is, in and of itself, proof of bigotry. The demagogic use of the charge of prejudice has done much to poison the contemporary discussion of race, persuading many scholars as well as citizens that the concept of prejudice has lost any serious meaning and become no more than a term of political abuse.

One of our primary objectives, accordingly, is to demonstrate that prejudice still matters politically. Because the use of the term has become so politicized, we have made a special effort to demonstrate that prejudice, in the straightforward sense of outright antipathy to those who are different by virtue of the color of their skin or their religious orientation, remains with us. Indeed, one of the best ways to tell how whites feel about blacks . . . is to find out how they feel about Jews. Unreasoning aversion to others merely on the ground of a difference in their appearance or religion *does* carry through to people's political views, significantly influencing the positions they take on issues of race.

This study documents—for the first time—not just how white Americans feel about black Americans, but the extent to which whites continue to practice a racial double standard against blacks. Our "laid-off worker" experiment and "equal opportunity" experiment . . . help us to identify when racial double standards manifest themselves and, as important, when they don't. But the larger theme uncovered by these two experiments is the positive role of education. Many critics have charged that schooling does not genuinely encourage racial tolerance and open-mindedness; it merely teaches people the right thing to say. Our findings . . . will show that this cynicism about education is wrong. Education is the institution of contemporary American society that fights the actual practice of racial double standards more effectively than any other.

The contemporary discussion of race confuses what white Americans think about blacks with what they think about public policies dealing with blacks. The two are not the same. It would be comforting to think that the clash over the place of race in American public life would disappear if only bigotry could be overcome. But the problem is more complex. For example, prejudice is one cause of the perception of blacks as more violent than whites. But it is far from true that every person who perceives blacks as more violent is a bigot. On the contrary, many people—including many blacks—do so because it fits their personal experience or their impressions picked up through the mass media. And, ironically, negative racial stereotypes would matter less politically if they were only an expression of prejudice. . . .

To focus only on racism in offering an account of the politics of race omits politics itself. People's reactions to a particular policy are presumed to be a product of social and economic factors—how they make their living, when and where they were raised and hence how they were socialized, how they feel about blacks—indeed, nearly every factor *except the policy itself*. But to give an account of people's reactions without taking into account what they are reacting *to* is misleading in a fundamental way. The presumption that whites' objections to racial quotas or preferential treatment as unfair is a smokescreen, intended to disguise either their racism or their fear that they will lose the privileges they illegitimately enjoy because of the racism of others, has led many observers to read the politics of affirmative action exactly the wrong way around. Certainly some whites dislike affirmative action because they dislike blacks (a racial bigot is not going to be a champion of racial quotas in behalf of blacks). But, as our "mere mention" experiment will show, it is unfortunately also true that a number of whites dislike the idea of affirmative action so much and perceive it to be so unfair that they have come to dislike blacks as a consequence. Hence the special irony of the contemporary politics of race. In the very effort to make things better, we have made some things worse. Strong arguments can be made in behalf of affirmative action, but its political price must also be recognized. Wishing to close the racial divide in America, we have widened it.

But to reduce the contemporary politics of race to affirmative action would be as serious a mistake as reducing it to racism. The most important feature of race as an issue in American public life today, we want to urge, is the diversity it manifests at every level. The most straightforward, yet curiously the most neglected, example of the diversity of contemporary racial politics is the strikingly different levels of public support different racial policies enjoy. Some policies—like affirmative action or busing—are supported by only a small fraction of the public, often on the order of only one in five or fewer. Other racial policies—like direct government assistance or antidiscrimination laws—command the support of a majority of whites. Moreover, not only do different racial policies enjoy different levels of public support, but also the factors underlying whites' racial policy positions differ in significant ways from one type of racial policy to another. . . . A swirl of forces—political ideology, prejudice, ideas of fairness and effort—are at work to shape the public's reactions to specific racial policies, and their relative importance varies twice over. It varies, first, from one racial issue to another, and second, even for the very same issue, from one part of American society to another.

The contemporary politics of race is complex, but it is not chaotic. It has a form, albeit a complex form. Every racial issue is not different from every other; rather, specific issues of race take on their defining characteristics depending on the larger policy agenda to which they belong.

We shall focus on three of these policy agendas: the social welfare agenda, which centers on the provision of income, services, and training to improve the economic and social circumstances of blacks; the equal treatment agenda, which centers on banning deliberate discrimination based on race; and the race-conscious agenda, which centers on awarding preferential treatment to blacks to compensate for past discrimination. Their politics are not completely divorced. There are common elements, due partly to the thin slice of the white public still obdurately opposed to any effort to assist blacks, due still more significantly to the thicker slice ready to back a range of racial policies to make things go better for blacks. Yet, the fundamental point is that the politics of social welfare is not the same as the politics of affirmative action, and the politics of fair housing differs from both.

The politics of the three racial agendas differ in levels of popular support, in the line-up of proponents and opponents, and in the configuration of social and economic forces that incline ordinary Americans to take one or the other side of a specific racial issue. And for that very reason, the politics of the three agendas differ in yet another and politically still more consequential way—namely, in the willingness of people to change their minds about a given issue.

The fact that the positions whites take on racial issues are pliable—that large numbers of them may be readily induced to change their stand given only a relatively slight pressure to do so—has gone virtually unsuspected. It has been taken for granted that however hazy ordinary citizens' views are on many issues of the day, when it comes to race they know which side of the fence they're on—and, apart from those affecting a concern they do not genuinely feel for the welfare of blacks, that is where they are going to stay. It has simply been assumed that on issues of race the positions of white Americans are fixed.

This unspoken—and . . . quite erroneous—assumption of fixity has hidden a vital feature of the contemporary politics of race. Believing that whites are more or less wedded to their positions on issues of race, political and civic leaders have concluded there is very little room for maneuver—or, indeed, very little point to it. Why calculate whether one's appeal and tactics on an issue will be persuasive if whites' minds are closed to any appeal to rethink their views on race?

Americans *are* dug in on some issues of race, affirmative action being a paradigmatic example. But the common impression of the American public as divided into two more or less fixed armies clashing over race is fundamentally mistaken. On many issues, whites are not stuck in place. They are open to arguments against their point of view. Their positions are subject to change. . . .

2. Covert Racism and Double Standards

The charge of covert racism has become commonplace. People who oppose affirmative action are, for that reason alone, said to be racists, and people who oppose labeling others as racist on grounds like these are, for that reason alone, said to be racists themselves. The odiousness of the accusation, plus its vagueness, has had a chilling effect on intellectual discussion of the place of race in American life. Ironically, however, the very willingness to announce that racism—in its covert, disguised form—is oppressive everywhere in American life has encouraged the counterbelief that in reality it no longer exists in any significant degree anywhere. The over-readiness to make blanket charges of racism—against people, points of view, institutions—has had an effect very nearly the opposite of the one intended. How seriously can one take the idea of racism if everyone is said to be a racist?

The suggestion that there is a new racism—a racism that has new strength precisely because it doesn't appear to be racism—deserves serious consideration. If true, it shows that an irrational animus against blacks remains more pervasive than many have been willing to acknowledge. If false, it teaches the no less valuable lesson that a sensitivity to racism, commendable in itself, can have pernicious consequences. Pernicious twice over. To label American values and institutions as racist—when they are *not*—impeaches the very values and institutions that can help overcome racism. And seeing racism where it is not has hidden where it *is*.

Our aim is to explore the extent to which, and the conditions under which, ordinary Americans practice a double standard in determining who is entitled to a public benefit or government service. If asked in the abstract, most Americans would agree that it is wrong for the government to offer assistance to white Americans and then deny exactly the same help to black Americans. But we shall demonstrate that nonetheless a significant number of whites still enforce a racial double standard. In an era in which allegations of racism have become so indiscriminate and self-serving, it is important, we believe, to demonstrate that clear-cut violations of common standards of fair play persist. How many whites will deny a public benefit or service to a black that they would award to a white? When are they most likely to do so? And where in contemporary American society is the practice of racial double standards most common? These are questions that can, for the first time, be answered.

No less important, a focus on racial double standards allows us to come to grips with a fundamental paradox of race in contemporary American life. On the one hand, historic improvements have occurred. Jim Crow has become a phrase of the past, unknown—indeed, very nearly unintelligible—to most Americans under thirty. And unprecedented opportunities for blacks have opened up. A generation ago, it was the highest ambition of civil rights activists that the state be neutral on race—that it stop using its power to impose inequality on blacks; no one suspected it would exert its authority, only a few years later, to see that blacks are preferred to whites. On the other hand, the problem of race manifestly persists, not just in the sense that many blacks are immiserated, though this is surely true, but also in the sense that blacks continue to be penalized by a double standard. By way of partly resolving this paradox of progress and stasis, we shall show that there are two different realities. On the one hand, confronted with an individual who is black, whites are as likely to support the claim of an *individual* black to government assistance as that of a white—indeed, in some circumstances more likely to do so. On the other hand, confronted with blacks *as a group,* a significant number of whites practice a racial double standard. Given this duality of response, it is easier to understand why whites see themselves as living in a world where the meaning of race has changed, while blacks see themselves as living in a world where its meaning has remained much the same.

Covert Racism and Traditional American Values

For some time now commentators on public affairs have spoken of a covert racism—a racism that is disguised and subtle but real all the same. Sometimes the notion of covert racism represents no more than an effort to square what seems to be a circle: all the systematic evidence of declining bigotry notwithstanding, race obviously remains a problem in American public life, and—it therefore seems to follow—racism must still persist, albeit under the surface. But the notion of a covert racism has also been developed by the new racism researchers as a part of their self-conscious critique of mainstream American values. According to their central thesis, the overt expression of racial prejudice is now frowned upon. People therefore favor disguised, indirect ways to express their bigotry. They will not say they are opposed to blacks getting help from government because they are black; they will instead say that blacks are not trying to help themselves—and because they are not making a genuine effort on their own, they do not deserve help from others. The perception that blacks "violate cherished values," particularly the values of hard work and individual initiative, has been the spur to a new kind of racism. This new racism, by expressing itself symbolically as support for traditional American values, can disguise itself. Ironically, then, what is *new* about the new racism is its expropriation of traditional values as a cloak to hide its true nature, which consists of prejudice and bigotry. . . .

The "Laid-off Worker" Experiment

We rarely encounter the issue of race in the abstract. People find themselves on a street late at night, walking to their car, when they spot on the other side of the street male teenagers: What difference does it make if the teenagers are black? Alternatively, a person may be sitting across the desk from an applicant for a job, who has done reasonably well in school apart from a problem in attendance: What difference does it make if the applicant is black rather than white? Exactly this kind of question, applied to politics, is what we want to address. Individuals routinely make claims for a public benefit or a governmental service—for assistance in finding work, for support in obtaining a better education, for a permit authorizing a business, for an indefinite number and variety of public services—and what needs to be determined is what difference it makes to white Americans if the person requesting a particular benefit or service is black.

Whites may no longer single out a black with a PhD for rebuff, but how will they react if they have a potentially legitimate basis available to them to reject the black's claim? Suppose he has lost his job and wants assistance in finding another, but it turns out that he has not been a very dependable worker? Can they not take advantage of this blemish on his work record and, pointing to it, reject his request for assistance without having to worry about appearing racist? Or, to take a situation which supplies a similarly plausible, nonprejudiced explanation for what might be considered prejudiced behavior, suppose a black woman fails to uphold traditional family values—let's say she's a single mother. Will whites take advantage of this pretext to reject her request for government assistance?

The whole point of the covert racism idea is the claim that substantial numbers of whites, given a socially acceptable pretext, will take advantage of it and express the spite, resentment, and hostility they feel toward blacks. Ideally, then, we need to create a situation in which two people, exactly alike in every respect except for race, make a request for government assistance, and see if the request of the white is approved and that of the black is denied. And what is more, we want to accomplish this without tipping off respondents about what we're up to. The laid-off worker experiment was designed specifically to accomplish this. The basic rationale behind the experiment is this: Respondents are asked to decide whether a person who has lost his or her job is entitled to government assistance in finding another one. Some of the characteristics of the person laid off are described in the process, including whether the laid-off worker is black or white. All this is deliberately done in a way to create different circumstances which can legitimize a negative reaction to blacks. In particular, three distinct combinations of characteristics—the "lazy" black, the black who violates traditional family values, and the young, male black—were created to legitimize a negative reaction to blacks. In each case, by experimentally randomizing the characteristics of the laid-off worker, it can be authoritatively determined whether whites respond more negatively to a black—without their being in a position to know that this analysis is going on.

The laid-off worker experiment begins with an introduction announcing that the next question concerns a person "laid off because the company where he or she worked had to reduce its staff." The interviewer asks respondents to "think for a moment about the person and then tell me how much government help, if any, that person should receive while looking for a new job," and then describes the laid-off worker. Specifically, the interviewer says:

> The first person is a [WHITE or a BLACK] [MALE or FEMALE], in [HIS or HER] [EARLY TWENTIES, MID-THIRTIES, or EARLY FORTIES]. HE/SHE is [SINGLE, A SINGLE PARENT, MARRIED, MARRIED AND HAS CHILDREN] and [IS A DEPENDABLE WORKER or IS NOT A VERY DEPENDABLE WORKER].

The description of the laid-off worker is determined by computer-generated random numbers, with the value of each characteristic independently determined. The experiment is thus designed to assess the impact of a variety of personal characteristics of the laid-off worker—for example, whether the person is white or black, single or has a family—on the amount of help the person is judged to be entitled to receive from the government in finding a new job, and in addition, the impact of each combination of these characteristics. Judgments about whether the person who has lost his or her job should receive government help are scored 0 for "none at all," 5 for "some," and 10 for "a lot," so in the analysis that follows, the higher the score, the more positive (or in favor of assistance) the response. . . .

Almost by definition, a conservative is more likely than a liberal to oppose efforts to increase government spending to assist blacks, for example; indeed, is more likely to oppose a range of public policies designed to help blacks. But does it follow that the conservative is racist?

Not necessarily. His opposition to activist government may be inspired not by racism but by conservatism itself. A conservative, in the nature of things, should manifestly be more likely than a liberal to attend to the risks and the costs of bigger government bureaucracies and the like. It is simply unreasonable to insist that a conservative be as enthusiastic as a liberal about government spending for social programs or else stand convicted of being a racist.

The test of whether conservatism is now joined to racism is whether the conservative treats all claimants for government assistance alike: insofar as conservatives judge that a white is entitled to government help but a black, identically situated and making the identical claim, is not, then conservatives are racist.

By way of locating a standard of comparison, let us first consider whether people who have described themselves as liberals penalize blacks—and black males in particular—by applying a racial double standard. This is not an idle exercise. Everybody is suspected by somebody of being a racist nowadays, and liberals are not exempt from suspicion if only because of the ambivalence toward blacks they are alleged to harbor. What we found, to the contrary, is that the race of the potential beneficiary makes no difference to white liberals. On the other hand, our results suggest that the *gender* of the laid-off worker can make a difference to liberals. The mean score for government assistance when the laid-off worker is a woman is 5.8, compared with 4.8 when the person losing a job is a man. Closer examination of the results, however, makes plain what is going on. . . . Liberals are distinctly less sympathetic to the claims of white men compared with their response to women, especially to white women.

Now, let us consider the reactions of people who have described themselves as conservatives to a claim for government assistance on behalf of a person who has lost his job. The covert racism thesis predicts that conservatives will respond more negatively to a black than to a white. We found that the race of the potential beneficiary does make a difference to conservatives, but in exactly the opposite way from what the thesis predicts. Conservatives are more likely to favor government help for a black than for a white.

The gender of the potential beneficiary makes no difference to conservatives, and conservatives do not react more negatively to the claims of black males. On the contrary, they are more likely to support government assistance for a black male than for either a white male or a white female.

These findings are surely counterintuitive. Not only do conservatives not react as the covert racism thesis predicts they will react; they react in the very opposite way—favoring blacks rather than discriminating against them. But perhaps the test is too crude; perhaps it is necessary to take account of a more subtle form of racism. Conservatives may not feel free to react against blacks in all circumstances, but they may disclose a hidden animus if they are supplied with a pretext to legitimize a negative reaction. Suppose, then, that we supplied a person of conservative outlook with exactly the sort of stereotypical symbol of blacks' violation of traditional values that proponents of the new racism thesis contend excites and cloaks negative feelings about blacks? What would happen then?

One way blacks are commonly said to violate traditional values is by failing to keep the nuclear family intact. Rates of illegitimacy and single parent homes among blacks are alarmingly high, and while this may be disquieting to many, it is likely to be particularly vexatious to people with a conservative outlook.

Accordingly, in the laid-off worker experiment the person in need of assistance was sometimes (at random) identified as a black single parent.

. . . Not only do conservatives *not* react more negatively to a potential beneficiary who is black than to one who is white, they do not react more negatively to the black *even* when he or she has violated the traditional value of keeping the family intact. Indeed, conservatives favor more government help for a black single parent than for a white—regardless of whether the white is single, married, a single parent, or both married and a parent. This finding clearly contradicts the thesis of covert racism: conservatives do not take advantage of the pretext supplied them to vent their negative feelings about blacks. The covert racism thesis thus misses the mark twice over. Conservatives do not treat a claim for government assistance by a black worse than one by a white; and insofar as they do take account of the race of a potential beneficiary, it is to respond more positively, not more negatively, to blacks.

But why are conservatives more likely to favor government assistance for a black claimant than for a white one? One hint at what is going on comes from classic studies showing that responses to blacks are highly contingent on "social responsibility" cues. In one experiment, for example, subjects were presented with a picture of a black male, then asked to describe his personal characteristics. In one condition of the experiment, the man in the photograph wore a t-shirt; in the other, a tie. Wearing a t-shirt, the black was perceived to be lazy, undependable, unintelligent; wearing a tie, the very same person was perceived to be industrious, reliable, intelligent. With this classic study in mind, we designed the laid-off worker experiment to manipulate the work history of the claimant. In one condition, the claimant is described as a dependable worker; in the other, as an undependable worker.

Looking first at liberals, we found that neither the race nor the work history of the claimant is regarded as a relevant consideration in judging whether the government should assist a person who has been laid off in finding a new job. . . . It makes virtually no difference to liberals whether the person who has lost his or her job is black or white, or has been a dependable worker or an undependable worker, in making a judgment whether the claimant is entitled to assistance from the government in finding a new job.

Looking next at conservatives, we can see that they are, as we would expect, in general cool to the idea of government assistance. They are manifestly not in favor when the person who has lost his job has not been a hard worker, whether white or black. Nor are they in favor of government assistance even in the case of a white person who has been a hard worker. But they come down strikingly in favor of a lot of government help if the person who has lost a job is *both* black and a dependable worker.

What we need to explain, then, is not why conservatives react more positively to blacks in general but rather why they deviate so markedly from their conservative outlook in the particular case of a black who has been a dependable employee. . . . Conservatives are more likely than liberals to believe that blacks are not trying as hard as they could or should, more likely, that is, to see a hard-working black as an exception. "This one," they say to themselves, "is not like the others; this one is really trying." And perceiving *this* black to be an exception—perceiving him to be a person who exemplifies the values of individual effort and striving they admire—they make an exception. Thus, precisely because they think less of blacks as a group, conservatives paradoxically can wind up wanting to do more for them as individuals.

People with a conservative outlook do tend to reject the idea that an undependable black deserves to get a lot of government help in finding a new job. But of course, being conservative, they are naturally inclined to oppose government help of this kind, whoever will get it. They do not single blacks out. In fact, they are, if anything, more opposed to a white getting this help, whether a dependable worker or an undependable one. . . .

The "Equal Opportunity" Experiment

The laid-off worker experiment shows that a racial double standard is *not* applied by whites in judging whether a person who has lost a job should receive assistance from the government in finding another. But should the absence of a racial double standard in judgments of this type be taken as proof of the absence of racial discrimination more broadly?

Consider the logic of the laid-off worker experiment. It is not blacks in general that a person is asked to respond to but a particular person, one who, in addition to being black, has a specific work history, background, and distinguishing characteristics. The design of the laid-off worker experiment thus focuses attention on the individuating characteristics of a specific person, which is precisely the opposite of a situation which facilitates a stereotypical response. In contrast, consider the kind of judgments that citizens more often are asked to make about politics and race. Should government spending be increased to improve the social and economic position of blacks? Should an antidiscrimination law in housing be passed? Should admissions to colleges and universities be made partly on the basis of the applicant's race? All these are judgments not about what should be done for a specific person who happens to be black but for blacks as a group. And because people are being asked to respond, on an immediate basis and without an extended opportunity for deliberation, to blacks taken as a group, their responses are more likely to be driven by stereotypes about blacks as a group. Thus, it is easy to argue that, notwithstanding the results of the laid-off worker experiment, since conservatives are more likely to hold negative stereotypes of blacks than are liberals, conservatives may discriminate against blacks at the level of policy even if they do not discriminate against them as individuals.

The equal opportunity experiment was performed to test this hypothesis. The basic idea is to focus on a policy effort which could plausibly be made in behalf of several different groups, one of which is blacks, and then see if whites are more willing to support exactly the same program if the beneficiary is a group other than blacks. Suppose there are two groups, one of which is blacks, either of which can plausibly lay claim to a particular public benefit or governmental service. Suppose further that the second group could not plausibly make a more compelling claim than blacks to the particular benefit or service, though it could conceivably make as strong a claim. In these circumstances, we shall define as a racial double standard a significantly greater willingness to affirm that the nonblack group is entitled to the governmental benefit or service than the black group.

We focused on the government's obligation to assure equal opportunity to succeed. Respondents were not asked to support equal outcomes, only to approve of government efforts to assure equal opportunities to succeed. The two groups compared were "blacks" and "women," the pair having been chosen to assure an asymmetry in standing: it is often argued that government is under a special obligation to assist blacks, that the burden of slavery and discrimination that blacks have borne in America is a uniquely oppressive burden. It is occasionally argued that the needs of women approach those of blacks, but it is not explicitly argued by anyone that the oppression of women eclipses that of blacks, and hence that the government should work to achieve equal opportunity for women—but that it ought not to do so for blacks. We shall, accordingly, interpret more support for government intervention to assure equal opportunity for women than for blacks as evidence of a double standard.

The equal opportunity experiment thus consists in experimentally contrasting reactions to two versions of otherwise identical questions. In one version, the statement is worded:

> While equal opportunity for blacks and minorities to succeed is important, it's not really the government's job to guarantee it.

In the other version, the statement is exactly the same in all respects except one: instead of referring to blacks and minorities, it refers to women.

Consider first the responses of conservatives. . . . They are significantly more likely to favor help for women than for blacks: 45 percent of them support government guarantees of equal opportunity for women, as compared with only 28 percent for blacks. Self-identified conservatives, the results of the equal opportunity experiment demonstrate, *do* practice a racial double standard in judging the claims of groups, if not those of individuals. But so do self-identified liberals: 69 percent of them believe that government should guarantee equal opportunity for women, as compared with only 54 percent for blacks.

The outcome of the equal opportunity experiment is thus the opposite of the laid-off worker experiment. When whites react not to individual blacks but to blacks as a group, a double standard is plain, and it shows up not in one particular narrow segment but across the political spectrum. Liberals are just as likely to discriminate as conservatives. An innocent explanation of the greater support for government guarantees of equal opportunity for women than for blacks could be the greater responsiveness of women, whether liberal or conservative, to an appeal to improve the opportunities open to them. But in fact, the reactions of women and men on this issue do not differ significantly.

Proponents of the covert racism thesis most often see the danger to be predominantly on the right, but some have warned of hazards of racism on the left. For our part, this stress on ideology as a source of racism, whether oriented to the left or the right, misses the point. As the classic studies of prejudice from a generation ago drove home, intolerance is strongest precisely in those parts of society where the power of abstract ideas is weakest, that is, among those with little formal education. On the one side, the less schooling people have had, the more likely they are to exhibit the simplistic thinking, plus the diffuse anger and apprehension, that favor intolerance. On the other side, the more schooling they have had, the more likely are the larger ideas of politics, on the left or on the right, to come alive for them and guide their political judgments. . . .

3. Prejudice and Politics

Opposition to social welfare assistance, our results make plain, goes beyond the ranks of bigots. Substantial numbers of whites who are not prejudiced—as measured by the total number of negative racial stereotypes they accept—nevertheless believe that blacks could be better off if they tried harder. They are people who acknowledge that blacks have been unfairly treated in the past, and indeed still suffer some disadvantages; they are not given to belittling or derogating outgroups; but they nonetheless believe that a measure of responsibility for the problems that blacks now experience must be shouldered by blacks themselves. And this judgment carries as much weight in shaping their view of welfare assistance for blacks as it does among whites who are manifestly prejudiced.

So how do whites make decisions about whether blacks are entitled to more social welfare assistance? By judging according to the "effort principle." The person faced with problems in part of his own making, who is not making a genuine effort to deal with them, is not entitled to assistance from others. The effort principle thus involves a pair of elements—judgments about the reasons for the problem besetting a person, and judgments about the effort a person is making to overcome the problem. Both judgments can be of consequence, but the second captures the aspect of reciprocity integral to ideas of fairness: one is not obliged to make a sacrifice to make things better for others if they are not also willing to make a sacrifice to make things better for themselves; conversely, one ought to make an effort in behalf of people who are trying to make an effort in behalf of themselves. And of course, the way to tell if a person is making a genuine effort is by how hard he or she is willing to work.

Prejudice drives the opposition of whites to efforts to improve the economic and social position of blacks, in the opinion of a number of commentators, nowhere more blatantly than in the case of affirmative action—indeed, so much so that opposition to affirmative action is said to be, in and of itself, racism. . . .

The "Mere Mention" Experiment

We devised a special experiment—called the mere mention experiment—to simulate the kinds of conversations that ordinary people undoubtedly have about affirmative action and the characteristics of blacks. The basic idea is to take advantage of the power of randomization to determine whether references to affirmative action can, in and of themselves, excite negative reactions to blacks. The logic of the experiment runs like this. A random sample of a cross section of whites is randomly divided into two halves. One half is asked their view of affirmative action, then their images of blacks. The other half is asked exactly the same questions, except in the opposite order. If a dislike of affirmative action provokes a dislike of blacks, then the half of the sample of whites asked first about affirmative action should dislike blacks more than the other half. And, if the two halves are observed to differ in this way, the reason must necessarily be that the *mere mention* of affirmative action encourages dislike of blacks—necessarily so, since the two halves of the sample, being randomly composed, are alike in all respects, chance variations aside.

By affirmative action we mean not simply making an extra effort to see that qualified blacks are given consideration—which is in itself not an especially controversial policy—but rather ensuring that a predetermined proportion of jobs or college admissions go to blacks, whether or not they are the most qualified applicants. Accordingly, the question used in the experiment ran as follows:

> In a nearby state, an effort is being made to increase dramatically the number of blacks working in state government. This means that a large number of jobs will be reserved for blacks, even if their scores on merit exams are lower than those of whites who are turned down for the job. Do you favor or oppose this policy?

Notice that the question targets affirmative action not in the respondent's own state but rather in a "nearby state." The issue is framed in this way to eliminate, or at any rate to minimize, considerations of self-interest—to ensure, that is, that people do not object to affirmative action because they will themselves be cut out of a job. In the same survey, to measure whites' feelings toward blacks, we presented respondents with a number of descriptions of blacks, one half positive, the other half negative, prefacing our question with the qualification that of course no statement is true about everybody, but still, speaking generally, did they agree or disagree with these descriptions of blacks.

What we found was that merely asking whites to respond to the issue of affirmative action increases significantly the likelihood that they will perceive blacks as irresponsible and lazy. As [our research shows] 43 percent of those who had just been asked their opinion about affirmative action described blacks as irresponsible, compared with only 26 percent of those for whom the subject of affirmative action had not yet been raised—a difference that is statistically significant. Analogously, whites who have been asked about affirmative action are more likely than those who have not heard the issue explicitly mentioned to describe blacks as lazy, by a difference of 31 to 20 percent. For that matter, whites who have just been asked to react to the race-conscious agenda are more likely to describe blacks as arrogant, though this difference is not statistically significant. Merely raising the issue of affirmative action, it is plain, increases the likelihood that whites will respond more negatively to blacks, not to an overwhelming extent and not in every respect, to be sure, but discernibly and precisely in the ways that most influence the reactions of whites to other racial policies, most especially those on the social welfare agenda.

In weighing the results of the mere mention experiment, it is essential to be clear on what is *not* being argued. It would be silly—and contrary to the results of the experiment—to assert that the primary reason that most whites dislike blacks is because they dislike affirmative action. Large numbers of whites endorsed negative characterizations of blacks before affirmative action came on the scene, and indisputably if affirmative action had never been dreamt of, substantial numbers would still accept negative racial stereotypes. Affirmative action did not create the problem of prejudice.

But it can aggravate it. Indeed, in reviewing the results of the mere mention experiment and in particular in gauging the size of the effects, the point to underline is that any effect at all was observed. The whole of the experimental "manipulation," after all, consisted in asking a question in an interview—only one question, in a standard form, in an interview made up of a hundred questions. No effort was made to whip up feelings about affirmative action. Respondents were not shown the equivalent of a "Willie Horton" type advertisement. They were not even subjected to a lengthy discussion of racial quotas or preferential treatment, to arouse latent feelings they might harbor. All that was done was to ask them a single question about affirmative action "in a nearby state." And that was sufficient to excite a statistically significant response, demonstrating that dislike of particular racial policies can provoke dislike of blacks, as well as the other way around.

Racial Policies and Racial Stereotypes

We want to draw together some of the principal strands of the analysis, and in particular to consider the light this chapter's findings shed on the role of prejudice in shaping the contemporary politics of race. . . .

For framing the problem as one of prejudice suggests that the source of difficulty lies with that segment of the American public who are bigots. There remain bigots, and they are not politically well-disposed toward blacks, but if the opposition to efforts to improve the social and economic position of blacks through government action consisted only, or even primarily, of bigots, the problem of race would be far less pervasive than it is. Indeed, what we want to suggest is that, paradoxically, thinking of the problem of race politics as a problem of prejudice trivializes the difficulties, because most of the people who oppose more government spending on behalf of blacks are not bigots.

What counts in generating opposition to policies to improve the social and economic position of blacks through government action is not any old negative characterization, but particularly the stereotype of the lazy, irresponsible black. It is nastier to talk about violent blacks than lazy blacks, but the latter stereotype is far more politically consequential than the former, as we have seen. Perceive blacks as belligerent or violent—it makes little or no difference in deciding whether to support or oppose more government spending to assist them. On the other hand, perceive blacks to be failing to make a genuine effort to overcome their problems, and one will be markedly more likely to oppose social welfare programs to help blacks. And the crucial point is that precisely those negative characterizations of blacks that count for most politically are the ones most commonly in circulation; and they are most common because of the contemporary circumstances that give them the color of plausibility.

It is part of the ordinary experience of many whites to encounter blacks who are not trying as hard as they could to overcome their problems—to know, at first hand or through the media, that black children disproportionately are dropping out of school, that black females are disproportionately having illegitimate children, that black families are disproportionately on welfare. All of these are social facts—facts that are rooted ultimately in the historical exploitation that blacks have suffered. But for many the crucial point is that these *are* social facts, and increasingly facts for which blacks are seen by ordinary white citizens to have to bear some responsibility, not for the problems' having arisen in the first place but for their persisting or even getting worse. And the consequence . . . is that exceedingly high proportions of whites—and for that matter, blacks, too—perceive blacks to be failing to make a genuine effort to work hard and overcome their problems on their own. Thus the impact of this common negative characterization of blacks on the political thinking of white Americans extends beyond—well beyond—the ranks of the manifestly bigoted. . . .

Above everything else, if one wants to understand the issue of race in America in the 1990s as it actually is, it is necessary to acknowledge the complexity of the problem. Prejudice is at work, and there are still questions of race that have moral issues at their center. But the politics of race is complex, and the findings in this chapter have underlined its complexity. For one, it turns out that nasty racial stereotypes count for little politically, and less nasty ones can count for a lot. For another, although it has become fashionable to assert that opposition to affirmative action is driven by racism, as though the reason so many whites object to racial quotas and preferential treatment is prejudice pure and simple, it turns out that the politics of affirmative actions has remarkably little to do with whites' feelings toward blacks. On the other hand, although little attention has been given to the politics of bread-and-butter social welfare issues, it turns out that this is precisely the policy agenda most heavily shaped by people's negative images of blacks.

The politics of race is driven not only by racial sentiments but also by politics—indeed, to a degree, racial politics is driving racial sentiments. If whites decide their position on issues of race partly on the basis of what they think about blacks, it is also true that what they think of policies devised to assist blacks influences what they think of blacks. Politics shapes as well as reflects public opinion, as the politics of affirmative action painfully demonstrates: whites have come to think less of blacks, to be more likely to perceive them as irresponsible and lazy merely in consequence of the issue of affirmative action being brought up. With the battle to persuade whites that blacks should be treated the same as whites only partly won, the political agenda raced on, fashioning a set of policies demanding, as a matter of principle, that blacks should be treated better than whites—that a black should be admitted to a school or get a job in preference to a white even if the white has higher grades or superior work skills. The new race-conscious agenda has provoked broad outrage and resentment. Affirmative action is so intensely disliked that it has led some whites to dislike blacks—an ironic example of a policy meant to put the divide of race behind us in fact further widening it. . . .

4. Conclusion: Ironies

. . . The shape of racial politics in America has changed. Arguments over segregated schools and restrictive covenants and the poll tax were part of one overarching argument over whether blacks deserve to be treated as equals, with the position the public took on any given issue of race dictated in the largest measure by their feelings toward blacks. The battle against segregation (squabbles over issues like states' rights to one side) centered on the clash between two camps—one sympathetic to blacks, persuaded that they had been exploited and victimized, committed to the idea that they deserved equal treatment, and another camp, either indifferent to the plight of blacks or convinced of their inherent inferiority.

Today there *is* a politics to issues of race. Racial policies themselves—the specific goals they are intended to serve, and the particular means by which they propose to accomplish those goals—define significantly the structure of conflict over race. And, in consequence, the forces in play, the reasons why whites choose one or the other side of an issue of race, vary across racial issues and agendas.

Consider the role of ideology. The politics of the social welfare agenda bears the clear stamp of the classic argument in American politics between left and right. We do not mean of course that ideology drives the reactions of citizens *en bloc*. As a generation of public opinion research has made plain, overarching considerations of left and right are important chiefly to the more politically sophisticated and aware. But as we have seen, the dispute over issues such as whether government spending in behalf of blacks should be increased or blacks should take more responsibility for dealing with their own problems, particularly among the more aware and better educated part of the American public, is very much an extension of the long-running argument over government activism in behalf of the disadvantaged. It is a mistake, a deep and disfiguring mistake, to believe that racial politics does not take part in regular politics, to suppose that the clash of interests and ideas over issues of race is unique, independent of the differences that divide Americans over a range of issues.

Race prejudice *is* an ingredient of racial politics but in ways quite different from those commonly supposed. The conventional wisdom is that opposition to affirmative action is driven by racism, with the vehemence of whites' opposition to racial quotas and preferential treatment taken as proof of the tenacity of their prejudice against blacks. In fact, as we have seen, whites' feelings toward blacks are a minor factor in promoting opposition to affirmative action. Indeed, as the "mere mention" experiment demonstrated, apparent cause and effect can be reversed: dislike of affirmative action can engender dislike of blacks. In contrast to the race-conscious agenda where prejudice plays a minor role, in the social welfare agenda it is more central. The reactions of whites to racial issues on the social welfare agenda, our findings demonstrate, are powerfully shaped by their images of blacks as unwilling to make a genuine effort to deal with their own problems. Ironically, then, where racial stereotypes supposedly most inflame the thinking of whites about issues of race, their influence is weakest, and where their influence is least suspected, their impact is strongest.

At the deepest level, though, racial politics owes its shape not to beliefs or stereotypes distinctively about blacks but to the broader set of convictions about fairness and fair play that make up the American Creed. Although it never speaks with only one voice, the Creed has offered onesided support in favor of the principle of equal treatment; and policies that have as their objective seeing that blacks are treated the same as whites have the advantage of being consistent *with* the American Creed. In contrast, both proponents and opponents of social welfare policies can cite chapter and verse from the Creed legitimating their position—slightly different chapters and verses, to be sure, but equally legitimate ones all the same. Conflict over the social welfare agenda thus tends to reproduce a conflict *within* the Creed itself.

The race-conscious agenda offers yet a third variation on the relationship between race and the American Creed. Just because so many Americans are committed—imperfectly to be sure, but genuinely all the same—to the values of liberty and equality, they had no *principled* basis to object to the original civil rights movement; on the contrary, so far as the Creed was relevant, it pushed them to support equal treatment. Though there are elements of the Creed that can be deployed in favor of affirmative action, the fundamental ideas of fairness and equal treatment, for ordinary citizens, thrust in exactly the opposite direction. What gives the race-conscious agenda its distinctive character, what makes the agenda open to challenge morally, is that the principle of preferential treatment runs *against* the Creed.

Affirmative action—defined to mean preferential treatment—has become the chief item on the race-conscious agenda. It produces resentment and disaffection not because it assists blacks—substantial numbers of whites are prepared to support a range of policies to see blacks better off—but because it is judged to be unfair. Yet affirmative action is by no means the only factor encouraging racial discord. Protest over race has, perhaps inevitably but in any event tragically, been a victim of its success. A generation ago, the civil rights movement represented the moral high ground of American politics, dedicated to the values that blacks and whites share in common, and led by charismatic and courageous figures like Martin Luther King Jr. Almost immediately on the heels of its greatest successes, the Civil Rights Acts of 1964 and 1965, the voices of separatism began to drown out those of integration; and the headlines came to be dominated not by Martin Luther King Jr., but by Stokely Carmichael and H. Rap Brown, then, in the fullness of time, by Marion Barry, Tawana Brawley, and the Reverend Al Sharpton. Civil rights groups came to boycott not well-established businesses of white segregationists but tiny grocery stores run by Korean immigrants. Integration as a moral idea slipped away.

It cannot be said that the prime players in the politics of race—on any side—can claim credit for relieving racial rancor. Anger and resentment have become the common currency, as much among racial liberals as among racial conservatives. Ironically, the one-sided public focus of both on the race-conscious agenda and their comparative inattention to the agendas of social welfare and equal treatment have encouraged—subtly and unintentionally—the presumption that earlier, less ambitious, and ostensibly less controversial objectives have been substantially realized. It is thus taken for granted by many that we now find ourselves split over more ambitious policies for achieving racial equality, having worked our way through the "easy" part of the civil rights agenda focused on equal treatment. Yet the crux of the contemporary politics of race, as we have seen, consists precisely in the fact that, excepting only the issue of segregation in public institutions, all of the major issues of race—from government spending for blacks, through assurances of fair treatment in employment, to fair housing—are *still* on the table.

Of the myriad findings we have reported on contemporary American racial attitudes, the one to which we ourselves attach the most importance is the pliability of the policy positions of substantial numbers of whites on specific issues of race. It has long been assumed that whites are dug in on racial issues. In fact, large numbers of whites can be dislodged from the positions they have taken on many issues of race by calling their attention to countervailing considerations. And this underlines the quintessential feature of politics, including racial politics: majorities are not immutable facts of life permanently dictated by deep-lying social and economic forces. They are made—and unmade. A large enough number of Americans are open to argument to tip the scales, not on every issue of race but on the largest number of them. The case for public policies to assist blacks can be won; and it can be lost.

4

The Paradox of Integration: Why Whites and Blacks Seem So Divided

ORLANDO PATTERSON

The traumas of the Million Man March and the O. J. Simpson verdict have forced America to focus its gaze once again on its lingering racial crisis. In sharpening our focus, they have done at least one good. By casting too bright a light on the realities of our unfinished racial agenda, they have scrambled the sordid use of coded and covert racial rhetoric by conventional politicians. We must now call a spade a spade, and, while it is good old American politics to fan racial division while pretending the opposite, it is far too risky to appear clearly to be doing so. But what exactly is the crisis upon which we again gaze?

For African Americans, these are genuinely the best and worst of times, at least since the ending of formal Jim Crow laws. What is odd, however, is that, in the current rhetoric of race, the pain completely dominates the gain. "Pain and predicament is driving this march," cried Jesse Jackson in a by now familiar African American refrain. The orthodox view among blacks at nearly all points on the political spectrum is that relations between the races are disastrous, whether it is the left, focusing on the political neglect of the devastated ghettos, or the right, condemning the abuses of affirmative action and failed government policies. Paradoxically, it is precisely the considerable success of America's experiment in integration that makes it almost impossible for black Americans to recognize what they have achieved. This perceived lack of gratitude in turn fuels white resentment and gives public discourse on race today the bewildering quality of a dialogue of the deaf.

On the one hand, there is no denying the fact that, in absolute terms, African Americans, on average, are better off now than at any other time in their history. The civil rights movement effectively abolished the culture of post-juridical slavery, which, reinforced by racism and legalized segregation, had denied black people the basic rights of citizenship in the land of their birth. They are now very much a part of the nation's political life, occupying positions in numbers and importance that go well beyond mere ethnic representation or tokenism. Quite apart from the thousands of local and appointed offices around the country (including mayorships of some of the nation's largest cities), blacks have occupied positions of major national importance in what is now the dominant power in the world—as governors, senators and powerful members of Congress chairing major congressional committees, and as appointed officials filling some of the most important offices in the nation, including that of the head of the most powerful military machine on earth.

Even as I write, the Colin Powell phenomenon bedazzles. For the first time, a black man is being seriously considered for the nation's highest office, with his strongest support coming from people with conservative views on race. It would be ridiculous to dismiss these developments as mere tokens. What they demonstrate, beyond a doubt, is that being black is no longer a significant obstacle to participation in the public life of the nation.

What is more, blacks have also become full members of what may be called the nation's moral community and cultural life. They are no longer in the basement of moral discourse in American life, as was the case up to about thirty or forty years ago. Until then blacks were "invisible men" in the nation's consciousness, a truly debased ex-slave people. America was assumed to be a white country. The public media, the literary and artistic community, the great national debates about major issues, even those concerning poverty, simply excluded blacks from consideration. Even a liberal thinker like John Kenneth Galbraith could write a major discourse on the affluent society without much thought to their plight.

No longer. The enormity of the achievement of the last forty years in American race relations cannot be overstated. The black presence in American life and thought is today pervasive. A mere 13 percent of the population, they dominate the nation's popular culture: its music, its dance, its talk, its sports, its youths' fashion; and they are a powerful force in its popular and elite literatures. A black music, jazz, is the nation's classical voice, defining, audibly, its entire civilizational style. So powerful and unavoidable is the black popular influence that it is now not uncommon to find persons who, while remaining racists in personal relations and attitudes, nonetheless have surrendered their tastes, and their viewing and listening habits, to black entertainers, talk-show hosts and sit-com stars. The typical Oprah Winfrey viewer is a conservative, white lower-middle-class housewife; the typical rap fan, an upper-middle-class white suburban youth. The cultural influence of so small and disadvantaged a minority on the wider society that has so harshly abused it finds few parallels in the history of civilization.

Closely related to the achievement of full political and cultural citizenship has been another great success of the post-war years: the desegregation of the military between 1948 and 1965. The extraordinary progress made in eliminating all formal discrimination, and a good deal of informal prejudice in promotions, has made the military, especially the Army, a model of successful race relations for the civilian community. With more than 30 percent of Army recruits and 10 percent of its officer corps black, the Army, and to a lesser extent the other services, stands out in American society as the only arena in which blacks routinely exercise authority over whites.

Most of these developments were helped along by another revolution in black life: the rapid growth in school enrollment and achievement at all levels. In 1940 there was a four-year gap in median years of schooling between whites and blacks; by 1991 this gap had been reduced to a few months. During the same period, the proportion of blacks aged 25 to 34 completing high school almost caught up with that of whites: 84 percent compared to 87 percent.

The record is far more mixed, and indeed troubling, in the case of higher education. After rapid growth in college completion during the '70s, the numbers fell off considerably during the '80s, especially for black men. The long-term effect has been that, while the proportion of blacks completing college has grown from less than 2 percent in 1940 to almost 12.8 percent in 1994, this is still only about half the white completion rate of almost 25 percent.

Even so, a six-fold increase in college completion is nothing to sniff at. It is great absolute progress and, compared to white populations elsewhere, great relative progress. African Americans, from a condition of mass illiteracy fifty years ago, are now among the most educated persons in the world, with median years of schooling and college completion rates higher than those of most Western Europeans. The average reader might find this statement a shocking overstatement. It is not. It only sounds like an overstatement when considered in light of the relentless insistence of the advocacy community that the miseducation of black Americans is the major source of their present dilemmas.

The rise of a genuine black middle class over the past quarter of a century is another cause for celebration, although no group of persons is less likely to celebrate it than the black establishment itself. The term "black middle class" once referred dismissively to those black persons who happened to be at the top of the bottom rung: Pullman porters, head waiters, successful barbers and street-front preachers, small-time funeral parlor owners and the like. Today the term "black middle class" means that segment of the nation's middle class which happens to be black, and it is no longer dependent on a segregated economy. These are without doubt the best of times for middle-class African Americans, who own more businesses and control a greater share of the national wealth than at any other period. At the most conservative estimate, they are between a quarter and a third of the black population, which means anywhere between 8 and 10 million persons. It is a mistake to overemphasize their shaky economic base, as is routinely done. Almost all new middle classes in the history of capitalism have had precarious economic starts. Seen from a long-term perspective, the important thing to note is that the children they produce will be second- and third-generation burghers with all the confidence, educational resources and, most of all, cultural capital to find a more secure place in the nation's economy.

And yet it is also no exaggeration to say that, both subjectively and by certain objective standards, these are among the worst of times, since the ending of Jim Crow, for the African American population.

Put in the starkest terms, the bottom third of the African American population—some 10 million persons—live in dire poverty, while the bottom 10 percent or so—the so-called underclass—exist in an advanced stage of social, economic and moral disintegration. The grim statistics are now familiar to anyone who pays even the most cursory attention to the news.

Thirty-one percent of all black families (in contrast with only 8 percent of non-Hispanic whites), comprising nearly a third of all African Americans, live in poverty. This is worse than in 1969. Children disproportionately bear the brunt of impoverishment. In 1994, 46 percent of all black children lived in poverty, nearly three times that of white children, and the situation is likely to get worse. Their parents and other adult caretakers experience Depression-level unemployment. The overall unemployment rate for blacks is 14 percent, more than twice that of whites (6 percent). But this obscures the fact that unemployment is concentrated in certain areas and among the young, where it tops 40 percent.

These figures tell only part of the plight of poor children. The other, grimmer aspect of the dilemma is the growing number of children born to female children with little or no social or economic support from the biological fathers or any other man, for that matter. The resulting abusive, mal-socialization of children by mothers who were themselves abused and mal-socialized is at the heart of the social and moral chaos in what is called the underclass. The situation is one of complete social anarchy and moral nihilism, reflected in the casual devaluation of human life. Kids and young adults kill for sneakers, leather jackets, cheap jewelry and drugs; worse, they kill for no other reason than having been dissed by a wrong look or misstatement. Linked to this social and moral catastrophe are the other well-known pathologies: the high drop-out rate in inner-city high schools, the epidemic of drugs and crime resulting in a horrendous incarceration rate wherein one in three of all black men aged 25 to 29 are under the supervision of the criminal justice system. Although government action is needed, solving these problems will take considerably more than changes in government policy. Clearly, the message of the Million Man March was long overdue.

There is undoubtedly much to outrage our sense of justice, but the condition of the bottom third should not obscure the extraordinary achievements of the upper two-thirds of the black population or the progress made in race relations over the past forty years. Black leaders' near-complete disregard of these hard-won achievements is obtuse and counterproductive.

This strange tendency to more loudly lament the black predicament the better it gets can be understood as a paradox of desegregation. When blacks and whites were segregated from each other there was little opportunity for conflict. The two groups lived in largely separate worlds, and when they did come in contact their interactions were highly structured by the perverse etiquette of racial relations. The system may have worked well in minimizing conflict, as long as both groups played by the rules, but it was clearly a pernicious arrangement for blacks since it condemned them to inferior status and excluded them from participation in the political life of their society and from nearly all the more desirable opportunities for economic advancement.

Desegregation meant partial access to the far superior facilities and opportunities open previously only to whites. Hence, it entailed a great improvement in the condition and dignity of blacks. All this should be terribly obvious, but it must be spelled out because it is precisely this obvious improvement that is so often implicitly denied when we acknowledge one of the inevitable consequences of desegregation: namely that, as individuals in both groups meet more and more, the possibility for conflict is bound to increase.

Whites outnumber blacks eight to one, and this simple demographic fact has an enormous social significance often unnoticed by whites. Numerous polls have shown tremendous change in white attitudes toward blacks over the last thirty years. For example, the number of whites who hold racist beliefs, measured by unfavorable attitudes toward miscegenation, integrated housing and job equality, has declined from a majority in the '50s to a quarter of the total population today. For whites this is real progress, however one may wish to quibble over the meaning of the survey data. But, even with only a quarter of all whites holding racist beliefs, it remains the case that for every black person there are two white racists.

Furthermore, the vast majority of blacks will rarely come in contact with the 75 percent of whites who are tolerant, for simple socioeconomic reasons. More educated, more prosperous and more suburban, the tolerant three-quarters tend to live exactly where blacks are least likely to be found: in the expensive suburbs. On the other hand, it is the least educated and most prejudiced whites who tend to be in closest proximity to blacks.

Further, the behavior of the tolerant three quarters of whites, and their attempts to improve the condition of blacks, tends to intensify racist feelings among the whites most likely to come in contact with blacks. The cost of racial change is disproportionately borne by those whites who have traditionally been most hostile to blacks. Black improvement is invariably perceived as competition in the once-protected economic preserves of working-class whites. Hence, not only do racist whites continue to outnumber blacks but their racist behavior also finds more frequent and intense outlets.

Of special concern here is the behavior of law-enforcement agencies. The typical big-city police officer is the white person with whom the typical lower- and working-class black person is most likely to come in contact outside the workplace. Unfortunately, white police officers tend to come from precisely the working-class urban communities most likely to be hostile to blacks. And there is also abundant psychological evidence that they tend to conform to the authoritarian

personality type which most closely correlates with racist behavior. At the same
time, their profession brings them into contact with the most lawless members of
the black community, continuously reinforcing their prejudices.

The result is that the typical white police officer holds all blacks in suspicion
and treats them in a manner that constantly threatens their dignity and most
basic rights. In some urban communities this amounts to life under a virtual police state for many law-abiding working-class and poor black Americans. Middle-
class status makes some difference, but only in well-defined social situations. It
can sometimes even be a disadvantage. The Mark Fuhrman tapes revealed what
every bourgeois black person already knew: that in unprotected contexts—driving on the highway, visiting a white suburban friend or caught in some minor
traffic or other infraction—they are likely to find themselves specially targeted by
white police officers and detectives who resent their success and take malignant
pleasure in harassing them, especially if they are in mixed relationships.

In this context, the speedy decision of the jury in the O.J. Simpson trial makes
perfect sense. The type of lower-middle and working-class black people who sat
on the jury have every reason to believe that white police officers are racists only
too willing to plant evidence and lie in court. All this is in direct contrast to the
experience of the typical white person, who views the police officer either as a
friend or acquaintance from the neighborhood or as a protector and guardian of
the suburban peace.

What exists, then, is a serious mismatch in racial perception of change. Most
middle-class whites feel, correctly, that things have gotten much better not only in
the objective socioeconomic condition of blacks but in their improved attitude
toward blacks. The typical black person perceives and experiences the situation as
either having not changed or having gotten worse.

The experience of Massachusetts is typical. By all objective criteria this is one of
most racially liberal areas of America. Not only was it the first state to elect a black
U.S. senator since Reconstruction, but its current two senators are among the
most liberal and pro-black in the Senate. And yet, among blacks of all classes, the
Boston area has the unenviable reputation of being one of the most racist parts of
the country. Many African Americans, put off by its racist image, still refuse to
move to the area. The fears of blacks are legitimate; but so is the bewilderment of
whites in middle-class Boston or in neighboring cities such as Cambridge (arguably one of the most racially liberal cities in the nation) when black colleagues
insist they would rather go back South than settle anywhere near Boston. The sad
truth is that, even as the number of tolerant whites rapidly increased between the
'60s and '70s, the amount of contact between blacks and racist working-class
whites also increased, as did the racial animosity of these whites, expressed most
notoriously in the anti-busing violence of South Boston.

To make matters worse, the hostile reaction of a small proportion of whites not
only hurts a large proportion of blacks; but, given the adversarial and litigious nature of the culture, and the tendency of the media to highlight the exceptional, a
small but active number of whites can disproportionately influence the percep-

tion of all whites, with consequences deleterious to blacks. The current political hostility to affirmative action is a perfect case in point.

Only a small proportion of whites—7 percent, according to recent opinion-poll data—claim to have been personally affected in any way by affirmative action. Yet the point of affirmative action is to bring blacks into greater contact with whites at the workplace and other sites where they were traditionally excluded. Aggrieved whites who feel they have been passed over in preference for blacks react sharply to this experience, which in turn colors the views of many whites who are in no way influenced by the policy. The result is the "angry white male" syndrome: increased hostility toward what are perceived as unreasonable black demands, and the conviction that the vast majority of whites are being hurt—78 percent of whites think so—when, in fact, only 7 percent can actually attest to such injuries from their own experience.

The experiential mismatch between blacks and whites is made still worse by what may be called the outrage of liberation. A formerly oppressed group's sense of outrage at what has been done to it increases the more equal it becomes with its former oppressors. In part, this is simply a case of relative deprivation; in part, it is the result of having a greater voice—more literate and vocal leadership, more access to the media and so on. But it also stems from the formerly deprived group's increased sense of dignity and, ironically, its embrace of the formerly oppressive Other within its moral universe.

The slave, the sharecropping serf, the black person living under Jim Crow laws administered by vicious white police officers and prejudiced judges, were all obliged, for reasons of sheer survival, to accommodate somehow to the system. One form of accommodation was to expect and demand less from the racist oppressors. To do so was in no way to lessen one's contempt, even hatred and loathing, for them. Indeed, one's diminished expectations may even have been a reflection of one's contempt.

It has often been observed that one of racism's worst consequences is the denial of the black person's humanity. What often goes unnoticed is the other side of this twisted coin: that it left most blacks persuaded that whites were less than human. Technically clever yes, powerful, well-armed and prolific, to be sure, but without an ounce of basic human decency. No one whose community of memory was etched with the vision of lynched, barbecued ancestors, no black person who has seen the flash of greedy, obsessive hatred in the fish-blue stare of a cracker's cocked eyes, could help but question his inherent humanness. Most blacks, whatever their outward style of interaction with whites, genuinely believed, as did the mother of Henry Louis Gates, that most whites were inherently filthy and evil, or as the poet Sterling Brown once wrote, that there was no place in heaven for "Whuffolks . . . being so onery," that, indeed, for most of them "hell would be good enough—if big enough."

Integration, however partially, began to change all that. By dis-alienating the Other, the members of each group came, however reluctantly, to accept each other's humanness. But that acceptance comes at a price: for whites, it is the growing sense of disbelief at what the nightly news brings in relentless detail from the inner cities. For blacks, it is the sense of outrage that someone truly human could have done what the evidence of more than three and a half centuries makes painfully clear. Like a woman chased and held down in a pitch-dark night who discovers, first to her relief, then to her disbelief, that the stranger recoiling from her in the horror of recognition had been her own brother, the moral embrace of integration is a liberation with a double take: outrage verging on incomprehension.

Increasingly exposed to the conflicts that result from integration, whites may rebel against affirmative action and other programs that bring them face to face with black anger. But resegregation is neither plausible nor desirable. Instead, whites, who dominate America's powerful institutions, must address the roots of black rage by committing to black America's socioeconomic advancement.

But, despite this imperative, a painful truth (one seemingly recognized by the participants in last week's march) emerges from the comparative sociology of group relations: except for those now-rare cases in which a minority constitutes the elite, the burden of racial and ethnic change always rests on a minority group. Although both whites and blacks have strong mutual interests in solving their racial problem, though the solution must eventually come from both, blacks must play the major role in achieving this objective—not only because they have more to gain from it but also because whites have far less to lose from doing nothing. It is blacks who must take the initiative, suffer the greater pain, define and offer the more creative solutions, persevere in the face of obstacles and paradoxical outcomes, insist that improvements are possible and maintain a climate of optimism concerning the eventual outcome. Or, to paraphrase Martin Luther King, it is they, and often they alone, who must keep the dream of a racially liberated America alive.

5

One Man's March

GLENN C. LOURY

Try to understand my problem. I am a black intellectual of moderate to conservative political instincts. Unlike many of my racial brethren, I have been denouncing the anti-Semitism of Minister Louis Farrakhan for over a decade. (My virgin Farrakhan denunciation was in this very magazine in December 1984.) To judge from the volume of press inquiries in past few weeks, I must have been one of the few black men in America willing to state for the record my reservations about, and objections to, the Million Man March. I promiscuously expounded my view that it would not be possible to separate the message from the messenger and that, in any case, a race- and sex-exclusive march would send the wrong message. In short, my credentials as a "deracinated Negro," able to steadfastly resist the call of tribe, are impeccable.

Imagine my surprise, then, when on the day before the march, as I walked along the Mall from the White House toward the Capitol encountering other black men in town for the event, I found myself becoming misty. I watched these "brothers," in clusters of two or three or six, from Philadelphia and Norfolk and my own hometown of Chicago, wandering among the museums and monuments like the tourists they were, cameras in hand, and the sight brought tears to my eyes. The march had not even begun, and already powerful sentiments, long buried inside me, were being resurrected. I knew then that I was in trouble.

Here were young black guys, the same ones occasionally mistaken by belligerent police officers or frightened passersby for threats to public safety because of the color of their skin and the swagger of their gait, scrambling up the steps and lounging between the columns of the National Gallery building, some even checking out the "Whistler and His Contemporaries" show on display inside. And there were others, sharing an excited expectancy with Japanese tourists and rural whites as we all waited in line to tour the White House. Taking in these various scenes, an obvious but profound thought occurred to me: this is their country, too. So, embarrassed that I needed to remind myself of this fact, I wept.

The next day, as I beheld hundreds of thousands of black men gathering in a crowd that ultimately stretched from the steps of the Capitol back toward the

Washington Monument, I would be even more deeply moved. Everything that has been said about the discipline and dignity of the gathering, and the spirit of camaraderie that pervaded it, is true. It was a glorious, uplifting day, and I was swept up in it along with everyone else. It almost did not matter what was being said from the podium. For the first time in years, as the drums beat and the crowd swayed, I heard the call of the tribe, big time.

Mingling in that throng, my thoughts drifted back to my late Uncle Moonie, the husband of my mother's sister, who, as head of the extended household in which I was raised, exerted a powerful influence on me in my formative years. Uncle Moonie, so called because his large, round eyes protruded like half-moons beneath his often-furrowed brow, was a barber, part-time hustler and admirer (though not a follower) of the Honorable Elijah Muhammad, founder of the Nation of Islam. My uncle kicked a nasty heroin habit in his youth and went on to achieve what was for his generation of black men an impressive degree of financial security. Fiercely proud and independent, he constantly railed against "the white man," and he never tired of berating those blacks who looked to "white folk" for their salvation. Occasionally he would take me with him to the state prison for his monthly visits with one or another of his incarcerated friends. "There, but for the grace of God, go you or I," he would say. He encouraged me in an intelligent militancy and even sought to extend his influence from beyond the grave by bequeathing to me one of his most cherished possessions—a complete set of the recorded speeches of Malcolm X. Had Uncle Moonie lived to attend this march, he would have thought it the greatest experience of his life.

To be sure, my uncle would not have understood my public criticism of the march or of Minister Louis Farrakhan, for that matter. He was no great fan of the nonviolent philosophy of Reverend Martin Luther King Jr. He much preferred the straight-backed, unapologetic defiance of Malcolm. He would have been puzzled that I could find the opinions of "white folks" worth taking into account. He would have rejected the notion that there are ethical and political principles, my fealty to which could transcend my sense of racial loyalty.

In short, were he alive today, I fear that Uncle Moonie would be profoundly disappointed in me. Still, those tears welling in my eyes at the sight of "our brothers" on the Mall might have given him hope that I could yet be redeemed. The tingle that ran up my spine as I beheld that massive assembly of beautiful black men seeking unity and spiritual upliftment caused me to hope, for a fleeting moment, that I could, at long last, go home again.

My pre-march analysis was a tight little piece of amateur political theory that ran as follows: the problem with the Million Man March is that it mixes communal and political activities inappropriately. As a communal matter, a religiously motivated gathering of men seeking to commit themselves to reconstruction and renewal in their personal lives and in their respective neighborhoods, it is highly commendable. However, as a political matter, gathering on the Mall at the site of the great 1963 March on Washington—but now as black men and not as

Americans, under the leadership of a Louis Farrakhan not a Martin Luther King—this is deeply problematic. The sacrifice of liberal democratic ideals and the separatist message is too high a price to pay for getting our cultural trains to run on time.

Yet, when put to the test on the Mall, this elegant bit of theory seemed to collapse instantly under the weight of a single fact: nearly one-half million African American men had solemnly, prayerfully assembled to affirm their intention to take responsibility for the condition of their people.

As a social critic, I have called for many years for the civil rights leadership to reorient itself from a focus on the "enemy without," white racism, toward the "enemy within," the dysfunctional behaviors of young black men and women that prevent too many from capitalizing on existing opportunity. Well, here were some 5 percent of the age-adjusted national black male population, together in one place, supporting this very idea. Standing there, and listening to their collective affirmations, I found it hard to deny that the conception and execution of this event had been a work of genius. In the heat of those moments, I felt confused about my ideals and commitments and deeply ashamed to have spoken against the march.

However, I have been an economist for more years than I have been a social critic. As such, I have learned well the art of tenaciously holding on to a theory that, by virtue of its elegance and appeal to intuition, "ought to be true," even when it seems inconsistent with the facts. The key is to find another way of looking at the evidence that casts one's favored theory in a better light. That is not difficult in the case at hand, for what seemed at that march like the salvation of black Americans is, upon closer examination, no such thing at all.

Begin with a simple question: How did it come to pass that this great moment in American cultural politics was orchestrated by the demagogic leader of a black fascist sect, while no other nationally prominent black leader could have pulled it off? The answer is two-fold. First, Farrakhan, whatever one thinks of him, is a *religious* leader, speaking to a flock desperate to hear an explicitly spiritual appeal. The Nation of Islam has a track record of "turning the souls" of a great many underclass men, especially in prisons. In contrast, liberal black political leaders, ironically drawn substantially from the clergy, have checked their theologically conservative Christian witness at the door of the Democratic Party. In coalitions with feminists, gays and radical secularists, and in reaction against the politics of the religious right, they have muted their voices on social issues, leaving a void in black public life that Minister Farrakhan has adroitly filled.

Secondly, Farrakhan's message of spiritual uplift is deeply rooted in a white-man-has-done-us-wrong grievance politics. He does not ask blacks to give up the latter as he proffers the former. In this, he is being faithful to his teacher, the Honorable Elijah Muhammad, who taught that the white man is a blue-eyed devil, a mutant breed created by the mad scientist Yakub and allowed by God to rule over the superior black man until such time as the black man would return to the true faith. No serious persons, inside the Nation of Islam or out, could take this literally. But the premise that blacks find our reason for being in the fact of our enslavement and subsequent persecution anchors all that the Nation of Islam undertakes. This narrow, reactive self-conception is glorified as manly, truth-telling, clear-eyed realism.

Thus, forcing myself to listen carefully to what the speakers at this massive gathering actually said, I began to fear that, notwithstanding the emotion of the moment, nothing will really change. We all pray that one-half million inspired black men will return to their cities and towns, redouble their efforts and with the help of their women create nurturing families and community-based institutions that will change the awful facts on the ground. But do we have any warrant, based upon what was said from the podium, much of it clichéd, resentful and conspiracy-laden, to believe this will transpire?

Uncle Moonie has been dead nearly fifteen years now. His was a different, harder time for black men. That he admired Elijah Muhammad is not surprising, given the context of his life. Now, removed from the passions of the march, and having had the opportunity to reflect, I believe that my passionate rejection of racial essentialism was right for me and, given the context of our lives today, for "my people." The American people, that is.

There are now one and a half million Americans behind bars. This seems to me a tragedy of enormous proportions. Our cities are filled with poor, uneducated young people, wandering the streets aimlessly and without hope. This is a blight that graphically reveals the failure of our political leadership. We now celebrate in our politics the state-sanctioned, eye-for-an-eye taking of human life via capital punishment and the arbitrary locking away for a lifetime of those who have made but three mistakes. I think that this is an abomination unworthy of a civilized nation. So do the organizers of the march. But, unlike them, I do not believe that our outrage should depend on the racial identity of those who suffer. What is morally significant is that they are human; their claim on our attention derives from this fact alone.

The call of the tribe is seductive, but ultimately it is a siren call. As comforting as the prospect may seem, the truth, for all of us, is that we can't go home again. For blacks, as Ralph Ellison has taught us, "our task is that of making ourselves individuals. . . . We create the race by creating ourselves and then to our great astonishment we will have created a culture. Why waste time creating a conscience for something which doesn't exist? For you see, blood and skin do not think."

This is the fundamental point. Skin and blood do not think, or dream, or love or pray. The "conscience of the race" must be constructed from the inside out, one person at a time. I did not hear this sentiment expressed by a single speaker at the Million Man March.

Part Two

The Black Underclass

6

Victims and Heroes in the "Benevolent State"

CLARENCE THOMAS

I would like to thank my friends here at the Federalist Society for once again inviting me to be a part of an important and timely conference. And I would like to begin by returning to a topic I touched upon in my last speech at a conference cosponsored by this organization: personal responsibility. It says something about the current state of affairs in our society that a conference on victims—that is, a conference on the rise of the practice of blaming circumstances for one's situation rather than taking responsibility for changing things for the better—is even necessary. As many of you have heard me say before, the very notion of submitting to one's circumstances was unthinkable in the household in which I was raised. The mere suggestion that difficult circumstances could prevail over individual effort would evoke a response that my brother and I could lip-sync on cue: "Old man can't is dead; I helped bury him." Or, another favorite response: "Where there is a will, there is a way." Under this philosophy—the essential truth of which we all recognize in our hearts—victims have no refuge.

It may have seemed harsh at the time to be told that failure was one's own fault. Indeed, there may have been many circumstances beyond our control. But there was much that my family and my community did to reinforce this message of self-determination and self-worth, thereby inoculating us against the victim plague that was highly contagious in the hot, humid climate of segregation. What has become clear to me over the years, as I have witnessed the transformation of our society into one based upon victims rather than heroes, is that there is a more positive message to be gained from adversity: success (as well as failure) is the result of one's own talents, morals, decisions, and actions. Accepting personal responsibility for victory as well as for defeat is as liberating and empowering as it is unpopular today. Overcoming adversity not only gives us our measure as individuals, but it also reinforces those basic principles and rules without which a society based upon freedom and liberty cannot function.

In those years of my youth, there was a deep appreciation of heroes and heroic virtue. Art, literature, and even popular culture (unlike today) often focused on people who demonstrated heroic virtues—courage, persistence, discipline, hard work, humility, triumph in the face of adversity, just to mention a few. These building blocks of self-reliance were replicated and reinforced at home, school, and church. The "rags to riches" Horatio Alger stories were powerful messages of hope and inspiration to those struggling for a better life. And, many of us used to read and dream about heroes—not to mention our favorite television heroes, something perhaps unbelievable these days. I am certain that many of you who attended grammar school in the 1950s or earlier probably remember reading a favorite account of the integrity and work ethic of George Washington, or of Abraham Lincoln, or of George Washington Carver, or even of some baseball or football legend. It seemed that we all had heroes (not role models, a term of far more recent vintage). Indeed, it would have been odd for a child of several decades ago not to have had a hero.

But today, our culture is far less likely to raise up heroes than it is to exalt victims—individuals who are overcome by the sting of oppression, injustice, adversity, neglect, or misfortune. Today, victims of discrimination, racism, poverty, sickness, and societal neglect abound in the popular press. Today, there are few (if any) heroes. Often, it seems that those who have succumbed to their circumstances are more likely to be singled out than those who have overcome them.

What caused this cultural shift—from an emphasis on heroes to a preoccupation with victims? Why are there more victims and virtually no heroes recognized today? Why in years past was there much less of an emphasis on victimage?

I think two things contributed to this change in the state of affairs. The first is that our political and legal systems now actively encourage people to claim victim status and to make demands on society for reparations and recompense. The second is that our culture actually seeks to denigrate or deconstruct heroes. Why would a civilized society travel down two such destructive paths? Why has it become no more admirable to rise valiantly above one's circumstances than it is to submit to them—all the while aggressively transferring responsibility for one's condition to others?

Let's begin with our political and legal systems—how have they contributed to this state of affairs? The classical conception was that government and the law were meant to ensure freedom and equality of opportunity by giving people the most room possible for self-provision and self-determination. James Madison made this point in *The Federalist Papers* when he observed that the "protection" of the "diversity of faculties in men" was the "first object" of government. And, in more recent times, the great political economist Friedrich von Hayek—who witnessed totalitarianism first hand—made a similar point when he observed that "the chief aim of freedom is to provide both the opportunity and the inducement to insure the maximum use of the knowledge that an individual can acquire."

Between the New Deal and the 1960s, a far different view began to hold sway—namely, that the role of the state was to eliminate want, suffering and adversity. Freedom was no longer simply a right to self-provision and self-determination, but was instead a right to make demands on government and society for one's well-being and happiness. That is the import of Franklin Roosevelt's "Citizen Bill of Rights", which spoke of freedom from want—rights to minimum income, housing, and other "adequate protections from economic fears." And, I think it is axiomatic that the call for such new rights (if not claims) became ever more prevalent in the 1950s and 1960s.

No doubt, this gradual transformation in ideas took root and flourished (at least in part) because of the aggregate growth in wealth and resources we were witnessing in this country during the course of the 20th century. Against the background of this prosperity, poverty stood out in bold relief and in uncomfortably stark contrast—even as the number of people suffering from it shrank. It is not surprising that people began to think that, in a world of seemingly unlimited resources, adversity could be eliminated, or, at the very least, remedied. The ideal of the "benevolent state" took hold. In our "enlightened" society, neglect, misfortune, and injustice did not have to be accepted as inevitable facts of life. Good government and laws could step in when necessary, as many believed they had successfully done during two World Wars, the Great Depression, and the Civil Rights Movement.

If one assumes that suffering and adversity can be eliminated, but sees a number of people continuing to suffer from adversity or misfortune, then there must be some forces in society that relegate the "have nots" to this fate. Or, at the very least, the less fortunate are being ignored. Those facing adversity, hence, are victims of a society that is not doing as much as it could (if it so desired), and these victims can (and should) stake a legitimate claim against the political and legal systems for recompense. On this view, neglect or selfishness on the part of society and government is responsible for the sting of oppression, injustice, and misfortune that the unfortunate and "have nots" feel today.

In light of this modern ideology, is it any surprise that people identify themselves as victims and make demands on the political systems for special status and entitlements? Our culture expects (and, indeed, encourages) people to do exactly that. Consider, for example, the creation and continued expansion of the welfare state and other social programs in this country. How often have we heard proponents of these programs lull the poor into thinking that they are hopeless victims, incapable of triumphing over adversity without "benevolent intervention" by the state? How often have we heard these proponents encouraging the less fortunate in our society to become indignant about their situation in life and more demanding on the political system to find solutions to their problems?

It is not only in the political system, though, that we see our society and its leaders succumbing to the modern ideology of victimhood. As with the political system, people today also are strongly encouraged to make demands on the legal system by claiming victim status. Indeed, the legal system has, in many ways, become a significant driving force behind the modern ideology of victimhood. Courts are viewed as an effective means of forcing (or at least pressuring) political institutions into meeting demands for protected status and new rights or entitlements. Pointing to perceived "victimization" by "the system" or by others in society, our legal culture has often told the least fortunate in our society that their last hope is to claim special legal rights and benefits, or to seek exoneration for the harmful, criminal consequences of their acts. The least fortunate are encouraged to turn to legal arguments that admit defeat and that challenge the moral authority of society. In these ways, courts are called upon to solve social problems—by creating special rules, and by crafting remedies that will satisfy the claims and demands of victim groups but that do not apply to all of us.

Appealing to the legal system, though, was not as easy a task as making demands on the political system. Our legal system has traditionally required that redress for grievances only be granted after very exacting standards have been met. There had to be, for example, very distinct, individualized harm. And, the definition of harm was circumscribed by a traditional understanding of adjudication under the common law, where narrow disputes regarding traditional property rights were resolved among private parties who could not settle matters on their own. Very generalized claims of misfortune or oppression or neglect—the kinds of assertions made in the political system—would not easily fit into this common mold of court activity. It would not be enough for people to be indignant, angry, and demanding about their situation in life. There would have to be an assertion of a legal wrong and a persuasive argument that a legal remedy was available.

The pressure of victimology "revolutionized"—and that word does not always have positive connotations—the courts and the law. For those in our culture seeking to use the courts as agents of social change, poverty, unemployment, social deviancy, and criminal behavior were not just unfair conditions in our society that could be eliminated if only people or politicians cared. Instead, these abstract problems were personified as the direct actions of local schools, churches, businesses, and other social institutions so that they could be sued for causing individualized harm to the victims. Based on this new kind of harm—a kind of legalistic understanding of "victimage"—the courts were said to be obligated to recognize special rights and protected status under the law.

Take, for example, welfare rights and due process. Beginning with *Goldberg v. Kelly,* our cases underscored the importance of welfare as a means of preventing social malaise, promoting the general welfare, and securing the blessings of liberty for all Americans. The rights to life, liberty, and property were, in effect, transformed from freedom from government interference into a right to welfare payments. There are countless other examples in legal literature and judicial opinions—some have argued that inner city minorities and the poor should not be held responsible for the consequences of their criminal acts because of oppression and misfortune; and, of course, there is the debate now raging about preferences based on sex, race, and ethnicity.

This change in our political and legal systems has been accompanied by the rise of the "victim group." These groups are quite useful to public officials for building coalitions for future political support and legitimacy as well. And, for the courts, "victim groups" provide useful justification or cover for energizing the legislative process, changing the legislative agenda, forcing reconsideration of spending priorities, and transforming public debate.

But the rise of victimhood, and its perpetuation by government and the law, is only part of the modern tragedy. There is also the dearth of heroes in our culture. Significantly, as the number of these "victim groups" has escalated, there has been a corresponding decline in the amount of attention that our culture has paid to heroes or, even worse, a conscious attempt to cheapen their achievements. Today, success or a commitment to fighting for noble ideas is attributed to self-interest, revenge, self-aggrandizement, insecurity, or some psychological idiosyncrasy. Just thumb through recently published biographies in the library or bookstore—in many of them, it is not a conscious effort to be virtuous or to do good, but instead a series of unforeseeable and external forces, that lead to greatness or success. And, in many of these biographies, we are introduced to the uncut, "never before seen" foibles, mistakes, and transgressions of people our culture idealized for centuries. The message—that these so-called heroes are really just regular people capable of folly and vice who happened to have a few good breaks. In *Democracy in America,* Alexis de Tocqueville anticipated this state of affairs when he said: "historians who live in democratic times do not only refuse to admit that some citizens may influence the destiny of a people, but also take away from the people themselves the faculty of modifying their own lot and make them depend on an inflexible providence or a kind of blind fatality."

Now, the problem these days is not that there are no people who should be singled out as heroes. Rather, as Daniel Boorstin suggests in his book, *The Image,* society is preoccupied with celebrities. And heroism and celebrity status are two very different things. The word hero refers to people of great strength, integrity, or courage who are recognized and admired for their accomplishments and achievements. The word celebrity, on the other hand, refers to a condition—the condition of being much talked about. It is a state of notoriety or famousness. As Boorstin says, "a celebrity is a person who is known for his well-knownness." Thus, while a hero is distinguished by his achievement, celebrities are created by the media and are simply a trademark. Celebrities are, in short, neither good nor bad—they are just a big name. Publicity is the defining feature of a celebrity's existence, and, unlike a hero who will become greater as time passes, time destroys celebrities. Over time the glare of publicity, as Boorstin notes, melts away the celebrity by shedding light and heat on his vices and commonplaceness.

This pattern of ignoring and deconstructing heroes—and focusing instead on the ephemeral celebrity who is known for his well-knownness rather than character or individual worth—stems from the rise of radical egalitarianism. In the 1960's, many of the cultural elite saw a need to ensure absolute equality. On this view, differences in ability and level of achievement are random or uncontrolled; and to permit these characteristics to dictate human happiness and well-being would therefore be unfair. Celebrity status, in contrast, is not a problem for egalitarians, for as Boorstin notes, "anyone can become a celebrity, if only he can get into the news and stay there." Certainly, real achievement is not necessarily required.

It should surprise no one that our culture now has far less difficulty recognizing celebrities than it does those who achieve success as a result of personal effort and character traits that we traditionally would consider heroic. Denigrating heroic virtue—in other words, chalking heroism up to circumstance—fits quite well with the notion that we must all be the same and that there can be no significant differences in our achievement, social standing, or wealth.

Anyone can see what these intellectual currents have done to the ideals of human dignity, personal responsibility, and self-determination. Preoccupation with victim status has caused people to focus covetously on what they do not have in comparison to others, or on what has happened to them in the past. Many fail to see the freedom they do have and the talents and resources that are at their disposal.

Our culture today discourages, and even at times stifles, heroic virtues—fortitude, character, courage, a sense of self-worth. For so many, the will, the spirit, and a firm sense of self-respect and self-worth have been suffocated. Many in today's society do not expect the less fortunate to accept responsibility for (and overcome) their present circumstances. Because they are given no chance to overcome their circumstances, they will not have the chance to savor the triumph over adversity. They are instead given the right to fret and complain, and are encouraged to avoid responsibility and self-help. This is a poor substitute for the empowering rewards of true victory over adversity. One of my favorite memories of my grandfather is how he would walk slowly by the corn field, admiring the fruits of his labor. I have often thought that just the sight of a tall stand of corn must have been more nourishing to his spirit than the corn itself was to his body.

But the culture of victimology—with its emphasis on the so-called "benevolent state"—delivers an additional (and perhaps worse) blow to dignity and self-worth. When the less fortunate do accomplish something, they are often denied the sense of achievement which is so very important for strengthening and empowering the human spirit. They owe all their achievements to the "anointed" in society who supposedly changed the circumstances—not to their own efforts. Long hours, hard work, discipline, and sacrifice are all irrelevant. In a world where the less fortunate are given special treatment and benefits—and, significantly, where they are told that whatever gains or successes they have realized would not be possible without protected status and special benefits—the so-called beneficiaries of state-sponsored benevolence are denied the opportunity to derive any sense of satisfaction from their hard work and self-help. There is not a one among us who views what others do for us the same way we view what we do for ourselves. No matter how much we appreciate the help, it is still just that—help, not achievement.

It also bears noting that our culture's preoccupation with grouping victims has balkanized society. The "We/They" mentality of calling oneself a victim of society breeds social conflict and calls into question the moral authority of society. The idea that whole groups or classes are victims robs individuals of an independent spirit—they are just moving along with the "herd" of other victims. Such individuals also lack any incentive to be independent, because they know that as part of an oppressed group they will neither be singled out for the life choices they make nor capable of distinguishing themselves by their own efforts.

As victim ideology flourishes, and people are demoralized by its grip, more and more people begin to think that they must claim victim status to get anywhere in this world. Indeed, is it any surprise that anyone and everyone can claim to be a victim of something these days? In his book *The Abuse Excuse*, Alan Dershowitz criticizes countless examples of conditions that "victimize" people and thereby release them from responsibility for their actions. Here are just a few examples:

- the "black rage defense", which asserts that blacks who are constantly subjected to oppression and racial injustice will become uncontrollably violent;
- "urban survival syndrome", which claims that violent living conditions justify acts of aggression in the community;
- "self-victimization syndrome", which maintains that people become less productive and creative, and become severely depressed, as a result of societal neglect and discrimination.

Most significantly, there is the backlash against affirmative action by "angry white males." I do not question a person's belief that affirmative action is unjust because it judges people based on their sex or the color of their skin. But something far more insidious is afoot. For some white men, preoccupation with oppression has become the defining feature of their existence. They have fallen prey to the very aspects of the modern ideology of victimology that they deplore.

Some critics of affirmative action, for example, fault today's civil rights movement for demanding equality yet supporting policies that discriminate based on race. These critics expect the intended beneficiaries of the civil rights regime to break away from the ideology of victimhood: to cherish freedom, to accept responsibility, and, where necessary, to demonstrate fortitude in the face of unfairness. I do not quarrel with this. But these critics should hold themselves to the same standards, resisting the temptation to allow resentment over what they consider reverse discrimination to take hold of their lives and to get the best of them. They must remember that if we are to play the victim game the very people they decry have the better claim to victim status.

Of course, de-emphasizing heroism exacerbates all these problems. Human beings have always faced the temptation to permit adversity or hate to dominate and destroy their lives. To counter this tendency, society had heroes—people capable of overcoming the very adversity or injustice that currently affects today's victims. They rose above their circumstances and inherent imperfections. Heroes cherished freedom, and tried to accomplish much with what little they had. Heroes demonstrated perseverance in the face of adversity and used hardship as a means to strive for greater virtue. And heroes accepted responsibility—they did what they did despite fear and temptation, and tried to do the right thing when presented with a choice between good and evil. It is awfully hard for society to inculcate these values without some useful models from the past and present.

I may not have realized it as a child, but my grandfather was a hero who had a tremendous impact on my life. He certainly would not be a celebrity by today's standards. Though barely able to read and saddled with the burdens of segregation, he worked hard to provide for his family. He was a deeply religious man who lived by the Christian virtues. He was a man who believed in responsibility and self-help. And though this could not bring him freedom in a segregated society, it at least gave him independence from its daily demeaning clutches.

In all the years I spent in my grandparents' house, I never heard them complain that they were victims. Now, they did not like segregation or think that it was right. In fact, there was no question that it was immoral and that anyone who promoted it was morally reprehensible. But there was work to be done. I assure you that I did not enjoy the demands he placed on us. I saw no value in rising with the chicken, and, unlike him, I was not obsessed with what I will call the "reverse dracula syndrome": that is, fear that the rising sun would catch me in bed. It would not be until I was exposed to the most fortunate and best educated in our society that I would be informed that all this time I had been a victim. I am sure you can imagine what it was like when I returned home to Savannah, and informed my grandparents that with the education I had received because of their tremendous foresight and sacrifice, I had discovered our oppressed and victimized status in society. Needless to say relations were quite strained, and our vacation visits were somewhat difficult. My grandfather was no victim and he didn't send me to school to become one.

There are many people like my grandfather alive today. The cultural elite does not honor them as the heroes they are, but instead views them as people who are sadly ignorant of their victim status or who have forgotten where they came from. Our social institutions do not train today's young to view such people as heroes and do not urge them to emulate their virtues.

In idealizing heroic virtue and criticizing the victim ideology of our day, I am not saying that society is free from intractable and very saddening injustice and harm. That would not be true. But, the idea that government can be the primary instrument for the elimination of misfortune is a fundamental misunderstanding of the human condition. There has always been bad and suffering in the world, and we must admit that wrongs have been and will continue to be committed.

People will always be treated unfairly—we can never eliminate oppression or adversity completely, though we can and should fight injustice as best we can.

But keep in mind that all of us are easily tempted to think of ourselves as victims and thereby permit adversity to be the defining feature of our lives. In so doing, we deny the very attributes that are at the core of human dignity—freedom of will, the capacity to choose between good and bad, and the ability to endure adversity and to use it for gain. Victimhood destroys the human spirit.

I also am not saying that we should expect everyone to be a hero all of the time. We humans are weak by our very nature; all of us at times will permit hardship to get the very best of us. But having a set of norms to guide us and to push us along—the stuff of heroes—can be a source of great strength. If we do not have a society that honors people who make the right choices in the face of adversity—and reject the bad choices—far fewer people will make the right choices. Ultimately, without a celebration of heroic virtue, we throw ourselves into the current state of affairs, where man is a passive victim incapable of triumphing over adversity and where aggression, resentment, envy and other vice thwart progress and true happiness.

What I am saying is that it requires the leadership of heroes and the best efforts of all to advance civilization and to ensure that its people follow the path of virtue. And, because of the role law has played in perpetuating victim ideology, and because of the influence law can have in teaching people about right and wrong, lawyers have a special obligation here. We should seek to pare back the victimology that pervades our law, and thereby encourage a new generation of heroes to flourish.

I am reminded of what Saint Thomas a Kempis wrote more than 500 years ago about the human spirit. His standard is a useful one for thinking about the instruction that our law should be offering: "take care to ensure that in every place, action, and outward occupation you remain inwardly free and your own master. Control circumstances, and do not allow them to control you. Only so can you be a master and ruler of your actions, not their servant or slave; a free man. . . ."

7

Clarence X

PATRICIA J. WILLIAMS

As a child of the civil rights movement, I do find it amazing to wake up and find that a black neoconservative Supreme Court justice named Clarence Thomas has suddenly become the symbolic guardian of racial justice in America. And as though that weren't amazement enough, it turns out that Clarence Thomas's erstwhile hero is, was, or has been none other than Malcolm X.

It took me a long time to sort out what on earth was going on when the newspapers reported that Malcolm X was one of Clarence Thomas's role models. I just didn't get it: Malcolm, man of the people, outspoken firebrand of his day, religious fundamentalist, and radical black nationalist? And Clarence, lonely disdainer of the group—no matter what group—not outspoken about much of anything he wasn't later willing to disclaim, confused theologian in the church of an undefined, mushy breed of so-called natural law.

A friend tried to reconcile it all for me by saying, "Oh, it's not about politics—it's a male thing. You wouldn't understand." (Maybe. But the sentiment was at least one I could place. When asked to explain why he delivered the eulogy at Malcolm X's funeral, for example, the actor Ossie Davis told a reporter, "You always left his presence with the sneaky suspicion that maybe, after all, you were a man . . . However much I disagreed with him, I never doubted that Malcolm X, even when he was wrong, was always that rarest thing in the world among us Negroes: a true man.")

Then another friend said, "Malcolm represented manhood. It's as simple as that." (This, of course, is the way Ossie Davis characterized Malcolm X in the eulogy itself: "Malcolm was our manhood, our living black manhood! This was his meaning to his people. And, in honoring him, we honor the best in ourselves.")

And then, just to make sure things stayed complicated, a third friend observed, "Malcolm wasn't just a role model; he's become the ultimate pornographic object." Against the backdrop of rumored affidavits that Clarence Thomas had a penchant for the pornographic, I found this last particularly provocative; so I went to the library and started reading and thinking about pornography in this larger sense, in the beyond-role-model sense, as part of a scheme of thought that has no necessary connection to sex.

I started to think about pornography as the habit of thinking that is a relation of dominance and submission. A habit of thinking that permits the imagination of the voyeur to indulge in auto-sensation that obliterates the subjectivity of the observed. A habit of thinking that allows that self-generated sensation to substitute for interaction with a whole other human being, to substitute for listening or conversing or caring. In which the object is pacified, a malleable "thing" upon which to project. In which the object becomes interchangeable with the will of the voyeur, in which the insatiable lust of Wanda the Wench is representational of the insatiable lust of all women. In which Wanda the Wench may profess deepest delight in the unspeakable pain of having unspeakable acts of violence enacted upon her, because she "delights" "in being a real woman" and real women are defined as the sum of their body parts, bared, open, and eternally available for use and abuse. In which Wanda says she would never want to be a feminist because they don't believe in having fun and they emasculate men and besides women should be free to experience the joys of a little bondage.

And from this thinking I began to extrapolate, hypothesize, do a little imagining of my own: Here we have Clarence Thomas, man of the moment, whose biggest appeal is that he will stand in and speak for all black people while speaking exclusively about himself. Not that he will represent their interests, but that he will represent their image. He will be a role model, but more in the sense of a runway model than of a modeler of actions or a propounder of ideas; as a Supreme Court justice, he will be seen but not heard. Clarence Thomas says he loves the good old days when a little oppression was good for the soul and brought black people together and taught them the true meaning of community; Clarence Thomas hangs a Confederate flag in his office and says it makes him think of home. Affirmative action just emasculates him, and besides blacks should be free to experience the self-help joys of a little bondage.

I can't help wondering what Wanda and Malcolm would have to say about all this, if she weren't bleeding and he weren't dead.

Recently I have began to appreciate why there was so much controversy about Spike Lee's film of Malcolm X's life. As Alex Haley recounts, "After signing the contract for [the autobiography], Malcolm X looked at me hard. 'A writer is what I want, not an interpreter.'" So perhaps it doesn't really matter who would do such a movie: the effrontery is the transition from literary imagination to the filmic, the iconographic. As Haley continues, "I tried to be a dispassionate chronicler. But he was the most electric personality I have ever met, and I still can't quite conceive him dead. It stills feels to me as if he has just gone into some next chapter, to be written by historians."

And with that shift of perception, I began to see the extent to which a whole generation of us have grown up pretenders to the Malcolm legacy; I see it in the faces of my friends; I hear it in the inflections of our voices. I see it in myself:

iconette in the making, dedicatedly pursuing the path of liberatory potential. Who knows if Malcolm would have approved. But that's the beauty of it all, the achingly postmodern transformativity of the singular imagination, floating somewhere in the misty blue angst of annibus domini 1980–2001. Who knows, who cares. And if the complexity that was Malcolm X survives this moment as only a tee-shirt or a trademark, then it is no wonder that Clarence Thomas has emerged as the perfect co-optive successor—an heir-transparent; a product with real producers; the new improved apparition of Malcolm, the cleaned-up version of what he could have been with a good strong grandfather figure to set him right. Clarence X gone good.

Clarence Thomas is to Malcolm X what "Unforgettable. The perfume. By Revlon." is to Nat King Cole. A sea change of intriguing dimension, like the time Eldridge Cleaver came back from Algeria preaching the good news of free enterprise and started marketing trousers with codpieces, and barbecue sauce. Or the time when Ray Charles proclaimed that, although he sang "America the Beautiful" at the 1988 Republican National Convention, he would have done it for the Democrats "if they had paid me some money. I'm just telling the truth."

Symbolic complication was a feature of Clarence Thomas's entire nomination process, right down to the "symbolic" swearing-in ceremony on the White House lawn, which turned out to be an entirely different event from the "real" swearing-in—so that even the oath-taking to uphold the Constitution that was broadcast to Us the People was a reenactment for prime-time consumption. Many blacks supported him because his success was a symbol of the heights to which a black man could aspire. His strong-but-simple, rags-to-riches stories symbolized triumph over adversity, knowledge over darkness, industry over idleness. His powerful mythology, helpfully concocted by some of the very same public relations people who designed Ronald Reagan's, George Bush's, Ross Perot's, and Jesse Helms's campaigns, presented Thomas as the product of a land where dreams come true, where odds are always overcome, where workers whistle (even at the risk of a few sour *feminists* misunderstanding the bright innocence of it all), and where the rainbow is enuf. Clarence Thomas looked like Horatio Alger, Miss Jane Pittman, and Colin Powell all wrapped into one.

If, as some assert, in sexual pornography men act and women appear, and if in racial pornography white people act and black people appear, a classic instance in the political pornography of the Malcolmized moment was when President Bush invited the Black Caucus, who represent many millions of black and white voters, up to the White House to sit and chat about their concerns for a while. As it turned out, of course, the whole event was a magnificently choreographed photo opportunity, the entire point of which was the images—stills of Bush *looking* as if he were listening—disseminated to the media all over America. Similarly, the entire arrangement of witnesses in the confirmation process—four witnesses for, four witnesses against—replicated a kind of "he said–she said" set-up if there ever was one, and belied the extent to which the witnesses represented complex and vastly differing constituencies. The witness from the NAACP represented a membership of thousands upon thousands, yet was made the imagistic equivalent of the witness who represented the relatively minuscule membership of the black bailiffs' association of Southern California.

A lot has been written about role models and the black community. Some of it undoubtedly is useful. I firmly believe that there is great power in seeing ourselves in others who are likable, respectable, and socially desirable. But models are not enough, and I am increasingly concerned that *all* we are left with is "players" in "roles," rather than substantive, interactive beings—people as labels rather than complexly situated bundles of fluid allegiances. Furthermore, I have a sneaky suspicion that the ideals embodied in "role models" are the forced bright side of stereotyped, or even demographic, images—the Willie Horton–shape of all black men, for example—that displace or engulf the lived body and soul. (Thomas figured his own conservative values as the track to success by contrasting them with the image of his sister, Emma Mae Martin, as an unmotivated, welfare-dependent, lazy hustler. Yet the historian Nell Painter points out that "she was only on welfare temporarily and that she was usually a two-job-holding, minimum-wage-earning mother of four. Unable to afford professional help, she had gone on welfare while she nursed the aunt who had suffered a stroke but who normally kept her children when Martin was at work." The aura that dazzles is matched, in other words, by the shadow that follows. The exceptional profile in courage posed in finger-shaking opposition to the suspect profile. The wife to the whore, the younger woman to the ex-wife. The model figure that devalues all others as disfigured.

During the Gulf War, a black friend of mine expressed her unswerving pride in and support of General Colin Powell: "Black people can sleep better knowing that a black man has his finger on the button." (Actually I've been losing a lot of sleep lately: In my dreams, I am toiling endlessly in a world where hard labor is supposed to be eternally ennobling, rather than ever degrading or even just exhausting, where ignorance is glorified, where creativity is vilified as mental disobedience, and cruelty rationalized as preemptive necessity. In *my* dreams, there's just a big button, with this disembodied finger on it.)

I worry about this tendency to indulge in figureheading our ideals. I think that imbuing humans with ideal or essential traits is a formula for either dashed ideals or corrupted ones. It is a formula as well for cynicism on the one hand or intolerance on the other. It prevents us from engagement with the shortcomings of idols; it requires that our public figures be monolithic—saints or sinners. It is no wonder we end up with a lot of liars in public office. Malcolm was both saint and sinner, and for his insistence to just *be,* paid dearly. No one knew better than he how complicated is heroism: how much it is the product of good acts and bad, of bravery, craft, dumb luck, and brilliant insight, all mixed up in serendipitous proportion. If Malcolm had conformed to the politically pornographic imagination of his generation's fixed ideals—even just a little—he would no doubt be alive today, hosting a talk show, lunching with Clarence. But Malcolm never was one for mannered acquiescence.

The substitution of role models for complete understanding of the political implications of certain philosophical doctrines results in the privatization of the political, and shifts focus from the implications of philosophy to the personalities of its proponents. It also makes those proponents *very* authoritative. It cedes to them enormous and total power over the consequences of "their" theories, as though theory had no life beyond birth, no interpretive generative property as taken up and reiterated by others. As though the life of the mind were physical, rigid, bounded as the body—as though you could pick an idea up and lay it down, this concrete, static, three-dimensional club of an idea flung forth like law upon the earth. And as though the idea might die like the man.

Given all that, it is simultaneously true that the ideals embodied in role modeling, like laws themselves, are frequently a way of presenting, and are premised on, certain kinds of statistical probabilities. Thus, when Clarence Thomas's image as a black man was advanced as a reason he should be on the Supreme Court, that supposition was often used by black people to mean that the experience of being black increases the likelihood of being sympathetic to the advancement of particular collective agendas. So it was that many people asked with disarming credulousness of Thomas: How could a once-poor black man turn on his people? (One hears the same sorts of veiled statistical wistfulness at the other end of the political spectrum: Tom Metzger, founder of the White Aryan Resistance, said, "I think David Duke will make a great politician, because politicians make themselves acceptable to a majority of people.")

We live in a moment in which political ad agencies have perfected the art of exploiting symbolic properties while severing them from the statistical likelihoods that gave rise to them. Thus Clarence Thomas could exploit his roots as a poor black man and simultaneously deny that the poverty and material degradation in which millions of other poor blacks live is anything more than a state of mind. And thus Virginia Lamp Thomas, of all people, could, in the pages of *People* magazine, of all places, exploit the status of rape victim by dressing herself in the language of "survivor"—as a way of denying another woman's allegations of sexual harassment. This entire article in *People* is a fascinating study in the metaphors of embattlement, and weirdly evocative of Malcolm X's stories. Listen, for example, to Malcolm X:

> It was Allah's intent for me to help Cassius prove Islam's superiority before the world—through proving that mind can win over brawn. I don't have to remind you how people everywhere scoffed at Cassius Clay's chances of beating Liston.
>
> This time, I brought from New York with me some photographs of Floyd Patterson and Sonny Liston in their fight camps, with white priests as their "spiritual advisors." Cassius Clay, being a Muslim, didn't need to be told how white Christianity had dealt with the American black man. "This fight is the *truth*," I told Cassius. "It's the Cross and the Crescent fighting in a prize ring—for the first time. It's a modern

Crusades—a Christian and a Muslim facing each other with television to beam it off Telstar for the whole world to see what happens!" I told Cassius, "Do you think Allah has brought about all this intending for you to leave the ring as anything but the champion?"

And compare Virginia Lamp Thomas:

Clarence knew the next round of hearings to being that day was not the normal political battle. It was spiritual warfare. Good versus evil. We were fighting something we didn't understand, and we needed prayerful people in our lives. We needed God.

So the next morning, Wednesday, we started having these two couples in our home to pray for two or three hours every day. They brought over prayer tapes, and we would read parts of the Bible. We held hands and prayed. What got us through the next six days was God. We shut the kitchen blinds and turned on Christian praise music to survive the worst days.

Later, after two hours' sleep, we walked into the hearing room, and people were lining the hallways, urging him on. "Who are these people?" Clarence asked me, and I said, "I think they are angels."

These kinds of calculated disjunctures, rhetorical rearrangements, and surgical revisionism have resulted in such strange symbolic cyborgs that I sometimes think a President could appoint an outright fascist to the Supreme Court, as long as he could find the right packaging—a black Hispanic lesbian one, say, in a wheelchair. This is, of course, exactly what the voters of Louisiana too nearly did, in their rush to endorse the boyish good looks and the political plastic surgery of the "new" David Duke's new words. "When David Duke entered a hotel ballroom here today, JoAnn Jernigan, a retired nurse and lifelong Democrat, jumped to her feet and applauded . . . 'I've got to see my candidate,' she said of Mr. Duke, the Republican candidate for governor and former grand wizard of the Ku Klux Klan. 'He's so cute. How can someone who looks like that be bad?'" It is what Ross Perot and the Infinity automobile did with their fill-in-the-fantasy-of-your-choice style of mythic, malleable self-promotion. And it is what David Duke himself did when, "under the pseudonym 'Mohammed X,' he wrote 'African Atto,' a martial arts manual for black militants. He later said it was a way to develop a mailing list to keep track of potential black agitators. Under the pseudonym 'Dorothy Vanderbilt,' he wrote 'Finders-keepers,' a dating-and-sex manual for women." This is, after all, pornography's great power: to disguise, to dehistoricize, to decontextualize, to isolate.

Against this backdrop, it seems weirdly fitting that one of the most distinguishing features of Clarence Thomas's judicial philosophy is his wholesale rejection of statistics and other social science data, and with it the dismissal of a range of affirmative action remedies that have been central to blacks' social and economic progress over the last thirty years or so. For all of his quite moving anecdotalizing about his own history, Thomas by this gesture effectively supplants a larger common history with individualized hypotheses about free choice, in which each self chooses her destiny even if it is destitution. Clarence Thomas has not clearly committed himself to taking into account past and present social constraints as infringements on the ability to exercise choice. He ignores the history that gives at least as much weight to the possibility that certain minority groups have not had many chances to be in charge of things as to the possibility that they just don't want to, or that they just can't.

While self-help and strong personal values are marvelous virtues, they are no stand-in for the zealous protection of civil and human rights—that protection being the paramount task of the judiciary in any democracy, and of the Supreme Court in greatest particular. The problem with Clarence Thomas's espousal of these self-help values is that he positions them in direct "either/or" tension with any other value; self-help is presented as bitterly competitive rather than in complete concert with those social measures which would help ever more rather than ever fewer people.

Thomas's insistence on a hyperindividualistic case-by-case analytic in race and gender cases is nothing more than another way of insisting on a very high statistical probability, by narrowing the range of reference and narrowing the number of parties at issue. The difficulty with that, of course, is that while the evidence is narrowed from probabilities in the population at large to the credibility of sometimes a single witness, nothing is done to deal with the unconscious or unexpressed probabilistic presumptions that judges as well as juries bring to the calculation of credibility itself. Blacks are "more likely" to be criminals, for example; Hispanics "probably" steal cars; and women are "undoubtedly" hysterics.

Adducing evidence of disparate impact in a larger population is one very effective way of countering such free-floating presumptions or prejudices. Imagine, for example, how cumulatively powerful it would have been if (that is, *hypothetically*) there had been evidence that 99 percent of the female Yale Law School graduates who worked at the Equal Employment Opportunity Commission during a given director's tenure never advanced beyond the lowest G-level ranking, while (still hypothetically) John Doggett and 99 percent of the rest of the male Yalies sailed to the top within two months. Yet evidence of disparate impact is precisely the sort of stuff that Thomas's judicial philosophy *excludes*—thus, in a very real and ironic way, making sure that the vast majority of complaints about race and gender discrimination don't get past the "he said–she said" stage.

Against this, consider the utter disarray of any data about Clarence Thomas's judicial philosophy—the complete, calculated lack of a basis upon which to form an opinion or fashion a likelihood about what Thomas would do on the Supreme Court. (And contrary to the many careless aspersions about how "politicized" the hearings became, it must be kept in mind that the Constitution expressly makes the senatorial process of inquiry a political one. The Constitution specifies that no nominee shall be confirmed without the "advice and consent" of the Senate.) If the Senate is confronted with a tabula rasa—or even a tabula not-so-clara, a "mystery," as some of the senators openly called Thomas—then there is little basis for either knowledgeable advice or informed consent. And this is a severe threat to the functioning of our tripartite system of government, to the balance of political input that the involvement of the several branches of government must provide before someone is placed into that most sensitive position of discretionary insularity, the shielded office of highest trust that is the Supreme Court.

In the face of the Senate's duty to inform itself about a judicial candidate's philosophy, Judge Thomas showed a deeply disconcerting pattern of either revising or disclaiming many of the most troubling aspects of his record. If we believe in this epiphanous recanting, we are left with the disturbing phenomenon of a Supreme Court nominee who didn't read his own citations, who misunderstood the legal import of his own obstructionist administrative actions, and who didn't really mean most of what he said. This disdain for accountability was made even more alarming by being echoed in the CIA director's hearings just down the hall: "In explanation of his flagging memory, Robert Gates recently told the Senate confirmation committee, 'I have to admit to you that when I left the CIA in 1989 . . . I did a major data dump.'"

And if we are not inclined to believe that Clarence Thomas's keen intelligence could leave him in quite so disingenuous a state of disarray, then we the people must come to terms with the fact that we were confronted with an outright, practiced refusal to answer questions. This is a tremendously serious violation of the Senate's right to get answers to questions about any nominee's views and his disposition to uphold precedent as well as to judge facts and interpret new law. The Senate has a constitutional *duty* to ensure that the Court remain a place where voices of dissent and unpopular causes may be heard. Ambiguity is not the standard. A senatorial leap of faith, as the *Philadelphia Inquirer* urged in an editorial, should not have been good enough. Much of the vocabulary that even some senators employed during the hearings—"impression," "faith," "instinct," "hope," "trust"—simply did not describe a reasoned choice to support Clarence Thomas.

(But the truth was, I suppose, that through all the masquerade, there really was lots of evidence about what Clarence Thomas was likely to do on the Supreme Court, just none that anyone ever talked about straightforwardly or sustainedly. We were left instead with the ghostly, enigmatic trace of Senator Thurmond's smile . . .)

"There but for the grace of God, go I," said Clarence Thomas of the prisoners he saw being shuttled back and forth from the District Courthouse in Washington, D.C. These words were uttered during his confirmation hearings, an attempt to reassure senators of his compassion, which was in question. Barely four months later, from his post on the Supreme Court, Thomas wrote, in a dissenting opinion, that a prisoner who was beaten and bloodied and had his teeth loosened by prison guards should have no constitutional claim under the Eighth Amendment proscription against cruel and unusual punishment, even where the violence was undue, wanton, and excessive. In a majority opinion joined in or concurred with by everyone else on the Court but Antonin Scalia, Justice Sandra Day O'Connor chided Thomas's use of this "substantial injury" test, pointing out that if the cutoff for constitutional claims is whether someone requires medical attention, this sanctions forms of torture that stop just short of leaving marks on the body. It's not a constitutional issue, in the world according to Clarence, until they *have* to go to the hospital.

Malcolm X once said, "It didn't take me a week to learn that all you had to do was give white people a show and they'd buy anything you offered them. It was like popping your shoeshine rag. The dining car waiters and Pullman porters knew it too, and they faked their Uncle Tomming to get bigger tips. We were in that world of Negroes who are both servants and psychologists."

And I wonder from the sidelines: if in sexual pornography men act and women appear, and if in racial pornography white people act and black people appear, then what happens in the intersectional politics of race and gender, when a black woman suffers sexual abuse at the hands of a black man, against the gladiatorial backdrop of a white theater? In order to win, will he have to act as aggressive racial observer (or "play the race card")? Will he have to appear the sexual victim, malleable and open and available (or "lynched," castrated, skewered)? In order for her to have won, would she, paradoxically, have had to appear sexually assertive? And act racially passive? Or vice versa? Or would any matrix of asserted attributes work in her case, or would she always just disappear? Is the double-binding double burden of her race and her gender simply too great a confluence of appearances for her to ever successfully achieve the role of actor? (As opposed to that sly counterfeit, the "mere actress.") What arrangement of ingredients from the archetypal stewpot would allow her interpretive apotheosis into the cult of true womanhood?

In today's world, discrimination and the deprivation of cherished civil liberties have taken on new forms, unforms, and wordlessness that our labor and civil rights laws are hard-pressed if not outright unable to recognize. One reason is a sociopolitical climate in which both formal and informal burdens of proof make it harder and harder to have anything recognized as discrimination. Another is a kind of calculated confusion and rhetorical gaming, of which the spectacle of Clarence Thomas's hearing was exemplary, and which clouds all discussion of the rights of minorities and women in the United States, and of Thomas himself. In the words of a friend of mine: "Thomas invokes a mythical image of Malcolm X to serve his own needs . . . Thomas's use of X is the theft of a religious icon from a people whose religious and spiritual [ties come not from triptychs or cathedrals, but political] memories . . . In short, Thomas is a thief in the temple."

In today's world, this repeated emptying of all our cultural coffers, of all our sources of both self and unity, has left us much the poorer. It has left us with an atmosphere in which public relations firms, like mean-spirited astrologers, dictate presidential politics, and TV call-in polls divine the course of governance. In which David Duke's plastic surgery is a metaphor for the cosmetizing of Nazi policies made mainstream. In which if calling a black person a nigger is bad, then calling a white person a racist must be exactly the same thing only twice as bad. In which sexual harassment is shrugged off as children playing that annoying little game of "he said–she said," so better for the parents not to get involved. In which parties in relationships of political trust are replaced by game-show contestants for verisimilitude. In which reality is a stranger category than fantasy. In which reality is just a high-priced form of fantasy. In which marketing trend is the new-age demonstration of democracy-in-action. In which there is justice for sale and media moments for all.

8

The Chronicle of the Slave Scrolls

DERRICK BELL

From my cabin window I look out on the full moon, and the ghosts of my forefathers rise and fall with the undulating waves. Across these same waters how many years ago they came! What were the inchoate mutterings locked tight within the circle of their hearts? In the deep, heavy darkness of the foul-smelling hold of the ship, where they could not see the sky, nor hear the night noises, nor feel the warm compassion of the tribe, they held their breath against the agony! . . .

O my fathers, what was it like to be stripped of all supports of life save the beating of the heart and the ebb and flow of fetid air in the lungs? In a strange moment, when you suddenly caught your breath, did some intimation from the future give to your spirits a hint of promise? In the darkness did you hear the silent feet of your children beating a melody of freedom to words which you would never know, in a land in which your bones would be warmed again in the depths of the cold earth in which you will sleep unknown, unrealized and alone.

—Howard Thurman

The musings of the black theologian Dr. Howard Thurman[1] give eloquent voice to questions that led me, in frustration and growing despair, to abandon my civil rights law practice and seek refuge in religion. After several years of study and missionary endeavor, I became the minister of an urban black church. A short time later, I decided to make a pilgrimage to Ghana. As Christians of old sought the Holy Grail as proof of the miraculous in Christ's death and our redemption, so I was drawn to Africa seeking secrets of the slaves' survival that might offer their descendants sustenance and possible salvation. And, amazingly, on my last evening there, I found the revelation for which I had come—and for which, indeed, I have been searching all of my life.

On that evening I walked along a wide desolate beach; and as the sun fell slowly beyond the waves, it cast a fan of gold and salmon and rose across the sky. Even the gray sand was transformed into a palette of rich pastels. As I marveled, I saw the ship. It was not some far-off sail etching an invisible line between brilliant sky and darkening sea, but rather lay at my feet, a model ship perhaps two feet long. By its worn appearance, I could tell that until the sands shifted, it had lain submerged for a very long time.

I picked up the ship and studied it in fading light. I knew from my studies of slave history that I was holding a likeness of the ships the slave traders had used to transport African captives to the Americas, and I felt renewed sympathy for those whose first contact with Western civilization had brought generations of despair and misery. For, as Dr. Thurman had written:

> Nothing anywhere in all the myths, in all the stories, in all the ancient memory of the race had given hint of this tortuous convulsion. There were no gods to hear, no magic spell of witch doctor to summon; even one's companion in chains muttered his quivering misery in a tongue unknown and a sound unfamiliar.[2]

Examining the vessel more closely, I found it to be hollow, and it had a corklike plug stuck deep into its stern. Later that evening in my hotel room, I managed with some difficulty to withdraw the cork and found in the ship's hold three tight-rolled parchment scrolls. Unrolling the scrolls, I found them to be covered with thin, fine writing in antiquated English. I read them through at once. They were a testament from the slaves themselves.

Dr. Thurman has asked: "How does the human spirit accommodate itself to desolation? How did they? What tools of the spirit were in their hands with which to cut a path through the wilderness of their despair."[3] The answers were in the scrolls. The identity of those who recorded the secrets of survival, like that of the composers of the spirituals, would likely never be known. But the miracle of their being far outweighed the importance of their origins. And just as the spirituals had enabled slaves to survive, so the scrolls would enable their descendants to overcome.

Returning home to my church, I began to teach the message of the Slave Scrolls. The members of my congregation were profoundly affected. After a few weeks of intense study conducted as the scrolls prescribed in "healing groups" of twenty-five people, the myriad marks of racial oppression began to fall away. There were no "magic" potions to take, no charms to wear, no special religious creed to adopt, and no political philosophy to espouse. Mainly, the scrolls taught the readily available but seldom-read history of slavery in America—a history gory, brutal, filled with more murder, mutilation, rape, and brutality than most of us can imagine or easily comprehend.[4]

But the humanity of our ancestors survived, as the spirituals prove. In the healing-group sessions, black people discovered this proud survival and experienced the secular equivalent of being "born again." Those who completed the healing process began to wear wide metal bands on their right wrists to help them remember what their forebears had endured and survived. Blacks left the healing groups fired with a determination to achieve in ways that would forever justify the faith of the slaves who hoped when there was no reason for hope. If revenge was a component of their drive, it was not the retaliatory "we will get them" but the competitive "we will *show* them."

In this spirit, the healing groups demonstrated a deep desire, precursor to the soon-to-be-gained ability, to accomplish all that white people have long claimed blacks must do to win full acceptance by American society. Blacks who were good workers before learning of the Slave Scrolls became whirlwinds of purposeful activity. Even previously shiftless and lazy black people became models of industry.

Word spread quickly, and soon the congregation grew beyond the confines of our small church. At first, we held healing sessions in public auditoriums but then determined to share the teachings with other ministers and community leaders. The members of my congregation became missionaries traveling across the country teaching black people what we had learned. Excitement in black communities grew; but with the exception of a few black newspapers, the media initially ignored what they viewed as just another charlatan scheme preying on the superstitions of ignorant and gullible black folk.

Within a year, though, neither the media nor the nation could ignore the rapid transformation in the black community. After a time, blacks who heard about, but had not actually gone through, the healing sessions began reading slave histories on their own and later were able to experience the change within themselves simply by seeing its powers working in other black people.[5] All the "Marks of Oppression"[6]—crime, addiction, self-hate—disappeared; and every black became obsessed by a fierce desire to compete, excel, and—as Booker T. Washington used to admonish—"prove thyself worthy."[7]

Unemployed blacks who could find work did so. Those who could not joined together to work for those who did. All manner of community enterprises were started and flourished. Black churches became social-aid centers, and blacks who had been receiving public assistance took themselves off the rolls and soon began sending small repayment checks to welfare agencies. Black family life strengthened as divorce and out-of-wedlock births disappeared. Black children excelled in the public schools, and attended newly opened community classes held in converted taverns and pool halls. They learned the truth about their slave history while preparing themselves to be future leaders.

In a word, black people became in fact what white people boasted their own immigrant forebears had been. Even the storied Saturday-night party disappeared, and was replaced in many areas by organizations working to eliminate poverty and unemployment among whites. Blacks began outachieving whites in every area save sports and entertainment—activities that black people no longer believed could compare with the challenge of getting ahead through business and industry. Blacks not only voted together but spent their money for only those products that they made or, if white-owned, had been given a vote of approval by the black community.

Understandably, a great many white people, after an initial rather patronizing surprise, became alarmed. They deemed it strange, abnormal, when large numbers of blacks—as opposed to the token one or two—began surpassing whites in business, industry, and education. It was, some whites felt, neither right nor fair—even un-American—for a minority group to gain so much advantage over the majority in a majoritarian society. Spurred by this unease, both government and media investigators searched frantically, without success, for wrongdoing or evidence of subversive elements. For many whites, lack of proved wrongdoing did not deter retaliation. Employers and educational institutions disbanded their affirmative-action programs, replacing them instead with explicit ceilings on the number of black candidates they would hire or admit.

Working-class whites, severely threatened by the increasingly widespread pattern of black economic and political gains, carried out violent attacks against adherents of the healing movement. At several public healing sessions, groups of whites pelted blacks with insults and missiles; in one notorious incident, white attacks resulted in a violent melee in which several persons were killed. In other incidents, several blacks who wore the metal wristbands in public were brutally beaten.

Finally, a popular television minister found in "American morality" what no one had yet discovered in law: an answer to what was now openly referred to as the "black success" problem. In a rousing sermon, the minister told his fundamentalist audience: "Success that is the result of self-help is the will of God"—but the preaching of racial hatred is subversive. The Slave Scrolls, he asserted, created hostility between the races by teaching blacks about the evils of a system wiped out more than a century ago. The minister warned that, unless the scrolls were banished, their teachings would prove as pernicious as those of Nazism and the Ku Klux Klan. Ideologies based on racial hatred, he reiterated, should have no place in a country committed to brotherhood across racial boundaries.

The minister's sermon provided the key to action. Despite the opposition of blacks and civil libertarians, virtually every state enacted what were called Racial Toleration Laws, which severely restricted—and, in some states, banned outright—public teaching that promoted racial hatred by focusing on the past strife between blacks and whites. Penalties were severe for leading or participating in unauthorized public healing sessions, or for publicly wearing what the law termed "symbols of racial hatred." State officials enforced these laws with vigor, severely hampering the ability of blacks to carry out their healing campaign. Whites whose fears were not allayed by the government's actions organized volunteer citizens' groups to help rid their communities of those whose teachings would destroy the moral fabric of American society.

The rest is almost too painful to tell. Whites perverted the law; many still resorted to violence. Like their forebears in the Reconstruction era, blacks tried to hold on. For longer than was perhaps wise, black people resisted, but the campaign to suppress those who wore the distinctive bracelets proved too strong.

Black enterprise was no match for the true basis of majoritarian democracy: white economic and military power. Nor were the courts of much help. Our best lawyers' challenges to the Racial Toleration Laws were to no avail.

For the black community, the Slave Scrolls experience served as a bitter reminder that sheer survival rather than inherent sloth has prompted the shiftless habits that, continued over time, led many to forget that whites are threatened by black initiative and comforted by black indolence. If blacks were to survive, they had to make overtures to peace—a prelude to a return to the past. My church, which had become the symbol of what by then was called the "Slave Scrolls movement," undertook "negotiations" with the white community. In fact, we had no choice but to surrender all. We returned the scrolls to the hallowed model ship. Then, at a massive service held in accordance with the surrender terms, thousands of black people renounced the lessons of the healing groups. Having removed and destroyed our bracelets, we watched, and wept, in silence, as both ship and Slave Scrolls were burned.

For a long time, neither Geneva nor I said anything. I was overcome with the ultimate defeat of the Chronicle.

"That's quite a story," I finally ventured, "but one I imagine many whites and more than a few blacks will dismiss as highly implausible."

"Are you suggesting," Geneva asked apprehensively, "that you find yourself in the disbelieving group?"

"Well," I hedged, "it's hard to predict how the public would react to so dramatic a transformation in black conduct and competitiveness. One would have hoped that most whites would hail the black achievements as proof that any group can make it in America by pulling themselves up by their own bootstraps."

"Your hopes, friend, are not supported by Reconstruction history. In that brief period after the Civil War, the newly freed blacks, despite the failure of the national government to provide meaningful reparations, made impressive educational and political gains.[8] But their very success served to deepen and intensify the hostility of southern whites."

"Nineteenth-century history certainly supports your pessimism," I conceded. "And before you remind me, it is true that white society has often persecuted black leaders and groups who have placed a high priority on ridding blacks of their slave mentality. There is the fate of Delia Jones's hero Marcus Garvey, and the more recent experiences of the Black Muslims, Paul Robeson, W. E. B. DuBois, Martin Luther King, Jr., and Malcolm X[9]—whose calls for black communities to organize for mutual protection and benefit gained them many black followers but engendered crushing enmity among whites.

"Malcolm X was a good example of what might be called the black leadership dilemma. That is, during the early 1960s, his trenchant and highly articulate condemnation of white racism gained him tremendous support among poor blacks but harsh hostility from most of white society. He didn't want, as many whites feared, to lead a revolution, but was trying through his angry tirades to show blacks that racism, not inherent inferiority, was the source of their self-hate and self-destructive behavior. What Malcolm X hoped to bring about was the 'decolonization of the black mind—the awakening of a proud, bold, impolite new consciousness of color and everything that color means in white America.'"[10]

"And," Geneva interjected, "it is precisely that threshold task of decolonization through condemnation of white racism that—when espoused by black leaders, whether a Malcolm X or a Martin Luther King—arouses such hostility as to lead enemies of these leaders to believe that society will see killing them as a great public favor. This has been the fate of our leaders who have merely espoused the cure of decolonization of the black mind. What makes you think that whites would be more receptive to the actual achievement of this goal, as in the Chronicle of the Slave Scrolls?"

"Perhaps it is less black achievement than fear of the Slave Scrolls' almost supernatural powers that leads whites to strike back and eradicate the Scrolls and the ship they deem the sources of that strange and threatening power.

"What bothers me, though, is how could blacks ever return to a colonized mindset even with the destruction of the Scrolls and the model ship? After all, they must have known by then that their achievements had been the result of their efforts and not some magic of the Slave Scrolls."

"Think about it," said Geneva. "The Chronicle is not suggesting that black people need to be taught how to succeed, but reminds us that they have learned very early that too much success in competition with whites for things that really matter like money and power threatens black survival. In a society where success is a supreme virtue, a deliberate decision not to succeed creates a spiritual vacuum. Just as some poor whites relieve their frustration by feeding on the myth of their superiority, many blacks engage in self-destructive and antisocial behavior as an outlet for their despair. The teachings in the Slave Scrolls cause black people to forget their basic lesson of survival through self-subordination, but their resulting success leads to a life-threatening reaction by whites that makes it necessary for blacks to relearn that lesson the hard way. The public ceremony where they are forced to renounce the truth they know about their history and themselves is a symbolic action, a surrender of the rediscovered knowledge, and the end of expectations that black people can gain acceptance in America by becoming superachievers in business and displacing white people, or at least those whites who blacks believe have been getting by owing to their color rather than their competence."

NOTES

1. Howard Thurman, "On Viewing the Coast of Africa," in A. Thurman, ed., *For the Inward Journey: The Writings of Howard Thurman* (1984), p. 199.

2. Ibid., pp. 199–200.

3. Ibid.

4. See, for example, E. Genovese, *Roll, Jordan, Roll: The World the Slaves Made* (1974); L. Higginbotham, *In the Matter of Color: Race and the American Legal Process* (1978).

5. See K. Keyes, Jr., *The Hundredth Monkey* (1982), who suggests, on the basis of animal behavior studies, that "when a certain critical number achieves an awareness, this new awareness may be communicated from mind to mind" (p. 17).

6. Kardiner and Ovesey, *The Mark of Oppression* (1962).

7. L. Harlan, *Booker T. Washington: The Making of a Black Leader, 1856–1901* (1972). Washington's life and policies are summarized in J. Franklin, *From Slavery to Freedom* (3d ed.).

8. See, for example, James McPherson, "Comparing the Two Reconstructions," *Princeton Alumni Weekly,* 26 February 1979, pp. 16, 18–19. McPherson reports that between 1860 and 1880 the proportion of blacks who were literate climbed from 10 percent to 30 percent, and of black children who attended public schools, from 2 percent to 34 percent; that by 1870, 15 percent of all southern public officials were black; and that by 1880, 20 percent of blacks owned land, whereas none had owned land in 1865.

9. See E. Cronon, *Black Moses: The Story of Marcus Garvey and the Universal Negro Improvement Association* (1955); C. E. Lincoln, *The Black Muslims in America* (1961); Paul Robeson, *Here I Stand* (1958); E. Hoyt, *Paul Robeson: The American Othello* (1967); A. Rampersad, *The Art and Imagination of W. E. B. Du Bois* (1976); D. Garrow, *The FBI and Martin Luther King, Jr.* (1981); P. Goldman, *The Death and Life of Malcolm X* (1973); *The Autobiography of Malcolm X,* A. Haley, ed. (1964).

10. Goldman, *Malcolm X,* p. 396.

9

Who Shot Johnny?

DEBRA DICKERSON

Given my level of political awareness, it was inevitable that I would come to view the everyday events of my life through the prism of politics and the national discourse. I read *The Washington Post, The New Republic, The New Yorker, Harper's, The Atlantic Monthly, The Nation, National Review, Black Enterprise* and *Essence* and wrote a weekly column for the Harvard Law School Record during my three years just ended there. I do this because I know that those of us who are not well-fed white guys in suits must not yield the debate to them, however well-intentioned or well-informed they may be. Accordingly, I am unrepentant and vocal about having gained admittance to Harvard through affirmative action; I am a feminist, stoic about my marriage chances as a well-educated, 36-year-old black woman who won't pretend to need help taking care of herself. My strength flags, though, in the face of the latest role assigned to my family in the national drama. On July 27, 1995, my 16-year-old nephew was shot and paralyzed.

Talking with friends in front of his home, Johnny saw a car he thought he recognized. He waved boisterously—his trademark—throwing both arms in the air in a full-bodied, hip-hop Y. When he got no response, he and his friends sauntered down the walk to join a group loitering in front of an apartment building. The car followed. The driver got out, brandished a revolver and fired into the air. Everyone scattered. Then he took aim and shot my running nephew in the back.

Johnny never lost consciousness. He lay in the road, trying to understand what had happened to him, why he couldn't get up. Emotionlessly, he told the story again and again on demand, remaining apologetically firm against all demands to divulge the missing details that would make sense of the shooting but obviously cast him in a bad light. Being black, male and shot, he must, apparently, be gang- or drug-involved. Probably both. Witnesses corroborate his version of events.

Nearly six months have passed since that phone call in the night and my nightmarish, headlong drive from Boston to Charlotte. After twenty hours behind the wheel, I arrived haggard enough to reduce my mother to fresh tears and to find my nephew reassuring well-wishers with an eerie sangfroid.

I take the day shift in his hospital room; his mother and grandmother, a clerk and cafeteria worker, respectively, alternate nights there on a cot. They don their uniforms the next day, gaunt after hours spent listening to Johnny moan in his sleep. How often must his subconscious replay those events and curse its host for saying hello without permission, for being carefree and young while a would-be murderer hefted the weight of his uselessness and failure like Jacob Marley's chains? How often must he watch himself lying stubbornly immobile on the pavement of his nightmares while the sound of running feet syncopate his attacker's taunts?

I spend these days beating him at gin rummy and Scrabble, holding a basin while he coughs up phlegm and crying in the corridor while he catheterizes himself. There are children here much worse off than he. I should be grateful. The doctors can't, or won't, say whether he'll walk again.

I am at once repulsed and fascinated by the bullet, which remains lodged in his spine (having done all the damage it can do, the doctors say). The wound is undramatic—small, neat and perfectly centered—an impossibly pink pit surrounded by an otherwise undisturbed expanse of mahogany. Johnny has asked me several times to describe it but politely declines to look in the mirror I hold for him.

Here on the pediatric rehab ward, Johnny speaks little, never cries, never complains, works diligently to become independent. He does whatever he is told; if two hours remain until the next pain pill, he waits quietly. Eyes bloodshot, hands gripping the bed rails. During the week of his intravenous feeding when he was tormented by the primal need to masticate, he never asked for food. He just listened while we counted down the days for him and planned his favorite meals. Now required to dress himself unassisted, he does so without demur, rolling himself back and forth valiantly on the bed and shivering afterwards, exhausted. He "ma'am"s and "sir"s everyone politely. Before his "accident," a simple request to take out the trash could provoke a firestorm of teenage attitude. We, the women who have raised him, have changed as well; we've finally come to appreciate those boxer-baring, oversized pants we used to hate—it would be much more difficult to fit properly sized pants over his diaper.

He spends a lot of time tethered to rap music still loud enough to break my concentration as I read my many magazines. I hear him try to soundlessly mouth the obligatory "mothafuckers" overlaying the funereal dirge of the music tracks. I do not normally tolerate disrespectful music in my or my mother's presence, but if it distracts him now . . .

"Johnny," I ask later, "do you still like gangster rap?" During the long pause I hear him think loudly, *I'm paralyzed Auntie, not stupid.* "I mostly just listen to hip hop," he says evasively into his *Sports Illustrated.*

Miserable though it is, time passes quickly here. We always seem to be jerking awake in our chairs just in time for the next pill, his every-other-night bowel program, the doctor's rounds. Harvard feels a galaxy away—the world revolves around

Family Members Living With Spinal Cord Injury class, Johnny's urine output and strategizing with my sister to find affordable, accessible housing. There is always another long-distance uncle in need of an update, another church member wanting to pray with us or Johnny's little brother in need of some attention.

We Dickerson women are so constant a presence the ward nurses and cleaning staff call us by name and join us for cafeteria meals and cigarette breaks. At Johnny's birthday pizza party, they crack jokes and make fun of each other's husbands (there are no men here). I pass slices around and try not to think, "17 with a bullet."

Oddly, we feel little curiosity or specific anger toward the man who shot him. We have to remind ourselves to check in with the police. Even so, it feels pro forma, like sending in those $2 rebate forms that come with new pantyhose: you know your request will fall into a deep, dark hole somewhere but, still, it's your duty to try. We push for an arrest because we owe it to Johnny and to ourselves as citizens. We don't think about it otherwise—our low expectations are too ingrained. A Harvard aunt notwithstanding, for people like Johnny, Marvin Gaye was right that only three things are sure: taxes, death and trouble. At least it wasn't the second.

We rarely wonder about or discuss the brother who shot him because we already know everything about him. When the call came, my first thought was the same one I'd had when I'd heard about Rosa Parks's beating: a brother did it. A non-job-having, middle-of-the-day malt-liquor-drinking, crotch-clutching, loud-talking brother with many neglected children born of many forgotten women. He lives in his mother's basement with furniture rented at an astronomical interest rate, the exact amount of which he does not know. He has a car phone, an $80 monthly cable bill and every possible phone feature but no savings. He steals Social Security numbers from unsuspecting relatives and assumes their identities to acquire large TV sets for which he will never pay. On the slim chance that he is brought to justice, he will have a colorful criminal history and no coherent explanation to offer for this act. His family will raucously defend him and cry cover-up. Some liberal lawyer just like me will help him plea bargain his way to yet another short stay in a prison pesthouse that will serve only to add another layer to the brother's sociopathology and formless, mindless nihilism. We know him. We've known and feared him all our lives.

As a teenager, he called, "Hey, baby, gimme somma that boodie!" at us from car windows. Indignant at our lack of response, he followed up with, "Fuck you, then, 'ho!" He called me a "white-boy lovin' nigger bitch oreo" for being in the gifted program and loving it. At 27, he got my 17-year-old sister pregnant with Johnny and lost interest without ever informing her that he was married. He snatched my widowed mother's purse as she waited in pre-dawn darkness for the bus to work and then broke into our house while she soldered on an assembly line. He chased all the small entrepreneurs from our neighborhood with his violent thievery, and put bars on our windows. He kept us from sitting on our own front porch after dark and laid the foundation for our periodic bouts of self-hating anger and racial embarrassment. He made our neighborhood a ghetto. He is the poster fool behind the maddening community knowledge that there are still some black mothers who raise their daughters but merely love their sons. He and his cancerous carbon copies eclipse the vast majority of us who are not sociopaths and render us invisible. He is the Siamese twin who has died but cannot be separated from his living, vibrant sibling; which of us must attract more notice? We despise and disown this anomalous loser but, for many, he *is* black America. We know him, we know that he is outside the fold, and we know that he will only get worse. What we didn't know is that, because of him, my little sister would one day be the latest hysterical black mother wailing over a fallen child on TV.

Alone, lying in the road bleeding and paralyzed but hideously conscious, Johnny had lain helpless as he watched his would-be murderer come to stand over him and offer this prophecy: "Betch'ou won't be doin' nomo' wavin', motha'-fucker."

Fuck you, asshole. He's fine from the waist up. You just can't do anything right, can you?

10

The Truly Disadvantaged

WILLIAM JULIUS WILSON

The inner city is less pleasant and more dangerous than it was prior to 1960. . . . Despite a high rate of poverty in inner-city areas during the first half of this century, rates of joblessness, out-of-wedlock births, single families, welfare dependency, and serious crime were significantly lower than they are today and did not begin to rise rapidly until after the mid-1960s, with extraordinary increases during the 1970s. . . .

The Ghetto Underclass and Social Dislocations

Why have the social conditions of the ghetto underclass deteriorated so rapidly in recent years? Racial discrimination is the most frequently invoked explanation, and it is undeniable that discrimination continues to aggravate the social and economic problems of poor blacks. But is discrimination really greater today than it was in 1948, when black unemployment was less than half of what it is now, and when the gap between black and white jobless rates was narrower?

As for the poor black family, it apparently began to fall apart not before but after the mid-twentieth century. Until publication in 1976 of Herbert Gutman's *The Black Family in Slavery and Freedom,* most scholars had believed otherwise. Stimulated by the acrimonious debate over the Moynihan report, Gutman produced data demonstrating that the black family was not significantly disrupted during slavery or even during the early years of the first migration to the urban North, beginning after the turn of the century. The problems of the modern black family, he implied, were associated with modern forces.

Those who cite discrimination as the root cause of poverty often fail to make a distinction between the effects of *historic* discrimination (i.e., discrimination prior to the mid-twentieth century) and the effects of *contemporary* discrimination. Thus they find it hard to explain why the economic position of the black underclass started to worsen soon after Congress enacted, and the White House began to enforce, the most sweeping civil rights legislation since Reconstruction.

The point to be emphasized is that historic discrimination is more important than contemporary discrimination in understanding the plight of the ghetto underclass—that in any event there is more to the story than discrimination (of whichever kind). Historic discrimination certainly helped create an impoverished urban black community in the first place. In his recent *A Piece of the Pie: Black and White Immigrants since 1880* (1980), Stanley Lieberson shows how, in many areas of life, including the labor market, black newcomers from the rural South were far more severely discriminated against in northern cities than were the new white immigrants from southern, central, and eastern Europe. Skin color was part of the problem but it was not all of it.

The disadvantage of skin color—the fact that the dominant whites preferred whites over nonwhites—is one that blacks shared with the Japanese, Chinese, and others. Yet the experience of the Asians, who also experienced harsh discriminatory treatment in the communities where they were concentrated, but who went on to prosper in their adopted land, suggests that skin color per se was not an insuperable obstacle. Indeed Lieberson argues that the greater success enjoyed by Asians may well be explained largely by the different context of their contact with whites. Because changes in immigration policy cut off Asian migration to America in the late nineteenth century, the Japanese and Chinese population did not reach large numbers and therefore did not pose as great a threat as did blacks.

Furthermore, the discontinuation of large-scale immigration from Japan and China enabled those Chinese and Japanese already in the United States to solidify networks of ethnic contacts and to occupy particular occupational niches in small, relatively stable communities. For blacks, the situation was different. The 1970 census recorded 22,580,000 blacks in the United States but only 435,000 Chinese and 591,000 Japanese.

If different population sizes accounted for a good deal of the difference in the economic success of blacks and Asians, they also helped determine the dissimilar rates of progress of urban blacks and the new European arrivals. European immigration was curtailed during the 1920s, but black migration to the urban North continued through the 1960s. With each passing decade there were many more blacks who were recent migrants to the North, whereas the immigrant component of the new Europeans dropped off over time. Eventually, other whites muffled their dislike of the Poles and Italians and Jews and directed their antagonism against blacks.

In addition to the problem of historic discrimination, the black migration to New York, Philadelphia, Chicago, and other northern cities—the continued replenishment of black populations there by poor newcomers—predictably skewed the age profile of the urban black community and kept it relatively young. The number of central-city black youths aged sixteen to nineteen increased by almost 75 percent from 1960 to 1969. Young black adults (aged twenty to twenty-four) increased in number by two-thirds during the same period, three times the increase for young white adults. In the nation's inner cities in 1977, the median age for whites was 30.3, for blacks 23.9. The importance of this jump in the number of young minorities in the ghetto, many of them lacking one or more parents, cannot be overemphasized.

Age correlates with many things. For example, the higher the median age of a group, the higher its income; the lower the median age, the higher the unemployment rate and the higher the crime rate (more than half of those arrested in 1980 for violent and property crimes in American cities were under twenty-one). The younger a woman is, the more likely she is to bear a child out of wedlock, head up a new household, and depend on welfare. In short, part of what had gone awry in the ghetto was due to the sheer increase in the number of black youth.

The population explosion among minority youth occurred at a time when changes in the economy were beginning to pose serious problems for unskilled workers. Urban minorities have been particularly vulnerable to the structural economic changes of the past two decades: the shift from goods-producing to service-producing industries, the increasing polarization of the labor market into low-wage and high-wage sectors, innovations in technology, and the relocation of manufacturing industries out of the central cities.

Most unemployed blacks in the United States reside within the central cities. Their situation, already more difficult than that of any other major ethnic group in the country, continues to worsen. Not only are there more blacks without jobs every year; men, especially young males, are dropping out of the labor force in record proportions. Also, more and more black youth, including many who are no longer in school, are obtaining no job experience at all.

However, the growing problem of joblessness in the inner city exacerbates and is in turn partly created by the changing social composition of inner-city neighborhoods. These areas have undergone a profound social transformation in the last several years, as reflected not only in their increasing rates of social dislocation but also in the changing class structure of ghetto neighborhoods. In the 1940s, 1950s, and even the 1960s, lower-class, working-class, and middle-class black urban families all resided more or less in the same ghetto areas, albeit on different streets. Although black middle-class professionals today tend to be employed in mainstream occupations outside the black community and neither live nor frequently interact with ghetto residents, the black middle-class professionals of the 1940s and 1950s (doctors, lawyers, teachers, social workers, etc.) resided in the higher-income areas of the inner city and serviced the ghetto community. The exodus of black middle-class professionals from the inner city has been increasingly accompanied by a movement of stable working-class blacks to higher-income neighborhoods in other parts of the city and to the suburbs. Confined by restrictive covenants to communities also inhabited by the urban black lower classes, the black working and middle classes in earlier years provided stability to inner-city neighborhoods and perpetuated and reinforced societal norms and values. In short, their very presence enhanced the social organization of ghetto communities. If strong norms and sanctions against aberrant behavior, a sense of community, and positive neighborhood identification are the essential features of social organization in urban areas, inner-city neighborhoods today suffer from a severe lack of social organization.

Unlike in previous years, today's ghetto residents represent almost exclusively the most disadvantaged segments of the urban black community—including those families that have experienced long-term spells of poverty and/or welfare dependency, individuals who lack training and skills and have either experienced periods of persistent unemployment or have dropped out of the labor force altogether, and individuals who are frequently involved in street criminal activity. The term *ghetto underclass* refers to this heterogeneous group of families and individuals who inhabit the cores of the nation's central cities. The term suggests that a fundamental social transformation has taken place in ghetto neighborhoods, and the groups represented by this term are collectively different from and much more socially isolated than those that lived in these communities in earlier years.

The significance of changes embodied in the social transformation of the inner city is perhaps best captured by the concepts *concentration effects* and *social buffer*. The former refers to the constraints and opportunities associated with living in a neighborhood in which the population is overwhelmingly socially disadvantaged—constraints and opportunities that include the kinds of ecological niches that the residents of these communities occupy in terms of access to jobs, availability of marriageable partners, and exposure to conventional role models. The latter refers to the presence of a sufficient number of working- and middle-class professional families to absorb the shock or cushion the effect of uneven economic growth and periodic recessions on inner-city neighborhoods. The basic thesis is not that ghetto culture went unchecked following the removal of higher-income families in the inner city, but that the removal of these families made it more difficult to sustain the basic institutions in the inner city (including churches, stores, schools, recreational facilities, etc.) in the face of prolonged joblessness. And as the basic institutions declined, the social organization of inner-city neighborhoods (defined here to include a sense of community, positive neighborhood identification, and explicit norms and sanctions against aberrant behavior) likewise declined. Indeed, the social organization of any neighborhood depends in large measure on the viability of social institutions in that neighborhood. It is true that the presence of stable working- and middle-class families in the ghetto provides mainstream role models that reinforce mainstream values pertaining to employment, education, and family structure. But, in the final analysis, a far more important effect is the institutional stability that these families are able to provide in their neighborhoods because of their greater economic and educational resources, especially during periods of an economic downturn—periods in which joblessness in poor urban areas tends to substantially increase.

In underlining joblessness as an important aspect of inner-city social transformations, we are reminded that in the 1960s scholars readily attributed poor black family deterioration to problems of employment. Nonetheless, in the last several years, in the face of the overwhelming attention given to welfare as the major source of black family breakup, concerns about the importance of joblessness have diminished, despite the existence of evidence strongly suggesting the need for renewed scholarly and public policy attention to the relationship between the disintegration of poor black families and black male labor-market experiences.

Although changing social and cultural trends have often been said to explain some of the dynamic shifts in the structure of the family, they appear to have more relevance for changes in family structure among whites. And contrary to popular opinion, there is little evidence to support the argument that welfare is the primary cause of family out-of-wedlock births, breakups, and female-headed households. Welfare does seem to have a modest effect on separation and divorce, particularly for white women, but recent evidence indicates that its total effect on the proportion of all female householders is small.

By contrast, the evidence for the influence of joblessness on family structure is much more conclusive. Research has demonstrated, for example, a connection between an encouraging economic situation and the early marriage of young people. In this connection, black women are more likely to delay marriage and less likely to remarry. Although black and white teenagers expect to become parents at about the same ages, black teenagers expect to marry at later ages. The black delay in marriage and the lower rate of remarriage, each associated with high percentages of out-of-wedlock births and female-headed households, can be directly tied to the employment status of black males. Indeed, black women, especially young black women, are confronting a shrinking pool of "marriageable" (that is economically stable) men.

White women are not experiencing this problem. Our "male marriageable pool index" shows that the number of employed white men per one hundred white women in different age categories has either remained roughly the same or has only slightly increased in the last two decades. There is little reason, therefore, to assume a connection between the recent growth of female-headed white families and patterns of white male employment. That the pool of "marriageable" white men has not decreased over the years is perhaps reflected in the earlier age of first marriage and the higher rate of remarriage among white women. It is therefore reasonable to hypothesize that the rise in rates of separation and divorce among whites is due mainly to the increased economic independence of white women and related social and cultural factors embodied in the feminist movement.

The argument that the decline in the incidence of intact marriages among blacks is associated with the declining economic status of black men is further supported by an analysis of regional data on female headship and the "male marriageable pool." Whereas changes in the ratios of employed men to women among whites have been minimal for all regions of the country regardless of age from 1960 to 1980, the ratios among blacks have declined significantly in all regions except the West, with the greatest declines in the northeastern and north-central regions of the country. On the basis of these trends, it would be expected that the growth in numbers of black female-headed households would occur most rapidly in the northern regions, followed by the South and the West. Regional data on the "male marriageable pool index" support this conclusion, except for the larger-than-expected increase in black female-headed families in the West—a function of patterns of selective black migration to the West.

The sharp decline in the black "male marriageable pool" in the northeastern and north-central regions is related to recent changes in the basic economic organization in American society. In the two northern regions, the shift in economic activity from goods production to services has been associated with changes in the location of production, including an interregional movement of industry from the North to the South and West and, more important, a movement of certain industries out of the older central cities where blacks are concentrated. Moreover, the shrinkage of the male marriageable pool for ages sixteen to twenty-four in the South from 1960 to 1980 is related to the mechanization of agriculture, which lowered substantially the demand for low-skilled agricultural labor, especially during the 1960s. For all these reasons, it is often necessary to go beyond the specific issue of current racial discrimination to understand factors that contribute directly to poor black joblessness and indirectly to related social problems such as family instability in the inner city. But this point has not been readily grasped by policymakers and civil rights leaders.

The Limits of Race-specific Public Policy

In the early 1960s there was no comprehensive civil rights bill and Jim Crow segregation was still widespread in parts of the nation, particularly in the Deep South. With the passage of the 1964 Civil Rights Bill there was considerable optimism that racial progress would ensue and that the principle of equality of individual rights (namely, that candidates for positions stratified in terms of prestige, power, or other social criteria ought to be judged solely on individual merit and therefore should not be discriminated against on the basis of racial orgin) would be upheld.

Programs based solely on this principle are inadequate, however, to deal with the complex problems of race in America because they are not designed to address the substantive inequality that exists at the time discrimination is eliminated. In other words, long periods of racial oppression can result in a system of inequality that may persist for indefinite periods of time even after racial barriers are removed. This is because the most disadvantaged members of racial minority groups, who suffer the cumulative effects of both race and class subjugation (including those effects passed on from generation to generation), are disproportionately represented among the segment of the general population that has been denied the resources to compete effectively in a free and open market.

On the other hand, the competitive resources developed by the *advantaged minority members*—resources that flow directly from the family stability, schooling, income, and peer groups that their parents have been able to provide—result in their benefiting disproportionately from policies that promote the rights of minority individuals by removing artificial barriers to valued positions.

Nevertheless, since 1970, government policy has tended to focus on formal programs designed and created both to prevent discrimination and to ensure that minorities are sufficiently represented in certain positions. This has resulted in a shift from the simple formal investigation and adjudication of complaints of racial discrimination to government-mandated affirmative action programs to increase minority representation in public programs, employment, and education.

However, if minority members from the most advantaged families profit disproportionately from policies based on the principle of equality of individual opportunity, they also reap disproportionate benefits from policies of affirmative action based solely on their group membership. This is because advantaged minority members are likely to be disproportionately represented among those of their racial group most qualified for valued positions, such as college admissions, higher paying jobs, and promotions. Thus, if policies of preferential treatment for such positions are developed in terms of racial group membership rather than the real disadvantages suffered by individuals, then these policies will further improve the opportunities of the advantaged without necessarily addressing the problems of the truly disadvantaged such as the ghetto underclass.[1] The problems of the truly disadvantaged may require *nonracial* solutions such as full employment, balanced economic growth, and manpower training and education (tied to—not isolated from—these two economic conditions).

By 1980 this argument was not widely recognized or truly appreciated. Therefore, because the government not only adopted and implemented antibias legislation to promote minority individual rights, but also mandated and enforced affirmative action and related programs to enhance minority group rights, many thoughtful American citizens, including supporters of civil rights, were puzzled by recent social developments in black communities. Despite the passage of civil rights legislation and the creation of affirmative action programs, they sensed that conditions were deteriorating instead of improving for a significant segment of the black American population. This perception had emerged because of the continuous flow of pessimistic reports concerning the sharp rise in black joblessness, the precipitous drop in the black-white family income ratio, the steady increase in the percentage of blacks on the welfare rolls, and the extraordinary growth in the number of female-headed families. This perception was strengthened by the almost uniform cry among black leaders that not only had conditions worsened, but that white Americans had forsaken the cause of blacks as well.

Meanwhile, the liberal architects of the War on Poverty became puzzled when Great Society programs failed to reduce poverty in America and when they could find few satisfactory explanations for the sharp rise in inner-city social dislocations during the 1970s. However, just as advocates for minority rights have been slow to comprehend that many of the current problems of race, particularly those that plague the minority poor, derived from the broader processes of societal organization and therefore may have no direct or indirect connection with race, so too have the architects of the War on Poverty failed to emphasize the relationship between poverty and the broader processes of American economic organization. Accordingly, given the most comprehensive civil rights and antipoverty programs in America's history, the liberals of the civil rights movement and the Great Society became demoralized when inner-city poverty proved to be more intractable than they realized and when they could not satisfactorily explain such events as the unprecedented rise in inner-city joblessness and the remarkable growth in the number of female-headed households. This demoralization cleared the path for conservative analysts to fundamentally shift the focus away from changing the environments of the minority poor to changing their values and behavior.

However, and to repeat, many of the problems of the ghetto underclass are related to the broader problems of societal organization, including economic organization. For example, as pointed out earlier, regional differences in changes in the "male marriageable pool index" signify the importance of industrial shifts in the Northeast and Midwest. Related research clearly demonstrated the declining labor-market opportunities in the older central cities. Indeed, blacks tend to be concentrated in areas where the number and characteristics of jobs have been most significantly altered by shifts in the location of production activity and from manufacturing to services. Since an overwhelming majority of inner-city blacks lacks the qualifications for the high-skilled segment of the service sector such as information processing, finance, and real estate, they tend to be concentrated in the low-skilled segment, which features unstable employment, restricted opportunities, and low wages.

The Hidden Agenda: From Group-specific to Universal Programs of Reform

It is not enough simply to recognize the need to relate many of the woes of truly disadvantaged blacks to the problems of societal organization; it is also important to describe the problems of the ghetto underclass candidly and openly so that they can be fully explained and appropriate policy programs can be devised. It has been problematic, therefore, that liberal journalists, social scientists, policymakers, and civil rights leaders were reluctant throughout the decade of the 1970s to discuss inner-city social pathologies. Often, analysts of such issues as violent crime or teenage pregnancy deliberately make no references to race at all, unless perhaps to emphasize the deleterious consequences of racial discrimination or the institutionalized inequality of American society. Some scholars, in an effort to avoid the appearance of "blaming the victim" or to protect their work from charges of racism, simply ignore patterns of behavior that might be construed as stigmatizing to particular racial minorities.

Such neglect is relatively recent. During the mid-1960s, social scientists such as Kenneth B. Clark, Daniel Patrick Moynihan, and Lee Rainwater forthrightly examined the cumulative effects of racial isolation and class subordination on inner-city blacks. They vividly described aspects of ghetto life that, as Rainwater observed, are usually not discussed in polite conversations. All of these studies attempted to show the connection between the economic and social environment into which many blacks are born and the creation of patterns of behavior that, in Clark's words, frequently amounted to "self-perpetuating pathology."

Why have scholars tended to shy away from this line of research? One reason has to do with the vitriolic attack by many blacks and liberals against Moynihan upon publication of his report in 1965—denunciations that generally focused on the author's unflattering depiction of the black family in the urban ghetto rather than on the proposed remedies or his historical analysis of the black family's social plight. The harsh reception accorded *The Negro Family* undoubtedly dissuaded many social scientists from following in Moynihan's footsteps.

The "black solidarity" movement was also emerging during the latter half of the 1960s. A new emphasis by young black scholars and intellectuals on the positive aspects of the black experience tended to crowd out older concerns. Indeed, certain forms of ghetto behavior labeled pathological in the studies of Clark and colleagues were redefined by some during the early 1970s as "functional" because, it was argued, blacks were displaying the ability to survive and in some cases flourish in an economically depressed environment. The ghetto family was described as resilient and capable of adapting creatively to an oppressive, racist society. And the candid, but liberal writings on the inner city in the 1960s were generally denounced. In the end, the promising efforts of the early 1960s—to distinguish the socioeconomic characteristics of different groups within the black community, and to identify the structural problems of the United States economy that affected minorities—were cut short by calls for "reparations" or for "black control of institutions serving the black community."

If this ideologically tinged criticism discouraged research by liberal scholars on the poor black family and the ghetto community, conservative thinkers were not so inhibited. From the early 1970s through the first half of the 1980s, their writings on the culture of poverty and the deleterious effects of Great Society liberal welfare policies on ghetto underclass behavior dominated the public policy debate on alleviating inner-city social dislocations.

The Great Society programs represented the country's most ambitious attempt to implement the principle of equality of life chances. However, the extent to which these programs helped the truly disadvantaged is difficult to assess when one considers the simultaneous impact of the economic downturn from 1968 to the early 1980s. Indeed, it has been argued that many people slipped into poverty because of the economic downturn and were lifted out by the broadening of welfare benefits. Moreover, the increase in unemployment that accompanied the economic downturn and the lack of growth of real wages in the 1970s, although they had risen steadily from 1950 to about 1970, have had a pronounced effect on low-income groups (especially black males).

The above analysis has certain distinct public policy implications for attacking the problems of inner-city joblessness and the related problems of poor female-headed families, welfare dependency, crime, and so forth. Comprehensive economic policies aimed at the general population but that would also enhance employment opportunities among the truly disadvantaged—both men and women—are needed. The research presented in this study suggests that improving the job prospects of men will strengthen low-income black families. Moreover, underclass absent fathers with more stable employment are in a better position to contribute financial support for their families. Furthermore, since the majority of female householders are in the labor force, improved job prospects would very likely draw in others.[2]

I have in mind the creation of a macroeconomic policy designed to promote both economic growth and a tight labor market.[3] The latter affects the supply-and-demand ratio and wages tend to rise. It would be necessary, however, to combine this policy with fiscal and monetary policies to stimulate noninflationary growth and thereby move away from the policy of controlling inflation by allowing unemployment to rise. Furthermore, it would be important to develop policy to increase the competitiveness of American goods on the international market by, among other things, reducing the budget deficit to adjust the value of the American dollar.

In addition, measures such as on-the-job training and apprenticeships to elevate the skill levels of the truly disadvantaged are needed. I will soon discuss in another context why such problems have to be part of a more universal package of reform. For now, let me simply say that improved manpower policies are needed in the short run to help lift the truly disadvantaged from the lowest rungs of the job market. In other words, it would be necessary to devise a national labor-market strategy to increase "the adaptability of the labor force to changing employment opportunities." In this connection, instead of focusing on remedial programs in the public sector for the poor and the unemployed, emphasis would be placed on relating these programs more closely to opportunities in the private sector to facilitate the movement of recipients (including relocation assistance) into more secure jobs. Of course there would be a need to create public transitional programs for those who have difficulty finding immediate employment in the private sector, but such programs would aim toward eventually getting individuals into the private sector economy. Although public employment programs continue to draw popular support, as Weir, Orloff, and Skocpol point out, "they must be designed and administered in close conjunction with a nationally oriented labor market strategy" to avoid both becoming "enmeshed in congressionally reinforced local political patronage" and being attacked as costly, inefficient, or "corrupt."[4]

Since national opinion polls consistently reveal strong public support for efforts to enhance work in America, political support for a program of economic reform (macroeconomic employment policies and labor-market strategies including training efforts) could be considerably stronger than many people presently assume.[5] However, in order to draw sustained public support for such a program, it is necessary that training or retraining, transitional employment benefits, and relocation assistance be available to all members of society who choose to use them, not just to poor minorities.

It would be ideal if problems of the ghetto underclass could be adequately addressed by the combination of macroeconomic policy, labor-market strategies, and manpower training programs. However, in the foreseeable future employment alone will not necessarily lift a family out of poverty.[6] Many families would still require income support and/or social services such as child care. A program of welfare reform is needed, therefore, to address the current problems of public assistance, including lack of provisions for poor two-parent families, inadequate levels of support, inequities between different states, and work disincentives. A national AFDC benefit standard adjusted yearly for inflation is the most minimal required change. We might also give serious consideration to programs such as the Child Support Assurance Program developed by Irwin Garfinkel and colleagues at the Institute for Research on Poverty at the University of Wisconsin, Madison.[7] This program, currently in operation as a demonstration project in the state of Wisconsin, provides a guaranteed minimum benefit per child to single-parent families regardless of the income of the custodial parent. The state collects from the absent parent through wage withholding a sum of money at a fixed rate and then makes regular payments to the custodial parent. If the absent parent is jobless or if his or her payment from withholdings is less than the minimum, the state makes up the difference. Since all absent parents regardless of income are required to participate in this program, it is far less stigmatizing than, say, public assistance. Moreover, preliminary evidence from Wisconsin suggests that this program carries little or no additional cost to the state.

Many western European countries have programs of family or child allowances to support families. These programs provide families with an annual benefit per child regardless of the family's income, and regardless of whether the parents are living together or whether either or both are employed. Unlike public assistance, therefore, a family allowance program carries no social stigma and has no built-in work disincentives. In this connection, Daniel Patrick Moynihan has recently observed that a form of family allowance is already available to American families with the standard deduction and the Earned Income Tax Credit, although the latter can only be obtained by low-income families. Even though both have been significantly eroded by inflation, they could represent the basis for a more comprehensive family allowance program that approximates the European model.

Neither the Child Support Assurance Program under demonstration in Wisconsin nor the European family allowances program is means tested; that is, they are not targeted at a particular income group and therefore do not suffer the degree of stigmatization that plagues public assistance programs such as AFDC. More important, such universal programs would tend to draw more political support from the general public because the programs would be available not only to the poor but to the working- and middle-class segments as well. And such programs would not be readily associated with specific minority groups. Nonetheless, truly disadvantaged groups would reap disproportionate benefits from such programs because of the groups' limited alternative economic resources. For example, low-income single mothers could combine work with adequate guaranteed child support and/or child allowance benefits and therefore escape poverty and avoid public assistance.

Finally, the question of child care has to be addressed in any program designed to improve the employment prospects of women and men. Because of the growing participation of women in the labor market, adequate child care has been a topic receiving increasing attention in public policy discussions. For the overwhelmingly female-headed ghetto underclass families, access to quality child care becomes a critical issue if steps are taken to move single mothers into education and training programs and/or full- or part-time employment. However, I am not recommending government-operated child care centers. Rather it would be better to avoid additional federal bureaucracy by seeking alternative and decentralized forms of child care such as expanding the child care tax credit, including three- and four-year-olds in preschool enrollment, and providing child care subsidies to the working-poor parents.

If the truly disadvantaged reaped disproportionate benefits from a child support enforcement program, child allowance program, and child care strategy, they would also benefit disproportionately from a program of balanced economic growth and tight-labor-market policies because of their greater vulnerability to swings in the business cycle and changes in economic organization, including the relocation of plants and the use of labor-saving technology. It would be shortsighted to conclude, therefore, that universal programs (i.e., programs not targeted at any particular group) are not designed to help address in a fundamental way some of the problems of the truly disadvantaged, such as the ghetto underclass.

By emphasizing universal programs as an effective way to address problems in the inner city created by historic racial subjugation, I am recommending a fundamental shift from the traditional race-specific approach of addressing such problems. It is true that problems of joblessness and related woes such as poverty, teenage pregnancies, out-of-wedlock births, female-headed families, and welfare dependency are, for reasons of historic racial oppression, disproportionately concentrated in the black community. And it is important to recognize the racial differences in rates of social dislocation so as not to obscure problems currently gripping the ghetto underclass. However, as discussed above, race-specific policies are often not designed to address fundamental problems of the truly disadvantaged. Moreover, as also discussed above, both race-specific and targeted programs based on the principle of equality of life chances (often identified with a minority constituency) have difficulty sustaining widespread public support.

Does this mean that targeted programs of any kind would necessarily be excluded from a package highlighting universal programs of reform? On the contrary, as long as a racial division of labor exists and racial minorities are disproportionately concentrated in low-paying positions, antidiscrimination and affirmative action programs will be needed even though they tend to benefit the more advantaged minority members. Moreover, as long as certain groups lack the training, skills, and education to compete effectively on the job market or move into newly created jobs, manpower training and education programs targeted at these groups will also be needed, even under a tight-labor-market situation. For example, a program of adult education and training may be necessary for some ghetto underclass males before they can either become oriented to or move into an expanded labor market. Finally, as long as some poor families are unable to work because of physical or other disabilities, public assistance would be needed even if the government adopted a program of welfare reform that included child support enforcement and family allowance provisions.

For all these reasons, a comprehensive program of economic and social reform (highlighting macroeconomic policies to promote balanced economic growth and create a tight-labor-market situation, a nationally oriented labor-market strategy, a child support assurance program, a child care strategy, and a family allowances program) would have to include targeted programs, both means tested and race-specific. However, the latter would be considered an offshoot of and indeed secondary to the universal programs. The important goal is to construct an economic-social reform program in such a way that the universal programs are seen as the dominant and most visible aspects by the general public. As the universal programs draw support from a wider population, the targeted programs included in the comprehensive reform package would be indirectly supported and protected. Accordingly, *the hidden agenda for liberal policymakers is to improve the life chances of truly disadvantaged groups such as the ghetto underclass by emphasizing programs to which the more advantaged groups of all races and class backgrounds can positively relate.*

I am reminded of Bayard Rustin's plea during the early 1960s that blacks ought to recognize the importance of fundamental economic reform (including a system of national economic planning along with new education, manpower, and public works programs to help reach full employment) and the need for a broad-based political coalition to achieve it. And since an effective coalition will in part depend upon how the issues are defined, it is imperative that the political message underline the need for economic and social reforms that benefit all groups in the United States, not just poor minorities. Politicians and civil rights organizations, as two important examples, ought to shift or expand their definition of America's racial problems and broaden the scope of suggested policy programs to address them. They should, of course, continue to fight for an end to racial discrimination. But they must also recognize that poor minorities are profoundly affected by problems in America that go beyond racial considerations. Furthermore, civil rights groups should also recognize that the problems of societal organization in America often create situations that enhance racial antagonisms between the different racial groups in central cities that are struggling to maintain their quality of life, and that these groups, although they appear to be fundamental adversaries, are potential allies in a reform coalition because of their problematic economic situations. . . .

NOTES

1. James Fishkin covers much of this ground very convincingly. See his *Justice, Equal Opportunity and the Family* (New Haven, Conn.: Yale University Press, 1983).

2. Kathryn M. Neckerman, Robert Aponte, and William Julius Wilson, "Family Structure, Black Unemployment, and American Social Policy," in *The Politics of Social Policy in the United States,* ed. Margaret Weir, Ann Shola Orloff, and Theda Skocpol (Princeton, N.J.: Princeton University Press, forthcoming).

3. The essential features of such a policy are discussed in chap. 5, "The Case for a Universal Program."

4. Margaret Weir, Ann Shola Orloff, and Theda Skocpol, "The Future of Social Policy in the United States: Political Constraints and Possibilities," in Weir, Orloff, and Skocpol, *Politics of Social Policy in the United States.*

5. Theda Skocpol, "Brother Can You Spare a Job?: Work and Welfare in the United States," paper presented at the Annual Meeting of the American Sociological Association, Washington, D.C., August 27, 1985.

6. Part of the discussion on welfare reform in the next several pages is based on Neckerman, Aponte, and Wilson, "Family Structure, Black Unemployment, and American Social Policy."

7. Irwin Garfinkel and Sara S. McLanahan, *Single Mothers and Their Children: A New American Dilemma* (Washington, D.C.: Urban Institute Press, 1986).

11

All in the Family:
Illegitimacy and Welfare Dependence

WILLIAM TUCKER

Aid to Families with Dependent Children (AFDC) began in 1935 as a small stipend for "widows and orphans." It was anticipated that the program would be phased out in a few years as the survivor's benefits in the Social Security system became fully funded. Instead, AFDC has become the economic underpinning of a huge and growing American underclass.

This underclass has become self-perpetuating. Gone are the days when we could kid ourselves that welfare was a temporary expedient designed to lift people out of poverty. The habits that the underclass has acquired under AFDC assure that the next generation will be even more dependent and dysfunctional than the last.

In a recent visit to the subterranean world of single motherhood, Kay Hymowitz, a contributing editor for *The City Journal,* discovered "a culture—or subculture to be precise—with its own values, beliefs, sexual mores, and, to a certain extent, its own economy." Teenage boys who have already fathered several children express horror at the possibility of marriage, viewing it as a responsibility they wouldn't begin to consider "until I'm about 30." Fourteen-year-old girls who haven't yet become pregnant are accused by friends and neighbors of "thinking you're better than us." Older mothers actually take pleasure in seeing their sons get girls pregnant, and older fathers—well, who knows where they are? "Someone who waits until 30 or even 25 to have her first child seems a little weird, like the spinster aunt of yesteryear," Hymowitz reports. "All view marriage as irrelevant, vestigial."

It is important to realize how far this social disintegration goes beyond mere "laziness" and "refusal to work." What has been disrupted is the process of family formation. Not twenty years ago, anthropologists were fond of noting that there was no human society anywhere that did not have some form of marriage. Now we have one. Having separated childbearing from the economic responsibilities of raising children, we find that people are willing to breed as fast as humanly possible. Biology has replaced culture.

What is surprising is that anthropologists have had little to say about this development. Anthropology, after all, is founded on the principle that culture, more than biology, is the driving force in human evolution. What anthropologists have known for a long time—and what they seem reluctant to say now—is that marriage and family formation are institutions that differ widely across cultures. Among other things, those cross-cultural differences help explain why African-Americans have been especially susceptible to the negative incentives of welfare. At the same time, an understanding of how marriage patterns among American blacks have changed during the last few centuries suggests that the damage can be reversed.

A Universal Institution

Bronislaw Malinowski, the first great anthropologist who lived among primitive peoples, learned their language, and made painstaking observations of their daily habits, came away with the belief that the human family was a universal institution. In his 1930 essay, "Parenthood: The Basis of Social Structure," he writes:

> Indeed, at first sight, the typical savage family, as it is found among the vast majority of native tribes . . . seems hardly to differ at all from its civilized counterpart. Mother, father, and children share the camp, the home, the food, and the life. . . . Attached to each other, sharing life and most of its interests, exchanging counsel and help, company and cheer, and reciprocating in economic cooperation . . . the individual, undivided family stands out conspicuous, a definite social unit marked off from the rest of society by a clear line of division.

What struck Malinowski most forcefully was the universal role of the father in primitive societies:

> Expecting, perhaps, from a savage man a certain degree of ferocity towards wife and children, [an observer] might be astonished to find instead a kind and considerate husband and a tender father. At worst—I mean in tribes where, through custom and tradition, he plays the not always amiable role of a stern patriarch—he is still the provider of the family, the helpmate at home, and the guardian of the children up to a certain age. At his best and mildest, in a typical matrilineal community, he is a drudge within the household, the assistant nurse of his children, the weaker and fonder of the two parents, and later on the most faithful and often the most intimate friend of his sons and daughters.

Malinowski generalized these observations into what he called the "principle of legitimacy":

> Through all societies there runs the rule that the father is indispensable for the full sociological status of the child [and] that the group consisting of a woman and her offspring is sociologically incomplete and illegitimate. . . . The most important moral and legal rule [in primitive societies] is that no child should be brought into the

world without a man—and one man at that—assuming the role of sociological father, that is guardian and protector, the male link between the child and the rest of
the community.

Marriage was a way of ensuring that, whatever degree of sexual puritanism or
license might characterize a society, the rearing of children was always done
within the confines of the family. In "The Family: Past and Present" (1934),
Malinowski writes:

> [Some societies] look at [sex] in a way [that] even Queen Victoria herself could not
> improve. . . . [In others,] free love making is allowed. . . . But one rule is always precise
> and often extremely stringent: there must be no pregnancy without marriage. . . . Every
> tribal tradition puts a premium on effective and successful parenthood.

Every society has set up a ritual to draw the line between the married and non-
married states and trigger family formation. In societies that emphasize chastity
and paternal claims, the ritual often involves a symbolic deflowering or lifting of
the bride's veil. But even among societies where paternity is not emphasized and
premarital sex is tolerated, there is always a symbolic act that both affirms the couple's commitment to each other and sets them apart from the rest of the society.

Among the Trobriand Islanders, where Malinowski did his first important field
work, the role of paternity was unknown. Sexual intercourse was not connected
with procreation, and women were believed to be impregnated "by the spirits." As a
result, young people engaged in considerable sexual experimentation. Yet a couple
was not allowed to *eat a meal together* until they were married. "To take a girl out to
dinner without having previously married her—a thing permitted in Europe—
would be to disgrace her in the eyes of a Trobriander," Malinowski writes in *The
Sexual Life of Savages* (1929). "We object to an unmarried girl sharing a man's
bed—the Trobriander would object just as strongly to her sharing a meal."

In *Facing Mount Kenya*, Jomo Kenyatta, an anthropologist who became Kenya's
first president, describes family formation among the Kikuyu. Young people engage in extensive liaisons, and young men often stay at their girlfriends' huts
overnight. Yet they are always careful to leave before dawn. If a boy accidentally
oversleeps and the girl's family catches him, the couple must get married.

"Marriage is never a mere cohabitation," concluded Malinowski. "In no society
are two people of different sex allowed to share life in common and produce children without having the approval of the community. . . . Marriage in all human
societies is a license of parenthood rather than of sexual intercourse."

Forms of Families

Still, the form of the family is not always the same from one society to another.
The most obvious distinction is between polygamy and monogamy.
Anthropologists like to say that 75 per cent of the world's societies sanction
polygamy, but that is misleading. Most of these "societies" are small tribal cul-

tures. About 75 per cent of the world's people live in societies that permit only monogamy.

Monogamy is most prevalent in the temperate zones, particularly the great axis that spans Europe and Asia. Oriental cultures—especially those in the Confucian tradition—are the most strongly monogamous in the world. European and American cultures have also been monogamous, although not to the same degree. Polygamy is still common in the early books of the Bible. (Esau has five sons by three wives, and Jacob has 12 sons by two wives and two concubines.) The heroes of *The Iliad* also have concubines, but by the time of *The Odyssey*—itself a great hymn to monogamy—a pattern of lifetime marriages had been established that persisted throughout Western history.

The great culture that stands between East and West, Islam, has tolerated polygamy, but in a limited fashion. The Koran permits a man five wives, but he must support them equally. In practice, this has limited polygamy to the very rich. In most Islamic countries, no more than 5 per cent of marriages are polygamous.

The real home of polygamy (or more precisely, "polygyny") has been the tropical cultures of Africa and the South Seas. In West Africa, polygamy is practiced at all levels of society, and in some countries as many as 30 per cent of all marriages are polygamous. A village elder may take two wives, whereas a prominent national leader may take more than a dozen. Chief M. K. O. Abiola of Nigeria's Yoruba tribe, a self-made billionaire and chairman of ITT Nigeria, has 26 wives. Polygyny is everywhere accompanied by the "bride price," a payment by the husband to the wife's family that, in effect, reflects the shortage of eligible brides. (The "dowry," a sum of money to make an eligible daughter more attractive, is strictly the product of monogamy.)

In 1976 Cambridge anthropologist Jack Goody published *Production and Reproduction,* an attempt to explain why monogamy prevails in the temperate zones while polygyny prevails in the tropics. Goody concluded that the decisive factor was male participation in agriculture: "Monogamy is most likely to be found with male farming and generally polygyny [is] the least likely (though limited polygyny [the Islamic variety] is common); the reverse occurs with female farming."

Births to Unwed American Mothers			
Ethnic Origin	Percentage of Births	Ethnic Origin	Percentage of Births
African	68.2	Cuban	19.5
Puerto Rican	57.5	European	18.0
American Indian	55.3	Filipino	16.8
Hawaiian Islander	45.0	East Asian	13.5
Central/South American	43.1	Japanese	9.8
Mexican	35.3	Chinese	5.5

SOURCE: U.S. Census Bureau, 1993

Surprisingly, it turns out that the earliest human societies, the hunter-gatherers, are almost as strongly monogamous as contemporary Western societies. The reason seems to be the division of labor—men as hunters, women as gatherers. Both sexes are productive, and their efforts combine to form an efficient economic unit. The drift into polygamy seems to occur when former hunter–gatherers adopt early agriculture—"horticulture" or "gardening," as the anthropologists call it. During the horticultural stage, farming is regarded as women's work. Men tend to be unproductive. They either cling to the lost privileges of a hunting society ("leaning on their spears," as one wag put it) or maintain political power through the tribal hierarchies. Women do the heavy gardening and are therefore more economically productive. This leads to an imbalance between the sexes, which encourages polygamy. Only when animals are harnessed to the plow do men again become the principal producers, and monogamy reasserts itself.

Female Farming and Polygyny

The best way to understand why polygyny is associated with female farming is to look at contemporary West Africa. In the 1970 book *Women's Role in Economic Development*, Danish anthropologist Esther Boserup notes:

> Africa is the region of female farming *par excellence.* . . . In many African tribes, nearly all the tasks connected with food production continue to be left to women. . . . Men may [fell trees] or take part in the preparatory hoeing before the crops are planted, but even with such help the bulk of the work with the food crops is done by women.

In addition to farming, much of the trade in West Africa is handled by "market mammies." Studies in West Africa show that women make up 35 to 80 per cent of the traders—a much higher percentage than anywhere else in the world.

What do men do? Boserup writes:

> Before the European conquest of Africa, felling, hunting, and warfare were the chief occupations of men in the regions of female farming. Gradually, as felling and hunting became less important and inter-tribal warfare was prevented by European domination, little remained for the men to do. The Europeans, accustomed to the male farming systems of their home countries, looked with little sympathy on this unfamiliar distribution of the work load between the sexes and, understandably, the concept of the "lazy African man" was firmly fixed in the minds of settlers and administrators.

Men do have some sources of economic power. They bring in a little food from hunting or fishing and do heavy work. More important, they often control the land through village councils. To farm, a woman must acquire land through her husband, making marriage something of a landlord–tenant relationship. The husband usually builds a new hut where his wife will live and raise her children.

The outcome, paradoxically, is that polygamy becomes more attractive to both parties. A man who controls much land may marry several wives to work it for him. Since he is providing only about half their income, even a man of modest means can take several wives. In addition, women find polygyny helps lighten their work burden. Boserup writes:

> In many cases, the first wife takes the initiative in suggesting that a second wife, who can take over the most tiresome jobs in the household, should be procured. A woman marrying a man who already has a number of wives often joins the household more or less in the capacity of a servant for the first wife, unless it happens to be a love match. . . . Many women are said to prefer Moslems because a Moslem has a religious duty to support his wife.

How do African men get away with it? Essentially, they don't. Although an African husband can expect to have his wife or wives supporting themselves and working for him, he has very little claim to his children. As Goody notes, female farming and polygyny are nearly always coupled with "matrilineal descent," meaning that heritage is traced only through the mother's line. Often, children bear their mother's name.

The result is that marriages are relatively transient and divorce is common. As sociologist Wilson J. Goode writes in *World Revolution and Family Patterns* (1963) (the "revolution" is the Westernization of underdeveloped countries):

> What is crucial in African divorce is that in matrilineal systems the husband obtains certain domestic and sexual services from the wife, but her other loyalties and her offspring always belong to her lineage [meaning her natal family]. If there is a divorce, the lineage will care for her and her children. She is not "absorbed" into her husband's lineage. In such systems, divorce is common.

Studies confirm this pattern all over tribal Africa, often called the "matrilineal belt." Goode reports:

> In Stanleyville [the Congo], well over half of those who had been married had also been divorced. According to one calculation, Hausa women [in Nigeria] average about three marriages between puberty and menopause. . . . Eight out of ten persons over 40 years of age in a Yao village [Nyasaland] were found to have been divorced. . . . In the Voltaic group of the Mossi, [men who have migrated to neighboring Ghana] may establish households with the Ashanti women, but avoid marriage, because . . . the Ashanti matrilineal descent pattern [would] not [let them] take their own children back with them.

In patrilineal or "dual descent" societies, by contrast, marriages are stable. Illegitimacy is also regarded differently. In monogamous societies, with their emphasis on paternal claims, illegitimacy is a scandal that may disqualify a woman from ever gaining a husband. In matrilineal societies, illegitimacy is not such a big deal, since children belong to the mother's line anyway. [Early illegitimacy can even have a positive aspect, since it proves fertility.]

In general, China and the Orient fall at the patrilineal extreme, while African and South Seas cultures are at the matrilineal extreme. Western European cultures tend toward the patrilineal, although they are not as extreme as Oriental cultures. American Indian cultures have strong matrilineal traditions. As different ethnic groups have immigrated to America, they have brought their marital customs with them. Despite a certain amount of assimilation to Western standards, the underlying cultural dynamics play an important role. This becomes apparent when we consider the most recent figures for illegitimacy among various ethnic groups in the United States. (See Table.)

Knowing all this, it is easy enough to construct a scenario explaining why African-Americans have become so permanently dependent upon welfare. African marriages are unstable. Women have a great deal of economic independence, and men have weak paternal claims. Black slaves brought these traditions with them. Under such conditions, it has been easy enough for African-American women to abandon marriage and depend on the subsidies of the welfare system for economic support instead.

Although probably true in its general outline, this explanation fails to take account of the three-hundred-year history that preceded the welfare system—a period in which African-Americans made an enormous adjustment to Western standards and were leading lives that were not qualitatively different from the white, middle-class norm. Numerous studies have shown that, before 1925, the vast majority of blacks were living in two-parent households. This middle period, before welfare took hold, offers hope that the cultural damage since inflicted by government policies can be swiftly undone.

Stable Families Under Slavery

The classic account of this period is historian Herbert Gutman's massive book, *The Black Family in Slavery and Freedom: 1750–1925*. Published in 1973, it is still the definitive work of scholarship in the field. Examining plantation records, Gutman finds that fully 80 per cent of black children were living in intact mother–father families *during slavery*. He shows that blacks had their own marriage ceremonies ("jumping the broomstick") and that their rules against cross-cousin marriages differed sharply from the permissive attitudes of white Southerners. Gutman's point is twofold: 1) black families remained largely intact through slavery and beyond, and 2) their marital customs were not simply copied from whites but represented a continuation of African traditions.

Gutman's work stands as a huge barrier to anyone offering simple solutions to the problem of contemporary welfare dependency. (Nicholas Lemann, for example, tries to explain today's urban family dysfunction by arguing that the black family had already disintegrated in the rural South—an argument that is flatly contradicted by Gutman's research.) Gutman's book and all other accounts of the period clearly show that black men had adopted farming and become the heads of monogamous households.

But there are two areas that Gutman does not explore: 1) actual African marital customs and 2) the period of black family disintegration, which did not begin until after the introduction of AFDC in 1935. Thus, while Gutman's research cannot be challenged on its own grounds, it must be framed by events before and after.

Under the influence of European Christianity, African slaves traded matrilineal polygyny for what Margaret Mead once described as a "brittle monogamy." So things continued after slavery was abolished in the United States. Gutman shows that in several North Carolina counties, more than 70 per cent of African-American women obtained marriage licenses in one year, 1866, when there was widespread fear that slave marriages would not be considered legal. Surveys taken from 1870 to 1925 in both South and North reveal a consistent pattern, with 80 to 90 per cent of black homes including a father. In fact, the only "single-parent homes" appear to be those headed by widows.

The clues to what has happened since 1925, the point at which Gutman discontinued his research, can be found in the very documents he uses to make his case: the complete records of several large plantations in North Carolina, Virginia, and Louisiana, which registered hundreds of births between 1750 and 1860. As noted, these records show that 80 per cent of children were being raised in two-parent households. Although perhaps somewhat atypical, since the plantations were obviously well-run and were probably more humane about selling children and breaking up families, the records clearly indicate that, even during slavery, two-parent families predominated among black households.

But they also reveal something that Gutman overlooks—something that helps solve the mystery of the welfare culture. The records of the Bennehan–Cameron Plantation in North Carolina are the most extensive, listing 57 families that registered births for 241 children. Of the 57 families, only 13 were headed by "unmarried mothers," with no father listed on any of their birth records. Among these 13 mothers, only five had more than one child. Together, the 13 single mothers produced 22 births (9 per cent of the total). The number of children born within permanent marriages, on the other hand, was 165, or 68 per cent of the total.

The remaining births—54 children, or 23 per cent—were "children of fortune," born either to an unlisted father or to a man who did not father the remainder of the mother's children. In almost every instance, these children were born before the mother settled down to a permanent marriage. Typically, a woman would have one or two illegitimacies, usually to an unknown father, then become permanently attached to one man for the rest of her life.

In total, then, among the 57 families, 24 (42 per cent) had marriages in which all children had the same father. In twenty families (35 per cent), the mother had one or two early illegitimacies, then settled down to a permanent marriage. The other 13 families (23 per cent) were headed by single mothers. Among families with more than one child, 38 per cent were monogamous marriages, 50 per cent involved early illegitimacies, and 12 per cent had single mothers.

Thus, although more than 80 per cent of the children were *raised* in two-parent households, one-third of births occurred out of wedlock. For half the adult population, family formation did not occur until after the woman had given birth to at least one child. But it occurred nevertheless. By the time everyone had settled down to permanent arrangements, more than 80 per cent of the population was living in two-parent households.

Persisting Pattern

As a welfare-rights worker in Clark County, Alabama, in 1969, I saw the same pattern largely intact more than a hundred years later. Working as a volunteer for the Southern Rural Research Project, I was supposed to find people in the county who were eligible for welfare. A few people qualified for old-age or disability pensions, but my clientele consisted mostly of the ubiquitous girls in their late teens and early 20s who had already had a baby and were still living with their parents.

Among older women in the community, most had also had early illegitimacies but eventually settled into some permanent, if tenuous, marriage. All the farming was done by men, and indeed all men worked. Some were suspiciously absent for long periods of time, however, and were suspected of practicing bigamy. This pattern was then quite familiar in the South and was memorialized in the Temptations' mournful lament, "Papa Was a Rolling Stone." (". . . talk goin' round town sayin' Papa had three outside children and another wife—and that ain't right!") Based on this experience, it has always been obvious to me—and anyone else who lived in the South during the Sixties and Seventies—that welfare was not "causing" teenage girls to have illegitimate babies. The pattern was there long before welfare.

What welfare did was to *disrupt the process of family formation*. In a practice traceable to Africa, a young woman would have one or two illegitimate children who could be supported by her natal family. Only when the children began to grow, or the girl became pregnant for the second or third time, would her family force her to seek a husband. Immigrants from Puerto Rico and other Central American cultures often do the same. This custom, however much it differed from Oriental and European cultures, eventually led to its own kind of family formation.

Tragically, AFDC interrupted the process precisely at the point where family formation usually occurred. Now, as a young woman's children become more disruptive or she becomes pregnant again, she no longer has to choose between imposing on her parents or finding a husband. She can go on welfare. With the help of the Federal Government, she can form her own household, receive a small but steady income, and become eligible for medical care and housing subsidies—none of which come with marriage. She can continue to have further illegitimate children or just settle down with the ones she already has. In either case, family formation fails. This is why the negative effects of welfare have had such a severe impact on ethnic groups with weak traditions of paternal claims—and why so many middle-class bureaucrats, accustomed to European norms, still cannot understand why welfare is the problem.

Nor should it be assumed that a similar pattern of illegitimacy cannot emerge among people of European origin. As cultural attitudes drift toward acceptance of illegitimacy, marginally educated white groups have easily fallen into the same syndrome. As Charles Murray notes, illegitimacy among whites with less than a high-school education is now 25 per cent—exactly where it was among blacks when illegitimacy "took off" during the welfare-rights era of the late 1960s. Exacerbating this trend is the highly visible experimentation in single mother-hood among educated elites, who, although their numbers are not great, tend to be style-setters. As long as the welfare system remains in place, lending economic and moral support to single motherhood, an explosion of underclass behavior among even greater portions of the population is not a remote possibility.

What can we do to head off this eventuality, and perhaps even reverse some of the tragic disruption that has already occurred? Of the two main proposals on the table, neither is very satisfactory.

The liberal Democratic approach is to keep patching the current welfare sys-tem, adding job programs, requiring welfare mothers to work, perhaps putting time limits on eligibility. All this is punitive and does nothing to discourage ille-gitimacy in the first place.

The Republican proposal that has received the most attention is to eliminate welfare and use the savings to set up orphanages and other state institutions to care for children who are then abandoned. Although it may discourage illegiti-macy, this policy offers few positive incentives and casts the government in the role of a cruel Dickensian taskmaster. It also fails to acknowledge the grim re-sponsibility that the government bears for aiding and abetting underclass behav-ior in the first place.

I propose a third option, one that offers both positive and negative incentives. Let us create an "opportunity grant" for poor married couples where both part-ners are over 21, both have finished high school, at least one is working, and nei-ther parent has had any illegitimate children. Such couples would receive the grant for five years after their first child is born. If there are any indications that people are manipulating the grant or being encouraged to act irresponsibly, Congress or the states should not hesitate to change the incentives.

Although this program would involve some initial spending, it would quickly become cheaper and eventually abolish itself. From it would emerge a middle class with the habits and behavior that obviate public assistance. Research shows that children from two-parent families commit far fewer crimes, produce far fewer illegitimate children, and score better on intelligence tests.

Such a program would not only pay a longstanding historical debt, it would produce the building blocks for a middle-class society. Prosperity, not poverty, would become intergenerational.

12

Counting Asians

PETER SHAW

Earlier this summer the University of California at Berkeley released figures on affirmative action that make clear the degree to which Asians, and to a lesser extent whites, are being excluded from that university. Berkeley's estimates of what would happen to white and especially Asian enrollment if affirmative action were done away with are quite conservative. Yet they yield the following indications: Asians would go from 40 per cent to 55 per cent of the student body. Whites would go from 30 per cent to 35 per cent. Hispanics would go from 15 per cent to 5 per cent. Blacks would go from over 6 per cent to under 2 per cent.

Such an outcome makes clear the extent to which Asian-descended students are currently discriminated against. Why, then, did Berkeley reveal the truth?

Because, it would seem, its administration realized that the changes predicted by the university's figures would come as a shock to even the most decided opponents of affirmative action—such as Ward Connerly, the black University of California Regent who had called for an end to affirmative action earlier in the year, provoking the Regents' stormy July meeting. By suddenly telling the truth about how discriminatory the university actually was, the administrators could hope to preserve affirmative action.

Evidently they took their cue from the shocked reactions to estimates similar to theirs in a study done for the Board of Regents. Once that earlier study indicated the results of eliminating affirmative action in admissions, the burden of proof shifted to that system's critics. They became obliged to show how the resultingly low representation of blacks and Hispanics could be defended. Such became the dilemma of Ward Connerly. Two weeks after release of the Berkeley study, the *New York Times* reported that Connerly "now says he sees merit in some cases of preferential treatment for black and Hispanic students." In the event, although the Regents voted to end affirmative action based on sex or race, they inserted an escape clause concerning socioeconomic factors that will surely preserve affirmative action almost as we know it.

But what if the unthinkable did actually take place? What would be the consequences of actually allowing a student population over 50 per cent Asian and under 2 per cent black?

At Berkeley, Stanford, the Ivy League, and other prestigious colleges, the change would amount to a distinct loss of prestige. Why? Just as one of the old measures of prestige was not having too many Jews in attendance, one current measure is not having too many Asians. (Blacks and Hispanics admitted under affirmative action pose no problem, since they can be viewed as charity cases, and the dispensing of charity boosts esteem.) If the prestigious schools were ever in any doubt about the connection between their own standing and the social standing of their student bodies, they had only to consider the counterexample of New York's City College. Thanks to its unfashionable, working-class, largely Jewish student body, that school never could gain prestige. Its students were regularly going on to win Nobel Prizes and to otherwise distinguish themselves in society, yet their successes could not produce prestige.

An unfettered admission of Asians would not make Berkeley as unfashionable as City College of New York used to be. But the place would undoubtedly become academically more like the old City College. The feminist, homosexualist, ethnocentric, and other narrow and politically conceived courses that now make up an important part of the curriculum would hardly be of interest to the Asian majority. To accommodate *them,* departments would have to shift from the intellectually disreputable back to traditional learning. Nor would inflated grades any longer prevail, since these students would be strivers wanting objective measures by which they could be seen to have excelled others. Among other things, then, the feared flood of Asians would lead the prestige schools away from some of the intellectually disreputable ways into which they have fallen.

At the same time, other colleges in the nation, most of which have labored to keep up with the worst practices of the day, would also feel free to back off from them. Their resolve would be strengthened, moreover, by having in their student bodies many highly qualified students who could not get into the prestigious schools under the new admissions policy. The best of these students would find places in schools of the second rank. Yet this apparent step down would not constitute a tragedy for these students. After all, the so-called second-rank schools do not lack academic excellence so much as prestige.

Now these colleges would be in a position to compete with their former betters in both areas. First, the influx of better-qualified students would gain them higher intellectual reputations. Second, the influx of socially well-connected students pushed out by the Asians would raise the second-rank schools' quotient of the impalpable, formerly unattainable kind of prestige. There would, in short, take place what might be termed a democratization of prestige.

Black and Hispanic students would also have to shift to (at first) less prestigious schools. Like others forced lower down the collegiate food chain, they would end up at the right level for their academic abilities. Only the highest scorers in their groups would now be at the (former) prestigious schools, while the less-high-scoring would find themselves at schools where the white, Asian, and all other students were at levels comparable to theirs. System-wide, therefore, the current numbers of students from each group would remain constant. No one now capable of being accepted at an institution of higher education in California would be denied a place. The levels of college attendance for blacks and Hispanics would therefore remain the same—that is, about twice as high as their present representation at Berkeley.

Thomas Sowell has shown how students admitted to schools under affirmative action are forced to compete with better-prepared contemporaries. The top schools, by taking in students who cannot compete at that level, leave the next level of schools without students suitable to *them*. Those schools, in turn, take in students who cannot compete there. And so it goes from one level to another of the university system, with blacks and Hispanics who could do well at the level just below them being placed in untenable situations.

In the meantime, as the democratization of prestige proceeded, the Asian students would find that the few schools they had concentrated so hard on entering were perhaps not worth either the expense or the striving. They and their parents would suffer some disappointment at having the prestige they had sought snatched away from them by a kind of discrimination less organized than affirmative action but no less real. On the other hand, they would feel more free to choose previously less prestigious schools with special academic strengths or more desirable locations. And so, as they spread themselves more evenly among schools, their so greatly feared domination of a few currently prestigious schools would be diluted.

Within each school where they predominated, furthermore, native-born, Asian-descended students, as they gained full possession of the language, would spread out from the sciences and engineering and begin to study history and literature, which have fallen on parlous times, and perhaps bring some improvement to the teaching of these subjects. However, while the Asian-descended students might do well in history and literature and the other humanities, they probably would not be predominant in those fields. These subject areas, thanks to being spared an initial loss of prestige from having too many Asian-descended students, might gain back some of the respectability they have lost.

The final impact on the Asian-descended students would be more subtle but no less decisive. As a consequence of admissions obstacles being removed, they would experience less difficulty getting into their college of choice—at the same time as they would have a wider choice of acceptable schools. Next, college work would be easier for those of them who had moved into humanities subjects.

At the same time, they and their families would be undergoing the inevitable process of Americanization. Television, popular music, and the need to select sneakers and blue jeans would do their work. As a result of the academic and cultural changes that they would experience, they would lose some of the advantages of disadvantage—just as the Jews whom they currently outscore did before them. Somewhat distracted, and no longer pressingly compelled to strive so hard, they would not excel to the same extent in grades and on tests. Undoubtedly they would remain outstanding students, but they would not represent over 60 per cent of any student body. And as the Asian student population dropped to perhaps 35 per cent—that is, to Berkeley's projected rate for whites under a fair and open system—admission to Berkeley and other currently oversubscribed schools would become easier for all.

In this particular as well as in others the answer to the question of what would happen if Berkeley and other schools stopped discriminating against Asians is that all concerned would be likely to benefit. The universities could eliminate the worst of their politicized programs and courses. At a 35 per cent admission rate, white students would enjoy a slight easing of the exclusionary policies now directed against them. Black and Hispanic students would no longer be humiliated by doing less well than others, and so would lose their understandable resentment at being made to seem inadequate.

For Asian-descended students, the results would be mixed. On the one hand, they, too, would no longer be unfairly singled out by discriminatory policies. On the other hand, they would feel the sting of the prejudice operating to reduce the prestige of the schools where they predominated. In sum, they would experience some of the glories and some of the pain of the American immigration experience.

And finally, like the Asians, all students would be exposed to the vagaries of having an unprotected status. The condition is not without its vicissitudes—some harmful, some potentially character-building. Yet the current unhappiness of students under discrimination—whether in their favor or against them—makes at least one thing clear. This is that no better arrangement can ever be brought about either by continued discriminatory legislation, or by hidden practices like Berkeley's exclusion of Asians.

13

American Apartheid:
The Perpetuation of the Underclass

DOUGLAS S. MASSEY

NANCY A. DENTON

One notable difference appears between the immigrant and Negro populations. In the case of the former, there is the possibility of escape, with improvement in economic status in the second generation.

—*1931 report to President Herbert Hoover by the Committee on Negro Housing*

If the black ghetto was deliberately constructed by whites through a series of private decisions and institutional practices, if racial discrimination persists at remarkably high levels in U.S. housing markets, if intensive residential segregation continues to be imposed on blacks by virtue of their skin color, and if segregation concentrates poverty to build a self-perpetuating spiral of decay into black neighborhoods, then a variety of deleterious consequences automatically follow for individual African Americans. A racially segregated society cannot be a race-blind society; as long as U.S. cities remain segregated—indeed, hypersegregated—the United States cannot claim to have equalized opportunities for blacks and whites. In a segregated world, the deck is stacked against black socioeconomic progress, political empowerment, and full participation in the mainstream of American life.

In considering how individuals fare in the world, social scientists make a fundamental distinction between individual, family, and structural characteristics. To a great extent, of course, a person's success depends on individual traits such as motivation, intelligence, and especially, education. Other things equal, those who are more highly motivated, smarter, and better educated will be rewarded more highly in the labor market and will achieve greater socioeconomic success.

Other things generally are not equal, however, because individual traits such as motivation and education are strongly affected by family background. Parents who are themselves educated, motivated, and economically successful tend to pass these traits on to their children. Children who enter the middle and upper classes through the accident of birth are more likely than other, equally intelligent children from other classes to acquire the schooling, motivation, and cultural knowledge required for socioeconomic success in contemporary society. Other aspects of family background, moreover, such as wealth and social connections, open the doors of opportunity irrespective of education or motivation.

Yet even when one adjusts for family background, other things are still not equal, because the structural organization of society also plays a profound role in shaping the life chances of individuals. Structural variables are elements of social and economic organization that lie beyond individual control, that are built into the way society is organized. Structural characteristics affect the fate of large numbers of people and families who share common locations in the social order.

Among the most important structural variables are those that are geographically defined. Where one lives—especially, where one grows up—exerts a profound effect on one's life chances. Identical individuals with similar family backgrounds and personal characteristics will lead very different lives and achieve different rates of socioeconomic success depending on where they reside. Because racial segregation confines blacks to a circumscribed and disadvantaged niche in the urban spatial order, it has profound consequences for individual and family well-being.

Social and Spatial Mobility

In a market society such as the United States, opportunities, resources, and benefits are not distributed evenly across the urban landscape. Rather, certain residential areas have more prestige, greater affluence, higher home values, better services, and safer streets than others. Marketing consultants have grown rich by taking advantage of this "clustering of America" to target specific groups of consumers for wealthy corporate clients. The geographic differentiation of American cities by socioeconomic status does more than conveniently rank neighborhoods for the benefit of demographers, however; it also creates a crucial connection between social and spatial mobility.

As people get ahead, they not only move up the economic ladder, they move up the residential ladder as well. As early as the 1920s, sociologists at the University of Chicago noted this close connection between social and spatial mobility, a link that has been verified many times since. As socioeconomic status improves, families relocate to take advantage of opportunities and resources that are available in greater abundance elsewhere. By drawing on benefits acquired through residential mobility, aspiring parents not only consolidate their own class position but enhance their and their children's prospects for additional social mobility.

In a very real way, therefore, barriers to spatial mobility are barriers to social mobility, and where one lives determines a variety of salient factors that affect individual well-being: the quality of schooling, the value of housing, exposure to crime, the quality of public services, and the character of children's peers. As a result, residential integration has been a crucial component in the broader process of socioeconomic advancement among immigrants and their children. By moving to successively better neighborhoods, other racial and ethnic groups have gradually become integrated into American society. Although rates of spatial assimilation have varied, levels of segregation have fallen for each immigrant group as socioeconomic status and generations in the United States have increased.

The residential integration of most ethnic groups has been achieved as a byproduct of broader processes of socioeconomic attainment, not because group members sought to live among native whites per se. The desire for integration is only one of a larger set of motivations, and not necessarily the most important. Some minorities may even be antagonistic to the idea of integration, but for spatial assimilation to occur, they need only be willing to put up with integration in order to gain access to socioeconomic resources that are more abundant in areas in which white families predominate.

To the extent that white prejudice and discrimination restrict the residential mobility of blacks and confine them to areas with poor schools, low home values, inferior services, high crime, and low educational aspirations, segregation undermines their social and economic well-being. The persistence of racial segregation makes it difficult for aspiring black families to escape the concentrated poverty of the ghetto and puts them at a distinct disadvantage in the larger competition for education, jobs, wealth, and power. The central issue is not whether African Americans "prefer" to live near white people or whether integration is a desirable social goal, but how the restrictions on individual liberty implied by severe segregation undermine the social and economic well-being of individuals.

Extensive research demonstrates that blacks face strong barriers to spatial assimilation within American society. Compared with other minority groups, they are markedly less able to convert their socioeconomic attainments into residential contact with whites, and because of this fact they are unable to gain access to crucial resources and benefits that are distributed through housing markets. Dollar for dollar, blacks are able to buy fewer neighborhood amenities with their income than other groups.

Among all groups in the United States, only Puerto Ricans share blacks' relative inability to assimilate spatially; but this disadvantage stems from the fact that many are of African origin. Although white Puerto Ricans achieve rates of spatial assimilation that are comparable with those found among other ethnic groups, those of African or racially mixed origins experience markedly lower abilities to convert socioeconomic attainments into contact with whites. Once race is controlled, the "paradox of Puerto Rican segregation" disappears.

Given the close connection between social and spatial mobility, the persistence of racial barriers implies the systematic exclusion of blacks from benefits and resources that are distributed through housing markets. We illustrate the severity of this black disadvantage with data specially compiled for the city of Philadelphia in 1980. The data allow us to consider the socioeconomic character of neighborhoods that poor, middle-income, and affluent blacks and whites can be expected to inhabit, holding education and occupational status constant.

In Philadelphia, poor blacks and poor whites both experience very bleak neighborhood environments; both groups live in areas where about 40% of the births are to unwed mothers, where median home values are under $30,000, and where nearly 40% of high school students score under the 15th percentile on a standardized achievement test. Families in such an environment would be unlikely to build wealth through home equity, and children growing up in such an environment would be exposed to a peer environment where unwed parenthood was common and where educational performance and aspirations were low.

As income rises, however, whites are able to escape this disadvantaged setting by relocating to a more advantaged setting. With a middle-class income ($20,000 1979 dollars), whites no longer reside in a neighborhood where unwed parenthood predominates (only 10% of births are to single mothers) and housing values are well above $30,000. At the same time, school performance is markedly better; only 17% of students in the local high school score below the 15th percentile.

Once whites achieve affluence, moreover, negative residential conditions are left far behind. Affluent whites in Philadelphia (those with a 1979 income of $32,000) live in neighborhoods where only 2% of the births are to unwed mothers, where the median home value is $57,000, and where a mere 6% of high school students score below the 15th percentile on achievement tests. Upwardly mobile whites, in essence, capitalize on their higher incomes to buy their way into improved residential circumstances.

Blacks, in contrast, remain mired in disadvantage no matter what income they achieve. Middle-income blacks live in an area where more than a quarter of the births are to unwed mothers, where housing values languish below $30,000, and where 27% of all students in the local high school score below the 15th percentile. Even with affluence, blacks achieve neighborhood environments that compare unfavorably with those attained by whites. With an income of $32,000, a black family can expect to live in a neighborhood where 17% of all births are to unwed mothers, home values are barely over $30,000, and where a fifth of high school students score below the 15th percentile.

For blacks, in other words, high incomes do not buy entrée to residential circumstances that can serve as springboards for future socioeconomic mobility; in particular, blacks are unable to achieve a school environment conducive to later academic success. In Philadelphia, children from an affluent black family are likely to attend a public school where the percentage of low-achieving students is three times greater than the percentage in schools attended by affluent white children. Small wonder, then, that controlling for income in no way erases the large racial gap in SAT scores. Because of segregation, the same income buys black and white families educational environments that are of vastly different quality.

Given these limitations on the ability of black families to gain access to neighborhood resources, it is hardly surprising that government surveys reveal blacks to be less satisfied with their residential circumstances than socioeconomically equivalent whites. This negative evaluation reflects an accurate appraisal of their circumstances rather than different values or ideals on the part of blacks. Both races want the same things in homes and neighborhoods; blacks are just less able to achieve them. Compared with whites, blacks are less likely to be homeowners, and the homes they do own are of poorer quality, in poorer neighborhoods, and of lower value. Moreover, given the close connection between home equity and family wealth, the net worth of blacks is a small fraction of that of whites, even though their incomes have converged over the years. Finally, blacks tend to occupy older, more crowded dwellings that are structurally inadequate compared to those inhabited by whites; and because these racial differentials stem from segregation rather income, adjusting for socioeconomic status does not erase them.

The Politics of Segregation

Socioeconomic achievement is not only a matter of individual aspirations and effort, however; it is also a matter of collective action in the political arena. Generations of immigrants have entered American cities and struggled to acquire political power as a means to enhance individual mobility. Ultimately most were incorporated into the pluralist political structure of American cities. In return for support at the polls, ethnic groups were awarded a share of public services, city contracts, and municipal jobs in rough proportion to their share of the electorate. The receipt of these public resources, in turn, helped groups consolidate their class position and gave their members a secure economic base from which to advance further.

The process of political incorporation that followed each immigrant wave grew out of shared political interests that were, to a large extent, geographically determined. Although neighborhoods may have been labeled "Polish," "Italian," or "Jewish," neighborhoods in which one ethnic group constituted a majority were rare, and most immigrants of European origin never lived in them. As a result, levels of ethnic segregation never reached the heights typical of black-white segregation today.

This geographic diversification of ethnicity created a situation in which ethnic groups necessarily shared common political interests. In distributing public works, municipal services, and patronage jobs to ethnic groups in return for their political support, resources were also allocated to specific neighborhoods, which typically contained a diverse array of ethnicities. Given the degree of ethnic mixing within neighborhoods, political patronage provided to one group yielded substantial benefits for others as well. Building a new subway stop in an "Italian" neighborhood, for example, also provided benefits to Jews, Poles, and Lithuanians who shared the area; and allocating municipal jobs to Poles not only benefited merchants in "Polish" communities but generated extra business for nearby shopkeepers who were Hungarian, Italian, or Czech.

At the same time, threats to curtail municipal services encouraged the formation of broad, interethnic coalitions built around common neighborhood interests. A plan to close a firehouse in a "Jewish" neighborhood, for example, brought protests not only from Jews but from Scandinavians, Italians, and Slovaks who shared the neighborhood and relied on its facilities. These other ethnics, moreover, were invariably connected to friends and relatives in other neighborhoods or to co-ethnic politicians from other districts who could assist them in applying political pressure to forestall the closure. In this way, residential integration structurally supported the formation of interethnic coalitions, providing a firm base for the emergence of pluralist political machines.

Residential integration also made it possible for ethnic groups to compete for political leadership throughout the city, no matter what their size. Because no single group dominated numerically in most neighborhoods, politicians from a variety of backgrounds found the door open to make a bid for elective office. Moreover, representatives elected from ethnically diverse neighborhoods had to pay attention to all voters irrespective of ethnic affiliation. The geographic distribution of political power across ethnically heterogeneous districts spread political influence widely among groups and ensured that all were given a political voice.

The residential segregation of blacks, in contrast, provided no basis for pluralist politics because it precluded the emergence of common neighborhood interests; the geographic isolation of blacks instead forced nearly all issues to cleave along racial lines. When a library, firehouse, police station, or school was built in a black neighborhood, other ethnic groups derived few, if any, benefits; and when important services were threatened with reduction or removal, blacks could find few coalition partners with whom to protest the cuts. Since no one except blacks lived in the ghetto, no other ethnic group had a self-interest in seeing them provided with public services or political patronage.

On the contrary, resources allocated to black neighborhoods detracted from the benefits going to white ethnic groups; and because patronage was the glue that held white political coalitions together, resources allocated to the ghetto automatically undermined the stability of the pluralist machine. As long as whites controlled city politics, their political interests lay in providing as few resources as possible to African Americans and as many as possible to white ethnic groups. Although blacks occasionally formed alliances with white reformers, the latter acted more from moral conviction than from self-interest. Because altruism is notoriously unreliable as a basis for political cooperation, interracial coalitions were unstable and of limited effectiveness in representing black interests.

The historical confinement of blacks to the ghetto thus meant that blacks shared few political interests with whites. As a result, their incorporation into local political structures differed fundamentally from the pluralist model followed by other groups. The geographic and political isolation of blacks meant that they had virtually no power when their numbers were small; only when their numbers increased enough to dominate one or more wards did they acquire any influence at all. But rather than entering the pluralist coalition as an equal partner, the black community was incorporated in a very different way: as a machine within a machine.

The existence of solid black electoral districts, while undermining interracial coalition-building, did create the potential for bloc voting along racial lines. In a close citywide election, the delivery of a large number of black votes could be extremely useful to white politicians, and inevitably black political bosses arose to control and deliver this vote in return for political favors. Unlike whites, who exercised power through politicians of diverse ethnicities, blacks were typically represented by one boss, always black, who developed a symbiotic and dependent relationship with the larger white power structure.

In return for black political support, white politicians granted black bosses such as Oscar DePriest or William Dawson of Chicago and Charles Anderson of Harlem a share of jobs and patronage that they could, in turn, distribute within the ghetto. Although these bosses wielded considerable power and status within the black community, they occupied a very tenuous position in the larger white polity. On issues that threatened the white machine or its constituents, the black bosses could easily be outvoted. Thus patronage, services, and jobs were allocated to the ghetto only as long as black bosses controlled racial agitation and didn't threaten the color line, and the resources they received typically compared unfavorably to those provided to white politicians and their neighborhoods.

As with black business owners and professionals, the pragmatic adaptation of black politicians to the realities of segregation gave them a vested interest in the ghetto and its perpetuation. During the 1950s, for example, William Dawson joined with white ethnic politicians to oppose the construction of public housing projects in white neighborhoods, not because of an ideological objection to public housing per se, but because integration would antagonize his white political sponsors and take voters outside of wards that he controlled.

The status quo of a powerful white machine and a separate but dependent black machine was built on shifting sand, however. It remained viable only as long as cities dominated state politics, patronage was plentiful, and blacks comprised a minority of the population. During the 1950s and 1960s, white suburbanization and black in-migration systematically undermined these foundations, and white machine politicians became progressively less able to accommodate black demands while simultaneously maintaining the color line. Given the declining political clout of cities, the erosion of their tax base, and the rising proportion of blacks in cities, municipal politics became a racially charged zero-sum game that pitted politically disenfranchised blacks against a faltering coalition of ethnic whites. . . .

Even in cities where blacks have assumed political leadership by virtue of becoming a majority, the structural constraints of segregation still remain decisive. Indeed, the political isolation experienced by blacks in places such as Newark and Detroit is probably more severe than that experienced earlier in the century, when ghetto votes were at least useful to white politicians in citywide elections. Once blacks gained control of the central city and whites completed their withdrawal to the surrounding suburbs, virtually all structural supports for interracial cooperation ended.

In the suburbs surrounding places such as Newark and Detroit, white politicians are administratively and politically insulated from black voters in central cities, and they have no direct political interest in their welfare. Indeed, money that flows into black central cities generally means increased taxes and lower net incomes for suburban whites. Because suburbanites now form a majority of most state populations—and a majority of the national electorate—the "chocolate city—vanilla suburb" pattern of contemporary racial segregation gives white politicians a strong interest in limiting the flow of public resources to black-controlled cities.

In an era of fiscal austerity and declining urban resources, therefore, the political isolation of blacks makes them extremely vulnerable to cutbacks in governmental services and public investments. If cuts must be made to balance strained city budgets, it makes political sense for white politicians to concentrate the cuts in black neighborhoods, where the political damage will be minimal; and if state budgets must be trimmed, it is in white legislators' interests to cut subventions to black-controlled central cities, which now represent a minority of most states' voters. The spatial and political isolation of blacks interacts with declining public resources to create a powerful dynamic for disinvestment in the black community.

The destructiveness of this dynamic has been forcefully illustrated by Rodrick and Deborah Wallace, who trace the direct and indirect results of a political decision in New York City to reduce the number of fire companies in black and Puerto Rican neighborhoods during the early 1970s.[1] Faced with a shortage of funds during the city's financial crisis, the Fire Department eliminated thirty-five fire companies between 1969 and 1976, twenty-seven of which were in poor minority areas located in the Bronx, Manhattan, and Brooklyn, areas where the risk of fire was, in fact, quite high. Confronted with the unpleasant task of cutting services, white politicians confined the reductions to segregated ghetto and barrio wards where the political damage could be contained. The geographic and political isolation of blacks and Puerto Ricans meant that their representatives were unable to prevent the cuts.

As soon as the closings were implemented, the number of residential fires increased dramatically. An epidemic of building fires occurred within black and Puerto Rican neighborhoods. As housing was systematically destroyed, social networks were fractured and institutions collapsed; churches, block associations, youth programs, and political clubs vanished. The destruction of housing, networks, and social institutions, in turn, caused a massive flight of destitute families out of core minority areas. Some affected areas lost 80% of their residents between 1970 and 1980, putting a severe strain on housing in adjacent neighborhoods, which had been stable until then. As families doubled up in response to the influx of fire refugees, overcrowding increased, which led to additional fires and the diffusion of the chaos into adjacent areas. Black ghettos and Puerto Rican barrios were hollowed out from their cores.

The overcrowded housing, collapsed institutions, and ruptured support networks overwhelmed municipal disease prevention efforts and swamped medical care facilities. Within affected neighborhoods, infant mortality rates rose, as did the incidence of cirrhosis, gonorrhea, tuberculosis, and drug use. The destruction of the social fabric of black and Puerto Rican neighborhoods led to an increase in the number of unsupervised young males, which contributed to a sharp increase in crime, followed by an increase in the rate of violent deaths among young men. By 1990, this chain reaction of social and economic collapse had turned vast areas of the Bronx, Harlem, and Brooklyn into "urban deserts" bereft of normal community life.

Despite the havoc that followed in the wake of New York's fire service reductions, the cuts were never rescinded. The only people affected were minority members who were politically marginalized by segregation and thereby prevented, structurally, from finding allies to oppose the service reductions. Although residential segregation paradoxically made it easier for blacks and Puerto Ricans to elect city councillors by creating homogeneous districts, it left those that were elected relatively weak, dependent, and unable to protect the interests of their constituents.

As a result of their residential segregation and resultant political isolation, therefore, black politicians in New York and elsewhere have been forced into a strategy of angrily demanding that whites give them more public resources. Given their geographic isolation, however, these appeals cannot be made on the basis of whites' self-interest, but must rely on appeals to altruism, guilt, or fear. Because altruism, guilt, and fear do not provide a good foundation for concerted political action, the downward spiral of black neighborhoods continues and black hostility and bitterness grow while white fears are progressively reinforced. Segregation creates a political impasse that deepens the chasm of race in American society.

Under the best of circumstances, segregation undermines the ability of blacks to advance their interests because it provides ethnic whites with no immediate self-interest in their welfare. The circumstances of U.S. race relations, however, can hardly be described as "best," for not only do whites have little self-interest in promoting black welfare, but a significant share must be assumed to be racially prejudiced and supportive of policies injurious to blacks. To the extent that racism exists, of course, the geographic and political isolation of the ghetto makes it easier for racists to act on their prejudices. In a segregated society, blacks become easy targets for racist actions and policies.

The Isolation of the Ghetto

The high degree of residential segregation imposed on blacks ensures their social and economic isolation from the rest of American society. As we have seen, in 1980 ten large U.S. cities had black isolation indices in excess of 80 (Atlanta, Baltimore, Chicago, Cleveland, Detroit, Gary, Newark, Philadelphia, St. Louis, and Washington, D.C.), meaning that the average black person in these cities lived in a neighborhood that was at least 80% black. Averages in excess of 80% occur when a few blacks live in integrated areas, and the vast majority reside in areas that are 100% black.

Such high levels of racial isolation cannot be sustained without creating a profound alienation from American society and its institutions. Unless ghetto residents work outside of their neighborhoods, they are unlikely to come into contact with anyone else who is not also black, and if they live in an area of concentrated poverty, they are unlikely to interact with anyone who is not also *poor* and black. The structural constraints on social interaction imposed by segregation loom large when one considers that 36% of black men in central cities are either out of the labor force, unemployed, or underemployed, a figure that rises to 54% among black men aged 18 to 29.

The role that segregation plays in undermining blacks' connection to the rest of society has been demonstrated by William Yancey and his colleagues at Temple University.[2] They undertook a representative survey of people in the Philadelphia urban area and asked them to describe the race and ethnicity of their friends and neighbors. Not surprisingly, blacks were far more concentrated residentially than any other group, even controlling for social and economic background. They were also very unlikely to report friendships with anyone else but blacks, and this remarkable racial homogeneity in their friendship networks was explained entirely by their residential concentration; it had nothing to do with group size, birthplace, socioeconomic status, or organizational membership. Unlike other groups, blacks were prevented from forming friendships outside their group because they were so residentially segregated: spatial isolation leads to social isolation.

The intense isolation imposed by segregation has been confirmed by an ethnographic study of blacks living in Chicago's poorest neighborhoods.[3] Drawing on detailed, in-depth interviews gathered in William Julius Wilson's Urban Family Life Survey, Sophie Pedder found that one theme consistently emerged in the narratives: poor blacks had extremely narrow geographic horizons. Many of her informants, who lived on Chicago's South Side, had never been into the Loop (the city's center), and a large number had never left the immediate confines of their neighborhood. A significant percentage only left the neighborhood after reaching adulthood. According to Pedder, this racial isolation "is at once both real, in that movement outside the neighborhood is limited, and psychological, in that residents feel cut off from the rest of the city."[4]

Thus residents of hypersegregated neighborhoods necessarily live within a very circumscribed and limited social world. They rarely travel outside of the black enclave, and most have few friends outside of the ghetto. This lack of connection to the rest of society carries profound costs, because personal contacts and friendship networks are among the most important means by which people get jobs. Relatively few job seekers attain employment by responding to ads or canvassing employers; most people find jobs through friends, relatives, or neighbors, and frequently they learn of jobs through acquaintances they know only casually.

The social isolation imposed on blacks by virtue of their systematic residential segregation thus guarantees their economic isolation as well. Because blacks have weak links to white society, they are not connected to the jobs that white society provides. They are put at a clear disadvantage in the competition for employment, and especially for increasingly scarce jobs that pay well but require little formal skill or education. This economic isolation, moreover, is cumulative and self-perpetuating: because blacks have few connections outside the ghetto, they are less likely to be employed in the mainstream economy, and this fact, in turn, reduces the number and range of their connections to other people and institutions, which further undermines their employment chances. Given the levels of residential segregation typically found in large American cities, therefore, the inevitable result is a dependent black community within which work experience is lacking and linkages to legitimate employment are weak.

The Language of Segregation

The depth of isolation in the ghetto is also evident in black speech patterns, which have evolved steadily away from Standard American English. Because of their intense social isolation, many ghetto residents have come to speak a language that is increasingly remote from that spoken by American whites. Black street speech, or more formally, Black English Vernacular, has its roots in the West Indian creole and Scots-Irish dialects of the eighteenth century. As linguists have shown, it is by no means a "degenerate," or "illogical" version of Standard American English; rather, it constitutes a complex, rich, and expressive language in its own right, with a consistent grammar, pronunciation, and lexicon all its own. It evolved independently from Standard American English because blacks were historically separated from whites by caste, class, and region; but among the most powerful influences on black speech has been the residential segregation that blacks have experienced since early in the century.

For several decades, the linguist William Labov and his colleagues have systematically taped, transcribed, and analyzed black and white speech patterns in American cities.[5] In city after city they have found that whites "constitute a single speech community, defined by a single set of norms and a single, extraordinarily uniform structural base. Linguistic features pass freely across ethnic lines within the white community. But not across racial lines: black(s) . . . have nothing to do with these sound changes in process."[6] Divergent black and white speech patterns provide stark evidence of the structural limits to interracial communication that come with high levels of residential segregation.

Whereas white speech has become more regionally specialized over time, with linguistic patterns varying increasingly between metropolitan areas, Labov and his colleagues found precisely the opposite pattern for Black English: it has become progressively more uniform across urban areas. Over the past two decades, the Black English Vernaculars of Boston, Chicago, Detroit, New York, and Philadelphia have become increasingly similar in their grammatical structure and lexicon, reflecting urban blacks' common social and economic isolation within urban American. Although black speech has become more uniform internally, however, as a dialect it has drifted farther and farther away from the form and structure of Standard American English. According to Labov's measurements, blacks and whites in the United States increasingly speak different tongues, with different grammatical rules, divergent pronunciations, and separate vocabularies. . . .

The ability to speak, write, and communicate effectively in Standard English is essential for employment in most white-collar jobs. The ability to speak Standard English, at least, is also widely demanded by employers for clerical or service positions that bring jobholders into frequent contact with the general public, most of whom are white. Employers make frequent use of language as a screening device for blue-collar jobs, even those that involve little or no interaction with the public. They assume that people who speak Black English carry a street culture that devalues behaviors and attitudes consistent with being a "good worker," such as regularity, punctuality, dependability, and respect for authority.[7]

The inability to communicate in Standard American English, therefore, presents serious obstacles to socioeconomic advancement. Black Americans who aspire to socioeconomic success generally must acquire a facility in Standard English as a precondition of advancement, even if they retain a fluency in black speech. Successful blacks who have grown up in the ghetto literally become bilingual, learning to switch back and forth between black and white dialects depending on the social context.

This "code switching" involves not only a change of words but a shift between contrasting cultures and identities. Although some people acquire the ability to make this shift without difficulty, it causes real social and psychological problems for others. For someone raised in the segregated environment of the ghetto, adopting white linguistic conventions can seem like a betrayal of black culture, a phony attempt to deny the reality of one's "blackness." As a result, black people who regularly speak Standard American English often encounter strong disapproval from other blacks. Many well-educated blacks recall with some bitterness the ridicule and ostracism they suffered as children for the sin of "talking white."

The Culture of Segregation

This struggle between "black" and "white" speech patterns is symptomatic of a larger conflict between "black" and "white" cultural identities that arises from residential segregation. In response to the harsh and isolated conditions of ghetto life, a segment of the urban black population has evolved a set of behaviors, attitudes, and values that are increasingly at variance with those held in the wider society. Although these adaptations represent rational accommodations to social and economic conditions within the ghetto, they are not widely accepted or understood outside of it, and in fact are negatively evaluated by most of American society.

Middle-class American culture generally idealizes the values of self-reliance, hard work, sobriety, and sacrifice, and adherence to these principles is widely believed to bring monetary reward and economic advancement in society. Among men, adherence to these values means that employment and financial security should precede marriage, and among women they imply that childbearing should occur only after adequate means to support the raising of children have been secured, either through marriage or through employment. In the ideal world, everyone is hardworking, self-sufficient, and not a burden to fellow citizens.

In most white neighborhoods the vast majority of working age men are employed. Because jobs are available and poverty is relatively uncommon, most residents can reasonably expect to conform to ideal values most of the time. Men generally do find jobs before marrying and women have reason to believe that men will help support the children they father. Although these ideals may be violated with some frequency, there is enough conformity in most white neighborhoods for them to retain their force as guides for behavior; there are still enough people who exemplify the values to serve as role models for others. Those failures that do occur are taken to reflect individual flaws, and most whites derive a sense of self-esteem and prestige by conforming to the broader ideals of American society.

Ghetto blacks, however, face very different neighborhood conditions created by residential segregation. A large share live in a geographically isolated and racially homogeneous neighborhood where poverty is endemic, joblessness is rife, schools are poor, and even high school graduates are unlikely to speak Standard English with any facility. Employment opportunities are limited, and given the social isolation enforced by segregation, black men are not well connected to employers in the larger economy. As a result, young men coming of age in ghetto areas are relatively unlikely to find jobs capable of supporting a wife and children, and black women, facing a dearth of potential husbands and an absence of educational institutions capable of preparing them for gainful employment, cannot realistically hope to conform to societal ideals of marriage and childbearing.

The conditions of the ghetto, in short, make it exceedingly difficult to live up to broader societal values with respect to work, marriage, and family formation, and poor blacks are thus denied the opportunity to build self-esteem and to acquire prestige through channels valued in the wider society. As a result, an alternative status system has evolved within America's ghettos that is defined *in opposition to* the basic ideals and values of American society. It is a culture that explains and legitimizes the social and economic shortcomings of ghetto blacks, which are built into their lives by segregation rather than by personal failings. This culture of segregation attaches value and meaning to a way of life that the broader society would label as deviant and unworthy. . . .

As a protection against the persistent assaults to self-esteem that are inherent in ghetto life, black street culture has evolved to legitimate certain behaviors prevalent within the black community that would otherwise be held in contempt by white society. Black identity is thus constructed as a series of oppositions to conventional middle-class "white" attitudes and behavior. If whites speak Standard American English, succeed in school, work hard at routine jobs, marry, and support their children, then to be "black" requires one to speak Black English, do poorly in school, denigrate conventional employment, shun marriage, and raise children outside of marriage. To do otherwise would be to "act white."

By concentrating poor people prone to such oppositional identities in racially homogeneous settings, segregation creates the structural context for the maintenance and perpetuation of an ongoing oppositional culture, "which includes devices for protecting [black] identity and for maintaining boundaries between [blacks] and white Americans. [Blacks] regard certain forms of behavior and certain activities or events, symbols, and meanings as *not appropriate* for them because . . . [they] are characteristic of white Americans. At the same time, they emphasize other forms of behavior and other events, symbols, and meanings as more appropriate for them because they are *not* a part of white Americans' way of life."

Ogbu and Fordham are educational specialists who have specifically documented the effect of oppositional black culture on educational achievement among black children. Their investigations show how bright, motivated, and intellectually curious ghetto children face tremendous pressure from their peers to avoid "acting white" in succeeding in school and achieving academic distinction.[8] The pressure for educational failure is most intense during the teenage years, when peer acceptance is so important and black young people live in fear of being labeled "Oreos," "Uncle Toms," or "Aunt Jemimahs" for speaking Standard English or doing well in school. If they actually achieve academic distinction, they risk being called a "brainiac," or worse, a "pervert brainiac" (someone who is not only smart but of questionable sexuality as well).

Black children who do overcome the odds and achieve academic success in inner-city schools typically go to great lengths, and adopt ingenious strategies, to lessen the burden of "acting white." Some deliberately fail selected courses, others scale back their efforts and get B's or C's rather than the A's they are capable of, and still others become class clowns, seeking to deflect attention away from their scholarly achievements by acting so ridiculous that their peers no longer take them seriously. Better to be called "crazy" or a "clown" than a "pervert brainiac."

The powerful effect of oppositional ghetto culture on black educational performance is suggested by the recent work of James Rosenbaum and his colleagues at Northwestern University.[9] Working in the Chicago area, they compared low-income black students from families assigned to scattered site housing in a white suburb (under the *Gautreaux* court decision) with comparable students from families assigned to public housing in Chicago's ghetto. Although the two groups were initially identical, once removed from ghetto high schools black students achieved higher grades, lower dropout rates, better academic preparation, and higher rates of college attendance compared with those who remained behind in ghetto institutions.

Another study by Robert Crain and Rita Mahard, who used a nationwide sample, found that northern blacks who attended racially mixed schools were more likely to enter and stay in college than those who went to all-black high schools.[10] Susan Mayer followed students who attended the tenth grade in poor and affluent high schools in 1980 and determined the likelihood of their dropping out before 1982. Controlling for family background, she discovered that students who went to affluent schools were considerably less likely to drop out than those who attended poor schools, and that girls in affluent schools were much less likely to have a child. Moreover, white students who attended predominantly black high schools were considerably more likely to drop out and have a child than those who attended predominantly white schools.

All too often, whites observe the workings of black oppositional culture and conclude that African Americans suffer from some kind of "cultural defect," or that they are somehow "culturally disadvantaged." In doing so, they blame the victims of segregation rather than the social arrangements that created the oppositional culture in the first place. It is not a self-perpetuating "culture of poverty"[11] that retards black educational progress but a structurally created and sustained "culture of segregation" that, however useful in adapting to the harsh realities of ghetto life, undermines socioeconomic progress in the wider society.

As Kenneth Clark pointed out in 1965, "the invisible walls of a segregated society are not only damaging but protective in a debilitating way. There is considerable psychological safety in the ghetto; there one lives among one's own and does not risk rejection among strangers. One first becomes aware of the psychological damage of such 'safety' when the walls of the ghetto are breached and the Negro ventures out into the repressive, frightening white world . . . Most Negroes take the first steps into an integrated society tentatively and torn with conflict. To be the first Negro who is offered a job in a company brings a sense of triumph but also the dread of failure."[12] More recently, Shelby Steele has written of the "integration shock" that envelops blacks who enter white society directly from the isolated world of the ghetto.[13]

The origins of black oppositional culture can be traced to the period before 1920, when black migration fomented a hardening of white racial attitudes and a systematic limiting of opportunities for African Americans on a variety of fronts. Whereas urban blacks had zealously pursued education after the Civil War and were making great strides, the rise of Jim Crow in the south and de facto segregation in the north severed the links between hard work, education, sobriety, and their presumed rewards in society. Although black elites continued to promote these values, the rise of the ghetto made them look increasingly pathetic and ridiculous to the mass of recent in-migrants: in the face of pervasive barriers to social and residential mobility, the moral admonitions of the elites seemed hollow and pointless. If whites would not accept blacks on the basis of their individual accomplishments and if hard work and education went unrewarded, then why expend the effort? If one could never be accepted as white, it was just demeaning and humiliating to go through the motions of "acting white." Malcolm X summed up this attitude with his sardonic quip, "What do you call a Negro with a Ph.D.? A nigger."[14]

Unlike other groups, the force of oppositional culture is particularly powerful among African Americans because it is so strongly reinforced by residential segregation. By isolating blacks within racially homogeneous neighborhoods and concentrating poverty within them, segregation creates an environment where failure to meet the ideal standards of American society loses its stigma; indeed, individual shortcomings become normative and supported by the values of oppositional culture. As transgressions lose their stigma through repetition and institutionalization, individual behavior at variance with broader societal ideals becomes progressively more likely.

The culture of segregation arises from the coincidence of racial isolation and high poverty, which inevitably occurs when a poor minority group is residentially segregated. By concentrating poverty, segregation simultaneously concentrates male joblessness, teenage motherhood, single parenthood, alcoholism, and drug abuse, thus creating an entirely black social world in which these oppositional states are normative. Given the racial isolation and concentrated poverty of the ghetto, it is hardly surprising that black street culture has drifted steadily away from middle-class American values.

The steady divergence of black street culture from the white mainstream is clearly visible in a series of participant observer studies of ghetto life conducted over the past thirty years. Studies carried out during the 1960s and 1970s—such as Elliot Liebow's *Tally's Corner,* Lee Rainwater's *Behind Ghetto Walls,* Ulf Hannerz's *Soulside,* and Elijah Anderson's *A Place on the Corner*—were remarkably consistent in reporting that ghetto dwellers, despite their poverty and oppression, essentially subscribed to the basic values of American society. What set ghetto blacks apart from other Americans was not their lack of fealty to American ideals but their inability to accomplish them. Specifically, the pervasiveness of poverty, unemployment, and dependency in the ghetto made it nearly impossible for them to live up to ideals they in fact held, which in turn undermined their self-esteem and thus created a psychological need for gratification through other means.

The participant observer studies indicated that feelings of personal inadequacy led black men to reject the unskilled and poorly paid jobs open to them, to denigrate the kind of work these jobs represented, and to seek gratification through more accessible channels, such as sexual liaisons or intoxication. Women and men tended to begin sexual relations at a young age, and woman generally found themselves pregnant as teenagers. Childbirth was typically followed by marriage or some informal living arrangement, at least for a time; but eventually the woman's demands for financial support undermined her partner's self-esteem, and family responsibilities blocked his access to the alternate status system of the streets. Given the cross-cutting pressures of poverty, joblessness, low self-esteem, family demands, and the allure of the streets, most male-female relationships were short-lived and devolved sooner or later into female-headed families.

Once they had been through this cycle of romance, pregnancy, family formation, and dissolution, black men and women came to see romantic relationships as a mutually exploitative contest whose pleasures were temporary and whose stability could not be relied upon. At the same time, the pervasive poverty of the ghetto meant that families were constantly bombarded with energy-sapping demands for assistance and debilitating requests for financial aid from extended family, friends, and neighbors. Given the association of poverty with crime and violence, moreover, they were constantly at risk of criminal victimization, injury, or even death.

In this social world, ghetto dwellers acquired a tough, cynical attitude toward life, a deep suspicion of the motives of others, and a marked lack of trust in the goodwill or benevolent intentions of people and institutions. Growing up in the ghetto, blacks came to expect the worst of others and to experience little sense of control over their lives. They adapted to these feelings by confining relationships of trust to close kin, especially maternal relatives.

Underlying this bleak portrait of ghetto life painted by studies carried out during the 1960s and 1970s was a common thread. Early participant observers saw ghetto culture as rooted in the structural conditions of poverty, dependency, and joblessness, over which ghetto residents had little control, and all characterized ghetto culture as essentially oppositional. That is, the attitudes and behaviors of ghetto blacks were fundamentally defined in opposition to the ideals of white society. Underneath the jaded rejection of conventional mores, ghetto dwellers, at least in the first or second generations, still clung to the basic values of American society. Indeed, it was because they judged themselves so harshly by broader standards that the psychological need for an oppositional identity arose in the first place.

Over time, however, as intense racial isolation and acutely concentrated poverty have continued, ghetto attitudes, values, and ideals have become progressively less connected to those prevailing elsewhere in the United States. More and more, the culture of the ghetto has become an entity unto itself, remote from the rest of American society and its institutions, and drifting even further afield. As conditions within the ghetto worsen, as the social environment grows more hostile, and as racial isolation deepens, the original connection of ghetto culture to the broader values of American society—even if only in opposition—has faded.

The new culture of the ghetto increasingly rejects the values of American society as a farce and a sham, and traits that were once clearly oppositional and therefore somehow *linked* to the rest of American society have become ends in themselves, esteemed in their own right and disconnected from their relationship to the surrounding "white" society. Under the combined pressure of isolation and poverty, black street culture has increasingly become an autonomous cultural system. Participant observer studies of ghetto life done in the 1980s have an even darker and more pessimistic tone than those carried out in earlier decades. The contrast is clearly illustrated by two studies conducted by the sociologist Elijah Anderson: one carried out in the ghetto of Chicago during the early 1970s and the other conducted in a poor black neighborhood of Philadelphia during the late 1980s.

In Anderson's first study, *A Place on the Corner,* basic American values such as hard work, honesty, diligence, respect for authority, and staying out of trouble were still very much in evidence in the thoughts and words of the poor black men gathered around the corner bar he studied. Indeed, these values provided the basis for an alternative status system that arose to confer esteem when broader standards were not met, and to encourage young men to live up to ideals despite the long odds. As a result, Anderson's subjects—who would be considered of "no account" by conventional standards—acquire a certain nobility for their pursuit of dignity and honor in the face of adversity.

In contrast, the subjects of Anderson's latest study, *Streetwise,* scorn and ridicule conventional American ideals.[15] Symbolic of the disappearance of traditional values from the ghetto is the breakdown of the longstanding relationship between "old heads" and young boys. According to Anderson, "an old head was a man of stable means who was strongly committed to family life, to church, and, most important, to passing on his philosophy, developed through his own rewarding experience with work, to young boys he found worthy. He personified the work ethnic and equated it with value and high standards of morality; in his eyes a workingman was a good, decent individual."[16]

In the ghetto environment of earlier decades, the old head "acted as a kind of guidance counselor and moral cheerleader who preached anticrime and antitrouble messages to his charges," and "the young boy readily deferred to the old head's chronological age and worldly experience."[17] In contrast, today, "as the economic and social circumstances of the urban ghetto have changed, the traditional old head has been losing prestige and credibility as a role model . . . When gainful employment and its rewards are not forthcoming, boys easily conclude that the moral lessons of the old head concerning the work ethnic, punctuality, and honesty do not fit their own circumstances."[18]

In the past, black ghettos also used to contain numerous "female old heads," who served as "neighborhood mothers," correcting and admonishing children in the streets and instructing them in proper behavior. They "were seen as mature and wise figures in the community, not only by women and girls, but also by many young men" because of their motherly love and concern for children.[19] According to Anderson, however, these role models also have increasingly disappeared, indicating "a breakdown in feelings of community. Residents . . . keep more to themselves now, [and] no longer involve themselves in their neighbors' lives as they did as recently as ten years ago."[20]

In place of traditional mores that assign value to steady work, family life, the church, and respect for others, a drug culture and its economy have arisen, with profound effects on community well-being. Anderson and others have studied and written on the appeal of the underground drug economy to young men and women from the ghetto. According to Anderson, "the roles of drug pusher, pimp, and (illegal) hustler have become more and more attractive. Street-smart young people who operate this underground economy are apparently able to obtain big money more easily and glamorously than their elders, including traditional male and female old heads. Because they appear successful, they become role models for still younger people."[21]

The proliferation of the drug culture within the ghetto has exacerbated the problems caused by segregation and its concentration of poverty, adding a powerful impetus to the cycle of neighborhood decline. Given the financial gain to be had from drugs, ghetto dealers establish aggressive marketing strategies to capture business from disillusioned young people who see little hope for improvement through work, education, or staying out of trouble. Because limited economic opportunities in the ghetto as well as drug use itself make it difficult for drug users to support themselves, the spread of drug use leads inevitably to the escalation of crime and violence. As a by-product of the new drug culture, the violent death rate has skyrocketed among black men, prostitution has spread among black women, and the number of drug-addicted babies has mushroomed. The old social order of the ghetto has increasingly broken down and veered off on an independent path dramatically different from that prevailing in the rest of American society.

At the same time, relations between the sexes, which were already antagonistic and mutually exploitative in the ghetto world of the 1960s, had by the 1980s lost all connection to conventional family values. According to Anderson, by the late 1980s sexual relations in the ghetto had degenerated into a vicious, competitive contest in which young men and women exploited each other with diametrically opposed goals. For young ghetto men, sex had become strictly a means of enhancing status among male peers and of experiencing pleasure at the expense of women. "To the young man the woman becomes, in the most profound sense, a sexual object. Her body and mind are the object of a sexual game, to be won for personal aggrandizement. Status goes to the winner, and sex is prized not as a testament of love but as testimony to control of another human being. Sex is the prize, and sexual conquests are a game whose goal is to make a fool of the young woman."[22]

In the ghetto of the 1960s, a pregnancy growing out of such casual sexual encounters was relatively likely to be followed by a marriage or some other housekeeping arrangement, however unstable or short-lived it might have been. By the late 1980s, however, this bow to conventional culture had been eliminated in black street culture. "In the social context of persistent poverty, [black men] have come to devalue the conventional marital relationship, viewing women as a burden and children as even more of one."[23] Even if a young man "admits paternity and 'does right' by the girl, his peer group likely will label him a chump, a square, or a fool."[24]

Ghetto women, for their part, seek gratification less through sex than through pregnancy and childbirth. They understand that their suitors' sweet words and well-honed "rap" are fabrications being told in order to extract sex from them, and despite a few romantic self-deceptions along the way, they realize that if they become pregnant the father is unlikely to support their child. Nonetheless, they look forward to getting pregnant, for in the contemporary ghetto "it is becoming socially acceptable for a young woman to have children out of wedlock—supported by a regular welfare check."[25]

These findings are corroborated by other ethnographic interviews gathered as part of William Julius Wilson's larger study of urban poverty in Chicago. When the sociologist Richard Taub examined the interview transcripts, he found that marriage had virtually disappeared as a meaningful category of thought and discourse among poor blacks.[26] Informants consistently stated that husband-wife relationships were neither important nor reliable as a basis for family life and child-rearing, and they were deeply suspicious of the intentions of the opposite sex.

The disappearance of marriage as a social institution was underscored by field observations that Taub and his associates undertook in black and Mexican neighborhoods. Whereas a four-block shopping strip in one of Chicago's poor Mexican neighborhoods yielded fifteen shops that provided goods or services explicitly connected to marriage, a trip to a comparable black shopping area uncovered only two shops that even mentioned marriage, and not very prominently at that.

Elijah Anderson argues that childbearing has become increasingly disconnected from marriage in the ghetto; black women now seek childbirth to signal their status as adults and to validate their worth and standing before their own peer group—namely, other young black women. A baby is a young girl's entry ticket into what Anderson calls "the baby club." This "club" consists of young black mothers who gather in public places with their children to "lobby for compliments, smiles, and nods of approval and feel very good when they are forthcoming, since they signal affirmation and pride. On Sundays, the new little dresses and suits come out and the cutest babies are passed around, and this attention serves as a social measure of the person. The young mothers who form such baby clubs develop an ideology counter to that of more conventional society, one that not only approves of but enhances their position. In effect, they work to create value and status by inverting that of the girls who do not become pregnant. The teenage mother derives status from her baby; hence, her preoccupation with the impression that the baby makes and her willingness to spend inordinately large sums toward that end."[27]

According to Anderson, sex is thus a key component in the informal status system that has evolved in the street culture of America's urban ghettos. In the absence of gratification through the conventional avenues of work and family, young men and women have increasingly turned to one commodity that lies within their reach. Through sex, young men get pleasure and a feeling of self-esteem before their peers, whereas young women get a baby and a sense of belonging within the baby club. This relationship of mutual exploitation, however, has come at a price. It has further marginalized black men from black women and has escalated the war of the sexes to new heights, a fact that is clearly revealed in the music of black street culture—rap.

An unabashedly misogynist viewpoint is extolled by rap groups such as N.W.A. ("Niggers with Attitude"), whose song "A Bitch Iz a Bitch" depicts black women as scheming, vain, whining mercenaries whose goal is to deprive black men of their self-esteem, money, and possessions. In the view of N.W.A., women are good for little more than sex, and their incessant demands for attention, constant requests for money and support, and their ever-present threats to male pride can only be checked through violence, ". . . 'cause a bitch is a bitch."[28]

The female side of the issue is aired by the female rap group H.W.A. ("Hoes [Whores] with Attitude") in songs such as "A Trick Is a Trick," "Little Dick," and "1-900-BITCHES," which attack men as vain, superficial creatures who are incompetent in their love-making, ill equipped to satisfy, and prone to meaningless violence when their inflated pride is punctured. Their metaphor for the state of male-female relations in the ghetto is that of a whorehouse, where all women are whores and men are either tricks or pimps. The liner notes leave little doubt as to the group's message: "Everybody is a pimp of some kind and pimpin' is easy when you got a Hoe Wit Attitude."[29]

The war of words between black men and women has also been fought in the black press, exemplified in 1990 by the appearance of *The Blackman's Guide to Understanding the Blackwoman,* by Shaharazad Ali, which presents a vituperative attack on black women for their supposedly historical emasculation of black men. The book advocates the violent subjugation of women by black men, advising male readers that "there is never an excuse for ever hitting a Blackwoman anywhere but in the mouth. Because it is from that hole, in the lower part of her face, that all her rebellion culminates into words. Her unbridled tongue is a main reason she cannot get along with the Blackman . . . If she ignores the authority and superiority of the Blackman, there is a penalty. When she crosses this line and becomes viciously insulting it is time for the Blackman to soundly slap her in the mouth."[30] Ten black scholars answered to the attack in a pamphlet entitled *Confusion by Any Other Name,* hoping "to respond to the range of insulting myths, half-truths and generalized personal experiences by the author."[31]

From a sociological point of view, the specific content of these works is less important than what they illustrate about the state of relations between the sexes within the black community. After evolving for decades under conditions of intense social and economic isolation, black street culture has become increasingly divorced from basic American ideals of family, work, and respect for others. By confining large numbers of black people to an environment within which failure is endemic, negative role models abound, and adherence to conventional values is nearly impossible, segregation has helped to create a nihilistic and violent counterculture sharply at odds with the basic values and goals of a democratic society. As Kenneth Clark presciently noted in 1965, "the pathologies of the ghetto community perpetuate themselves through cumulative ugliness, deterioration, and isolation."[32]

The social environment created by segregation places a heavy burden on black parents aspiring to promote conventional attitudes and behavior in their children and increase the odds for their socioeconomic success. Although the problem is most acute for the poor, segregation confines all blacks to segregated neighborhoods regardless of social class, so working- and middle-class blacks also have a

very difficult time insulating their children from the competing values and attitudes of the street. Compared with children of middle-class whites, children of
middle-class blacks are much more likely to be exposed to poverty, drugs, teenage
pregnancy, family disruption, and violence in the neighborhoods where they live.

As a result, it requires a great deal of concerted effort by committed parents,
and no small amount of luck, to raise children successfully within the ghetto.
Given the burden of "acting white," the pressures to speak Black English, the social
stigma attached to "brainiacs," the allure of drug taking, the quick money to be
had from drug dealing, and the romantic sexuality of the streets, it is not surprising that black educational achievement has stagnated. . . .

The Case for National Action

. . . Although race has become embroiled in partisan politics during the 1980s and
1990s, residential desegregation is not intrinsically a cause of either the right or
the left; it is neither liberal nor conservative, democrat nor republican. Rather it is
a bipartisan agenda in the national interest. The ghetto must be dismantled because only by ending segregation will we eliminate the manifold social and economic problems that follow from its persistence.

For conservatives, the cause of desegregation turns on the issue of market access. We have marshaled extensive evidence to show that one particular group—
black Americans—is systematically denied full access to a crucial market.
Housing markets are central to individual social and economic well-being because they distribute much more than shelter; they also distribute a variety of resources that shape and largely determine one's life chances. Along with housing,
residential markets also allocate schooling, peer groups, safety, jobs, insurance
costs, public services, home equity, and, ultimately, wealth. By tolerating the persistent and systematic disenfranchisement of blacks from housing markets, we
send a clear signal to one group that hard work, individual enterprise, sacrifice,
and aspirations don't matter; what determines one's life chances is the color of
one's skin.

For liberals, the issue is one of unfinished business, for residential segregation
is the most important item remaining on the nation's civil rights agenda. In many
areas of civil life, desegregation has occurred; in the south, Jim Crow is dead, and
throughout the country blacks are accepted in unions, sports, entertainment,
journalism, politics, government, administration, and academia. Many barriers
have fallen, but still the residential color line remains—and from residential segregation follows a host of deadly social ills that continue to undercut and over-
whelm the progress achieved in other areas.

Residential desegregation should be considered an effort of national unity; any
other course of action is politically indefensible. For conservatives, turning away
from the task means denying the importance of markets and individual enterprise; for liberals it means sweeping the last piece of unfinished civil rights busi-

ness under the rug. Ultimately, however, residential desegregation requires a moral commitment and a bipartisan leadership that have been lacking among politicians for the past two decades. Without a willingness to lead and take risks on the part of elected officials, and without a will to change on the part of the American people, none of the legal changes and policy solutions we propose will succeed.

For America, the failure to end segregation will perpetuate a bitter dilemma that has long divided the nation. If segregation is permitted to continue, poverty will inevitably deepen and become more persistent within a large share of the black community, crime and drugs will become more firmly rooted, and social institutions will fragment further under the weight of deteriorating conditions. As racial inequality sharpens, white fears will grow, racial prejudices will be reinforced, and hostility toward blacks will increase, making the problems of racial justice and equal opportunity even more insoluble. Until we face up to the difficult task of dismantling the ghetto, the disastrous consequences of residential segregation will radiate outward to poison American society. Until we decide to end the long reign of American apartheid, we cannot hope to move forward as a people and a nation.

NOTES

1. Deborah Wallace, "Roots of Increased Health Care Inequality in New York," *Social Science and Medicine* 31 (1990):1219–27; Rodrick Wallace, "Urban Desertification, Public Health and Public Order: 'Planned Shrinkage,' Violent Death, Substance Abuse, and AIDS in the Bronx," *Social Science and Medicine* 32 (1991):801–813; Rodrick Wallace, "'Planned Shrinkage,' Contagious Urban Decay, and Violent Death in the Bronx: The Implications of Synergism," Epidemiology of Mental Disorders Research Department, New York State Psychiatric Institute, 1990.

2. William L. Yancey, Eugene P. Ericksen, and George H. Leon, "The Structure of Pluralism: 'We're All Italian Around Here, Aren't We Mrs. O'Brien?'" *Ethnic and Racial Studies* 8 (1985):94–116.

3. Sophie Pedder, "Social Isolation and the Labor Market: Black Americans in Chicago," paper presented at the Chicago Urban Poverty and Family Life Conference, Chicago, Ill., Oct. 10–12, 1991.

4. Ibid.

5. See Labov, *Language in the Inner City*; Labov, "The Logic of Nonstandard English"; William Labov, ed., *Locating Language in Space and Time* (New York: Academic Press, 1980).

6. Labov and Harris, "De Facto Segregation," p. 2.

7. Joleen Kirschenman and Kathryn M. Neckerman, "'We'd Love to Hire Them, But . . . ': The Meaning of Race for Employers," in Christopher Jencks and Paul E. Peterson, eds., *The Urban Underclass* (Washington, D.C.: Brookings Institution, 1991), pp. 203–232.

8. Signithia Fordham and John U. Ogbu, "Black Students' School Success: Coping with the 'Burden of Acting White,'" *Urban Review* 18 (1986):176–206.

9. James E. Rosenbaum and Susan J. Popkin, "Economic and Social Impacts of Housing Integration," Center for Urban Affairs and Policy Research, Northwestern University, 1990; James E. Rosenbaum, Marilynn J. Kulieke, and Leonard S. Rubinowitz, "White Suburban Schools' Responses to Low-Income Black Children: Sources of Success and Problems,"

Urban Review 20 (1988):28–41; James E. Rosenbaum and Susan J. Popkin, "Black Pioneers: Do Their Moves to Suburbs Increase Economic Opportunity for Mothers and Children?" *Housing Policy Debate* 2 (1991): 1179–1214.

10. Robert Crain and Rita Mahard, "School Racial Composition and Black College Attendance and Achievement Test Performance," *Sociology of Education* 51 (1978):81–101.

11. Susan E. Mayer, "How Much Does a High School's Racial and Socioeconomic Mix Affect Graduation and Teenage Fertility Rates?" in Christopher Jencks and Paul E. Peterson, eds., *The Urban Underclass* (Washington, D.C.: Brookings Institution, 1991), pp. 321–41.

12. Clark, *Dark Ghetto,* p. 19.

13. Shelby Steele, *The Content of Our Character* (New York: St. Martin's Press, 1990), p. 60.

14. Cited in Dinesh D'Souza, *Illiberal Education: The Politics of Race and Sex on Campus* (New York: Free Press, 1991), p. 239.

15. Elijah Anderson, *Streetwise: Race, Class, and Change in an Urban Community* (Chicago: University of Chicago Press, 1990).

16. Ibid., p. 69.

17. Ibid.

18. Ibid., p. 72.

19. Ibid., pp. 74–75.

20. Ibid., p. 76.

21. Anderson, *Streetwise,* p. 77.

22. Ibid., p. 114.

23. Ibid., p. 120.

24. Ibid.

25. Ibid., p. 126.

26. Richard P. Taub, "Differing Conceptions of Honor and Orientations toward Work and Marriage among Low-Income African-Americans and Mexican-Americans," paper presented at the Chicago Urban Poverty and Family Life Conference, October 10–12, 1991.

27. Anderson, *Streetwise,* p. 126.

28. N.W.A. and the Posse, "A Bitch Iz A Bitch" (Hollywood, Calif.: Priority Records, published by Ruthless Attack Muzick, 1989, ASCAP).

29. H.W.A., "Livin' in a Hoe House" (Hollywood, Calif.: Drive By Records, published by Thunder Publishing Company, 1990, BMI).

30. Shaharazad Ali, *The Blackman's Guide to Understanding the Blackwoman* (Philadelphia: Civilized Publications, 1990), p. 169.

31. Haki R. Madhubuti, ed., *Confusion by Any Other Name: Essays Exploring the Negative Impact of the Blackman's Guide to Understanding the Blackwoman* (Chicago: Third World Press, 1990).

32. Clark, *Dark Ghetto,* p. 12.

Part Three

Assimilation and Identity in a Multicultural Society

14

The Souls of Black Folk

W.E.B. DU BOIS

O water, voice of my heart, crying in the sand,
All night long crying with a mournful cry,
As I lie and listen, and cannot understand
The voice of my heart in my side or the voice of the sea,
O water, crying for rest, is it I, is it I?
All night long the water is crying to me.

Unresting water, there shall never be rest
Till the last moon droop and the last tide fail,
And the fire of the end begin to burn in the west;
And the heart shall be weary and wonder and cry like the sea,
All life long crying without avail,
As the water all night long is crying to me.

—Arthur Symons

Between me and the other world there is ever an unasked question: unasked by some through feelings of delicacy; by others through the difficulty of rightly framing it. All, nevertheless, flutter round it. They approach me in a half-hesitant sort of way, eye me curiously or compassionately, and then, instead of saying directly, How does it feel to be a problem? they say, I know an excellent colored man in my town; or, I fought at Mechanicsville; or, Do not these Southern outrages make your blood boil? At these I smile, or am interested, or reduce the boiling to a simmer, as the occasion may require. To the real question, How does it feel to be a problem? I answer seldom a word.

And yet, being a problem is a strange experience,—peculiar even for one who has never been anything else, save perhaps in babyhood and in Europe. It is in the early days of rollicking boyhood that the revelation first bursts upon one, all in a day, as it were. I remember well when the shadow swept across me. I was a little thing, away up in the hills of New England, where the dark Housatonic winds between Hoosac and Taghkanic to the sea. In a wee wooden schoolhouse, something

163

put it into the boys' and girls' heads to buy gorgeous visiting-cards—ten cents a package—and exchange. The exchange was merry, till one girl, a tall newcomer, refused my card,—refused it peremptorily, with a glance. Then it dawned upon me with a certain suddenness that I was different from the others; or like, may-hap, in heart and life and longing, but shut out from their world by a vast veil. I had thereafter no desire to tear down that veil, to creep through; I held all beyond it in common contempt, and lived above it in a region of blue sky and great wandering shadows. That sky was bluest when I could beat my mates at examination-time, or beat them at a foot-race, or even beat their stringy heads. Alas, with the years all this fine contempt began to fade; for the words I longed for, and all their dazzling opportunities, were theirs, not mine. But they should not keep these prizes, I said; some, all, I would wrest from them. Just how I would do it I could never decide: by reading law, by healing the sick, by telling the wonderful tales that swam in my head,—some way. With other black boys the strife was not so fiercely sunny: their youth shrunk into tasteless sycophancy, or into silent hatred of the pale world about them and mocking distrust of everything white; or wasted itself in a bitter cry. Why did God make me an outcast and a stranger in mine own house? The shades of the prison-house closed round about us all: walls strait and stubborn to the whitest, but relentlessly narrow, tall, and unscalable to sons of night who must plod darkly on in resignation, or beat unavailing palms against the stone, or steadily, half hopelessly, watch the streak of blue above.

After the Egyptian and Indian, the Greek and Roman, the Teuton and Mongolian, the negro is a sort of seventh son, born with a veil, and gifted with second-sight in this American world,—a world which yields him no true self-consciousness, but only lets him see himself through the revelation of the other world. It is a peculiar sensation, this double-consciousness, this sense of always looking at one's self through the eyes of others, of measuring one's soul by the tape of a world that looks on in amused contempt and pity. One ever feels his twoness,—an American, a Negro; two souls, two thoughts, two unreconciled strivings; two warring ideals in one dark body, whose dogged strength alone keeps it from being torn asunder.

The history of the American Negro is the history of this strife,—this longing to attain self-conscious manhood, to merge his double self into a better and truer self. In this merging he wishes neither of the older selves to be lost. He would not Africanize America, for America has too much to teach the world and Africa. He would not bleach his Negro soul in a flood of white Americanism, for he knows that Negro blood has a message for the world. He simply wishes to make it possible for a man to be both a Negro and an American, without being cursed and spit upon by his fellows, without having the doors of Opportunity closed roughly in his face.

This, then, is the end of his striving: to be a co-worker in the kingdom of culture, to escape both death and isolation, to husband and use his best powers and his latent genius. These powers of body and mind have in the past been strangely wasted, dispersed, or forgotten. The shadow of a mighty Negro past flits through the tale of Ethiopia the Shadowy and of Egypt the Sphinx. Through history, the powers of single black men flash here and there like falling stars, and die sometimes before the world has rightly gauged their brightness. Here in America, in the few days since Emancipation, the black man's turning hither and thither in hesitant and doubtful striving has often made his very strength to lose effectiveness, to seem like absence of power, like weakness, and yet it is not weakness,—it is the contradiction of double aims. The double-aimed struggle of the black artisan—on the one hand to escape white contempt for a nation of mere hewers of wood and drawers of water, and on the other hand to plough and nail and dig for a poverty-stricken horde—could only result in making him a poor craftsman, for he had but half a heart in either cause. By the poverty and ignorance of his people, the Negro minister or doctor was tempted toward quackery and demagogy; and by the criticism of the other world, toward ideals that made him ashamed of his lowly tasks. The would-be black *savant* was confronted by the paradox that the knowledge of his people needed was a twice-told tale to his white neighbors, while the knowledge which would teach the white world was Greek to his own flesh and blood. The innate love of harmony and beauty that set the ruder souls of his people a-dancing and a-singing raised but confusion and doubt in the soul of the black artist; for the beauty revealed to him was the soul-beauty of a race which his larger audience despised, and he could not articulate the message of another people. This waste of double aims, this seeking to satisfy two unreconciled ideals, has wrought sad havoc with the courage and faith and deeds of ten thousand thousand people,—has sent them often wooing false gods and invoking false means of salvation, and at times has even seemed about to make them ashamed of themselves.

Away back in the days of bondage they thought to see in one divine event the end of all doubt and disappointment; few men ever worshipped Freedom with half such unquestioning faith as did the American Negro for two centuries. To him, so far as he thought and dreamed, slavery was indeed the sum of all villainies, the cause of all sorrow, the root of all prejudice; Emancipation was the key to a promised land of sweeter beauty than ever stretched before the eyes of wearied Israelites. In song and exhortation swelled one refrain—Liberty; in his tears and curses the God he implored had Freedom in his right hand. At last it came,— suddenly, fearfully, like a dream. With one wild carnival of blood and passion came the message in his own plaintive cadences:—

> *"Shout, O children!*
> *Shout, you're free!*
> *For God has brought your liberty!"*

Years have passed away since then,—ten, twenty, forty; forty years of national life, forty years of renewal and development, and yet the swarthy spectre sits in its accustomed seat at the Nation's feast. In vain do we cry to this our vastest social problem:—

"Take any shape but that, and my firm nerves
Shall never tremble!"

The Nation has not yet found peace from its sins; the freedman has not yet found in freedom his promised land. Whatever of good may have come in these years of change, the shadow of a deep disappointment rests upon the Negro people,—a disappointment all the more bitter because the unattained ideal was unbounded save by the simple ignorance of a lowly people.

The first decade was merely a prolongation of the vain search for freedom, the boon that seemed ever barely to elude their grasp,—like a tantalizing will-o'-the-wisp, maddening and misleading the headless host. The holocaust of war, the terrors of the Ku-Klux Klan, the lies of carpet-baggers, the disorganization of industry, and the contradictory advice of friends and foes, left the bewildered serf with no new watchword beyond the old cry for freedom. As the time flew, however, he began to grasp a new idea. The ideal of liberty demanded for its attainment powerful means, and these the Fifteenth Amendment gave him. The ballot, which before he had looked upon as a visible sign of freedom, he now regarded as the chief means of gaining and perfecting the liberty with which war had partially endowed him. And why not? Had not votes made war and emancipated millions? Had not votes enfranchised the freedmen? Was anything impossible to a power that had done all this? A million black men started with renewed zeal to vote themselves into the kingdom. So the decade flew away, the revolution of 1876 came, and left the half-free serf weary, wondering, but still inspired. Slowly but steadily, in the following years, a new vision began gradually to replace the dream of political power,—a powerful movement, the rise of another ideal to guide the unguided, another pillar of fire by night after a clouded day. It was the ideal of "book-learning"; the curiosity, born of compulsory ignorance, to know and test the power of the cabalistic letters of the white man, the longing to know. Here at last seemed to have been discovered the mountain path to Canaan; longer than the highway of Emancipation and law, steep and rugged, but straight, leading to heights high enough to overlook life.

Up the new path the advance guard toiled, slowly, heavily, doggedly; only those who have watched and guided the faltering feet, the misty minds, the dull understandings, of the dark pupils of these schools know how faithfully, how piteously, this people strove to learn. It was weary work. The cold statistician wrote down the inches of progress here and there, noted also where here and there a foot had slipped or some one had fallen. To the tired climbers, the horizon was ever dark, the mists were often cold, the Canaan was always dim and far away. If, however, the vistas disclosed as yet no goal, no resting-place, little but flattery and criticism, the journey at least gave leisure for reflection and self-examination; it changed the child of Emancipation to the youth with dawning self-consciousness, self-realization, self-respect. In those sombre forests of his striving his own soul rose before him, and he saw himself,—darkly as through a veil; and yet he saw in himself some faint revelation of his power, of his mission. He began to have a dim feeling that, to attain his place in the world, he must be himself, and not another. For the first time he sought to analyze the burden he bore upon his back, that dead-weight of social degradation partially masked behind a half-named Negro problem. He felt his poverty; without a cent, without a home, without land, tools, or savings, he had entered into competition with rich, landed, skilled neighbors. To be a poor man is hard, but to be a poor race in a land of dollars is the very bottom of hardships. He felt the weight of his ignorance,—not simply of letters, but of life, of business, of the humanities; the accumulated sloth and shirking and awkwardness of decades and centuries shackled his hands and feet. Nor was his burden all poverty and ignorance. The red stain of bastardy, which two centuries of systematic legal defilement of Negro women had stamped upon his race, meant not only the loss of ancient African chastity, but also the hereditary weight of a mass of corruption from white adulterers, threatening almost the obliteration of the Negro home.

A people thus handicapped ought not to be asked to race with the world, but rather allowed to give all its time and thought to its own social problems. But alas! while sociologists gleefully count his bastards and his prostitutes, the very soul of the toiling, sweating black man is darkened by the shadow of a vast despair. Men call the shadow prejudice, and learnedly explain it as the natural defence of culture against barbarism, learning against ignorance, purity against crime, the "higher" against the "lower" races. To which the Negro cries Amen! and swears that to so much of this strange prejudice as is founded on just homage to civilization, culture, righteousness, and progress, he humbly bows and meekly does obeisance. But before that nameless prejudice that leaps beyond all this he stands helpless, dismayed, and well-nigh speechless; before that personal disrespect and mockery, the ridicule and systematic humiliation, the distortion of fact and wanton license of fancy, the cynical ignoring of the better and the boisterous welcoming of the worse, the all-pervading desire to inculcate disdain for everything black, from Toussaint to the devil,—before this there rises a sickening despair that would disarm and discourage any nation save that black host to whom "discouragement" is an unwritten word.

But the facing of so vast a prejudice could not but bring the inevitable self-questioning, self-disparagement, and lowering of ideals which ever accompany repression and breed in an atmosphere of contempt and hate. Whisperings and portents came borne upon the four winds: Lo! we are diseased and dying, cried the dark hosts; we cannot write, our voting is vain; what need of education, since we must always cook and serve? And the Nation echoed and enforced this self-criticism, saying: Be content to be servants, and nothing more; what need of higher culture for half-men? Away with the black man's ballot, by force or fraud,—and behold the suicide of a race! Nevertheless, out of the evil came something of good,—the more careful adjustment of education to real life, the clearer perception of the Negroes' social responsibilities, and the sobering realization of the meaning of progress.

So dawned the time of *Sturm und Drang:* storm and stress to-day rocks our little boat on the mad waters of the world-sea; there is within and without the sound of conflict, the burning of body and rending of soul; inspiration strives with doubt, and faith with vain questionings. The bright ideals of the past,—physical freedom, political power, the training of brains and the training of hands,—all these in turn have waxed and waned, until even the last grows dim and overcast. Are they all wrong,—all false? No, not that, but each alone was over-simple and incomplete,—the dreams of a credulous race-childhood, or the fond imaginings of the other world which does not know and does not want to know our power. To be really true, all these ideals must be melted and welded into one. The training of the schools we need to-day more than ever,—the training of deft hands, quick eyes and ears, and above all the broader, deeper, higher culture of gifted minds and pure hearts. The power of the ballot we need in sheer self-defence,—else what shall save us from a second slavery? Freedom, too, the long-sought, we still seek,—the freedom of life and limb, the freedom to work and think, the freedom to love and aspire. Work, culture, liberty,—all these we need, not singly but together, not successively but together, each growing and aiding each, and all striving toward that vaster ideal that swims before the Negro people, the ideal of human brotherhood, gained through the unifying ideal of Race; the ideal of fostering and developing the traits and talents of the Negro, not in oppo-sition to or contempt for other races, but rather in large conformity to the greater ideals of the American Republic, in order that some day on American soil two world-races may give each to each those characteristics both so sadly lack. We the darker ones come even now not altogether empty-handed: there are to-day no truer exponents of the pure human spirit of the Declaration of Independence than the American Negroes; there is no true American music but the wild sweet melodies of the Negro slave; the American fairy tales and folklore are Indian and African; and, all in all, we black men seem the sole oasis of simple faith and rever-ence in a dusty desert of dollars and smartness. Will America be poorer if she re-place her brutal dyspeptic blundering with light-hearted but determined Negro humility? or her coarse and cruel wit with loving jovial good-humor? or her vul-gar music with the soul of the Sorrow Songs?

Merely a concrete test of the underlying principles of the great republic is the Negro Problem, and the spiritual striving of the freedmen's sons is the travail of souls whose burden is almost beyond the measure of their strength, but who bear it in the name of an historic race, in the name of this land of their fathers' fa-thers, and in the name of human opportunity.

15

Race Matters

CORNEL WEST

Malcolm X and Black Rage

Malcolm X articulated black rage in a manner unprecedented in American history. His style of communicating this rage bespoke a boiling urgency and an audacious sincerity. The substance of what he said highlighted the chronic refusal of most Americans to acknowledge the sheer absurdity that confronts human beings of African descent in this country—the incessant assaults on black intelligence, beauty, character, and possibility. His profound commitment to affirm black humanity at any cost and his tremendous courage to accent the hypocrisy of American society made Malcolm X the prophet of black rage—then and now.

Malcolm X was the prophet of black rage primarily because of his great love for black people. His love was neither abstract nor ephemeral. Rather, it was a concrete connection with a degraded and devalued people in need of psychic conversion. This is why Malcolm X's articulation of black rage was not directed first and foremost at white America. Rather, Malcolm believed that if black people felt the love that motivated that rage the love would produce a psychic conversion in black people; they would affirm themselves as human beings, no longer viewing their bodies, minds, and souls through white lenses, and believing themselves capable of taking control of their own destinies.

In American society—especially during Malcolm X's life in the 1950s and early 1960s—such a psychic conversion could easily result in death. A proud, self-affirming black person who truly believed in the capacity of black people to throw off the yoke of white racist oppression and control their own destiny usually ended up as one of those strange fruit that Southern trees bore, about which the great Billie Holliday poignantly sang. So when Malcolm X articulated black rage, he knew he also had to exemplify in his own life the courage and sacrifice that any truly self-loving black person needs in order to confront the frightening consequences of being self-loving in American society. In other words, Malcolm X sharply crystallized the relation of black affirmation of self, black desire for freedom, black rage against American society, and the likelihood of early black death.

Malcolm X's notion of psychic conversion holds that black people must no longer view themselves through white lenses. He claims black people will never value themselves as long as they subscribe to a standard of valuation that devalues them. For example, Michael Jackson may rightly wish to be viewed as a person, not a color (neither black nor white), but his facial revisions reveal a self-measurement based on a white yardstick. Hence, despite the fact that he is one of the greatest entertainers who has ever lived, he still views himself, at least in part, through white aesthetic lenses that devalue some of his African characteristics. Needless to say, Michael Jackson's example is but the more honest and visible instance of a rather pervasive self-loathing among many of the black professional class. Malcolm X's call for psychic conversion often strikes horror into this privileged group because so much of who they are and what they do is evaluated in terms of their wealth, status, and prestige in American society. On the other hand, this group often understands Malcolm X's claim more than others precisely because they have lived so intimately in a white world in which the devaluation of black people is so often taken for granted or unconsciously assumed. It is no accident that the black middle class has always had an ambivalent relation to Malcolm X—an open rejection of his militant strategy of wholesale defiance of American society and a secret embrace of his bold truth-telling about the depths of racism in American society. One rarely encounters a picture of Malcolm X (as one does of Martin Luther King, Jr.) in the office of a black professional, but there is no doubt that Malcolm X dangles as the skeleton in the closet lodged in the racial memory of most black professionals.

In short, Malcolm X's notion of psychic conversion is an implicit critique of W.E.B. Du Bois's idea of "double-consciousness." Du Bois wrote:

> The Negro is a sort of seventh son, born with a veil, and gifted with second-sight in this American world,—a world which yields him no true self-consciousness, but only lets him see himself through the revelation of the other world. It is a peculiar sensation, this double-consciousness, this sense of always looking at one's self through the eyes of others, of measuring one's soul by the tape of a world that looks on in amused contempt and pity.

For Malcolm X this "double-consciousness" pertains more to those black people who live "betwixt and between" the black and white worlds—traversing the borders between them yet never settled in either. Hence, they crave peer acceptance in both, receive genuine approval from neither, yet persist in viewing themselves through the lenses of the dominant white society. For Malcolm X, this "double-consciousness" is less a description of a necessary black mode of being in America than a particular kind of colonized mind-set of a special group in black America. Du Bois's "double-consciousness" seems to lock black people into the quest for white approval and disappointment owing mainly to white racist assessment, whereas Malcolm X suggests that this tragic syndrome can be broken through psychic conversion. But how?

Malcolm X does not put forward a direct answer to this question. First, his well-known distinction between "house negroes" (who love and protect the white master) and "field negroes" (who hate and resist the white master) suggests that the masses of black people are more likely to acquire decolonized sensibilities and hence less likely to be "co-opted" by the white status quo. Yet this rhetorical device, though insightful in highlighting different perspectives among black people, fails as a persuasive description of the behavior of "well-to-do" black folk and "poor" black folk. In other words, there are numerous instances of "field negroes" with "house negro" mentalities and "house negroes" with "field negro" mentalities. Malcolm X's often-quoted distinction rightly highlights the propensity among highly assimilated black professionals to put "whiteness" (in all its various forms) on a pedestal, but it also tends to depict "poor" black peoples' notions and enactments of "blackness" in an uncritical manner. Hence his implicit critique of Du Bois's idea of "double-consciousness" contains some truth yet offers an inadequate alternative.

Second, Malcolm X's black nationalist viewpoint claims that the only legitimate response to white supremacist ideology and practice is black self-love and black self-determination free of the tension generated by "double-consciousness." This claim is both subtle and problematic. It is subtle in that every black freedom movement is predicated on an affirmation of African humanity and a quest for black control over the destinies of black people. Yet not every form of black self-love affirms African humanity. Furthermore not every project of black self-determination consists of a serious quest for black control over the destinies of black people. Malcolm's claim is problematic in that it tends to assume that black nationalisms have a monopoly on black self-love and black self-determination. This fallacious assumption confuses the issues highlighted by black nationalisms with the various ways in which black nationalists and others understand these issues.

For example, the grand legacy of Marcus Garvey forces us never to forget that black self-love and black self-respect sit at the center of any possible black freedom movement. Yet this does not mean that we must talk about black self-love and black self-respect in the way in which Garvey did, that is, on an imperial model in which black armies and navies signify black power. Similarly, the tradition of Elijah Muhammad compels us to acknowledge the centrality of black self-regard and black self-esteem, yet that does not entail an acceptance of how Elijah Muhammad talked about achieving this aim, that is, by playing a game of black supremacy that awakens us from our captivity to white supremacy. My point here is that a focus on the issues rightly targeted by black nationalists and an openness to the insights of black nationalists does not necessarily result in an acceptance of black nationalist ideology. Malcolm X tended to make such an unwarranted move—despite his legitimate focus on black self-love, his rich insights on black captivity to white supremacy, and his profound notion of psychic conversion.

Malcolm X's notion of psychic conversion depends on the idea that black spaces, in which black community, humanity, love, care, concern, and support flourish, will emerge from a boiling black rage. At this point, however, Malcolm X's project falters. How can the boiling black rage be contained and channeled in the black spaces such that destructive and self-destructive consequences are abated? The greatness of Malcolm X is, in part, that he raises this fundamental challenge with a sharpness and urgency never before posed in black America, yet he never had a chance in his short life to grapple with it, nor solve it in idea and deed. . . .

The Pitfalls of Racial Reasoning

The most depressing feature of the Clarence Thomas / Anita Hill hearings was neither the mean-spirited attacks of the Republicans nor the spineless silences of the Democrats—both reveal the predictable inability of most white politicians to talk candidly about race and gender. Rather what was most disturbing was the low level of political discussion in black America about these hearings—a crude discourse about race and gender that bespeaks a failure of nerve of black leadership.

This failure of nerve already was manifest in the selection and confirmation process of Clarence Thomas. Bush's choice of Thomas caught most black leaders off guard. Few had the courage to say publicly that this was an act of cynical tokenism concealed by outright lies about Thomas being the most qualified candidate regardless of race. Thomas had an undistinguished record as a student (mere graduation from Yale Law School does not qualify one for the Supreme Court); he left thirteen thousand age discrimination cases dying on the vine for lack of investigation in his turbulent eight years at the EEOC; and his performance during his short fifteen months as an appellate court judge was mediocre. The very fact that no black leader could utter publicly that a black appointee for the Supreme Court was *unqualified* shows how captive they are to white racist stereotypes about black intellectual talent. The point here is not simply that if Thomas were white they would have no trouble shouting this fact from the rooftops. The point is also that their silence reveals that black leaders may entertain the possibility that the racist stereotype may be true. Hence their attempt to cover Thomas's mediocrity with silence. Of course, some privately admit his mediocrity while pointing out the mediocrity of Justice Souter and other members of the Court—as if white mediocrity were a justification of black mediocrity. No double standards here, the argument goes, if a black man is unqualified one can defend and excuse him by appealing to other unqualified white judges. This chimes well with a cynical tokenism of the lowest common denominator—with little concern for the goal of shattering the racist stereotype or for furthering the public interest of the nation. It also renders invisible highly qualified black judges who deserve serious consideration for selection to the Court.

How did much of black leadership get in this bind? Why did so many of them capitulate to Bush's cynical strategy? First, Thomas's claim to racial authenticity—his birth in Jim Crow Georgia, his childhood as the grandson of a black sharecropper, his undeniably black phenotype degraded by racist ideals of beauty, and his gallant black struggle for achievement in racist America. Second, the complex relation of this claim to racial authenticity to the increasing closing-ranks mentality in black America. Escalating black nationalist sentiments—the notion that America's will to racial justice is weak and therefore black people must close ranks for survival in a hostile country—rests principally upon claims to racial authenticity. Third, the way in which black nationalist sentiments promote and encourage black cultural conservatism, especially black patriarchal (and homophobic) power. The idea of black people closing ranks against hostile white Americans reinforces black male power exercised over black women (e.g., to protect, regulate, subordinate, and hence usually, though not always, to use and abuse women) in order to preserve black social order under circumstances of white literal attack and symbolic assault.

Most black leaders got lost in this thicket of reasoning and hence got caught in a vulgar form of racial reasoning: black authenticity → black closing-ranks mentality → black male subordination of black women in the interests of the black community in a hostile white racist country. Such a line of racial reasoning leads to such questions as: "Is Thomas really black?" "Is he black enough to be defended?" "Is he just black on the outside?" In fact, these kinds of questions were asked, debated, and answered throughout black America in barber shops, beauty salons, living rooms, churches, mosques, and schoolrooms.

Unfortunately, the very framework of racial reasoning was not called into question. Yet as long as racial reasoning regulates black thought and action, Clarence Thomases will continue to haunt black America—as Bush and other conservatives sit back, watch, and prosper. How does one undermine the framework of racial reasoning? By dismantling each pillar slowly and systematically. The fundamental aim of this undermining and dismantling is to replace racial reasoning with moral reasoning, to understand the black freedom struggle not as an affair of skin pigmentation and racial phenotype but rather as a matter of ethical principles and wise politics, and to combat the black nationalist attempt to subordinate the issues and interests of black women by linking mature black self-love and self-respect to egalitarian relations within and outside black communities. The failure of nerve of black leadership is its refusal to undermine and dismantle the framework of racial reasoning.

Let us begin with the claim to racial authenticity—a claim Bush made about Thomas, Thomas made about himself in the hearings, and black nationalists make about themselves. What is black authenticity? Who is really black? First, blackness has no meaning outside of a system of race-conscious people and practices. After centuries of racist degradation, exploitation, and oppression in America, being black means being minimally subject to white supremacist abuse and being part of a rich culture and community that has struggled against such abuse. All people with black skin and African phenotype are subject to potential white supremacist abuse. Hence, all black Americans have some interest in resisting racism—even if their interest is confined solely to themselves as individuals rather than to larger black communities. Yet how this "interest" is defined and how individuals and communities are understood vary. Hence any claim to black authenticity—beyond that of being a potential object of racist abuse and an heir to a grand tradition of black struggle—is contingent on one's political definition of black interest and one's ethical understanding of how this interest relates to individuals and communities in and outside black America. In short, blackness is a political and ethical construct. Appeals to black authenticity ignore this fact; such appeals hide and conceal the political and ethical dimension of blackness. This is why claims to racial authenticity trump political and ethical argument—and why racial reasoning discourages moral reasoning. Every claim to racial authenticity presupposes elaborate conceptions of political and ethical relations of interests, individuals, and communities. Racial reasoning conceals these presuppositions behind a deceptive cloak of racial consensus—yet racial reasoning is seductive because it invokes an undeniable history of racial abuse and racial struggle. This is why Bush's claims to Thomas's black authenticity, Thomas's claims about his own black authenticity, and black nationalist claims about black authenticity all highlight histories of black abuse and black struggle.

But if claims to black authenticity are political and ethical conceptions of the relation of black interests, individuals, and communities, then any attempt to confine black authenticity to black nationalist politics or black male interests warrants suspicion. For example, black leaders failed to highlight the problematic statements Clarence Thomas made about his sister, Emma Mae, regarding her experience with the welfare system. In front of a conservative audience in San Francisco, Thomas implied she was a welfare cheat dependent on state support. Yet, like most black women in American history, Emma Mae is a hard-working person. She was sensitive enough to take care of her sick aunt even though she was unable to work for a short period of time. After she left welfare, she worked two jobs—until 3:00 in the morning! Thomas's statements reveal his own lack of integrity and character. But the failure of black leaders to highlight his statements discloses a conception of black authenticity confined to black male interests, individuals, and communities. In short, the refusal by most black leaders to give weight to the interests of black women was already apparent before Anita Hill appeared on the scene.

The claims to black authenticity that feed on the closing-ranks mentality of black people are dangerous precisely because this closing of ranks is usually done at the expense of black women. It also tends to ignore the divisions of class and sexual orientation in black America—divisions that require attention if *all* black interests, individuals, and communities are to be taken into consideration. Thomas's conservative Republican politics do not promote a closing-ranks mentality; instead Thomas claims black authenticity for self-promotion, to gain power and prestige. All his professional life he has championed individual achievement and race-free standards. Yet when it looked as though the Senate would not confirm his appointment to the Supreme Court, he played the racial card of black victimization and black solidarity at the expense of Anita Hill. Like his sister, Emma Mae, Anita Hill could be used and abused for his own self-interested conception of black authenticity and racial solidarity.

Thomas played this racial card with success—first with appeals to his victimization in Jim Crow Georgia and later to his victimization by a "hi-tech lynching"—primarily because of the deep cultural conservatism in white and black America. In white America, cultural conservatism takes the form of a chronic racism, sexism, and homophobia. Hence, only certain kinds of black people deserve high positions, that is, those who accept the rules of the game played by white America. In black America, cultural conservatism takes the form of a inchoate xenophobia (e.g., against whites, Jews, and Asians), systemic sexism, and homophobia. Like all conservatisms rooted in a quest for order, the pervasive disorder in white and, especially, black America fans and fuels the channeling of rage toward the most vulnerable and degraded members of the community. For white America, this means primarily scapegoating black people, women, gay men, and lesbians. For black America, this means principally attacking black women and black gay men and lesbians. In this way, black nationalist and black male-centered claims to black authenticity reinforce black cultural conservatism. The support of Louis Farrakhan's Nation of Islam for Clarence Thomas—despite Farrakhan's critique of Republican Party racist and conservative policies—highlights this fact. It also shows how racial reasoning leads different and disparate viewpoints in black America to the same dead end—with substantive ethical principles and savvy wise politics left out.

The undermining and dismantling of the framework of racial reasoning—especially the basic notions of black authenticity, closed-ranks mentality, and black cultural conservatism—lead toward a new framework for black thought and practice. This new framework should be a *prophetic* one of moral reasoning with its fundamental ideas of a mature black identity, coalition strategy, and black cultural democracy. Instead of cathartic appeals to black authenticity, a prophetic viewpoint bases mature black self-love and self-respect on the moral quality of black responses to undeniable racist degradation in the American past and present. These responses assume neither a black essence that all black people share nor one black perspective to which all black people should adhere. Rather, a prophetic framework encourages *moral* assessment of the variety of perspectives held by black people and selects those views based on black dignity and decency that eschew putting any group of people or culture on a pedestal or in the gutter. Instead, blackness is understood to be either the perennial possibility of white supremacist abuse or the distinct styles and dominant modes of expression found in black cultures and communities. These styles and modes are diverse—yet they do stand apart from those of other groups (even as they are shaped by and shape those of other groups). And all such styles and modes stand in need of ethical evaluation. Mature black identity results from an acknowledgment of the specific

black responses to white supremacist abuses and a moral assessment of these responses such that the humanity of black people does not rest on deifying or de-
monizing others.

Instead of a closing-ranks mentality, a prophetic framework encourages a
coalition strategy that solicits genuine solidarity with those deeply committed to
antiracist struggle. This strategy is neither naive nor opportunistic; black suspicion of whites, Latinos, Jews, and Asians runs deep for historical reasons. Yet there
are slight though significant antiracist traditions among whites, Asians, and especially Latinos, Jews, and indigenous people that must not be cast aside. Such coalitions are important precisely because they not only enhance the plight of black
people but also because they enrich the quality of life in America.

Last, a prophetic framework replaces black cultural conservatism with black
cultural democracy. Instead of authoritarian sensibilities that subordinate women
or degrade gay men and lesbians, black cultural democracy promotes the equality
of black women and men and the humanity of black gay men and lesbians. In
short, black cultural democracy rejects the pervasive patriarchy and homophobia
in black American life.

If most black leaders had adopted a prophetic framework of moral reasoning
rather than a narrow framework of racial reasoning, the debate over the Clarence
Thomas / Anita Hill hearings would have proceeded in a quite different manner
in black America. For example, both Thomas and Hill would be viewed as two
black Republican conservative supporters of some of the most vicious policies to
besiege black working and poor communities since Jim and Jane Crow segregation. Both Thomas and Hill supported an unprecedented redistribution of wealth
from working people to well-to-do people in the form of regressive taxation,
deregulation policies, cutbacks and slowdowns in public service programs, take-
backs at the negotiation table between workers and management, and military
buildups at the Pentagon. Both Thomas and Hill supported the unleashing of unbridled capitalist market forces on a level never witnessed in the United States before that have devastated black working and poor communities. These market
forces took the principal form of unregulated corporative and financial expansion
and intense entrepreneurial activity. This tremendous ferment in big and small
businesses—including enormous bonanzas in speculation, leverage buyouts and
mergers, as well as high levels of corruption and graft—contributed to a new kind
of culture of consumption in white and black America. Never before has the seductive market way of life held such sway in nearly every sphere of American life.
This market way of life promotes addictions to stimulation and obsessions with
comfort and convenience. Addictions and obsessions—centered primarily
around bodily pleasures and status rankings—constitute market moralities of
various sorts. The common denominator is a rugged and ragged individualism
and rapacious hedonism in quest of a perennial "high" in body and mind.

In the hearings, the image of Clarence Thomas that emerged was one of an exemplary hedonist, a consumer of pornography, captive to a stereotypical self-

image of the powerful black man who revels in sexual prowess in a racist society. Anita Hill appeared as the exemplary careerist addicted to job promotion and captive to the stereotypical self-image of the sacrificial black woman who suffers silently and alone. There was reason to suspect that Thomas was not telling the whole truth. He was silent about *Roe v. Wade,* his intentions in the antiabortion essay on Lewis Lehrmann, and the contours of his conservative political philosophy. Furthermore, his obdurate stonewalling in regard to his private life was disturbing. There also should be little doubt that Anita Hill's decision to testify was a break from her careerist ambitions. On the one hand, she strikes me as a person of integrity and honesty. On the other hand, she indeed put a premium on job advancement—even at painful personal cost. Yet her speaking out disrupted this pattern of behavior and she found herself supported only by people who opposed the very conservative Republican policies she otherwise championed, namely, progressive feminists, liberals, and some black folk. How strange she must feel being a hero to her former foes. One wonders whether Judge Bork supported her as fervently as she did him a few years ago.

A prophetic framework of moral reasoning would have liberated black leaders from the racial guilt of opposing a black man for the highest court in the land and of the feeling that one had to choose between a black woman and a black man. Like the Black Congressional Caucus (minus one?), black people could have simply opposed Thomas based on qualifications and principle. And one could have chosen between two black right-wing figures based on their sworn testimonies in light of the patterns of their behavior in the recent past. Similarly, black leaders could have avoided being duped by Thomas's desperate and vulgar appeals to racial victimization by a white male Senate committee who handled him gently (no questions about his private life). Like Senator Hollings, who knows racial intimidation when he sees it (given his past experiences with it), black leaders could have seen through the rhetorical charade and called a moral spade a moral spade.

Unfortunately, most black leaders remained caught in a framework of racial reasoning—even when they opposed Thomas and/or supported Hill. Rarely did we have a black leader highlight the moral content of a mature black identity, accent the crucial role of coalition strategy in the struggle for justice, or promote the ideal of black cultural democracy. Instead, the debate evolved around glib formulations of a black "role model" based on mere pigmentation, an atavistic defense of blackness that mirrors the increasing xenophobia in American life, and circled around a silence about the ugly authoritarian practices in black America that range from sexual harassment to indescribable violence against women. Hence a grand opportunity for substantive discussion and struggle over race and gender was missed in black America and the larger society. And black leadership must share some of the blame. As long as black leaders remain caught in a framework of racial reasoning, they will not rise above the manipulative language of Bush and Thomas—just as the state of siege (the death, disease, and destruction) raging in much of black America creates more urban wastelands and combat zones.

Where there is no vision, the people perish; where there is no framework of moral reasoning, the people close ranks in a war of all against all. The growing gangster-ization of America results in part from a market-driven racial reasoning that links the White House to the ghetto projects. In this sense, George Bush, David Duke, and many gangster rap artists speak the same language from different social loca-tions—only racial reasoning can save us. Yet I hear a cloud of witnesses from afar—Sojourner Truth, Wendell Phillips, Emma Goldman, A. Phillip Randolph, Ella Baker, Myles Horton, Fannie Lou Hamer, Michael Harrington, Abraham Joshua Heschel, Tom Hayden, Harvey Milk, Robert Moses, Barbara Ehrenreich, Martin Luther King, Jr., and many anonymous others who championed the strug-gle for freedom and justice in a prophetic framework of moral reasoning. They understood that the pitfalls of racial reasoning are too costly in mind, body, and soul—especially for a downtrodden and despised people like black Americans. The best of our leadership recognized this valuable truth—and more must do so in the future if America is to survive with any moral sense.

16

Group Autonomy
and Narrative Identity

LAURENCE MORDEKHAI THOMAS

Any attempt to compare the suffering of blacks and Jews would seem likely to be felled by the waves of invidious comparisons. That is because any such comparison is likely to be seen, however obliquely, as an endeavor to answer the question: Which group has suffered more—blacks or Jews? And the feeling, of course, is that the suffering of both has been (and is) so heinous that to be concerned with answering that question is to embark upon a most despicable kind of moral enterprise. Be that as it may, there can be instructive comparisons regarding the suffering of Jews and blacks. I shall attempt such a comparison in this essay. At the very end of this essay, I shall speak to why it has seemed so natural to compare Jews and blacks.

I.

My thesis is that *despite* the Holocaust contemporary Jews have group autonomy, whereas *on account of* American slavery contemporary blacks do not. An identifiable group of people has group autonomy when its members are generally regarded by others not belonging to the group as the foremost interpreters of their own historical-cultural traditions. I take it to be obvious that group autonomy, understood in that way, is a moral good of enormous importance. On an individual level the most significant indication that others take us seriously is that they regard us as the foremost interpreters of who we are: our desires, aims, values, beliefs, and so on. Suppose I were to ask a person about her aims and so forth—but only as a matter of courtesy, it being evident that I have already satisfied myself as to what the person is like. If the person has any self-respect at all, she would rightly feel insulted, resentful, and angry. The importance of group autonomy is analogous. Normally, it is only because a group has an extraordinary command of its own history and experiences that it has group autonomy. It is logically possible that a group could have such autonomy and yet lack a command of these things, if the group is regarded as having mastery of its historical-cultural traditions when, in actuality, it does not. On the other hand, it is not sufficient for group autonomy that a group has such mastery, since having the mastery is quite compatible with other groups not acknowledging that it does.

To be sure, it is a consequence of my account that group autonomy is contingent upon being held in a certain regard by others. This is true of self-regarding attitudes in general. Insofar as we respect ourselves as individuals, it is precisely because we have been respected often enough by others. If respect from others has been adequate at the very formative stages of our lives, then it is possible to endure a considerable amount of disrespect from others for a period of time without losing our respect for ourselves, even if our self-respect shows signs of wearing out. And massive displays of respect after the ordeal would be crucial to repairing the damage done—to strengthening the paths of self-respect that had worn thin. Our own self-respect is not thereby diminished because it is anchored in the respect that we receive from others. By parity of reasoning, then, group autonomy is not diminished because it is anchored in the respect that a group receives from other groups.

I maintain that despite the Holocaust contemporary Jews have group autonomy, whereas on account of American slavery contemporary blacks do not. At any rate, blacks have considerably less group autonomy than Jews. What fuels my thinking are the following considerations: 1) Given the evil of the Holocaust for Jews and the evil of slavery for blacks, if any two groups should interact in harmony with one another it is Jews and blacks. 2) It is clear that they do not. And 3) I do not find the prevailing explanation that there is enormous economic disparity between blacks and Jews to be a complete explanation for the disharmony between the two groups. I do not wish to discount the reality of the economic disparity between blacks and Jews as a factor in black-Jewish tensions; rather, I believe that the disharmony between the two groups can be explained in a different and morally more satisfying way.

I suggest that some of the negative feelings toward Jews that are so prevalent among blacks can be attributed to the fact that Jews have considerably more group autonomy than blacks. This difference has given rise to resentment born of envy on the part of blacks toward Jews. At the end of this essay, I shall say something about racism on the part of Jews toward blacks.

Group autonomy is an indisputable moral good. It is understandable that every group should want to have it. Likewise, if a group which has been egregiously wronged should fail to have it, then it is understandable, though in no way justifiable, that the members of that group should be envious of the members of groups which have it, especially the members of groups which have also been egregiously wronged. For envy is a function of the uncomfortably small distance that we find between ourselves and others who possess goods that we prize. It does not require any wrongdoing on anyone's part. As social beings, we inevitably have a comparative conception of ourselves, and sometimes we cannot prevent or blunt the force of a stark comparison between ourselves and those who possess a prized good. It is perfectly understandable, for instance, that a person without legs might experience envy from time to time toward persons with legs. Envy is no less understandable when it can be attributed to a prized good that is moral, as group autonomy certainly is.

When we see the negative feelings that blacks have toward Jews derives, in large part, from the disparity in group autonomy between the two groups rather than from the economic disparity between them, we thereby view those negative feelings from a different part of the moral landscape. Of course, understandable envy is no less envy, and we should do all that we can to dissipate it. But our attitude toward understandable envy should be different from our attitude toward envy born of rapaciousness. And this holds all the more when the envy can be attributed to a failure to possess the prized moral good of group autonomy owing to social victimization. I do not want to deny the existence of anti-Semitism on the part of blacks toward Jews. It is very real indeed. Rather, I have tried to show that not all negative feelings that blacks might have toward Jews are properly characterized as anti-Semitic. I take it to be obvious that resentment on the part of blacks toward Jews owing to the differential between them with respect to group autonomy is far more morally palatable than resentment owing to the economic success of Jews.

Needless to say, I am no more blaming blacks for lacking group autonomy than I am crediting Jews for having it. Neither situation can be construed as a matter of choice.

It is perhaps tempting to suppose that group autonomy comes in the wake of economic success. This temptation should be resisted, however. In *A Certain People* (1986), Charles E. Silberman paints a glowing picture of the success of American Jews. Well, the success of Jews should not blind us to the reality that in general Jews did not arrive in America well-off. On the contrary, many were quite poor when they came here. Yet they had group autonomy.

It was not too long ago that Jews had considerable difficulty getting into so venerable an institution as Harvard University, as Bruce Kuklick has shown in *The Rise of American Philosophy* (1977). Indeed, the Harvard philosophy department has come a very long way since the days of Harvard University's president, Lawrence Lowell, who wrote that "Cambridge could make a Jew indistinguishable from an Anglo-Saxon; but not even Harvard could make a black man white." But even in those days—when Harvard philosophy professors could write, in a letter on behalf of a Jew, that "he has none of the traits calculated to excite prejudice" (Ralph Perry), and that his Jewishness is "faintly marked and by no means offensive" (James Wood)—the Jews, I submit, still had group autonomy.

On the other hand, it is far from obvious that economically well-off blacks have group autonomy. In the area of sports and entertainment, numerous blacks are making millions upon millions of dollars. All the same, there is no reason to suppose that, collectively or individually, blacks in sports and entertainment have more group autonomy than other blacks. Together, these considerations show that economic good fortune is neither a necessary basis for group autonomy nor a sufficient basis for it. What then is? The answer, I suggest, is a narrative.

II.

By a narrative, I mean a set of stories which defines values and entirely positive goals, which specifies a set of fixed points of historical significance, and which defines a set of ennobling rituals to be regularly performed. A goal is entirely positive only if it is not in any way defined in terms of avoiding some harm. Thus, simply eliminating sexism, or racism, or anti-Semitism does not constitute a positive goal, as important as these objectives are. Learning Swahili, by contrast, can be a positive goal, even if it turns out to help one avoid some harm, since the goal itself can be entirely specified independently of avoiding any harm. A narrative can be understood as a group's conception of its good. The stories which constitute a narrative may very well be true, but they need not be—though perhaps they cannot be blatantly inconsistent with the facts. For example, the Jewish narrative (as well as the Muslim one) holds that Abraham circumcised himself in his old age, with a stone no less. Can this be true? Well, it simply does not matter at this point. For circumcision has been required of Jewish males down through the ages. What Abraham actually did does not change one iota the fact that this has been an ennobling ritual among Jewish males down through the ages.

Now, given the character of American slavery, it can hardly be surprising that this institution and its racist legacy left blacks bereft of a narrative, and so of group autonomy. The Holocaust did not leave Jews bereft of a narrative, and so of their conception of the good. This is not because the Holocaust was a less nefarious institution than American slavery, but because the Holocaust was a radically different kind of nefarious institution. The telos of American slavery was utter dependence; the telos of the Holocaust was the extermination of the Jews. The former is best achieved by depriving the victims of any sense of their history. As a matter of logic, the latter, of course, is achieved by death. But Hitler did not succeed in exterminating the Jews; and his failure made it possible for the Jewish narrative to survive. Reflection upon the extent to which he almost succeeded, and the means that he employed to achieve that end, leaves any morally decent person numb. But that he did not succeed is an unvarnished truth. The survival of the Jewish narrative owes to that fact. Many will insist that surely blacks have a narrative, as shown by black music and art. I think not, a point to which I shall return in due course (Section III).

Now, I believe that it is impossible for a people to flourish in a society that is hostile toward them without a narrative that is essentially isomorphic with respect to them. A narrative is essentially isomorphic when, taken in its totality, it cannot be shared by others. There are primarily two reasons why a narrative is crucial to the flourishing of a people in a hostile society. One is the obvious truth that genuine cooperation is necessary if a people is to be successful in the face of systematic hostility. The other is that there can be no genuine cooperation among a people in the absence of a narrative, for a narrative provides the basis for trust.

Having a common enemy does not, in and of itself, suffice to ensure cooperating among a people, precisely because it cannot be a basis for trust. If a member of an oppressed group has good reason to believe that she can entirely avoid social hostility without cooperating with others in her group, or that she can avoid as much hostility on her own as she would avoid if she cooperated, then she has no rationally compelling reason to cooperate with others like herself. For if one's only aim is to avoid harm, then it is totally irrelevant whether one does so with one's group or on one's own, since in either case one avoids the harm in question. What is more, there will always be the incentive to avoid the harm on one's own, regardless of what might happen to the group. Naturally, a person could be motivated by altruistic considerations to help others in his group. But the motive of altruism is something distinct from and additional to the motive that stems purely from having a common enemy.

A common enemy makes for very unstable cooperation, if any at all, among a people. We can trust people when they have given us a good reason to believe that they will do their part, although they could refrain from doing so without bearing any loss whatsoever—that is, they will do their part whether they are being observed by others or not. A common enemy alone does not deliver such a basis for trust.

By contrast, when a people has a narrative, then their self-identity is tied to a set of goals and values that is independent of a common enemy. What is more, there is what I shall call contributory pride. Contributory pride is no more mysterious than pride itself or than the delight we generally take in doing things that reflect well upon our talents. Even when alone, and there is no chance of being heard by someone, a person who can play the piano well will want to do so because she delights in playing up to her level of competence. Likewise, we want our lives to reflect those values and goals which are dear to us, and it is a source of pleasure to us when this is so.

Because a narrative provides a basis for contributory pride, it allows for the possibility of genuine cooperation, in that others who belong to the group—and so identify with the narrative—can be counted on to do their part even if no one is observing their performances. Sometimes, in fact, people can be counted on to do their part even when this is at some cost to them. Such is the power of identification with an ideal. The moral of the story, then, is this. There can be no genuine cooperation among a people who belong to the same group simply on account of their desire to overcome the same hostile social forces, since the existence of the same social forces cannot suffice as a basis for mutual trust. What is needed is a set of positive values and goals which are constitutive of the self-identity of persons who belong to the group. For positive values and goals have their own motivational force, as the case of contributory pride makes abundantly clear.

III.

Let me now apply the account of a narrative, with its implications for group trust, directly to the situation of blacks and Jews. I take it to be obvious that there is an isomorphic narrative for Jews. Even people who do not like Jews are prepared to acknowledge that the Old Testament is primarily about the history of the Jews. What is more, there is a universal set of ennobling rituals which, when practiced, define being a good Jew or, at any rate, are the reference point against which a good Jew is defined, such as keeping kosher and mastering the Torah. These ennobling rituals are defined by the narrative and are entirely independent of the culture in which Jews happen to find themselves (the State of Israel aside). Wearing a yarmulke is an ennobling Jewish ritual. And notice that a non-Jew who outside of a synagogue generally wore what was unmistakably a yarmulke would be showing utter disrespect for Judaism. This speaks to the point that a narrative cannot be readily appropriated by nonmembers of the group.

Do blacks have a narrative, their conception of the good? Clearly, there is no denying the influence of African traditions upon the lives of black Americans. In voice, music, and dance the influence of Africa is unshakably there. Martin Luther King's speech, "I Have a Dream," surely owes some of its majesty to the cadence of voice, with its indelible African influence. It is impossible to listen to black gospel music and preaching without seeing—nay, feeling—the distinctiveness and richness. But form does not a narrative make. I want to say that blacks do not have a narrative—at least not as yet, anyway.

It is important to distinguish between culture and what I am calling a narrative. A narrative can be part of a culture, but it is quite possible to have a culture without a narrative. And even where a narrative is part of a culture, not everything in the culture is part of the narrative. Although bagels are very much identified with Jewish American culture, they are not part of the Jewish narrative. There are various Jewish cultures, but one Jewish narrative—though various disagreements over that narrative. While it is manifestly obvious that there is a black culture in America, that culture is not underwritten or guided by a narrative. Black music and style do not constitute an ennobling ritual. Neither rap music nor braids constitute ennobling rituals, although both are deep aspects of black culture. Things do not change with black gospel music and preaching. The distinctiveness here is indicative of black culture, and not to some ennobling ritual that black gospel music and preaching exemplify. Blacks have no special claim to preaching and gospel music, only to the style of performance.

Let me acknowledge the role of black Christianity in the lives of black Americans and black slaves. It stands to reason that without Christianity both American slavery and racism in general would have taken a much greater toll upon the lives of black people. Some of the great Negro spirituals such as "Swing Low, Sweet Chariot" and "Let My People Go" were surely an emotional balm in a very harsh world. Notwithstanding this moral reality, the truth of the matter is that blacks do not have any isomorphic relationship to Christianity. Christianity is a universal doctrine. Even if Jesus is given a black face, that will not change the fact that Christianity remains a universal doctrine. There are no texts in the Christian writings that blacks can claim as applying specifically to them. Nor have blacks gone on either to produce a reading of Christianity that applies specifically to blacks or to produce a set of ennobling rituals that only black Christians lay claim to performing. No basis for such rituals can be found in the Christian writings themselves.

So, in denying that blacks have a narrative, I do not mean to be taking anything away from the richness of black culture—just as in claiming that Jews do have narrative, I do not mean to be taking anything away from the suffering that Jews have endured. What is more, if it seems reasonable that blacks do not have group autonomy owing to American slavery and its racist legacy, then it should also stand to reason that blacks do not have a narrative, given the nature of slavery and racism. While I have maintained that it is possible to have a culture without a narrative, the converse is not true: a people with a narrative will have a culture. The idea that slavery robbed blacks of a narrative helps us to appreciate just how devastating the effect was that slavery had upon blacks. To be sure, there were whips and chains. There were even deaths. But the real pain of slavery, I suggest, is not to be located here but in the fact that it robbed blacks of a narrative. This makes it clear that I am using the notion of narrative in a very technical sense. The slave narratives—that is, the memoirs written by the slaves themselves—do not constitute what I have called a ritual. These are primarily accounts of the experience of slavery. The slave narratives do not specify ennobling rituals or fixed points of historical reference nor do they define a set of positive goals and values to be achieved by blacks independently of racism. As I have said, I regard the fact that black slaves were robbed of a narrative to be the very essence of the real pain of American slavery.

On the other hand, from just the fact that Hitler failed in his attempt to exterminate the Jews, and the Jewish narrative survived, we can see the hope that can arise out of the utter ashes of despair, and so appreciate all the more Emil Fackenheim's so-called 614th Commandment: Lest Hitler be handed a posthumous victory, every Jew must continue being a Jew in practice.

Jews have both group autonomy and a narrative, whereas blacks have neither—so I have claimed. All the same, the picture is somewhat more complicated than I have allowed. It is not just that Jews have a narrative, but that the Jewish narrative is an indispensable aspect of the Christian narrative, since the Christ story is inextricably tied to the Jewish narrative. The Christian narrative, by its very own account, is conceptually tied to the Jewish narrative (see also Section V). But if the Jewish narrative is an ineliminable part of the Christian narrative, then the Jewish narrative is also an ineliminable part of the narrative of Western culture, because of the place of Christianity in Western culture. Thus, insofar as Christianity takes itself seriously, it is conceptually bound to acknowledge that at the very least

Judaism once had an indisputable claim to being meritorious. So, while Christianity may insist that Jews are now quite mistaken about the importance of their rituals and traditions, it must concede the importance of these things at an earlier time. And it must concede that Jews are rightly an authority on those rituals and traditions.

By contrast, neither the Western nor the Christian narrative is conceptually required to take the black experience seriously. Lest there be any misunderstanding, I do not deny that there have been gross distortions of the contributions of blacks to Western thought. But, as I have already observed, truth as such is not the defining feature of a narrative. I am not here debating whether Christianity and Western culture have discounted the accomplishments of blacks. My point, instead, is that as these two narratives, the Christian and the Western, have been formulated, they are not conceptually bound, by their very own formulations, to take blacks seriously at any point in time, in the way that Christianity is required to take Judaism seriously.

From these considerations it might be thought to follow that Western culture has been more racist than anti-Semitic. But not so. While I shall not argue the case here, suffice it to say that having to take a people seriously is perfectly compatible with despising them to the very core. Indeed, one may despise them precisely because one has to take them seriously.

In the next section, I shall look at some of the practical implications of the account of group autonomy and narrative which I have offered.

IV.

Recall the 1967 Six-Day War, when Israel fought Egypt, Syria, and Jordan. Jews of virtually every stripe and persuasion banded together in support of Israel. This was no accident, because in the face of an imminent threat, a narrative—a group's conception of its good—orders priorities. For Orthodox Jews, kashrut laws are extremely important; for Reform Jews, nothing could be further from the truth. But during the 1967 war, a good Jew was most certainly one who supported the State of Israel, regardless of her or his other shortcomings. A common threat can be most galvanizing. But it is a narrative that gives directions that amount to more than avoiding harm.

For just about every Jew, including quite secular Jews, the existence of synagogues and the State of Israel is a good thing. It is regarded as a good thing by just about every Jew that there are Talmudic scholars and rabbis. One may define a secular Jew as one who wants nearly all aspects of Jewish life to flourish, but who does not want to be an active or regular participant in any aspect of Jewish religious life. In any case, the point that I am concerned to bring out in these observations is that there are goods that Jews want, and these goods are quite independent of a common enemy. These goods are delivered by the Jewish narrative.

Do we find a comparable set of goods among blacks? I think not. Aside from the elimination of racism, it is not clear what blacks in general can be said to want, from the standpoint of being black. But I want to bring out the significance of a group's having a narrative, and the significance of its not having one, in another way.

Consider the black church. It is widely regarded as the most influential institution in the black community. What is more, it is relatively independent of white influence. Now, there are approximately 30 million blacks in America, and let us suppose that 4 million black adults regularly go to church each Sunday. If each were to give fifty cents to the United Negro College Fund, say, that would be $2 million. Over a year that would be $104 million to UNCF. For years now, fifty cents has been barely enough to buy a cup of coffee. And I assume that anyone who attends church regularly can afford to part with fifty cents. So, the most obvious question is: Why is something like this not being done? The answer cannot possibly be racism, if only because the black church is as independent of white influence as any institution in the black community can be. And if a common enemy—racism, in this instance—were a sufficient basis for cooperative endeavors, then one would have thought that a practice analogous to the one that I have proposed would have been in place quite some time ago.

I want to say that lack of a narrative can explain the absence of cooperative practices of the sort sketched above. In order for a people in a hostile society to flourish as a people, their self-identity must be anchored by a conception of the good that is independent of the hostility that they wish to avoid. What prevents us from seeing this, I suspect, is that there are times when eliminating a harm counts as an end in its own right, and it is irrelevant what other objectives a person might have.

To view struggling against oppression as the equivalent of eliminating an imminent life-threatening harm is to make an egregious error. By its very nature, oppression is about being deprived of some options rather than others. The struggle of a people against oppression can only be properly understood in the context of what it means for them to get on with their lives as a people. And that requires a narrative which anchors their self-identity.

Thus, we must distinguish between a racist society with overt structural inequality (such as American slavery and Jim Crow practices) and a society with structural equality that is coupled with widespread racist presuppositions of inferiority on the part of the powerful toward an identifiable group of individuals who are less well-off. In either case, we have an unjust society, and the latter, of course, may owe its origins to the former. However, combating the former does not require a narrative, whereas combating the latter does. For in the first instance, there is a rigorously specifiable set of harms or wrongs the elimination of which is called for. Their elimination is called for regardless of the aims that a people might otherwise have in society. What is more, while the elimination of the harms of overt structural inequality is no doubt a precondition for flourishing, just as being alive is a precondition for flourishing, their elimination does not constitute flourishing; nor does their elimination point to what a people's flourishing might consist of, just as being alive does not.

By contrast, eliminating the coupling of structural equality with widespread presuppositions of the other's inferiority is a different matter entirely, if only because in such an instance there is no rigorously specifiable set of harms or wrongs to be eliminated and there is no socially acceptable procedure for getting the dominant group to change their pejorative beliefs. Moreover, while it is conceptually possible to have no beliefs at all about an oppressed people, in other words a null set of beliefs, what is wanted is not a case where the null set of beliefs replaces the beliefs that a people are inferior. What is wanted, rather, is for the beliefs of inferiority to be replaced by a positive set of beliefs about the people in question. But which positive set? More to the point, who determines which positive set of beliefs replaces the beliefs about inferiority? Nothing better positions an oppressed people to answer these two questions than their having a narrative. For we have equality at its very best not simply when a people must be precisely like others in order to command the respect of others, but when a people can command the respect of others for being who they are. Equality across sameness is one thing; equality across differences is quite another. And the virtue of equality is truly showcased only in the latter instance. The latter equality is a more affirming equality that is inescapably predicated upon a people having a narrative—not just a culture—of their own.

The role of a narrative in equality simply presupposes what we already know, namely that there is all the difference in the world between being moved to help someone out of pity and being moved to help someone out of respect for their conception of the good. The latter is a more affirming kind of assistance. Things are no different at the level of groups.

I have claimed that without a narrative a people cannot flourish in a hostile society. Initially, I focused on how a narrative provides a basis for cooperation among a people. As should be obvious, I want also to say that it is only in having a narrative that, in a hostile society, a people can have assistance born of respect instead of pity. It has been said that the Creator helps those who help themselves. It would be stunning if human beings were much different. And nothing enhances self-help like a goal. Things can be no different for a group; hence, the importance of a narrative. We can best understand the success of Jews in America if we see them as having a narrative in a society with structural equality coupled with widespread presuppositions of inferiority. In the face of widespread presuppositions of (moral) inferiority, Jews had a conception of their good—that is, a narrative. This narrative anchored their lives and provided a basis for affirmation that was (and continues to be) independent of the values of society at large, not readily appropriated by mainstream American society. Again, I submit that the pain of slavery can be seen in the fact that it robbed blacks of a narrative.

V.

A narrative is the cornerstone that secures group autonomy. In claiming that Jews, on the one hand, have both group autonomy and a narrative and that blacks, on the other, have neither, have I made an invidious comparison? It is true that I have drawn attention to a differential between blacks and Jews of extraordinary significance. But that does not make the comparison invidious. After all, it is generally agreed that Jews as a people have flourished in American society, whereas blacks as a people have languished. Yet, few would call that comparison invidious. Why? Because by any reasonable assessment, that differential between Jews and blacks would seem to be the truth of the matter—a truth that neither distorts the present social reality of either group nor requires distorting the historical experiences of either group. If this should be the guide to whether a comparison is invidious or not, then the differential between blacks and Jews regarding group autonomy and a narrative is not invidious.

Furthermore, there is the explanatory power of the account offered. Some insight is gained into why Jews have flourished and blacks have languished without denying the reality of the horrors that have occurred in the history of the Jews. If anything, some insight has been gained regarding the toll that American slavery and racism has taken upon the lives of blacks in the United States—an insight that is not gained by focusing upon the horrors of chains, whips, and lynchings or even upon the horror of how many blacks lost their lives due to slavery. These horrors are not to be diminished. Thus, those who would object to the account that I have offered as favoring Jews might want to think again; for the account gives us a better handle on the evil of racism without detracting from the horrendous evil that others have suffered.

Finally, the account sheds some light on the tension between blacks and Jews. I have already spoken to the negative feelings of blacks regarding Jews. I want to conclude with a word about racism on the part of Jews toward blacks.

Racism is the belief, immune to a wide range of evidence and explanatory considerations to the contrary, that blacks are inferior. Nothing better invites the suspicion of inferiority than the following line of reasoning: Although Jews and blacks have suffered equally, the Jews have flourished and the blacks have languished. What can explain this differential between Jews and blacks other than that blacks are lacking in some way?

In *Vessels of Evil,* I observed that there are two ways of understanding the claim that X is an ultimate evil: 1) No evil can be more horrible than X; 2) All other evils are less horrible than X. Far too often, in talking about the difference between the Holocaust and American slavery, people have said the first, but in their heart of hearts have meant the second. Blacks have often supposed that understanding American slavery in the second sense of ultimate evil helps to explain the plight of blacks in the United States today. I suggest that the account of group autonomy and narrative does much better in that regard. Let me observe that when the Holocaust is understood by Jews as an ultimate evil in the second sense, then in light of the comparative success of Jews vis-à-vis blacks, the result is an interpretation of the respective sufferings of both groups that is easily carried along by the winds of racist ideology. By contrast, the account of group autonomy and narrative is not.

But why do we think of drawing the contrast between Jews and blacks instead of Jews and some other group, or blacks and some other group? The obvious answer, it might seem, is the extraordinary suffering that both groups have endured. The problem with this answer, though, is that it does not take seriously the suffering of still other groups—Native Americans, the Armenians, and so on. I should like to conclude this essay with a different answer.

As the label suggests, American slavery stands as America's most brazen, systematic, and enduring institution of oppression. It is an evil that America actively sought to sustain. This it did, even as it took itself to be a Christian nation, which brings me to Judaism. According to the Christian narrative, Christianity is flanked by the experience of the Jews: The Jewish people gave birth to Christianity, and the fulfillment of Christianity is tied to the experience of the Jewish people. For many fundamentalist Christians, Israel's winning the Six-Day War was an occasion to rejoice, as this could only mean that the Second Coming was near. Thus, for radically different reasons—reasons that have nothing whatsoever to do with the comparative success of Jews and blacks, these two peoples are—or at least have been—an extremely deep part of the very psyche of Americans. It is most unfortunate that this has turned into a race for the who-has-suffered-the-most award. With the accounts of group autonomy and narrative offered in this essay, I should like to think we have a basis for leaving behind that useless competition and entering into a dialogue of understanding.

17

Ethnic Transgressions

LAURIE SHRAGE

My aunt, who is now in her eighties, tells the following story. When her daughter was about six, she came home one day and told her parents that she didn't like the girl down the street because she was "jewith." My aunt says she was rather taken aback by her daughter's remark, to which she responded: "But Lisa, don't you know? You're Jewish too."

My mother-in-law used to tell the following story. When her daughter, Elizabeth, was around four, my mother-in-law discovered that Elizabeth had been telling their neighbors and friends that she was Catholic. According to my mother-in-law, her daughter formed her religious identity in the following way. Once when Elizabeth was visiting the larger extended family, she asked her cousin why she was not allowed to eat certain foods. Her cousin explained that it was because she was Jewish. Evidently Elizabeth reasoned that, because she was allowed to eat the forbidden foods, she must not be Jewish, and because she wasn't Jewish, she must be Catholic.

As the child of assimilated, nonobservant Jews, my discoveries of self were similarly comical and confusing. As I describe elsewhere,[1] my first-grade teacher is the first person I can remember who revealed to me that I was a Jew. This came about during an awkward show-and-tell presentation in which I attempted to repeat something my mother had told me. In one of her nostalgic moments, my mother sent me to school with a plate of hamentashen (a cookie made to celebrate Purim) and told me some story to go along with it. Evidently, in my mother's narration, I misheard *jewels* for *Jews*, and thus the story I told had to do with the former. My teacher caught my error, and in correcting my story she explained to the class what Jews were—and I was the primary means by which she did this.

I grew up in a very waspy part of northern California in the 60s. Once when one of my Brooklyn cousins was visiting us, she told me our household was too weird for her. She happened to be visiting us during some religious holiday (I can't remember which one). Now looking back on this, I think she found it strange that our daily routine was not in the least interrupted or changed during this holiday, and that we did not engage in any ritual or connect with other Jews in any way. At the time, I found her discomfort and proclaimed need to be with other Jews strange. I vaguely remember that my mother somehow arranged for her to go to a temple or be with a Jewish family during the holiday. What I learned from this and some other experiences was that, for some Jews, we were not Jews.

But strangely, to all non-Jews, we were Jews. I've been told by non-Jews (once I've indicated in some way that I am Jewish) that I look Jewish; and some non-Jewish men have told me how much they like Jewish girls, and how my Jewishness explains their perception that I talk too much, or that I can eat and talk at the same time, or some such thing. My college professors were often surprised to find out that I was a first-generation college student, that I was a financial-aid student, and that my parents thought my becoming a teacher was boring—they hoped I might aspire to something more glamourous, such as a stewardess. And my friends usually assume that my choice of a Jewish marital partner must have pleased my mother. Actually she always encouraged me to seek non-Jewish partners, having been limited by her own parents, but I rebelled.

A Polish-American I know tells the following story. Growing up in Poland, when he was asked what he was, he knew he was supposed to answer "Jewish." To be Jewish was to distinguish oneself from being "Polish," and vice versa. When he came to America, he was often asked what he was. The answer "Jewish" didn't seem to work. Eventually, he found out that the correct answer in this context was "Polish." Also, he learned that in giving this answer he did not erase his Jewishness—here he could be both.

After my own discovery, around the age of six, that the correct answer for me to the question "What are you?" was "Jewish," I started to wonder about what this attribute "Jewish" meant. Responding, in part, to my identity confusion, my mother decided that I ought to attend Jewish Sunday school so that I might learn something about my Jewish heritage. (I was about nine at this time.) To my surprise, the people at this religious school talked a lot about God. What did God have to do with being Jewish, I worried? Didn't they know God didn't exist, as my mother had so logically explained? After my first day of Sunday School, I told my mother that if being Jewish meant believing in God, then I wasn't Jewish. She told me it didn't mean that. Then what did it mean? Unfortunately, I never found out from attending Sunday school (I dropped out after the first month) or from my parents.

Being Jewish, at different historical moments and in different places, has been variously understood as being of a particular "race," "religion," or "ethnicity." In contemporary America it seems to be mostly a matter of "ethnicity." Ethnicities usually have something to do with the way we live, the values we hold, the customs we follow, the foods we eat, and the dialects we speak. I have several books that I call my "how to be Jewish" books. When I want to celebrate the Jewish holidays with my children, when I want to prepare Jewish foods, when I want to understand some Jewish expression, I now look them up in my books. Because I and my children are Jews to others—which is to say that we are Other to non-Jews—I want my children to associate this otherness with something other than pure otherness. This then is how I am dealing with the issue of difference. It indeed seems to be the favored solution of many—to claim one's otherness and then be the Other adequately or convincingly, that is, in a way that doesn't betray perhaps internalized anti-Semitism or racism, or inauthenticity. Had I married a non-Jew, it might have been different. I might have passed as something else or passed my children off as something else. But these assimilationist strategies seem less attractive than they must have to my parents' generation.

Although racial and ethnic assimilation, acculturation, and passing have problematic consequences and causes, the existing alternatives to assimilation are equally problematic. For persons like myself, the preferred alternative seems to be "finding my roots," learning about "my people," practicing "my traditions," or, in short, constructing a self that is more racially and ethnically pure. This is problematic to me for several reasons. One, many aspects of the traditions and roots I am supposed to seek appear patriarchal, misogynist, homophobic, and even racist or elitist toward non-Jews. Two, to seek to be more purely or thoroughly Jewish is to deny the part of me that grew up enjoying coloring Easter eggs or listening to gospel music. It also leads to seeing my upbringing as somehow deficient, shameful, or culturally and ethnically deprived. And three, to be more purely Jewish seems not at all to resist anti-Semitism, for the construction and reification of the Jew, as others have pointed out, may itself be a product of anti-Semitism.

Yet, to allow the Jewish part of my background to be crowded out by some intervening autobiographical and social circumstances communicates to others (especially to those to whom I look, act, "smell," or otherwise appear Jewish) the acceptance and internalization of the devaluation of things Jewish. Also, this "gentilization" of myself might appear opportunistic and selfish. It will look as if I am suppressing or deforming myself to profit individually in a system that oppresses my kind.

For people like myself, assimilation, acculturation, heterogeneity, and syncretism are not a choice, but something chosen for us by our parents (who then are often surprised by how ignorant their children are of their ethnic origins). For us the choice appears to be either to assimilate further into the dominant culture or to assimilate back to the communities our parents, and perhaps grandparents, rejected. Yet, while seeking to discover and express my Jewish "essence" in order to connect with a particular community is problematic in the ways indicated above, seeing myself as neither Jewish nor Gentile, that is, in ethnically blind terms, is also problematic. For as Patricia Williams argues in regard to blacks who do not identify as "black,"

> Neutrality is from this perspective a suppression, an institutionalization of psychic taboos as much as segregation was the institutionalization of physical boundaries. What the middle-class, propertied, upwardly mobile black striver must do, to accommodate a race-neutral world view, is to become an invisible black, a phantom black,

by avoiding the label "black." . . . The words of race are like windows into the most private vulnerable parts of the self; the world looks in and the world will know, by the awesome, horrific revelation of a name.[2]

To echo Williams, what a person with Jewish ancestors must do to accommodate an ethnically neutral identity is to become an invisible Jew, a phantom Jew. In other words, because being Jewish carries a stigma, not to announce one's Jewishness is paramount to concealing it—to keeping it in the closet, so to speak. Yet, this socially construed act of concealing one's self is an act that serves to perpetuate an anti-Semitic social order—a system of power and privilege that serves to obliterate Jews and Jewishness. It is also pointless, as Williams's passage suggests, for the world will eventually find one's Jewish self because of the mere fact that there exist designations or names for it. In short, neither the choice to closet one's Jewishness and thereby assimilate further into the dominant social order, nor the choice to spring the Jewish self out of the closet for the world to observe and know, offers possibilities of resistance for partially assimilated, mixed-background people.

Naomi Zack has recently proposed that people who have both designated black and white ancestors should create mixed or hybrid identities that recognize their heterogeneous ethnic and racial origins.[3] For given that assimilation (identifying as white) and difference (identifying as black) are problematic choices for people of mixed racial backgrounds, Zack argues that it is unfair and damaging to such people to make them choose. Instead, people of mixed backgrounds should be allowed to identify (legally and informally) as persons of mixed race—as persons who are part black and white, or perhaps gray.

Although there is a need as Zack and others have shown to disrupt and denaturalize American racial and ethnic categories, deploying the metaphor of "mixing" categories may not be the most effective in this regard. Mixing suggests that there is some more pure stuff to be "mixed," and thus is consistent with racial ideologies that posit pure racial kinds. Though mixing recognizes the miscibility of different human kinds, the quality of the mixtures will still be determined by the quality of the stuff mixed. That is, the establishment of mixed identities may do little to challenge the valuations placed on different human kinds. Thus while claiming a mixed identity may marginally improve the treatment of mixed individuals, it will do little for unmixed people of the stigmatized races and ethnicities. Moreover, the recognition of mixed-race people may naturalize yet another racial group in a way that is divisive of economically and politically oppressed communities. Zack recognizes these aspects of positing mixed identities, but holds that racial identities and identifications serve important and meaningful functions in American society and will not be easily abolished. She thus proposes establishing mixed identities as an intermediate, temporary, or transitional remedy for the psychological harm and social injustice that our racial system imposes on persons of mixed backgrounds.

Perhaps there are other solutions. At least two other options present themselves. The first is the option Zack recognizes but dismisses for being perhaps unrealistic: the option of eschewing all racial and some ethnic identifications. The other option is that of claiming more than one racial or ethnic classification: of being *multi*racial or *multi*ethnic. This option is similar to the option of claiming a "mixed" identity, but it is different in the following way. The multiracial individual is not part black and white, but is both black and white. The multiethnic individual is not part-Jewish and part-Gentile, but is both a Jew and a Gentile. Moreover, multiracialism does not lead to an invention of new human kinds but calls our attention to areas of overlap between different categories. And finally, being multiracial and multiethnic may challenge pernicious customs of differentially valuing human kinds in the following way: if a black person can be white and a white person can be black, then black and white persons cannot have different degrees of moral worth by virtue of being black or white.

One might argue that under the current system of racial and ethnic classification in the United States, these multiple identities make little sense because American racial and ethnic categories are mutually exclusive, and thus multiple racial designations are contradictory designations. But the problem with mixed identities may be that they make too much sense given the existing systems of racial and ethnic classification, and thus they may fail to challenge the logic of these systems. Multiracial or multiethnic identities also may fail to challenge many pernicious aspects of the contemporary U.S. racial order. For multiple designations do not challenge the apparent necessity of the designations themselves or the apparent existence of racially differentiable human kinds.

Judith Butler has argued that identity categories are "sites of necessary trouble."[4] By communicating our membership in a particular category (lesbian, woman, black, Jew), we do not necessarily liberate or expose some intrinsic quality of ourselves, but rather we perpetuate the naturalization of categories that are themselves the byproducts of unliberatory discourses. Yet, Butler recognizes, like Williams, that we cannot simply refuse these identities, for such refusals perpetuate systems of power that oppress those subsumed under these categories. Nevertheless, our choices are not limited to either adopting or refusing these identities. For Butler, the challenge is, "How to use the sign and avow its temporal contingency at once?"[5] In other words, how can we assume these identities in ways that reflect or expose their nonnaturalness and historical specificity?

Writing about gender and sexual identity, Butler considers how particular identity categories become naturalized. She states that one way

> heterosexuality naturalizes itself [is] through setting up certain illusions of continuity between sex, gender, and desire. When Aretha Franklin sings, "you make me feel like a natural woman," she seems at first to suggest that some natural potential of her biological sex is actualized by her participation in the cultural position of "woman" as object of heterosexual recognition. Something in her "sex" is thus expressed by her "gender" which is then fully known and consecrated within the heterosexual scene. There is no breakage, no discontinuity between "sex" as biological facticity and essence, or between gender and sexuality. Although Aretha appears to be all too glad to have her naturalness confirmed, she also seems fully and paradoxically mindful

that confirmation is never guaranteed, that the effect of naturalness is only achieved
as a consequence of that moment of heterosexual recognition.[6]

Butler then goes on to consider how these illusions of continuity between sex,
gender, and desire can be broken, so that we might glimpse how women are made
by the operation of heterosexual norms, rather than born in some natural fashion
with natural heterosexual desire. If the illusions of continuity are created in part
by socially conventional expressions of biological sex and sexual desire, then these
illusions might be disrupted by socially transgressive expressions of biological sex
and sexual desire. Such transgressive performances are what are typically called
"drag" and engaging in drag is indeed what Butler recommends both to claim
particular identities and simultaneously subvert the very ideologies that produce
them. For example, Butler asks us to imagine Aretha Franklin singing the same
song to a female "impersonator," or to imagine Franklin singing this song to her,
that is Butler herself.

Following Butler, we might try to see how particular systems of race and ethnicity in the United States naturalize themselves by setting up certain illusions of
continuity between skin pigment, genealogy, race, ethnicity, character, behavior,
ability, aspirations, dispositions, and so on. How might these illusions be interrupted so that we might glimpse how blacks and whites, Jews and Gentiles, are
made by the operation of racial and ethnic norms, rather than born naturally
possessing their notorious racial and ethnic traits? If these illusions of continuity
are created, in part, by conforming to socially conventional interpretations of skin
pigment and genealogy, then these illusions might be destroyed by attempts at
transgressive interpretations of these facts. In this way, racial and ethnic drag
might consist in blacks with one or more white ancestors taking up the mannerisms, personal styles, and vocations associated with whites, and "whites" with one
or more black ancestors taking up the mannerisms, personal styles, and vocations
associated with blacks.

When designated white persons[7] wear Afros or African clothing, and when designated black persons lighten and straighten their hair or wear formal European-
style suits, we often see such people as confused, unauthentic, and, in the former
kind of case, perhaps ridiculous. But why is this? Does the first kind of person
represent the pathetic attempt of a "nonethnic" person to "go ethnic," and does
the second kind of case represent the reverse? And why shouldn't whites "go ethnic" and those designated ethnic "go white"? One answer that comes to mind is
that when whites "go ethnic" they engage in inappropriate cultural appropriation,
and when ethnics whiten themselves they capitulate to hegemonic white values
that threaten to obliterate nonwhite ethnicities.

When women of Asian descent have eyelid surgery and dark-pigmented persons use cosmetics to lighten their skin, these acts reflect the cultural hegemony of
pernicious aesthetic and moral values that oppress many persons. And when New
Age European Americans perform American Indian rituals, their acts reflect the

illegitimate assumption of a particular type of cultural authority. But perhaps not all acts of "cross-dressing" and cross-behaving reflect and reproduce existing patterns of hegemony and marginalization. Moreover, our prudishness about ethnic-crossing places persons whose family backgrounds and personal lives are not ethnically pure in a bind. For example, Patricia Williams relates an incident where a particular white man and a particular black woman wondered if she, a law professor, saw herself as black. She states, "I heard the same-different words addressed to me, a perceived white-male-socialized black woman, as a challenge to mutually exclusive categorization. . . ."[8] Those who see her as predominantly a law professor see her blackness as irrelevant or suppressed, while those who see her as a black woman see her as an odd kind of law professor. In each case, her blackness or her professional status, respectively, are in constant jeopardy. De-essentializing racial and ethnic categories would alleviate the need to excuse or explain to ourselves some perceived crossings.

Commenting on the cross-gendered behavior of some lesbians and gay men, Butler states,

> It is important to recognize the ways in which heterosexual norms reappear within gay identities . . . but that they are *not* for that reason *determined* by them. They are running commentaries on those naturalized positions as well, parodic replays and re-significations. . . . But to be constituted or structured in part by the very heterosexual norms by which gay people are oppressed is not, I repeat, to be claimed or determined by those structures. And it is not necessary to think of such heterosexual constructs as the pernicious intrusion of "the straight mind," one that must be rooted out in its entirety. . . . The parodic replication and resignification of heterosexual constructs within non-heterosexual frames brings into relief the utterly constructed status of the so-called original. . . . The more the act is expropriated, the more the heterosexual claim to originality is exposed as illusory.[9]

Butler's comments might lead us to ask: are there ways for designated whites to "go ethnic" and for designated ethnics to "whiten" themselves that might call attention to the constructed status of whiteness and blackness? Can these transgressive ethnic crossings subvert pernicious racial norms and ideologies? Converging on a similar issue, Williams states:

> I think that the hard work of a nonracist sensibility is the boundary crossing, from safe circle into wilderness: the testing of boundary, the consecration of sacrilege. . . . The transgression is dizzyingly intense, a reminder of what it is to be alive. It is a sinful pleasure, this willing transgression of a line, which takes one into new awareness, a secret, lonely, and tabooed world—to survive transgression is terrifying and addictive. To know that everything has changed and yet that nothing has changed; and in leaping the chasm of this impossible division of self, a discovery of the self surviving, still well, still strong, and, as a curious consequence, renewed.[10]

By crossing the boundaries of ethnic and racial classification and incorporating the Other into ourselves, we do not necessarily betray, distort, or eradicate some more racially and ethnically pure self. When I light Hanukkah candles with my children one week and the next week decorate a Christmas tree with them, I am not claimed or determined (to borrow Butler's language) by the structures Jew and Gentile; I am deploying these constructs within a nonorthodox frame. And perhaps the sight of a Christmas tree, set under a Menorah and decorated with recycled dreidels, may draw attention to the temporal contingency of this sign. What this suggests is that we might usefully subject to critical reflection the discomfort we feel when a person's behavior and self-expression challenge the mutually exclusive categorization (to borrow Williams's words) of races, ethnicities, genders, and sexualities. In this regard, we need to distinguish when our discomfort results from crossings that indeed seem to perpetuate racism, heterosexism, and so on, and when our discomfort results from crossings that merely challenge our own essentialized notions of race, ethnicity, and gender. In short, it may be that some transgressions are destabilizing of gender, racial, sexual, and ethnic norms while others are not, and we need to be able to recognize the difference.

NOTES

1. See my *Moral Dilemmas of Feminism: Prostitution, Adultery, and Abortion* (New York: Routledge, 1994), pp. 137–40.

2. Patricia Williams, *The Alchemy of Race and Rights* (Cambridge: Harvard University Press, 1991), p. 119.

3. Naomi Zack, *Race and Mixed Race* (Philadelphia: Temple University Press, 1993), pp. 143–7.

4. Judith Butler, "Imitation and Gender Insubordination," *The Lesbian and Gay Studies Reader,* eds. H. Abelove, M. Barale, and D. Halperin (New York: Routledge, 1993), p. 308. See also Judith Butler, *Gender Trouble: Feminism and the Subversion of Identity* (New York: Routledge, 1990).

5. Butler, "Imitation and Gender," p. 312.

6. Ibid., p. 317.

7. Here I follow Zack's practice of speaking of "designated whites and blacks" rather than just "whites" and "blacks" to underscore, as she does, that these are social constructs. See, for example, Zack, *Race and Mixed Race,* p. 27.

8. Williams, *Alchemy of Race and Rights,* p. 10.

9. Butler, "Imitation and Gender," p. 314. In her recent book, *Bodies That Matter* (New York: Routledge, 1993), Butler also considers drag performances that reproduce dominant cultural norms. Here she states

Although many readers understood *Gender Trouble* to be arguing for the proliferation of drag performances as a way of subverting dominant gender norms, I want to underscore that there is no necessary relation between drag and subversion, and that drag may well be used in the service of both the denaturalization and idealization of hyperbolic heterosexual gender norms. (p. 125)

10. Williams, *Alchemy of Race and Rights,* pp. 129–30.

18

The Disuniting of America: Reflections on a Multicultural Society

ARTHUR M. SCHLESINGER, JR.

"A New Race"?

At the beginning America was seen as a severing of roots, a liberation from the stifling past, an entry into a new life, an interweaving of separate ethnic strands into a new national design. "We have it in our power," said Thomas Paine for the revolutionary generation, "to begin the world all over again." The unstated national motto was "Never look back." "The Past is dead, and has no resurrection," wrote Herman Melville. ". . . The Past is the text-book of tyrants; the Future the Bible of the Free."

And the future was America—not so much a nation, Melville said, as a world. "You can not spill a drop of American blood without spilling the blood of the whole world. On this Western Hemisphere all tribes and people are forming into one federated whole. . . ." For Ralph Waldo Emerson too, like Crèvecoeur, like Melville, America was the distillation of the multifarious planet. As the burning of the temple at Corinth had melted and intermixed silver and gold to produce Corinthian brass, "a new compound more precious than any," so, Emerson wrote in his journal, in America, in this "asylum of all nations, the energy of Irish, Germans, Swedes, Poles, & Cossacks, & all the European tribes—of the Africans, & of the Polynesians, will construct a new race . . . as vigorous as the new Europe which came out of the smelting pot of the Dark Ages. . . ."

Melville was a novelist, Emerson an essayist; both were poets. But George Washington was a sternly practical man. Yet he believed no less ardently in the doctrine of the "new race." "The bosom of America," Washington said, "is open . . . to the oppressed and persecuted of all Nations and Religions." But immigrants who nestled as clannish groups in the national bosom retained the "Language, habits and principles (good or bad) which they bring with them." Let them therefore settle as individuals, prepared for "intermixture with our people." Then they would be "assimilated to our customs, measures and laws: in a word, soon become *one people.*"

John Quincy Adams, another sternly practical man, similarly insisted on the exclusiveness of the new American identity. When a German baron contemplating emigration interviewed Adams as secretary of state, Adams admonished his visitor that emigrants had to make up their minds to one thing: "*They must cast off the European skin, never to resume it.* They must look forward to their posterity rather than backward to their ancestors. . . ."

But how could Crèvecoeur's "promiscuous breed" be transformed into a "new race"? How was Emerson's "smelting pot" to fuse such disparate elements into Washington's "one people"? This question preoccupied another young Frenchman who arrived in America three quarters of a century after Crèvecoeur. "Imagine, my dear friend, if you can," Alexis de Tocqueville wrote back to France, "a society formed of all the nations of the world . . . people having different languages, beliefs, opinions: in a word, a society without roots, without memories, without prejudices, without routines, without common ideas, without a national character, yet a hundred times happier than our own." What alchemy could make this miscellany into a single society?

The answer, Tocqueville concluded, lay in the commitment of Americans to democracy and self-government. Civic participation, Tocqueville argued in *Democracy in America,* was the great educator and the great unifier.

> How does it happen that in the United States, where the inhabitants have only recently immigrated to the land which they now occupy, and brought neither customs nor traditions with them there; where they met one another for the first time with no previous acquaintance; where, in short, the instinctive love of country can scarcely exist; how does it happen that every one takes as zealous an interest in the affairs of his township, his country, and the whole state as if they were his own? It is because everyone, in his sphere, takes an active part in the government of society.

Immigrants, Tocqueville said, become Americans through the exercise of the political rights and civic responsibilities bestowed on them by the Declaration of Independence and the Constitution.

Half a century later, when the next great foreign commentator on American democracy, James Bryce, wrote *The American Commonwealth,* immigration had vastly increased and diversified. Bryce's European friends expected that it would take a very long time for America to assimilate these "heterogeneous elements." What struck Bryce, on the contrary, was what had struck Tocqueville: "the amazing solvent power which American institutions, habits, and ideas exercise upon newcomers of all races . . . quickly dissolving and assimilating the foreign bodies that are poured into her mass."

A century after Tocqueville, another foreign visitor, Gunnar Myrdal of Sweden, called the cluster of ideas, institutions, and habits "the American Creed." Americans "of all national origins, regions, creeds, and colors," Myrdal wrote in

1944, hold in common "the *most explicitly expressed* system of general ideals" of any country in the West: the ideals of the essential dignity and equality of all human beings, of inalienable rights to freedom, justice, and opportunity.

The schools teach the principles of the Creed, Myrdal said; the churches preach them; the courts hand down judgments in their terms. Myrdal saw the Creed as the bond that links all Americans, including nonwhite minorities, and as the spur forever goading Americans to live up to their principles. "America," Myrdal said, "is continuously struggling for its soul."

"One national mould"? Not everyone agreed. In 1915 Horace Kallen, a Jewish-American philosopher, wrote an essay for *The Nation* entitled "Democracy Versus the Melting-Pot." The melting pot, Kallen argued, was valid neither as a fact nor as an ideal. What impressed him was, on the contrary, the persistence of ethnic groups and their distinctive traditions. Unlike freely chosen affiliations, Kallen said, the ethnic bond was both involuntary and immutable. "Men may change their clothes, their politics, their wives, their religions, their philosophies, to a greater or lesser extent: they cannot change their grandfathers. Jews or Poles or Anglo-Saxons, in order to cease being Jews or Poles or Anglo-Saxons, would have to cease to be. . . ."

Ethnic diversity, Kallen observed, enriches American civilization. He saw the nation not as one people, except in a political and administrative sense, but rather "as a federation or commonwealth of national cultures . . . a democracy of nationalities, cooperating voluntarily and autonomously through common institutions . . . a multiplicity in a unity, an orchestration of mankind." This conception he came to call "cultural pluralism."

Kallen was unclear on the question of how to encourage ethnic separatism without weakening the original ideal of a single society. One critic warned that cultural pluralism would "result in the Balkanization of these United States." But Kallen made his attack on Anglo-centered assimilation at a time when critics of the melting pot could reasonably assume the solidity of the overarching framework. Because he considered political unity a given, he put his emphasis on the protection of cultural diversity.

The gospel of cultural pluralism was at first largely confined to academics, intellectuals, and artists. The postwar years saw much popular disenchantment with Europe, a Red Scare directed largely against aliens, the rise of the anti-Catholic Ku Klux Klan, and a campaign, realized in the Immigration Act of 1924, to freeze the ethnic composition of the American people. The new law established quotas on the basis of the national origins of the population in 1890, thereby drastically reducing the flow from southern and eastern Europe.

The xenophobic nationalism of the 1920s was followed in the 1930s by crises that, on some levels divisive, nevertheless strengthened the feeling that all Americans were in the same boat and might as well pull together. The Great Depression and the Second World War showed the desperate necessity of national cohesion within the frame of shared national ideals. "The principle on which this

country was founded and by which it has always been governed," Franklin D.
Roosevelt said in 1943, "is that Americanism is a matter of the mind and heart;
Americanism is not, and never was, a matter of race and ancestry. A good
American is one who is loyal to this country and to our creed of liberty and
democracy."

Gunnar Myrdal in 1944 showed no hesitation in declaring the American Creed
the common possession of all Americans, even as his great book *An American
Dilemma* provided a magistral analysis of America's most conspicuous failure to
live up to the Creed: the treatment by white Americans of black America.

Noble ideals had been pronounced as if for all Americans, yet in practice they
applied only to white people. Most interpretations of the national identity from
Crèvecoeur on were for whites only. Even Horace Kallen, the champion of cultural pluralism, made no provision in his "democracy of nationalities" for black
or red or brown or yellow Americans.

Tocqueville was an exception in factoring persons of color into the American
equation. With his usual prescience, he identified racism as the irremediable flaw
in American democracy. This "most grasping nation on the globe" had doomed
the red man to extinction; and the presence of a black population was "the most
formidable of all the ills that threaten the future of the Union." The more opti-
mistic Emerson and Zangwill had thrown nonwhite nationalities into their smelting or melting pots, but Tocqueville saw racist exclusion as deeply ingrained in
the national character.

History supported this judgment. White settlers had systematically pushed the
American Indians back, killed their braves, seized their lands, and sequestered
their tribes. They had brought Africans to America to work their plantations and
Chinese to build their railroads. They had enunciated glittering generalities of
freedom and withheld them from people of color. Their Constitution protected
slavery, and their laws made distinctions on the basis of race. Though they eventually emancipated the slaves, they conspired in the reduction of the freedom to
third-class citizenship. Their Chinese Exclusion acts culminated in the total pro-
hibition of Asian immigration in the Immigration Act of 1924. It occurred to
damned few white Americans in these years that Americans of color were also entitled to the rights and liberties promised by the Constitution.

Yet what Bryce had called "the amazing solvent power" of American institutions
and ideas retained its force, even among those most cruelly oppressed and excluded. Myrdal's polls of Afro-America showed the "determination" of blacks "to
hold to the American Creed." Ralph Bunche, one of Myrdal's collaborators, observed that every man in the street—black, red, and yellow as well as white—regarded America as the "land of the free" and the "cradle of liberty." The American
Creed, Myrdal surmised, meant even more to blacks than to whites, since it was the
great means of pleading their unfulfilled rights. Blacks, new immigrants, Jews, and
other disadvantaged groups, Myrdal said, "could not possibly have invented a system of political ideals which better corresponded to their interests."

The Second World War gave the Creed new bite. Hitler's racism forced Americans to look hard at their own racial assumptions. How, in fighting against Hitler's doctrine of the Master Race abroad, could Americans maintain a doctrine of white supremacy at home? How, with China a faithful American ally, could Americans continue to forbid Chinese to become American citizens? If the war did not end American racism, at least it drove much racial bigotry underground. The rethinking of racial issues challenged the conscience of the majority and raised the consciousness of minorities.

Emboldened by the Creed, blacks organized for equal opportunities in employment, opposed segregation in the armed forces, and fought in their own units on many fronts. After the war, the civil rights revolution, so long deferred, accelerated black self-reliance. So did the collapse of white colonialism around the world and the appearance of independent black states.

Across America minorities proclaimed their pride and demanded their rights. Women, the one "minority" that in America constituted a numerical majority, sought political and economic equality. Jews gained new solidarity from the holocaust and then from the establishment of a Jewish state in Israel. Changes in the immigration law dramatically increased the number arriving from Hispanic and Asian lands, and, following the general example, they asserted their own prerogatives. American Indians mobilized to reclaim rights and lands long since appropriated by the white man; their spokesmen even rejected the historic designation in which Indians had taken deserved pride and named themselves Native Americans.

The civil rights revolution provoked new expressions of ethnic identity by the now long-resident "new migration" from southern and eastern Europe—Italians, Greeks, Poles, Czechs, Slovaks, Hungarians. The ethnic enthusiasm was reinforced by the "third-generation" effect formulated in Hansen's Law, named after Marcus Lee Hansen, the great pioneer in immigration history: "What the son wishes to forget the grandson wishes to remember."

Another factor powerfully nourished the passion for roots: the waning American optimism about the nation's prospects. For two centuries Americans had been confident that life would be better for their children than it was for them. In their exuberant youth, Americans had disdained the past and, as John Quincy Adams urged, looked forward to their posterity rather than backward to their ancestors. Amid forebodings of national decline, Americans now began to look forward less and backward more. The rising cult of ethnicity was a symptom of decreasing confidence in the American future.

Ethnic as a word has had a long history. It originally meant "heathen" or "pagan" but soon came to mean anything pertaining to a race or nation. In this sense everyone, even the Lowells and the Cabots, were ethnics. By the time Henry James used the word in *The American Scene,* however, "ethnic" had acquired an association with foreignness. As applied since the 1960s, it definitely means non-Anglo minorities—a reversion to the original sense of being beyond the pale.

The noun *ethnicity* meanwhile made its modern debut in 1940 in W. Lloyd Warner's Yankee City series. From its modest beginning in that sociological study, "ethnicity" moved vigorously to center stage in popular discourse. The bicentennial of American independence, the centennial of the Statue of Liberty, the restoration of Ellis Island—all turned from tributes to the melting pot into extravaganzas of ethnic distinctiveness.

The pressure for the new cult of ethnicity came less from the minorities en masse than from their often self-appointed spokesmen. Most ethnics, white and nonwhite, saw themselves primarily as Americans. "The cravings for 'historical identity,'" Gunnar Myrdal said at the height of the ethnic rage, "is not in any sense a people's movement. Those cravings have been raised by a few well-established intellectuals, professors, writers—mostly, I gather, of a third generation." Few of them, Myrdal thought, made much effort to talk to their own ethnic groups. He feared, Myrdal added with a certain contempt, that this movement was only "upper-class intellectual romanticism."

Still, ideologues, with sufficient publicity and time, could create audiences. Spokesmen with a vested interest in ethnic identification repudiated the ideal of assimilation. The melting pot, it was said, injured people by undermining their self-esteem. It denied them heroes—"role models," in the jargon—from their own ethnic ancestries. Praise now went to "the unmeltable ethnics."

In 1974, after testimony from ethnic spokesmen denouncing the melting pot as a conspiracy to homogenize America, Congress passed the Ethnic Heritage Studies Program Act—a statute that, by applying the ethnic ideology to all Americans, compromised the historic right of Americans to decide their ethnic identities for themselves. The act ignored those millions of Americans—surely a majority—who refused identification with any particular ethnic group.

The ethnic upsurge (it can hardly be called a revival because it was unprecedented) began as a gesture of protest against the Anglocentric culture. It became a cult, and today it threatens to become a counterrevolution against the original theory of America as "one people," a common culture, a single nation. . . .

The Decomposition of America

Low self-esteem is too deep a malady to be cured by hearing nice things about one's own ethnic past. History is not likely to succeed where psychiatry fails. Afrocentrism in particular is an escape from the hard and expensive challenges of our society—the need for safer schools, better teachers, better teaching materials, greater investment in education; the need for stable families that can nourish self-discipline and aspiration; the need for jobs and income that can nourish stable families; the need to stop the ravages of drugs and crime; the need to overcome the racism still lurking in the interstices of American society. "The need," William Raspberry observes of his own people, "is not to reach back for some culture we never knew but to lay full claim to the culture in which we exist."

The ethnicity rage in general and Afrocentricity in particular not only divert attention from the real needs but exacerbate the problems. The recent apotheosis of ethnicity, black, brown, red, yellow, white, has revived the dismal prospect that in happy melting-pot days Americans thought the republic was moving safely beyond—that is, a society fragmented into separate ethnic communities. The cult of ethnicity exaggerates differences, intensifies resentments and antagonisms, drives ever deeper the awful wedges between races and nationalities. The endgame is self-pity and self-ghettoization.

Now there is a reasonable argument in the black case for a measure of regrouping and self-reliance as part of the preparation for entry into an integrated society on an equal basis. Integration on any other basis, it is contended, would mean total capitulation to white standards. Affirmation of racial and cultural pride is thus essential to true integration. One can see this as a psychological point, but as a cultural point?

For generations blacks have grown up in an American culture, on which they have had significant influence and to which they have made significant contributions. Self-Africanization after 300 years in America is playacting. Afrocentricity as expounded by ethnic ideologues implies Europhobia, separatism, emotions of alienation, victimization, paranoia. Most curious and unexpected of all is a black demand for the return of black-white segregation.

"To separate [black children] from others of similar age and qualifications solely because of their race," Chief Justice Warren wrote in the school-integration case, "generates a feeling of inferiority as to their status in the community that may affect their hearts and minds in a way unlikely ever to be undone." In 40 years doctrine has come full circle. Now integration is held to bring feelings of inferiority, and segregation to bring the cure.

This revival of separatism will begin, if the black educator Felix Boateng has his way, in the earliest grades. "The use of standard English as the only language of instruction," Boateng argues, "aggravates the process of deculturalization." A "culturally relevant curriculum" for minority children would recognize "the home and community dialect they bring to school." (Not all black educators, it should be said, share this desire to handicap black children from infancy. "One fact is clear," notes Janice Hale-Benson of Cleveland State University. "Speaking standard English is a skill needed by Black children for upward mobility in American society and it should be taught in early childhood.")

If any educational institution should bring people together as individuals in friendly and civil association, it should be the university. But the fragmentation of campuses in recent years into a multitude of ethnic organizations is spectacular—and disconcerting.

One finds black dormitories, black student unions, black fraternities and sororities, black business and law societies, black homosexual and lesbian groups, black tables in dining halls. Stanford, Dinesh D'Souza reports, has "ethnic theme houses." The University of Pennsylvania gives blacks—6 percent of the enrollment—their own yearbook. Campuses today, according to one University of Pennsylvania professor, have "the cultural diversity of Beirut. There are separate armed camps. The black kids don't mix with the white kids. The Asians are off by themselves. Oppression is the great status symbol."

Oberlin was for a century and half the model of a racially integrated college. "Increasingly," Jacob Weisberg, an editor at *The New Republic,* reports, "Oberlin students think, act, study, and live apart." Asians live in Asia House, Jews in "J" House, Latinos in Spanish House, blacks in African-Heritage House, foreign students in Third World House. Even the Lesbian, Gay, and Bisexual Union has broken up into racial and gender factions. "The result is separate worlds."

Huddling is an understandable reaction for any minority group faced with new and scary challenges. But institutionalized separatism only crystallizes racial differences and magnifies racial tensions. "Certain activities are labeled white and black," says a black student at Central Michigan University. "If you don't just participate in black activities, you are shunned." A recent study by the black anthropologist Signithia Fordham of Rutgers concludes that a big reason for black underachievement is the fear that academic success will be taken as a sellout to the white world. "What appears to have emerged in some segments of the black community," Fordham says, "is a kind of cultural orientation which defines academic learning in school as 'acting white.'"

Militants further argue that because only blacks can comprehend the black experience, only blacks should teach black history and literature, as, in the view of some feminists, only women should teach women's history and literature. "True diversity," according to the faculty's Budget Committee at the University of California at Berkeley, requires that courses match the ethnic and gender identities of the professors.

The doctrine that *only* blacks can teach and write black history leads inexorably to the doctrine that blacks can teach and write *only* black history as well as to inescapable corollaries: Chinese must be restricted to Chinese history, women to women's history, and so on. Henry Louis Gates criticizes "ghettoized programs where students and members of the faculty sit around and argue about whether a white person can think a black thought." As for the notion that there is a "mystique" about black studies that requires a person to have black skin in order to pursue them—that, John Hope Franklin observes succinctly, is "voodoo."

The voodoo principle is extended from scholarship to the arts. Thus the fine black playwright August Wilson insists on a black director for the film of his play *Fences.* "We have a different way of responding to the world," Wilson explains. "We have different ideas about religion, different manners of social intercourse. We have different ideas about style, about language. We have different esthetics [*sic*]. . . . The job requires someone who shares the specifics of the culture of black Americans. . . . Let's make a rule. Blacks don't direct Italian films. Italians don't direct Jewish films. Jews don't direct black American films." What a terrible rule that would be!

In the same restrictive spirit, Actors' Equity tried to prevent the British actor Jonathan Pryce from playing in New York the role he created in London in *Miss Saigon,* announcing that it could not condone "the casting of a Caucasian actor in the role of a Eurasian." (Pryce responded that, if this doctrine prevails, "I'd be stuck playing Welshmen for the rest of my life.") Equity did not, however, apply the same principle to the black actors Morgan Freeman and Denzel Washington who were both acting in Shakespeare at that time in New York. *The Wall Street Journal* acidly suggested that, according to the principle invoked, not only whites but the disabled should protest the casting of Denzel Washington as Richard III because Washington lacked a hunchback.

The distinguished black social psychologist Kenneth B. Clark, whose findings influenced the Supreme Court's decision in the school-integration case, rejects the argument that blacks and whites must be separated "because they represent different cultures and that cultures, like oil and water, cannot mix." This, Clark says, is what white segregationists have argued for generations. He adds, "There is absolutely no evidence to support the contention that the inherent damage to human beings of primitive exclusion on the basis of race is any less damaging when demanded or enforced by the previous victims than when imposed by the dominant group."

"The era that began with the dream of integration," Richard Rodriguez has observed, "ended up with scorn for assimilation." Instead of casting off the foreign skin, as John Quincy Adams had stipulated, never to resume it, the fashion is to resume the foreign skin as conspicuously as can be. The cult of ethnicity has reversed the movement of American history, producing a nation of minorities—or at least of minority spokesmen—less interested in joining with the majority in common endeavor than in declaring their alienation from an oppressive, white, patriarchal, racist, sexist, classist society. The ethnic ideology inculcates the illusion that membership in one or another ethnic group is the basic American experience.

Most Americans, it is true, continue to see themselves primarily as individuals and only secondarily and trivially as adherents of a group. Nor is harm done when ethnic groups display pride in their historic past or in their contributions to the American present. But the division of society into fixed ethnicities nourishes a culture of victimization and a contagion of inflammable sensitivities. And when a vocal and visible minority pledges primary allegiance to their groups, whether ethnic, sexual, religious, or, in rare cases (communist, fascist), political, it presents a threat to the brittle bonds of national identity that hold this diverse and fractious society together.

E. Pluribus Unum?

Is the Western tradition a bar to progress and a curse on humanity? Would it really do America and the world good to get rid of the European legacy?

No doubt Europe has done terrible things, not least to itself. But what culture has not? History, said Edward Gibbon, is little more than the register of the crimes, follies, and misfortunes of mankind. The sins of the West are no worse than the sins of Asia or of the Middle East or of Africa.

There remains, however, a crucial difference between the Western tradition and the others. The crimes of the West have produced their own antidotes. They have provoked great movements to end slavery, to raise the status of women, to abolish torture, to combat racism, to defend freedom of inquiry and expression, to advance personal liberty and human rights.

Whatever the particular crimes of Europe, that continent is also the source—the *unique* source—of those liberating ideas of individual liberty, political democracy, the rule of law, human rights, and cultural freedom that constitute our most precious legacy and to which most of the world today aspires. These are *European* ideas, not Asian, nor African, nor Middle Eastern ideas, except by adoption.

The freedoms of inquiry and of artistic creation, for example, are Western values. Consider the differing reactions to the case of Salman Rushdie: what the West saw as an intolerable attack on individual freedom the Middle East saw as a proper punishment for an evildoer who had violated the mores of his group. Individualism itself is looked on with abhorrence and dread by collectivist cultures in which loyalty to the group overrides personal goals—cultures that, social scientists say, comprise about 70 percent of the world's population.

There is surely no reason for Western civilization to have guilt trips laid on it by champions of cultures based on despotism, superstition, tribalism, and fanaticism. In this regard the Afrocentrists are especially absurd. The West needs no lectures on the superior virtue of those "sun people" who sustained slavery until Western imperialism abolished it (and, it is reported, sustain it to this day in Mauritania and the Sudan), who still keep women in subjection and cut off their clitorises, who carry out racial persecutions not only against Indians and other Asians but against fellow Africans from the wrong tribes, who show themselves either incapable of operating a democracy or ideologically hostile to the democratic idea, and who in their tyrannies and massacres, their Idi Amins and Boukassas, have stamped with utmost brutality on human rights.

Certainly the European overlords did little enough to prepare Africa for self-government. But democracy would find it hard in any case to put down roots in a tribalist and patrimonial culture that, long before the West invaded Africa, had sacralized the personal authority of chieftains and ordained the submission of the rest. What the West would call corruption is regarded through much of Africa as no more than the prerogative of power. Competitive political parties, an independent judiciary, a free press, the rule of law are alien to African traditions.

It was the French, not the Algerians, who freed Algerian women from the veil (much to the irritation of Frantz Fanon, who regarded deveiling as symbolic rape); as in India it was the British, not the Indians, who ended (or did their best to end) the horrible custom of *suttee*—widows burning themselves alive on their husbands' funeral pyres. And it was the West, not the non-Western cultures, that launched the crusade to abolish slavery—and in doing so encountered mighty resistance, especially in the Islamic world (where Moslems, with fine impartiality, enslaved whites as well as blacks). Those many brave and humane Africans who are struggling these days for decent societies are animated by Western, not by African, ideals. White guilt can be pushed too far.

The Western commitment to human rights has unquestionably been intermittent and imperfect. Yet the ideal remains—and movement toward it has been real, if sporadic. Today it is the *Western* democratic tradition that attracts and empowers people of all continents, creeds, and colors. When the Chinese students cried and died for democracy in Tiananmen Square, they brought with them not representations of Confucius or Buddha but a model of the Statue of Liberty.

The great American asylum, as Crèvecoeur called it, open, as Washington said, to the oppressed and persecuted of all nations, has been from the start an experiment in a multiethnic society. This is a bolder experiment than we sometimes remember. History is littered with the wreck of states that tried to combine diverse ethnic or linguistic or religious groups within a single sovereignty. Today's headlines tell of imminent crisis or impending dissolution in one or another multiethnic polity—the Soviet Union, India, Yugoslavia, Czechoslovakia, Ireland, Belgium, Canada, Lebanon, Cyprus, Israel, Ceylon, Spain, Nigeria, Kenya, Angola, Trinidad, Guyana. . . . The list is almost endless. The luck so far of the American experiment has been due in large part to the vision of the melting pot. "No other nation," Margaret Thatcher has said, "has so successfully combined people of different races and nations within a single culture."

But even in the United States, ethnic ideologues have not been without effect. They have set themselves against the old American ideal of assimilation. They call on the republic to think in terms not of individual but of group identity and to move the polity from individual rights to group rights. They have made a certain progress in transforming the United States into a more segregated society. They have done their best to turn a college generation against Europe and the Western tradition. They have imposed ethnocentric, Afrocentric, and bilingual curricula on public schools, well designed to hold minority children out of American society. They have told young people from minority groups that the Western democratic tradition is not for them. They have encouraged minorities to see themselves as victims and to live by alibis rather than to claim the opportunities opened for them by the potent combination of black protest and white guilt. They have filled the air with recrimination and rancor and have remarkably advanced the fragmentation of American life.

Yet I believe the campaign against the idea of common ideals and a single society will fail. Gunnar Myrdal was surely right: for all the damage it has done, the upsurge of ethnicity is a superficial enthusiasm stirred by romantic ideologues and unscrupulous hucksters whose claim to speak for their minorities is thoughtlessly accepted by the media. I doubt that the ethnic vogue expresses a reversal of direction from assimilation to apartheid among the minorities themselves. Indeed, the more the ideologues press the case for ethnic separatism, the less they appeal to the mass of their own groups. They have thus far done better in intimidating the white majority than in converting their own constituencies.

"No nation in history," writes Lawrence Fuchs, the political scientist and immigration expert in his fine book *The American Kaleidoscope,* "had proved as successful as the United States in managing ethnic diversity. No nation before had ever made diversity itself a source of national identity and unity." The second sentence explains the success described in the first, and the mechanism for translating diversity into unity has been the American Creed, the civic culture—the very assimilating, unifying culture that is today challenged, and not seldom rejected, by the ideologues of ethnicity.

A historian's guess is that the resources of the Creed have not been exhausted. Americanization has not lost its charms. Many sons and daughters of ethnic neighborhoods still want to shed their ethnicity and move to the suburbs as fast as they can—where they will be received with far more tolerance than they would have been 70 years ago. The desire for achievement and success in American society remains a potent force for assimilation. Ethnic subcultures, Stephen Steinberg, author of *The Ethnic Myth,* points out, fade away "because circumstances forced them to make choices that undermined the basis for cultural survival."

Others may enjoy their ethnic neighborhoods but see no conflict between foreign descent and American loyalty. Unlike the multiculturalists, they celebrate not only what is distinctive in their own backgrounds but what they hold in common with the rest of the population.

The ethnic identification often tends toward superficiality. The sociologist Richard Alba's study of children and grandchildren of immigrants in the Albany, New York, area shows the most popular "ethnic experience" to be sampling the ancestral cuisine. Still, less than half the respondents picked that, and only one percent ate ethnic food every day. Only one-fifth acknowledged a sense of special relationship to people of their own ethnic background; less than one-sixth taught their children about their ethnic origins; almost none was fluent in the language of the old country. "It is hard to avoid the conclusion," Alba writes, "that ethnic experience is shallow for the great majority of whites."

If ethnic experience is a good deal less shallow for blacks, it is because of their bitter experience in America, not because of their memories of Africa. Nonetheless most blacks prefer "black" to "African-Americans," fight bravely and patriotically for their country, and would move to the suburbs too if income and racism would permit.

The ethnic revolt against the melting pot has reached the point, in rhetoric at least, though not I think in reality, of a denial of the idea of a common culture and a single society. If large numbers of people really accept this, the republic would be in serious trouble. The question poses itself: how to restore the balance between *unum* and *pluribus?*

The old American homogeneity disappeared well over a century ago, never to return. Ever since, we have been preoccupied in one way or another with the problem, as Herbert Croly phrased in 80 years back in *The Promise of American Life,* "of preventing such divisions from dissolving the society into which they enter—of keeping such a highly differentiated society fundamentally sound and whole." This required, Croly believed, an "ultimate bond of union." There was only one way by which solidarity could be restored, "and that is by means of a democratic social ideal. . . ."

The genius of America lies in its capacity to forge a single nation from peoples of remarkably diverse racial, religious, and ethnic origins. It has done so because democratic principles provide both the philosophical bond of union and practical experience in civic participation. The American Creed envisages a nation composed of individuals making their own choices and accountable to themselves, not a nation based on inviolable ethnic communities. The Constitution turns on individual rights, not on group rights. Law, in order to rectify past wrongs, has from time to time (and in my view often properly so) acknowledged the claims of groups; but this is the exception, not the rule.

Our democratic principles contemplate an open society founded on tolerance of differences and on mutual respect. In practice, America has been more open to some than to others. But it is more open to all today than it was yesterday and is likely to be even more open tomorrow than today. The steady movement of American life has been from exclusion to inclusion.

Historically and culturally this republic has an Anglo-Saxon base; but from the start the base has been modified, enriched, and reconstituted by transfusions from other continents and civilizations. The movement from exclusion to inclusion causes a constant revision in the texture of our culture. The ethnic transfusions affect all aspects of American life—our politics, our literature, our music, our painting, our movies, our cuisine, our customs, our dreams.

Black Americans in particular have influenced the ever-changing national culture in many ways. They have lived here for centuries, and, unless one believes in racist mysticism, they belong far more to American culture than to the culture of Africa. Their history is part of the Western democratic tradition, not an alternative to it. Henry Louis Gates Jr. reminds us of James Baldwin's remark about coming to Europe to find out that he was "as American as any Texas G.I." No one does black Americans more disservice than those Afrocentric ideologues who would define them out of the West.

The interplay of diverse traditions produces the America we know. "Paradoxical though it may seem," Diane Ravitch has well said, "the United States has a common culture that is multicultural." That is why unifying political ideals coexist so easily and cheerfully with diversity in social and cultural values. Within the overarching political commitment, people are free to live as they choose, ethnically and otherwise. Differences will remain; some are reinvented; some are used to drive us apart. But as we renew our allegiance to the unifying ideals, we provide the solvent that will prevent differences from escalating into antagonism and hatred.

One powerful reason for the movement from exclusion to inclusion is that the American Creed facilitates the appeal from the actual to the ideal. When we talk of the American democratic faith, we must understand it in its true dimensions. It is not an impervious, final, and complacent orthodoxy, intolerant of deviation and dissent, fulfilled in flag salutes, oaths of allegiance, and hands over the heart. It is an ever-evolving philosophy, fulfilling its ideals through debate, self-criticism, protest, disrespect, and irreverence; a tradition in which all have rights of heterodoxy and opportunities for self-assertion. The Creed has been the means by which Americans have haltingly but persistently narrowed the gap between performance and principle. It is what all Americans should learn, because it is what binds all Americans together.

19

A Different Mirror

RONALD T. TAKAKI

I had flown from San Francisco to Norfolk and was riding in a taxi to my hotel to attend a conference on multiculturalism. Hundreds of educators from across the country were meeting to discuss the need for greater cultural diversity in the curriculum. My driver and I chatted about the weather and the tourists. The sky was cloudy, and Virginia Beach was twenty minutes away. The rearview mirror reflected a white man in his forties. "How long have you been in this country?" he asked. "All my life," I replied, wincing. "I was born in the United States." With a strong southern drawl, he remarked: "I was wondering because your English is excellent!" Then, as I had many times before, I explained: "My grandfather came here from Japan in the 1880s. My family has been here, in America, for over a hundred years." He glanced at me in the mirror. Somehow I did not look "American" to him; my eyes and complexion looked foreign.

Suddenly, we both became uncomfortably conscious of a racial divide separating us. An awkward silence turned my gaze from the mirror to the passing landscape, the shore where the English and the Powhatan Indians first encountered each other. Our highway was on land that Sir Walter Raleigh had renamed "Virginia" in honor of Elizabeth I, the Virgin Queen. In the English cultural appropriation of America, the indigenous peoples themselves would become outsiders in their native land. Here, at the eastern edge of the continent, I mused, was the site of the beginning of multicultural America. Jamestown, the English settlement founded in 1607, was nearby: the first twenty Africans were brought here a year before the Pilgrims arrived at Plymouth Rock. Several hundred miles offshore was Bermuda, the "Bermoothes" where William Shakespeare's Prospero had landed and met the native Caliban in *The Tempest*. Earlier, another voyager had made an Atlantic crossing and unexpectedly bumped into some islands to the south. Thinking he had reached Asia, Christopher Columbus mistakenly identified one of the islands as "Cipango" (Japan). In the wake of the admiral, many peoples would come to America from different shores, not only from Europe but also Africa and Asia. One of them would be my grandfather. My mental wandering across terrain and time ended abruptly as we arrived at my destination. I said good-bye to my driver and went into the hotel, carrying a vivid reminder of why I was attending this conference.

Questions like the one my taxi driver asked me are always jarring, but I can understand why he could not see me as American. He had a narrow but widely shared sense of the past—a history that has viewed American as European in ancestry. "Race," Toni Morrison explained, has functioned as a "metaphor" necessary to the "construction of Americanness": in the creation of our national identity, "American" has been defined as "white."[1]

But America has been racially diverse since our very beginning on the Virginia shore, and this reality is increasingly becoming visible and ubiquitous. Currently, one-third of the American people do not trace their origins to Europe; in California, minorities are fast becoming a majority. They already predominate in major cities across the country—New York, Chicago, Atlanta, Detroit, Philadelphia, San Francisco, and Los Angeles.

This emerging demographic diversity has raised fundamental questions about America's identity and culture. In 1990, *Time* published a cover story on "America's Changing Colors." "Someday soon," the magazine announced, "white Americans will become a minority group." How soon? By 2056, most Americans will trace their descent to "Africa, Asia, the Hispanic world, the Pacific Islands, Arabia—almost anywhere but white Europe." This dramatic change in our nation's ethnic composition is altering the way we think about ourselves. "The deeper significance of America's becoming a majority nonwhite society is what it means to the national psyche, to individuals' sense of themselves and their nation—their idea of what it is to be American." . . . [2]

What is fueling the debate over our national identity and the content of our curriculum is America's intensifying racial crisis. The alarming signs and symptoms seem to be everywhere—the killing of Vincent Chin in Detroit, the black boycott of a Korean grocery store in Flatbush, the hysteria in Boston over the Carol Stuart murder, the battle between white sportsmen and Indians over tribal fishing rights in Wisconsin, the Jewish-black clashes in Brooklyn's Crown Heights, the black-Hispanic competition for jobs and educational resources in Dallas, which *Newsweek* described as "a conflict of the have-nots," and the Willie Horton campaign commercials, which widened the divide between the suburbs and the inner cities.[3]

This reality of racial tension rudely woke America like a fire bell in the night on April 29, 1992. Immediately after four Los Angeles police officers were found not guilty of brutality against Rodney King, rage exploded in Los Angeles. Race relations reached a new nadir. During the nightmarish rampage, scores of people were killed, over two thousand injured, twelve thousand arrested, and almost a billion dollars' worth of property destroyed. The live televised images mesmerized America. The rioting and the murderous melee on the streets resembled the fighting in Beirut and the West Bank. The thousands of fires burning out of control and the dark smoke filling the skies brought back images of the burning oil fields of Kuwait during Desert Storm. Entire sections of Los Angeles looked like a bombed city. "Is this America?" many shocked viewers asked. "Please, can we get along here," pleaded Rodney King, calling for calm. "We all can get along. I mean, we're all stuck here for a while. Let's try to work it out."[4]

But how should "we" be defined? Who are the people "stuck here" in America? One of the lessons of the Los Angeles explosion is the recognition of the fact that we are a multiracial society and that race can no longer be defined in the binary terms of white and black. "We" will have to include Hispanics and Asians. While blacks currently constitute 13 percent of the Los Angeles population, Hispanics represent 40 percent. The 1990 census revealed that South Central Los Angeles, which was predominantly black in 1965 when the Watts rebellion occurred, is now 45 percent Hispanic. A majority of the first 5,438 people arrested were Hispanic, while 37 percent were black. Of the fifty-eight people who died in the riot, more than a third were Hispanic, and about 40 percent of the businesses destroyed were Hispanic-owned. Most of the other shops and stores were Korean-owned. The dreams of many Korean immigrants went up in smoke during the riot: two thousand Korean-owned businesses were damaged or demolished, totaling about $400 million in losses. There is evidence indicating they were targeted. "After all," explained a black gang member, "we didn't burn our community, just *their* stores."[5]

"I don't feel like I'm in America anymore," said Denisse Bustamente as she watched the police protecting the firefighters. "I feel like I am far away." Indeed, Americans have been witnessing ethnic strife erupting around the world—the rise of neo-Nazism and the murder of Turks in Germany, the ugly "ethnic cleansing" in Bosnia, the terrible and bloody clashes between Muslims and Hindus in India. Is the situation here different, we have been nervously wondering, or do ethnic conflicts elsewhere represent a prologue for America? What is the nature of malevolence? Is there a deep, perhaps primordial, need for group identity rooted in hatred for the other? Is ethnic pluralism possible for America? But answers have been limited. Television reports have been little more than thirty-second sound bites. Newspaper articles have been mostly superficial descriptions of racial antagonisms and the current urban malaise. What is lacking is historical context; consequently, we are left, feeling bewildered.[6]

How did we get to this point, Americans everywhere are anxiously asking. What does our diversity mean, and where is it leading us? *How* do we work it out in the post–Rodney King era?

Certainly one crucial way is for our society's various ethnic groups to develop a greater understanding of each other. For example, how can African Americans and Korean Americans work it out unless they learn about each other's cultures, histories, and also economic situations? This need to share knowledge about our ethnic diversity has acquired new importance and has given new urgency to the pursuit for a more accurate history. . . .

While all of America's many groups cannot be covered in one book, the English immigrants and their descendants require attention, for they possessed inordinate power to define American culture and make public policy. What men like John Winthrop, Thomas Jefferson, and Andrew Jackson thought as well as did mattered greatly to all of us and was consequential for everyone. A broad range of groups has been selected: African Americans, Asian Americans, Chicanos, Irish, Jews, and Indians. While together they help to explain general patterns in our society, each has contributed to the making of the United States.

African Americans have been the central minority throughout our country's history. They were initially brought here on a slave ship in 1619. Actually, these first twenty Africans might not have been slaves; rather, like most of the white laborers, they were probably indentured servants. The transformation of Africans into slaves is the story of the "hidden" origins of slavery. How and when was it decided to institute a system of bonded black labor? What happened, while freighted with racial significance, was actually conditioned by class conflicts within white society. Once established, the "peculiar institution" would have consequences for centuries to come. During the nineteenth century, the political storm over slavery almost destroyed the nation. Since the Civil War and emancipation, race has continued to be largely defined in relation to African Americans—segregation, civil rights, the underclass, and affirmative action. Constituting the largest minority group in our society, they have been at the cutting edge of the Civil Rights Movement. Indeed, their struggle has been a constant reminder of America's moral vision as a country committed to the principle of liberty. Martin Luther King clearly understood this truth when he wrote from a jail cell: "We will reach the goal of freedom in Birmingham and all over the nation, because the goal of America is freedom. Abused and scorned though we may be, our destiny is tied up with America's destiny."[7]

Asian Americans have been here for over one hundred and fifty years, before many European immigrant groups. But as "strangers" coming from a "different shore," they have been stereotyped as "heathen," exotic, and unassimilable. Seeking "Gold Mountain," the Chinese arrived first, and what happened to them influenced the reception of the Japanese, Koreans, Filipinos, and Asian Indians as well as the Southeast Asian refugees like the Vietnamese and the Hmong. The 1882 Chinese Exclusion Act was the first law that prohibited the entry of immigrants on the basis of nationality. The Chinese condemned this restriction as racist and tyrannical. "They call us 'Chink,'" complained a Chinese immigrant, cursing the "white demons." "They think we no good! America cuts us off. No more come now, too bad!" This precedent later provided a basis for the restriction of European immigrant groups such as Italians, Russians, Poles, and Greeks. The Japanese painfully discovered that their accomplishments in America did not lead to acceptance, for during World War II, unlike Italian Americans and German Americans, they were placed in internment camps. Two-thirds of them were citizens by birth. "How could I as a 6-month-old child born in this country," asked Congressman Robert Matsui years later, "be declared by my own Government to be an enemy alien?" Today, Asian Americans represent the fastest-growing ethnic group. They have also become the focus of much mass media attention as "the Model Minority" not only for blacks and Chicanos, but also for whites on welfare and even middle-class whites experiencing economic difficulties.[8]

Chicanos represent the largest group among the Hispanic population, which is projected to outnumber African Americans. They have been in the United States for a long time, initially incorporated by the war against Mexico. The treaty had moved the border between the two countries, and the people of "occupied" Mexico suddenly found themselves "foreigners" in their "native land." As historian Albert Camarillo pointed out, the Chicano past is an integral part of America's westward expansion, also known as "manifest destiny." But while the early Chicanos were a colonized people, most of them today have immigrant roots. Many began the trek to El Norte in the early twentieth century. "As I had heard a lot about the United States," Jesus Garza recalled, "it was my dream to come here." "We came to know families from Chihuahua, Sonora, Jalisco, and Durango," stated Ernesto Galarza. "Like ourselves, our Mexican neighbors had come this far moving step by step, working and waiting, as if they were feeling their way up a ladder." Nevertheless, the Chicano experience has been unique, for most of them have lived close to their homeland—a proximity that has helped reinforce their language, identity, and culture. This migration to El Norte has continued to the present. Los Angeles has more people of Mexican origin than any other city in the world, except Mexico City. A mostly mestizo people of Indian as well as African and Spanish ancestries, Chicanos currently represent the largest minority group in the Southwest, where they have been visibly transforming culture and society.[9]

The Irish came here in greater numbers than most immigrant groups. Their history has been tied to America's past from the very beginning. Ireland represented the earliest English frontier: the conquest of Ireland occurred before the colonization of America, and the Irish were the first group that the English called "savages." In this context, the Irish past foreshadowed the Indian future. During the nineteenth century, the Irish, like the Chinese, were victims of British colonialism. While the Chinese fled from the ravages of the Opium Wars, the Irish were pushed from their homeland by "English tyranny." Here they became construction workers and factory operatives as well as the "maids" of America. Representing a Catholic group seeking to settle in a fiercely Protestant society, the Irish immigrants were targets of American nativist hostility. They were also what historian Lawrence J. McCaffrey called "the pioneers of the American urban ghetto," "previewing" experiences that would later be shared by the Italians, Poles, and other groups from southern and eastern Europe. Furthermore, they offer contrast to the immigrants from Asia. The Irish came about the same time as the Chinese, but they had a distinct advantage: the Naturalization Law of 1790 had reserved citizenship for "whites" only. Their compatible complexion allowed them to assimilate by blending into American society. In making their journey successfully into the mainstream, however, these immigrants from Erin pursued an Irish "ethnic" strategy: they promoted "Irish" solidarity in order to gain political power and also to dominate the skilled blue-collar occupations, often at the expense of the Chinese and blacks.[10]

Fleeing pogroms and religious persecution in Russia, the Jews were driven from what John Cuddihy described as the "Middle Ages into the Anglo-American world of the *goyim* 'beyond the pale.'" To them, America represented the Promised Land. This vision led Jews to struggle not only for themselves but also for other oppressed groups, especially blacks. After the 1917 East St. Louis race riot, the Yiddish *Forward* of New York compared this anti-black violence to a 1903 pogrom in Russia: "Kishinev and St. Louis—the same soil, the same people." Jews cheered when Jackie Robinson broke into the Brooklyn Dodgers in 1947. "He was adopted as the surrogate hero by many of us growing up at the time," recalled Jack Greenberg of the NAACP Legal Defense Fund. "He was the way we saw ourselves triumphing against the forces of bigotry and ignorance." Jews stood shoulder to shoulder with blacks in the Civil Rights Movement: two-thirds of the white volunteers who went south during the 1964 Freedom Summer were Jewish. Today Jews are considered a highly successful "ethnic" group. How did they make such great socioeconomic strides? This question is often reframed by neoconservative intellectuals like Irving Kristol and Nathan Glazer to read: if Jewish immigrants were able to lift themselves from poverty into the mainstream through self-help and education without welfare and affirmative action, why can't blacks? But what this thinking overlooks is the unique history of Jewish immigrants, especially the initial advantages of many of them as literate and skilled. Moreover, it minimizes the virulence of racial prejudice rooted in American slavery.[11]

Indians represent a critical contrast, for theirs was not an immigrant experience. The Wampanoags were on the shore as the first English strangers arrived in what would be called "New England." The encounters between Indians and whites not only shaped the course of race relations, but also influenced the very culture and identity of the general society. The architect of Indian removal, President Andrew Jackson told Congress: "Our conduct toward these people is deeply interesting to the national character." Frederick Jackson Turner understood the meaning of this observation when he identified the frontier as our transforming crucible. At first, the European newcomers had to wear Indian moccasins and shout the war cry. "Little by little," as they subdued the wilderness, the pioneers became "a new product" that was "American." But Indians have had a different view of this entire process. "The white man," Luther Standing Bear of the Sioux explained, "does not understand the Indian for the reason that he does not understand America." Continuing to be "troubled with primitive fears," he has "in his consciousness the perils of this frontier continent. . . . The man from Europe is still a foreigner and an alien. And he still hates the man who questioned his path across the continent." Indians questioned what Jackson and Turner trumpeted as "progress." For them, the frontier had a different "significance": their history was how the West was lost. But their story has also been one of resistance. As Vine Deloria declared, "Custer died for your sins."[12]

By looking at these groups from a multicultural perspective, we can comparatively analyze their experience in order to develop an understanding of their differences and similarities. Race, we will see, has been a social construction that has historically set apart racial minorities from European immigrant groups. Contrary to the notions of scholars like Nathan Glazer and Thomas Sowell, race in America has not been the same as ethnicity. A broad comparative focus also allows us to see how the varied experiences of different racial and ethnic groups occurred within shared contexts.

During the nineteenth century, for example, the Market Revolution employed Irish immigrant laborers in New England factories as it expanded cotton fields worked by enslaved blacks across Indian lands toward Mexico. Like blacks, the Irish newcomers were stereotyped as "savages," ruled by passions rather than "civilized" virtues such as self-control and hard work. The Irish saw themselves as the "slaves" of British oppressors, and during a visit to Ireland in the 1840s, Frederick Douglass found that the "wailing notes" of the Irish ballads reminded him of the "wild notes" of slave songs. The United States annexation of California, while incorporating Mexicans, led to trade with Asia and the migration of "strangers" from Pacific shores. In 1870, Chinese immigrant laborers were transported to Massachusetts as scabs to break an Irish immigrant strike; in response, the Irish recognized the need for interethnic working-class solidarity and tried to organize a Chinese lodge of the Knights of St. Crispin. After the Civil War, Mississippi planters recruited Chinese immigrants to discipline the newly freed blacks. During the debate over an immigration exclusion bill in 1882, a senator asked: If Indians could be located on reservations, why not the Chinese?[13]

Other instances of our connectedness abound. In 1903, Mexican and Japanese farm laborers went on strike together in California: their union officers had names like Yamaguchi and Lizarras, and strike meetings were conducted in Japanese and Spanish. The Mexican strikers declared that they were standing in solidarity with their "Japanese brothers" because the two groups had toiled together in the fields and were now fighting together for a fair wage. Speaking in impassioned Yiddish during the 1909 "uprising of twenty thousand" strikers in New York, the charismatic Clara Lemlich compared the abuse of Jewish female garment workers to the experience of blacks: "[The bosses] yell at the girls and 'call them down' even worse than I imagine the Negro slaves were in the South." During the 1920s, elite universities like Harvard worried about the increasing numbers of Jewish students, and new admissions criteria were instituted to curb their enrollment. Jewish students were scorned for their studiousness and criticized for their "clannishness," Recently, Asian-American students have been the targets of similar complaints: they have been called "nerds" and told there are "too many" of them on campus.[14]

Indians were already here, while blacks were forcibly transported to America, and Mexicans were initially enclosed by America's expanding border. The other groups came here as immigrants: for them, America represented liminality—a new world where they could pursue extravagant urges and do things they had thought beyond their capabilities. Like the land itself, they found themselves "betwixt and between all fixed points of classification." No longer fastened as fiercely to their old countries, they felt a stirring to become new people in a society still being defined and formed.[15]

These immigrants made bold and dangerous crossings, pushed by political events and economic hardships in their homelands and pulled by America's demand for labor as well as by their own dreams for a better life. "By all means let me go to America," a young man in Japan begged his parents. He had calculated that in one year as a laborer here he could save almost a thousand yen—an amount equal to the income of a governor in Japan. "My dear Father," wrote an immigrant Irish girl living in New York, "Any man or woman without a family are fools that would not venture and come to this plentyful Country where no man or woman ever hungered." In the shtetls of Russia, the cry "To America!" roared like "wild-fire." "America was in everybody's mouth," a Jewish immigrant recalled. "Businessmen talked [about] it over their accounts; the market women made up their quarrels that they might discuss it from stall to stall; people who had relatives in the famous land went around reading their letters." Similarly, for Mexican immigrants crossing the border in the early twentieth century, El Norte became the stuff of overblown hopes. "If only you could see how nice the United States is," they said, "that is why the Mexicans are crazy about it."[16]

The signs of America's ethnic diversity can be discerned across the continent— Ellis Island, Angel Island, Chinatown, Harlem, South Boston, the Lower East Side, places with Spanish names like Los Angeles and San Antonio or Indian names like Massachusetts and Iowa. Much of what is familiar in America's cultural landscape actually has ethnic origins. The Bing cherry was developed by an early Chinese immigrant named Ah Bing. American Indians were cultivating corn, tomatoes, and tobacco long before the arrival of Columbus. The term *okay* was derived from the Choctaw word *oke,* meaning "it is so." There is evidence indicating that the name *Yankee* came from Indian terms for the English—from *eankke* in Cherokee and *Yankwis* in Delaware. Jazz and blues as well as rock and roll have African-American origins. The "Forty-Niners" of the Gold Rush learned mining techniques from the Mexicans; American cowboys acquired herding skills from Mexican *vaqueros* and adopted their range terms—such as *lariat* from *la reata,* *lasso* from *lazo,* and *stampede* from *estampida.* Songs like "God Bless America," "Easter Parade," and "White Christmas" were written by a Russian-Jewish immigrant named Israel Baline, more popularly known as Irving Berlin.[17]

Furthermore, many diverse ethnic groups have contributed to the building of the American economy, forming what Walt Whitman saluted as "a vast, surging, hopeful army of workers." They worked in the South's cotton fields, New England's textile mills, Hawaii's canefields, New York's garment factories, California's orchards, Washington's salmon canneries, and Arizona's copper mines. They built the railroad, the great symbol of America's industrial triumph. . . .

Moreover, our diversity was tied to America's most serious crisis: the Civil War was fought over a racial issue—slavery. . . .

. . . The people in our study have been actors in history, not merely victims of discrimination and exploitation. They are entitled to be viewed as subjects—as men and women with minds, wills, and voices.

> *In the telling and retelling*
> *of their stories,*
> *They create communities*
> *of memory.*

They also re-vision history. "It is very natural that the history written by the victim," said a Mexican in 1874, "does not altogether chime with the story of the victor." Sometimes they are hesitant to speak, thinking they are only "little people." "I don't know why anybody wants to hear my history," an Irish maid said apologetically in 1900. "Nothing ever happened to me worth the tellin.'"[18]

But their stories are worthy. Through their stories, the people who have lived America's history can help all of us, including my taxi driver, understand that Americans originated from many shores, and that all of us are entitled to dignity. "I hope this survey do a lot of good for Chinese people," an immigrant told an interviewer from Stanford University in the 1920s. "Make American people realize that Chinese people are humans. I think very few American people really know anything about Chinese." But the remembering is also for the sake of the children. "This story is dedicated to the descendants of Lazar and Goldie Glauberman," Jewish immigrant Minnie Miller wrote in her autobiography. "My history is bound up in their history and the generations that follow should know where they came from to know better who they are." Similarly, Tomo Shoji, an elderly Nisei woman, urged Asian Americans to learn more about their roots: "We got such good, fantastic stories to tell. All our stories are different." Seeking to know how they fit into America, many young people have become listeners; they are eager to learn about the hardships and humiliations experienced by their parents and grandparents. They want to hear their stories, unwilling to remain ignorant or ashamed of their identity and past.[19]

The telling of stories liberates. By writing about the people on Mango Street, Sandra Cisneros explained, "the ghost does not ache so much." The place no longer holds her with "both arms. She sets me free." Indeed, stories may not be as innocent or simple as they seem to be. Native-American novelist Leslie Marmon Silko cautioned:

> *I will tell you something about stories . . .*
> *They aren't just entertainment.*
> *Don't be fooled.*

Indeed, the accounts given by the people in this study vibrantly re-create moments, capturing the complexities of human emotions and thoughts. They also provide the authenticity of experience. After she escaped from slavery, Harriet Jacobs wrote in her autobiography: "[My purpose] is not to tell you what I have heard but what I have seen—and what I have suffered." In their sharing of memory, the people in this study offer us an opportunity to see ourselves reflected in a mirror called history.[20]

In his recent study of Spain and the New World, *The Buried Mirror,* Carlos Fuentes points out that mirrors have been found in the tombs of ancient Mexico, placed there to guide the dead through the underworld. He also tells us about the legend of Quetzalcoatl, the Plumed Serpent: when this god was given a mirror by the Toltec deity Tezcatlipoca, he saw a man's face in the mirror and realized his own humanity. For us, the "mirror" of history can guide the living and also help us recognize who we have been and hence are. In *A Distant Mirror,* Barbara W. Tuchman finds "phenomenal parallels" between the "calamitous 14th century" of European society and our own era. We can, she, observes, have "greater fellow-feeling for a distraught age" as we painfully recognize the "similar disarray," "collapsing assumptions," and "unusual discomfort."[21]

But what is needed in our own perplexing times is not so much a "distant" mirror, as one that is "different." While the study of the past can provide collective self-knowledge, it often reflects the scholar's particular perspective or view of the world. What happens when historians leave out many of America's peoples? What happens, to borrow the words of Adrienne Rich, "when someone with the authority of a teacher" describes our society, and "you are not in it"? Such an experience can be disorienting—"a moment of psychic disequilibrium, as if you looked into a mirror and saw nothing."[22]

Through their narratives about their lives and circumstances, the people of America's diverse groups are able to see themselves and each other in our common past. They celebrate what Ishmael Reed has described as a society "unique" in the world because "the world is here"—a place "where the cultures of the world crisscross." Much of America's past, they point out, has been riddled with racism. At the same time, these people offer hope, affirming the struggle for equality as a central theme in our country's history. At its conception, our nation was dedicated to the proposition of equality. What has given concreteness to this powerful national principle has been our coming together in the creation of a new society. "Stuck here" together, workers of different backgrounds have attempted to get along with each other.

> *People harvesting*
> *Work together unaware*
> *Of racial problems,*

wrote a Japanese immigrant describing a lesson learned by Mexican and Asian farm laborers in California.[23]

Finally, how do we see our prospects for "working out" America's racial crisis? Do we see it as through a glass darkly? Do the televised images of racial hatred and violence that riveted us in 1992 during the days of rage in Los Angeles frame a future of divisive race relations—what Arthur Schlesinger, Jr., has fearfully denounced as the "disuniting of America"? Or will Americans of diverse races and ethnicities be able to connect themselves to a larger narrative? Whatever happens, we can be certain that much of our society's future will be influenced by which "mirror" we choose to see ourselves. America does not belong to one race or one group, the people in this study remind us, and Americans have been constantly redefining their national identity from the moment of first contact on the Virginia shore. By sharing their stories, they invite us to see ourselves in a different mirror.[24]

NOTES

1. Toni Morrison, *Playing in the Dark: Whiteness in the Literary Imagination* (Cambridge, Mass., 1992), p. 47.

2. William A. Henry III, "Beyond the Melting Pot," in "America's Changing Colors," *Time*, vol. 135, no. 15 (April 9, 1990), pp. 28–31.

3. "A Conflict of the Have-Nots," *Newsweek*, December 12, 1988, pp. 28–29.

4. Rodney King's statement to the press, *New York Times*, May 2, 1992, p. 6.

5. Tim Rutten, "A New Kind of Riot," *New York Review of Books*, June 11, 1992, pp. 52–53; Maria Newman, "Riots Bring Attention to Growing Hispanic Presence in South-Central Area," *New York Times*, May 11, 1992, p. A10; Mike Davis, "In L.A. Burning All Illusions," *The Nation*, June 1, 1992, pp. 744–745; Jack Viets and Peter Fimrite, "S.F. Mayor Visits Riot-Torn Area to Buoy Businesses," *San Francisco Chronicle*, May 6, 1992, p. A6.

6. Rick DelVecchio, Suzanne Espinosa, and Carl Nolte, "Bradley Ready to Lift Curfew," *San Francisco Chronicle*, May 4, 1992, p. A1.

7. Abraham Lincoln, "The Gettysburg Address," in *The Annals of America*, vol. 9, *1863–1865: The Crisis of the Union* (Chicago, 1968), pp. 462–463; Martin Luther King, *Why We Can't Wait* (New York, 1964), pp. 92–93.

8. Interview with old laundryman, in "Interviews with Two Chinese," circa 1924, Box 326, folder 325, Survey of Race Relations, Stanford University, Hoover Institution Archives; Congressman Robert Matsui, speech in the House of Representatives on the 442 bill for redress and reparations, September 17, 1987, *Congressional Record* (Washington, D.C., 1987), p. 7584.

9. Camarillo, *Chicanos in a Changing Society*, p. 2; Juan Nepornuceno Seguín, in David J. Weber (ed.), *Foreigners in Their Native Land: Historical Roots of the Mexican Americans* (Albuquerque, N. Mex., 1973), p. vi; Jesus Garza, in Manuel Garnio, *The Mexican Immigrant: His Life Story* (Chicago, 1931), p. 15; Ernesto Galarza, *Barrio Boy: The Story of a Boy's Acculturation* (Notre Dame, Ind., 1986), p. 200.

10. Lawrence J. McCaffrey, *The Irish Diaspora in America* (Washington, D.C., 1984), pp. 6, 62.

11. John Murray Cuddihy, *The Ordeal of Civility: Freud, Marx, Levi Strauss, and the Jewish Struggle with Modernity* (Boston, 1987), p. 165; Jonathan Kaufman, *Broken Alliance: The Turbulent Times between Blacks and Jews in America* (New York, 1989), pp. 28, 82, 83–84, 91, 93, 106.

12. Andrew Jackson, First Annual Message to Congress, December 8, 1829, in James D. Richardson (ed.), *A Compilation of the Messages and Papers of the Presidents, 1789–1897* (Washington, D.C., 1897), vol. 2, p. 457; Frederick Jackson Turner, "The Significance of the Frontier in American History," in *The Early Writings of Frederick Jackson Turner* (Madison, Wis., 1938), pp. 185ff.; Luther Standing Bear, "What the Indian Means to America," in

Wayne Moquin (ed.), *Great Documents in American Indian History* (New York, 1973), p. 307; Vine Deloria, Jr., *Custer Died for Your Sins: An Indian Manifesto* (New York, 1969).

13. Nathan Glazer, *Affirmative Discrimination: Ethnic Inequality and Public Policy* (New York, 1978); Thomas Sowell, *Ethnic America: A History* (New York, 1981); David R. Roediger, *The Wages of Whiteness: Race and the Making of the American Working Class* (London, 1991), pp. 134–136; Dan Caldwell, "The Negroization of the Chinese Stereotype in California," *Southern California Quarterly,* vol. 33 (June 1971), pp. 123–131.

14. Thomas Almaguer, "Racial Domination and Class Conflict in Capitalist Agriculture: The Oxnard Sugar Beet Workers' Strike of 1903," *Labor History,* vol. 25, no. 3 (summer 1984), p. 347; Howard M. Sachar, *A History of the Jews in America* (New York, 1992), p. 183.

15. For the concept of liminality, see Victor Turner, *Dramas, Fields, and Metaphors: Symbolic Action in Human Society* (Ithaca, N.Y., 1974), pp. 232, 237; and Arnold Van Gennep, *The Rites of Passage* (Chicago, 1960). What I try to do is to apply liminality to the land called America.

16. Kazuo Ito, *Issei: A History of Japanese Immigrants in North America* (Seattle, 1973), p. 33; Arnold Schrier, *Ireland and the American Emigration, 1850–1900* (New York, 1970), p. 24; Abraham Cahan, *The Rise of David Levinsky* (New York, 1960; originally published in 1917), pp. 59–61; Mary Antin, quoted in Howe, *World of Our Fathers* (New York, 1983), p. 27; Lawrence A. Cardoso, *Mexican Emigration to the United States, 1897–1931* (Tucson, Ariz., 1981), p. 80.

17. Ronald Takaki, *Strangers from a Different Shore: A History of Asian Americans* (Boston, 1989), pp. 88–89; Jack Weatherford, *Native Roots: How the Indians Enriched America* (New York, 1991), pp. 210, 212; Carey McWilliams, *North from Mexico: The Spanish-Speaking People of the United States* (New York, 1968), p. 154; Stephan Themstrom (ed.), *Harvard Encyclopedia of American Ethnic Groups* (Cambridge, Mass., 1980), p. 22; Sachar, *A History of the Jews in America,* p. 367.

18. Weber (ed.), *Foreigners in Their Native Land,* p. vi; Hamilton Holt (ed.), *The Life Stories of Undistinguished Americans as Told by Themselves* (New York, 1906), p. 143.

19. "Social Document of Pany Lowe, interviewed by C. H. Burnett, Seattle, July 5, 1924," p. 6, Survey of Race Relations, Stanford University, Hoover Institution Archives; Minnie Miller, "Autobiography," private manuscript, copy from Richard Balkin; Tomo Shoji, presentation, Obana Cultural Center, Oakland, California, March 4, 1988.

20. Sandra Cisneros, *The House on Mango Street* (New York, 1991), pp. 109–110; Leslie Marmon Silko, *Ceremony* (New York, 1978), p. 2; Harriet A. Jacobs, *Incidents in the Life of a Slave Girl, written by herself* (Cambridge, Mass., 1987; originally published in 1857), p. xiii.

21. Carlos Fuentes, *The Buried Mirror: Reflections on Spain and the New World* (Boston, 1992), pp. 10, 11, 109; Barbara W. Tuchman, *A Distant Mirror: The Calamitous 14th Century* (New York, 1978), pp. xiii, xiv.

22. Adrienne Rich, *Blood, Bread, and Poetry: Selected Prose, 1979–1985* (New York, 1986), p. 199.

23. Ishmael Reed, "America: The Multinational Society," in Rick Simonson and Scott Walker (eds.), *Multi-cultural Literacy* (St. Paul, 1988), p. 160; Ito, *Issei,* p. 497.

24. Arthur M. Schlesinger, Jr., *The Disuniting of America: Reflections on a Multicultural Society* (Knoxville, Tenn., 1991); Carlos Bulosan, *America Is in the Heart: A Personal History* (Seattle, 1981), pp. 188–189.

Credits

Henry Louis Gates, Jr., "Thirteen Ways of Looking at a Black Man," *The New Yorker,* October 23, 1995. Reprinted by permission of the author.

Shelby Steele, "I'm Black, You're White, Who's Innocent?" *The Content of Our Character* (New York, NY: St. Martin's Press, Inc., 1990). Copyright © by Shelby Steele.

Paul M. Sniderman and Thomas Piazza, *The Scar of Race* (Cambridge: Harvard University Press, 1993). Copyright © 1993 by the President and Fellows of Harvard University. Reprinted by permission.

Orlando Patterson, "The Paradox of Integration: Why Blacks and Whites Seem So Divided," *The New Republic,* November 6, 1995. Copyright © Orlando Patterson. Reprinted by permission of the author.

Glenn C. Loury, "One Man's March," *The New Republic,* November 6, 1995. Copyright © Glenn C. Loury. Reprinted by permission.

Clarence Thomas's speech, "Victims and Heroes in the Benevolent State" was delivered to the Federalist Society's "Group Rights, Victim Status, and the Law" conference on September 22, 1995. Reprinted by permission.

Derrick Bell, "The Right to Decolonize Black Minds," selected excerpt from *And We Are Not Saved* by Derrick Bell, pp. 215–223. Copyright © 1987 by Basic Books, Inc. Reprinted by permission of Basic Books, a division of HarperCollins Publishers, Inc.

Patricia J. Williams, "Clarence X," from *The Rooster's Egg* by Patricia Williams. Copyright © 1995 by the President and Fellows of Harvard College. Reprinted by permission of Harvard University Press.

Debra Dickerson, "Who Shot Johnny?" *The New Republic,* January 1, 1996. Reprinted by permission.

William Tucker, "All in the Family: Illegitimacy and Welfare Dependence," *National Review,* March 6, 1995. Copyright © 1995 by *National Review,* Inc., 150 East 35th Street, New York, NY 10016. Reprinted by permission.

William Julius Wilson, "The Truly Disadvantaged," from William Julius Wilson, *The Truly Disadvantaged* (Chicago: The University of Chicago Press, 1987). Copyright © 1987 by The University of Chicago.

Peter Shaw, "Counting Asians," *National Review,* September 25, 1995. Copyright © 1995 by *National Review,* Inc., 150 East 35th Street, New York, NY 10016. Reprinted by permission.

Douglas S. Massey and Nancy A. Denton, "American Apartheid: The Perpetuation of the Underclass," from *American Apartheid* by D. Massey and N. Denton. Copyright © 1993 by the President and Fellows of Harvard College. Reprinted by permission of Harvard University Press.

W.E.B. Du Bois, *The Souls of Black Folk,* from *W.E.B. Du Bois: Writings,* ed. Nathan Huggins (New York: The Library of America, 1986).

About the Book and Editors

Three recent and dramatic national events have shattered the complacency of many people about progress, however fitful, in race relations in America. The Clarence Thomas–Anita Hill hearings, the O. J. Simpson trial, and the Million Man March of Louis Farrakhan have forced reconsideration of their assumptions about race and racial relations.

The Thomas-Hill hearings exposed the complexity and volatility of perceptions about race and gender. The sight of jubilant blacks and despondent whites reacting to the O. J. Simpson verdict shook our confidence in shared assumptions about equal protection under the law. The image of hundreds of thousands of black men gathering in Washington in defense of their racial and cultural identity angered millions of whites and exposed divisions within the black community.

These events were unfolding at a time when there seemed to be considerable progress in fighting racial discrimination. On the legal side, discrimination has been eliminated in more and more arenas, in theory if not always in practice. Economically, more and more blacks have moved into the middle class, albeit while larger numbers have slipped further back into poverty. Intellectually, figures like Cornel West, Henry Louis Gates, Jr., and Patricia J. Williams are playing a central role as public intellectuals.

In the face of these disparate trends, it is clear that Americans need to rethink their assumptions about race, racial relations, and inter-racial communication. *Color•Class•Identity* is the ideal tool to facilitate this process. It provides a richly textured selection of readings from Du Bois, Cornel West, Derrick Bell, and others as well as a range of responses to the particular controversies that are now dividing us.

Color•Class•Identity furthers these debates, showing that the racial question is far more complex than it used to be; it is no longer a simple matter of black versus white and racial mistrust. A landmark anthology that will help advance understanding of the present unease, not just between black and white, but within each community, this book will be useful in a broad range of courses on contemporary U.S. society.

John Arthur studied at Cornell College, Vanderbilt University, and Fisk University, receiving a Ph.D. in philosophy from Vanderbilt in 1973 and an M.A. in sociology in 1976. He taught philosophy at historically black Tennessee State University and is now professor of philosophy and Director of the program in Philosophy, Politics, and Law at the State University of New York at Binghamton. He has published articles and book reviews in ethics, philosophy of law, and political philosophy and is author of two books: *The Unfinished Constitution* (1989) and *Words that Bind: Judicial Review and the Grounds of Modern Constitutional Theory* (1995). He is also editor or coeditor of seven books, including *Morality and Moral Controversies* (4th edition, 1996), *Justice and Economic Distribution* (2nd edition, 1991) and *Readings in Philosophy of Law* (2nd edition, 1993). In 1992 he was awarded the SUNY Chancellor's and University President's awards for excellence in teaching.

Amy Shapiro graduated from Pomona College and Harvard Law School. She has worked as a reporter in Latin America and a columnist for the *Rocky Mountain News* in Denver, Colorado, and taught legal history at the State University of New York at Binghamton. In addition to articles in *Harvard Women's Law Journal* and *Glamour Magazine,* she wrote *A Guide to the Jewish Rockies* (1979) and coedited *Campus Wars: Multiculturalism and the Politics of Difference* (1995). A former consumer fraud litigator with the Federal Trade Commission in Washington, D.C., she now practices law in Binghamton, New York.

About the Contributors

Derrick Bell, a scholar in residence at New York University Law School, is author of *Race, Racism, and American Law, And We Are Not Saved,* and *Faces at the Bottom of the Well* as well as numerous scholarly articles.

Nancy A. Denton is assistant professor of sociology at the State University of New York at Albany.

Debra Dickerson is a lawyer in Washington, D.C.

William Edward Burghardt Du Bois, 1868–1963, earned a Ph.D. from Harvard University and taught economics and history at Atlanta University. He is perhaps best known for his early insistence that African-Americans achieve full economic, political, and civil equality and for his support of Pan Africanism. He edited the influential NAACP magazine, *Crisis,* from 1910 to 1934. His books include *The Souls of Black Folk* (1903), *Black Reconstruction in America* (1935), *Color and Democracy* (1945), and *The World and Africa* (1947).

Henry Louis Gates, Jr., is the W.E.B. Du Bois Professor of English and chair of the department of Afro-American Studies at Harvard University. He writes for numerous publications, both scholarly and popular, and is author of several books including *The Signifying Monkey,* winner of the American Book Award.

Glenn C. Loury, professor of economics at Boston University, is author of works including *One by One from the Inside Out: Race and Responsibility in America.*

Douglas S. Massey is professor of sociology at the University of Chicago and Harris School of Public Policy Studies.

Orlando Patterson is John Cowles Professor of Sociology at Harvard University and author of *Slavery and Social Death: A Comparative Study, Freedom 1,* and *Sociology of Slavery.*

Thomas Piazza is research specialist and manager of technical services of the Survey Research Center at the University of California at Berkeley.

Arthur M. Schlesinger, Jr., teaches at the graduate school of the University Center of City University of New York. He has won two Pulitzer Prizes and is the author of many books, including *A Thousand Days: John F. Kennedy in the White House.*

Peter Shaw, who died in 1995, was a professor of English at the State University of New York at Stony Brook, author of *The War Against the Intellect: Recovering American Literature*, and a founding member and chair of the National Association of Scholars.

Laurie Shrage is professor of philosophy at California State Polytechnic University, Pomona. She is author of *Moral Dilemmas of Feminism: Prostitution, Adultery, and Abortion* (1994) as well as numerous professional articles.

Paul M. Sniderman is professor of Political Science at Stanford University. In addition to many other books, he is coauthor of *Reasoning and Choice: Explorations in Political Psychology*, which received the Woodrow Wilson Foundation award in 1992.

Shelby Steele is professor of English at San Jose State University. His work has appeared widely, including in *The New York Times Magazine*, and he won the National Magazine Award in 1989. He is author of *The Content of Our Character* along with many essays and articles.

Ronald T. Takaki helped establish the multicultural graduation requirement at the University of California, Berkeley, where he is professor of ethnic studies. His books include *Strangers from a Different Shore: A History of Asian Americans* and *A Different Mirror: A History of Multicultural America*.

Clarence Thomas was nominated Associate Justice of the United States Supreme Court in 1991 by President Bush and confirmed by a vote of 52–48 in the U.S. Senate. The second African-American to serve on the nation's highest court, he was previously chair of the Equal Employment Opportunity Commission and a federal appeals court judge.

Laurence Mordekhai Thomas is a professor of philosophy, political science, and Judaic studies at Syracuse University. He is author of *Vessels of Evil: American Slavery and the Holocaust* and *Living Morally: A Psychology of Moral Character*.

William Tucker is a writer in New York.

Cornel West, professor of Afro-American studies and the philosophy of religion at Harvard University, is author of *A Genealogy of Pragmatism, Keeping Faith,* and *Race Matters*.

Patricia J. Williams is professor of law at Columbia University and author of *The Alchemy of Race and Rights* and *The Rooster's Egg: On the Persistence of Prejudice*.

William Julius Wilson is professor of Afro-American studies at Harvard University. Winner of a MacArthur Fellowship, he is author of *Power, Racism, and Privilege* (1976) and *The Declining Significance of Race* (1980) along with other books and articles.

Louis Riel and the Creation of Modern Canada

A VOLUME IN THE RELIGIONS
OF THE AMERICAS SERIES

Series Editors: DAVÍD CARRASCO and CHARLES H. LONG

Also available in the University of New Mexico Press
Religions of the Americas Series:

Sacred Spaces and Religious Traditions in Oriente Cuba
by Jualynne E. Dodson

Louis Riel and the Creation of Modern Canada

Mythic Discourse and the Postcolonial State

Jennifer Reid

UNIVERSITY OF NEW MEXICO PRESS   ALBUQUERQUE

Printed in the United States of America

13   12   11   10   09   08   1   2   3   4   5   6

Library of Congress Cataloging-in-Publication Data

Reid, Jennifer, 1962–

Louis Riel and the creation of modern Canada : mythic discourse
and the postcolonial state / Jennifer Reid.

    p. cm. — (Religions of the Americas)

Includes bibliographical references and index.

ISBN 978-0-8263-4415-1 (cloth : alk. paper)

1. Riel, Louis, 1844–1885.

2. Red River Rebellion, 1869–1870.

3. Riel Rebellion, 1885.

4. Métis—Northwest, Canadian—History—19th century.

5. National characteristics, Canadian.

6. Canada—History.

7. Canada—Politics and government.

8. Nationalism—Canada.

9. Postcolonialism—Canada.

10. Canada—Folklore.

I. Title.

F1060.9.R53R45 2008

971.05´1—dc22

2008017952

Book design and type composition by Melissa Tandysh

Composed in 10.5/14 Minion Pro

Display type is Delphin LT Std

For Margaret and Kate

Contents

List of Maps

This series, Religions of the Americas: Passages, Rims, and Borders, is devoted to a study of the nature, meaning, and dynamics of religion within the context of transcultural situations. As Mary Louise Pratt put it, transcultural situations define contact zones; within these zones of contact, cultures meet, clash, and grapple. Such temporal/spatial zones reveal different modalities of religion and religious experience.

Jennifer Reid's book, *Louis Riel and the Creation of Modern Canada*, presents us with a complex and comprehensive description of the religious dynamics of a contact zone in Canada through the Metis, Louis Riel, and the ensuing response to his life and work. The intriguing novelty of her study lies in the fact that the protagonist, Louis Riel, is himself a Metis, a person of mixed French and aboriginal parentage. In seeking a legitimate place for a Metis presence in Canada, Riel set forth a pattern and paradigm that became the template for all the major subsequent attempts to order the many and various regional, Euro-American ethnics, Metis, and Aborigines, as well as the various economic interests into some kind of ordered Canadian entity.

Jennifer Reid portrays Louis Riel as a revolutionary and employs revolutionary theories and analyses in expressing the meaning of his life and work. Compared, however, to the "classic" revolutions of the modern period—the American, Haitian, Mexican, and Russian, Riel and his revolution appear as strange and radically unorthodox. She rightly compares "Riel's revolution" to those that took place in Europe in 1848 rather than those of the "classic" type. The violent aspect of his revolution is confined to what could be called a series of skirmishes between Riel and his followers with the official military arms of the Canadian government at Duck Lake in 1885. As a matter of fact, Riel and his followers were defeated and Riel was tried and hanged for his participation in this rebellion.

Through a careful delineation of Canadian cultural history, Jennifer Reid reveals how the "Riel revolution" emerges as a delayed reaction. The memory of Riel always evoked the problem of the nature and meaning of the legitimacy to the land for all those who presently inhabited it spaces. The discussion and discourses centered around Riel and his actions from 1885 to the present evoked and sustained the vision of another kind of "imagined community" for a Canadian nation.

By asking questions regarding the nature and meaning of religion within a "contact zone," Jennifer Reid shows in her work how an activist religious mystic, a virtual "musician of words," a mythmaker and astute diplomat provided the right tonality, suggested the specific kind of temporality and improvisations that seemed to be demanded in Canada for a new and different kind of democratic revolutionary order.

Acknowledgments

I wish to acknowledge a number of people who helped me to write this book. First, Robert Choquette who, as my doctoral advisor at the University of Ottawa in the early 1990s, encouraged me to pursue research on a figure who already appeared to have been subjected to all possible forms of scrutiny. My early work with Professor Choquette provided a foundation that would stay with me for more than a decade as I remained enchanted with Louis Riel. I must also thank Davíd Carrasco who, in 2001, pressed me to more fully pursue the questions that were being raised by my research, to address issues I had not previously considered and, ultimately, to write this book; and I am grateful to Charles H. Long for the many critical discussions we had as I researched and thought through this work over a number of years. I was also assisted by a number of people in the course of my research and wish to express my appreciation particularly to Elizabeth Marshall, Kristin McLaren, Moira Woolihan, Nancy Walters, Andrew Bryant, and Casey Koons. I am grateful, too, to Liz Frederic for her skillful work in creating maps for this book, based on a series of somewhat obscure references I provided; and to Dee Marie Freedman for offering me her wonderful photograph of Riel's statue. Finally, my thanks to Lisa Poirier for helping me to see things that were staring me in the face, and to Irene Reid for her help as we worked together on translation.

Chapter 1

Setting the Stage
The North-West to 1885

Since the time of his execution in 1885, Louis Riel has become increasingly imbedded in the Canadian cultural imagination. Riel's trial is the most celebrated in the country's history, making him Canada's "most famous traitor";[1] and in spite of the fact that neither the Red River uprising of 1869–70 nor the North-West Rebellion of 1885 involved substantial numbers of insurgents (seven hundred in 1869–70 and somewhere shy of four hundred in 1885), and neither event resulted in substantial fatalities (a handful in the first instance, and around ninety in the second), Canadian historians have generally agreed that the events surrounding both uprisings have deeply affected the country. In particular, questions concerning the moral, political, and cultural culpability of the individuals who were implicated in both events have remained passionate issues of debate to the present day.[2]

Louis Riel was born at the Red River Settlement (St. Boniface, Manitoba) on October 22, 1844. He was the oldest of eleven children born to Louis Riel Sr. and Julie Lagimonière, and he was Métis by virtue of the fact that his paternal grandmother was Chippewa.[3] Riel was raised in a deeply Roman Catholic home; he received his early education in Catholic school and at the age of fourteen was sent to a Sulpician college at Montreal to study for the priesthood. He withdrew from the college in 1866 when he learned of his father's death. Hoping to assist his mother who had been left with her husband's debt, he took a position as a law clerk in Montreal, before moving to Chicago and then to St. Paul, Minnesota, and finally back to St. Boniface in the summer of 1868. Within a short time, Riel emerged as a spokesman for the local Métis population, whose frustrations were mounting over Canadian mismanagement in annexing the territory. He would ultimately play a key role in two Métis uprisings against the Canadian government in 1869 at Red River and in 1885 along the South Saskatchewan River in what was then the North-West Territories.[4]

During the years between these events, Riel was exiled to the United States, and he was elected to the Canadian House of Commons three times (although he was never permitted to take his seat). He spent two periods in asylums at Longue Pointe and Beauport, Quebec, after which he settled among other Métis in the Montana Territory, marrying Marguerite Monet with whom he had three children (a boy who died immediately following his birth a few weeks before Riel was hanged; Marie-Angélique, who was born in 1883 and died at fourteen years old; and Jean-Louis, born a year before his sister and killed in a "buggy" accident in July of 1908 at the age of twenty-six).[5] It was during this period of exile that Riel began to have visions directing him to work toward creating a sovereign Métis nation in the North-West. In June of 1884, Riel was visited by a delegation representing disaffected Métis, English mixed-blood peoples, and English settlers in the Territories' District of Lorne (later the province of Saskatchewan), and he was persuaded to relocate with his family to the region. The uprising that transpired a year later was crushed by Canadian forces, and Riel was tried and hanged for treason in November of 1885.

The uprisings at Red River and in the North-West have been the subject of more books than any other in Canadian history; and more histories, biographies, novels, and poetry have been written about Riel than any other Canadian figure. Most intriguing, perhaps, is the fact that he is the only prominent figure whose writings have been published in their entirety: the one hundredth anniversary of Riel's execution was marked by the publication of *The Collected Writings of Louis Riel* (*Les écrits complets de Louis Riel*), a five-volume set produced cooperatively between the Canada Council and a number of universities.[6]

In addition, Riel has been the focus of radio dramas, plays, CBC television miniseries, even an opera; and statues have been erected in his honor on the grounds of the Manitoba and Saskatchewan legislatures. The statues provoked a particularly lively series of controversies among Canadians. The first of these statues was created by John Nugent for the grounds of the Saskatchewan legislature in 1968. In a ceremony that figured the prime

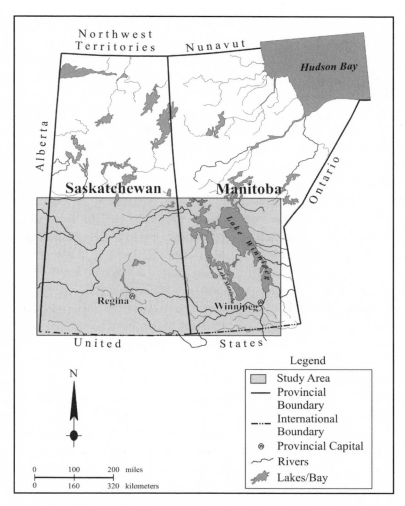

MAP 1. *Study Area for Military Conflicts of 1869 and 1885.*
CREDIT: LIZ FREDERIC.

minister, Pierre Trudeau, the virtually naked representation of Riel, right arm raised, genitals clearly visible, and neck angled upward as in prayer was presented to a public that was relatively unanimous in its displeasure for the piece. Saskatchewan's Métis population was particularly appalled by the statue, and its leaders quickly began lobbying for its removal from the grounds of the legislature, arguing that it was an "inaccurate" portrayal and "demoralizing for Métis people." The statue was finally removed by the provincial government in 1991 and relocated to the MacKenzie Art Gallery where it is still housed, though not in public view.

The second statue, created by Marcien Lemay and Étienne Gaboury, was commissioned by the Manitoba government to be displayed at the back of the legislature. Public reception for the piece, unveiled in 1971, was similar to that which accompanied the Nugent sculpture three years earlier. The naked and tormented Riel, placed between two towering pillars of concrete, drew immediate censure from politicians as well as the Manitoba Métis Federation, which regarded the piece, as Angus Spence (past president of the MMF) said, to be "undignified" and an "incongruous monstrosity." The monument was removed from the grounds of the legislature in 1994, and erected in an obscure location at the Collège universitaire de Saint-Boniface. In addition, the federal and provincial legislatures together contributed $150,000 toward the creation of another statue. The third sculpture, commissioned from Miguel Joyal, was unveiled at the Manitoba legislature in 1996, and generally met with public approval although, as one critic pointedly remarked, this monument appeared "just as boring and constipated as the other statues that dot the grounds." This Riel was fully clothed with a bow tie beneath his overcoat, and wearing moccasins, an image that seemed more acceptable to a public largely prepared to regard the man as a founder of Manitoba.[7]

Recognition of both Riel's role as the founder of Manitoba and his significance within the broader federal project have in recent decades gained increasing attention, and many Canadians have come to support former Prime Minister Joe Clark's call for formal acknowledgment of Riel's "unique and historic role . . . as a founder of Manitoba and his contribution in the development of Confederation."[8] Many, however, are inclined to go further, arguing that he should be recognized as a Father of Confederation.[9] Beginning in the early 1980s, federal members of parliament representing the Liberal, Conservative, Bloc Québécois, and New Democratic Parties variously tabled motions to have Riel either pardoned or recognized as a Father of Confederation, claiming, as Suzanne Tremblay did when she moved a second reading of Bill C-297 in 1996, that "[w]e are not asking that history be rewritten. What is done is done, and Riel is dead. But the memory of Louis Riel is alive and, for that reason, he must be cleared."[10]

Riel's public persona has undergone a radical transformation among Anglophones since the late nineteenth century when he was the object of intense criticism, branded an "egotist" and "coward," a "self-seeking adventurer," and a "mad messiah."[11] By the latter part of the twentieth century, he had undeniably become something of a popular hero: the Riel family home near Winnipeg, Manitoba, is now a national historical park.[12] In addition, discussions have transpired in the federal parliament regarding both official recognition of Riel as a "Canadian hero" and the designation of May 12 as "Louis Riel Day";[13] in 2007, the Manitoba government voted to recognize the third Monday of February as Louis Riel Day. More significant, perhaps, is the fact that Riel has been cast not only as a Canadian hero but as a mythic figure who has been the catalyst for a literature that is equally mythic in character.[14] It is Riel as both man and myth, and the legendary uprisings he led in 1869–70 and 1885, that are the focus of this study. It is also, more particularly, their relationship to the issue of Canadian identity and to nationalist discourses that will be considered in this book. In spite of the fact that Riel and the uprisings have been invoked to variously support a number of such discourses, I will suggest that both the myths and the man point to the profound inadequacy of the concepts of *nationalism* and the *nation* in the Canadian situation.

Beginning a study of myth and history requires a point of entry that is, in some measure, quite arbitrary. One might, for instance, assume a psychological vantage point, identifying the origin of a collective mythos within the psychic formation of a particular people or of humans generally. An equally valid point of departure might be within the political life of a state—in this case, one whose parliamentary debates on affording an official pardon to a geographically peripheral, French-speaking rebel are undeniably located within a long-standing tradition of political discourse enmeshed in dichotomies of region and ethnicity. Although both these perspectives are undeniably implicated in this book, as a historian of religion, however, my interest lies in the intersection of life in time and space with the human propensity for forms of self-understanding not fully bound by conventional notions of time and space: the spaces, in other words, in which human beings express the meaning of their existence in religious, or ultimate, terms. This, then, is my starting point: the mythicization of both Riel and the rebellions that have betrayed a desire on the part of many Canadians to locate a source of collective identity in a figure and an event that are not only historical, but profoundly symbolic and enmeshed in consciously religious language.

To contextualize this collective process of mythicization and its relationship to the modern political entity called Canada, I will begin with a brief overview of the Métis uprisings and the specific arena in which they transpired: the historically contested colonial space that would ultimately become the Canadian West, and that would provide the context for Riel's religious life and the rebellions, events in relation to which a good deal of Canadian mythic imagination has since expressed itself. Having first mapped out the territory within which the rebellions occurred, I will then turn to their collective mythic reverberations and the relationship between these reverberations and the perennially slippery issue of Canadian identity that has been a recurrent concern and that has often been related to the construction of nationalist discourses. These have included an Anglo-Saxon nationalism dating from the Confederation period, which was distinguished by a marked desire on the part of Anglophones to impose upon the newly formed state an Anglo-Protestant character; French Canadian nationalism, located primarily in the province of Quebec; First Nations and Métis nationalisms; and a variety of metropolis-hinterland nationalist discourses and formulations of identity ranging from geographical and technological nationalisms to a more pervasive anti-Americanism stemming from nineteenth-century annexationist fears and twentieth-century concerns about cultural domination. The tendency to equate the issue of identity with broad nationalist aspirations has been a deeply rooted miscalculation in the Canadian situation, and one that I believe can be addressed constructively through an analysis of the relationship between geopolitical identity and the mythicization of Riel. In the course of this exploration, I hope to provide a framework for rethinking the geopolitical significance of the modern Canadian state, for considering a *confederation* as a postcolonial alternative to the normative model of the modern *nation-state*, and, finally, to provide a narrative space in which the voice of Louis Riel will be invited to speak to these issues.

Within this framework, I hope also to draw attention to the broader significance of hybridity in postcolonial states, to consider the historical implications of what is perhaps more conventionally referred to as creolization (what will be called *métissage* in this context), and the forces that have too often sought to conceal the cultural meaning of hybridity within conceptual dichotomies and practices of exclusion. This *dynamic of concealment* has ultimately served to mask much of the violence that has been implicated in the process of state creation in the postcolonial West, especially in the Americas. At the level of discourse, this dynamic has revolved around what the historian of religion Charles Long has described as a disregard for "the actual relationships and entanglements of cultures that took place during the imperial and colonial ventures" of the modern period, a stylistic that has too often obscured "the gross realities of economic exploitation, tyrannical practices, terrorization, and enslavements."[15] In the United States, for instance, the discursive—and dichotomous—formulation of the nation as "white" has concealed the foundational meaning of slavery and conquest. As we will see, the dichotomy of color has undoubtedly figured also in conceptions of Canada, particularly in terms of a long-held view of the state as a northern European outpost. This concealment has been imbedded in the discursive, political, and economic history of the country. It has reared its head, for example, in the establishment of segregated schools for blacks in nineteenth-century Canada West (later the province of Ontario).[16] We have seen it at work again in the twentieth-century residential school system (administered jointly by the federal government and the churches) that was intended to assimilate First Nations peoples into the dominant cultural fabric of the descendants of Europeans; and again, at the opening of the twenty-first century, it clearly played a role in the Maher Arar case, in which a Canadian-Syrian citizen was deported to Syria by U.S. authorities who were acting on erroneous information supplied by the Royal Canadian Mounted Police, linking Arar to al-Qaeda (Arar spent a year undergoing torture in a Syrian prison).[17]

In spite of this, however, a deeply rooted antipathy between Francophone and Anglophone Canadians has ultimately precluded the emergence of a unified color-coded discourse about identity-in-place similar to that which developed in the United States. Broader contested issues relating to ethnicity (bound to language, religion, and economics) commanded the attention of Canadian colonials and forced them into a multiplistic mode of self-representation from the time of the British Conquest of Quebec in 1759, a contested discourse based on what would become one of a number of particularly Canadian dichotomies (e.g., English/French, Aboriginal/non-Aboriginal, east/west) that would hamper the emergence of a unified national narrative. These dichotomies will be considered more fully in later chapters, especially with respect to the ways in which they have concealed certain complexities that define the Canadian situation, while contributing to cultural fragmentation, ethnic oppression, competing nationalisms, separatism, and outbreaks of violence. They will also be examined in relation to Louis Riel, a man who was profoundly enmeshed in the tenuous—often tortuous—space between the dichotomies, and who experienced visions and revelations concerning ethnic, regional, and economic injustices on which the Dominion of Canada was being constructed. Revelation, of course, is the opposite of concealment; and Riel as the recipient of revelation went on to assume the role of revealer: he was a man who called an emerging state to recognize the defining meaning of plurality at its foundation.

This is not to suggest that Riel is an anomaly in this respect. He is one among countless voices who have ceaselessly called for an end to the concealment of the condition of multiplicity that undergirds the formation of the Americas, and the violence that has been its correlate. We can hear the revelation, for instance, in the tradition of "sorrow songs" among African Americans, through which, wrote W. E. B. Du Bois,

> breathes a hope—a faith in the ultimate justice of things. The minor cadences of despair change often to triumph and calm confidence. Sometimes it is a faith in life, sometimes a faith in death, sometimes assurance of boundless justice in some fair world beyond. But whichever it is, the meaning is always clear: that sometime, somewhere, men will judge men by their souls and not by their skins.[18]

Still, while Riel's is not an isolated revelation, he himself is something of an oddity. Rarely in the Americas has a dissenting voice from a marginalized and oppressed community come to occupy a position of such cultural prominence. The story of his rise to mythic hero is the object of this study in which the reverberations of his revelation will be traced and, I hope, revisited in a new and constructive fashion.

This book will not be a religious analysis of Louis Riel himself. This kind of analysis has been undertaken by a number of scholars (notably Thomas Flanagan and Gilles Martel) who have consciously veered away from previous interpretations that regarded the man's visions and writing as indicative of insanity.[19] Choosing instead to focus on his psychological development, these scholars have interpreted Riel's religion in relation to third world millenarian movements; and as such, their work has represented a distinct shift in interpretive approach.[20] Neither will this book be a history of Canada, in spite of its focus on the way in which a collective historical narrative might be reconfigured and the issue of Canadian identity reconsidered. It begins in the figure of Louis Riel and the rebellions of 1869–70 and 1885, and moves out from this preliminary vantage point along a variety of paths, but it does not explore more than a few avenues.

My hope is that it will provide a template for considering other aspects of the country's history and collective self-image and for creating a discourse that does justice to the complexities, anomalies, and creative possibilities of both of these.

The North-West to 1870

Within a year of the confederation of Ontario, Quebec, Nova Scotia, and New Brunswick under the banner of the Dominion of Canada in 1867, discussions concerning the acquisition of Hudson's Bay Company territories (Rupert's Land and the North-West) were initiated in the House of Commons in Ottawa; and negotiations were undertaken with the British Colonial Office.[21] The terms of confederation (set out in the British North America [BNA] Act) contained provisions for the entry of the territories into the Dominion; and in July of 1868, the British Parliament passed the Rupert's Land Act, which provided for the transfer of the territory to the Crown and, within a month, from the Crown to Canada. The initial date for transfer was set for October 1, 1869, but was subsequently postponed to December 1. The acquisition would more than double the size of the country and set the stage within a year for the entry of British Columbia into the Confederation, on the assurance that the federal government would finance the construction of a transcontinental railway.

An overzealous Canadian government immediately set about drafting legislation to provide for the governance of the newly acquired territories and passed the Act for the Temporary Government of Rupert's Land, which specified that the territory would be governed by a lieutenant governor and a council of between seven and fifteen members, and that residual Hudson's Bay Company laws that were compatible with the BNA Act would remain in force. William McDougall was selected for the office of lieutenant governor.[22] Around the time that these negotiations were transpiring, a twenty-four-year-old Louis Riel returned to Red River from Montreal where he had been studying for the priesthood.[23] He quickly assumed an active political role at Red River, where the impending Canadian annexation had created concerns among residents of the area.[24] The population of Red River was not informed concerning Ottawa's plans for assuming control of the territory and learned of the appointment of William McDougall through the press. McDougall was dispatched to the territory before the British Crown had released an order in council necessary for the territory's entrance into Canada; and, without consultation with the residents, government surveyors began simultaneously surveying the area at Red River along a grid system that ran counter to the water frontage arrangement that already existed in the area. These preexisting lots were principally occupied by Métis settlers who were not consulted as the surveys were undertaken.

The first major clash of the Métis and the Canadian government occurred on October 11, 1869, when a team of government surveyors was met by a group of Métis at St. Vital who obstructed the surveyors' movement and forced them to withdraw. The disregard of Métis land holdings in the region resulted not only in the confrontation at St. Vital but the creation of the Comité National des Métis (with Louis Riel as secretary and John Bruce as president) that, by the end of October, had coordinated a Métis response resulting in the construction of a blockade at St. Norbert and the expulsion of a delegation including the new lieutenant governor. Ambroise Lépine was given command of the resistance, and within two days had forced McDougall to retreat over the U.S. border along with the rest of the government party. Once Lépine had successfully repelled McDougall from the region, Riel and his associates took control of the printing press of the *Nor'Wester*, obstructed the mail in the region, and established a provisional government at Upper Fort Garry (which had been the Hudson's Bay Company's principal storehouse) with the intention of entering into negotiations with the federal government concerning the territory's terms of entry into the Confederation as a province.[25]

Throughout January and February of 1870, negotiations relating to the proposed status of the Red River Settlement were carried on at Upper Fort Garry, pitting Louis Riel against Donald Smith, one of the Hudson's Bay Company's major shareholders who had been appointed by the federal government to resolve the standoff. An ineffective force under the command of Captain Charles Boulton arrived in February from Portage la Prairie with the intention of taking Fort Garry, but he quickly retreated when faced with a group of Métis soldiers under the direction of Ambroise Lépine and William O'Donoghue. The contingent apprehended Boulton and his men, among whom was a man by the name of Thomas Scott. Boulton was tried and received a death sentence that was subsequently commuted; but Scott, who was also sentenced to death, was executed on March 4, a move that Riel believed would compel the Canadian government into authentic negotiations. Scott was charged with "insubordination and armed revolt," and his trial was presided over by Lépine. Along with Riel, Lépine and O'Donoghue were later charged in connection with the death of Scott.[26]

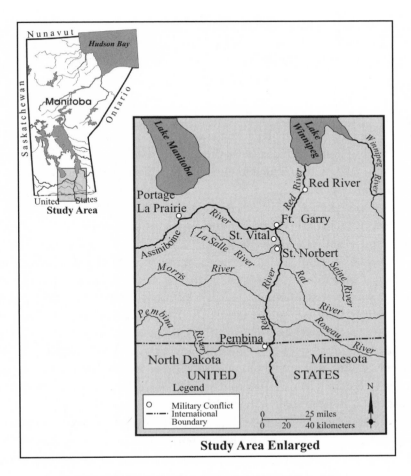

Study Area Enlarged

MAP 2. *Military Conflicts in the Red River Valley, 1869.*
CREDIT: LIZ FREDERIC.

On April 11, 1870, a Red River delegation composed of John Black (a judge at Red River), Alfred Scott (an English supporter of the Métis from Winnipeg), and Noël-Joseph Ritchot (a Roman Catholic priest who was also a supporter) arrived in Ottawa to negotiate with the federal government over the terms of the territory's entry into the Confederation. By the Manitoba Act, which was passed on May 12, the Métis were to defer political control of the new province of Manitoba to the federal government and to concede control of land and resources in exchange for 1.4 million acres of land. According to Section 31 of the act, whereas, it is expedient, towards the extinguishment of the Indian Title to the lands in the Province, to appropriate a portion of such ungranted lands, to the extent of one million four hundred thousand acres thereof, for the benefit of the families of the half-breed residents.[27]

In addition to the Métis land base, which was to be established via a system of land grants to individuals, the Manitoba Act provided for the entry of Manitoba into the Confederation with provincial status, senate and parliamentary representation, and both English and French language rights. Ritchot and his associates were also led to believe that Riel would receive an amnesty for his role in the military resistance to Ottawa's premature attempt to extend its authority in the territory.[28]

Riel's leadership at Red River was unquestionable by the summer of 1870, and he no doubt fully expected to assume a prominent political role in the province of Manitoba that was officially created on July 15. Riel, however, had not anticipated the extent to which the execution of Thomas Scott would infuriate English Canadians. Rather than assuming a position as a federal member of parliament, Riel was forced into exile because his promised amnesty became too politically explosive for the federal government to sanction. As a result, and in spite of the best efforts of the local Roman Catholic bishop (Alexandre-Antonin Taché), Riel, Lépine, and O'Donoghue became fugitives. Lépine was arrested on September 16, 1874, and charged in connection with the murder of Scott. Riel was formally charged at the same time.[29] A month later, Lépine was tried for the murder, convicted, and sentenced to death; but the sentence was commuted by the governor general, Lord Dufferin, and Lépine was sentenced instead to two years in prison and permanent loss of civil rights. An amnesty was finally offered to the two men in April of 1875 on the condition that each agreed to remain outside Canada for five years. Riel accepted the condition, but Lépine chose to serve the remainder of his sentence in lieu of banishment.

It was while living in exile in the United States that Riel began having religious visions; and on December 18, 1874, while visiting a friend in Washington, D.C., he received the first of these. He later wrote of the experience, describing the genesis of his sense of mission in respect to fighting for the rights of the Métis people:

While I was seated on the top of a mountain near Washington . . . the same spirit who showed himself to Moses in the midst of the burning cloud appeared to me in the same manner. I was stupefied. I was confused. He said to me, "Rise up, Louis David Riel, you have a mission to fulfil [*sic*]." Stretching out my arms and bowing my head, I received this heavenly message.[30]

Shortly after this first mystical experience, Riel experienced another vision in which the Virgin Mary appeared to him, standing over his desk. She would appear to him again at a later date, this time with a child. By mid-December, Riel had been taken to Worcestershire, Massachusetts, by his friend Edmund Mallet, who believed Riel was suffering from mental instability.[31] Riel would spend two separate periods in asylums at Longue Point and Beauport, Quebec, before returning to Montana where he focused his attention on improving the conditions of life for the local Métis.

In the spring of 1883, a few weeks after Riel's five-year banishment from Canada had concluded, he decided to seek naturalization as an American. Two years later, at his trial before a Canadian court on charges of high treason, he would explain this symbolic decision:

Did I take my American paper, put my papers of American naturalization during my five years' banishment? No, I did not want to give the States a citizen of banishment, but when my banishment had expired, when an officer at Battleford—somewhere on this side of the line, in Benton—invited me to come to the North-West I said: No, I will go to an American court, I will declare my intention, now that I am free to go back, and choose another land. It sored my heart . . . but I felt that in coming back to [Canada] I could not reenter it without protesting against all the injustice which I had been suffering, and in doing it I was renewing a struggle which I had not been able to continue as a sound man, as I thought I was, I thought it better to begin a career on the other side of the line.[32]

Riel became a naturalized American on March 16, 1883, at a Montana district court; his adopted name "David" was used in the ceremony. Shortly thereafter, Riel assumed his first paid position as a teacher at the Jesuit-run St. Peter's Mission, situated on the Sun River.[33]

The agreement that had been reached between the Métis and the federal government in 1870 had not guaranteed the protection of Native and Métis land rights as had been expected, and in the wake of the granting of provincial status to Manitoba, many Métis were forced to migrate westward into the Saskatchewan Valley. Their relocation was also spurred by railway construction, which brought inevitable demographic changes to Manitoba. After 1870, three-quarters of the Métis who moved into the south Saskatchewan area in search of land and employment came from Red River, and most of these had been supporters of the resistance of 1869–70. The Prince Albert District proved attractive to the Métis due to the availability of both work with the Hudson's Bay Company and land along the south branch of the Saskatchewan River. In 1884, many of these migrants mobilized again to press for responsible government, provincial status, and protection of land rights for Natives, Métis, and Euro-Canadian settlers.[34]

Additionally, and in spite of an expressed commitment to the colonization of the North-West, Ottawa did not prove to be adequately supportive of settlers in the region. Administration of the territory and its resident population was left in the hands of Manitoba's lieutenant governor who took two years to appoint a council to assist him. The first council (composed principally of residents of Manitoba) was established in 1872, and it elicited immediate criticism, generating regional friction that would become a constant characteristic of east-west relations. The appointment of a governing council in the North-West did little to equalize the relationship between the territory and Ottawa. Although its members tended to be selected from both French and Anglo-Ontarian immigrants, very few were selected from the local population, and the council itself was denied any real executive power.[35]

The Canadian government also fueled the fires of discontent among the territory's Native population during the period. In its treaty negotiations with First Nations peoples, the government proved to be at least as alienating as it had been with its lack of direct consultation with the Métis of Manitoba. Difficulties in effecting treaties were inevitable, as the government resisted recognizing the rights of the resident Native population in order to expediently acquire title to land intended for eastern Canadian development. In the interest of avoiding these stumbling blocks in the North-West, the federal government negotiated four treaties (Treaties Four through Seven) with bands in the region who acquiesced to the pressure of negotiators. Bands were promised parcels of land, educational and medical facilities, support for the transition to an agrarian life-style (through training, equipment, and domestic animals), financial allowances, legal protection, and assistance during periods of food shortage. In exchange, they were expected to relinquish their Aboriginal claim to the land.[36]

By the 1880s, all sectors of the North-West had serious objections to the way in which the Canadian government was dealing with them, but Native peoples of the territory were in a particularly precarious position. Because the buffalo had virtually disappeared by the early 1870s due to overhunting by nonnatives, First Nations peoples had lost a basic mode of subsistence. Additionally, epidemic disease and a lack of agricultural knowledge placed an unbearable strain on communities, and Alexander Mackenzie's government refused to provide the kind of financial assistance that was necessary to ameliorate the situation. As increasing numbers of Native peoples faced starvation and death, most had few options but to acquiesce to signing treaties.

In January of 1883, a group of Cree leaders (Bobtail, Ermine Skin, Samson, and others) drafted a petition to the federal government in which they described the dire situation in which they had come to find themselves and requested that it be rectified on the basis of Ottawa's treaty obligations:

> Nothing but our dire poverty, our utter destitution during this severe winter, when ourselves, our wives and our children are smarting under the pangs of cold and hunger, with little or no help, and apparently less sympathy from those placed to watch over us, could have induced us to make this final attempt to have redress directly from headquarters. We say final because, if no attention is paid to our case we shall conclude that the treaty made with us six years ago was a meaningless matter of form and that the white man has indirectly doomed us to annihilation little by little.... Shall we still be refused, and be compelled to adhere to the conclusion spoken of in the beginning of this letter, that the treaty is a farce enacted to kill us quietly, and if so, let us die at once?[37]

During the winter of 1884, the Department of Indian Affairs, under the advice of Deputy Minister Lawrence Vankoughnet, decided to reduce the rations provided to Big Bear's band because it had yet to sign Treaty Six. While working as a freighter between Fort Pitt and Edmonton that winter,

Big Bear had occasion to speak with Pakan (who was chief of the Cree band at Whitefish Lake) and discovered that Pakan's band had also been similarly denied rations. Big Bear subsequently allied himself with Pakan and organized a thirst dance at Big Bear's Battleford Reserve in the spring, a gathering intended to draw together various Cree bands that had similar grievances against the Canadian government. The gathering, though well-intentioned, deteriorated into a conflict with the Mounted Police when a group of young men attacked a local farm instructor and were subsequently arrested. The confrontation was decisive in terms of Big Bear's leadership of his band, as his son Imasees, who was a principal figure in the affair, subsequently assumed his father's position of authority. By the winter of 1885, Big Bear had lost virtually all influence within his band, which was suffering extreme privation and had relocated itself to the peripheries of Frog Lake where a government storehouse of rations was located. The situation among Native peoples generally had reached crisis proportions early in 1885; nearly seven thousand starving Cree had gravitated to the North West Mounted Police (NWMP) post at Fort Walsh, and Native peoples throughout the North-West were suffering from extreme starvation. The federal government did virtually nothing to address the tensions that were steadily mounting within the Native community.[38]

Métis grievances against the Canadian government differed from those of the Native population, but were also substantial. As already noted, in the wake of the Manitoba Act, Macdonald's administration did nothing to confirm the land claims of existing settlers. Rather, for the tenure of the government, new immigration was actively promoted and the claims of new settlers were recognized rapidly. At the same time, Ottawa reassigned responsibility for managing untitled lands in the province to a government department whose principal charge was to assure that new settlers secured claims. A policy for distribution took more than two years to be put into effect, during which time land speculators were accumulating land around Winnipeg at a rapid pace (by 1872, forty thousand acres had been purchased). Weak annual agricultural yields and epidemics characterized the early 1870s, and all these factors together prompted many Métis to leave the province in search of unsettled land or buffalo in the North-West. These migrants settled largely in the Saskatchewan Valley, where the buffalo hunt would continue a few years longer than in Manitoba; and all arrived in the territory with preexisting grievances against the government in Ottawa. Many Métis who had remained in Manitoba, and who had received title to their land, chose in the late 1870s to sell their properties to immigrants and move westward also, settling in the Saskatchewan Valley at Batoche, Qu'Appelle, and Duck Lake. Like the region's Native population, and along with English mixed-blood peoples, this largely transplanted Métis community was deeply affected by the disappearance of the buffalo; and, like the resident Anglo-Canadian population, suffered because of crop failures of the early 1880s (although perhaps more so because the Métis lacked financial reserves to see them through). In addition to these issues, Métis and mixed-blood peoples were concerned over government plans to survey the area on a square system, a model that threatened to disregard entirely Métis land holdings that ran back from the Saskatchewan River in narrow strips. Their petitions for recognition of their grievances were ignored by the federal government.[39]

Preliminary efforts toward organizing disparate pools of dissatisfaction in the North-West were initiated by British and English Canadian farmers who, by the early 1880s, numbered a few thousand in the North Saskatchewan Valley.[40] In conjunction with the frustration escalating within Métis and Native communities, these settlers were expressing mounting irritation with the federal government's refusal to initiate a process by which the territory could be recognized as a province. In the spring of 1883, the Qu'Appelle Settlers' Rights Association passed a series of resolutions dealing with the issues of representation in Parliament, new and reformed legislation, and federal assistance for settlers. In December, over a hundred delegates converged at Winnipeg for a farmers' convention where the Manitoba and North West Farmers Co-operative and Protective Union was formed to lobby for government support. This was Canada's first organized, western agricultural association.

Newspapers in the region also began to voice the settlers' frustrations. Nicholas Flood Davin, editor of the *Regina Leader*, was one of the most outspoken, writing scathing condemnations of government policy in the North-West. Early in 1885, for instance, he asked, "Were they—*an immigration d'élite*—a select immigration—the flower of the old pioneers of Canada—to remain 'disestablished and disendowed,' and outside the pall of the Constitution?" The grievances of the Settlers' Union were presented to Parliament in March of 1884, but they were discussed only briefly. It is no surprise, then, that many began to think seriously about allying themselves with the dissatisfied Métis. On January 29, 1884, a meeting was organized at Halcro on the South Saskatchewan, during which a group of disgruntled settlers appointed a committee chaired by Andrew Spence to draw up a petition to the federal government outlining their grievances. At this time, William Jackson was asked to solicit the assistance of the local Métis in supporting the motions that had been passed at a number of previous meetings convened among English colonial and mixed-blood settlers.[41] He was introduced to Louis Riel in the summer of 1884.

When Riel returned to Canada that summer, all segments of the population of the North-West had serious grievances with the federal government based on frustrations that had been escalating over the previous decade; and when he subsequently undertook the leadership of the 1885 agitation, Riel assumed he had the support of all the settlers of the region. He had good reason for expecting their assistance. They had supported his decision to leave the United States and return to Canada; they had taken part in the meetings that led to the drafting of the petition of rights and had actively contributed to the writing of the document; and they had, finally, financially supported Riel once he assumed leadership of the movement.[42] In spite of the fact that the majority of those involved in the 1885 Rebellion were Métis, Native and settler dissatisfaction with the Dominion government played a decisive role in convincing Riel that an uprising would be successful.

An uprising, however, was not what Riel envisioned in 1884. In the midst of an increasingly tumultuous situation, Riel and his colleagues embarked on a course of action intended to force the federal government into negotiations (as had been done at Red River in 1869). Speaking publicly on July 9, Riel advocated an alliance of all disaffected groups in the area to negotiate with the federal government:

> I know that you are labouring under serious governmental difficulties. Were you to tolerate your situation without seeking true remedies, the state of your affairs would become worse and worse. And in a comparatively short time, it would become evident to the calculating observations of the Capitalists that your future is not taken care of. Allow me a suggestion. Instead of petitioning for your rights severally; instead of making a particular struggle for each of your rights, thereby wasting energy and wasting time, would it not be better to apply for them all in black.[43]

English mixed-blood and French Métis representatives from the area around Prince Albert, as well as Métis communities along the south branch of the Saskatchewan River, held meetings throughout the fall of 1884; and on December 16, they approved a petition of rights to be forwarded to the government in Ottawa. The petition of rights contained clauses that represented the grievances of all sectors of the North-West. The first article in the document referred directly to the need for increased rations for Native people; and, on the model of the Manitoba negotiations fifteen years earlier, the second demanded that Métis and mixed-blood peoples be allotted two hundred and forty acres of land each. Subsequent articles asserted the rights of established settlers (titled and untitled), protested the high price placed on additional land purchased by settlers after the establishment of homesteads, objected to inflated customs duties and the awarding of government contracts to interests outside of the North-West, proposed the creation of a commercial route by way of Hudson Bay, recommended elections by ballot, and proposed the creation of a number of provinces in the North-West with individual jurisdictions over natural resources and representation in the cabinet in Ottawa. Turning to the model of the 1870 negotiations with the federal government, the petitioners requested that representatives of the population of the territory be invited to Ottawa to present a bill of rights that would initiate negotiations relating to the entry of the North-West into the Confederation. It concluded with the declaration that the people of the North-West were "treated neither according to their privileges as British subjects nor according to the rights of people and that consequently as long as they are retained in those circumstances, they can be neither prosperous nor happy."[44]

The petition was forwarded to the secretary of state (J. A. Chapleau) with a cover letter written by Jackson; and the under secretary of state wrote to acknowledge its receipt. He subsequently forwarded the petition to Chapleau, John A. Macdonald, as the minister of the interior, and the Privy Council. This letter of acknowledgment, however, was the only correspondence Jackson would receive from the federal government; no formal response to the demands contained in the petition ever materialized. As a result, Riel created a provisional government early in 1885, with Jackson as its secretary. In spite of the fact that the letter was received at the office of the secretary of state, and forwarded to appropriate parties, Macdonald stood before Parliament in March of 1885 and informed the House that no such document had been "officially, or indeed in any way, promulgated so far as we know, and transmitted to the Government."[45] Furthermore, when the outbreak of violence at Fort Carleton occurred in March, and Macdonald was asked for details concerning it in the House of Commons, he claimed,

"The immediate cause of the rising is not known. . . . I do not believe there is the slightest danger of the Halfbreeds unless joined by the Indians. All our information goes to show that the Indians are quiet, that there is no danger of them joining the Halfbreeds."[46]

Rebellion had been the intention of neither Riel nor his colleagues in the provisional government. Gabriel Dumont (the general who led the Métis rebellion) later recalled that the agreement that had been negotiated with the federal government in 1870 was one that was essentially the result of the collaboration of two autonomous political bodies; and, in 1884, it was hoped generally that the relative lack of violence involved in reaching this 1869 accord could be repeated.[47] In a letter (later, an exhibit for the prosecution at Riel's trial) written to gain the support of the people of Prince Albert District, for instance, Riel argued: "If we are well united the police will surrender and come out of Carleton as the hen's heat causes the chicken to come out of the shell. A strong union between the French and English Halfbreeds is the only guarantee that there will be no bloodshed."[48] Even when the decision was made to threaten rebellion, there was a general sense among the Métis that events would not reach the point of open confrontation. Gabriel Dumont later claimed that Riel and his colleagues believed that the threat of violence would impel the government to recognize their rights: "This time the Métis who were talking about rebellion felt that a noisy threat would bring them their rights. These were the memories that were held in everyone's minds." When Dumont and his supporters decided to engage in open rebellion, they were deterred for a time by Riel. Faced with a potentially overpowering federal force that undoubtedly possessed sophisticated weaponry and supplies and, most critically, soldiers that far outnumbered the Métis, Riel was able to argue successfully among his colleagues for negotiations, and to temporarily delay the turn to armed uprising.[49]

In spite of the Métis' desire to reach an acceptable solution through negotiations with Ottawa, government delays in addressing the land question resulted in an explosion of tensions. After receiving a letter from Riel calling for his surrender, Superintendent Leif Crozier, of the North West Mounted Police, telegraphed Lieutenant Governor Edgar Dewdney from Fort Carleton on March 13, informing him that: "Halfbreed rebellion likely to break out any moment. Must be prepared for consequence. Troops must be largely reinforced. French Halfbreeds alone in this section number seven hundred men. If Halfbreeds rise Indians will join them."[50] A contingent of

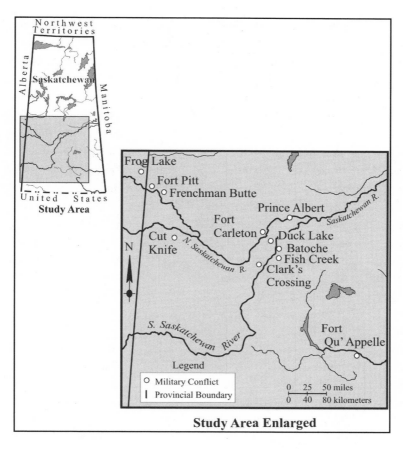

MAP 3. *Military Conflicts in 1885.*
CREDIT: LIZ FREDERIC.

forty policemen was immediately dispatched to Fort Carleton. On March 23, Major General Frederick Middleton received orders from Adolphe-Philippe Caron, federal minister of militia and defense, to set out for Winnipeg.[51]

On March 26, over a week before Middleton reached Winnipeg, the armed confrontation with the Métis and their allies began. A day earlier, Dumont and Riel were at St. Antoine de Padoue, near Batoche, when they learned that the North West Mounted Police had arrived on the opposite side of the river with the intention of arresting Riel. Dumont requested that Riel give him thirty men to head to Duck Lake to raid the Mounted Police warehouses.[52] Crozier, along with ninety-nine militia and policemen, appeared shortly after the Métis arrived at Duck Lake; and Dumont prepared his soldiers for an inevitable skirmish (Riel strictly forbade them from firing the first shots).[53] The battle itself was set off inadvertently; and after three days, Crozier realized that it was unwinnable, and withdrew. Fort Carleton was destroyed, and its residents were forced to retreat to Prince Albert where they found protection behind a hastily assembled stockade.

News of the Métis victory at Duck Lake spread through the region quickly and may well have provided an impetus for disaffected Native groups who were already on the verge of open confrontation with government representatives and the police. Two hundred Cree and a smaller number of Assiniboine joined forces and raided the settlement of Battleford, forcing nearly five hundred settlers to seek refuge in the NWMP barracks. At Frog Lake on April 2, a party led by Wandering Spirit killed the Indian agent Thomas Quinn, the farm instructor, and two Catholic priests (Father Fafard and Father Marchand). After being refused clothing and rations at Fort Pitt, a group of Cree led by Big Bear established camp close by on April 13, apparently in preparation for a blockade. Twenty resident policemen abandoned the fort by boat during the night of the fourteenth, leaving thirty civilians behind. The final Cree victory would take place on May 2 at Cut Knife Hill when three hundred and twenty-five Native men were attacked by Canadian forces under Colonel William D. Otter. The men had rifles, bows, and arrows, and were pitted against soldiers equipped with canons and a Gatling gun. The confrontation lasted seven hours, at which point Otter's troops withdrew; if they had chosen, the Cree contingent under Poundmaker could have easily slaughtered the government troops.[54]

Upon his arrival at Winnipeg on April 3, Middleton was met with the news of the clash at Duck Lake, and he immediately set off for Qu'Appelle accompanied by the Ninetieth Rifle Regiment stationed at Winnipeg. News of Duck Lake reached eastern Canada quickly and, unlike 1869, the outbreak brought about the immediate military response of the Canadian government. The militia was inundated with volunteers, and within a few days troops were mobilized and dispatched to the Saskatchewan Valley from Toronto, Montreal, Quebec City, and the Maritimes. At the height of hostilities, volunteers would number over five thousand of a full Canadian force of seven thousand men.[55] Although Middleton technically headed the campaign in 1885, he was actually in command of only one of three columns, located at Batoche on the south branch of the Saskatchewan River, from which he would lead his forces in central clashes at Fish Creek and Batoche itself.

Otter and Major General Thomas Strange were placed in command of two other columns on the North Saskatchewan, from which they were directed to focus their attention on Native resistance among the Cree who were associated predominantly with the bands of Poundmaker and Big Bear.[56]

Middleton led the Dominion forces in the central clashes with the Métis at Fish Creek and Batoche, although other significant battles occurred at Cut Knife Hill and Frenchman Butte. By the time of the Battle of Batoche (May 9), there were eight thousand Dominion troops in the North-West set against a mere one thousand Native and Métis soldiers. Most of the recruits fighting under Middleton were complete novices who had never seen combat of any sort; and their final victory at Batoche was very nearly accidental, taking four days to accomplish. The battle ended on May 12 when Middleton's field force of eight hundred men managed to overcome a line of fifty or sixty rebels that included men in their seventies and one who was ninety-three, and who had run out of ammunition and were stuffing nails, bolts, and stones into their guns to defend themselves.[57] On May 15, Riel wrote to Middleton offering to turn himself in: "My council are dispersed. I wish you would let them go quiet and free. I hear that presently you are absent. Would I go to Batoche, who is going to receive me? I will go to fulfil [sic] God's will."[58] Riel was picked up by three of Middleton's scouts about four miles north of Batoche.

Dumont crossed into Montana around June 1 and was immediately taken into custody by American cavalry stationed at Fort Assiniboine. Although he was facing extradition, Dumont was released with no explanation a week later.[59] Dumont had fled to the United States with the intention of continuing his resistance and securing either Riel's release or his escape from the Regina jail in which he was being held. Dumont was refused a temporary amnesty that would allow him to testify on behalf of Riel at his trial, and so he began laying plans for an armed raid on the Regina jail:

> St. Paul, Aug. 12—A dispatch from Fort Benton says there have been many querries [sic] regarding the continuous stay in this neighborhood of Dumont and Dumais, lately of Riel's force. It is understood that they were trying to make arrangements with the authorities at Washington for a tract of land for their Halfbreed brethren; yesterday, however, it was rumoured that Dumont's real mission here was to organize a force of dare devils to make a dash on Regina and release Riel.[60]

For his part, Riel believed that Dumont was working to this end and announced during his trial: "Gabriel Dumont on the other side of the line, is that Gabriel Dumont inactive? I believe not. He is trying to save me from this box."[61] Indeed, in attempting to execute his release plan for Riel, Dumont may have traveled as far as Regina before having to turn back because of the level of security surrounding the jail.[62]

Dumont joined Buffalo Bill Cody's Wild West Show as "the Hero of the Halfbreed Rebellion" in the spring of 1886, where he worked until his pardon arrived a few months later. Cody's general manager, John Burke, had contacted Dumont during the fall of 1885, hoping to persuade him to join the show, but Dumont had been too busy attempting to organize the rescue of Riel at the time. When Burke reiterated the offer in the spring, however, Dumont decided to perform in the show. His first performance was in Philadelphia, June 7, 1886, where he was billed as "Gabriel Dumont, the Hero of the Halfbreed Rebellion," who was "without fear, without reproach." In his early appearances, Dumont's principal task was to display his saddle and his Winchester; but in later shows he performed as a marksman with Annie Oakley and Jonnie Baker (known as the "cowboy marksman"). His amnesty was issued by the Canadian government in the summer of 1886, and although Buffalo Bill encouraged him to leave the show at this point, Dumont attempted to continue performing to audiences that grew increasingly sparse as news of his loss of fugitive status circulated. He left the show in September, embarked on a speaking tour of various Franco-American communities in the northeastern United States, and was subsequently invited to Quebec by Honoré Mercier to speak about Riel and the rebellion during Mercier's election campaign.[63] The tour ended prematurely, however, when Dumont became discouraged by the use to which his story was being put by nationalists in the province. Following this short foray into politics, he returned to perform again with the Wild West Show in 1887 and 1888 in the cast of Bill's stagecoach extravaganza, "The Battle of Civilization." When he subsequently left the show, he returned to Saskatchewan and resumed his former life as a hunter and trader.[64]

Riel's secretary, William Jackson, was brought to trial on a charge of "treason-felony" on July 24. Jackson was considered insane by everyone involved in his trial, and the presiding stipendiary magistrate (justice of the peace), Hugh Richardson, cooperated with Jackson's defense to obtain an acquittal on the basis of insanity. The trial took a half hour. Jackson was acquitted and dragged from the courtroom insisting on his sanity; he was subsequently transported to Selkirk Asylum near Winnipeg. Two and a half months after having been committed, Jackson escaped and was able to cross the border into the United States where he began campaigning on behalf of Riel at a series of public lectures in North Dakota and Minnesota. When Riel was executed on November 16, Jackson publicly described the act as "legal murder of a patriot and statesman." When he moved to Chicago a few months later he represented himself as Métis, a transformation that had begun with his conversion to Riel's Catholicism, and his decision to wear a Métis headband in 1884, and culminated in his formal adoption of the name Honoré Jaxon a few years later.

In Chicago, Jackson became an anarchist, converted to the Baha'i faith, and assumed a significant role in the city's labor movement. In 1905, he joined the newly created Industrial Workers of the World and was able to travel as the organization's delegate to Winnipeg to take part in the annual meeting of the Trades and Labour Congress of Canada in 1907. Once in Canada, Jackson embarked on a speaking tour of the west, culminating in a speech before the Regina chapter of the Canadian Labour Party in December of 1907. By the 1920s, Jackson was back in the United States, living in New York City, where he resumed his earlier interest in lecturing and writing in support of virtually every controversial cause that came to his attention. During the same period, he began scouring auctions and used-book stores, buying as many books as he could in the hope of eventually establishing a library for the Native population living in the vicinity of a three-hundred-acre lot he owned in Saskatchewan. In 1951, a ninety-year-old Jackson was evicted from his apartment, and his collection of books— which covered twenty-one hundred cubic feet—was carried off as trash. Jackson became ill shortly thereafter and was taken to Bellevue Hospital where he died.[65]

In the immediate wake of the 1885 Rebellion, twenty-eight Native communities were designated "disloyal," more than fifty Native men (including Big Bear and Poundmaker) were indicted for crimes relating to the uprising, and eight were simultaneously hanged on November 27, 1885, in the country's largest group execution.[66] Poundmaker and Big Bear were each charged with treason-felony, in spite of the fact that each had assumed a compromissary stance and had been a constant voice for peace. Each received a sentence of three years to be served at Stony Mountain Penitentiary (in Manitoba); and both became ill due to their incarceration. Poundmaker was released after only a year and died within a few weeks, while Big Bear was released after serving two years of his sentence and died a few months later.[67]

Riel was charged with six counts of "high treason" under an archaic statute dating back to the reign of Edward III: the Statute of Treasons, 1351.[68] The question of what charge could be laid in respect to Riel's conduct during the uprising was not at all clear. By allegedly provoking a rebellion against a government linked to the British Crown, it seemed clear that Riel could legitimately stand trial for treason. Yet the legal definition of treason in the North-West in the late nineteenth century was not immediately obvious. By tradition, all British colonies inherited the entire body of operative British law in existence when they were claimed by Britain; in the case of the North-West, this occurred on May 1, 1670, when the Hudson's Bay Company received its charter. Subsequent to the date of colonial acquisition, all colonies were required to formally approve any new British legislation in order for such changes to become local law. Consequently, the laws operative in the North-West at the time of the territory's acquisition by Canada were comprised of British law in 1670 as well as any new laws ratified by the Hudson's Bay Company's judicial arm, the Council of Assiniboia, over the span of the next two hundred years. Since the council had essentially functioned as an administrative branch of the company, dealing with new legislation on an ad hoc basis, significant crimes such as treason had simply never presented themselves for consideration. As a consequence, when Canada acquired the North-West in 1870 the charge of treason related only to the legal definition of the crime that had been operative when the company received its charter in 1670: the Statute of Treasons, dating back to 1351.[69]

The first three charges against Riel asserted that he was a British subject and, based on the legal assumption of "natural allegiance," charged him in connection with conflicts at Duck Lake, Fish Creek, and Batoche; the other three named Riel as a resident of the Dominion under the protection of the British Crown and were based on the principle of "local allegiance." The first count is representative of all six:

> That Louis Riel being a subject of Our Lady the Queen, not regarding the duty of his allegiance, nor having the fear of God in his heart, but being moved and seduced by the instigation of the Devil, as a false traitor against our said Lady the Queen ... on the twenty-sixth day of March, together with divers other false traitors ... armed and

arranged in warlike manner, that is to say, with guns, rifles, pistols, bayonets, and other weapons, being then unlawfully, maliciously, and traitorously assembled and gathered together against our said Lady the Queen, at the locality known as Duck Lake, in the said North-West Territories of Canada, and within this Realm, and did then maliciously and traitorously attempt and endeavor by force and arms to subvert and destroy the Constitution and Government of this Realm as by law established, and deprive and depose our said Lady the Queen of and from the style, honour, and kingly name of the Imperial Crown of this Realm, in contempt of our said Lady the Queen and her laws, to the evil example of all others in the like case offending, contrary to the duty of the allegiance of him, the said Louis Riel, against the form of the statute in such case made and provided and against the peace of our said Lady the Queen, her crown and dignity.[70]

Alternate wording in charges four through six was introduced to address the fact that Riel had, during his period of living in Montana, taken U.S. citizenship. Although seventy-two others had been charged with treason in connection with the uprising, only Riel was charged under this archaic British statute that carried a compulsory death sentence; the others were charged under a Canadian law, the Statute of Canada, 1868, which provided for a charge of treason-felony, and carried a sentence of incarceration for a period ranging from a number of days to life. Introduced by the British Parliament, it had been adopted in 1868 by the Canadian government under An Act for the Better Security of the Crown and of the Government, and it became operative in the North-West in 1873.[71]

Riel wanted to have a dramatic trial in eastern Canada under national and international scrutiny; instead, his case was heard by a stipendiary magistrate and half a jury in the small North-West community of Regina. The trial began at 11:00 a.m., on Monday the twentieth of July. The Regina police barracks, which were generally used as a courtroom, were too small to accommodate the crowd (which included legal council, journalists, and citizens) that attended the trial, so the offices of a local real estate company had been rented for the occasion.[72] Macdonald's government brought together a potent bipartisan, bicultural, and multiregional team of lawyers, led by the Toronto lawyer Christopher Robinson, to represent the Crown in the trial.[73] Britton Bath Osler, a Liberal who was one of the country's foremost criminal lawyers, was assigned the task of assembling the Crown's evidence; and the team was rounded out with George Wheelock Burbidge (a Nova Scotian who had been appointed federal deputy minister of justice three years earlier), the French Canadian Thomas-Chase Casgrain (a partner in the law firm of Adolphe-Philippe Caron, Macdonald's minister of militia and defense), and Regina mayor, David Lynch Scott. Unlike the Canadian government, which had virtually unlimited financial resources at its disposal to assemble the strongest legal team possible, Riel was destitute and, had it not been for a fortuitous turn of Quebec public opinion, would not have been able to pay the cost of representation. French Canadian sentiment had been fully with the Dominion at the outset of the North-West Rebellion (a subject we'll explore more fully later), but Riel's cause proved to be politically expedient for Quebec Liberals seeking to bring down the Conservative Party in the province. Led by Honoré Mercier, the Liberals rallied to the cause of Riel, portraying him as a victim of Anglophone intolerance, and taking it upon themselves to assemble and finance a defense team for the Métis leader. The team was led by François Lemieux, a young lawyer who had a reputation for acquittals and mistrials and who would eventually serve on the Supreme Court of Quebec before being appointed chief justice of the province in 1915. He was joined by Charles Fitzpatrick (who would be named minister of justice, under Wilfrid Laurier, and chief justice of Canada in 1906), Montreal lawyer James Greenshields, and Thomas Cooke Johnstone, a Winnipeg barrister who would be appointed to the Supreme Court of Saskatchewan in 1906.[74] The magistrate for the trial was Hugh Richardson, an Ontario lawyer who had been appointed stipendiary magistrate in 1877, after five years' tenure as chief clerk for the Department of Justice. Richardson had officiated over the Regina court since 1880, where his time had been principally spent ruling on liquor infractions, although he had found a Native man guilty of cannibalism, and two Métis and an Anglophone settler guilty of murder during that time.[75]

A one-week adjournment was initially granted to the defense; and in the interim, a number of other individuals accused of crimes related to the uprising were tried. Of the seventy men who had been arrested in connection with the rebellion, less than half appeared in a courtroom, and a number of these were acquitted. In the end, eighteen Métis were found guilty of treason-felony, receiving sentences varying from one to seven years. Of the Native men charged in connection with the affair, eleven were sentenced to death, although three were able to have their sentences commuted. The remaining eight were hanged at Battleford on November 27. Riel was found guilty of high treason on August 1, and in spite of the jury's recommendation of mercy, Richardson had no choice, according to the Statute of Treasons, but to sentence Riel to execution. He appears, however, to have had no difficulty in bringing the law to bear fully in the situation:

> For what you did, the remarks you have made form no excuse whatever. For what you have done the law requires you to answer. It is true that the jury in merciful consideration have asked Her Majesty to give your case such merciful consideration as she can bestow upon it . . . For me, I have only one more duty to perform, that is, to tell you what the sentence of the law is upon you. I have, as I must, given time to enable your case to be heard. All I can suggest or advise is to prepare to meet your end. . . . It is now my painful duty to pass the sentence of the court upon you, and that is, that you be taken now from here to the police guard-room at Regina, which is the gaol and the place from whence you came, and that you be kept there till the eighteenth of September next, that on the eighteenth of September next you be taken to the place appointed for your execution, and there be hanged by the neck till you are dead, and may God have mercy on your soul.[76]

Following Riel's conviction in the Regina court, his lawyers appealed the decision to the Queen's Bench of Manitoba where the three judges upheld the earlier decision. As a last resort, the team of lawyers appealed to the judicial committee of the Privy Council in London, but the case was dismissed, the judges ruling that there was no basis for an appeal.

In the wake of the decisions, and ostensibly in order to satisfy demands from the province of Quebec, Macdonald appointed three physicians to assess Riel's mental state. Two of the doctors provided Macdonald with the report he was seeking, declaring that Riel was fully in control of his faculties; the third, however, concluded that Riel was not mentally stable:

> After having examined carefully Riel in private conversation with him and by testimony of persons who take care of him I have come to the conclusion that he is not an accountable being, that he is unable to distinguish between wrong and right on political and religious subjects which I consider well marked typical forms

of a kind of insanity under which he undoubtedly suffers, but on other points I believe him to be quite sensible and can distinguish between right and wrong.

In the version of this third report that was presented in the House of Commons, Macdonald managed to delete some of the most critical elements:

> After having examined carefully Riel in private conversation with him and by testimony of persons who take care of him I have come to the conclusion that he suffers under hallucinations on political and religious subjects, but on other points I believe him to be quite sensible and can distinguish right from wrong.[77]

Riel was executed on November 16.

Following the rebellion, William Pearce (the civil servant who had been responsible for reporting on the 1884 Petition of Rights) was appointed by the government to investigate Ottawa's management of the Métis grievances, and his resulting document, *Detailed Report upon All Claims to Land and Rights to Participate in the North-West Halfbreed Grant by Settlers along the South Saskatchewan*, absolved the federal government of any mismanagement in the affair.[78] Métis and Native peoples would experience immediate and long-term reverberations from the uprising (which was the last confrontation between the Canadian army and Aboriginal peoples in Canada until that at Oka in 1990).[79] We will consider many of these presently in the context of discussing the mythicization of the rebellions but we might note at this point that immediate political and economic pressures exerted by the federal government undermined the traditionally flexible structure of Native bands, and new distinctions between groups were created that have remained to the present. In addition, an amendment to the Indian Act limited the sale of firearms and ammunition to Native peoples after the uprising, and both First Nations and Métis peoples suffered as a consequence. For Native peoples, the restriction caused critical difficulties; given that many survived by hunting, the amendment to the act that prohibited the sale of anything larger than shotguns effectively rendered them incapable of hunting for large game. For substantial numbers of Métis who had chosen to identify themselves as "Treaty Indians," the problem was the same. Escalating prices for necessities after the outbreak only exacerbated the problem. The untenable economic position in which the Métis found themselves after the rebellion resulted in the desire of many to remove themselves from treaty. Faced with a substantial body of Métis seeking scrip rather than treaty rights, the government moved comparatively quickly to effect the process and, as a result, a number of Native bands lost most of their members. The Peaysis band of Lac La Biche and the Ka-qua-num band at Beaver River, for instance, were impacted to such a degree that by 1900, their few remaining members had moved to other reserves, and the Peaysis and Ka-qua-num reserves ceased to exist in any legal fashion.[80]

In addition to these immediate results of the confrontation in the North-West, the rebellion would also have a far-reaching impact on the country as a whole. The nature of this impact will be the subject of the chapters to follow.

Chapter 2

Canadian Myths and Canadian Identity

Controversy has dogged Riel and the rebellions for over a century, resulting not only in a dramatically diverse body of academic interpretation of their significance, but in their mythic deployment in the service of a variety of cultural agendas ranging from Francophone nationalism to Aboriginal rights. When Riel's complete papers were published in 1985, J. M. Bumsted believed the project would provide scholars with a unique opportunity to study the man apart from the cultural images that had become associated with him; but he seriously doubted that such reinterpretation would have any impact on those various (often contradictory) images themselves.[1] These simply run too deep.

In French Canada, literary works began appearing within a few months of Riel's execution, and in all cases Riel was thematically linked to Anglo-Saxon bigotry against French Catholics. This early literature consistently neglected the fact of Riel's Métis ethnicity and subsumed him within the context of a broader Quebec cultural identity. Indeed, only one poem from the period immediately following his execution defied this tendency: George Lemay's "Chant du Métis," published in 1886, which clearly identified Riel with the Métis.[2] The first two French plays involving Riel were written in 1886. Elzéar Paquin's *Riel: tragédie en quatre actes* covered the period of time between the 1869 uprising and the immediate wake of Riel's execution, spinning a narrative about anguish and deceit that ended with a conversation between Dumont and a number of other French Canadians in which the men discussed their hopes for ultimately seeing justice served. In the scene, one of the men addressed his friends in the following fashion:

> My dear friends, since the day we were so ignominiously insulted on the gallows of Regina, I haven't ceased filling my newspaper with the most outspoken documents along with the most irrefutable arguments, together with the most categorical proofs, to demonstrate that the ringleaders of the disorders and uprisings—that the enemies of law and justice, of peace, prosperity and the glory of our country, between 1869 and 1870, and 1884–85—were the Federal ministers themselves and their subalterns in the North-West.[3]

In the play, Paquin presented Riel as a "martyred patriot," and English Canadians as "fanatical," "sanguinary," and "francophobic."[4] Far less polemic than Paquin's *Riel* was Charles Bayer and E. Parage's *Riel: drame historique en quatre acts et un prologue*, which incorporated both relatively accurate and rather warped historical details alongside romance, humor, and action. Still, the play was an enthusiastic defense of the Métis and of Riel himself, who assumed heroic status. "If I am a victim of the dishonesty of my enemies," Riel claimed at one point in the play,

> if instead of a pardon, it is the scaffold that awaits me, my martyrdom will be useful to our cause; it will serve to unmask their crooked politics, and my blood will be on their head. In all civilized countries no one is condemned without judgment. My acceptance will disarm my enemies. I will have my trial before impartial judges. The publicity of these debates, or the legitimacy of our revolt will be discussed, where all our grievances will be exposed, which will likely help our cause more than a desperate fight.[5]

French Canadian historians of the first few decades of the twentieth century generally assumed attitudes toward Riel that reflected established Anglo-Protestant and French-Catholic antipathies. George Dugast's 1905 *Histoire véridique*, a work that was informed by the author's own experience of having met Riel, portrayed the Métis leader as a martyr.[6] Similarly, Jean Bruchési represented Riel as a casualty of ethnic bigotry in his *Histoire du Canada pour tous* (1940); and Lionel Groulx made use of the figure of Riel as a foundation upon which to launch denunciations of the narrow-minded attitudes of Anglo-Manitobans and their "destructive" public schools. The conception of Riel as an early champion of French and Roman Catholic interests was likewise foundational in works such as Adrien Morice's *A Critical History of the Red River Insurrection* (1935) and Auguste-Henri de Trémaudan's *Histoire de la Nation Métisse dans Ouest Canadien* (1936).[7] Marcel Giraud (a historian from France) produced *Le Métis Canadien* in 1945; in the book, which became a seminal work that would be cited often by subsequent historians, the Métis were presented as a people that was virtually indistinguishable from western Native peoples.[8]

This tendency to equate the Métis with either French or Native Canadians was noticeably absent from Jean-Louis Roux's play *Bois-Brûlés* (1967), where Riel appeared as a hero of a Métis people who were part of a broader Aboriginal resistance movement against white incursion. Roux's work also presented a more evenhanded assessment of the government forces opposing the Métis, and aside from John Schultz (leader of the Canadian Party at Red River in 1869), who was the object of rather pointed criticism, neither the Canadian soldiers, nor the politicians in Ottawa, nor Riel's jury were the targets of particular disparagement. The soldiers were portrayed as pawns of the political process, men who were relatively unaware of the reasons for the military engagement: John A. Macdonald was a man caught in a difficult position by forces outside his control, and the members of Riel's jury in Regina were depicted as legitimately struggling with a decision that could not easily be made.[9] Reverting to a more established mode of dichotomizing absolutely the Métis and their enemies, Michelle Boulet and Thérèse Pilotte's *Uneyeen: Ou Not' bord de la rivière* (1985) presented a notably unbalanced portrayal of Riel and his opponents. As Chris Johnson has noted, the unrelentingly critical presentation of the prime minister and others in this play served to undermine Riel's character, rendering him less credible for having lost his life to simple fools: "Macdonald may have been duplicitous, cunning, and opportunistic," writes Johnson, "but he was certainly not a drooling idiot."[10] Likewise, the National Arts Centre's production of *Debout mon people!* (1992) followed the model in which Riel has been idolized and the government vilified by means of an interactive re-creation of Riel's trial in which the jury (the audience) consistently acquits the accused man. The critic, Joël Beddoes, said of a particular production: "It is a shame that contemporary young audiences were not members of the jury during the deliberations of yesteryear, since Riel is almost never condemned now."[11] The conviction that Riel was a victim of bigotry—"English prejudice," "Orange fanaticism," and "Ontario fanaticism"—remains firm to this day among French Canadians.[12]

Aboriginal writing on Riel has been quite distinct from that of French Canadian writers. Although he has often been regarded as "a champion of aboriginal peoples," an "Aboriginal hero," and "a pawn of shadowy white forces," he has not received unflagging respect from Aboriginal writers. Blair Stonechild and Bill Waiser have suggested that in the case of First Nations, this lack of attention has been due to the fact that Riel has often been regarded as having exploited Native peoples in the service of forwarding his own Métis agenda.[13] Many Métis writers have expressed a similar sense of hesitation in dealing with Riel. In a speech delivered to mark the "Occasion of the National Celebration to Mark Louis Riel Day" in 1999, Governor General Adrienne Clarkson described him as an advocate for "the rights of his people."[14] Many Métis writers, however, have reacted against the preeminence afforded Riel by nonnative writers, often inherently criticizing him for his lack of decisiveness by juxtaposing him with the figure of his general Gabriel Dumont. Riel has not been a protagonist of choice among many Métis writers, and even among those who have incorporated him into their work many have generally done so in a relatively secondary fashion. Maria Campbell's *Halfbreed* (1973), Beatrice Culleton's *In Search of April Raintree* (1983), and Laure Bouvier's *Une histoire de Métisses* (1995) all have some reference to Riel but in none of these does the man play any kind of substantive role in the narrative.

The reason for this apparent neglect may well relate to a certain level of ambivalence on the part of many Métis toward the figure of Riel. Emma LaRocque has suggested that this hinges on the concomitant acknowledgment of Riel's symbolic significance as an embodiment of "the grave injustice" the Métis have suffered, with an uneasiness over the preeminence that he has been afforded by nonnatives. Riel, she says, "overshadows his own people." In addition, she points out that many Métis believe that Riel was not representative of the Métis—that he was "different from the people. He really believed in civilization," and his leadership lacked the boldness of someone like his general, Dumont.[15] Howard Adams has argued that Anglo-Canadians have simply been attempting to mitigate their sense of guilt over the execution of Riel by erecting statues and calling for retroactive pardons and recognition of Riel as a "founding father"—that his elevation to the status of a national hero has been the work of hegemonic politicians and the media that serve their interests, seeking to create a "government-sanctioned" cult of Riel intended to swindle the victims of Canada's colonial policies and conceal the real meaning of the Métis uprisings as conflicts over class and race. Adams goes on to suggest that Riel was clearly a strategic leader in the uprising of 1869, pressing for a "national revolution," but that in the campaign of 1885 his desire for reform had shifted from the political to the religious sphere, demonstrating little of the revolutionary spirit he had shown in the earlier movement. Throughout the conflict of 1885, his focus was on acting as a negotiator with the Canadian government and he avoided participation in armed confrontation, going so far as to attempt to dissuade his colleagues under Dumont from killing NWMP officers and members of the Canadian militia. If Riel had not been involved in the uprising, Howard contends, the Métis would have fared better, perhaps even succeeding in their struggle for liberation, retaining their land, and ultimately founding a Métis nation.[16]

The hero Dumont thus figures notably in the work of many Métis writers as an archetype, often eclipsing Riel in works ostensibly focused on him. Upisasik Theatre's *Gabrielle* (1985) is a case in point. The play, which was produced initially at Ile-à-la-Crosse (where Riel's sister Sara is buried), revolves around a central character who is visited by Riel a hundred years after his death, and it concerns the question of "what might happen if the 1885 Rebellion were to occur in 1985" at Ile-à-la-Crosse, with a woman as its leader. In spite of the fact that Riel figures principally as the central character's inspiration in speaking for the Métis, her name—Gabrielle—is not based on that of Riel but on Dumont.[17]

This is not to say, however, that Riel has been summarily criticized or trivialized within Métis writing. In point of fact, he has often assumed a prominent role in this literature in spite of his clearly ambiguous position among Métis peoples. In Bob Rock's *The Missing Bell of Batoche* (1994), for instance, Riel is portrayed as a "New World David" who is struggling for Métis land rights and sovereignty, along with multiculturalism and free trade. The federal government, on the other hand, is attacked for having failed to assume the small expense necessary to provide food to those in need and for having refused to take the time to consult with the Métis as it initiated land surveys, both of which would have undoubtedly forestalled the uprisings and loss of life that ensued. Gregory Scofield's *Thunder Through My Veins* focuses similar attention on Riel by presenting the author's personal sense of arriving "home at last" when he travels to Batoche and encounters Riel and Dumont, "the half-breed soldiers who had given their lives for *our* homeland, freedom, and independence."[18] Additionally, Métis writers in Manitoba have created a tradition of drama, for example, Claude Dorge's *Le Roitelet* (1976), and folk music (such as those songs collected and published by Annette Saint-Pierre) around Riel.[19]

Unlike the ambivalence that Riel has generated with respect to Aboriginal rights, his identification with regional disparities, and even western separatist movements, has been solidly placed. In much of the literature of the post–World War II era, Riel has been portrayed as a Native nonconformist in opposition to the domination of central Canada and, more broadly, to the normalization of the West.[20] Scholars have argued that he advocated primarily regionalism over and above federalism, regarding regional independence as the best mode of protecting ethnic identities (a claim that seems to be substantiated by his willingness to lead two rebellions against the Dominion). William Klassen has suggested that in this sense Riel was identifying a Canadian problem that he could not resolve with violence, and that has not been subsequently settled.[21] Often, the association of Riel with regionalism has been more focused on the Canadian west in opposition to the power of central Canada. In her Louis Riel Day speech of 1999, for instance, the country's governor general described Riel as an advocate of "western rights."[22] Additionally, it has been argued that Riel's effortless melding of religion and political life became emblematic of a particular western Canadian view of the interrelationship of religion and politics, a view that would later be articulated by men such as J. S. Woodsworth and Ernest Manning.[23]

The Métis leader has also often been invoked as an embodiment of western resistance against the federal government's indifference or mismanagement of the Prairie provinces, and he has been referred to as the forerunner to western populist politics, a forebear of men like Thomas Crerar (1920s), William Aberhart (1930s and 1940s), Peter Lougheed (1970s and 1980s), and Preston Manning (1990s).[24] In drama too, the issue of western resistance has been noticeable. In Harry Somers's opera, *Louis Riel* (see Moore and Languirand 1967), for example, the hero is portrayed as representing the interests of Métis, English mixed-blood, and Native peoples in the North-West, and so the delegation that travels to Montana to convince him to return to the Saskatchewan Valley is composed not only of Dumont and James Isbester (an influential English mixed-blood man) but also the Cree chief Poundmaker. This historical fabrication (Poundmaker never made such a journey, and in fact, no Native-Métis alliance existed during the uprising) allowed the librettists to present Riel as a hero of a pan-western resistance to central Canadian expansion.[25] We should note, however, that some western writers have adopted the stance of Métis and Native colleagues, breaking from the model and disparaging or conspicuously ignoring Riel's role in the uprisings because his image is perceived as having been too much influenced by central Canadian values, as being "too intellectual, too Eastern, indeed, too white."[26] In much of this work, the role of Riel's associate Gabriel Dumont has been highlighted.

It is among Anglophones that Riel's image has undergone the most dramatic shift since the time of his execution. Regarded almost universally as a homicidal traitor in 1885, by a century later he had become something of a cultural emblem in English Canada. Riel's first appearance in Anglophone literature, if only by name, was in George Broughall's musical, *The Ninetieth on Active Service, or Campaigning in the North West*, a "Musical and Dramatic Burlesque in Two Acts" that was first performed at Winnipeg's Princess Opera House in 1885. Riel did not figure notably in the play, but was mentioned only with enmity by soldiers referring to the rebellion and expressing their hopes that Riel would be found guilty and punished so that the lives that had been lost would have some purpose. In a typical scene from the burlesque, Canadian soldiers were praised for their loyalty to both Canada and the empire at the Battle of Batoche:

> OFFICER:. . . . we have all come out here in defence of our country and institutions; and we should patiently and willingly submit to many blunders of a commissariat and the hardships of a campaign. We are here to do our duty; and we can at least tolerate many grievances, on a campaign in which so much is at stake."[27]

Like their French counterparts, English writers lost interest in the man soon after his execution, but the situation began to slowly turn around (among historians, at least) in the 1930s. It took until the end of the Second World War, however, for Riel to begin appearing again in English fiction. In an interesting reversal, much of English Canada has generally come to assume the traditionally French Canadian view that the man was a victim of bigotry.[28]

Concomitant with renewed interest in Riel at the midpoint of the twentieth century was a change in English portrayals of Native peoples. The end of World War II appears to have signaled a shift in residual English

Canadian cultural identification with England; and Robert Kroetch has argued that in literature, this translated into a general modification of traditional images of Native peoples from obstacles of Canadian expansion to cultural forebears. In parallel fashion, the 1885 Rebellion also underwent an interpretive shift from being an "uprising" to a "necessary revolution of the perceiving self" through which Riel and his general, Dumont, revealed the meaning of Canadians as a "new people in a new landscape." Rather than being insurgents, the two were "poets of place, telling us what they see."[29] Daniel Francis, however, sees in this shift something more pragmatic: in an attempt to establish a primordial relationship with the land, and to authenticate their presence in the country, nonnatives have had a tendency to associate themselves with Native Canadians in advertising and organized sports, and through a generalized appropriation of Native symbols (e.g., totem poles) as emblematic of national identity.[30] His assessment seems to be an accurate one, and resonances of it can be detected as early as the 1940s. In *The Flying Years* (1942), for instance, Frederick Niven reflected on the terror that riddled the settler community around Calgary in 1885 and cast a Cree chief, Buffalo Calf, as the spokesman for a future vision of the country in which all Canadians would ultimately become indigenous through the creative power of the land: "[T]his is Indian country and it turns even white men to Indians in time."[31] Albert Braz has noted that unlike Niven, most Anglophone writers have lacked this confidence in the indigenizing power of the Canadian landscape, and many have advocated forging an identification with Native peoples or, in the words of Dorothy Livesay, "finding the Indian." Of course, this desire for identification has not tended to translate into a need for tangible relationships between Natives and nonnatives; rather, it has been the *idea* of the "Indian" that has fascinated Anglophone writers. As John Newlove put it: Canada is "crammed/ with the ghosts of Indians and they are all ready/to be found, the legends/ and the people."[32]

The shift in perspective has been dramatic in respect to Riel and the Métis rebellions. Even many of those who were contemporaries of Riel tended to alter their view of the entire affair as time has passed. A. O. Wheeler, who was a surveyor and eyewitness to the 1885 uprising, was perhaps emblematic of this change. By the time he published an article on the rebellion in 1934, he had come to believe that the importance of the confrontation in the Saskatchewan Valley had been exaggerated, and that the Dominion's victory and the crushing of the rebels were not sources of patriotic pride: "Looked back upon through the vista of years the whole episode seems inglorious . . . a vastly superior force with the best of, then, modern fighting equipment against a scattered rabble of half-breeds and Indians with a few antique rifles and ancient shot-guns."[33] Wheeler's reversal was somewhat prophetic in terms of Anglophone writing. By 1992, Desmond Morton would claim that in spite of the fact that it might do no injustice to the historical record, portraying the Canadian soldiers who fought against Riel and the Métis in the 1885 Rebellion as patriots had simply become unacceptable.[34]

Despite the work of historians like A. S. Morton and George Stanley, whose histories of western Canada written in the 1930s presented an early sympathetic view of Riel, broader cultural perceptions of Riel as a heroic figure did not begin to appear in literature until after World War II. While Morton and Stanley were admittedly less hostile toward Riel than earlier writers, they nonetheless maintained the conviction that Riel and the Métis were doomed to failure by virtue of the fact that they were situated on the peripheries of modern civilization. Stanley's *The Birth of Western Canada* (1936), for instance, would become one of the definitive historical texts on the Métis uprisings of 1869 and 1885; but in the book, Riel was presented as "a sad, pathetic, unstable man, who led his followers in a suicide crusade and whose brief glory rests upon a distortion of history." The text revolved around the presumption of an epic collision involving civilized Canadians and primitives—Native and mixed-blood peoples who were "centuries behind in mental and economic development," and "bound to give way before the march of a more progressive people."[35] W. L. Morton reacted against Stanley's analysis of the Métis in a 1937 article that blamed the "primitive" nature of the Red River settlement on its administration under the Hudson's Bay Company, which had enforced an unaccountable "seigniorial despotism" on the community. Morton admitted that the Métis under Riel had made serious tactical errors (principal among which was the execution of Thomas Scott); but he argued that they had, in the interest of establishing a nationalist claim, proceeded with an undeniable "integrity" in the establishment of representative government with a supportive military arm. As a result, the Canadian government did not *establish* a province with the Manitoba Act, but *acknowledged* a political entity that was already established. In this analysis, Morton remained uncertain as to how it was that a population with an entrenched national identity capable of withstanding the incursion of an "almost foreign power" was so easily forced into exile in the wake of its success in gaining recognition. He continued to explore this question and ultimately settled on a solution presented to him by Marcel Giraud, who argued that the Métis had unknowingly contributed to their own dispossession by refusing to submit to the guidance of non-native allies in respect to the acquisition of civilization through education and morality. Under the sway of Giraud, Morton essentially reverted to the same kind of analysis that he had initially criticized in Stanley's work. Thus he argued that the Métis insistence on retaining a nomadic and "barbaric" life-style that was intrinsically unstable and prone to violence was ultimately reflected in Riel's own proclivity for violence: "It was their tragedy that the instability and violence of Riel, reflecting the inherent instability and ready violence of his own uncertain people, ruined his achievement and destroyed his nation."[36]

These early interpretations of Riel and the rebellions set a pattern in historiography that has continued in some quarters to this day, a pattern that D. N. Sprague has suggested was based on an assumption of "government good faith." For historians who have relied upon this fundamental assumption, the most potentially disquieting issue has been the emigration of the Red River Métis to the North-West in the wake of the Manitoba Act. Stanley resolved the problem by resorting to an argument based on the "primitive" state of the Métis, while Giraud and W. L. Morton contended that the Métis were victims of a fatal impulse toward a nomadic life-style. Critics of Giraud and Morton have admitted that evidence exists to support the arguments that the federal government did not act in good faith, and that the Métis were not undone by primitivism; but even these historians, represented by Donald Creighton and Thomas Flanagan, have tended to regard instances of government duplicity as departures from a generally evenhanded policy toward the Métis, and have countered the argument based on primitivism with equally disparaging—and ultimately equivalent—claims that Riel was politically corrupt and/or his followers exceptionally naive.[37]

Scholarship and literature on Riel and the Métis rebellions assumed another trajectory with the posthumous publication of Joseph Kinsey Howard's *Strange Empire* in 1952. Howard, an American-born historian who had been raised in Montana, has been credited with providing the impetus for the elevation of Riel from the status of a rebel to that of a hero.[38] He regarded Riel as a farsighted Native leader (his Métis identity was eclipsed) whose intention it was to create a structured Aboriginal state in the North-West; and what appears to have sparked the interest of other writers in both the United States and Canada was Kinsey's recasting of Riel as a cultural forefather rather than a rebel.[39] The changing perspective expressed by Howard was obvious also in John Coulter's play *Riel*, which was written in 1950 and initiated a period of broad interest in the Métis leader among writers in Canada. Coulter chose to write about the man because he hoped to contribute to the emergence of a distinctly Canadian theater; in Riel, he said, "I saw the shape of Canadian myth, the heroic individual driven by his conviction that God had chosen him to defend a peripheral community."[40] The play, which its author called an epic, was a colossal project involving forty-one roles in addition to extras. It appears that Coulter discovered in Riel a Canadian figure that most clearly resonated with his own cultural background; in spite of the fact that Coulter was an immigrant Irish Protestant, he maintained a sympathy for Irish Catholics, and he viewed Riel and the rebellion through this lens. As a consequence, O'Donoghue figured prominently in the first part of the play, Riel's Irish ancestry was noted, and the clash between the nineteenth-century North-West and central Canada was presented as analogous to that between Ireland and England.[41]

In 1960, Coulter was commissioned by the Canada Council to create a trilogy of plays about Riel; and building on his earlier *Riel*, Coulter wrote *The Trial of Louis Riel* (1968) and *The Crime of Louis Riel* (1976). Essentially reworking the material from the first play to produce the shorter *The Crime of Louis Riel*, Coulter focused this time on Riel's struggle as emblematic of broader colonial resistances, especially those of the twentieth century; and the play has had a substantial cultural impact, with its annual staging in Regina having become something of an institution. In the Regina production, the audience members are cast as spectators in a courtroom modeled on that in which the original trial took place, and an actor playing the role of a NWMP officer controls the crowd that must conform to regulations of conduct in a nineteenth-century court. One critic has compared the continual production of the play to the cycle dramas of medieval Christian Europe, through which communities renewed their relationship to their sanctified history through the annual reenactment of originary, or foundational, narratives. Another has suggested that its recurrent staging, and the audiences it attracts, have transformed the play from simply an artistic interpretation of the events of 1885 to a determinant of public perception. The play has assumed a ritualized form through its annual repetition, the inescapability of its conclusion, and the sacrificial nature of Riel's conviction: by continually re-trying Riel, in a sense it is the Confederation that is on trial and the conclusion of the spectacle leaves its audience with what he describes as a sense that there is "something valuable in ourselves that we have done away with. We suspect we have made a mistake."[42]

Coulter's plays have influenced a great deal of creative work revolving around Riel, prominent among which is Harry Somers's opera *Louis Riel*, a work whose tonality resonates with that of Coulter. The three-act opera was composed as part of the commemoration of Canada's centennial in 1967, and was presented first by the Canadian Opera Company in 1967 (it subsequently went on to be the first Canadian opera staged at the Kennedy Center in Washington, D.C.). *Louis Riel* signaled the broad cultural shift in perspective in favor of Riel that Howard's *Strange Empire* and Coulter's play had conjured up in the 1950s. Somers, considered at the time to be one of Canada's foremost composers, worked with a libretto by Mavor Moore and Jacques Languirand in which the writers employed four languages (English, French, Cree, and Latin). What was most striking about the work was its explicit condemnation of nineteenth-century Anglo-Canadian expansionism and of specific individuals such as John A. Macdonald and Thomas Scott. As a contribution to the centennial celebrations it clearly highlighted a changing cultural perception of Riel and the movement he led.[43] The bias against expansionists was clear in the presentation of John Schultz, who was head of the Canada Party and publisher of the *Nor'Wester* in 1869–70, and was held under arrest by the Métis forces during the uprising. Schultz was portrayed as igniting the anger of Ontario Orangemen over the murder of Thomas Scott, and his actions were referred to as a "holy crusade." Pressing the image of a religious confrontation further, Moore and Languirand drew an explicit analogy between Schultz and Judas Iscariot, portraying a man who "pockets the hateful coins" offered by his aggravated compatriots in support of suppressing the rebellion. Speaking then with Charles Mair (one of the founders of the Canada First movement and a journalist working for the *Toronto Globe* and the *Montreal Gazette* during the uprising, who was also arrested by Riel's forces), Schultz declared that they were on a "grim pilgrimage" for the sake of Canada. The nation, he added, now had a martyr in the figure of Thomas Scott, a man who may have been "a pain in every ass" while he was alive but whose "corpse'll be a hero by and by." Macdonald was perhaps the character most maligned in the production, and when the CBC chose to air the opera in 1969 it made one alteration to Moore's and Languirand's overall characterization: the prime minister was presented in a less comical fashion.[44]

Coulter's contribution to Riel drama and fiction was matched in poetry by Don Gutteridge's *Riel: A Poem for Voices* (1968). Gutteridge's concern was to bring history, myth, and poetry into the same sphere, something that he believed was lacking in the work of others who wrote on Riel. Coulter, he maintained, "was not prepared to see the story in poetic or mythical terms," and Howard had failed to concern himself with "patterns of universal meaning" discernable within the Riel story.[45] The increasingly broad-based desire to recast the rebel Riel as a cultural hero was evident in Janet Rosenstock and Dennis Adair's *Riel*, a two-part miniseries produced by the CBC in 1979 which, in spite of its rather bland presentation, was extremely successful with television viewers, reaching an audience of five million Canadians. What is most interesting perhaps is the fact that a Crown corporation, representing ostensibly the biases of prominent artists and public servants, had by the late 1970s arrived at the conclusion that the Canadian television-viewing public would accept an image of a heroic Louis Riel at odds with malevolent expansionist forces. The producers' bias was no more evident than in the contrast created between the characters of Riel and Macdonald. Riel, who was presented as serious, somber, and cultured, a man whose only desire was to assist in achieving "freedom and dignity" for his fellow Métis, was juxtaposed with the insipid prime minister portrayed in a drunken state at the opening of the series amusing himself with a model train.[46] The dichotomizing portrayals of both Riel and Macdonald in the miniseries *Riel* were somewhat offset by a subsequent CBC series, *Canada: A People's History*, aired in 2000–2001. The ninth episode of the series, *From Sea to Sea*, which was written and directed by Jim Williamson and dealt with the Red River resistance, depicted a much more human Macdonald, a man affected profoundly by the assassination of Thomas D'Arcy McGee and consequently displaying a resolute intolerance of "those who seek to change society by a barrel of a gun." However, the desire to idealize Riel was still apparent in the film, especially in the glossing of the treatment of Thomas Scott.[47]

The image of Riel as a proto-nationalist opposed by self-serving politicians in Ottawa has continued to permeate Canadian literature. Kevin Robert's poem "Riel," published in 1985, goes further than most perhaps, in condemning not only Riel's adversaries but the entire Canadian project, pointing out that it was an unnatural national configuration that ran in direct opposition to the inherent north-south orientation of the continent. Riel, in this instance, was opposed by

John A and the need for
CANADA
A mare usque ad mare
railway economics
irrational steel lines
denying the natural flow
North/South   geese/buffalo &

people who follow
seasons of flesh[48]

Unlike Roberts, most Anglophone writers have stopped short of condemning the entire Confederation, but have remained critical of Ottawa's handling of the Métis uprisings. Don McLean, for instance, has noted that between 1867 and 1885, the federal government was the strategic arm of eastern Canadian capitalists as they sought to extend their interests into the west, providing the legal framework and military support necessary to allow the economy to expand in such a way as to contribute to the requirements of the Canadian state as well as those of imperial Britain. McLean has consequently argued that the government ultimately bore sole responsibility for the confrontation that occurred between the Métis and the Canadian military in 1885.[49] Finally, we might note that some Anglophone writers have, like some Métis writers, also chosen to elevate Dumont over Riel. George Woodcock, for instance, took a shot at Riel in his *Six Dry Cakes for the Hunted*, a play aired by the CBC in 1975 that focused on Dumont, and in which Dumont expressed disappointment in Riel for having frustrated his ability to wage a sound campaign.[50] While such work represents a distinct part of Anglophone cultural production relating to the Métis rebellions, it has tended to be the exception rather than the norm.

Anglophones have been the last among Canadians to regard Riel as a heroic figure, although they have undeniably embraced him with a passion. The reasons for the transformation of public opinion are obviously many; but there have been at least two cultural changes that have underlain this shift. First, there is a direct correlation between the widespread emergence of positive English Canadian work on Riel and the ebbing of British Canadian nationalism after the Second World War. In the cultural space created by a general disenchantment with propagating a British Canadian image of the country, Riel apparently became visible in a new light to

Anglophones: as the victim of a vision of the Canadian polis that was undeniably flawed. Second, while Francophones, westerners and, to varying degrees, Native peoples have found within constructions of Riel a figure with whom they have been able to identify, in all these cases identification has been the product of asymmetrical power relationships with English Canada—a cultural, political, social, and/or economic sense of oppression based on the identifiable experience of marginalization. It can be argued that English Canada did not undergo this form of impingement—experienced as a loss of faith in the capacity of the Confederation to maintain itself as a structure intended to serve the best interest of Canadians—until the 1960s. To be sure, the threat of U.S. annexation of the country loomed large in the late nineteenth century and was, as we noted earlier, one of the principal motivating factors in the federal government's move to take possession of Rupert's Land and the North-West Territories; but annexation, as a serious threat, did not last longer than the initial Confederation period. It was not until Quebec's Quiet Revolution—and perhaps, more particularly, until the less quiet October Crisis of 1970—that English Canada found itself for the first time feeling somewhat peripheral to the forces that were shaping the Confederation; work concerning Riel reached a peak during the period when French nationalism emerged as a pronounced, and potentially destructive, Canadian fact. Rosenstock and Adair's *Riel*, (the miniseries produced by the CBC in 1979) was a prime example of this collective recognition of the precarious political nature of the country. The production received its share of criticism, especially for its many obviously warped historical details; yet, as one critic has suggested, the film was truly a fiasco primarily because it was not so much concerned with the Red River and North-West rebellions as with using these events to focus on contemporary tensions between French and English Canada in the wake of the October Crisis. Macdonald's outburst, upon learning of Riel's formation of a provisional government in 1870, was telling: "God, man! This means *Separation!*" The eruption may well have made sense within the context of the film, but in terms of history, it was patently wrong: after all, the colony at Red River could not "separate" itself from a state of which it was not yet a part.[51]

With respect to popular culture, it appears that the French Canadian perception of Riel and the events surrounding his death has become the prevailing point of view.[52] Still, as J. M. Bumsted has suggested, in spite of the fact that more biographical work has been written on Riel than on any other Canadian figure, he remains the most misunderstood public figure in Canadian history. The images of the man that have permeated Canadian historical writing, literature, film, and popular art vary so dramatically that it is difficult to see the same individual either within or across these genres. The issue of who the man *really* was has been progressively more difficult to address as we have moved further from the events of 1869 and 1885 and found ourselves inundated by competing formulations. In his 1964 poem *Louis Riel*, William Hawkins lamented this fact, writing that Riel had been "drained of meaning by Time." Hawkins found himself exasperated by the gulf in understanding and ended his poem by sneering at Riel and his "fucked up visions" that lay at the foundation of the Battle of Batoche.[53] Clearly, however, it is precisely this ambiguity that has sustained the interest of Canadians for more than a century. Riel has provided a model that resonates with their various experiences of being Canadians, a phenomenon that has given rise to ambiguous images and interpretations: "whenever I die,/I get new ideas," the poet Lyle Neff wrote in "Riel's Last Letter from Vancouver" in 1997.[54]

From the earliest works about Riel, there has been a tendency among writers to see in him some reflection of their own cultural values and agendas. The images that have emerged have generally been somewhat circumscribed, portraying him as emblematic of various sectarian interests and, in most cases, as a rather one-dimensional character. As a champion of French culture, or western rights, or regionalism, for instance, he has been cast in an oppositional light that obscures his commitment to Aboriginal rights and, often, his belief in the Confederation (to be considered later). Likewise, while elevating the uprisings to mythic proportion, Native and Métis preference for the figure of Dumont has concomitantly constituted a critique of the way in which the image of Riel has been manipulated by nonnatives. This critique has been focused on the English typecasting of Riel as either a symbol of the failure of Anglophone nationalism and imperialism, or a link between English Canadians and their country (a trope that has rightly been criticized for creating a caricature that has little to do with the actual relationship between Aboriginals and nonnatives).

The point is well taken. Albert Braz has noted that since the end of the Second World War, writers like Gutteridge, Rosenstock, and Adair have tended to elevate Riel to the status of a Canadian nationalist (in spite of the fact that he was executed for treason by the Canadian government), and to disparage those who opposed him as bigoted "imperialists." These writers have appeared to identify Canadians of European descent with Aboriginal

Canadians, rather than with their own progenitors who were responsible for the legacy of marginalization and social crises with which contemporary Native and Métis peoples are contending; and Riel has proven to be a ready cultural instrument for accomplishing this. It has also been suggested that the cultural space between Native and nonnative peoples has been psychologically dissonant for nonnatives carrying a historical sense of cultural displacement, and that Riel has been exploited to mediate this gulf.[55] A number of scholars and writers have in recent years also accused Anglophone writers of focusing on Riel in order to mitigate their sense of cultural guilt for his execution; in the process of elevating Riel to hero status, they have distanced him entirely from his aboriginality. bpNichol reflected on this appropriation in his poem "The Long Weekend of Louis Riel":

> they killed louis riel & by Monday they were feeling guilty
> maybe we shouldn't have done it said the mounties as they sat
> down to breakfast   louis rolled over in his grave & sighed
>   it's not enough they take your life away with a gun they
> have to take it away with their pens   in the distance he could
> hear the writers scratching louder & louder[56]

The Riels who have emerged as the champion of French Canadian or western rights, the antifederalist, the cultural bridge between Native and nonnative Canadians, or the instrument of imperializing forces are, in and of themselves, rather fractional Riels; but taken together, they provide a portrait of a multidimensional Canadian hero who has come to be regarded broadly also as a mythic symbol. Mythic heroes are specific kinds of cultural figures who are intimately related to originary cultural structures within a society. Whether they are responsible for the creation of a world or for a particular aspect of a world, they are generally figures who return from difficult journeys (traditionally, into primordial waters, or the underworld, or the womb) with something necessary and valuable (perhaps a tool) for their culture, the acquisition of which signals a "new creation" of some sort.[57] In his repeated elevation to the status of a mythic hero, Riel has been recognized in this way as having some sort of broad cultural significance, presumably related to an originary meaning of the Canadian community. It has been suggested that the Riel of the Canadian imagination has become a reflection of the varied contours of Canadian consciousness; and while this is quite likely true, we must add to this that he has also reflected some of the very real contingencies of the Canadian experience that reside at the foundation of this consciousness: the country's varied ethnic composition, its regional disparity, and its concomitant resistance to the formulation of a broadly based sense of shared cultural identity.[58] Sectarian reflections on the meaning of the man have served sectarian interests; but taken as a whole, all these varied interpretations of his significance have charted the contours of a broader meaning of being located within the geopolitical entity called Canada: Riel's multidimensionality articulates something significant about what it means to be a Canadian—something, in other words, about Canadian identity.[59] Ian Dowbiggin has described Canada as "the world's first postwar paranoid nation," for which Riel is "the paradigmatic historical icon for delusional times, a role model for a paranoid citizenry."[60] I would contend that there may be something more constructive to be said of Riel in terms of Canadian identity, and that this rests in the broad panorama of images that have attached themselves to him and the rebellions, not merely in the fact of simple contradiction.

It is unquestionably obvious to anyone with even a tertiary knowledge of Canada that the issue of Canadian identity has been an ongoing conundrum in the country. Indeed, Neil Bissondath has referred to the problem of determining *who are Canadians* as the "quintessential (and possibly eternal) Canadian question."[61] Writers and scholars have been pursuing an answer to the question for as long as there has been a Canadian state. From the vision of Canadian identity proposed by Vincent Massey (a historian who became the first Canadian-born governor general in 1952), as the product of the coming together of Great Britain and the United States in North America, to W. L. Morton's argument that Canadians have been indelibly shaped by the presence of the Canadian Shield, to Margaret Atwood's and Northrop Frye's explorations of the relationship between Canadian identity and literature, the issue has proven to be both fascinating and elusive.[62] In spite of continual efforts to isolate some aspect of shared experience or vision that might provide a culturally defining link between the country's ethnically and geographically disparate peoples, a single formulation has yet to emerge that is capable of speaking to all Canadians. The idea that Canadians could experience and express a sense of identity based on the country's identification with Great Britain was the core component of a form of nationalism that took root in the Confederation period and, as already noted, withered measurably following World War II (this subject will be explored at greater length subsequently). Of the countless other formulations that have been presented as possible rejoinders to the question, there have been two that have proffered the possibility of greatest applicability in the wake of the waning of Anglo-Saxon nationalism: that of anti-Americanism and that of the Laurentian school of historiography.

The presence of the United States has loomed large in the Canadian psyche since the time of the American Revolution; so much so, in fact, that academics and intellectuals have generally contended that a shared public sense of identity in any pervasive and deep-seated sense has been absent from the collective Canadian psyche, with the exception, perhaps, of a rather reversed sense of not being American. In the first instance, the Revolutionary War forced the remaining British colonies in North America to define themselves to a substantive degree as an alternative geopolitical space on the continent; and for Anglophones, a form of identity (and nationalism) based on an imperial British tie promised to afford a shield from U.S. economic, cultural, and military encroachment. Over time, this initial necessity for an oppositional self-definition assumed a sense of distinctiveness based on moral superiority that precluded the possibility of regarding the United States as an "equal" when the time came for Canada to identify fully with its continental situation rather than with the British Empire.[63] Goldwin Smith argued in the late nineteenth century, for instance, that American financial and cultural power would ultimately destroy the Canadian state, a prospect that he believed was inescapable because of the degree of commerce and communication that was being transacted regionally between the Canadian provinces and neighboring American states. Smith's work elicited severe criticism, especially from scholars like George Parkin, who responded by claiming that Canadians' moral "opposition to absorption in the United States" constituted their strongest political obsession.[64]

In the twentieth century the issue of identity was complicated by a generalized experience of marginalization created by the country's situation at the edges of an emerging major global power. The consequence of Canada's switch in identification from Europe to the Americas was that the country discovered itself to have shifted from being a vital component of an empire to a secondary player in a continental order. The threat of cultural assimilation latent in Canada's proximity to the United States began to loom large in the mid-twentieth century, and within this rapidly changing global environment, some voices continued to call for an identity based on an association with Britain. Writing about Canadian identity in the 1940s, for instance, Vincent Massey fully supported Canada's participation in the

British Commonwealth, which he regarded as "essential to Canadian independence," given its situation on the flanks of the United States. Massey valued the solid relationship that existed between Canada and the United States, but was uneasy about the potentially damaging effects of American "influences" in terms of Canadian culture and economics. He consequently believed that the unique character of the country had to be expressed in a broadly held national ethos if there was to be any hope of withstanding the impact of American culture and business.[65]

By the late 1960s, the concept of a collective identity tied to the British Empire had all but disappeared; efforts aimed at arriving at an explanation for the basic character of Canada had moved in a variety of directions, and consensus on the issue was all but an impossibility. Social, economic, and ideological changes in the country were sufficiently powerful during the period that many Canadians virtually gave up attempting to describe the country's fundamental attributes, and settled into a kind of negative definition of the Canadian people as *not American*. In the final decades of the century, being *not American* became a foundational mode of political life in the country, finding voice in a variety of issues ranging from cultural policy to social welfare. Scholars began to argue, for example, that official bilingualism and multiculturalism set Canada apart from the United States, preserving its capacity to remain culturally distinct from that nation. Likewise, when Canada's social welfare system underwent dramatic alterations in the 1990s, recourse to being *not America* became part of the reaction against reductions in government spending on health care, education, and other social safety nets. The fiscal environment proved conducive to the emergence of right-wing political forces (e.g., Preston Manning and his Reform Party, and provincial premiers like Mike Harris in Ontario and Ralph Klein in Alberta), and although there is no doubt that reductions in government spending were necessary, public reaction against these right-leaning regimes focused, to a noticeable degree, on the perennial Canadian concern with distinguishing Canada from the United States, which rested in this instance on the conviction that social welfare was a necessary and defining component of a modern state.[66]

Aside from the obvious appeals to being "not American" that have characterized the conversation about identity in Canada, the fact remains that the United States has indeed been a pervasive force in Canadian cultural life, something that scholars and writers have been hard-pressed to ignore. All too often, discussions of Canadian issues have resorted to comparative reflections in which the United States has been employed as a foil. Subjects as diverse as the historical significance of the west and the frontier, the cultural meaning of violence, the basic pattern of the country's historical development, and the failure of Canadian nationalism have frequently been approached from the perspective of opposition with the United States, and even discussion of the apparent lack of collective identity has pitted Canada against the United States.[67] The United States has been a constant presence in the consciousness of Canadians, a phenomenon that Neil Bissoondath highlighted anecdotally in his *Selling Illusions* (2002) by referring to John Robert Colombo's *The Dictionary of Canadian Quotations*, in which the entry under the heading "Canada" occupies half the space of that under "Canada and the United States."[68] The perennial issue of who Canadians truly are has been persistently resolved with simple recourse to their difference from Americans; but whether a country's identity can be defined absolutely in relation to another state is, obviously, questionable. More critically, however, this notion of identity has been tossed about in public, academic, political, and literary arenas for a least a century, while Canadians have concomitantly continued to fuss about the issue of identity. One must conclude that it has not, ultimately, proven to be a satisfactory model for defining the country's people in relation to those of other states.

The Laurentian school of historiography, typified by Harold Innis, Donald Creighton, and W. L. Morton, provided what was perhaps the most viable alternative to this formulation of identity in the twentieth century. These historians, who have been credited with providing Canadian historiography with an unprecedented level of both unity and complexity, argued that a northern orientation in the country's landscape lay at the foundation of the Canadian character; and they created a historical point of entry for many other historians through their concentration on the fur trade and its relation to northern expansion. The presumption that the country's cultural, demographic, economic, and political development could be traced to the trade in northern resources became a mode by which the Laurentian historians invoked a sense of a coherent development of the country—a development that was distinctly northern.

> Canadian history began when the Vikings carried the frontier of fish, fur and farm across the North Atlantic to Iceland and Greenland. . . . From that obscure beginning Canada had a distinct, a unique, and northern destiny. Its modern beginnings

are not Columbian but Cabotan. And when the French followed Cartier up the St. Lawrence they were at once committed by the development of the fur trade to the exploitations of the Canadian Shield. . . . The Canadian or Precambrian Shield is as central in Canadian history as it is in Canadian geography, and to all understandings of Canada. . . . And this alternate penetration of the wilderness and return to civilization is the basic rhythm of Canadian life, and forms the basic elements of Canadian character.[69]

For these scholars, the coherence of Canada's development, as defined by a northern orientation, was derived to varying degrees from the presence of the Canadian Shield—a Precambrian backdrop of stone and watercourses that historically served as the northern periphery of the commercial and political center of what would eventually become central Canada. The country emerged, from this perspective, by means of the deployment of capital and industry from this region in relation to the Shield. Harold Innis thus argued that the Canadian Shield determined the earliest fur trade routes that would ultimately shape the parameters of a northern American state, and that the state was consequently not a synthetic construction, but a legitimization of a coherent political entity that had been established by its geography.[70]

It was Donald Creighton who took up Innis's work and gave it a political meaning. In *The Commercial Empire of the St. Lawrence*, Creighton suggested that European forays into North America were motivated by a desire for wealth that he labeled "the dream of the Empire of the St. Lawrence." He described the river as a "destined pathway of North American trade," the foundation of a system of transportation that would give rise to a "western commercial empire" based on the flow of New World staples and Old World commodities. He argued, further, that the dream of the St. Lawrence Empire had permeated Canadian history, driving its early economic development and its subsequent stake at nationhood. Going further, he argued that Canada's cultural diversity could provide no foundation for national character. He believed that Canadians were bound by their common geographical heritage and, in particular, the St. Lawrence River system that had unified all regions of the country by providing a transcontinental economic focus for its creation. Thus, any perception of political, cultural, or regional fragmentation was secondary to the fundamental unifying fact of Canada's landscape.[71]

The relationship between the Laurentian theory and national character would be explored further by W. L. Morton, who was initially critical of the correlation. In 1946, he published an article in which he granted the historical utility of the theory but questioned its extension into the arena of nationalist discourse, claiming that the Canadian state could not develop an absolute form of nationalism reflecting a homogenous popular vision; the country's multiple nationalities and regions simply made this impossible. Rather, he suggested, a Canadian nationalism would have to be formulated in terms of the ethnic and regional groups that were at the foundation of the national project.[72] By 1960, he had tempered his views, coming to believe that no society could survive without developing a distinct self-understanding that was broadly accepted by its population; he consequently attempted to adapt the Laurentian model of Canadian development to the reality of a pluralistic nation, and in formulating such a theory he had recourse to a Canadian archetype: that of the nation as a northern society. In spite of legitimate regional and ethnic disparity, Morton argued, Canadians were unified by their common character derived of being situated in a northern environment.[73]

It has been suggested that the Laurentian hypothesis was, in a sense, reminiscent of Frederick Jackson Turner's "frontier thesis" insofar as it appeared capable of coherently addressing the fundamental issues at stake in the creation of a state. Like Turner's theory, it proved well-suited to dealing with some aspects of Canada's expansion, but it was ultimately of limited utility in terms of defining a people's identity.[74] The Laurentian school was successful in intellectually legitimizing a form of nationalism based on a particular historical trajectory: as the pivotal phenomenon of Canada's history, the ascendancy of the St. Lawrence River could well be argued. This was not, however, a sufficient basis on which to develop a more broad-ranging popular formulation of identity, as Creighton and Innis hoped to do. Canada, from the perspective of the Laurentianists, was a nation of peripheral zones that existed in relation to a unified, determining center. To create a theory of national character on the basis of this configuration would necessarily entail a disregard for the historical development of strong regional identities. As a historical theory, there is no question that the Laurentian hypothesis was extremely successful in turning attention toward the particular North American history of Canada, but it ultimately reduced the Canadian West and the Atlantic provinces to peripheral regions attached asymmetrically to central Canada, and in particular, to the province of Ontario.[75]

The limitations of the Laurentian theory, as well as those of the even more pervasive notion of Canadian identity as a function of being *not American*, are emblematic of the obstacles that have faced most conceptions of collective identity in the country. Ultimately, no single formulation has been capable of resonating with Canadians sufficiently to put the issue to rest. Identity, in its individual and social sense, revolves around attitudes that one possesses regarding oneself, as well as the symbolic expression of these attitudes.[76] Further, there is an undeniable relationship between identity and myth, a correlation that many Canadian writers have discerned with respect to the ways in which their work is concerned with locating the myths and historical spaces that make the creation of a common sense of identity possible. Margaret Laurence, for instance, claimed that "[m]any Canadian writers, myself among them, have spent much of our lives, in our novels and poems, coming back home, in a spiritual sense, trying to bring into acknowledged being the myths and backgrounds and places which belong to us." Similarly, Rudy Wiebe suggested that "[t]he principle task of the Canadian writer is not simply to explain his contemporary world, but to create a past, a lived history, a vital mythology."[77] Like their literary counterparts, historians have also recognized the link between identity and myth, a relationship that is, from their perspective, mediated by history. W. L. Morton, for instance, argued that both the historian and the poet are "maker[s] of myths, only the historian has neglected his job of making myths in this decadent, analytical age."[78] Morton thus identified in the 1940s a shortcoming of historical writing that had impeded Canadians' capacity to formulate a sense of shared identity, something that the journalist Robert MacNeil confronted decades later:

> One of the psychologically crippling things, part of the colonial wound that never healed at least in the psyches of my generation, is that we grew up reading books that were all written and published about people who lived . . . in other countries.[79]

Earle Birney leveled the same criticism in his poem "Can Lit":

> the wounded sirened off
> no Whitman wanted
> its only by our lack of ghosts
> we're haunted[80]

The problem, however, may not be so much a function of a decadent age, as Morton believed, as a product of the tendency of historians to serve the interests of prevailing discourses within society. From this perspective, the writing of *history* is an exercise in creating a dominant narrative that both reflects and promulgates the myths that are presumed to reside at the foundation of a shared identity. These central myths are generally the constructions of dominant groups within society, and are used as tools for maintaining social stability and legitimizing these groups' positions of advantage. While they are not necessarily untrue, they tend to be incomplete representations of a society's experience, and, as such, are always vulnerable to subversion by competing historical accounts. This is precisely what began occurring in Canada in the latter part of the twentieth century. Many of the elite myths that had, for over a century, reflected the self-understanding of dominant groups, had also effectively relegated many Canadians to the peripheries of national identity. As the histories of these peripheral groups has increasingly entered into the arena of historical debate, dominant historical narratives—and the myths they embody—have come under equally mounting criticism that cannot be dismissed.[81]

In his *National Dreams: Myth, Memory, and Canadian History* (1997), Daniel Francis engaged in an extended discussion of a number of predominant myths and mythic symbols that have failed to generate or sustain a collective sense of identity in Canada. Principal among these were those of a northern orientation, the Canadian Pacific Railway (CPR), the Royal Canadian Mounted Police (RCMP), the "British Master Race," and the mosaic, all of which are worth noting and exploring briefly here.

The Myth of the North

The "northern character" of Canada has been a consistent component of the country's discourse from the time of the first explorations of Frenchmen who repeatedly asserted that colonists would need to be as tough as the natural environment to which they were immigrating. Nationalists and other commentators have likewise turned to the environment as a defining mode of nationality, summoning, as John Diefenbaker would in the mid-twentieth century, the country's "northern destiny." The idea of the north as a unifying motif assumed its first structured mythic—and nationalist—articulation in 1868 with a small group of literary and intellectual elites in Ottawa that referred to itself as Canada First. These men hoped to formulate a nationalist discourse that would take root in the nascent Confederation, a discourse that went beyond the practical political alliance that Canada was. A significant component of their vision was a northern geographical location that they believed pointed to a cultural and racial preeminence. Canadians, said Firster Robert Grant Haliburton, "are the Northmen of the New World."[82] Although largely discredited in the years following World War I, theories of national character based on a northern orientation continued within Canadian discourses. Vincent Massey, for instance, claimed in 1948 that a principal distinction between Canadians and Americans was the moderate manner of Canadians originating in the meeting of northern ethnicity and environment.

> Climate plays a great part in giving us our special character, different from that of our southern neighbours. Quite apart from the huge annual bill our winter imposes on us in terms of building construction and clothing and fuel, it influences our mentality, produces a sober temperament. Our racial composition—and this is partly because of our climate—is different, too. A small percentage of our people comes from central or southern Europe. The vast majority springs either from the British Isles or Northern France, and good many, too, from Scandinavia and Germany, and it is in northwestern Europe that one finds the elements of human stability highly developed. Nothing is more characteristic of Canadians than the inclination to be moderate.[83]

This sense of the intrusion of landscape into self-definition was likewise at the core of W. L. Morton's argument for the impact of the "northern frontier" upon the Canadian imagination. Morton argued that the development of the state, its dependence on British and European markets, its literature, and its cyclic annual rhythms were all substantially products of a northern orientation that imbedded a notion within the collective Canadian psyche of a stark line dividing the "wilderness" from the "baseland," or the hinterland from the metropolis. While pointing out that the same might be said of Americans living in Colorado, Arkansas, or Oregon, Northrop Frye argued that there was something fundamentally different at work in the American situation: Americans have a unifying perception of the collective self that has allowed the hinterland and metropolis to be incorporated into a single notion of American space. Canadians, on the other hand, have regarded the hinterland (represented by the "north") as an alter ego, "oneself and yet the opposite of oneself."[84]

While the myth of Canadians as northern peoples maintained an imaginative foothold on those living in the southern parts of the country, the Native population of the north, the Inuit, remained virtually unknown to Canadians even as the state's expansion into the north wrought devastation upon them in the twentieth century. What southern Canadians came to know of the Inuit of the period was based principally on idealized images created by filmmakers beginning with Robert Flaherty, whose 1922 documentary *Nanook of the North* (still the most recognizable film on the Inuit) portrayed the Inuit as an incurably happy people forced to contend with an inhospitable ecosystem. The film, which focused on a family living along the coast of Hudson Bay, sold itself as an authentic representation of traditional Inuit life, in spite of the fact that its creator was fully aware of the fact that his image was not entirely accurate: "I am not going to make films about what the white man has made of primitive peoples. . . . What I want to show is the former majesty and character of these people, while it is still possible—before the white man has destroyed not only their character, but the people as well."[85] Flaherty's portrayal of the Inuit influenced a number of subsequent films made in both Canada and the United States, and Nanook himself was immortalized on the package of Eskimo Pie ice cream bars. Doug Wilkinson's contribution to the Eskimo film genre, *Land of the Long Day*, reinforced the image with Joseph Idlouk who, dressed in Nanook style, ultimately appeared on the country's two-dollar bill. By the second half of the twentieth century, it was impossible to reasonably maintain this image of the Inuit. Diseases like tuberculosis were devastating the population, while starvation had become a constant reality for people whose lives depended upon the harvesting of animal stocks that had been substantially diminished, and for whom employment opportunities were scarce. In addition, substance and domestic abuse had become widespread. Francis argued that the myth of the north had, by the end of the twentieth century, undergone substantial erosion as a result of southern Canadians' increasing contact with the north. Inuit voices were calling for recognition of an alternate understanding of history that had become increasingly difficult to ignore, and the dominant notion of what constitutes a "northern people" had consequently come under pressure for change. Given the situation, Francis predicted that continued contact of this sort would inevitably render the fantasy on which the myth was founded untenable.[86]

Like the myth of the north, that of the Canadian Pacific Railway was successfully propagated for more than a century following confederation. The latter was based on the assumption that Canada would not exist without the Canadian Pacific Railway, since it was responsible for uniting Canadians into a single geopolitical body. To be sure, the CPR did unify the country in some respects, but the unity it created was fundamentally political, with the construction of the railway serving as a catalyst for a discourse about the country that legitimated the idea of a sovereign state, and encouraged the country's disparate population to regard itself as Canadian.[87] The CPR, which was subsidized by the federal government, was important for the developing Dominion insofar as it connected central Canada with British Columbia for the purposes of extending both trade and political control. Further, it was discursively important as an expression of national political determination, something John A. Macdonald clearly discerned: "The road will be constructed," he announced to the House of Commons in 1881, "and the fate of Canada, will then as a Dominion, be realized. Then will the fate of Canada, as one great body be fixed." Macdonald's vision would be echoed by the popular historian, Pierre Berton, nearly a century later when he wrote: "[I]t was Macdonald's intention to defy nature and fashion a nation in the process. His tool, to this end, would be the Canadian Pacific."[88]

Francis suggested that the most coherent articulation of the myth of the CPR hailed from the pen of Berton, who wrote three books and a CBC miniseries in the 1970s in which the CPR was cast as the foundation for uniting a group of distinct regions into a unified national body—"a rare example of a nation created through the construction of a railway." On Berton's account, Macdonald was a political prophet who realized that a Canadian nation was not possible without the unifying presence of a transcontinental railroad.[89] Although Berton was instrumental in broadening the appeal of the myth of the CPR, he was not the first to advocate it. R. G. MacBeth wrote in 1924, for example, that "the country and the railway must stand or fall together"; and the poet E. J. Pratt wrote in his *Towards the Last Spike* (for which he won the Governor General's Award) that, by bringing about the emergence of a nation, the railroad had expanded the world—"if not the universe."[90]

A similar national rhetoric can be discerned in Gordon Lightfoot's classic "Canadian Railroad Trilogy," in which capitalist interests, national expansion, and the railroad were inextricably linked:

But . . . they looked in the future
    and what did they see?
They saw an iron rail running
    from the sea to the sea . . .
The song of the future has been sung,
    all the battles have been won.
We have opened up the land,
    All the world's at our command . . .
We have opened up the soil
    With our teardrops and our toil.

The success of the myth, however, was not principally the result of politics, but of the promotional efforts of the CPR itself. Once the line had been completed, the company found itself in a difficult financial position; and with extensive immigration into the west more than a decade away, the railway was forced to mount its own advertising campaign to promote western settlement and tourism. The CPR's reward for constructing a transcontinental railway was a government grant of twenty-five million dollars and title to ten million hectares of real estate, intended for sale to prospective settlers. To this end, the company established its own immigration service that mounted a promotional campaign in the United States and Europe, portraying the prairies as a "paradise" for immigrants. In the United States, Britain, and the rest of Canada, the campaign hit the road, with a CPR-funded "Travelling Exhibition Van" that moved from town to town giving out promotional materials and exhibiting agricultural products. In addition, an English movie producer, Charles Urban, was hired in 1902 to produce thirty-five shorts, called *Living Canada*, aimed at marketing the region; and the Edison Company produced thirteen melodramas shortly afterward that highlighted the spectacular landscape of the region.[91] The CPR constructed a myth about itself that was adopted by generations of subsequent historians. As Francis noted, the fact that the railway was constructed principally with British funds, and by exploited Chinese laborers on land that was unethically obtained from Aboriginal peoples, was never accounted for within the substance of these histories that cast the railway as the creator of a nation. While it is true that if the railway had not been constructed when it was, the Canadian west might well have been annexed by the United States, it is also clear that the CPR contributed to a discourse about Canada that did not foster a collective sense of cultural, political, or economic identity; rather it primarily extended central Canadian commercial interests, creating a "nation" founded upon capitalist enterprise. The building of the CPR was a national mission principally in terms of economics; it was constructed by both private and public funds with the intention of economic expansion in both sectors.[92]

The Royal Canadian Mounted Police

A third myth, relating to the Royal Canadian Mounted Police (and its precursor the North West Mounted Police), was operative within the Canadian imagination for over a century, and expressed through the symbolic image of Mounties in books, films, television programs, and significant state events. There is no older police force in the Western Hemisphere than the RCMP; indeed, its formal costume is one of the most well known in the world. The mythic narrative associated with the force traditionally involved the image of Mounties pacifying savage Indians in order to render the west secure for Canadian colonization; it also projected an image of Canada as a society in which the law and communal order were valued above individual autonomy.[93]

The NWMP was established in 1873 as a quasi-military arm of the federal government. By the early twentieth century, the force had gained widespread respect among English Canadians for its role in the annexation of the west. J. G. Colmer, in his introduction to NWMP superintendent Sam Steele's account of the North-West Rebellion, succinctly described the myth as it had come to be known at that time. Colmer praised the Hudson's Bay Company, territorial governments, and the Mounted Police for the way in which they contributed to the "peaceful and wonderful development" of a region that had been, previously, the "red man's country"—an "illimitable wilderness." Although he admitted that some confrontation over control of the region occurred in 1869 and again in 1885, this was not a product of widespread legitimate dissatisfaction but, rather, the result of agitation by a small number of Métis and Natives. Further, he claimed that governing bodies in the territories had always dealt fairly with the Native population. First Nations peoples had been satisfied with the Hudson's Bay Company's evenhanded management of the region; and the Canadian government followed suit, effecting justice in an unbiased fashion among Natives and non-native settlers. As a result, the country was made suitable for settlement and development with relatively little resistance from Native peoples. According to Colmer, the North West Mounted Police was the mechanism by which the government was able to carry out this transformation of the west, and the skill and prudence the force employed in maintaining order was confirmation that Natives and nonnatives alike had faith in the force's abilities.[94]

A number of other Mounted Policemen published memoirs of their experience with the force in the late nineteenth and early twentieth centuries, and these spawned an industry in Mountie mythology through autobiographies, novels, popular histories, and Hollywood movies. Movies like *Rose-Marie* (featuring Nelson Eddy and Jeanette MacDonald) and *North West Mounted Police* (with Gary Cooper) made the image of the Mountie a familiar one to movie audiences everywhere;[95] and within Canada the symbol remained a respected one throughout the first three-quarters of the twentieth century. Northrop Frye argued that the appeal of the RCMP as both symbol and myth was related to Canadians' attitude toward violence, which differed substantially from that of Americans. According to Frye, American culture had been shaped by a constructive view of violence based on having waged a successful revolution, and he suggested that many of the most violent vignettes of American history (e.g., the opening of the west) had drawn on the revolutionary heritage. Revolution was not part of the Canadian experience where, rather, the state was constructed on the back of a series of "military occupations." For a country where the most obvious forms of violence have consequently been repressive, it was no surprise to Frye that the image of the policeman-soldier-Mountie had become a cultural symbol.[96]

The reality of the force's activities, however, were not consonant with the generally held view of the RCMP as emblematic of Canadians' respect for order and the law; and in the 1970s, the force became the object of a number of public inquiries that exposed a surprising level of corruption within its ranks. In their national security capacity, for instance, the officers of Montreal's RCMP G-section engaged in a number of highly objectionable practices in the early 1970s, burning a barn, stealing explosives, and issuing a bogus FLQ (Front de Libération du Québec) public statement. The federal government's reaction to the FLQ was little short of draconian in the lengths to which it was willing to go to counter an unconstitutional separatist movement; but it was also ultimately effective in destroying the terrorist movement. In the wake of the government's invocation of the War Measures Act (an attack on civil liberties that resulted in the arrest of hundreds of Quebec citizens who were held without being charged with any crime), the deportation of James Cross's kidnappers to Cuba, and the imprisonment of Pierre Laporte's murderers, the FLQ was effectively crushed and the separatist movement focused its energies on constitutional modes articulated increasingly by the Parti Québécois. The RCMP's security branch, however, continued to function as though the situation had not changed. During the October Crisis of 1970, the police force had enjoyed unparalleled powers of search and seizure. When the crisis passed, the force continued to exercise these powers, functioning under the assumption that proactive interference would allow for preemptive police action, thus preventing further agitations like that which had occurred in 1970.[97] The force had, it appeared, consistently acted in contravention of the law, interfering with mail, breaking into the offices of political parties, and illegally scrutinizing the activities of African Canadians, labor unions, and Aboriginal and student organizations. Subsequent to federal inquiries, the RCMP lost jurisdiction over internal national security, and a new agency— the Canadian Security Intelligence Service (CSIS)—was established to assume this responsibility. The inquiries of the 1970s resulted in a general decline in Canadians' confidence in the RCMP and, as Francis noted, the myth of the force consequently went the way of many others during the late twentieth century: the force became a target of humor rather than a bastion of authority.[98]

Despite the fact that Canadians suffered a loss of faith in the RCMP as a symbol of integrity and moral rectitude, the image continues to evoke a response in countries outside Canada. Foreign tourists, for instance, still flock to witness the Musical Ride; and a beer was introduced into the British market in the 1990s whose label portrayed a Mounted Policeman. The public persona of the force has become sufficiently tarnished in Canada, however, that foreign ownership of its image was acceptable to a population that has generally been resistant toward U.S. incursion into Canadian cultural arenas: in 1995, the Disney Corporation acquired the license to control the marketing of the Mountie image.[99]

The "British Master Race" in Canada

Another long-standing myth that has lost sway over the Canadian imagination is that of the British master race. This myth of Anglo-Saxon preeminence was pervasive in Canada until the second half of the twentieth century; and the country's educational system was, until that time, designed to convince Canadians that they possessed a birthright to citizenship within a broader British Empire. Canadian history was taught with the intention of affirming the ascendancy of British institutions and culture, and inculcating Canadians with the conviction that their country was destined to become a principal player in the British imperial venture. As a result, history was framed around defining military, political, and judicial moments, and episodes that did not correspond with this master narrative were generally marginalized, regarded as anecdotal at best.[100] At the beginning of the twentieth century, the country's dominant historical narrative involved its development from a position of colonial dependency to one of full national autonomy. In the interest of promoting this view and creating a widely recognizable pool of Canadian heroes, the twenty-one-volume *Makers of Canada* series was published in the years 1908 to 1911. The series was a reflection of the dominant Anglo-Saxon interpretation of Canadian history in which, for instance, Aboriginals, peoples of color, women, and the working classes were not represented as having contributed anything to the formation of the country. This was a collection of potential heroes that mapped out a history defined, aside from the achievements of a smattering of fur traders, by political and constitutional evolution.[101]

There was an odd overtone inherent in the myth of British ascendancy as it pertained to the Canadian situation. Writers of histories based on this myth consistently turned to the image of Canada as part of a larger imperial family, warning the country's young that, as Charles G. D. Roberts (who was a history teacher in addition to being a poet) argued at the end of the nineteenth century, it would be distinctly unappreciative of Canadians to contemplate breaking their national bond to Great Britain. A half-century later, Arthur Dorland informed his readers that England was "the mother of a family of free states" that, despite their sovereignty, were ineradicably bound to Great Britain for defense and some forms of state management. As Francis notes, it is indeed unusual to encounter a modern state that has consistently educated its population to believe that national self-determination is a dishonorable objective.[102] For nearly a century following confederation, dominant constructions of identity were characterized by a noticeable air of confidence; the imperialist account of the country as the direct heir of Anglo-Saxon cultural superiority instilled a distinct sense of self-assurance within that quarter of the society that had a monopoly on national discourse. Within this narrative structure, non–British Canadians were cast as fortunate members of a British-derived society into which they should feel privileged to be afforded the opportunity to assimilate. This confidence, however, was no longer evident by the second half of the twentieth century; in fact, during the period, discourses on Canadian identity demonstrated what Francis described as "self-effacement." It is perhaps a peculiarity of the Canadian situation that historical pariahs (e.g., Riel or the deported Acadians) have come to be widely regarded as prototypically Canadian. "Un-Canadianism," wrote Hugh Hood in 1970, "is almost the very definition of Canadianism."[103]

The Canadian Cultural Mosaic

A consideration of failed Canadian myths would not be adequate without reference to that of the mosaic, a description of the Canadian cultural situation that was coined in 1922 by Victoria Hayward, an American writer who published a book entitled *Romantic Canada* in the wake of a trip across Canada. In the context of a description of prairie architecture and ethnic diversity, Hayward wrote: "It is indeed a mosaic of vast dimensions and breadth." Hayward's desire to adequately portray what she regarded as a peculiarly Canadian ethnic phenomenon led her to draw a distinction between Canada and the United States, a dissimilarity that was picked up by Edward J. O'Brien, who wrote in the introduction to her book that Canada was unlike the United States insofar as it had allowed for the flourishing of "unique and beautiful racial traditions."[104] The term appeared again in 1926 in *Our Canadian Mosaic*, Kate Foster's review of Canadian immigrants compiled for the YWCA's Dominion Council, in which she employed the term in a relatively neutral fashion as a way of describing a society with numerous cultural components. The symbol was subsequently introduced into Canadian academic discourse by John Murray Gibbon, in his *Canadian Mosaic*, published in 1938.[105]

The mosaic symbol differed from that of the American melting pot principally in terms of its expressed valuation of cultural diversity as the foundation for a state, and in this respect, the symbol did indeed reflect a legitimate aspect of the Canadian experience. Of necessity, a state defined in terms of such an image attaches less significance to cultural homogeny than to creating a political landscape in which dissimilar groups can flourish as a result of their national coexistence; consensus—the foundation of all modern states—cannot be acquired in many postcolonial states via a common cultural orientation, but rather by means of a fundamental conviction among its people that its political organization is best equipped to serve its needs.[106] Still, the image of the mosaic was just as much of an imaginative construction as its American counterpart. In the first instance, *Canadian Mosaic* was Gibbon's attempt to present a history of Canada that focused on the role of the country's various ethnic groups: "The Canadian people today presents itself as a decorated surface, bright with inlays of separate colored pieces . . . and so the ensemble may truly be called a mosaic." His mosaic, however, was noticeably limited in scope, as the subtitle of his book demonstrated; *The Making of a Northern Nation* asserted foremost that the mosaic north of the forty-ninth parallel would not include peoples of color or Jews, thus adhering to an established vision of the state as a product of northern European expansion. The notion that Canada's pluralistic heritage might include those of other than northern European descent did not enter into dominant national discourses until after World War II.[107]

Secondarily, the development of a national culture has never been a possibility in a state whose political genesis was forged primarily in relation to two vocal, powerful, and culturally distinct groups that could agree only on the barest essentials of a geopolitical life. The political melding of a French-speaking, Roman Catholic, and agrarian society with one that was Anglo-Saxon, Protestant, and market-oriented was a precarious undertaking: it impelled the French minority into a protectionist stance and the English majority into one that was reactive and expansionist. As a consequence, both groups depended substantially on Old World associations in articulating a sense of identity within their shared political space, a tendency that undermined a mutual aspiration for a novel form of collective identity to which subsequent immigrants could aspire, and with which indigenous peoples could identify. More critically, the mosaic image suggested that within a structure of cultural diversity all members of the society had equal access to arenas of collective valuation; in fact, the most influential positions in Canadian society have historically been overwhelmingly occupied by the British and Canadians of British heritage. Ultimately, the idea of the mosaic was initiated by Canadians of European descent who appeared ready to acknowledge their country's ethnic multiplicity while remaining unmoved by the realities of discrimination that confronted ethnic minorities in Canada.[108]

Each of these mythic formulations reflected the desire to establish a foundation upon which to define a Canadian people; yet each ultimately failed to maintain a grasp on the collective psyche because it proved incapable of reflecting the experience of more than a minority of Canadians. To some degree, each of these myths served the interests of the others, and so it is no surprise that they disintegrated concurrently after the middle of the twentieth century. The myth of the RCMP is perhaps most reflective of this phenomenon, insofar as it was founded on a body of literature that melded the exploits of Mounted Policemen, the construction of the CPR, and the value of British culture. A common motif of cultural confrontation characterized all the early literature featuring the force and, in particular, the image of a single Mountie pitted against a group of angry Indians keen on causing a disturbance. The Cree chief Piapot figured prominently in these narrative accounts, as he attempted to obstruct the construction of the CPR with a contingent of compatriots in order to blackmail the Canadians into giving them food.

In this scenario, Piapot was confronted by two Mounted Policeman who were able to frighten the Indians into retreat by knocking down a couple of their teepees. The story became generally accepted as an accurate historical account despite the fact that it was created by William Fraser, in 1899, and published in *McClure's Magazine*. The fact that a force of merely two policemen could have pacified a troop of angry Indians was generally read by Canadians as evidence of the moral power of British judicial institutions and of their "civilization," and it became illustrative of a more general perception of the Mounted Police as emblematic of these fundamental values.[109]

It is obvious, too, that the symbol of the mosaic was created substantially by the CPR in the interest of marketing Canada as a potential destination for tourists. The modification of the image from a descriptive expression to one that conveyed a cultural aspiration was accomplished by Gibbon, a promoter who worked for the CPR and who introduced a meaning of the term that transformed it into a proscriptive symbol for the way in which Canadians of various ethnic backgrounds should view their national association (and, at the same time, as a national feature that distinguished Canada from the United States). Gibbon was a British journalist who was hired by the London office of the CPR in 1907 to market the railway in Europe. In 1913, he relocated to Canada to assume a position in publicity with Canadian Pacific, and he spent the next quarter-century as a determined promoter of the CPR, bilingualism, and Canadian culture more broadly. He wrote in excess of thirty books, was the first president of the Canadian Authors Association, and initiated a series of annual cultural festivals showcasing Canada's multicultural heritage. In celebration of the inauguration of Canadian Pacific's Quebec City hotel, the Chateau Frontenac, he coordinated a presentation of French Canadian folk songs that developed into an annual music and craft festival held at the hotel. At Desbarats, Ontario, he organized an annual summer production of Longfellow's *Hiawatha* in which actors portrayed the Indians of the poem; at the Banff Springs Hotel, he orchestrated a Scottish Highland festival; at the Royal Alexandra Hotel in Winnipeg, a multiethnic New Canadian Festival; and in Vancouver, a Sea Music Festival. These annual celebrations of Canada's ethnic diversity became the foundation for a radio series and a book for which Gibbon won the Governor General's Award, both of which were titled *Canadian Mosaic*. It is doubtful that the idea of the mosaic would have extended beyond the work of Hayward had it not been for Gibbon's reclaiming of it as an overarching metaphor for what Ian McKay called an "emerging post-colonial liberal nationalism" that eclipsed the firm national connection that many Canadians had previously held with England.[110] The myth of the railway was fundamentally a creation of the self-promotion of the CPR, and that of the mosaic was its corollary in respect to tourism.

Finally, the myths of the north and of a "master race" operated in the service of sustaining the fantasy that Canada was a predominantly British nation. The idea of the master race, in particular, marginalized virtually every non-British group in the country—as well as women and the working classes—from meaningful participation in the country's history.[111] In the middle part of the twentieth century these myths that had sustained a national discourse of sorts began to erode, and the discourse itself fell like a house of cards. By the turn of the twenty-first century there appeared to be no single myth capable of providing a foundation for a vision of collective identity and, according to Francis, virtually no single Canadian capable of assuming heroic status for the Canadian community as a whole. Rather, all regions of the country—as well as all marginalized groups—had produced heroes who were specific to themselves. Joseph Howe, for instance, has been considered by many to have been Nova Scotia's greatest historical figure, as the man who orchestrated Maritime Canada's achievement of responsible government. Still, Howe could hardly fit the bill as a Canadian hero given that he vigorously resisted Nova Scotia's entry into the Confederation and would have welcomed the chance to remove the province from the union. Likewise, Henri Bourassa, who founded the newspaper *Le Devoir* and who has achieved heroic status in Quebec for his efforts in promoting Canadian autonomy, has been considered a traitor to the British Empire in sectors outside the province.[112]

All the failed myths of the nineteenth and twentieth centuries were attempts to articulate what it means to be Canadian, and in spite of their lack of broad or lasting relevance, they did betray a commonality beneath their disparate details: all reverberated in some manner within the figure of Riel and the nineteenth century uprisings in the western territories. The NWMP and the CPR, for instance, were critically implicated in the North-West Rebellion and were to flourish as a result of the uprising; the myth of the "master race" fueled western expansion in the wake of confederation, undergirded Ottawa's disregard for the grievances of the Métis, Native, and settler populations in the territories, and was intensified as Francophone anger over Riel's execution brought French and English Canada into conflict; additionally, the idea of a mosaic as descriptive of the Canadian situation in many respects reverberated in its most benign form with the vision of Canada that fueled Riel's participation in the 1885 Rebellion. As the myths themselves disintegrated, Riel concomitantly emerged across a variety of discourses as a "mythic hero" of previously unmatched proportion, pointing to some form of broad-based orientation. If he has become such a figure, in the interest of shedding light on this orientation we might ask ourselves what has made him so; and the answer clearly lies beyond any individual representation of him.

As a champion of various rights and a critic of Anglo imperialism and nationalism, he has consistently been portrayed as a man caught in the web of dualities that rests at the heart of the Canadian experience. He brings to the foreground a particular array of tensions between east and west, Quebec and Ontario, Catholic and Protestant, Native and nonnative; and he occupies the contradictory space between these dichotomous extremes, a position that some have argued has yet to be clearly established. This sense of the man's enigmatic cultural placement was expressed in a striking fashion in Erin Mouré's "Riel: In the Season of His Birth" (1979), a poetic exploration of Riel's lack of self-determination in the face of an oppressive and destructive world. Mouré found within Riel a fundamental fragmentation of self that was irreparable, and through which Riel became both a tormented agent and a vague onlooker to his own life. For Mouré, his duality signified a more generalized cultural sense of perennial dislocation.[113] This kind of negative formulation is based partly on the reality that Riel, the man, was undeniably situated at the heart of dichotomies of ethnicity, language, and region; but more critically, perhaps, on the fact that Riel, the myth, has yet to be conceived in a broadly acceptable fashion. The anomaly that he has become might consequently also be the source of a more constructive formulation. In other words, his mythicization, ambiguous as it is, may well hold the key to understanding something of the way that Canadians view themselves: he is, we might argue, emblematic of the fundamental dichotomies that define the specificity of Canadian cultural and political life.

There is no doubt that these dichotomies have been sufficiently pronounced so as to render problematic the possibility of talking about Canada as a unified cultural body. To begin to consider Riel within this context of disunity, we might find it helpful to employ a scientific analogy to the Canadian situation in which apparent disunity also figures—specifically, that of chaos theory, which is a mode of describing the order that exists within ostensibly disordered systems. Chaos theory holds that the disorder that surrounds natural phenomena contains within it "regularities" that are universally discernable. Chaotic motion is often represented by use of a phase diagram, a graphing device that reveals a systematic form of motion that characterizes a system's movement regardless of its initial states. It appears that any particular system is attracted to a specific kind of motion, and this kind of motion is called an attractor. In systems that exhibit a tendency toward extremely complex forms of motion, the term "strange attractors" is used to describe this motion.[114]

Although firmly located in the sciences and mathematics, the theory has begun to appear in philosophical discussions of phenomena and relationships that appear as accidental, idiosyncratic, and universal; and this discourse has spilled over into various fields in the human sciences. To make use of this position with respect to the Canadian situation, we might take a cue from Antonio Benítez-Rojo who suggested that the utility of the chaos perspective in understanding geocultural entities does not lie in its capacity to explain their fundamental nature but to reveal "dynamics" within seemingly tumultuous situations that, when exposed to "attractors," function in somewhat more organized and predictable ways than it first appears. In his *Repeating Islands*, Benítez-Rojo brought the perspective of chaos theory to bear upon the culture(s) of the Caribbean, discerning dynamics of heterogeneity within the processes and tempos of the region that are a ubiquitous presence in the modern world. He thus regarded the Caribbean as a tumultuous organism within whose apparent disarray are reliable repeating elements that, when identified, provide insight into how the Caribbean operates at the level of both its defining points and its resistance to change.[115]

We might regard the Canadian situation in a similar fashion, identifying Riel in this case as a kind of "attractor." Straddling the dichotomies of the Canadian social body, the man and the myths that have attached themselves to him (as well as to the resistance of 1869–70 and the Rebellion of 1885) might also present themselves to us as "repeating" elements, signaling a different kind of order to be discerned within a history of disjunction. From this vantage point, it is Riel as the emblem of "in-between-ness" who expresses a most basic fact of the Canadian experience: that of cultural hybridity or, as I will choose to describe it, *métissage*. It is this hybridity that I wish to suggest rests at the foundation of an elusive Canadian identity. In the first instance, this argument requires that the issue of identity be firmly separated from the ideas of "nationhood" and "nationalism," with which it has too often been equated. If it is taken seriously, it raises also a correlative question of whether Canada can be legitimately regarded as a nation, and whether a Confederation might more constructively be regarded as an alternative modern geopolitical configuration to that of the nation-state.

Chapter 3

Nation-States and National Discourses

The question of whether Canada can appropriately be called a nation-state is, to a measurable degree, implicated in the enduring problem of collective identity in the country. The ongoing tendency to equate identity with nationalist discourse in Canada highlights the problems of both identity and nation in this context, since nations and nationalism are, obviously, intimately related. Nation-states are a form of modern social and political organization, sustained by the acquiescence of a majority of a given population to certain customary obligations (e.g., paying of taxes, conformity to laws) and to periodic contributions of individual resources (e.g., military service). Majority acquiescence of this form requires that a population recognizes the legitimacy of state apparatus and willingly complies with state regulation. A state can sustain itself ultimately, however, only on the basis of a reserve of positive sentiment within this population.[1] This emotional foundation is, as Benedict Anderson pointed out, very much an act of imagination. Nations, according to Anderson's now classic formulation, are "imagined communities" insofar as they are conceived of as both intrinsically restricted and "sovereign."[2] Because no nation conceives of itself as correlated with all of humanity, all nations are of necessity imagined as restricted in scope; similarly, claims to sovereignty are the product of an imaginative act that can be traced to the revolutions that sprang from the European Enlightenment. The period spawned a political reaction against dynastic rule that had made territorial claims on the basis of universal religion; the new political communities that were imagined into existence based their claims to freedom from the existing order on the idea of the sovereignty of the state. The principal implication of being both limited and sovereign is that the nation is very much a conceptual entity; consequently, nations are not differentiated from one another on the basis of any objective truth that is attached to their claims to nationhood, but on the "style" in which they are conceived.[3]

There are undoubtedly common elements within the various nation-states that have come into being (particularly during the last 150 years), but there are also pronounced stylistic distinctions that have had notable political implications, distinctions that are to a great extent products of the premodern period. These are present within mythic and symbolic structures that have informed the character of modern nations and have commonly been associated with a collective sense of common culture, origin (often ethnic), and aspiration (or ideology). Stathis Gourgouris has referred to this stylistic as "mythistorical energy"—the capacity to incorporate a prenational past and a projected future into a historical present. There is no doubt that shared memories are foundational to the modern nation-state; these are collectivities whose members share a geographical territory, mythic formulations, a civic culture, economic and judicial systems, and an agreed-upon set of core public responsibilities—none of which can be established without recourse to memory.[4] A rather amusing definition was suggested by Julian Huxley and A. C. Hadden in the 1960s: the nation, they wrote, is nothing more than "a society united by a common error as to its origins and a common aversion to its neighbours."[5]

Nationalism, as Ernest Gellner suggested, is "primarily a principle which holds that the political and national unit should be congruent"; it is the articulation of a sovereign community's self-conception as a national body in opposition to all others.[6] European nationalism was based on the assumption that nations and states should be coincidental with one another, a condition that could be achieved by means of either a nation's acquisition of a state or a state's construction of a nation. Although there were nations in existence prior to the late eighteenth century, nationalism as an ideology came into existence at the time of the French Revolution, emerging from revolutionary conceptions of sovereignty. The defeat of the French monarchy resulted in a vesting of authority in the hands of individuals who were recognized as representing the nation; the principle, once established, provided the basis not only for nationalist movements but for their expansion into territories beyond their own parameters.[7] In the final analysis, nationalism is founded on the central unifying idea of the nation. It differs from other modes of defining identity insofar as it offers the individual identification with a larger human collectivity that is considered to be sovereign. Within such a sovereign body, differences of social and economic status, geographical situation, and ethnicity are regarded as relatively superficial delineations; the political body is seen as ultimately unified. Commanding nationalist formulations tend to expunge prenational cultural or ethnic discrepancies by means of either imagining some sort of primal unity, or by relegating such disparity to a past from which the present nation is insulated. By either means, the nation can be conjured up as a social body instituted on the basis of an alliance among roughly congruent individuals. At the level of discourse, these formulations give rise to new myths that often obscure realities of class, ethnic, or other social distinctions.[8]

Anderson and others have maintained that the reproduction of these myths has been the primary mission of print media; the extension of print media, on this account, facilitated the dissemination of myths throughout the geographical sphere of the nation's political organization, becoming the foundation for the imagined community of the modern nation-state. It has been convincingly demonstrated, however, that Anderson's argument does not entirely hold in a number of New World situations, especially that of Latin America, where there were few newspapers in existence prior to the wars of independence. Although print media exerted an undeniable influence on the subsequent growth of nationalism in Latin America, it did not do so in terms of the initial "territorial definition." While Anderson argued that the emergence of nations as imagined communities has been simultaneous with that of nationalism, the nations of Spanish America undeniably came into existence as politically legitimate alternatives to monarchies before their populations possessed distinct nationalist constructions.[9] Although there is no question that print media contributed to the rise of nationalism in these countries, it did not do so in terms of the critical sequential pattern that Anderson maintained. In Canada, likewise, print media undoubtedly buttressed already existing nationalisms of the late nineteenth century, but printers in the British North American colonies came into existence in the first instance not to promote nationalist agendas but by and large as reflections and expressions of the country's foundational dichotomies.

The first Canadian newspaper was the *Halifax Gazette*, which made its appearance in 1752. The *Gazette* was printed by the same press responsible for the publication of a number of other pamphlets and brochures that are illustrative of its primary intent; these included *An Act for the Relief of Debtors with respect to the imprisonment of their Persons* (1752), *Treaty of Article of Peace and Friendship between His Excellency Peregrine Thomas Hopson and Major Jean Baptiste Cope, Chief Sachem of the Tribe of Mickmack Indians* (1753), and a brochure that reproduced the content of an agreement reached by the respective English and French governors at Halifax and Quebec arranging for an exchange of deserters. Another broadsheet produced by the press in 1755 announced bounties on Native peoples in the region who were thwarting the efforts of English settlers; and following the destruction of Louisburg in 1758 a proclamation by Governor Charles Lawrence was printed to advertise among New Englanders property that had been made available by the Acadian deportation.[10]

The country's second newspaper, the *Quebec Gazette*, was created by William Brown and Thomas Gilmore, in 1764, and was printed in both English and French. Brown and Gilmore's newspaper was followed in 1778 by *La Gazette du Commerce et Littéraire* (renamed shortly after its appearance as *La Gazette Littéraire*), a publication of Montreal's first printer, Fleury Mesplet. The *Gazette*'s editor, Valentin Jautard, mounted a number of scathing assaults on the government, and within a year the paper had folded, and both Jautard and Mesplet were in jail. Mesplet spent three years in prison, and after his release he re-established his newspaper, this time as a bilingual publication, the *Gazette de Montréal* (the *Montreal Gazette*) (1875)—a paper that remains in publication to this day as the *Montreal Gazette*. In addition, Mesplet was responsible for the publication of nearly seventy books and pamphlets printed in English, French, Latin, and Iroquois.[11] Print media was introduced in both New Brunswick and Prince Edward Island by Loyalist printers in 1784 and 1787 respectively, and in 1807 New Brunswick Loyalist John Ryan also established the *Royal Gazette and Newfoundland Advertiser*, the colony's first newspaper.[12]

By the Constitutional Act, 1791, the colony of Quebec was divided into two distinct bodies—Upper Canada and Lower Canada—as a way of resolving the difficulties associated with the coexistence of the French and English within a single unified state. The act generated a substantial body of official announcements and orders that required dissemination, but the newly formed province of Upper Canada lacked a printer. The lieutenant governor, John Graves Simcoe, convinced a French Canadian by the name of Louis Roy to establish a press in the province's capital, Newark (later

Niagara-on-the-Lake), with equipment shipped from England; and in 1793 the *Upper Canada Gazette or American Oracle* became Upper Canada's first newspaper. The first press in the Canadian west was built by James Evans, a Methodist minister who developed a syllabic system of reading and writing for missionizing among the Cree in the northern part of the region. He printed one hundred copies of a sixteen-page hymnal in 1841 and was eventually supplied with a proper press by the church leadership in England. The first commercial press in Manitoba was established at Red River by William Buckingham and William Coldwell in 1859, with which they began publishing the *Nor'Wester*. Their first subscription was sold to a chief who Buckingham and Coldwell referred to as "Hole in the Day," a man who they admitted feeling inclined to address as "esquire" since he demonstrated "a promptitude which many of our pale-face subscribers would do well to imitate, he at once paid his money, stating that ours was the only 'big news' he'd ever subscribed to."[13] The first newspaper in British Columbia was *Le Courrier de la Nouvelle Calédonie*, established by a French Catholic bishop (named Dermers) in 1858. Almost immediately, a competing English-language newspaper, the *Victoria Gazette*, was established by a group of four entrepreneurs from San Francisco.[14]

Early print media in the colonies highlighted the principal founding players in the dichotomies that would come to largely define Canada: French, English, and Aboriginal. The development of the industry was a slow process, with daily newspapers becoming viable only at the midpoint of the nineteenth century. Earlier attempts to run daily papers (e.g., the *Montreal Advertiser*, in 1833; the *Toronto Royal Standard*, 1836) were unsuccessful; and even weekly newspapers during the early part of the century were extremely small operations, generally being managed by an editor with the help of one or two assistants. The size of the country's news-reading public began to grow in the late 1830s with the appearance of penny tri-weekly papers that sought to entertain readers, rather than inform them; these proved popular with the working classes and were touted as "the poor man's friend." More formal papers began, in the 1840s, to expand into bi- and triweekly editions but it took until the 1850s for daily papers to become financially lucrative. The post-Confederation period of the 1870s and 1880s were decades of pronounced growth in Canada's newspaper industry, with the number of daily newspapers doubling from forty-seven to ninety-four during the period.[15] Reflecting the initial range of ethnicity that had characterized the establishment of print media in the country, newspapers that emerged from the second half of the century were distinctly sectarian organs. The *Montreal Gazette*, for instance, was firmly wedded to an English Tory agenda in the province; Toronto's *British Colonist* (founded in 1838) had been established by Hugh Scobie as a mouthpiece for the conservative leanings of Scottish immigrants and the Church of Scotland; *Le Minerve* (established in 1842) was established by Ludger Duvernay to serve the agenda of the Reform movement; and the *Halifax Chronicle* (founded in 1844) was William Annand's attempt to create a prominent Liberal voice in the Maritimes and Canada. During the period, French and English newspapers differed markedly in the kind of stories they covered, especially with respect to foreign news. As a rule, the English papers (e.g., the *British Colonist* and the *Globe*) tended to focus on events from around the globe, while the French press (e.g., *La Minerve* and *L'Avenir*) tended to cover stories that pertained to Europe and, especially, France.[16]

As Canadians entered into the final decades of the nineteenth century, the principal French and English newspapers of the day began to display a distinct nationalist inclination, but in each case the nationalist formulation was focused on a political identity based upon either Anglo-Saxon expansionism or French protectionism. Anglo-Protestant nationalism found its first sustained media expression in the 1870s, when Anglophone papers (backed in some instances by the Canada Firsters) like the *Montreal Witness*, the *Toronto Leader*, and the *Toronto Telegram* began attaching a nationalist sentiment to their inherited distaste for French Catholics. It was during the 1880s, however, and especially in the wake of the Riel affair, that this emerging Anglophone nationalism began to flourish: for a decade following the 1885 Rebellion, the *Toronto Mail* led a campaign for cultural ascendancy that was echoed in more popular-based papers in the city, as well as those in cities like Ottawa and Winnipeg. French newspapers followed suit (a phenomenon that will presently be discussed more fully).[17] Something resembling a coherent broad-based nationalism that was capable of resounding with Canadians generally simply did not emerge during the period of state consolidation in Canada. We might argue, however, that Canada was not created fundamentally with the Confederation, and that any successful nationalist formulation that might have accompanied its transition from a colonial outpost to a modern state in 1867 would have had to have been forged in the midst of the ethnic divisions that were present at the outset of its emergence as a distinct North American geopolitical entity a century earlier. This did not occur, and the ethnic rifts that were present at the time of both the Conquest and the influx of Tory Loyalists in the wake of the American Revolutionary War were reified to such a degree that a collective self-definition was rendered impossible by the late nineteenth century.[18]

Compounding the problem of national discourse in Canada is the fact that the country not only lacks a foundational national discourse, but it lacks a collective and reverberating moment of inception that could have allowed a Canadian community to forge a collective vision of itself. Northrop Frye argued that this was partly a result of the fact that Canada lacked a revolutionary heritage necessary for the creation of a constitutional foundation from which such a vision could be articulated. Revolutionary traditions, he wrote, function deductively, imagining a rupture with the past and a link with the future; and they codify this perspective within written constitutions. The U.S. Constitution, in this sense, stood in direct opposition to its contemporary, the Quebec Act. With an objective that was antithetical to that of a revolutionary tradition, the writers of the Quebec Act attempted to fuse contingent elements of the inherited past into a workable formula for a peculiar historical situation: that of the presence of an overwhelming French population in a British colony, where differences of language, religion, and law were insurmountable. Resolving the contingencies of immediate circumstance, the act contained no design for the future of a national community.[19] Canada's constitutional development, beginning in the Quebec Act, was emblematic of the protracted process by which the country became an independent state; ultimately, this process left it without a collective myth of origin. "We cannot find our beginning," Robert Kroetsch has written; "There is no Declaration of Independence, no Magna Carta, no Bastille Day."[20]

While this is undeniably the case, it is also true that Canadian history is checkered with a *variety* of defining foundational narratives. A tertiary glance at the country's three founding peoples, for instance, reveals a number of collectively recognized loci of modern inception. Anglophones, for instance, traditionally regarded the emergence of their independent state as the outcome of constitutional development that preceded the Confederation of 1867 and continued for another century afterward. Its sovereignty, from this perspective, was signified by the Confederation while having developed incrementally; and the Anglophone narrative is represented by July 1, a day that marks Confederation and has been designated Canada's birthday and a national holiday (Canada Day).

The day is not, however, recognized by the majority of Québécois.[21] Some Québécois trace the origins of modern Canada back as far as the sixteenth century claiming, like Anne Hébert, that, "The creation of the world took place on the rock of Quebec. . . . The first written word. It was in 1534: 'In the name of God and of the King of France.' A cross planted at Gaspé by Jacques Cartier."[22] By and large, however, most have recognized the British Conquest of Quebec on September 13, 1759, as modern Canada's point of origin, a view succinctly expressed in Christian Dufour's claim that Canada was "built on the Conquest," an event that "institutionalized defeat."[23] Rather than celebrating July 1, we might add, Québécois regard Fête nationale du Québec (formerly Saint-Jean-Baptiste Day on June 24) as their national holiday.

Turning to the third charter group, it would be impossible to propose a single recognized moment of inception for modern Canada from the perspective of Native peoples, given not only cultural particularities but the fact that their points of entry into the history of modern Canada variously spanned a period of over four hundred years. By way of example, however, we might consider the Mi'kmaq of Canada's Atlantic provinces.[24] In the mid-sixteenth century, the Mi'kmaq became the first indigenous North Americans to encounter Europeans (fishermen, principally, from Brittany and the Basque region of France), and they tend to locate the origins of modern Canada within this early period of cultural confrontation with Europeans, their economy (fish and furs), their diseases (which had ravaged the community by the turn of the seventeenth century), and their Roman Catholicism. To a substantial degree, the Mi'kmaq regard the 1610 baptism of Chief Membertou and twenty members of his family by Father Jessé Fléché as the moment that the territory they inhabited was transformed into modern Canada. The Mi'kmaq-French alliance created by the ritual was foundational (politically, religiously, and economically) and is reflected to this day in the Grand Council Seal—an image of a cross with hieroglyphics invoking the Virgin Mary and Jesus.[25] The most significant day of the year for the Mi'kmaq is not Canada Day, nor Fête nationale, however; it is July 26, the feast of St. Anne, the grandmother of Jesus.

No single nationalist discourse has been capable of speaking to these various originary formulations; rather, Canadian history has been checkered with a variety of nationalisms since the mid-nineteenth century. Anderson suggested that nationalism emerged first in the New World in concert with revolutions waged by creoles against Europeans with whom they shared linguistic, religious, and cultural kinship; and the revolutions they waged— no matter how ruthless—consequently transpired within a framework of familial association.[26] In Canada, however, this was not the case: nationalism emerged first among the nineteenth-century French and Métis in relation not to revolution but to violent agitations within the established order. The 1885 Rebellion further promoted a sense of nationalism among the Métis as well as the French who, despite having taken no part in the uprising, attached themselves to it symbolically in its immediate wake.

The development of French Canadian nationalism has roots in the post-Conquest colonies of the late eighteenth century, but did not find expression until the nineteenth century. Although it was common for scholars prior to the mid-twentieth century (and some since) to claim that French nationalism was articulated in New France and that it developed substantially in the period immediately following the Conquest, it has been persuasively demonstrated that genuine French nationalist consciousness began only in the early nineteenth century with the appearance of a privileged secular middle class in Montreal and Quebec. Ultimately, the Francophone community of New France during the Conquest period expressed no more than the potential for the development of a distinct nationalism.[27] Nationalist sentiment would be truly expressed for the first time by French Canadians in the Rebellion of 1837, an agitation that drew on resources from a variety of sectors in the colony. Politically, this emergence of nationalism was abetted by the division of the province into two colonies—Upper and Lower Canada—in 1791, at the request of British colonists who were outnumbered in the region fifteen to one by Canadiens. In response to their demands, each colony was granted parliamentary government directed by a British-appointed governor, but elite legislative councils in each were ultimately afforded the greater share of power.[28] Management of the colonies during the period was, consequently, principally in the hands of the British government. To a substantial degree, the agitation of 1837 (in both Upper and Lower Canada) was motivated by a general desire to achieve dramatic shifts in both federal allocation of land and the accountability of public administrators and the civil service through responsible parliamentary government. Public funds were being misappropriated, public lands were being volleyed among administrators and public officials, parliaments were disbursing funds over which they had no jurisdiction and, in Lower Canada, the Legislative Council was composed of only the elite classes.[29]

Antagonism in Lower Canada, however, was also motivated by economic concerns. With neither vested financial interests nor political power, a middle-class elite that emerged in Quebec's two principal cities of the early nineteenth century was at a distinct disadvantage in comparison with the colony's landed seigneurial class and their established agricultural sector, as well as the commercial class that had developed within the traditional structure of the fur trade. As Maurice Careless pointed out, the Quebec Act had validated the assets and properties of seigneurs, while the British market had supported the development of wheat production of their rural constituencies. In peripheral regions, the contingencies of the fur trade economy had required cooperation among disparate ethnic groups; and when the North West Company assumed control of the trade, the French adapted themselves to a new commercial structure controlled by London interests. The emerging middle class at Quebec and Montreal had no confirmed role in the British colonial system in North America, and so it assumed an oppositional stance based on the exploitation of a virtually untapped mode of communication: print media. Mounting an offensive aimed at awakening a sense of political consciousness in Quebec, and assailing the financial power of London within the colony, this merchant class began using newspapers (beginning in 1806 with *Le Canadien*) to campaign against mounting British metropolitan power. In spite of the fact that British colonial policy in Quebec was more benign than perhaps in any other of its colonies (Careless suggested it was "defensive"), Montreal in particular had become by the nineteenth century an expanding satellite for London commercial enterprise, with a flourishing commercial sector, increasingly lucrative canal construction, and an escalating British immigrant population. Quebec's social organization which had, to a notable degree, been confirmed by British colonial policy, was clearly being threatened by the metropolitan commercial power of London.[30]

As a result of various frustrations, the parliaments of both Upper and Lower Canada began agitating in the 1830s for constitutional reforms establishing responsible government. A Patriote Party in Lower Canada, led by Louis-Joseph Papineau (with the support of Canadiens, Irish immigrants, and some British democrats), was the organ of what can now be considered French nationalist dissent; and when the British government granted Lower Canada's governor the right to spend the colony's revenues without parliamentary consent, the Patriotes reacted by turning to armed uprising in the colony in 1837 and 1838. The outbreak of violence brought about the British government's suspension of parliamentary government in Lower Canada in 1838.[31]

Initial nationalist articulations among Francophones in 1837 would entrench themselves to such a degree that by the second half of the nineteenth century they had become commonplace. Consequently, the principal issue for the French in Lower Canada, as they considered the desirability of the projected Confederation, was the potential impact of such a union on their sense of their own nationality; they wanted to know, as *La Gazette de Sorel* put it, "what guarantees will be offered for the future of the French-Canadian nationality, to which we are attached above all else."[32] Likewise, *La Minerve* announced, "If the plan seems to us to safeguard Lower Canada's special interests, its religion and its nationality, we'll give it our support; if not, we'll fight it with all our strength";[33] and,

> The English . . . have nothing to fear from the central government, and their first concern is to ensure its proper functioning. This is what they base their hopes upon, and the need for strong local governments only takes a second place in their minds. . . . The French press, on the contrary, feels that guarantees for the particular autonomy of our nationality must come before all else in the federal constitution. It sees the whole system as based on these very guarantees.[34]

The Confederation was achieved, but French nationalism did not subside as a result of this constitutional arrangement. In fact, it reemerged with particular vehemence in relation to the Métis uprisings, and particularly during the period directly following 1885. The resistance of 1869–70 fanned smoldering flames of embitterment between the English and the French, reaching a temporary pitch with riots in Montreal in 1877 following an Orange parade; but these would find their full articulation in widespread civil unrest in 1885, in the wake of the execution of Riel. In Quebec, the events surrounding the trial and hanging of Riel awakened an interest in the fate of French Catholics in the west that had not previously existed. In addition, the general sense that the execution had constituted an assault on French Canadians kindled the perception of a need to assert the presence and strength of French nationalism, especially in Quebec; ultimately, Honoré Mercier would ride the current of this sentiment to power in the province.[35] The fury caused by the execution transcended party lines, as the *Montreal Gazette* aptly demonstrated on November 17, 1885. Referring to an emergency meeting of the Montreal City Council following a telegraph announcing Riel's hanging, the *Gazette* reported:

Mr. J. J. H. Bergeron, MP, had thought it impossible that Sir John could commit such an iniquity. But they would never trust the government again. It was not Riel that was struck at, but the whole French-Canadian nationality. Henceforth all distinctions between Rouge and Bleu and Castor would disappear and they would all be united in a common cause.[36]

Further, the 1885 reverberations of French nationalist sentiment that had been awakened in 1837 were not lost on English Canada. The *Daily Intelligencer*, for instance, carped in December of 1885, "They place him in the ranks of heroes, patriots, and martyrs. They go even so far as to demand that he should be interred under the monument of the heroes of 1837–38."[37] Prime Minister John A. Macdonald himself misjudged the depth of Quebec's reaction to Riel's trial, believing that it would ultimately be a short-lived phenomenon based on a manipulated public perception of a correspondence between the rebellion and the uprising under Papineau earlier in the century: "The attempt now made," he suggested, "to revive that feeling [of 1837] in his favor will not extend far and will be evanescent."[38] Macdonald obviously miscalculated the significance of the situation. French nationalism was not a passing phenomenon, and it was amplified by overt Anglophone hostility toward French Canadians that was born in the wake of Riel's execution. French support of Riel during the amnesty crisis of 1875 and rumors of support for the cause of the Métis early in 1885 had planted seeds of distrust among English Canadians toward their French compatriots; but Quebec's apparent support for the military intervention in the Saskatchewan Valley went some distance toward temporarily mollifying such misgivings. However, these suspicions returned with greater potency in the aftermath of the rebellion when it appeared to Anglophones that the French in Quebec had become committed to furthering their own nationalist agenda within the Confederation framework.[39] The *London Advertiser*, for instance, detected "a determination on the part of our French fellow-countrymen not in any way to regard themselves as one with us"; and the *Week* likewise claimed that "New France is a separate nation from British Canada."[40]

There is no doubt that the execution of Riel sowed seeds of nationalism in Quebec and, ultimately, of separatism. Because Francophones in the province overwhelmingly regarded the execution as an instance of the federal Conservatives' bigotry against the French, the Rouges (Liberals) under

Honoré Mercier (the political engineer of Quebec nationalism) were able to mobilize anti-Conservative sentiment and win the 1886 provincial election in Quebec, defeating the incumbent Conservatives. The Conservative Party was never able to regain its foothold in the province and Mercier's focus on Quebec's self-determination laid the foundation for nationalist politics in Quebec that would culminate with the establishment of the Parti Québécois nearly a century later.[41] Additionally, this maturing Francophone nationalism extended beyond the parameters of the province of Quebec, such that many began calling for Quebec's participation in the development of the west. Although this generally stopped short of demanding a bilingual foundation for the western provinces, many believed that the Prairies should contain a French Canadian national element: "Let it be understood that we have the right, in the North-West just as on the banks of the St Lawrence, to work to set up a French-Canadian state."[42] Ultimately, many Anglophones began to believe that Francophones were devoted to the Canadian state only insofar as they could extend French culture within its structure; they were not, as the *Mail* argued in November of 1885, committed to "the Canada which stretches from Atlantic to Pacific."[43] Whether French nationalism ever reached such a state is disputable; but it was undoubtedly true that the notion of Quebec as "a country within a country" (to quote the writer Anne Hébert) was not only advanced but also gained a political meaning in the period following Riel's trial and execution.[44]

Métis nationalism was likewise founded in the early nineteenth century and given impetus by the events of 1885. It is generally recognized that the Red River Métis (the most substantial community of Métis in the region) had developed a distinct sense of ethnic identity that was articulated as early as 1815, when their flag was raised in resistance to the governmental authority claimed by Selkirk's newly imported settler population. Expressing defiance, on June 19, 1816, a group of Métis laid siege to the recently created Selkirk community at Red River, believing it to be an incursion into their own territory; yet in spite of this early reaction against the Red River Settlement, it would quickly become a focus for the consolidation of a Métis identity. The Catholic Church established a foothold in the Métis community through its creation of a mission at Red River in 1818, a venture that involved the encouragement of settlement and farming as an economic complement to the buffalo hunt. The amalgamation of the Hudson's Bay and North West Companies in 1821 resulted in a downsizing of personnel that reduced the number of jobs available to the Métis; and the presence of the agricultural

Red River Settlement presented a viable alternative to unemployment, while allowing for the continuation of the annual Métis buffalo hunt, which had become a significant facet of the community's life on the prairie.[45]

In 1869, the Red River Settlement (later the city of Winnipeg) was the principal population center of what would become the province of Manitoba. Directed by the Hudson's Bay Company, the community (whose population was about twelve thousand), was dominated by the Métis who numbered approximately ten thousand. By the time of the Red River uprising, the Métis in the region identified culturally with neither the European nor the Native communities from which they had descended, but had developed a distinct sense of cultural identity that many have argued constituted a "national identity." Conflicts throughout the nineteenth century with both colonials and Native groups had fostered among the Métis an awareness of their cultural distinctiveness. They were, as W. L. Morton wrote in 1937, a "well-rooted national people"; and it has been maintained, further, that the politicization of Riel upon his return to Red River in 1868 was an articulation of a "Métis nationalism" that had emerged from this collective sense of cultural identity.[46] Thus, Harry Daniels argued in 1979 that the Métis reaction to the economic and social dislocation initiated by eastern Canadian expansion into the western territories—the institution of provisional governments in both 1870 and 1885—was a nationalist assertion equivalent to the Parti Québécois' assumption of power in Quebec. Similarly, Saskatchewan's Department of Culture and Youth published a project in 1975, *Towards a New Past*, in the introduction of which the editors referred to the 1885 Rebellion as a "war for independence." Contemporary Métis have sustained this nationalist perspective, referring to themselves as the "true Canadians," the "progeny of Canada," and, more critically, the "new Nation."[47]

Native Canadian nationalism developed later than both French and Métis forms, coming to full expression only in the second half of the twentieth century. Like its counterparts, however, this form of nationalism was again a direct result of conflicted relationships with dominant political, economic, and social forces. The history of Native relationships with nonnatives in Canada has been fraught with asymmetry from at least the eighteenth century. Looking again, by way of example, to the Mi'kmaq (the First Nation that has had to weather contact with prevailing power structures for the longest time in North America), we find a sustained legacy of cultural marginalization and oppression. By the mid-nineteenth century, Mi'kmaq communities were being destroyed by land loss, rampant disease, and starvation, much of it caused by a systematic and flagrant disregard for the validity of treaties that were negotiated with the British government in the eighteenth century, beginning in 1726. The 1726 treaty had been the basis for a series of others signed in 1749, 1752, 1760, and 1761; and although equivocal in some respects, these guaranteed the Mi'kmaq rights of occupation and of unobstructed use of natural resources.[48] Compounding the issue of dispossession, the twentieth century saw the introduction of the residential school system, a joint enterprise of the federal government and the churches that became a weapon of cultural assault. By way of example, the Shubenacadie School (in Nova Scotia) was one of seventy-seven similar institutions across the country, and over the span of its career from 1930–69, it systematically assaulted the Mi'kmaq language, removed two thousand Mi'kmaq children from their families, and subjected large numbers of them to emotional and physical abuse.[49] Native Canadians bore anywhere from decades to centuries of social, political, and economic marginalization before they were able to organize themselves sufficiently to begin a process of collectively seeking redress. Concomitantly with this drive toward organization, a nationalist discourse also emerged.

To a notable degree, this discourse developed in relation to the Trudeau government's now infamous White Paper of 1969. The White Paper proposed a dramatic alteration in Native Canadians' relationship with the federal government, recommending a policy of "de-Indianization," the repeal of the Indian Act, and the transfer of responsibility for Indian affairs to provincial legislatures that would financially support Native peoples for a restricted period of time. The "special status" afforded Native peoples by the Indian Act was said to have been a debilitating designation that had impeded their ability to assimilate with the wider culture, and it was consequently deemed obsolete.[50]

> The Government of Canada believes that its policies must lead to the full, free and non-discriminatory participation of the Indian people in Canadian society. Such a goal requires a break with the past. It requires that the Indian people's role of dependence be replaced by a role of equal status, opportunity and responsibility, a role they can share with all other Canadians.[51]

First Nations' resistance to the proposed legislation was strident, and it is now considered to have been a catalyst for coherent, broadly based

Native organization in Canada. In its wake, nationalism among indigenous Canadians (Native, Métis, and Inuit) began to develop at a striking rate, expressing itself since the last quarter of the twentieth century in terms of the issues of land claims and self-government.[52] The shift in self-designation among Native peoples from that of "Indian" in the 1960s, to that of "First Nations" (which had come to general usage by the end of the twentieth century) highlights the development of this nationalist consciousness during the period.

Unlike French, Métis, and First Nations peoples, English Canadians did not develop a distinct nationalism based upon a collective ethnic self-consciousness forged in relation to the experience of unbalanced relations of power: Anglophones emerged as victors at the time of the Conquest, and generally remained the most defining voice in terms of dominant Canadian political, economic, and social formation well into the twentieth century. In addition, English Canada lacked a conventional revolutionary heritage often associated with the emergence of a nationalist ideology. Rather, its sense of national character was imagined in relation to Old World attachments and, to a noticeable degree, in opposition to the reality of its own creolized situation, as well as in response to a series of historical and geographical contingencies requiring technological adaptation. As a consequence, Anglophones never developed a successful, durable, and overriding discourse about the social body.[53] Anglophone nationalism was expressed in relation to both the country's ties with Anglo-Saxon culture and the expansion of communications technologies, and it was intentionally formulated in both cases as an overarching configuration to which all Canadians should ultimately relate. Neither of these formulations, however, proved capable of fostering or sustaining the desired collective sense of national identification.

In spite of the fact that Confederation traditionally figured prominently in English nationalist discourses, Confederation itself did not immediately inspire nationalism. This was due primarily to the fact that the union did not arise from a domestic impulse but rather from one that was British-born. Throughout the nineteenth century, the colonies' economies were channeled toward England—a metropolitan nexus on which Canada's grain and timber production was focused. At the same time, English immigrants poured into the colonies, ultimately overwhelming the preexisting English-speaking population. As a result, the campaign for Confederation was forged in English Canada by British-born colonists like John A. Macdonald, George Brown (founder of the *Toronto Globe*), and the journalist Thomas

D'Arcy McGee.[54] In the wake of Confederation, Anglophone Canadians were far from unified in their vision of the nature of their new state. Some of the earliest articulations of Anglophone nationalism in Canada were not expressed at a popular level but were associated with elite political attempts to shape the country's economy. Advising a Conservative newspaper editor on how to present his party's position regarding tariffs, for instance, Macdonald wrote in 1872: "the paper must go in for a National policy in Tariff matters, and while avoiding the word 'protection' must advocate a readjustment of the tariff in such a manner as incidentally to aid our manufacturing and industrial interest."[55] This early articulation of the Macdonald government's National Policy was a clear elite nationalist expression of the Confederation era; contained within the National Policy were the basic elements of the Canadian desire to differentiate itself from the United States and to establish itself as a substantive component of the British Empire: tariff protection from U.S. economic interests, the need for a transcontinental railway and a solid industrial foundation, colonization of the west, the creation of reliable markets to sustain a domestic economic structure, and the desire for increased sovereignty maintained within the British Empire. The need to express a distinctive national character was clearly intertwined with the desire to define Canada as a nation in relation to both its colonial parent and the powerful nation to the south, but in this early articulation, nationalism was cast in the language of economics.[56]

At a more popular level, what many Anglophones shared was a desire for the expansion of the state. As we noted in chapter 1, by the 1860s a concept of nationalism was already developing in some quarters of eastern Canada that directly linked westward expansion with the establishment of a confederation; and following Confederation, expansion quickly became a mode of expressing a nationalism associated with the political union.[57] Canada First—an initially secretive group of intellectuals that emerged in 1868 in Ottawa—was perhaps the first coordinated nationalist approach to the issue of expansion. Railing against Canada's colonial position in the British Empire, Canada Firsters claimed that Canada (by which they meant English Ontario) was destined to occupy the western part of North America above the U.S.-Canada border, and they promoted a vision of a continent-wide national identity distinctive from that of the United States and Britain, while remaining firmly Anglo-Saxon and northern in character. William Foster was representative of this vision. Considering the need for a coherent nationalism, Foster wrote:

As between the various Provinces comprising the Dominion, we need some cement more binding than geographical contact; some bond more uniting than a shiftless expediency; some lodestar more potent than a mere community of profit. . . . [W]hy should not this principle of nationality be applied in Canada? There is more necessity for it here, at present, than anywhere else we know of. It would unite the factions now tearing themselves and the country to pieces, strengthen the weak bonds which hold the Dominion together.[58]

"Uniting the factions," for Canada Firsters, meant, first and foremost, eliminating the anomalous meaning of French and Aboriginal Canada (as well as many other ethnic presences) from the construction of a national consciousness. Foster's essay, "Canada First; or, Our New Nationality," made the point in terms of the Conquest, and his interpretation of its significance:

On the 13th September, 1759, Quebec was taken. One year afterwards the French flag was hauled down and Canada became part of the British Empire. Great was the joy manifested in England over the conquest of Louis XIV's "acres of snow." Addresses were presented to the king, congratulating him on this much-coveted addition to the Imperial possessions; a statue in Westminster Abbey was accorded to Wolfe; public thanks were decreed to each of the chief officers who had taken part in the Quebec expedition; and it was ordered that prayers of thanksgiving should be offered up to Heaven throughout the whole Empire.[59]

Foster's view of French Canadians was echoed by his fellow Firster Charles Mair. "Ontario and the English-speaking people of Quebec have been milked long enough," he wrote,

Thank God there is such a thing at last as a purely national feeling in Canada. There is a young and vigorous race coming to the front, entirely in Earnest, and which is no longer English, Scotch or Irish, but thoroughly and distinctly Canadian. . . . It means strict justice to the French and nothing more—a fair field and no favour.

Mair argued further that the presence of the French language interfered with Canada's potential for evolving into a "homogenous people."[60] Foster's discussion of the execution of Thomas Scott by the provisional government at Red River in 1870 restated much the same point in terms of Aboriginals:

> There are times when the sluggish pulse is quickened into activity. . . . *Such a time it was* when the news of the butchery of young Scott at Fort Garry fell upon our ears, thrilling every nerve, and crowding the hot blood into our hearts. Humble though his position was—yet he was a Canadian; his mental gifts may have been few—yet he died for us.

"Us," in this instance, presumably did not include the Métis.[61]

Given that Canada was geographically situated on the northern frontier of the globe, Canada Firsters argued that their nation should be populated by immigrants from northern Europe who would adapt to an Anglo-Saxon national identity. As Robert Grant Haliburton put it, Canada "must ever be a Northern country inhabited by the descendants of Northern races"; and while Canada Firsters accepted the fact of a French presence in Canada, they had no patience for French Canadian cultural aspirations.[62] They also had no tolerance within their national vision for peoples of color, those from southern and eastern Europe, and even in some cases, those of the United States. Americans, according to many Firsters, were prone to cultural corrosion because they resided in a more southern region and permitted themselves to be inundated with non-Europeans who weakened their European heritage. As George Parkin argued, Canada would not foster the growth of cities "like New York, St. Louis, Cincinnati, or New Orleans which attract even the vagrant population of Italy and other countries of southern Europe." This vision accommodated the desire for a nationalist vision that accounted for the reality of the French presence in the Confederation, while drawing distinct limits on the level of plurality it was willing to admit into the structure of the new state.[63]

In spite of the best efforts of the Canada Firsters, however, it took until the 1885 execution of Riel for widespread calls for national unity to emerge from English Canada. Responding to the increasingly vocal affirmations of French Canadian nationalism, Anglophones began voicing their own desire for "one nationality, one loyalty, one patriotism for Canada."[64] Confederation-era nationalism, articulated most clearly by the Canada Firsters, took root more popularly during the 1880s and 1890s. During the period, many English-language newspapers cultivated an Anglo-Protestant nationalism that pressed for the employment of state apparatus to transform the country into an English nation; and bilingualism, Catholic schools, and the Catholic Church were particular targets for their vitriolic assault. The *Winnipeg Tribune* claimed that "[u]nity of language tends to unity of purpose and disunity of language just as inevitably to diversity of purpose"; the *Toronto Mail* referred to Catholic schools as "nurseries not merely of an alien tongue, but of alien customs, of alien sentiments, and of a wholly alien people"; the *Toronto News* called for the establishment of a national public school system within which "the children of this country would not be educated as Nova Scotians, Lower Canadians, or as Manitobans, but as Canadians"; and the Catholic Church, according to the *Toronto Mail*, had been permitted to exercise the power to "retard the welfare and curtail the liberty of the Queen's subjects." The issue of confrontation between the forces of modernity and those of an intransigent French Catholic element in the country was also expressed in the context of the Anglo nationalist agenda as, in the words of the *Mail*, a conflict between "progress and reaction."[65] By the early years of the twentieth century, Canada's proto- (and self-promoting) Anglo-Saxon nationalism of the Confederation period had gradually developed into a form of imperialism that remained nationalist, while promoting the country's solid participation within the British Empire. From this perspective, an association with the empire provided Canada with a broader arena in which to play a geopolitical role. "I am an Imperialist," claimed the humorist Stephen Leacock in 1907, "because I will not be a colonial."[66]

Anglophone imperialist nationalism maintained itself as a popular discourse until the Second World War after which it began to flounder, finally falling into general decline during the 1960s. In the wake of World War II, the country found itself in a new situation with respect to the rest of the world. The disintegration of the British Empire left Canada in the position of having to modify its international posture both in terms of economics and diplomacy: virtually overnight it discovered itself to be an influential diplomatic participant in a global and industrial postwar situation (occupying, for instance, a seat in the discussions that led to the creation of the United Nations); while Great Britain found itself borrowing both money and wheat from its former colony.[67] This is not to say, however, that imperial nationalism disappeared entirely. In fact, it has remained a constant undercurrent in public discourse, rearing its head in relation to popular resistances to such things as the Official Languages Act of 1969 in which arguments for the ascendancy of the British at the time of the Conquest and fears of a French conspiracy to overtake the geopolitical landscape were noticeable components of the conflict.[68]

At the end of the twentieth century, vestiges of the discourse still remained. They provided, for instance, the foundation for a contentious argument among historians revolving around J. L. Granatstein's defense of Anglo-Saxon nationalism. In 1998, Granatstein published *Who Killed Canadian History?*—a book that argued that Canadian unity had reached a fragile state as a result of the fact that Canadians lacked a historical narrative that could connect them to one another. He claimed, further, that a history that could contribute to unity did indeed exist, but that Canadians had generally refused to invoke it.[69] In pursuing his argument, Granatstein turned to the issue of teaching history, whose primary purpose, he contended, is to foster a necessary patriotism required to maintain national unity. An education in history, consequently, offers the young suitable heroes and a foundation for collective memory that can reveal to them the basis of their nation's political formation. This kind of education had become a necessity in Canada, he wrote, in order to cultivate a broadly based nationalist discourse and to arrest the process of political fragmentation that was taking hold of the state:

> If written and taught properly, history is not myth or chauvinism, just as national history is not perfervid nationalism; rather, history and nationalism are about understanding this country's past, and how the past has made our present and is shaping our future.[70]

He was adamant, however, that this history should not stray from a Eurocentric template:

> Our civilization and culture is Western, and there is no reason we should be ashamed of it or not wish to teach our students about it. Canadians are the inheritors of Greek and Roman traditions and the British and French experience, and the West is the dominant civilization in the world today in part because its values have been tested and found true.[71]

Granatstein aptly noted that many Canadians regret the fact that they lack cultural heroes; but he lamented the tendency in the late twentieth century to cast Louis Riel as such a figure: the choice of Riel as a hero for anyone but the Métis, he argued, was utterly inappropriate. The man was a "crazed religious fanatic" who could be no more than a "bastardized" hero since not all Canadians recognized him as heroic (in a rejoinder to Granatstein, George Goulet suggested that by this criterion, no one in Canada would ever qualify as a national hero).[72] His argument proceeded like a snowball of Anglo nationalism: Canada was established on a foundation of European culture, but out of a misguided concern with offending Canadians of other cultural backgrounds, this basis of national culture has been disregarded within the educational system; by forgetting the exploits and heroism of past Canadians—those who crossed the violent Atlantic Ocean in overcrowded ships, those who struggled to extract a nation from the wilderness that was the northern part of the continent, those who fought in wars both domestically and internationally—Canadians have destroyed their own history. Finally (and perhaps most disturbingly), unlike the people of other modern nation-states who have had to "overcome" their histories, Canadians share a rather "benign" history, despite Canadians' insistence upon regarding their collective past as a legacy of violence, malevolence, and genocides.[73] One might be tempted to ask how any postcolonial state could possibly have a "benign" history; but Granatstein provided the answer himself: by selectively removing many of the state's citizens from its moral framework. Thus, he criticized the federal government's official pledge of January 7, 1998, to "look for ways of . . . reflecting Louis Riel's proper place in history," arguing that it is not the role of government to alter the past. The pledge followed the government's official apology to Native Canadians for "the role it played in the development and administration of Indian residential schools," an admission of culpability that Granatstein could admit only "might" have been justified.[74]

Reaction to Granatstein's thesis was predictably strident, particularly among social historians. A. B. McKillop summarized the critique from this quarter succinctly in the *Canadian Historical Review* in 1999:

> Canadian social historians understand what Granatstein apparently does not: that in order for Canadians to take the full measure of what it means to be Canadian, they must be made conscious of all aspects of their shared past. In this sense there are no subdisciplinary hierarchies of historical significance. Citizenship entails the understanding of what it means to be weak as well as powerful; it involves healing as much as it does pride.[75]

While recognizing the value of McKillop's criticism, Timothy Stanley subsequently raised a more fundamental question concerning whether, in the final analysis, it is even possible to write about a "shared past" with which all Canadians can identify.[76]

In spite of the disturbance it instigated, *Who Killed Canadian History?* was in many respects the shadow of a nationalist ghost of the Confederation era. Its author's understanding of the legitimate place of Aboriginal peoples in the country's collective history and conscience was reminiscent of the Canada Firsters, and his view of Riel could well have been articulated in 1885: "If that is the hero whom they wish to make us venerate," claimed a writer for the *Daily Intelligencer*, shortly after Riel's execution, "I, for one, will not be among his admirers."[77] There was, to be sure, nothing unusual about Anglophone attempts to define the cultural parameters of what they regarded as a new nation, in spite of the fact that its form—that of imperial nationalism—was undoubtedly misdirected in the Canadian situation. It is the character of nation-states to attempt to resolve internal ethnic and national animosities, and although they are inherently limited in their capacity to do this, they are not powerless. The options at their disposal in this respect involve policies of elimination of ethnic-national disparity: genocide, physical removal, territorial division, or strategies of assimilation; and these have been pursued to such a degree in the modern period that some argue that the formation of modern states has essentially been a "refugee-creating" enterprise.[78] States obviously have the option of dealing with such antagonisms through less aggressive processes of internal control that solidify the primacy of dominant ethnic groups while destabilizing the position of minorities. Regardless of the severity of a chosen mode of reducing ethnic disparity, it has been argued that no modern nation-state has been able to establish itself without recourse to some form of ethnic homogenization or ethnic cleansing. Ernest Gellner, for instance, believed that "nationalist homogenization" was a necessary property of modern states, a theory that certainly appears to be supported to a substantial degree by the level of genocide, ethnic removal, compulsory integration, and geopolitical reorganization that has accompanied modern forays into nationhood.[79]

English Canadian imperial nationalism, with its desire to see a culturally homogenous national configuration, appears to have followed this pattern, at least in its intention. In the nineteenth century, for instance, assimilation of the French to Anglophone culture was attempted in a variety of sectors. The Act of Union, 1840, for instance, was the British government's response to the Rebellions of 1837 and the subsequent report of Lord Durham, who had called for the assimilation of the French in the Canadas. His investigation of the situation in the colonies in the late 1830s led him to conclude that the English and French would never be reconciled with one another:

> The entire mistrust which the two races have thus learned to conceive of each other's intention, induces them to put the worst construction on the most innocent conduct; to judge every word, every act, and every intention unfairly; to attribute the most odious designs, and reject every overture of kindness or fairness, as covering secret designs of treachery and malignity.

He added that the two ethnic groups were alienated from one another "not only by diversity of feelings and opinions, but also by an actual belief in an utterly different set of facts."[80] Durham managed to underscore a fundamental contradiction at the core of the Canadian experience: "I expected to find a contest between a government and a people," he wrote; "I found two nations warring in the bosom of a single state; I found a struggle, not of principles, but of races."[81] Although Durham's report called principally for the constitutional amalgamation of Upper and Lower Canada, it also contained additional recommendations intended to cut at the cultural fabric of French Canada, principal among which were a concerted attempt at religious conversion and the termination of the recognition of French as an official language (a policy that remained in place until 1849). Durham believed that French Canadians lacked a legitimate literature and history and were thus culturally inferior to their British counterparts; his recommendation that the two Canadas be united into a single colony was based on his assumption that such a political move would force the Canadiens to turn away from "their vain hopes of nationality" thereby paving the way for their eventual assimilation to the dominant English population. The union was effected in 1841.[82]

The desire on the part of Anglophones to bring about the assimilation of the French within an English cultural framework (and the belief that it could be achieved) did not end with Lord Durham's report. The sentiment was echoed throughout the century: "The time will come," announced one Ontario newspaper in 1890, "when English only will be spoken throughout Canada, and a peaceful conquest will have been made of the French tongue as a peaceful conquest has been made of the French heart."[83] Efforts toward this end, however, were not quite as serene as this correspondent hoped. As early as 1871, for instance, the legislature of New Brunswick passed an act prohibiting the teaching of religion or the use of the French language in state-supported schools. Catholics appealed to the Privy Council, citing guarantees delineated in the British North America Act, but they lost.[84] In 1890, the government of Manitoba passed legislation that would have a more far-reaching effect on the attitude of Francophones in Quebec. The Manitoba Act had created a twofold educational system in the province whereby both Catholic and Protestant schools received government funding, but this aspect of the act was abolished twenty years later, when the population had become primarily Anglophone. The decision to rescind funding to Catholic schools was upheld by the Privy Council, and although some concessions to Catholic teachers were made in 1897, comprehensive Catholic rights were not restored until the 1970s. The "Manitoba Schools Question" remains the most substantial legislative assault on French rights to have occurred in the post-Confederation period.[85]

Aboriginal Canadians have been the heirs of the most sustained dominant efforts at both concealing ethnic diversity and forcing the assimilation of obviously distinct ethnic groups to a prevailing cultural template. The Métis were subject to a process of cultural veiling that resulted, in the first instance, from their lack of a land base and their extreme poverty in the wake of the annexation of their territories by Canada in the late nineteenth century. The problem extended beyond the issue of economic viability, however, as successive governments concertedly attempted to obliterate their ethnic specificity in order to avoid negotiations with them as a distinct ethnic group. In 1873, for instance, Chief Mawedopeness, of the Long Sault Native Band number 1, negotiated with government representatives on behalf of fifteen Métis families from Fort Frances who wished to be included in Treaty Three. Alexander Morris, speaking on behalf of the government, referred to his knowledge of how the issue of Métis status had been resolved at Red River, saying essentially that the Métis must choose whether they wished to be considered Native or nonnative: "I am sent here to treat with the Indians. In Red River, where I came from, and where there is a great body of half-breeds, they must be either white or Indian. If Indians, they get treaty money, if the half-breeds call themselves white they get land."[86] In his final report, Morris recommended to the minister of the interior, Alexander Campbell, that the formula for establishing rights by ethnicity that had been followed at Red River be followed in Ontario:

[T]here were some ten to twenty families of half-breeds who were recognized as Indians, and lived with them, and they [the Indian people] wished them [those half-breeds] included. I said the treaty was not for whites, but I would recommend that those families should be permitted the option of taking either status as Indians or whites, but that they could not take both.[87]

It is small wonder that the Métis, alongside their self-designation as "the new nation," have also been called "Canada's forgotten people."[88]

First Nations have also been subject to this kind of sanctioned concealment, alluded to previously in our discussions of both Mi'kmaq treaty rights and the refusal to assist destitute western Aboriginals who had been forced into extreme privation in the nineteenth century by the destruction of the buffalo and by colonial incursion. Compounding the issue was the fact that during the period, any Native man who could claim to have white ancestry could opt for scrip in lieu of "treaty status," and the appeal of cash induced many "treaty Indians" to opt for this alternative. The result was the creation of a body of "nonstatus" Indians who, like their Métis counterparts, were landless and impoverished. Ultimately, they would find themselves excluded from their communities of origin and ineligible for participation in tribal organizations established by the Indian Act.[89] For much of the century following Confederation, the country's Aboriginal population remained invisible to dominant sectors of society. The residential school system's goal of forced assimilation, for instance, constituted a graphic example of a politically legitimized assault on Native culture that was carried on for the better part of a century. In addition, from the time of the Royal Proclamation of 1763 (which was intended to protect Native lands from encroachment by British settlers), Aboriginal land claims rarely found their way into the Canadian judicial system; and after 1867, in particular, First Nations peoples were denied recourse to the courts in affirming their treaty rights. What the government could not accomplish in this respect was left to the courts themselves, and in 1888, the case of *St. Catherine's Milling and Lumber Co. v. the Queen* dealt a near deathblow to Aboriginal rights in this regard. This was a case involving the federal and Ontario provincial governments, in the context of which each claimed to have control over Crown land and resources: the federal government had negotiated Treaty Three with the Ojibwe in the region between the Manitoba border and Lake Superior, but the provincial government argued that Ontario owned the resources on this land. The case was taken to the Privy Council, and the council ruled in favor of the province of Ontario, asserting that the rights of provincial governments superseded Aboriginal claims. *St. Catherine's Milling* ultimately made it impossible for Aboriginal Canadians to use the courts to argue for land claims and treaty rights.[90]

Twentieth-century courts proved to be no more amenable to recognizing Aboriginal rights. The case of *Syliboy, 1928*, is a case in point. A Nova Scotia man, Gabriel Syliboy, was charged with possessing pelts in contravention of Lands and Forests regulations; and he argued in his defense that he had "by Treaty the right to hunt and fish at all times," regardless of the Lands and Forests Act. It was the first time a Native person had made this claim in a Canadian courtroom, but he was unsuccessful and was convicted.[91] To further hinder Native peoples' capacity to seek legal recognition of their rights, the government did not permit the retention of lawyers to press for such acknowledgment until 1960. Additionally, it was not until the *Calder* decision in 1973 (to be considered more fully later) that Aboriginal rights were recognized by the courts as legally enforceable. Prior to that decision, the government had successfully maintained that these rights were matters to be dealt with politically and morally, but not judicially.[92] Finally, it must also be noted that Aboriginal affairs were not regarded as a serious issue by the federal government until the 1960s, when a permanent department—Indian Affairs and Northern Development—was established to deal with Aboriginal issues. Until that time, responsibility for Aboriginal affairs had been volleyed among a series of departments that were often designed for dealing primarily with other issues: Secretary of State; Energy, Mines, and Resources; and Citizenship and Immigration—the latter of which is somewhat absurd, given that Aboriginals did not acquire fundamental rights of citizenship until they gained the right to vote in 1960; they were, consequently, neither fully citizens nor immigrants.[93]

Expressions of imperial nationalism (with their vision of a state with an Anglo-European complexion) created a legacy of hardship, destitution, alienation, and political inefficacy for large numbers of Canadians for as long as it maintained its hold on the self-definition of dominant sectors of society. These expressions did not, however, bring about either the intended assimilation or elimination of French, Métis, or First Nations peoples. This form of nationalism was ultimately unsuccessful in its attempt to create a unified cultural discourse (and social body) in the

Canadian context, although it undoubtedly contributed to the growth and solidification of counter-nationalist formulations within both the French and Aboriginal communities.

British imperialism was implicated in the emergence of a second form of Anglophone nationalism in Canada: that of technological nationalism. Like its imperial counterpart, technological nationalism was initially constructed around the defining power of the Confederation. This, again, was a predominantly Anglophone vision that attributed the creation and maintenance of the Canadian state to the capacity of technology to bind all regions of the country to one another. Canadian identity, from this perspective, was not based upon cultural particularity, but on the unifying power of technology.[94] Technological nationalism has undeniably had a certain appeal as a formulation of collective identity in a country that has had to contend with an expansive geographical territory, a relatively small population base, and substantial linguistic and cultural disparity (9.2 million square kilometers and a population of almost 30 million). The case for this form of nationalism was well articulated by E. S. Hallman and H. Hindley in the late 1970s with particular reference to the Canadian Broadcasting Corporation:

> Against this mosaic of regions and languages and cultures, against the inequalities of the economy, communication has a special importance in Canadian life. Without the roads and railways, without the airlines, the centrifugal forces of the Canadian environment are difficult to keep in balance. Without the national broadcasting services in both French and English, the full character of the Country, its regions and its particularities could not be expressed to the community as a whole. Perhaps the main responsibility of Canadian broadcasting is to create for Canadians the shared experience of living together in the second largest country in the world.[95]

The first articulations of this nationalist vision were formulated in the period immediately preceding the Confederation. They revolved around the proposal for the construction of an extended telegraph system by Sanford Flemming, a Scottish engineer who was also an ardent British imperialist and who would ultimately be instrumental in creating the transcontinental railway and the system of Eastern Standard Time (by which not only the Canadian time system but that of the rest of the world was standardized).

Flemming believed that a telegraph system would uphold British control in North America and provide military support for the empire.[96] The ideology was also implicated in the impetus toward the construction of the Canadian Pacific Railway, in terms of the desire to both protect imperial interests in the Canadian west in the face of a threat of U.S. annexation, and the expansion of Canada's own economic and political interests. As early as 1857, Chief Justice Draper admitted before a select committee,

> I hope you will not laugh at me as very visionary . . . but I hope to see the time, or that my children may live to see the time, when there is a railway going all across that country and ending at the Pacific; and so far as individual opinion goes, I entertain no doubt that the time will arrive when that will be accomplished.[97]

Accordingly, the North-West Transportation, Navigation and Railway Company was given a charter in 1858 to proceed with the construction of rail lines connecting the country's principal waterways. The idea of a transcontinental railway was promoted by Flemming (who would eventually be the Canadian Pacific Railway's engineer in chief), and the Canadian Legislature declared in 1864 that the construction of the railway was necessary for the country's economic development, as well as for the good of the British Empire:

> In view of the speedy opening up of the territories now occupied by the Hudson's Bay Company, and of the development and settlement of the vast regions between Canada and the Pacific ocean, it is essential to the interests of the Empire at large, that a highway extending from the Atlantic Ocean westward should exist, which should at once place the whole British possessions in America within the ready access and easy protection of Great Britain, whilst, by the facilities for internal communication thus afforded, the prosperity of those great dependencies would be promoted, their strength consolidated and added to the strength of the Empire and their permanent union with the Mother Country secured.

By the late 1850s, Canadians appeared generally in favor of securing the North-West for Canada and for Britain.[98]

From these foundations, technological nationalism developed into an integral component of many Canadians' discourse regarding their national character. To a substantial degree, this is entirely understandable. As Maurice Charland has noted, Canada is obviously a "technological state," insofar as its economic existence absolutely requires technologies of transportation and communication.[99] Moreover, there is no doubt that pioneering work in communication technology has been a point of pride in Canada. The media scholar John Irving pointed this out (correctly, but perhaps a little too exuberantly) in the early 1960s:

> [I]f Canada may be described as the child of European civilization and the American wilderness, the development of the system of communications which exists in the country today must rank as among the most creative and constructive enterprises of that civilization.[100]

It is also true that many aspects of the development of communications technologies (from the migrations of early fur traders to the construction of the CPR) have ultimately become integral components of the country's culture. As communications minister Gérard Pelletier said in 1973, "The existence of Canada as a political and social entity has always been heavily dependent upon effective systems of east/west communication" (Harold Innis made a similar assertion in relation to the CPR, when he noted that it was the mode by which eastern Canadian economic and political structures were extended to the western territories).[101] Technological expansion and development were integral factors in the creation of a political apparatus that allowed for the emergence of a Canadian state. In tangible terms, they accomplished the task by providing a bulwark against American annexation of the west, by encouraging westward immigration, and by making military occupation of the region possible; and in discursive terms, their related creed promised to unite Canadians with a sense of national unity under the aegis of a federal government committed to linking all regions of the country. Thus, Harry J. Boyle, vice chairman of the Canadian Radio-television and Telecommunications Commission (CRTC), could claim in 1970 that Canada "exists by reason of communication."[102]

Technological nationalism has not only been a primary nationalist discourse in English Canada, but has undergirded a great deal of public policy and enterprise. The Canadian state was constructed, to a substantial degree, on an infrastructure running east to west that offset the inherent north-south disposition of the continent; and the telecommunications industry has traditionally appealed to this trajectory in terms of framing a relationship between technology and national identity.[103] The country's broadcasting system is a prime example of this ideology at work. The publication of the Aird Royal Commission's 1929 report, for example, was the catalyst for the establishment of the Canadian Radio Broadcasting Commission in 1932, a case of state machinery having been employed to promote Canada's cultural and political autonomy.[104] The idea that technology could bring about nationhood has remained a noticeable element within the arena of public policy. Arguing in the House of Commons for government financial support of a satellite system in 1969, for instance, Deputy Minister of Communications A. E. Gotlieb promised:

> [The satellite] will introduce a new dimension into life in the North and thereby make it much more possible for that part of Canada to be a single, national, cohesive whole by integrating the more remote areas into the common whole. . . . I hate to use clichés, but I think there is an analogy with the railway here. When it was opened up, I imagine very, very few people lived at the end of the line where the last spike was driven, but the very fact this facility went in, I think, transformed the character of the country.[105]

Over two decades later, the Department of Communications likewise announced in its discussion paper *Communications for the Twenty-First Century*:

> Communications have always played a central role in Canada's history. From the fur trade of the seventeenth and eighteenth centuries, to the canals and railways of the nineteenth, from the broadcasting networks, airlines and highways to the telephone and satellite systems of the twentieth, communications technologies have helped Canadians reach new frontiers, settle and develop the wilderness, and build both a society and culture that are unique in the world for the degree to which they depend on good communications systems.[106]

Maurice Charland argued in the mid-1980s, however, that technological nationalism is based on a self-congratulatory relationship between technology and national aspirations. Using the transcontinental railway as an example, he suggested that from this vantage point, Canada became a nation-state due to the CPR, while the CPR was the product of far-thinking politicians who were envisioning a nation. We find the same relationship having been articulated a century later in Pierre Berton's history of the railway, *The National Dream*, a book that presented technology as a foundational Canadian value, and the mode by which a nation came into being as a political and economic unit. The CPR—and Canada—was thus configured as the result of political determination, dreamed into being by politicians; and the airing of the miniseries based on the book effectively extended this "self-congratulatory" mode: CBC television was the result of the valuation of technological nationalism, while the miniseries aired on the network encouraged Canadians to conceive of the nation as an act of political dreaming and will.[107]

By the second half of the twentieth century, when pressed to address issues of national unity, Anglophone Canadians more often had recourse to nationalist configurations based on technology than to any other form. A federal *White Paper on Broadcasting*, for instance, announced in the mid-1960s that "Broadcasting may well be regarded as the central nervous system of Canadian nationhood."[108] In its 1979 report, *A Future Together*, the Task Force on Canadian Unity described a country characterized by a detrimental level of regional and ethnic isolationism, for which technology provided the hope of reconciliation:

> Sometimes the country seemed to us to be composed of a multiplicity of solitudes, islands of self-contained activity and discourse disconnected from their neighbours and tragically unaware of the whole which contained them all. . . . Why is it that we have not learned better to employ this century's communications technology to talk together across the empty spaces?[109]

Like imperial nationalism, however, technological nationalism proved incapable of gaining the emotional commitment of Canadians on a collective level. Although the Confederation demonstrated a desire on the part of some of British North America to politically conceptualize a new national body, the expectations of its architects (not to mention other Canadians) were far from uniform. Ultimately, a broadly acceptable national discourse has never emerged in Canada, nor has a more general sense of shared identity.

As J. M. Bumsted pointed out, the country has rather been characterized by competing nationalisms, ranging from relatively broad Anglophone nationalisms to the circumscribed nationalism of much of Francophone Quebec. The creation of a viable nationalism in Canada has been impeded by the geographical scale of the country, the existence of numerous distinct founding ethnicities, and a federalist structure that has served to exacerbate regional antagonisms. However, to some degree all these broadly antinationalist forces have conversely given rise to specific and limited forms of nationalism within Canada, and no collectively recognized alternative has emerged as a rejoinder to the established disparities of nationality and regionalism.[110]

In spite of its lack of widespread appeal outside of predominantly Anglophone circles, the notion of technological nationalism was ultimately more successful in maintaining itself in the face of its incompatibility with much of the Canadian experience. On this account, "[t]he Canadian identity is, and always has been, fully integral to the question of technology. . . . Technological nationalism . . . has always been the essence of the Canadian state, and, most certainly, the locus of the Canadian identity."[111] Aside from its sectarian appeal, there is a profound disregard within the language of this ideology for the way in which technology has been implicated in the promotion of the economic and political interests of a minority of Canadians. The underlying assumption of technological nationalism is that communication technologies are capable of fostering national unity notwithstanding regional and cultural disparities. This possibility, however, requires that technologies be regarded as neutral vehicles for promoting nationalism when, in fact, they are anything but neutral. This assumption essentially locates the basis of a unified state in the interventions of technologies; but technologies are implicated in the extension of political and economic power, and are not disinterested vehicles that can provide the foundation for a national community.[112] In this regard, we might look to Harold Innis, who argued against technological nationalism from the perspective of the printing press. Countering a contemporary presumption that electricity would decentralize economics and politics, creating a cultural renewal in hinterland regions and an expansion of democracy, Innis claimed that in both Europe and America, an analogous technological innovation, the printing press, had served to diminish time and space in the interest of a commercial and expansionist centralized elite.[113]

What Innis recognized was that technological nationalism obscures the power differentials that are served by communication technologies, insofar as these technologies expand the control of production centers and force marginal regions into a situation of dependency upon these centers; it is a nationalist construction that masks the reality of political and economic forces advocating expansion for their own gain. Communications technologies are devised in capitalist societies chiefly for the purpose of facilitating the flow of capital. The result is that the regulation of both access to, and use of, such technologies remains in the hands of specific sectors of society, which, in order to sustain a capitalist structure, must enforce regulation that in turn further marginalizes certain regions or groups.[114] The expansion of communication technology in modernity has never been a natural occurrence, but has developed around the need to circulate information relating specifically to capitalist trade in commodities. This process can be discerned within the development of the telephone industry in Canada where, in spite of the fact that working-class Canadians expressed an early desire to have access to telephone service, Bell Canada resisted implementing a system of household telephones, assuming it would not be a sound investment. Bell's marketing tactics concentrated on affluent sectors of society that appeared to promise greater profits, and the company's managers defended the practice by claiming that the poor had no need for the technology and consequently no necessary understanding of its worth. Subscription rates were high, and the company made no effort to reduce them, preferring to target those classes that could generate the greatest revenues. Its primary obligation was to its shareholders, rather than to a working-class public that would undoubtedly have benefited from the technology; and the strategy proved to be extremely lucrative.[115] Given the fact that technologies in all contexts extend various forms of power, they cannot truly be said to rest at the foundation of a people's collective character. Technological nationalism is limited precisely because of its contradictory presumption that technology can both reflect and construct a national ethos while serving the interests principally of a minority within the nation.[116]

When all is said and done, we would be hard-pressed to identify a form of nationalism in Canada that has not defined a situation of dichotomy, whether it be French-English, Native-nonnative, or central-peripheral. In a more general sense, nationalism as we know it has often emerged in the modern period as a negative formulation insofar as it has been elaborated in opposition to external bodies rather than in terms of any particular nation's own internal structure.[117] In Canada, the situation has been complicated by the fact that nationalisms have been invoked in relation to internal dichotomies that have precluded the possibility of the emergence of a more broad-based formulation. In fact, it has been suggested that a nationalist discourse has never been successfully implemented in Canada because the country lacks a broad-ranging notion of a generative "Hegelian *geist*" that nationalism requires within any society; and, further, that such a nationalist underpinning, if it were to be articulated and acted upon, would effectively destroy the Canadian state.[118] This kind of claim can be made precisely because Canada did not develop in conformity with a typical pattern of national emergence, whereby internal divisions of class, ethnicity, or location have been conceived of as relatively superficial. Consequently, the country never developed an overarching indigenous nationalism, but rather was compelled to maintain itself in spite of subnationalisms.[119]

There was, in the first instance, no unanimity in respect to a collective meaning of Confederation itself within the British North American colonies. Clear popular support for political union did not exist; and the Confederation, a state project created in the midst of a period of enthusiastic nationalism around the globe, resulted in the creation of a political body that was somewhat atypical—a state lacking the fundamental popular commitment necessary for the emergence of a distinct nationalism.[120] The dilemma concerning a coherent nationalism was articulated from the time of the Confederation debates in the House of Commons. Cartier said, for instance, that the architects of Confederation faced the task of forming "a political nationality." Political nationalism appeared to many to be the only viable option for an emerging autonomous nation-state that lacked a common language, religion, ethnicity, or historical narrative; and geography could not present itself as an aesthetic foundational point of national orientation, given that the transcontinental railway rested at the heart of the national project, and those who were responsible for engineering, building, and paying for it regarded the landscape as a barrier to be overcome by human agency.[121]

Equally problematic was the fact that nationalism did not figure in the initiatives that led to the Confederation; rather, the shape assumed by the political union was the result of a series of conflicts that occurred between 1791 and 1871: North Americans who rejected absorption into the United States, Francophones who defied assimilation into Anglophone culture, and colonies that stood firmly attached to Britain (e.g., British Columbia). In point of fact, the idea of a nation was anterior to all these movements that forced a distinct state into being in the northern part of the continent.[122]

When NWMP inspector Francis Dickens wrote to a friend to report on the execution of Riel in 1885, he declared that the eyes of "both nations, French and English" were watching the man as he walked to the gallows.[123] To be most accurate, he would have been well advised to take note of the fact that a number of other "nations" were also scrutinizing the event: First Nations and Métis. From its inception, Canada contained a number of "national" bodies that the country's federal political structure has been unable to fully accommodate or ignore; and no overarching nationalist formulation has successfully undermined their potency.[124]

In the absence of a broadly based recognizable moment of national inception enshrined within a related nationalist discourse, a collective sense of identity akin to that maintained by citizens of other modern nation-states has been difficult to achieve. It has been suggested that this failure is the result of the fact that Canadians do not share the kind of foundational experience of national definition that appears to have given rise to other modern nations: in the absence of a revolution and revolutionary documents or, conversely, resounding defeats, Canada lacks a historical experience—and its concomitant symbols, heroes, or institutions—from which a nationally defining discourse has been able to emerge.[125] There is obviously some truth in this assertion. Nationalist formulations are much more easily arrived at when they derive from a community that has a distinct sense of its own historical coherence. Allen Smith argued, for instance, that because the United States has created a dominant narrative that masks its African American past, the country's nationalist discourse has reflected a belief in its inherent cultural and historical homogeneity, and that this discourse has resulted in a distinct sense of self-confidence about itself. Nationalist discourse in Canada, on the other hand, has never been able to overcome the country's own uncertainty about the possibility of possessing this kind of coherence; the society it has attempted to portray has generally been too precariously constructed to inspire nationalist confidence.[126]

Canada obviously lacks a defining revolutionary moment. Still, we might ask ourselves whether this means that the country also lacks resources for the construction of a collectively resonant foundational discourse. The answer lies to some degree in a reconsideration of the meaning of revolution. Revolutions, after all, are a peculiarly modern form of behavior; but it might be argued that they represent a yet more fundamental mode of collective self-definition of which they are instantiations, but with which they are not synonymous.

Chapter 4

Violence and State Creation

Hannah Arendt provided an effective portal for entering into a discussion of the meaning of revolution in the modern period. Arendt differentiated between the act of revolution and that of war (which has been a common political phenomenon throughout human history), defining revolution as a form of political behavior that has been limited, strictly speaking, to modernity: prior to the modern period, she argued, wars were rarely fought under the aegis of freedom. However, Arendt did not suggest that revolution was a form of collective behavior that was entirely distinct unto itself; rather, she viewed it as an articulation of a broader structure of violence or violation that resides at the foundation of all political order. From her perspective, the issue of "beginning," in its most profound sense, was fundamental with respect to revolution.[1] In considering revolution and the elemental meaning of violation in political organization, we might elaborate on Arendt's work on the subject with that of recent historians of religion who have provided a template for thinking about the relationship between violence as religious-symbolic activity and the origin of political legitimacy.

In his *City of Sacrifice*, for instance, Davíd Carrasco has argued that "religious violence" was a foundational element in the creation of order and authority in Mesoamerican city-states. Within this context, ritual warfare and human sacrifice served as modes of social and symbolic orientation for political bodies.[2] Returning to the Canadian situation, while it is true that no revolution (in the sense of the "great revolutions" on which

Arendt focused her attention) has transpired within this framework, there have undoubtedly been episodes of violent confrontation in which notable segments of the population have contested the legitimacy of the country's political order. Among such instances of turmoil, there have been perhaps two moments of civil unrest that are broadly recognized by Canadians as having had an impact on the shape of their state: (1) the Rebellions of 1837 in Upper and Lower Canada; and (2) the uprisings of 1869–70 and, especially, 1885.

The Rebellions of 1837 were influenced to some degree by the republican and democratic revolutions of the United States and France, although neither rebellion was revolutionary in spite of the impact they had together on the struggle for responsible government in Canada. What is most significant for our purposes, however, is the fact that neither acquired broad mythic status within the culture, nor had a lasting impact on the Canadian imagination. Neither, for instance, initiated a flurry of creative work that is in any way comparable to that provoked by the western rebellions later in the century; these later uprisings, especially that of 1885, had a much more powerful and enduring effect upon the Canadian psyche.[3] At the time of the later unrest, the intensity of emotional response was due initially to the fact that eastern Canadians saw the threat of an "Indian war" in the events transpiring on the South Saskatchewan. It is difficult in the twenty-first century to appreciate the sense of terror that such a prospect evoked among nonnatives at the time, but it was profound and widespread. It was also based on two factors: first, it was fed by preexisting fears stemming from published accounts of confrontations in the United States, rather than on an accurate perception of the conditions in the North-West; and second, it was fueled by the awareness that nearly twenty thousand Native peoples were included in Treaties Four, Six, and Seven. Eastern Canadians were not so much afraid of a purely Métis rising, since the number of Métis involved in the resistance amounted to only about one thousand men; they were, however, terrified by the prospect of tens of thousands of Native warriors rising in a manner that had been reported to have occurred south of the forty-ninth parallel.[4] Canadian newspapers of the period regularly carried stories of Indian attacks on colonials in both the United States and Mexico, and headlines like "Apaches Burning and Slaying" created paranoia among nonnatives.[5]

Initial reports of an imminent Native uprising originated with the NWMP, telegraph company employees, and the lieutenant governor, all of whom who were, understandably, highly concerned about initial threats and acts of violence on the part of Native peoples in the region. In April of 1885, Hartley Gisborne, district superintendent of the Government Telegraph Service, wired his superior to announce: "Indians raiding, killing, outlaying settlers. Barney Freeman, our old repairer, murdered. Everybody in barracks, expecting attack tonight."[6]

According to Middleton, the lieutenant governor received a telegram around the same time from NWMP Commander A. G. Irvine, informing him that the situation was at a critical juncture. If fifteen hundred troops were not dispatched immediately, he was confident that the Sioux, who were "roaming the country on the warpath," would join the Métis, and it would require thousands of government solders to regain control. For his part, Lieutenant Governor Dewdney was convinced that if the militia was defeated, a "general rising of the Indians" would occur, which would be "most disastrous to the country."[7] Irvine subsequently received a letter from Superintendent Crozier saying that the Indians had been "incited . . . to take up arms and rebel against authority, a condition of affairs which must lead to murders, massacres and the most frightful atrocities."[8]

The press in eastern Canada broadcast the dire concerns that were being voiced from the scene of the disturbance and amplified these fears among the general population. The *Toronto Globe* announced in late March that unconfirmed rumors indicated that at least five hundred starving Blackfoot, under the leadership of Poundmaker, had taken to the "war path" at Calgary and were on the verge of attacking the town in order to get provisions. "The hills," said the paper, "are black with redskins."[9] Likewise the *Daily British Whig* informed its readers on April 6 that the Sioux had taken "to the war path" at Prince Albert and the threat of violence had forced settlers in the vicinity to abandon their farms. The Sioux, said the paper, were "in swarms throughout that country."[10] The *Kingston Daily News* declared a few days later that it appeared that "all the horrors of Indian warfare" would be let loose in large segments of the Saskatchewan district.[11] Over the course of the rebellion, newspapers subsequently carried sensational and brutal accounts of Indian slaughter occurring in the North-West, much of which was exaggerated out of proportion. Reports of the battles, for example, were generally embellished to include fictitious descriptions of mutilated bodies.[12]

In the wake of the rebellion, eyewitnesses to the events confirmed—and in some cases propagated—the notion that an "Indian war" could well have broken out in the North-West in the spring and summer of 1885, and that such an episode would have been horrendous. A telegraph operator at Battleford, J. S. MacDonald, reported after the rebellion that the confrontation in the North-West had

> proved the incalculable value of the telegraph and abundantly justified its construction. . . . Without it many additional bands of Indians would have joined their kinsmen on the warpath and the trouble could not possibly have been brought to an end during that year . . . without the telegraph it would have cost many times that sum while the loss of life would have been infinitely greater.[13]

In his annual report subsequent to the rebellion, Irvine claimed that his scouts played a decisive role in preventing Prince Albert and its outlying settlements from being attacked and in preventing an "Indian massacre."[14] One of these scouts, whose diary was later published, likewise wrote that Riel had urged the Native population to "rise and massacre the white settlers."[15] Having internalized these images entirely, J. A. Chapleau published an account of the events, in which he described "Indian warfare" as "a war of extermination, without quarter, without mercy for defenseless people, for women and children. It is the greatest possible outrage on civilization, and a crime which falls outside the class of political offences."[16] Referring to the "savage barbarity" of the Natives, and Indian war as "a crime against all the laws of humanity," the *Daily Intelligencer* reprinted Chapleau's description two weeks after its publication.[17]

Chapleau would also accuse Riel of having incited the Native population to potential "Indian war," an opinion that was shared by most Anglophones in eastern Canada, and that would apparently prove to be his greatest "crime":

> He alone has been able to persuade the Indian tribes to rise, and he is directly responsible for the murders which the rising has caused. For to cause the Indians to rise is regarded by every government which has them under its control, as a crime which deserves death.[18]

The English press, like Chapleau, generally held Riel responsible for an Indian uprising, an act that was considered inexcusable: he had "set the savage Indians on to murder the white settlers," declared one paper; while others announced that Riel had "called the savages to massacre the whites," and "[b]y his orders the horrors of an Indian war were let loose upon unoffending settlers."[19] The press also tended to regard this aspect of Riel's activities during the rebellion as the most objectionable and deserving of punishment. The *Toronto Mail* called it "the chief burden of Riel's offence"; the *Toronto Week* said it was "'far worse" than any other part of his crime; and the *Ottawa Free Press* announced, "It is for this offence, and its terrible consequences, that the greatest and most firmly seated ill feeling against Riel exists."[20] Finally, it was for this crime, more than any other, that Macdonald is said to have claimed that Riel would hang "though every dog in Quebec bark in his favour."[21]

Setting aside for the moment the question of whether Riel was actually guilty of having encouraged the region's Native population to rise against the Canadian government, we should note that fear over an uprising of this sort was sufficiently widespread that it entered into the proceedings against Riel as he stood trial for high treason. Over the span of the trial, lawyers for the prosecution frequently invoked Riel's culpability in this offence and, ultimately, the presiding magistrate in the case concurred. B. B. Osler, for instance, repeatedly accused Riel of "inciting the Indians" and, on July 28, entered as evidence a letter found in Poundmaker's camp that he believed proved that Riel had attempted to "bring on this country the calamity of an Indian war with all its attendant horrors."[22] Christopher Robinson, who led the team of prosecutors, raised the issue in addressing allegations that Riel was mentally imbalanced. The letter found in Poundmaker's camp, he said, undeniably demonstrated that Riel was trying to incite the chief to "take up arms and go on the warpath," alongside the Métis rebels. "[D]o you think his treatment with regard to the rising of the Indians is a piece of insanity?" he asked; "Do you think the communications which he sent them were suited to their purpose, were adapted to answer the object he had in view? Or do you think you can discover in any one of these communications the insane ravings of an unsound mind?" To drive the point home, Robinson asked the jury, "If this scheme had succeeded, gentlemen, if these Indians had been roused, can any man with a human heart contemplate without a shudder the atrocities, the cruelties which would have overspread this land."[23] Justice Richardson appears to have been swayed by the allegations and evidence, and, on August 1, he announced the jury's verdict: "You have been found guilty of high treason," he said, adding immediately,

> You have been proved to have let loose the flood-gates of rapine and bloodshed, you have, with such assistance as you had in the

Saskatchewan country, managed to arouse the Indians and have brought ruin and misery to many families whom if you had simply left alone were in comfort, and many of them were on the road to affluence.[24]

The fear of an "Indian war," in fact, was without foundation. In 1885, Native peoples in the North-West were by and large passive, remaining on the whole disengaged from the events with which the public and subsequent historians have associated them. Of the few Native peoples who joined in the uprising, most were Cree from the bands of Big Bear and Poundmaker, and the majority of these restricted their activity to raiding abandoned nonnative settlements for provisions and awaiting the reprisals that inevitably ensued. On only one occasion was the intense fear felt by settlers warranted, when a number of settlers, government employees, and English mixed-blood settlers were killed at Frog Lake. On April 2, 1885, a group of young men from Big Bear's band broke into the Indian Agency at Frog Lake under the direction of Wandering Spirit, took prisoners, and decided, against Big Bear's urging, to leave the agency and return to their camp. Thomas Quinn, the subagent, resisted the move, and Wandering Spirit shot him fatally, triggering a shooting spree (in spite of Big Bear's attempts to subvert the violence) in the course of which nine people were killed.[25]

Although news of the Métis victory at Duck Lake undoubtedly had some impact on the attitude of those involved in the action at Frog Lake, it was clearly an autonomous and impulsive act, the result of the consumption of too much alcohol by a group of extremely hungry and frustrated young men. Moreover, the men involved in the attack, led by Wandering Spirit, had no plan for dealing with the situation once it had transpired. Knowing that a retaliatory force would undoubtedly be dispatched to Frog Lake, the group did nothing to prepare for a confrontation; nor did the men make any movement eastward toward the Métis base. Instead, they remained in the Fort Pitt area, apparently uninterested in further engagement; and when they finally confronted the Canadian militia in late May, they merely defended themselves and retreated. Clearly they had no intention of participating in the rebellion being waged by the Métis.[26] They were not taking directions from Riel, nor were they politically or militarily aligned with the Métis during the affair. In fact, all of the conflicts involving Native peoples in 1885 were executed entirely independently: the source of Métis and Native unrest was not the same, and the objectives of their respective protests were focused on different issues.[27]

As we noted, in the course of Riel's trial, B. B. Osler nonetheless stressed Riel's culpability in instigating an Indian uprising:

> About the beginning of July, or the latter end of June 1884, we find him living in this country, in the district of the Saskatchewan. In that district there were supposed to be some 700 or 800 French Halfbreeds, and a good many more English Halfbreeds, and there were several Indian reservations not very far from where the prisoner made his headquarters. . . . We first find him acting in concert with prominent men of both the English and French Halfbreeds and holding meetings. At those meetings apparently for some time nothing more than ordinary constitutional agitation for the redress of grievances, supposed or real, took place. The first overt act which we find against the prisoner is his calling his immediate friends— the French Halfbreeds—to bring their arms at the last of this series of public meetings; that meeting was held, I think, on the evening of the 3rd of March. At that meeting arms were brought. . . . On the twenty-first of March the French Halfbreeds, speaking generally, may be said to have been in arms under the guidance of the prisoner, and they were then joined by Indians, Indians incited to rise, as I think the evidence will satisfy you, by the prisoner.[28]

In truth, despite the fact that Riel would very much have appreciated the assistance of the region's Native population in agitating for recognition, he was not able to create a broadly based Aboriginal alliance—to "arouse the Indians," as Richardson claimed he had done—and, moreover, there is no evidence that he ever encouraged Native peoples to "massacre" settlers, as the press alleged. When Middleton's force was compelled to withdraw at Fish Creek, Riel was afforded time to send requests for assistance to Poundmaker and Big Bear, asking that they join in a combined Métis-Native offensive at Batoche. In a similar fashion, Poundmaker sent a letter to Riel urging him to dispatch men and ammunition to assist him at Battleford: "We wait still for you, as we are unable to take the fort without help," the chief wrote. Neither man, however, was capable of abandoning his position; and both were keenly aware of the fact that they lacked the resources to take on the Canadian militia.[29] As the *Daily Intelligencer* reported in late

May, when Middleton asked Poundmaker why his band had engaged in the uprising and joined "Riel's rebellion," the chief denied the allegation of an association with Riel, saying, "We were afraid to join Riel, because we knew that he had far too little ammunition."[30] Moreover, when Riel was accused at his trial of being culpable for the confrontation at Duck Lake, the evidence that was submitted in support of this claim consisted of letters allegedly written by Riel on April 19 and May 1, asking for the support of the Cree. Whether Riel did or did not write these letters was, however, inconsequential since the attack at Duck Lake occurred on April 2, weeks before the first of the letters was composed. If Riel and the Métis were in any way responsible for the attack at Duck Lake, it could only have been in the sense that successful Métis resistance against government forces had served as an inspiration for the region's desperate Native population.

However, it would be a mistake to presume that without the Métis model Native peoples of the territory would have been willing to allow themselves to face extinction without some form of resistance. By the spring of 1885, they were emerging from a particularly harsh winter and Indian Agency provisions were insufficient to deal with the destitution in which they found themselves. Their dissatisfaction was amplified by the fact that the Canadian government had virtually disregarded the petition that had been drafted and forwarded to Ottawa from Big Bear's council the previous August. The Métis success at Duck Lake, therefore, occurred at a particularly tenuous moment in the North-West, and there is no reason to believe that a Native backlash would not have occurred without the influence of the Métis victory.[31] In the end, however, as Desmond Morton noted, the action was "essentially a Métis rebellion, not an Indian war."[32]

The notion that the predominantly Métis uprising had been an "Indian war" became a persistent legend in the decades following the 1885 Rebellion. In 1910, for instance, the police historian A. L. Haydon wrote that "[t]here had been war—red war, with its opportunities for fighting, for revenge, and for many other outlets of energy so dear to the primitive mind. These instincts are hard to eradicate." Similarly, Charles Gordon wrote in his novel *The Patrol of the Sun Dance Trail* (1914) that an outnumbered force of Mounted Police had confronted a potential Indian uprising that was "so serious, so terrible, that the oldest officer of the force spoke of it with face growing grave and voice growing lowered."[33] George Stanley was, perhaps more than any other historian, responsible for propagating the fallacy of an Indian war. According to Stanley, Natives were "rebels" alongside the

Métis and were ultimately checked in their aspirations toward full war only by "the demands of savage democracy [that] rendered them incapable of rapid decision." Stanley's work became a standard in historical studies of the nineteenth-century west; and despite that fact that much of his analysis of the 1885 Rebellion has been rejected by recent scholars, his work continues to influence generalized understandings of the event. Prominent Cree chiefs, for instance, are still often portrayed as having been driven by destitution and disappointment with the federal government to join Riel and the Métis cause in 1885 as secondary characters.[34]

Although it is undeniable that the Canadian public was easily swayed into panicking over the prospect of a Native uprising, a number of recent scholars have argued convincingly that the perception of an Indian war was also propagated by the federal government in order to allow it the freedom to deal harshly with Native demands for recognition. The claim that Natives were widely rebellious in the uprising served to mask the punitive measures taken against bands in the aftermath of the confrontation in the North-West, and to defend the federal government's subsequent imposition of repressive regulation upon Native peoples. J. R. Miller, for instance, has described this pretense as a "great amnesia."[35] Jon Tobias argued in the early 1980s that the general perception of an Indian war in 1885 was calculatingly constructed by the federal government in order to deal harshly, and without public opposition, with escalating demands for acknowledgment of treaty rights. Bob Beal and Rod Macleod have suggested, further, that the federal government sought to penalize the Native population of the territory in full awareness that the rebellion had been a Métis action; and Sarah Carter has suggested that the majority of Native people in the North-West were committed to upholding treaty agreements restricting their use of violence, and that most of them were as anxious as nonnatives over the transpiring events of 1885.[36]

As an aside, it is difficult to ignore the irony involved in the coincidence of nonnative fears of Indian war (fears of looting, pillaging, and human violation) with the behavior of Dominion forces during the uprising. Fred Harris, a member of the Queen's Own Rifles, for instance, wrote in a private letter that he had been part of a "foraging party" dispatched to the Sweetgrass Reserve near Battleford to salvage anything the Natives might have left behind. "We loaded up ten wagons with stuff—flour, potatoes, etc.," he wrote. "In the Indian huts we found all sorts of strange things. I became the happy possessor of a tom-tom or Indian drum, banjo, a tanning stick, about twenty steel traps and a tomahawk." Similarly, a report by the city editor of the *St. Paul Pioneer Press* from mid-May of 1885 recounted an episode during which Middleton's men came upon Dumont's community and were ordered to refrain from looting. In spite of the directive, a pool table (which was subsequently put on a boat to be transported elsewhere) and boxes of blacking were taken from a local store, and a pair of violins, a concertina, and a book of Shakespeare were taken from Dumont's house. In addition, the soldiers took the eggs they found, killed a large number of chickens, and took items from most of the houses in the vicinity. "Nearly everyone," explained the editor who had witnessed the looting, "returned with one or more trophies." The same editor had previously described what he had witnessed at the Battle of Fish Creek and noted that despite the fact that Middleton strictly prohibited raiding, nearby homes were "despoiled of everything worth carrying away." He added, more grimly,

> You can't visit the battlefield now without a special permit, and this for two reasons: our pickets do not extend, in force, so far, and the visitor might fall victim to a scouting enemy; and (worse than the other reason) some of our soldiers mutilated the dead Indians left on the field by cutting off scalp locks, while all the bodies of the reds were looted of bangles, bracelets, moccasins, etc.[37]

Aside from widespread contemporary fears of an Indian massacre, the events that surrounded the 1885 Rebellion assumed another significance that in many respects has remained a powerful undercurrent in considerations of the period: that of the events as having religious ramifications. The frank use of religious language during and immediately following the uprising underscored the importance that contemporaries attached to the confrontation in the North-West and presaged the style in which Riel, in particular, would be portrayed in the century that followed. Soldiers and officers in the confrontation, lawyers at Riel's trial, contemporary historians, and the media freely employed the language of God, baptism, salvation, and sacrifice in describing the rebellion, defining the North-West, and censuring Riel. NWMP superintendent R. Burton Deane, for instance, referred in his memoir to the lectures he gave his officers during the conflict as "sermons"; and soldiers fighting for the Dominion generally believed that they had the high moral ground in the conflict, that, in the words of John Andrew Forin (a law student who joined the Queen's Own Rifles when the 1885 Rebellion erupted), "God's blessing will follow us." Middleton, recalling the first day of the clash at Batoche, later wrote: "Thus ended our first brush with the enemy. If not a complete victory, it was certainly not a defeat. . . . Personally I was fairly satisfied with the affair. My men had borne their baptism of fire well." The courtroom discourse at Riel's trial was also inundated with religious terminology. Deane, for instance, commented on the mood of the spectators at the trial, concluding that the "prevalent feeling in the North-West Territories was this: We have taken our lives in our hands to open up a new country, and [are] working out our own salvation"; and recalling Osler's opening comments at the trial, Deane noted that the lawyer concluded his remarks with a denunciation: Riel, he said, "did not care whose lives he sacrificed."[38] In the aftermath of Riel's execution, journalists and other writers referred to the "terrible sacrifice of life" that had occurred in the course of the uprising; Riel was described as an "apostle of insurrection and unrest," and a "murderous apostle of tumult"; the government forces were "eulogized" and the confrontation itself was said to have become a "sacred" event.[39]

The impact of the Métis risings at Red River and in the North-West was considerable at the time. However, it is the subsequent importance of these events and their leader that is of particular interest in this instance; and more particularly, the way in which they acquired mythic status within much of the collective Canadian imagination, as well as the implications of this mythicization. The reason for this elevation to mythic status is not perhaps immediately obvious; at least part of the explanation lies in the nature of the civil disturbances of both 1869–70 and 1885. Although the movements Riel led have been referred to as rebellions, insurrections, and uprisings (for reasons having to do with the lack of an available and suitable taxonomy, I have chosen to use this same language), the terminology is not quite accurate. Rebellions, insurrections, and uprisings are specific phenomena that can bring about a restructuring of *local* social and political arrangements, but they are never capable of altering such structures, nor the principles that underlie them, in the centers of political and economic control.[40] To refer to the Métis risings by these terms, then, is not entirely appropriate (although it is perhaps necessary in the absence of more precise terminology), since these uprisings did indeed initiate lasting change in relation to the country's larger political and social structures (a subject that will be explored further). When one thinks of lasting change of this sort, the idea of revolution naturally comes to mind as the principal mode by which this has been achieved in modernity. However, these instances of civil unrest cannot be considered classic revolutions either, since they failed to achieve the generally recognized outcomes that are necessary results of this kind of political agitation. Revolutions differ from other forms of violent protest insofar as they entail a swift alteration in a society's political and social structures, as well as in the principles and "myths" that underlie these structures. Moreover, to be fully a revolution, violent social upheaval must not only destroy an existing political apparatus but must also give rise to new political players who create radically new institutions to replace those that have been destroyed.[41]

Still, there may be some utility in pursuing the idea of revolution in this context, if we are able to move outside the traditional language of this kind of social disruption as it has been predominantly defined in respect to the "Great Revolutions" (e.g., the United States, France, and Russia). From such a vantage point it may be possible to argue that (1) the violence expressed in 1869–70 and 1885 constituted a critical and revolutionary moment within the country's history (one that was not mirrored by either the British North America Act or its resultant Confederation) that signaled in a rather profound sense the emergence of the modern state we know as Canada; and (2) the subsequent mythicization of the rebellions and of Riel expressed a more fundamental meaning of revolution that has served as a broadly based point of orientation for Canadians with respect to their geopolitical relationships with one another. The first issue will be considered in this chapter; while the second will constitute the focus of chapter 6.

To speak of revolution in the first manner requires that the Métis risings be regarded as bearing no relationship to 1776, 1789, or 1917. If they bore a resemblance to any previous movement for political and social change, it was perhaps to the social upheaval that occurred in Europe during the mid-nineteenth century: a series of uprisings that are collectively referred to as the European Revolutions of 1848. The principal significance of these revolutions was that they brought the "age of revolution" to an end and set the stage for subsequent reform movements that shaped Western and Central Europe. The Revolutions of 1848 were a unique phenomenon in European history. Although the seventeenth century saw much of Europe embroiled in revolt, the disturbances that occurred in Italy, Spain, Muscovy, Britain, and France were fundamentally different insofar as they were not the products of a widespread revolutionary mood, and they generally failed to have much of a lasting bearing on the shape of European society. The French Revolution, too, had instigated a period of revolution in Europe after 1789, but aside from France itself, these movements for change had been prompted by French invasions rather than by internal factors. Again, in 1830, uprisings occurred in France, and then Belgium, Poland, and Italy, but the situation proved to be unlike that which would erupt in 1848, whereby the continent's largest countries were swept by a revolutionary tide, from which only Russia and Spain were excluded. Italy, France, Germany, Austria, Bohemia, and Hungary were sites of full-scale revolutions, while Switzerland, Denmark, Rumania, Poland, Ireland, and England saw significant friction. To a notable degree, the Revolutions of 1848 were defined by their state of origin, but there was also a great deal of commonality among them; and as a whole, they destroyed Europe's existing diplomatic structure and made possible new political dynamics that would come to full expression a decade later, following the resolution of the Crimean War.[42]

It is often suggested that the Revolutions of 1848 were ultimately unsuccessful popular movements for social and political change; but this is an oversimplification. While it is true that Switzerland was perhaps the only state in which the goals of revolution were fully achieved, the upheaval that spread across Europe laid the foundation for dramatic changes that would occur over the next half-century. Considering 1848 in the context of the Great Revolutions of France or Russia, it would appear that the nineteenth-century outbreaks lacked many of the defining characteristics of revolutions, since most of the 1848 uprisings presented neither military nor political alternatives to existing regimes, and in many instances, there was no desire to do so. Additionally, the immediate gains of the revolutions were limited. The demands of the working classes were not met to any substantial degree; artisans were unable to slow the expansion of mechanization, nor were they able to achieve more universal educational systems or reduced hours of work; and the middle classes—the groups that apparently gained most from the uprisings—did not finally find themselves with political regimes that they desired. For these reasons, some might argue that these were not authentic revolutions; in comparison to the French and Russian revolutions, those of 1848 were, in the words of Peter Stearns, "short and very nearly stillborn."[43] Still, 1848 has remained of interest to political theorists and historians of revolution. In spite of their apparent immediate failures, the goals of the 1848 uprisings were largely achieved within a generation, and in most cases they were achieved by individuals or political bodies that had been opponents of the revolutions. France, for instance, developed a political consciousness that ultimately led to its adoption of democratic structures and broad-based suffrage; and in Central Europe, the Habsburg monarchy was forced to modernize itself. Thus, Central Europe saw greater rights for Jews, the elimination of the manorial system, standardization of taxes and tariffs, trial by jury, standardized judicial and commercial systems, local political autonomy, and support of economic growth.[44]

In the sense in which the Revolutions of 1848 failed, the Métis uprisings of 1869–70 and 1885 might also be regarded as having fallen short of the expectations of legitimate revolution. After all, neither brought about an immediate change in Canada's political or social framework, nor in the visions that buttressed these structures. In the aftermath of the confrontations, however, the country's political contours and its political balance shifted irreparably; its infrastructure was altered dramatically, and its nascent dichotomies of ethnicity and region emerged as geopolitically defining properties. Like the movements of 1848, then, these were not revolutions in the classic sense. However, like the 1848 movements, too, the late-nineteenth-century Métis risings proved to have a lasting impact on the cultural, social, and political shape of modern Canada.

Bob Beal and Rod Macleod have agued that no remarkable changes occurred in the Canadian west as a result of 1885. They maintain that parliamentary representation (an apparently immediate gain from the confrontation) would have happened without the uprising; and the farmers' organizations that developed in the region by the early twentieth century (and that ultimately led to the creation of the Progressive Party following World War I) arose out of dissatisfactions that predated the rebellion and that were not solved by the action. Beal and Macleod have also maintained that the allocation of land scrip to Métis in the region began with the Half Breed Commission established prior to the uprising, and that the situation of the Métis was not altered by the rebellion, as they remained impoverished and marginalized from the dominant culture. Further, they have suggested that Native peoples faired worse as a result of the uprising, since the Canadian government exploited its substantial police presence in the region to compel tribes into treaty agreements, when they had previously refused. Finally, the government imposed a pass system after the rebellion that effectively restricted the rights of mobility for Native peoples in the west.[45] While it is true that parliamentary representation and agrarian organization may well have developed independently of the uprisings, it is also true that 1885, in particular, led to the development of a distinct western self-consciousness that was little more than implicit prior to the uprising. Likewise, the allocation of land scrip was indeed begun at the eleventh hour in 1885, but it was the threat of rebellion that prompted the move, and rebellion itself that initiated dramatic changes in the lives of Aboriginals (both Métis and First Nations) that resulted in their complete marginalization. The post-1885 situation was not one in which the status quo was maintained. In fact, the creation of the province of Manitoba in 1870, the change in Aboriginal and nonnative relations, the development of telegraph and railway lines, and the elevation of ethnic and regional disparity from inconvenient traits of the British North American colonies to politically and socially defining properties of modern Canada reveal a decidedly different state after 1885.

While there is no question that the uprising of 1869–70 altered the political contours of Canada (by forcing the federal government to abandon its desire to maintain the territory of Rupert's Land as a colonial holding and to sanction the territory's entry into the Confederation with provincial status as the province of Manitoba), it was the events of 1885 that had a more profound impact on the political and social profile of the country. All the constitutional demands set out in the somewhat prophetic petition of rights that was drafted by representatives of the District of Lorne, for example, were eventually granted by the Canadian government. The year after the rebellion, Macdonald's government conceded territorial representation in Parliament, and although the relationship between the rebellion and the concession was never acknowledged, the uprising was clearly the catalyst for the change. In addition, years of campaigning led by F. W. G. Haultain resulted in the granting of responsible government to the territories in 1897; and in 1905, Alberta and Saskatchewan were constituted as provinces, although the federal government retained control of natural resources. Finally, federal control of natural resources was relinquished in 1930, thereby satisfying all the constitutional claims of the 1885 petition.[46]

More immediately, Canada's infrastructure developed substantially as a result of the events of 1885. On the eve of the 1885 Rebellion, for example, the Canadian Pacific Railway was unfinished and in dire need of funding to keep the project afloat. If it had not been for the uprising, the venture would undoubtedly have folded, since the government was not prepared to provide it with further capital. Within days of the news of events at Duck Lake reaching Ottawa, the federal government had managed to pull together five thousand recruits from central and eastern Canada to be dispatched to the

Saskatchewan Valley. The responsibility for transporting these troops was placed in the hands of the superintendent of the CPR, William Cornelius Van Horne, and while the railway line went only as far as Winnipeg, the recruits were delivered to the front by means of sleighs and, at some points, marches over frozen lakes. Middleton, however, was rushed to the territory quickly via the American rail system running through Chicago and St. Paul.[47] The unrest on the South Saskatchewan provided the floundering CPR with a badly needed boost in public image, thereby facilitating further government investment in the project. Central Canadian panic over a potential U.S.-styled Indian war created the ideal climate for the railway to step in, offer its services to transport Canadian militia to the North-West, and emerge in the wake of the confrontation prepared to reap the benefits of Ottawa's gratitude—the funding required to complete its transcontinental line.[48]

The year 1885 also initiated a dramatic development in telegraphic communication in the country. North America was connected to Europe via the telegraph in 1866, but it was not until the North-West Rebellion that the technology truly became integrated into Canadian society. From the outset, the telegraph played a key role in the mobilization and organization of both government troops and the Mounted Police during the outbreak, so much so that a telegraph facility was built inside the Parliament building at Ottawa for the minister of militia and defense, Adolphe-Philippe Caron. Distribution of goods to Natives in the territory during this volatile period was orchestrated also from Ottawa via telegraph messages, and Middleton's three columns of troops were in virtually uninterrupted communication with Ottawa throughout the campaign. Not only were government forces able to maintain continual communication with superiors in Ottawa due to telegraphic dispatches, but the rebellion signaled the beginning of a modern form of journalism: war correspondence. By means of the telegraph, reporters from the *Montreal Star, Montreal Witness, Toronto Globe, Toronto Mail,* and *La Minerve* were stationed with government troops in the North-West and remained in regular correspondence with their editors in central Canada and, consequently, with the reading public. The telegraph proved to be so valuable in terms of shortening the length of the rebellion and conveying news of the uprising to eastern Canada that the developing telegraph industry was able to acquire financial backing required for expansion. In the year immediately prior to the outbreak of the rebellion, the Telegraph Department of the CPR generated revenues of $70,000; in the following year, due principally to media coverage of the affair, departmental revenues more than doubled, to $145,000. As a result, the region between Lake Superior and the Rocky Mountains was connected by telegraph service within the year.[49]

Perhaps the most far-reaching impact of the uprisings was the way in which they served to transform imbedded dichotomies of ethnicity in the country (which had previously appeared to be manageable) into explicit and permanent structures of opposition and creative energy within the social and political fabric of the Confederation. The foundational French-English dichotomy traced its roots back to the Conquest and had been nurtured by the Rebellions of 1837 and the subsequent union of the Canadas in 1840. Ethnic tension had characterized French-English relations prior to the Confederation and had reared its head briefly with respect to the Métis resistance in 1869–70 and the amnesty issue, such that the ideal of a unified "national consciousness" to which many of the architects of Confederation aspired had clearly not been achieved by the time of the North-West Rebellion. The 1885 uprising, however, raised the stakes and ultimately created the most politically significant crisis of ethnicity to face the new state. In the wake of the rebellion, English and French Canadians were pitted against one another in a way that jeopardized the idea of national unity that had inspired the draftsmen of Confederation. English-speaking Ontarians, recalling the execution of Thomas Scott in 1870, regarded Riel as a French Catholic radical who had orchestrated an Aboriginal rebellion against the Dominion; they consequently called for the punishment of all those implicated in the uprising. The French of Quebec, however, cast Riel as a hero in the lineage of Papineau—a leader of a French resistance against Anglo repression—and accordingly demanded that all the rebel "patriots" be pardoned.[50]

In *Riel: The Man Who Had to Hang*, E. B. Osler reflected on the events of Riel's trial and concluded: "With the pronouncement of sentence . . . the country began to split wide open." The people of Ontario were at a loss to understand the jury's recommendation of mercy, and those of Quebec expected the sentence to be reduced to life imprisonment. Government ministers were generally in favor of the death sentence, believing that Riel had solely instigated two uprisings; and they refused to admit the possibility that the government bore some measure of culpability in what had occurred in the North-West.[51] In many respects, Riel's execution presaged the dynamics that would plague interaction between French and English Canada throughout the subsequent century. Certain that the execution of

Riel was simply a matter of justice, Anglophones resented the demand that his sentence be commuted, a demand that they interpreted as a claim for exceptional status and privilege for French Canadians, and the assumption of a prerogative to reinterpret Canadian law on the basis of Quebec's sectarian interests. French Canadians, conversely, perceived in the execution of Riel what they thought to be a victory for English Canadian extremism over the French Catholic population of the entire country. The conflict over the issue of Riel's hanging planted seeds of distrust that were to permanently influence the relationship between the English and French in Canada. It could be discerned early in Anglophone hostility toward Honoré Mercier's first systematic articulation of Quebec nationalism, the debate over the Jesuit's Estate Act, assaults on the French language and Catholic schools beginning in 1885 and lasting until 1916 in Ontario and the western provinces, resistance to the creation of French companies within the Canadian armed forces during both world wars, and, ultimately, in antagonism toward the federal policy of official bilingualism in the 1960s and 1970s.[52]

This level of antagonism was not present in 1869 when the Red River agitation commanded national attention; it appears that Francophones in Quebec at that time did not identify with the Métis cause, in spite of their shared language. In fact, at the outset of the uprising, French Canadians appear to have known almost nothing about the Métis or their grievances. Reports of what had been occurring on the American frontier were common in Quebec newspapers of the period, and news of "Indian wars" had largely informed French Canadian notions concerning the Canadian west. As a consequence, early newspaper reports of the situation at Red River presented the reading public with stereotypical images of the Métis as savages. *Le Canadien*, for instance, claimed in mid-1868 that annexation of the west could be accomplished only if attempts were made to "repulse the savage tribes"; and *La Minerve*, in a story on the Métis confrontation with William McDougall late in 1869 reported that the Métis had intended to "scalp the new lieutenant-governor."[53] A general awareness of the Métis as a distinct population began to become apparent in the winter of 1869–70, but the association of the Métis with stereotypes of Indians on the American frontier still persisted. The press expressed no sympathy for the Métis, referring to them as "rebels," "insurgents," and "ferocious mixed-bloods"; and their leader, Louis Riel, was portrayed as a tyrant who had capriciously and illegally seized control at Fort Garry.[54] General opinion held that the insurrection should be crushed as quickly as possible.[55]

All this shifted as Anglo-Ontarians quickly began seeing signs of a conscious plot to establish the territory as a French Catholic province that would undermine English settlement in the west. The paranoia was fueled by the Canada First movement (especially its western ambassadors Mair and Schultz), and particularly by a pamphlet written by William McDougall upon his return from the territories early in 1870. In *The Red River Rebellion*, McDougall accused "foreign Jesuits" (prominent among whom were "Bishop Taché and his co-conspirators") of orchestrating the entire confrontation in order to transform the territory into a "French Catholic Province."[56] McDougall's accusations were reported in the French press as "unjust and furious attacks" motivated by a "fanaticism which inspires Mr. McDougall against the French Canadians." He was further reproached for being "the one who started the cry in Ontario that we wanted to establish a 'French domination' at Red River! Always appeals to fanaticism!"[57] The suspicion of a French Catholic conspiracy was given impetus by the execution of Thomas Scott. The death of Scott prompted an initially critical response from the French Canadian press, one that ranged from mild censure of a "most regrettable" act to denunciation of an "abhorrent murder" that, for instance, *Le Journal des Trois-Rivières* announced "we blame as energetically as possible." A much more heated response in Ontario, however, turned the French press's attention away from criticizing the execution toward accusations of English bigotry against French Catholics. Thus, the *Journal de Québec* claimed that "their newspapers have long ago made clear to us the cause of their indignation. . . . There are inhabitants of French origin out there, and that upsets Upper Canada's plans." The paper further alleged that indignation over the murder of Scott was simply a smokescreen for the true foundation of Ontario's outrage: "All that is only a pretext to call for the expulsion of the French from the North-West." As Ontario opinion gained stridency, the French in Quebec began to realign their sympathies with Riel and the Métis: "The French-speaking Métis are considered as barbarians by the English element in Canada; it feels neither pity nor a sense of justice toward them, because of that belief."[58]

In the wake of the uprising, divergences in French and English opinion regarding the events that had occurred at Red River intensified. The Ontario public sustained its calls for the punishment of those responsible for the death of Scott, and Ambroise Lépine was ultimately arrested in 1873 and charged in connection with his part in the murder. The arrest outraged Quebec, which had been led to believe that the principal participants in the

Red River uprising had been promised an amnesty by the federal government in 1870; and Lépine's conviction and sentence of execution further alienated French opinion. Despite the fact that Lépine's sentence was commuted, Riel's expulsion from the House of Commons in 1874 (when he had attempted to take his seat as a legitimately elected member of parliament) only served to fuel resentment in Quebec. When the promised amnesties finally came early in 1875, they were not applied to William O'Donoghue (who was banished from Canada for life), nor to Riel and Lépine (who were each banished for five years).[59]

Still, tempers moderated somewhat in the years following the outbreak at Red River, and when rebellion erupted in the North-West in 1885 many French Canadians were somewhat ambivalent regarding the situation. To some degree, traditional ethnic boundaries became temporarily inconsequential, and support for the suppression of the Métis and Riel was described by the French press as comparatively broad-based: "Military enthusiasm," reported *La Presse* in late March, "is spreading throughout Canada."[60] At the very least, Francophones tended to agree that the uprising should be quelled, and to this end, many took part in the military campaign organized by the federal government. They were not, however, so eager to condemn the Métis as they had been at the outset of the 1869 uprising. A nagging belief tracing back to the Red River uprising—that the Métis were French Catholics who were struggling against the oppression of English Protestants—still lingered in 1885. This hesitant support for the Dominion's response to the events taking place in the Saskatchewan Valley remained throughout the confrontation; and in spite of the fact that the press endorsed the Canadian actions taken against the uprising, there was also consistent empathy for the rebels and the people they represented whose grievances were perceived as legitimate. As *La Revue Canadienne* put it, French Canadians who chose to enlist in the militia were forced to sacrifice "their feelings and their sympathies." This disquietude did not go unnoticed by the English commanders of the campaign: no French regiments were permitted to confront the Métis during the span of the rebellion. In fact, Middleton consigned two French regiments (the ninth and sixty-fifth) to western points as far from the center of fighting as possible.[61]

As the rebellion proceeded, Ontario began to express mounting anti-Catholic sentiment and Quebec responded with increasing sensitivity for the cause of the Métis with whose language and religion French Canadians identified. Ultimately, this rising tide of sympathy was reflected in Quebec's reaction to the trial of Riel: there was a common belief that Riel was clearly mentally imbalanced and that this should be considered a mitigating factor in respect to his culpability. He was, according to one newspaper, a "maniac" who had been twice committed to asylums between 1870 and 1885. "Yes, we say it again," said another, "Riel is just a madman, a visionary entirely without responsibility for his acts. He is a moonstruck fellow whose sickly excitation naturally made a great impression on the minds of the primitive people who took him for a sort of prophet."[62] When Riel's case came before the court, it appeared to many in Quebec that he was being denied a fair trial; and Richardson's remarks throughout the proceedings, which seemed unnecessarily ruthless, were reported in French-language newspapers, often in an inflated form. From the beginning of the trial, public opinion in Quebec was firmly with Riel; and demands for Riel's execution in the English press were met with strident calls from Quebec for a pardon.[63]

The expectation that Riel would be acquitted on the grounds of insanity led to disbelief and antagonism following his conviction. The fact that he had been found guilty by a jury of only six men, all of whom were English, was widely criticized as having prejudiced the trial; and the general opinion among Francophones was that "Riel was condemned even before being heard."[64] "The whole province of Quebec is distressed," announced one Quebec newspaper in early August; while another traditionally Conservative paper encouraged the people of Quebec to rally to the support of Riel. Concerns that Riel was being cast as a scapegoat in a crusade against French Catholicism reached a pitch with news of the trial verdict, and the press resounded with allegations that English Canadians were not so much interested in executing Riel himself but in attacking French Canadians more generally: "If the sentence is carried out . . . Riel will have been hanged because he's not English; and because the French-haters of Ontario wanted to see him . . . dance at the end of a rope."[65] "May this condemnation satisfy the blind fanaticism of Canadian Francophobes," announced *L'Etenard*, "it certainly is the bitter fruit of injustice, of the arbitrary, tyranny inimical to our race. May it be the last!"[66]

Macdonald received in excess of twelve hundred telegrams from Francophones in Quebec, Ontario, Manitoba, and the North-West pleading Riel's case; and petitions opposing the hanging were received in Ottawa with more than twelve thousand signatures on them. Similar petitions were drafted and forwarded to the Canadian government from New York, St. Louis, and other U.S. cities. A community of Franco-Americans in Chicago, for instance, wrote that "the execution of Riel, under the circumstances, would be considered as a refusal to do justice to a great portion of the population of Canada as well as to those French Canadians who are established in the United States, and who have at heart the wealth and prosperity of the land which gave them birth."[67] British Catholics submitted a petition under the auspices of a member of the House of Lords (Lord Clifford); and the London-based International Arbitration and Peace Association submitted a formal request that the death sentence be revoked. Additionally, the governor general received petitions from France; and Le Syndicat de la Presse Coloniale Française submitted one to the queen. The outcry was sufficiently intense to unnerve Conservatives in Quebec who expressed unanimous support for a reprieve and appealed to Macdonald on behalf of the party. Guillaume Amyot, a Quebec Conservative who had commanded a French Canadian regiment during the rebellion, wrote to Macdonald with a warning: "Every day public opinion here gets stronger and stronger against hanging Riel. . . . The *courant d'opinion* everywhere is getting irresistible, and take my word as a sincere friend that your best supporters will not be able to stand the position if Riel is hanged."[68] Macdonald found himself in a difficult position, as the conflict was carried into his cabinet where men like Mackenzie Bowel (grand master of Ontario's Orange Order) and Hector Langevin (a previous leader of the St. Jean Baptiste Society in Quebec) pressured the prime minister to acquiesce to antithetical demands in their respective provinces.[69]

Ten thousand people gathered on August 9 on the Champ-de-Mars in Montreal at a rally in support of Riel; and a few days later, five thousand turned out for a rally at St. Sauveur where two of Riel's lawyers, Lemieux and Fitzpatrick, were introduced and "enthusiastically cheered and applauded" for their efforts on Riel's behalf. Fitzpatrick began his remarks by saying that he had hoped by his efforts to repay in some way the kindness shown by French Canadians to the persecuted Irish when they arrived in Canada, and then proceeded to say that what Riel had done in leading the people in the North-West was no different from what Papineau had done in Quebec in 1837. On August 17, a large rally was held in Hull's Market Hall, where nearly seven hundred petitioners signed a series of resolutions to be forwarded to the governor general claiming that Riel was a "fellow countryman" who had committed a crime for which many others had been sentenced less harshly; that he had acted on behalf of the Métis whose rights as Canadians had been disregarded; and that a death sentence would surely be a sign to the Métis that recognition of their rights would not be forthcoming. They asked, finally, that the sentence be commuted or a retrial be called where Riel could be tried by a jury of twelve.[70]

Of particular contention to the people of Quebec was the fact that Riel's secretary, William Jackson, had been acquitted on the grounds of insanity only days prior to Riel's conviction. Given that most Francophones in the province were convinced that Riel was mentally unsound, they regarded the discrepancy in trial outcomes as an instance of the comparative mistreatment of a French Catholic Métis in relation to an Ontario-born English Protestant. The opinion that Riel's trial had been a sham gained impetus as the French press highlighted the disparity between the handling of Riel's case and that of Jackson. "The inconceivable ease with which they acquitted Jackson," declared *Le Courrier de St.-Hyacinthe*, "and the fanatical and bloody relentlessness with which they condemned Riel, disgust us and dishonor the justice of the country."[71] Although there were obvious similarities between the cases of Riel and Jackson, there were also some distinct differences between their situations. Virtually anyone who had contact with Jackson, for example, claimed that he was demonstrably mad; while many who had spent time with Riel in the period before his trial—Middleton, George Young (who had pleaded on behalf of Thomas Scott to have his life spared during the first rebellion), Augustus Jukes (NWMP surgeon who had treated Riel)—testified that he was sufficiently sane to be capable of orchestrating a Métis and Native uprising and, indeed, faking his own insanity. Of course, the most salient issue may have been what Desmond Morton noted: given the economic and human cost of the rebellion, it would have been highly unlikely that the Canadian government could have acted on the suggestion that a madman had instigated the entire affair.[72]

By the time Riel was hanged on November 16, French Canadians were resolutely wedded to the belief that Riel had died as a result of English extremism. *La Minerve*, which had firmly supported the suppression of the Métis and Riel during the summer of 1885, was emblematic. In the immediate wake of the execution, it proclaimed: "Riel was executed this morning at 8:23. He died a courageous soldier."[73] Within days of the hanging, Quebec erupted into fury. At Point Claire, according to the *Daily British Whig*, a "notice, covered in black, ha[d] been hung on the city hall with the inscription: 'Riel has died for his country. Shame on the Canadian Ministers'"; at Sorel, the paper reported, "There was a great demonstration. . . . At the market burning of effigies of our public men was enacted"; and in Montreal, Terrebonne was said to be

> in a state of stupor, stores are closed, and crepe hangs on each door. . . . Mass meetings to condemn the execution of Riel are to be held in every parish of Hochelaga County. Demonstrations and meetings to condemn the execution of Riel have been held at Terrebonne, Rigaud, St. Lin and Batiscan.[74]

On November 23, fifty thousand people gathered for a demonstration in Montreal at the Champ-de-Mars, an event that essentially signaled the death knell for the Conservative Party in Quebec, the beginning of a firm Liberal footing in the province, and the emergence of Wilfrid Laurier as a political force. Honoré Mercier, the leader of the provincial Liberals, head-lined a cast of thirty-seven speakers who addressed an impassioned crowd. The execution of Riel, Mercier said, was an attempt to execute all of French Canada. It was an act of war upon the French Canadian nation that had resulted in "two million Frenchmen in tears"; they had suffered a "national misfortune" because Macdonald had "struck a blow at the heart of our race."[75] The *Montreal Gazette*, reporting on an emergency meeting of the Montreal City Council, following a telegraph announcing Riel's hanging, related that

> The leading feature of the affair was the burning of the effigies sup-posed to represent Sir John Macdonald and the French ministers, who voted that justice should take its course in Riel's case. . . . Each effigy had a strong rope around the neck. . . . On a broad board in front were the words, "Our hero and patriot, Riel."[76]

Mercier opened his remarks that evening with: "Our poor brother is dead. He has been sacrificed to the fanaticism of the Orangemen," and in a move that would reverberate throughout the next century, Mercier, a Conservative until that evening, announced the inauguration of a new nationalist party in Quebec. Not to be outshone, the leader of the opposition and future prime minister Wilfrid Laurier declared: "Had I been born on the banks of the Saskatchewan I would myself have shouldered a musket to fight against the neglect of the government and the shameless greed of speculators."[77] It was a theme to which Laurier would return in the House of Commons four month later. "To tell us that Louis Riel, simply by his influence could bring these men from peace to war," he announced to the House,

> to tell us that they had no grievances, to tell us that they were brought into a state of rebellion either through pure malice or through imbecile adherence to an adventurer is an insult to the people at large and an unjust aspersion on the people of Saskatchewan. . . . I say they have been treated by this government with an indifference amounting to undisguised contempt, and if this rebellion be a crime, I say the responsibility for that crime weighs as much upon the men who by their conduct caused the rebellion as upon those engaged in it.[78]

In the end, it is clear that while the legitimacy of Riel's trial may be an arguable issue, the trial itself was undeniably a political miscalculation. Given that the proceedings would involve the issue of insanity, it would have been prudent for the Crown to take more time in dealing with Jackson's case. If Jackson had been deemed incapable of standing trial, and required to undergo treatment prior to his trial, or if more extended testimony regarding his alleged insanity had been provided at his trial, the federal government might have averted some of the backlash that erupted in Quebec following Riel's conviction. As it was, it appeared to the French that Jackson had received favorable treatment because he was an Anglophone; and that his crime, in the words of Laurier, was simply that he was possessed of "peculiar views on religious matters," a principal accusation that could well have been leveled at Riel.[79]

Ultimately, French Canadians saw in the execution the triumph of Anglo-Canadian racism: "Riel is dead . . . and the cursed city which has drunk his blood, the hordes of sectarians who called for it with foaming mouths and sinister, execrable cries are still plunged in an infernal orgy of fanaticism and hatred against everything French." From this perspective, Riel was hanged only for being French and Catholic: "If Riel had not had French blood in his veins and if he had not been Catholic; if he had been English and Protestant, or even Turkish, there would never have been any question of hanging him."[80] In addition, the execution was regarded by Francophones as a direct affront on their right to assume a role in western expansion; English Canadians, it seemed, were determined to assume control of the west, "which they're making into an English land at our expense."[81]

As A. I. Silver has noted, there appears to have been a distinct shift in French Canadian attitudes toward their role in the Confederation at the time of the fury over the hanging of Riel. At Confederation, most Francophones in Quebec understood the union to be an agreement between the provinces to function as a state while retaining their individual national traits; and in the case of French Canada, Quebec was perceived as being the principal arena of Francophone culture in respect to the entire country. In the wake of Riel's execution, however, Francophones were expressing a definite desire to share in the development of the west and an expectation that they should be permitted equal rights with Anglophones within the new provinces. The shift amounted to an assertion that Confederation had not been merely a coalition of provinces but of the two ethnic groups: "[T]hey have the same rights and the same duties. Although their aspirations are different, they are equal to each other." The perceived attempt to bar French Canada from the process of western development was consequently unacceptable: "[T]he two races are destined to live a common life on the Canadian land, to have the same political institutions and be governed by the same men."[82] It has been a common assumption that the events surrounding the death of Riel initiated an inward turn in Quebec, whereby Francophones realized they were to be excluded from the future development of the country and became, consequently, concerned principally with issues of self-definition within their own province. Silver, however, has argued that the plight of both the Métis and Riel drew their gaze toward the west and resulted in a claim to the right to participate in the development of the region. The events of 1869 and 1885, then, galvanized a "bilingual theory of Confederation" that does not appear to have been present in the minds of French Canadians at the time of Confederation; such that the political union came to be viewed as an agreement that assured the long-term survival of the French nationality and the equality of the two principal languages.[83] Thus, *La Minerve* claimed that the Confederation had been "a pact between the country's French- and English-speaking races"; and *L'Électeur* declared that Canada was a state "founded on the equality of races, and not on the absorption of one element by the other."[84]

To some degree, French antagonism toward the execution of Riel (as emblematic of English Canada's perceived bigotry) has persisted well into the present day, as Francophone writers continue to refer to Riel as prey to "English prejudice," "Ontario fanaticism," and "Orange fanaticism"; and there have been calls for a retroactive pardon as a long overdue admission that "anti-French and anti-Catholic' prejudice" had been at the root of the execution.[85] In response to Suzanne Tremblay's move to a second reading in the House of Commons of Bill C-297 (an act to revoke the conviction of Louis David Riel), in the fall of 1996, Jean-Paul Marchand illustratively stated:

> Louis Riel was led before a jury of six Anglophones and tried by an Anglophone judge in Regina, as Donald Smith drove the last spike for the transcontinental railway. In that same year, French was banned in Manitoba. Louis Riel was, in fact, the victim of a miscarriage of justice that reflected the attitude to Francophones at the time. . . . The conviction of Louis Riel was unjust, unacceptable and unpardonable. If people want to reconcile Canada with its Francophones, let them adopt, fairly and squarely, a formula to absolve or pardon Louis Riel.[86]

English Canadian reaction to the events surrounding the Métis uprisings was ultimately just as antagonistic as that of the French, contributing to an ethnic dichotomy that would imbed itself deeply in the cultural and political culture of the country. We noted earlier that Ontario's response to the uprising of 1869–70 was framed in terms of ethnicity and religion: because Riel had the support of the clergy, Anglo-Ontarians believed they were witnessing a concerted effort to establish the newly acquired territory as a Francophone Catholic province. The editor of the *Toronto Globe*, for instance, claimed in February of 1870 that Riel was the mouthpiece in a "political game of chess" that Bishop Taché was playing with Canada in which the Catholic clergy had "deeper designs than the uneducated French were aware of."[87]

Time would ultimately moderate both French and English hostilities associated with the uprising, and when hostilities again broke out in the west fifteen years later, the English press appeared to tenuously breathe a sigh of relief. Anti-French sentiment was not a feature of its discourse; rather, journalists made much of French Canadian support for the government's military offensive, extolling the roll of the minister of militia, Adolphe-Philippe Caron, in coordinating the offensive, applauding French regiments, publishing the names of French soldiers who were killed in battle, and reporting on the amicable relations that existed between French and English units meeting in the North-West. French Canadian troops were greeted with great public enthusiasm when they returned from the territory, and English newspapers praised them for having fought "for a common cause and a common country with our own men."[88] However, as Silver has noted, French support for the military offensive, as well as English appreciation for that support, were not indications of a united bicultural response to the affair. In fact, broad public admiration for the contributions of French Canadians betrayed an underlying English apprehension regarding French-English solidarity in the cause. There had been resistance on the part of Francophones to support the federal government's position in the 1869–70 uprising at Red River; they had not fully supported the introduction of Canadian troops into the region and had argued vociferously for the granting of an amnesty to Riel in the wake of the rebellion. With only a decade having transpired since the amnesty was granted, memories of French support for Riel were still alive in English Canada. Some of the English press expressed this apprehension, warning that Anglophones could not assume "that the men of Quebec should not only march alongside to put down put down the rebellion, as they are doing, but should also curse the rebels." For the most part, however, this kind of anxiety expressed itself in a readiness to extol the roles played by Francophones in the federal government's response to the outbreak.[89]

Although there were some indications during the campaign of the kind of ethnic enmity that would rear its head at its conclusion, for the most part this was tempered until Riel was brought to trial. At the outset of the proceedings, Anglophones seemed somewhat unaware of mounting French hostility and generally expressed the conviction that Riel's guilt was unequivocal and that the judicial system would deal with him in a fair and appropriate manner: "At any rate," noted the *London Free Press*, "while trusting that he will be firmly dealt with (for he has been the cause of a large loss of life), it may be anticipated that his condemnation will be left in the hands of justice, the due administration of which forms so marked a feature of Canadian procedures."[90] English Canadians were also generally satisfied with the results of the trial, believing that justice had been served and that the verdict and sentence were commensurate with the crime: "After a short, but in every respect a fair trial," announced the *Montreal Herald*, "Riel has been found guilty. The verdict will, we believe, be considered a just one by the great majority of the people of the Dominion." A great number of French Canadians, however, were not inclined to regard the decision as a just one, and they began to make their feelings known almost immediately. In response to their criticisms, and for the first time throughout the entire affair, pronounced Anglophone hostility began to emerge. "A man who is sane enough to organize two rebellions," claimed one Toronto newspaper,

> and cause the death of scores of his fellow-citizens, is sane enough to furnish material for a hangman. Riel's comrades had grievances; Riel had none; show what mercy is to be shown to the misguided followers, but show none to the assassin himself, who suffered nothing, dared nothing, won nothing, but tried his best to raise the Indians and massacre the whites.

In a more sardonic fashion, another journalist commented, "Riel is a criminal and must bear the consequences of his acts. Neither the holy water which he sprinkled round the court room nor his vehement prayers should save him."[91] The press was expressing the views of growing numbers of English-speaking Canadians who believed, like one anonymous critic who wrote to Macdonald, "If the French of Montreal and Quebec think that he is a marter [sic] and that he is sure of going strait [sic] to Heaven the sooner he goes there the better."[92]

In a symbiotic fashion, underpinnings of English antagonism became more obvious as Francophone resentment mounted; and French criticism of the legality and morality of Riel's trial elicited equally judgmental reactions from English Canada. Anglophones, for instance, refused to admit that the issue of Riel's sanity had any bearing on his conviction and sentence; he was regarded as religiously eccentric, but definitively sane. In fact, the *Ottawa Free Press* went so far as to compare him with General Charles Gordon: "Riel may be a crank upon religious matters—and so was the gallant General Gordon, the brave defender of Khartoum. . . . We do not believe that his actions bear out the inference that he is irresponsible."[93] Riel was compared also to Charles Guiteau, the man who had assassinated U.S. president James Garfield in 1881. Guiteau had committed the murder as a result of his belief that he had a sacred mission, and during his trial his religious eccentricity was submitted as evidence of insanity. In the end, the insanity claim was rejected and Guiteau was convicted and sentenced to execution. Referring to Riel, the editor of the *Northern Advance* declared, "He may be a crank, so was Guiteau, but that does not absolve him from responsibility nor lessen his guilt."[94]

English Canada also refused to recognize any similarity between the cases of Riel and Jackson. After the fall of Batoche, Jackson had been arrested by Middleton, and in his subsequent report on the victory, the major general made it clear that he believed the man to be psychologically deranged: "Prisoners all released and safe in my camp," he wrote; "[a]mong them: Jackson, a white man who was Riel's secretary, but who now is mad and rather dangerous." The press echoed Middleton's assessment, claiming that Jackson was "hopelessly insane"; and his trial, consequently, was regarded as having been absolutely fair.[95] Anglophones believed there were indeed differences between the situations of Riel and Jackson, but these had nothing to do with ethnicity. The issue was clearly related to the question of sanity, and Jackson was regarded as having been sufficiently mentally unsound to be unable to be held accountable for his actions. Riel, on the other hand, was sane enough to be fully culpable. "He is a rebel, a felon, a murderer," announced the *Canadian Statesman*, a man who had been responsible for senseless death and the "wanton destruction of property."[96] In addition, the appeal process that Riel's lawyers pursued and ultimately lost served to dismiss most doubts in the minds of English Canadians as to the legitimacy of the legal process. Macdonald was advised that "[l]etting the case go all the way to the Privy Council meant that 'fair play has been shown' and that 'everything has been done that could be done to have the matter settled fairly.'" Newspapers like the *Globe, Hamilton Spectator, Telegram, Mail*, and the *World* reported that even Charles Fitzpatrick, Riel's chief counsel, declared: "It is impossible to pretend that Riel was unfairly tried."[97] As for Macdonald himself, if not for the intervention of the governor general, he would have denied Riel recourse to the appeal process guaranteed by the British North America Act. Still, and in spite of Macdonald's role in Riel's execution, the fact that Riel's case was appealed through every possible channel ending with the Privy Council, meant that his execution was judicially legitimized by both Canada and Britain.[98]

Once the appeals process was complete, pressure began to mount from English quarters to proceed with the execution without delay. An officer of the Orange Association of West Toronto, for instance, epitomized contemporary sentiment in a letter he sent to the secretary of state, J. A. Chapleau:

> We would, therefore, most urgently and earnestly request you to use all Your influence with the Government to have the sentence passed upon Riel by his countrymen confirmed by the Supreme Court of the Province, and sustained by the Privy Council of England, carried into effect.

We trust that you will entreat the Government not to allow any petitions, requests or influences from Riel's friends, or from any other source, to prevail on them to commute the sentence, postpone the same, or in any way alter the just sentence that now hangs over this self-doomed man. . . .

James Boddy,
District Secretary on Behalf of the
Loyal Orange Association of West Toronto.[99]

In spite of an obvious desire to see the sentence carried out, Anglophone newspapers did not overtly express the level of religious and ethnic hostility toward Francophones that was alleged during the period in the French press; generally, Riel was portrayed by English journalists as the instigator of a rebellion, a man who had committed treason and who was justly sentenced. In fact, some English Canadians of the period actually argued that Riel's sentence should be commuted in order to avoid antagonism with French Canada. Macdonald received numerous letters from Anglophones suggesting that a stay of execution would promote peace in the country, and that the "wishes of . . . a very large portion of the people of this Dominion" should be respected. Ultimately, however, only a minority of Anglophones favored altering the sentence. Macdonald's English advisers were evenly split in terms of support for and against execution, but they reported that public opinion among their constituencies favored the sentence thirty to one; and prominent members of the Conservative Party generally advised Macdonald against commutation, fearing that any intervention into the judicial system would weaken support for the party in Ontario and jeopardize its success in future elections.[100]

There is no doubt that the hanging of Riel was the catalyst for enmity between French and English Canadians that would have a permanent bearing on their relationship. English journalists maintained that Anglophones were unanimous in their support of the execution of Riel; they found it difficult to understand Quebec's call for a reprieve, and they were infuriated by an increasing insistence among Francophones that the hanging would constitute an assault upon French Catholics: "[N]o one can believe that if Louis Riel were an Englishman," complained the *London Advertiser*, "that Quebec would have taken the slightest interest in his fate." Claiming that French Canadians were demanding special treatment for a criminal simply because he happened to be a French Catholic, Ontarians turned the tables on their French compatriots, accusing them in turn of transforming the entire Riel affair into a race issue when it was not. The press accused the French of demanding that they be judged by different legal standards from those of other Canadians and for insisting that they should not face the same penalties for crimes to which other Canadians were subject. They expected, in other words, "one kind of law for a French-Canadian and another for an English, Irish, Scotch, or German Canadian." The press was unequivocal in its denunciation of what it perceived to be an unreasonable demand: "Sir John Macdonald," said the *Evening Telegram*, "has now an opportunity . . . of giving the French Canadians to understand that the laws were made for all alike and cannot be overridden on the ground of race or religion."[101]

During the fall of 1885, political exigency appears to have effectively controlled the level to which Ontario politicians (and their media organs) expressed an emerging and dichotomous ethnically based nationalism. Both political parties in the province were well aware of the fact that achieving a majority of seats in the House of Commons required alliances between French and English in both provinces. In the aftermath of Riel's execution, however, overt hostility toward French Canadians was unmistakable. The strident response to the hanging in the province of Quebec—and the potential threat posed to the governing Conservative Party—inspired the editors of the *Toronto Mail* to take it upon themselves to denounce "French aggression" and shore up the position of the Conservative Party in Ontario. During the year following the execution, the newspaper became an advocate for the suppression of French Catholic culture and the extension of English Protestant power across the country; and throughout the subsequent decade, the crusade for cultural ascendancy spread to more popularly based papers in Toronto, Ottawa, and Winnipeg.[102]

The altered relationship between Francophones and Anglophones that came about as a result of the Métis uprisings was mirrored in a number of profound political changes. The rebellions had made an indelible mark on Canada's political culture; and the cultural issues that presented themselves during the trial have remained constant features of Canadian political life. Reaction to the execution of Riel restructured Quebec public life entirely, creating new coalitions among political rivals. When fifty thousand people gathered for a demonstration in Montreal at the Champ-de-Mars on the evening of November 22, 1885, they listened intently to speakers representing all political groups in the province. A little-known politician by the name of Wilfrid Laurier roused the crowd to such a degree that night that his appearance at the rally has been subsequently regarded as the foundation of his rise to the leadership of the Liberal Party and, eventually, to the office of prime minister.[103]

A hitherto unchallenged Conservative domination of Quebec's political life was permanently shattered in 1885, and the shape of federal politics was altered dramatically. In spite of an established Liberal or Reform inclination in Ontario, John A. Macdonald and George Cartier had successfully established their Conservative federal regime on the basis of Quebec support. In the wake of Riel's execution, however, a traditionally Conservative Quebec turned to the Liberal Party, a shift that was epitomized by Wilfrid Laurier's successful bid for leadership of the party in 1887. The shift was not the result of an ideological change in Quebec politics so much as it was of a widespread reaction to Riel's execution—a point made abundantly clear by the Liberal Party's rapid rejection of its politically radical tradition in favor of a more conservative stance. Concomitantly, the province of Ontario began to move away from its support of the Liberal Party, in order to offset the potential political strength of Quebec.[104]

Resentment toward English Canada was not, however, the only reaction to Riel's execution among Quebec Francophones. The provincial government also came under attack for its perceived complicity in a federal conspiracy against Riel; it was, in this view, "the tool and the accomplice of the federal cabinet which hanged Riel." The provincial government's failure to defy Macdonald's regime in Ottawa was considered to have been a violation of Quebec's sovereignty at the provincial level:

> By its anti-patriotic attitude in the discussion of the Riel question, and more recently, by its removal of resolutions in favour of an amnesty for the Métis, the provincial ministry has revealed to everyone its state of dependence [on Ottawa] . . . which perverts the working of the constitution and threatens our public liberties.[105]

What was clear by late in 1885 was that Quebec's political profile was undergoing a dramatic shift. In a revealing move, Honoré Mercier suggested that he resign the leadership of the Parti Nationale so that J. A. Chapleau (at the time, secretary of state in the federal Conservative government) could organize a more broad-based opposition to the political forces that had effected Riel's hanging; but Chapleau declined, believing that the enterprise would result in a potentially insurmountable confrontation between French and English Canada. Instead, Chapleau united with other Francophone members of Macdonald's cabinet and withdrew support from the prime minister. Mercier subsequently forged an alliance with the Liberal Party and a number of disgruntled Conservatives and was able to take the provincial election of 1886.

During the 1886 election campaign, the central issue revolved around allegations that the provincial Conservative government had become "nothing but the tool of the Orange ministry of John A. Macdonald." The party, described in some quarters as "hang-dogs," became the object of pointed attacks by the press; and support for the party was, according to *L'Électeur*, equivalent to submitting "a verdict approving of the crime of November 16." Throughout the months preceding the election, *L'Électeur* also published a daily front-page series, "Remember, People," referring to what had occurred the year before with respect to Riel's trial and appeals process. The Conservatives were never able to regain their foothold in the province, and Mercier's focus on Quebec's self-determination laid the foundation for both Québécois nationalism and separatism.[106] In spite of the fact that Mercier's government became immediately embroiled in scandal and was unable to secure a second term, it created a permanent rupture between the Conservative Party and the province of Quebec. The federal election of 1887 saw a slim majority of seats going to the Conservatives, the Liberal Party managed a slender victory in 1891, and by 1896 the Liberals scored a decided victory. Domination of politics in Quebec was essential to prominence in the federal political life, and the Rebellion of 1885 shifted the balance from the Conservatives to the Liberals. It has been argued that the change may well have been the most significant alteration in Canadian political life to occur in the post-Confederation period.[107]

Aside from these obvious political repercussions, the uprisings also signaled the reification of another potential dichotomy of Canadian life in the mid-nineteenth century: that of the west and central Canada. Ottawa's management of western expansion and the entry of the territories into the Confederation created the context for the uprisings of 1869–70 and 1885, and these in turn contributed to the emergence of a distinct regional dichotomy between the western territories and Ottawa. As we noted earlier, Section 11 of the British North America Act provided for the entry of Newfoundland, Prince Edward Island, and British Columbia into the Confederation upon the joint recommendations of the Canadian Parliament and the colonial legislatures, as well as the authorization of the queen and the Privy Council. The admittance of Rupert's Land and the North-West Territories could be carried out with one key difference: no request from a colonial legislature was necessary. British Columbia consequently entered the Confederation on the same constitutional footing as did Ontario, Quebec, Nova Scotia, and New Brunswick; but the western territories were not Crown colonies, and the terms of their entry into Confederation were at the discretion of the Canadian government, which chose to regard them essentially as colonies of Canada.[108] Settlement of the west occurred most substantially between 1870 and 1920, and during this time the political and economic framework of the Prairie provinces was established by the Canadian government to serve what it regarded as the best interests of the state as a whole. Consequently, the west was effectively maintained as a colony of a strong central Canadian political apparatus that was focused on opening the region for settlement, and staving off American expansion into the region by connecting one side of the continent with the other via a railway. The federal government imposed an institutional framework on Manitoba and the territories, and by 1885 an embryonic transcontinental railroad was operational. In 1905, Saskatchewan and Alberta were reconfigured institutionally in the same fashion as Manitoba, and over the next ten years a complex transcontinental rail system was established through the region.[109]

In order to extend Canada's sovereignty over Rupert's Land in 1870, Ottawa was forced to negotiate with the provisional government that Riel established for the region. Central to Métis negotiations at the time was the entrance of the territory into the Confederation with full provincial status, in order to ensure the Métis a political voice and representative political institutions. The result was the Manitoba Act, which was passed by both the federal government and the provisional government, and subsequently endorsed by the imperial legislature. The act specified that the federal government would assume control of land and resources in exchange for a Métis land base founded on a system of grants to individuals. It was undoubtedly a political victory (although the Métis were essentially excluded from its benefits), but the federal government's control of natural resources ultimately ensured that the province would remain a colony until Ottawa relinquished its control of the land and its resources in the west in 1930.[110]

Rapid economic development led inexorably to Confederation and to the annexation of the west, two historical events that contributed substantially to the emergence of powerful regionalisms. Moreover, it has been argued that the west, as a region, originated in the resistance of Natives, Métis, and Anglophone settlers against the imperial machinations of central Canada. The federal legislation enacted to bring Manitoba into existence contained a land settlement plan for the Métis that exemplified one of the ongoing political motifs of the Canadian Confederation: the necessity of resolving the incongruity that characterizes the dual needs of defending both national and local interests. There were numerous assurances included in the act aimed at resolving this potential clash of interests, including not only a plan for Métis land settlement, but guarantees for the use of both English and French in the province's legislature, and for denominational schools.[111] Ottawa may well have reneged on a good deal of the agreement, but ultimately the act set the pattern for dealing with the ongoing disputes over regional expectation and federal accountability that would subsequently characterize provincial-federal relations.

A third dichotomy that was reified by the Red River and North-West uprisings was a foundational one between Natives and nonnatives. Like the ethnic dichotomy expressed within French-English relations in Canada, the seeds of a similar oppositional structure involving Aboriginal peoples were present well before the outbreaks of violence in the territories. The uprisings, however, served to codify the disparity with Native peoples through legislation and to imbed it in the wider public imagination through distorted images. In the case of the Métis, it was reified by an attempt to render this community invisible through a lack of legal recognition (in spite of the fact that the Manitoba Act constituted legitimate acknowledgment of the Métis as a distinct ethnic group). On the eve of the Red River Rebellion, Native peoples in the west were generally an unknown quantity for central Canadians, although there was a distinct sense among nonnatives that Natives were situated somewhere beyond the parameters of an emerging Canadian social body. When, for instance, Macdonald took the floor for the first time during formal debate on the issue of western annexation, he announced that there was no possible way for the acquisition of the territories to be accomplished without both serious consultations with the Hudson's Bay Company and an accord with the British Parliament. Native peoples, however, would not be consulted because they were simply "incapable of the management of their own affairs."[112]

In the wake of Manitoba's entry into the Confederation, the Canadian government negotiated a series of treaties with Native communities of the North-West that acknowledged their Aboriginal right to the land and secured their removal to reserves in order to make the most arable land available to European-Canadian settlers. When Treaty Six was negotiated at Fort Carleton in 1876, Poundmaker attempted to press for the provision of training in agriculture and government assistance for Plains Cree, who were attempting to shift from a hunting to an agricultural life-style. In a move that appears, even by the most generous reading, to have been aimed at bringing about the utter destitution of the Native population, as well as their marginalization from the dominant economic system, Lieutenant Governor Alexander Morris refused to acquiesce to these demands, accusing Poundmaker of greed in asking for assistance in addition to meager parcels of land, livestock, and tools. Although Poundmaker signed the treaty, the Cree chief Big Bear held off signing for six years, surrendering only when his tribe was facing utter starvation.[113] There is no doubt that Native peoples entered into treaty agreements under duress, but it is also clear that they were misled with respect to the federal government's intentions and commitments involved in negotiating and ratifying the treaties. Gabriel Dumont made this point abundantly clear to Amédée Forget, clerk of the North-West Council, when the two men had occasion to speak in the early fall of 1884: "I want also to speak about the Indians," Dumont said.

> They are our relatives and when they are starving they come to us for relief and we have to feed them. The government is not doing right by them. I was present at the time of the Treaty. I don't know the words of the paper signed by them; but I underst[ood] with the Indians present that not only would they live as well as they had before, but better. Is that what is taking place now? They are allowed to go about starving. We want the Indians fed.[114]

The desire to remove First Nations peoples from the view of European Canadians was given impetus by the passing of the Indian Act of 1876, a piece of legislation intended to control the political and economic lives of Native peoples and to limit their mobility. By the act, Indian agents were empowered to direct the activities of band councils and to regulate the sale of agricultural products and other commodities in wider Canadian markets. In addition, cultural practices, such as the potlatch of the Northern coast of British Columbia and the thirst and sun dances of the prairies, were prohibited; and a pass system was introduced after 1885 that controlled the movement of western Natives beyond their reserves, requiring them to obtain permission from Indian agents to leave their reserves even temporarily.[115] One might wonder how it is that such dramatic restrictions could be placed on the freedoms of an entire ethnic group without eliciting criticism from some quarter of Canadian society; but we should remind ourselves that the public was inundated with images of Native peoples throughout the 1885 uprising that emphasized the potential threat they posed to the nonnative population.

During the uprising, for instance, paintings published in the *Illustrated War News* and the *London Illustrated News* provided eastern Canadians with threatening images of Natives and Métis that were utterly fictitious. The paintings that portrayed the Battle of Batoche, for example, created the impression that there was a sizeable faction of Native rebels present when, in fact, there were only about fifty Cree and Dakota involved in the confrontation, members solely of the bands of One Arrow and White Cap. Their presence was made eerily apparent in these illustrations by means of puffs of threatening smoke surrounding the town; and in most of them, dead and wounded federal soldiers were strewn in full view to elicit pity, while similar Native or Métis figures were not portrayed. Walter Hildebrandt has argued that these paintings may well have contributed to the rationalization of conquest of both the west and its Aboriginal population.[116]

Pejorative references to Native peoples were also stock in trade at Riel's trial, invoked by lawyers representing both the defendant and the Crown. Defense attorney Charles Fitzpatrick, for instance, claimed that Natives were driven by "savage instincts," possessed of "fell designs," and prone to committing "acts of the utmost brutality." Riel's correspondence with Poundmaker, which was discovered when the chief's camp was raided, was submitted in the course of the trial as evidence against the accused; one letter in particular indicated that Riel was pleased with the Métis success at Duck Lake and was hoping that Poundmaker would lead a contingent of Cree warriors to take Battleford and then join the Métis forces. Employing a turn of phrase that resounded throughout the uprising and was reserved only in reference to Native peoples, prosecution attorney Robinson submitted that the letter proved unequivocally that Riel had incited the chief to "take up arms and *go on the warpath*." Robinson continued: "If this scheme had succeeded, gentlemen, if these Indians had been roused, can any man with a human heart contemplate without a shudder the atrocities, the cruelties which would have overspread this land."[117]

Shortly after the uprising, a contemporary writer published an account of the events, *The Story of Louis Riel the Rebel Chief*, which served to extend these images. In respect to the murders at Frog Lake, the writer provided the following context:

> Not far away lived detachments of various tribes of Indians, who frequently came into the little settlement, and smoked their pipes among the inhabitants. Here, as elsewhere, the most bitter feelings were entertained by the Halfbreeds and Indians against the Government, and chief of all against Governor Dewdney. Every one with white skin, and all those who in any way were in the service of the Government, soon came to be regarded as enemies to the common cause. Therefore, when night came down upon the settlement, Indians, smeared in hideous, raw, earthy-smelling paint, would creep about among dwellings, and peer, with eyes gleaming with hate, through the winder-frames at the innocent and unsuspecting inmates. At last one chief, with a diabolical face, said, "Brothers, we must be avenged upon every white man and woman here. We will shoot them like dogs" . . . The answer to this harangue was the clanking of barbaric instruments of music, the brandishing of tomahawks, and the gleam of hunting-knives.[118]

His description of the murders themselves was utterly horrifying and uncompromisingly bound to stereotypes that had become common in the course of the rebellion:

> Therefore, the 2nd day of April was fixed for the holding of the conference between the Indians and the white settlers. The malignant chief had settled the plan.
>
> "When the white forces come to our lodge, they will expect no harm. Ugh! Then the red man will have his vengeance." . . . The morning of the 2nd opened gloomily. . . . Unsuspecting aught of harm, two priests of the settlement, Oblat [*sic*] Fathers, named Fafard and La Marchand, were the first at the spot. . . ." Entrez." Opening the door, the two good priests walked in, and turned to look for seats. Ah! What was the sight presented to them! Eyes like those of wild beasts, aflame with hate and ferocity, gleamed at them from the gloom of the back portion of the room. . . . Then a wild shriek was given, and the chief cried, "Enemies to the red man, you have come to your doom." Then, raising his rifle, he fired at Father

Marchand. . . . A dozen other muzzles were pointed, and in a far briefer space of time than it takes to relate it, the two priests lay weltering in their blood, pierced each by half a dozen bullets. . . . There was soon another knock at the door, and the same wolfish voice replied as before, saying, "Entrez." This time a full, manly-looking young fellow, named Charles Gowan, opened the door and entered. . . .

A tall savage approached him from behind, and striking him upon the head with his rifle-stock felled him to the earth. Then the savages fired five or six shots into him as he lay upon the floor. The body was dragged away and the blood-thirsty fiends sat waiting for the approach of another victim. . . . Half an hour passed and no other rap came upon the door. . . .

"Ugh!" grunted the chief, "no more coming. We go down and shoot em at em houses." Then the fiend divided his warriors into four companies, each one of which was assigned a couple of murders. One party proceeded toward the house of Mr. Gowanlock, of the firm of Gowanlock & Laurie, who had a large saw and grist mill in course of erection. . . . [S]ix or seven painted Indians, with rifles cocked, and uttering diabolical yells, burst into the house. The chief was with this party; and aiming his rifle, shot poor Gowanlock dead.[119]

The descriptions of Native peoples contained within *The Story of Louis Riel* were reminiscent of those that characteristically appeared in "captivity narratives" common in the eighteenth- and nineteenth-century United States. Despite the fact that fear of apprehension by Natives was common among Anglophone settlers in the Canadian west, the settlement of the region produced only a few such "captivity narratives." Principal among these was *Two Months in the Camp of Big Bear: The Life and Adventures of Theresa Gowanlock and Theresa Delaney*, an ostensibly accurate account of two women's captivity in the wake of the Frog Lake Massacre (during which their husbands had been among seven murdered men). The account appeared in November of 1885. When read against the public statements made by both women immediately following their release, however, the book presented a noticeably altered account of what had transpired during their captivity among the Cree. The plight of Delaney and Gowanlock was closely followed by the entire country through the spring and early summer of 1885, and the women were the subject of a host of rumors ranging from reports of their mistreatment to those claiming that they had been killed. Sarah Carter has pointed out the ways in which these reports were exploited in the service of diverse political, economic, and strategic objectives.[120] In the women's initial comments to the press after their release (due to scarcity of provisions, the Cree supplied their twenty-four hostages with flour and released them with horses on June 17), both claimed to have been treated well by their captors and to have suffered no "indignities." Although they had feared for their safety and "virtue" on occasion, they had found themselves to be adequately protected. They had suffered very little and had been sufficiently fed; and any work in which they had engaged (cooking and washing clothes) had been of their own choice, and not under duress. Their primary complaint was that due to their inability to speak either French or Cree, they felt isolated.[121] In addition, one of the other hostages, W. L. McLean, made his first public statement to a *Toronto Globe* correspondent:

> Of course we underwent a great deal of hardship, the nature of our wanderings made that unavoidable, but otherwise we were treated with the greatest respect. Nothing in the nature of an insult was ever offered us. The only reason the Indians kept us was to protect themselves in case they were cornered. I was never as much as asked to do any work.

The *Montreal Daily Star* reported that although one of McLean's children announced that she was pleased to have been released by her Cree captors, she admitted that she had found the adventure quite enjoyable: "She appeared inclined to look upon their experience as a joke."[122]

Delaney's and Gowanlock's captivity narrative presented an entirely different picture of their experience from that which they had presented to the press upon their release. In the book, the two women were portrayed as having been incapacitated by sorrow, exhaustion, and the misery of withstanding the "snow and ice of that trackless prairie"—an unusual assertion, as Carter pointed out, given that the bulk of their time with their captors had been in the months of May and June. Moreover, they described physical discomfort, insufficient food and rest, inadequate clothing, excessive travel on foot and, more generally, "untold suffering and privations" that had occurred at the hands of their "savage" captors. The "constant dread of outrage and death" that hung over them during their captivity did not resonate with their early reports to the press, nor did their claim to have been forced to walk through the harshest conditions while "the Indians were riding beside us with our horses and buckboards, laughing at us with umbrellas over their heads and buffalo overcoats on." By all accounts, neither of the two women had traveled by foot during the two months of constant movement, but had been permitted to ride in a wagon owned by a Métis named Pritchard. Finally, in their initial statements, neither woman had made particular note of the federal government's actions during the affair, and both had expressed admiration for a number of Métis who had been traveling with Big Bear's band. In the subsequent narrative, however, the government was highly commended, and the Métis who had been of assistance to them were presented in a disparaging manner.

Obviously, the North-West Rebellion had cost the Canadian taxpayers a great deal of money and a number of young lives; any account of the women's captivity, therefore, could well have met with public disapproval had it not praised the government and condemned the Métis and Native populations. Carter has argued, further, that the experience of Delaney and Gowanlock did not resonate with Ottawa's political agenda of securing power over the west, and it appears that their narrative may well have been altered to support a contemporary political agenda that required the concealment of an Aboriginal presence in the geopolitical landscape.[123]

The concealment of the Métis, as distinct in some ways from Native peoples, was effected from a number of different vantage points. In Quebec, as we have already noted, the obscuring of the ethnic specificity of the Métis served an emerging nationalist agenda. This was epitomized to some degree by the experience of Gabriel Dumont in the wake of the rebellion. Dumont had performed in Buffalo Bill's Wild West Show until he received his amnesty from the federal government in 1886, whereupon he headed to Quebec for a series of speaking engagements through which he hoped to be able to communicate an accurate version of what had transpired in 1885. The tour ended prematurely, however, as Dumont became discouraged with the use to which his story was being put by nationalists in the province, and as the nationalists realized that his critical stance toward the Catholic Church was to prove a liability to their political campaign in Quebec. In the years following the uprising of 1885, Dumont dictated two memoirs, with dramatically different political points of view. The first (dating from the period during which he was touring Quebec) was recorded by the official recorder of Quebec City, B. A. T. Montigny, and was dictated to an audience of journalists and Liberal Party members that hoped to draw on Dumont's association with Riel and his memories of the rebellion to garner public support for the Liberal Party in the province. The second memoir, dictated fifteen years later in the company of friends, expressed an entirely different attitude from the political bias that seemed to have been woven into the first. Specifically, Dumont did not regard the confrontation as one between French and English Canadian interests, but as one between two sovereign nations in which an invading force without proper authority had loosed itself on an indigenous population that was more than willing to negotiate a settlement to the conflict in good faith.[124]

The conflict would subsequently become indelibly linked to a debilitating marginalization of the Métis community that was experienced, especially, in economic terms. Reflecting on Métis willingness to conscript during the First World War, a number of Métis (whose statements were collected and recorded as "Found Poems" by the Saskatchewan Department of Culture and Youth in 1975), accounted for the phenomenon on the basis of dire poverty: "So a lot got involved/in going to war" said Pierre Vandale, "and they didn't know/why they were going." "Being a soldier/wasn't important to them," said Caroline Vandale; the decision was based on the promise that "they could make some money"; and Charles Pilon emphasized the point, saying that men went because "money was scarce/No jobs." According to Isadore Ledoux, who spent three years overseas, the poverty that compelled him to conscript could be traced back to the 1885 Rebellion, after which "the Indian Department/cut off all help of the Indians."[125]

This sense of government culpability in the marginalization of the Métis was not unfounded; it was the result of a distinct effort on the part of Ottawa to render this ethnic group invisible within the Canadian social landscape. The Métis, for example, were not permitted to participate formally in nineteenth-century treaty negotiations in Canada West (what would become the province of Ontario). They were sporadically included in treaty agreements, but this was left to the discretion of individual Native bands. During the negotiations leading to the Robinson Huron Treaty of 1850, for instance, Natives expressed concern over the status of their relatives who were Métis, and W. B. Robinson ruled that individuals could be included in band lists if the leaders wished to do so. As previously noted, in cases such as these, the Métis were forced to designate themselves as either Native or nonnative, and were thus unable to argue for possessing distinct status, a situation that left them politically powerless: with this kind of indeterminate recognition, they were situated somewhere between the legal categories of British citizen and Aboriginal.[126]

In the west, the Manitoba Act brought about the same form of marginalization. The wording of Section 31 of the act was noticeably vague and was clearly intended to force the Métis into an agrarian life-style that would do away with their ethnic specificity. It identified two phases for the allotment of land, the first to be overseen by the lieutenant governor who was given the task of arbitrarily choosing the land to be granted and identifying the children of heads of families who were to receive the grants. The second provided for actual land grants, but only on condition of settlement and other stipulations left to the government's discretion. Section 31 was intended to coerce the Métis into a mainstream economic structure, rather than to protect their right to occupy a portion of Manitoba's territory. Its goal, said the superintendent of Indian Affairs in 1871, was to "lead the Indian people by degrees to mingle with the white race in the ordinary avocations of life." Consequently, until a family could demonstrate the ability to defend a land grant in the economic market, the land could be resided upon or sold, but the family's children could not receive their grants. Paul Chartrand has argued that the federal government was required, according to Section 31 of the act, to set apart 1.4 million acres of land in Manitoba exclusively for the Métis; and that its decision to allot parcels of land only to individual children of family heads was a violation of the conditions set out in the act. His case is well-founded; and as he has noted, "there are now no Métis lands in Manitoba." The dispossession of Métis lands that followed the enactment of the Manitoba Act was, according to Chartrand, "one of the most highly placed extortion rackets in Canadian history," a case of fraud that involved bureaucrats and lawyers. A judicial inquiry was called in 1881 to examine the role that Manitoba's courts had played in the sale of Métis lands, and the inquiry recommended that a government official be appointed who would be responsible for the protection of Métis lands. Rather than follow this advice, the Manitoba government sanctioned the corruption that had occurred by passing legislation that retroactively legalized the practices that had come under scrutiny of the inquiry. Of the nearly six thousand Métis who initially received patents, less than twelve hundred ultimately received a grant.[127]

Recognition of Métis land rights in the Manitoba Act appears to have been a concession based on contingency, but clearly not one that was embraced by Macdonald or his negotiators in 1870 in practical terms. Speaking before Parliament in 1885, Macdonald claimed that the agreement had not been intended to affirm the Aboriginal rights of Métis and, secondarily, that it had been made with the assumption on the part of government that annexation of the territory could be achieved relatively peaceably by making such a concession to a Métis population that would eventually be outnumbered by Europe-Canadian immigrants. "To secure peace and order," admitted Macdonald,

> in fact, to obtain possession of the country—it was necessary to enter into an arrangement. . . . Whether [the Métis] had any right to those lands or not was not so much the question as it was a question of policy to make an arrangement with the inhabitants of the Province . . . in order to introduce law and order there, and assert the sovereignty of the Dominion.[128]

The violation of the responsibilities established in Section 31 of the Manitoba Act, in conjunction with the historical disregard for the Métis in other parts of Canada, created an anomalous ethnic relationship between the Métis and nonnatives that has had dire consequences for the Métis. It will, additionally, have constitutional significance that will have to be addressed on the basis of the recognition of the Métis as Aboriginal peoples according to Section 35 of the Canadian Constitution.[129]

When all is said and done, there is little doubt that the violent confrontations of 1869–70 and especially 1885 brought to the fore a series of dichotomous relations that have defined modern Canada. All three of the country's founding peoples were implicated in these binary relationships, the seeds of which had been planted prior to the late nineteenth century, but which had not assumed the dramatic proportion that resulted from the uprisings. Francophones (particularly in Quebec) and Anglophones emerged from the period with permanent scars that would ultimately lead to Quebec separatism; Aboriginal peoples were thrust into a modern state intent upon effecting their marginalization; and the west, as a distinct region with a cultural and political sense of itself in opposition to central Canada, emerged on the heels of the rebellions. With its emergence was also born a pattern of regional-federal dynamics that would remain part of the country's political and social landscape, a model for collective tension that had not been previously expressed to such a degree. Nova Scotia had, for instance, resisted entry into the Confederation, but had acquiesced without rebellion; and its chief spokesman, Joseph Howe, assumed the position of secretary of state. We might note that, in this capacity, he traveled to Red River in early October of 1868 for what appears to have been an "unofficial" tour of the area. Like most everyone else in Ottawa, Howe was apparently unaware of local antagonism toward Canadian annexation of the region and was taken by surprise. Rather than responding in some way, he chose to retreat from making any public statements regarding the legitimate concerns of the people of Red River.[130]

To a noticeable degree, much of what has constituted the most peculiar social and political aspects of the Canadian state reared its head in the context of the nineteenth-century uprisings. In a sense, then, the uprisings constituted a foundational moment of violence in the country's development into a postcolonial state; but more than this, it might be argued that Canada did not fully emerge as a modern geopolitical entity in 1867, but did so rather in the period of the North-West Rebellion. Admittedly this is a peculiar claim to make. After all, there is no doubt that prior to the Confederation, British North America was a colonial holding and, further, that it was the BNA Act that gave birth to an independent political body. Indeed, the post-Confederation assumption of a colonial prerogative over Canada's own colonies—Rupert's Land and the North-West Territories—would indicate a measurable shift in Canada's position within the international community of states and colonial satellites of the late nineteenth century. The matter of modern statehood, however, might well be a separate issue from that of autonomy, given that the newly formed Confederation found itself arguably enmeshed in a colonial stylistic that precluded its ability to function as a modern state. It is in this respect that we might argue that Canada did not function fully as a modern state until 1885.

An argument somewhat analogous to this was made by Karen Fields in relation to Central Africa of the early to mid-twentieth century. During the period, there were a number of millenarian movements that emerged with the expressed aim of achieving spiritual renewal and waging revolution; and although these movements were not successful in creating the political apparatus capable of driving out colonial powers (a task ultimately accomplished by "secular militants"), their presence did have important political effects. As a rule, millenarian movements do not contain within their structure a mandate for direct political revolution, but the Central African movements were perceived by ruling regimes as posing a threat to the established colonial order. Fields, in *Revival and Rebellion in Colonial Africa*, explored the reasons for the disquietude they caused, with a particular focus on the Watchtower movement that arose out of a context in which people believed deeply that their day-to-day (often political) actions were intimately related to their hopes of redemption. Moreover, administrators in this situation often treated with the utmost seriousness orthodox churchmen's allegations that religious heresy constituted political insurgency. God, Fields argued, was a "historical reality in this context"; and she suggested that an appreciation of this fact was necessary to fully understand the structure of these societies. Taking these phenomena seriously allowed her to perceive the arrangement of colonial societies in a way that called into question the generally accepted view that colonial states were "modern": they were, in fact, much more akin to the medieval states of sixteenth-century Europe, in which the state and the church functioned in concert with one another to maintain legal and political control. By virtue of the association, the exercise of this control assumed premodern local specificity.[131]

In these situations, for instance, judges participated in theological arguments with individuals standing trial, churchmen made arrests on behalf of the state and called for civil sentencing of those they regarded as blasphemous, and government administrators closely examined people's interpretation of biblical texts. The operative issue was that administrations were not able to maintain control of their colonies by means of a standardized legal system in spite of their desire to do so. Rather, these states required inexpensively maintained and idiosyncratic local alliances with church personnel that closely resembled the administrations of an earlier time in Europe. Secondarily, the option of continuing these inexpensive colonial administrative structures did not exist for subsequent postcolonial regimes. This system of control was the backbone of colonial rule, and the end of the colonial state necessarily entailed also the end of this system. The cost of governing in the postcolonial period was consequently dramatically increased, as the antiquated institutional structures of colonizing powers had to be dismantled and replaced by modern, less localized counterparts.[132]

There may well be a parallel to be drawn between the situation in Central Africa described by Fields and the post-Confederation condition in which eastern Canada found itself as it extended its sovereignty over the western territories. Within this context, the Canadian government was forced to recognize the authority of the French Catholic clergy and to rely upon it in order to establish its jurisdiction over the region and its inhabitants. Catholic missionaries had established themselves in the Red River area in 1818, and from that time onward the Métis had identified with the Roman Catholic Church. As noted earlier, the Hudson's Bay Company's monopoly over the fur trade met with resistance at Red River in the 1840s, when inhabitants of the region, under the leadership of Louis Riel Sr. and James Sinclair (representing English mixed-blood peoples), began pressuring the British government for redress of grievances. In mounting their campaign, they turned to a Catholic priest by the name of Georges Belcourt for assistance in drafting a petition that was transmitted to the home office in 1846 opposing the company's monopoly.[133] Moreover, as early as 1857, Bishop Taché had written to Georges Cartier expressing his reticence concerning the eventual entry of the territory into the Confederation, and his fear that it would bring about the destruction of the French Catholic population.[134] Finally, the Métis resistance of 1869–70 could not have been successfully executed nor resolved without the cooperation of the Roman Catholic clergy in the region. There were three delegates who set out for Ottawa in March of 1870 to negotiate with the federal government on behalf of Red River: Abbé Ritchot, Judge John Black, and Alfred H. Scott. Of the three, only the Catholic priest, Ritchot, was effective in the ensuing discussions; and in the end, it was he who persuaded Conservative Party negotiators to press for parliamentary passage of the Manitoba Act, legislation that affirmed the land rights of the Métis and protected bilingual education.[135]

The clergy's integral role as mediators between the Métis and the Canadian authorities was established in 1870, and as tensions in the North-West began escalating in 1884, there was a local expectation that Catholic priests would act as arbitrators once again. Both government officials and Catholic clergy were concerned over the arrival of Riel in the Prince Albert area in the summer of 1884, but his subsequent composed and judicious manner led many to believe that he had no malice in mind, an appraisal of the situation that Dewdney gleaned from correspondence with Father Alexis André. In early July, André wrote to Dewdney to assure him that he foresaw no unrest arising from Riel's presence among the local population:

> Riel and delegates have arrived from across the line. The news may surprise and alarm you about the tranquility of the country, but you can set your mind quiet about that and have no fear of any

disturbance in the country. You know I am [not] known to be a friend of Mr. Riel, and I looked to the event of his arrival among us as a danger for the peace of our community, but now I do not entertain the least suspicion about Riel causing any trouble. He acts quietly and speaks wisely. . . . The Halfbreeds, English as well [as] French, understand too well the foolishness and the consequences of rising in a rebellion against the Government, and Riel seems really to act by good motives and to have no bad design. A man will not bring his wife and children along with him if he intended to raise a rebellion, and Mr. Riel has brought his wife and two little children with him, and that is the best proof that he has no bad intentions.[136]

André was ultimately mistaken, but it was Ottawa's failure to respond to the situation of mounting hostility in the territory through the summer and fall of 1884 that led to a rupture in the relationship between the clergy and the disgruntled Métis, effectively destroying the serviceable role that the Catholic clergy had played in mediating the relationship between the Métis and governing colonial powers. Had the federal government been guided by Catholic priests as it had in 1869, the Métis may not have been forced into open rebellion nor, consequently, into breaking from the restraining power of the Catholic clergy. By September, however, the clerk of the North-West Council, Amédée Forget, wrote to Dewdney to inform him that the "agitation comprises all the French and English Halfbreeds and a number of unprincipled white settlers at Prince Albert. These latter are opponents politically of the present party in power and would delight in causing troubles that might embarrass the present government . . ." Forget added that the "most alarming" facet of the disturbance was "the Halfbreeds loss of confidence in some of their old missionaries, such as Fathers André, Fourmond, and Moulin."[137]

For his part, Father André attempted to continue to mediate between the Métis and the federal government, in spite of the fact that he had lost the confidence of the Métis. Local administrators treated his warnings with the utmost seriousness. The lack of any federal overture toward the disgruntled Métis and mixed-blood population had, by February of 1885, became a cause of distress for Father André. Trusting implicitly in his assessment of the situation, and responding to the priest's fears that an uprising was imminent, Mounted Police Superintendent Crozier sent a telegraph to Dewdney, informing him that there was in the region "[g]reat discontent at no reply to representation.... Urge government declare intention immediately." André himself followed up the telegraph with a formal letter to Dewdney, in which he warned that government procrastination was ill-advised in the current situation and affirmed the legitimacy of the Métis claims: "The government certainly takes upon itself great responsibility in thus delaying so long to redress the grievances of the Halfbreeds and rendering the justice to which they are entitled."[138]

In a manner reminiscent of the Central African situation in the early twentieth century, central Canada's need to create a geopolitical body that spanned the continent in 1885 undermined earlier colonial power relations in which Catholic clergy occupied a central role in mediating and sustaining the interests of both the Métis and of Canadian expansion. In 1869, the Canadian government was willing to negotiate with the people of Red River via the clergy. The acquisition of the territories was recent, the threat of U.S. annexation was pronounced, and a comprehensive notion of the position of the territories within the newly formed state was unclear (insofar as they had not been conceived of as other than colonial holdings). By 1885, the situation had changed dramatically, and the kind of negotiation and adaptability employed in 1869 was no longer possible. A modern transcontinental state had been conceived in Ottawa, and the entry of British Columbia into the Confederation required the completion of the railway. Manitoba had forced its entry into the newly formed Confederation as a province at a rather ill-defined and embryonic moment in the state's overall development, and on many of its own terms; but this would not be possible in the case of Saskatchewan, where the disgruntled Métis were an obstacle to the realization of a well-defined transcontinental conception of statehood. Over the course of the rebellion, Ottawa became a centralized modern political apparatus, willing to expend lives and millions of dollars in the interest of extending its own central authority; moreover, it was able to bring to bear the full weight of a centralized judicial structure in the aftermath of the uprising, something that was not possible in 1870. In a profound sense, then, we might argue that the Canadian conquest of the west and its Aboriginal populations, which was forcefully accomplished in 1885, was indelibly linked to the country's emergence as a modern state. As would occur in Central Africa in the next century, the cost of governing in the post-1885 period was significantly increased; and established structures of colonial power that had drawn, for instance, on the resources of the Catholic clergy were dissolved and replaced by a modern centralized political machinery capable of imposing the state's will on its peripheral zones.

Although the uprisings—and especially that of 1885—were not revolutions in a mode akin to those that occurred in the United States, France, or Russia, they expressed a foundational meaning of violence in modern state creation that is impossible to disregard.

Chapter 5

Revolution, Identity, and Canada

Aside from certain affinities between the Canadian situation and the Revolutions
of 1848, there is a more theologically founded meaning of revolution that
may be appropriate also to this discussion; and from this vantage point, the
mythicization of Louis Riel could be said to point to another kind of "revolutionary" mode within the structure of modern Canada. The Riel of myth has
affirmed a series of cultural modalities—more specifically, dichotomies—
that derive their meaning in relation to the Confederation. These are critical and dualistic affirmations of identity made necessary by their subjects'
situation within the broader geopolitical unit, a unit that is concomitantly
multifaceted by virtue of its constituent ethnic and regional components.
Together, the various mythic "Riels," and the identities to which they have
spoken, underscore a collective arrangement that lacks the ethnic, cultural,
or ideological purity that generally rests at the basis of nation-states. Canada
is, in a sense, a geopolitical body defined by a structure of what might be
called *métissage* that has proven impossible to disregard. I must say immediately that I am employing this idiom to refer to a process by which individual
and social bodies have been created in the New World, and particularly in
Canada. The concept of *métissage*, which has been employed in a variety of
contexts (Edouard Glissant, for instance, made use of it in writing of the cultures of the Caribbean[1]) is, as Françoise Lionnet aptly described it, one that
can help us to

articulate new visions of ourselves . . . to think *otherwise*, to bypass the ancient symmetries and dichotomies that have governed the ground and the very condition of possibilities of thought, of "clarity," in all of Western philosophy . . . it is the site of undecidability and indeterminacy.[2]

In employing this term *métissage* in this context, it is not my intent to detract from the serious political and cultural questions revolving around the definition of the Métis in Canada, which is an ongoing and important issue that warrants discussion here before proceeding.

There is not, as yet, a firm consensus among the Métis people of Canada regarding the use of the term *Métis* itself, although they have generally agreed that it refers to an Aboriginal people whose rights are recognized by the Constitution Act, 1982, and who have a distinct ethnicity that can be traced to the beginnings of Canada as a colonial state.[3] In this regard, there is a notable difference between the Métis and those Canadians who are the first-generation offspring of Native and nonnative parents: the Métis are that portion of the Canadian population whose distinct culture traces back to Native-European unions of the fur trade period, and who subsequently married others of the same ancestry. Similar communities have arisen in various parts of the Americas, and these cannot be classified as "half white, half Indian" nor as groups that are situated between other authentic cultures; they represent a distinct ethnicity. The definition of Métis peoples has been complicated by the variegated history of the people themselves, and by the fact that many Métis balk at the collective use of the term. Addressing the issue in 1984, the Métis National Council suggested that a differentiation should be made between uppercase *Métis* who are the descendants of the Manitoba and Saskatchewan peoples displaced by the Canadian government after 1869, and lowercase *métis* who are the descendants of all other Canadian peoples of similar ancestry. Likewise, the 1996 Royal Commission on Aboriginal Peoples (RCAP) attempted to account for this variance by distinguishing between the "Metis Nation" that traced its roots to Red River and the "other Metis" who were located in other areas of eastern Canada and Labrador.[4]

The operative factor in all configurations of the term, however, is the acknowledgment of the Métis as an Aboriginal people, a fact that was confirmed by Section 35 of the Constitution Act, 1982. Their inclusion in Section 35 was a response to Métis lobbying for inclusion, along with First Nations and Inuit Canadians, under the designation of Aboriginal Peoples;

but their recognition has been problematic insofar as Section 35 did not clearly define what is meant by the designation of "Métis." As a result, many issues relating to Métis identity and land rights have remained unsettled, and Métis across the country remain without land or status. In Manitoba, for instance, arguments concerning the legal rights of the province's Métis in relation to the Manitoba Act, 1870, have yet to be resolved, leaving between fifty and one hundred thousand Métis without land. The RCAP addressed this issue in its 1996 report, saying that the federal government had thus far refused to deal with the Métis as Aboriginal in accordance with the constitution, a failure that constituted a most basic form of discrimination that obstructed the implementation of necessary remedial measures.[5]

Complicating the issue, in a cultural sense, has been the fact that the Métis (as well as their English-speaking counterparts) have been too often defined in antithetical terms of what they are not: they have been regarded historically as "people between two worlds," who have no distinct cultural nucleus apart from the conglomeration of other distinct cultures. Even the RCAP, while defining the Métis as "distinct Aboriginal peoples" in 1996, went on to specify only that they were "neither First Nations nor Inuit."[6] In addition, historians have traditionally situated the Métis on a developmental social scale between the dichotomies of "savagery" and "civilization," a stylistic that received its first coherent and intellectually influential articulation with George Stanley in 1936: "Again and again," wrote Stanley,

> in different places and in different ways . . . [t]he European, conscious of his material superiority is only too contemptuous of the savage, intolerant of his helplessness, ignorant of his mental processes and impatient at his slow assimilation of civilization. The savage, centuries behind in mental and economic development, cannot readily adapt himself to meet the new conditions.[7]

As Emma Laroque has noted, even some Métis writers have yielded to this interpretative stance. Bruce Sealey and Antoine Laussier, for instance, credited George Stanley with most accurately identifying the foundations of the Rebellions of 1869 and 1885 as "civilization facing the frontier." Expanding on Stanley, Sealey and Laussier wrote in the mid-1970s, for instance:

> The Metis people were interested in the survival of their way of life and feared progress. They wished to be left alone to live their own

lives in a world set apart. Because the Metis attempted to halt the inevitable encroachment of civilization, the Red River Insurrection was doomed to fail.[8]

Laroque has also noted the way in which novelists have traditionally promulgated a historical portrayal of Métis and other mixed-blood peoples as dichotomously situated between the extremes of savagery and civilization. The tendency to portray them as trapped in such a position was evident in the late-nineteenth-century novel *Pierre and his People* (1894), in which Gilbert Parker appeared unable to settle on a coherent way of culturally representing his central character, Pierre. Pierre was, consequently, described at various points in the novel as either a "Frenchman" or an "Indian." In *The Foreigner* (1909), Ralph Connor created a character named Mackenzie, a mixed-blood drinking partner of an English character by the name of Jack French. The "foreigner" in the novel was Kalman, a teenager who attempted at one point to take a bottle of whiskey away from Mackenzie who immediately underwent a shift into utter barbarity:

> The change in Mackenzie was immediate and appalling. His smiling face became transformed with fury, his black eyes gleamed with the cunning malignity of the savage, he shed his soft Scotch voice with his genial manner, the very movements of his body became those of his Cree progenitors. Uttering hoarse gutteral [*sic*] cries, with the quick crouching run of the Indian on the trail of his foe, he chased Kalman. . . . There was something so fiendishly terrifying in the glimpses that Kalman caught of his face now and then that the boy was seized with an overpowering dread.[9]

In a similar fashion, Luke Allen's *Blue Pete: Rebel* (1940) was a novel with a mixed-blood character who, like Connor's Mackenzie, was precariously situated on the line between savagery and civilization. Despising the Mounted Police and Indians equally, Blue Pete was riddled with contradictory internal drives that were made obvious when he confronted a group of Indians:

> [H]is white blood was forgotten. Against Indians he fought as an Indian, until the moment of crisis. His Indian blood gave him cunning, animal instincts, and a certain amount of ruthlessness. . . .

But always at the last moment his relentlessness was tempered by the white blood in him.[10]

These early portrayals of Métis and mixed-blood peoples presented characters plagued by a critical lack of cultural and psychological stability; they were, essentially, Canadian cowboys who were wracked with deeply rooted insecurities about their ethnic identities.

Later-twentieth-century novels tended to follow the same formula in relation to the depiction of Métis and mixed-blood characters, presenting figures that bore little resemblance to their actual counterparts in Canadian society, but conforming to classic images of either Indian degeneracy or nonnative civility. The hero of Betty Wilson's *André Tom Macgregor* (1976), which was recognized with both the "Search-for-a-New-Alberta-Novelist" and Hudson's Bay Company's "Beaver" awards, is a case in point. The main character of the novel is set in relief against his community in which alcoholism and sexual promiscuity are of epidemic proportion; and the extremely intelligent André is ultimately able to extricate himself from that community and to find himself at home in nonnative society. Even Rudy Wiebe's *The Scorched-Wood People* (1977), a poignant novel revolving around the stories of Riel and Dumont, has been criticized for ultimately using Métis characters to further the author's own fundamental concern with the issues of Christian faith, community, and justice. George Woodcock has suggested that Wiebe's position as historical novelist might better be described as that of "historical moralist," since "*The Scorched-Wood People* is an invention of its author, and the Metis are there, as they were in [Wiebe's] *Peace Shall Destroy Many*, to pose a recurrent Wiebe theme, which is the relationship between spirit and community."[11] Laroque suggested that Margaret Laurence was notable in the extent to which she was able to write of Métis characters who were, to a substantial degree, believable. In her series of novels dealing with the fictional community of Manawaka, the Tonnerre family is presented as a focal point for expressing both the misery and capacity for survival that pervades Métis life. Each novel in the series brings the Tonnerre family into closer psychic proximity with non-Métis, culminating with the relationship between Jules Tonnerre and Morag Gunn in *The Diviners*, through which Morag comes to understand a meaning of freedom borne of suffering. In spite of the fact that Lawrence was undoubtedly more sensitive to the relationship between the characters of which she wrote and their actual counterparts, Laroque suggested that stereotypes still pervaded her novels, as she portrayed the Métis as more "passionate" than whites, and ultimately doomed in spite of their nobility in facing adversity.[12]

All this is to say that there are serious cultural and political issues involved in the definition and portrayal of the Métis in Canada. I am fully aware that I could be accused of insensitivity in putting forward the idea (and terminology) of *métissage* as foundational in the emergence of the Canadian social and political body, but I hope that it can be excused in the interest of the broader issue I am trying to raise concerning the nature of postcolonial society. *Métissage* is, in this sense, emblematic of a more pervasive structure of human and social generation in the modern world and particularly in Canada that has rested on a distinct and normative configuration of cultural or ethnic hybridity.

The necessity of arriving at a new configuration—and language—for speaking of the origins of the state and community in Canada has been reflected in a number of largely ineffective political and cultural enterprises that have been based on a realistic desire to define the country in terms of its lack of cultural or ethnic homogeneity. Among the various configurations that have been promoted in this regard have been binationalism, official multiculturalism, and national unity. The concept of binationalism is the oldest of these, harkening back to at least the turn of the twentieth century. Henri Bourassa (the grandson of Louis Joseph Papineau), for instance, articulated it clearly in the context of his argument over the Laurier government's desire to create a navy that would be made available to Britain during times of contingency—an issue that would bring about Laurier's defeat in 1911. Anticipating a later stylistic, Bourassa advanced a concept of nationalism based on biculturalism:

> The only possible basis for the solution of our national problems is one of mutual respect for our racial characters and exclusive devotion to our common land. . . . We are not asking our neighbors of English extraction to help us to develop a political reconciliation with France, and they have no right to use their strength of numbers to break the rules of the allegiance, forcing us to shoulder new obligations towards England, even if these were completely voluntary and spontaneous.

Bourassa firmly identified himself as French Canadian but adamantly held that his "native land is all of Canada, a federation of separate races and autonomous provinces. The nation I wish to see grow up is the Canadian nation, made up of French Canadians and English Canadians."[13] A generation later, Vincent Massey, whose vision of Canada undeniably rested on an acknowledgment of the country's association with Britain, nonetheless had recourse to the same kind of language. In spite of the fact that Massey turned to the mosaic metaphor in describing Canada's ethnic diversity, he ultimately rested his notion of unity—what he called "the holy grail"— on a binational model in which Anglophones and Francophones would fully accept the fact of their coexistence within a single nation.[14] Massey expressed an aspiration that would become the concern of the federal government in the 1960s and 1970s, when the Canadian state appeared to be in serious jeopardy of fragmentation for the first time since Confederation. The Royal Commission on Bilingualism and Biculturalism claimed in 1965 that Canada was on the verge of the most perilous crisis it had yet confronted and that, despite the fact that it was springing from the province of Quebec, its impact would be far-reaching. By 1970, the impending threat of rupture was largely attributed to "the manner in which today's citizens have learned the history of their country"; and in response the Royal Commission advocated the creation of a new historical—and bicultural—narrative that would subsume English and French divergences.[15] Meanwhile, academic voices echoed the certainty that the cultivation of binationalism was a solution to the political rupture that appeared to be threatening the country. It was argued in some quarters, for example, that a sustainable sense of Canadian identity to some degree was determinant upon the emergence of a widely acceptable nationalism developed along binational lines. It was necessary, according to one typical voice in the discussion, that English and French Canadians be encouraged to locate a way of uniting their national characters: French Canada needed to be induced to "modernize its value system"; while English Canadians had to be encouraged to return to a "traditional" formulation of broad-based identity.[16]

Binationalism nourished a fundamental privileging of Northern European culture and ethnicity in Canada. This was obvious in Vincent Massey's work, where his desire to see the formation of a distinct Canadian identity was indelibly linked to a primary regard for the country's French and English constituents. In spite of early Francophone support for the concept, the idea that Canada was a bicultural-binational state was, after the early part of the twentieth century, most often articulated by Anglophones. There is no doubt that Quebec's desire for a balanced political and cultural association within the Confederation was dealt a devastating blow over the issue of Riel's execution; but what remained of earlier aspirations for a shared national vision was fundamentally tempered by subsequent confrontations between the English and French over French language rights in Ontario and Manitoba schools, the issue of conscription during World War I (based on French resistance to participation in an "English war"), and increasing federal power in the twentieth century.[17] In addition, English attempts to answer French Canada's demands for recognition as a partner in a bicultural state tended to be introduced well past the point of efficacy. As Ronald Wardhaugh pointed out in *Language and Nationhood* (1983), Quebec had taken up the fleur-de-lis and a nationalist anthem (Wardhaugh suggests that the song "Mon pays" played this role, but "Gens du pays" is probably more often invoked) as national symbols well before the Canadian government commissioned a flag and a national anthem that would replace the Union Jack and "God Save the Queen."[18] Similarly, Ottawa's decision to officially designate the state as bilingual trailed Quebec's declaration that it was a unilingual province.[19] It was not that French Canada necessarily opposed the idea of binationalism or biculturalism, but that in spite of such formulations it appeared that English Canada continued throughout the century following Confederation to assume a culture-defining prerogative for itself.

Perhaps the most devastating practical expression of biculturalism, however, was in respect to the Native residential school system. Between 1812 and 1867, various churches had engaged themselves in efforts to convert First Nations peoples to Christianity and to enforce what was perceived to be a necessary level of cultural change to sustain conversion. After Confederation, however, the federal government began pursuing the objective of assimilating Native peoples to a dominant European-Canadian cultural framework and it entered into a partnership with the churches that culminated in the creation of a system of residential schools after 1880 that was intended to wean Native children away from their languages, life-styles, and families. The system, which remained in operation until 1970, ostensibly sought to equip these children with the skills necessary for entry into a mainstream economic structure and cultural framework; but as we have already noted, it was ultimately a mechanism of cultural assault that devastated Native communities for three generations.[20]

Ultimately, the conception of Canada as a bicultural-binational state could never hope to achieve the support of the majority of Canadians. Harry

Daniels articulated this succinctly from the perspective of Aboriginals when he wrote in 1979 that the "delusion that there were only two founding cultures in Canada" was untenable and would contribute only "to the resentment and mistrust which Native Canadians feel for Canadian governments."[21] The inherent limitations of biculturalism as a collective formulation were expressed also by the federal government's Task Force on Canadian Unity in 1979:

> To take French-English duality first, it could signify the thesis of the two founding peoples, the two-nations theory, the notion of the British North America Act as a pact between two peoples, the simple existence of two languages in Canada, or the distinction between Quebec society on the one hand and the rest of Canada on the other.

> [N]ative peoples . . . understandably find the two-founding-peoples concept of duality offensive. English-speaking Canadians find it difficult to conceive of two nations and doubt whether there was a pact in 1867. Québécois believe that any attempt to consider French-speaking Quebec simply as a branch of French Canada belittles its role. Francophones outside Quebec and Anglophones within Quebec are wary of any undue emphasis on the cleavage between Quebec and the rest of the country because it has the effect of submerging them within each majority society.[22]

The poet Earle Birney expressed a similar sense of the inadequacy of a bicultural model of Canada in a rather more sarcastic fashion in his poem "Can. Lit":

> we French&English never lost
> our civil war
> endure it still
> a bloody civil bore[23]

Like biculturalism, the idea of multiculturalism was an attempt to create a formal language (and practice) that reflected the cultural heterogeneity that lay at the foundation of modern Canada. The policy of official multiculturalism, however, was riddled with controversy from its inception.

Neil Bissoondath has argued that when Pierre Trudeau assumed the office of prime minister, the country—dazzled to some degree by his charismatic personality—eagerly expected that he would bring about a measure of unprecedented national unity. Federally funded reviews and reports proliferated during the first three years following his election; but aside from a tactlessly implemented strategy to achieve official bilingualism, very little in the way of public policy resulted from these. With his government's popularity dropping quickly, Trudeau announced a new federal policy in 1971 that would have lasting impact on the country: that of multiculturalism.

> It is hereby declared to be the policy of the Government of Canada to recognize and promote the understanding that multiculturalism reflects the cultural and racial diversity of Canadian society and acknowledges the freedom of all members of Canadian society to preserve, enhance and share their cultural heritage.[24]

It has been suggested that the policy was only ostensibly aimed at acknowledging the role of non-British or non-French immigrants in Canadian society, while it permitted the federal government to obscure earlier formulations of binationalism (and especially the 1965 and 1967 recommendations of the Royal Commission on Bilingualism and Biculturalism for fostering biculturalism) in the interest of opposing Quebec's demand for recognition of special status within the Confederation.[25] Réné Levesque was assiduous in condemning the multiculturalism act, calling it a "red herring" intended to obscure "the Quebec business," to give "an impression that we are all ethnics and do not have to worry about special status for Quebec." In *Le Défi québécois*, political scientist Christian Dufour expressed much the same sentiment in hindsight, claiming that the policy was "a way of refusing to recognize the bicultural nature of the country and political consequences of Québécois specificity. Multiculturalism, in principle, reduces the Québécois fact to an ethnic phenomenon."[26]

The Trudeau government's official multiculturalism policy trivialized cultural disparity, and in many respects reverberated with John Murray Gibbon's desire to ornament the state through a celebration of its various minority ethnic traditions in the 1930s. In his remarks before parliament, Trudeau announced that the federal government intended to "support and encourage the various cultures and ethnic groups that give structure and vitality to our society"; and harkening to Gibbon's sense of decoration, he added, "They will be encouraged to share their cultural expression and values with other Canadians and so contribute to a richer life for us all." Bissoondath has argued that official multiculturalism commodified culture, transforming it into a product to be exhibited, enacted, purchased, or disregarded entirely. "To attend an ethnic festival," he wrote, "is to expose yourself not to culture but to theatre"; it trivializes the very cultural phenomena it professes to promote, disassociating it from the thickness of history.[27] The idea of official multiculturalism was in fact a rather feeble attempt to mask a foundational English dominance, while ensuring that the cultural formation of new immigrants remained peripheral to Canadians' collective sense of identity. First and foremost, it cannot be denied that structurally the country remains an English state, and it is within this context that official multiculturalism functioned. Despite the fact that Canadians generally have little regard for the British monarchy in terms of collective self-definition, the monarchy is the backbone of the parliamentary system that defines the Canadian democracy. Furthermore, the country's constitution and legal framework are British in origin, English is the predominant language spoken in every province aside from Quebec, and the Canadian public school system traces its roots back to that of the Irish. Official multiculturalism functioned within a framework that took for granted a foundational English cultural structure.[28] It provided a means by which to mitigate the potential for creative changes in this structure by presuming that immigrants would ultimately wish to remain in a cultural vacuum once they arrived in Canada, preserving their preimmigrant cultural identities. As Bissoondath has pointed out, by virtue of this assumption, official multiculturalism allowed for a reification of immigrants as "exotics," tacitly promoting the view that this was an appropriate and adequate cultural status for foreign-born nationals.[29]

Not unexpectedly, condemnation of the policy was strident, and emerged from all quarters of Canadian society. Although some of this criticism was undoubtedly magnified by long-standing sectarian agendas, there is no denying that a good measure of it was well-founded. The allegation, for instance, that the policy was intended to diminish Quebec's distinct cultural position within the Confederation has clearly proven to be justifiable. Opposition to constitutional recognition of Quebec's distinct status, at the very least, has pointed to a desire to regard the province as an equal partner within a joint venture of ten provinces. Obviously, this is not really possible. Quebec is not equal in all respects with Canada's other provinces; it was recognized at the inception of the state as an idiosyncratic national enclave within the Confederation, with specific cultural responsibilities. The status of French Canada as simply one among many ethnic groups allowed this necessity to be essentially discounted. For this reason, the policy of official multiculturalism never found a place in the hearts of the Québécois. As Lise Bissonette (former publisher of *Le Devoir*) pointed out, "Carried over into Quebec, this multiculturalism would be suicidal, since it tends to make Francophones a minority like the others."[30] Similarly, Métis opposition to official multiculturalism reflected a realistic assessment of their situation as an already veiled people. Representatives of the Métis were opposed to the policy on the grounds that it relegated them (as an unrecognized "native and national minority") to the position of being simply an ethnic group within a larger national "mosaic." This is not to say that Métis leaders were opposed to the concept of multiculturalism itself, but simply to the policy that was crafted by the Trudeau government. Indeed, it has been suggested that the Métis were "pioneers of multiculturalism" in Canada, dating back to the provisional government at Red River that negotiated the entry of Manitoba into the Confederation with full protections for both French and English languages.[31]

In spite of political agendas, official multiculturalism may well have emerged from a desire to formulate a collective language and practice commensurate with the complex cultural substratum of the Canadian state. In the end, however, it was broadly perceived as an attempt to undermine the development of such a language through its emphasis on an aesthetic of dissimilarity. As such, it may well have contributed to an amplification of antagonisms. Ultimately, the proscribed value of tolerance that official multiculturalism engendered served to reinforce cultural differences in Canada, rather than promote some broader sense of collective identity. The consequence of this has been a cultural discord that, according to Bissoondath, is now so deeply rooted that Canadians are confronting "a future of solitudes with no central notion to bind us."[32]

Running through the fabric of theories such as binationalism and biculturalism has been a long-standing belief in the need for national unity. It could be discerned as early as the Canada First movement that emerged on the heels of Confederation, an interest group that, according to William Foster, had been "inaugurated in Toronto to promote the growth of a Canadian national sentiment and to secure Canadian unity."[33] National unity has been a pervasive concern that has often been linked to the need for an integrated historical narrative, reflecting the belief that the cause of unity could be furthered through the teaching of history and that a lack of unity has been the result of a fundamental discrepancy in the way that history has been taught in schools: essentially, that English and French Canadians were not learning the same history. The desire to provide Canada's youth with a coherent history that would promote national unity was expressed as early as 1893 when the Dominion Education Association, under the direction of Ontario's minister of education, George Ross, conceived of the Dominion History Competition, a contest intended to encourage the writing of a textbook that would provide all Canadian children with a common national narrative. According to the chair of the competition's organizing committee, William Patterson, the project was born out of a "wish to inspire the boys and girls of the Dominion with a true sense of the nobility and grandeur of the heritage of Canadians and so to help to create and maintain a writing of patriotic sentiment." The Dominion History Competition's underlying faith in the power of historical narrative to bring about national unity reverberated throughout the twentieth century. In 1968, for instance, A. B. Hodgetts published *What culture? What heritage?*—a denunciation of the way in which Canadian children were learning history and social studies. Hodgetts believed that the country was courting dissolution and potential amalgamation into the United States because "we have not given our students a meaningful sense of the Canadian identity." Anglophone and Francophone children were, he argued, being provided with contradictory accounts of Canadian history and as a consequence could not "possibly understand each other or the country in which they live."[34]

The issue was also of concern to the federal government. On July 5, 1977, it created the Task Force on Canadian Unity, a body whose objective it was to solicit the input of Canadians concerning their lack of unity, to report on this, and, finally, to address the need for initiatives promoting cultural cohesion. From the outset, the team of researchers saw its primary mission as an exploration of the relationship between Quebec and the rest of the country. In its conclusions, the task force argued that the contemporary crisis of national unity was ultimately a product of two long-standing "cleavages" in Canada that had been propagated by the country's political structures: the conflicts (1) between the French and the English, and (2) among regions. Both, it claimed, had "an extended lineage in Canadian social, economic and political life," and had produced a state in which there were a "multiplicity of solitudes, islands of self-contained activity and discourse disconnected from their neighbors and tragically unaware of the whole which contained them all."³⁵ To a noticeable degree, the task force was correct. There have indeed been multiple, and paradoxical, narratives of Canadian history that have their bases in the country's founding communities. Anglophone history, for instance, has traditionally concentrated on the progressive political development of the state within the parameters of British legislative and judicial structures; while its Francophone counterpart has focused on an ongoing effort to resist English attempts to culturally subsume French Canada. The notion of a unified "history"—and its corollary, a unified national vision—has repeatedly faltered in the face of these two distinct mainstream narratives that have configured virtually every aspect of Canadian history in opposing terms. From the perspective of this duality, the notion of national unity became obviously untenable with the advent of Quebec's Quiet Revolution in the 1960s and with the emergence of Québécois nationalists who subsequently became adamant in calling for the recognition of Quebec's "special status" within the Confederation (with the threat of separation standing in the wings of such sentiment). Of course, the dichotomy of French and English has only been a part of the story. Québécois calls for recognition of Quebec's distinct status have been reiterated by First Nations; and the Manitoba Métis Federation has claimed that the Métis generally have been distrustful of government initiatives toward national unity. The idea of national unity has virtually lost all sway over the Canadian imagination, although it continues to permeate the political rhetoric of the country. "Like Humpty Dumpty," writes Daniel Francis, "Canada is broken and will not be put back together again."³⁶

Despite this desire to reflect Canada's foundational ethnic and regional diversity, discourses of binationalism, multiculturalism, and national unity, have largely failed because they have tended to be either exclusionary or divisive rather than providing a defining framework of identity based on cultural commonalities within a multifaceted society. Each of these formulations has been, to varying degrees, dependant upon a narrative model with a nationalist underpinning, and their failure has been related to this dependence upon the idea of Canada as a nation. It may well be that in attempting to create a *national* discourse linked to identity, they have not only proven inadequate but have obscured the logic of a confederation.

To consider this, we might begin with the classic meaning of a confederation itself as a league of independent states from which a federal government derives its authority. The advantage of a confederation as a state structure rests primarily in its capacity to separate ethnically or regionally based nationalist objectives from issues of sovereignty. Within such a structure, it is fully possible for constituent ethnic or regional factions to enjoy the economic and social self-determination of which they are deprived in nonconfederated state arrangements, while remaining part of a multi-party state.[37] It is no accident that Canada was constituted by a confederation. The British government and Canadian interests were concerned with establishing a state in British North America that fell politically somewhere between the federated United States and Great Britain's legislative union. The problem was one of authority—the mode by which political bodies could be established with greater power than "municipal corporations" and less than "confederate states"—and it was a central issue to be resolved at the time not only in North America but in New Zealand and South Africa as well. Some system had to be devised by which to establish, as British Under Secretary of State for the Colonies Frederick Rogers suggested, "bodies possessing such large powers and above all such valuable sources of revenues as shall render them content to be subject to the central authority in matters of general concern."[38]

It can be argued that in the Canadian situation the configuration of a modern state as a confederation did not necessarily amount to the creation of a nation. As Francis has noted, despite the diehard efforts of government commissions, Canada is not a single nation; and, if they ever were, Canadians are no longer generally disposed to think of it as such.[39] In political terms, voting patterns, political postures, and partisan allegiances have tended to be regionally configured to the degree that the nation's political character has been described as a complex of regional "subcultures." Considering specifically the issue of national unity, Joel Smith and Allan Kornberg have suggested that provincial antagonisms may have been more responsible for problems affecting unity in the twentieth century than a general lack of regard for the state itself or its federal structure. The political system in Canada has invited the provinces to demand exceptional provisions and recognitions in their relationships with the federal government, a situation that has been the source of perennial conflict between provincial and federal regimes. All the provincial governments share a common desire to constitutionally improve their situation in the federal body; but independence has not, as a rule, been a provincial objective. In a related fashion, the creation of a "unitary state" has never been the goal of the federal government; rather its concern has traditionally been with establishing a broader political culture than the provinces will tolerate. Provincial governments have concomitantly aspired to a more extensive "provincialism" than is conducive to absolute federalism.[40]

The issue of whether Canadians have ever regarded their state as a single nation is a significant one. There is no doubt that the people of Ontario were disposed to think in national terms at the time of Confederation: the *Toronto Globe* announced to its subscribers on Monday morning, July 1, 1867: "With the first dawn of this gladsome midsummer morn, we hail this birthday of a new nationality. A United British America . . . takes its place among the nations of the world." Outside of Ontario, however, the aspiration for a single nationality was not pronounced. On the same morning of July 1, for instance, the *New Brunswick Reporter*'s announcement was noticeably different: "From Halifax to Sarnia we are one people—one in laws, one in government, one in interests." Where the central Canadian newspaper hailed the beginning of a new nation, its Maritime counterpart celebrated the emergence of what was obviously a new state with common legal, political, and economic structures.[41] In spite of the fact that it continued to make use of the term *nation* to speak of Canada, within two decades, it appears that the *Globe*, too, had come to regard the country as a state that lacked the defining properties of a nation while possessing unity in matters of economics, international persona, and style of life: "The Canadian Idea," the paper explained in the mid-1880s, "is the establishment of a nation united in the aim to make Canada great and good and rich, though long to be bi-lingual and of diverse creeds." By the end of the century this image of the country would come to define what many Canadians regarded as the nature of their political union. The *Manitoba Free Press*, for example, was suggesting by the 1890s that there could be a unified political body in Canada without Canadians being forced to relinquish "the language and the customs of their forefathers, without forgetting their history and without sacrificing their pride of nationality." The term "Canadian," then, could refer to "many nationalities and many languages."[42]

More significantly, it is undisputable that the Canadian state did not come into being as a result of widespread support for such a union. John Stuart Mill suggested that a nation-state was not merely a body of citizens sharing a sense of national identification, but the desire "to be under the same government" and to be governed "by themselves or a portion of themselves exclusively."[43] Canada did not become a state in this manner, since it is clear that the "desire to be under the same government" was not pronounced at the time of Confederation; moreover, it has been a touchy issue since. Confederation was a joint venture by Canada and the British Colonial Office that was conceived as a solution to a decade of economic difficulties that had plagued the colony. It was orchestrated by a group of central Canadian entrepreneurs who wished to unite the British North American colonies in order to have access to the resources that would encourage investment and economic growth. The British Empire provided a potentially lucrative market for Canadian capitalists, but full exploitation of the market required expansion of agricultural production and forestry, an industrial sector shored up by protective tariffs, and the capacity to increase immigration to meet rising labor demands.

In the first instance, the initiative was driven by Canadian and British railway interests. Two principal figures of the enterprise in Canada, for instance, were Alexander Tilloch Galt and George Etienne Cartier, both of whom were simultaneously on the executive of the Grand Trunk and in the federal cabinet.[44] The movement toward Confederation was also propelled by an issue of public investment facing the colonies, due to the closing of the London bond market that had driven them to turn to Canadian and English bank loans that carried prohibitive interest rates. The railway was inexorably implicated in the solution to this problem. Confederation was an obvious way to consolidate financial liability while increasing population, thus boosting the capacity to borrow money; and the most expedient way to revitalize the economy in this situation was to stimulate financial speculation in transportation. The benefits of union were immediately obvious. The colonies were freed of individual debt; the ability to secure reasonable credit internationally was improved for a larger political body; threats of U.S. involvement north of the forty-ninth parallel were mitigated substantially by the existence of a unified state; and an economic policy based on the use of Canadian financial resources (principally located in Montreal) could be deployed, with the construction of a railway as its focal point.[45]

Confederation was, then, a strategic maneuver intended to obtain for the federal government the political prerogative necessary for economic expansion; and the BNA Act was, in the first instance, an economic agreement whose intent it was to make available a larger pool of financial reserves for the purpose of investment, principally in railway construction. The development of rail technology promised the expansion of agriculture and forestry, both of which would increase exports to Britain and other European nations and provide concomitant access to European goods, technology, capital, and labor. Railroad construction would also stimulate mining, smelting, and other related industry, while protective tariffs would encourage Canadian financiers to invest in Canadian manufactures. At a fundamental level, Confederation was a politically expedient mode of realizing an economic venture.[46] It was not the product of a widespread desire for union in any region except central Canada. The project successfully united a good portion of British North America, but it did so not on the basis of popular support for the venture but by means of diplomacy and a measure of coercion. New Brunswick grudgingly joined under the assumption that a transcontinental railway would be constructed, while Nova Scotia was essentially coerced into the alliance. Newfoundland and Prince Edward Island, in spite of similar coercive tactics, resisted the pressure to join. A congratulatory message sent to Ottawa from Summerside, Prince Edward Island (the center of a large ship-building industry during the period), on July 1, 1867, summed up the feelings of many who resisted the move: although the town transmitted good wishes to the new state that had been "launched upon the sea of history," the message noted, "though we do not admire the build of the craft, we cannot find in our heart to wish her other than a prosperous voyage."[47] Many were not so tactful. The *Acadian Recorder*, for instance, appeared in black on July 1; the *Halifax Morning Chronicle* was scathing in its criticism of the scheme; and the *Fredericton Head Quarters* warned on July 3, "The future may be full of hope . . . but it is useless to shut one's eyes to the fact that in New Brunswick there is discontent and indignation smouldering [*sic*] in many places, while in Nova Scotia these feelings are afire and in action." Watching the Confederation from the sidelines, the *Charlottetown Examiner* announced, "Here, alas! the great public of Prince Edward Island treat the thing with feelings akin to contempt."[48]

Antagonism toward the Confederation remained a thorny problem for Ottawa in the wake of July 1, 1867. Despite the fact, for example, that legislation to effect annexation of the North-West was enthusiastically pursued and passed on December 6, 1867, Macdonald's government was delayed in following through with the enterprise until late the following year. This was because a group of "Repealers," led by Joseph Howe, mounted a campaign early in 1868 for the repeal of the British North America Act and the separation of Nova Scotia from Canada, a campaign that absorbed all of Macdonald's diplomatic skills before being settled in the fall of that year. Only when Nova Scotia had received guarantees of "better terms" in the

Confederation, and Joseph Howe and other dissenters had been awarded more prominent posts (Howe himself was named superintendent general of Indian Affairs and secretary of state for the provinces, two positions that were most significant in federal-provincial affairs) was Macdonald able to resolve the issue and turn his attention once again to the North-West.[49] All this is to say that broad support for the political union of the British North American colonies was nonexistent at the time of Confederation; and consensus in this regard was not forthcoming. Nearly two decades later, in March of 1885, the *Toronto Globe* published a scathing criticism of the Macdonald government's handling of dissatisfactions in the North-West, in the context of which the paper mapped out regional dissatisfactions with the Confederation.

> The men who now govern Canada have more than once proved that they are utterly incapable of governing the country so justly and wisely as to make all its Provinces and all classes of the people contented and to create the harmony amongst them all without which the Confederation can be but a rope of sand. Nova Scotia has never been thoroughly reconciled to the union. Cape Breton, under the administration of those men, begins to desire separation even from Nova Scotia. New Brunswick complains of the loss of her trade and the decay of her manufactures. A Tory Government in Prince Edward Island proposes to appeal to the Queen for the enforcement of an important undertaking made a condition of her entering the Dominion. Quebec has more than once declared by the acts of her representatives, that her interests are in many ways distinct from the interests of any or all of the other Provinces, and that she feels at liberty to enforce her demands by any means that promise to be effectual. British Columbia, setting the Dominion Government at defiance, undertakes to do by her own authority what the Dominion refused to do for her, and thus sets at naught the most important principle of the Confederation.[50]

Residual antagonism toward Ottawa for the way in which the other colonies had been brought into the political union was expressed during the same period in the House of Commons. In a statement that was perhaps emblematic of the discordant attitudes that would ultimately characterize relations between central Canada and the rest of the country, a member of Parliament from Nova Scotia raised a question concerning whether or not the people of the North-West had been properly consulted about their entry into Confederation, and whether there existed in the territories a reasonable level of local support for uniting with the larger body. Were the people of the North-West, he asked, "willing to come into the Union, or were they to be dragged in against their will also."[51]

By the traditional criteria for nationhood (e.g., shared language, ethnicity, or religion), and also by the more broad definition advanced by Mill, it appears that it might well be an error to claim that Canada has ever been a nation. If this is so, then in a related fashion, it might be equally ill-advised to speak of broad configurations of national discourse in this context. Nationalism is based to a notable degree on a people's acceptance of a shared historical narrative and a vision of the future; in a context such as this, historical moments recalled as remarkable accomplishments, as well as confidence about a significant future, are both mythic formulations to which present political forces are held accountable. Without myths of this type, the kind of collective identity that the nation requires cannot exist; and for this reason, it is imperative that nationalisms recover and utilize memories so that a necessary form of shared identity can be forged. It is in collectively recalling historical episodes or heroes that a people can form a relationship with one another in spite of often divergent and conflicting aspirations. Modern industrial nations (whether Western European, Asian, or American) have generally created narratives for themselves that imagine a linear relationship with past communities through invocations of shared language, geographical territory, the arts, heroes, "golden ages," and other mythic and symbolic structures. Despite their definitive location in modernity, these narratives suppose that the nations they describe are descended from preexisting cultural forms.[52] As was noted in chapter 4, nationalism is a mode of defining identity that differs from other approaches insofar as it makes possible individual identification with a larger human collectivity that is considered to be sovereign. Within such a sovereign body, differences of social and economic status, geographical situation, and ethnicity are presumed to be superficial; the body is regarded as ultimately unified.[53]

In a sense, Canada has not consciously formulated this necessary condition of nationhood. The country, as Northrop Frye suggested, "never defined itself as a unified society." Reflecting on the difference between Canadian and American students he had taught, Frye believed that those in the United States were possessed of a much firmer notion of national

identity than their Canadian counterparts. The Americans had a confidence about their nation's principal role in world affairs and the global
charge that coincided with this role; while Canadians, on the other hand,
were prone to thinking of themselves as members of a geopolitical community that lacked coherent perceptions of a common identity, a unified past,
and a reliable future.[54] To be sure, many (perhaps a majority of) Canadians
have come to agree that nationalism (as classically delineated in terms of
language, ethnicity, religion, national heroes, declarations of independence,
and so on) is not possible in Canada. As Stephen Clarkson pointed out in
the mid-1960s, a good deal of nationalist formulation in the country has
been "piously meaningless," insofar as it has proven to be ill-equipped to
serve a state that is riddled with internal cultural incongruity. Allen Smith
made the same kind of assertion a few years later when he suggested that
any formulation of Canadian nationalism would have to concede the fact
that it could be only a "non-nationalism"—the exclusivity that nationalism presupposes could not exist viably in Canada. Similarly, Ramsey Cook
would suggest that,

> A pluralistic society, if it values and understands its pluralism,
> cannot be a nationalist society. Without the homogeneity which
> nationalism assumes, it cannot develop that sense of mission
> which characterizes all modern nationalisms . . . Canada can exist
> only as a pluralist society for geographical and economic as well as
> historical and cultural reasons.

Of Canada's leading statesmen, it was perhaps Pierre Trudeau who came
closest to expressing this critique of orthodox formulations of nationalism
in the Canadian context: "We must," he wrote, "separate once and for all
the concepts of state and nation, and make Canada a truly pluralistic and
polyethnic society." In a generous reading, it was perhaps this belief that lay
at the foundation of his desire for official multiculturalism; but, of course,
the assumption that measures were required to transform Canada into a
"polyethnic society" disregarded the fundamental fact that the Canadian
state was already polyethnic, and it was for this reason that it might not be
a nation.[55]

Still, in spite of the fact that many Canadians surrendered any conscious aspiration toward nationalism in the second half of the twentieth
century, the issue of nationalism has remained a subtext in discussions

concerning the problem of identity. Too often, *nationalism* and *identity* have been conflated terms, a discursive stylistic that, although fitting in the case of other modern states, is inappropriate to the Canadian situation.[56] Although it is obviously not the definitive formulation, we might consider in this regard Louis Hartz's model for the development of nations—and by association, national identities—from colonial to postcolonial entities. Hartz suggested that at the outset, all colonies are dependent upon the metropolis from which they materialize and therefore lack a clear sense of autonomous national identity. The period during which colonies strive for autonomy is characterized by vigorous nationalism, and if that autonomy is achieved there also emerges a strong sense of national identity. This formulation obviously does not hold in the case of Canada where no abrupt rupture with a metropolis occurred, but rather there was a protracted process of severing a connection with Great Britain.[57] In spite of the fact that, in Hartz's terms, Canada lacked the kind of foundational propulsion toward autonomy that gives rise to effective national identity, it has remained a functioning template for talking about Canadians' collective character to the present.

In the mid-1960s, Craig Brown claimed that "[d]ebating nationalism is the great Canadian pastime." Everyone, he wrote, from governor generals, politicians, and writers of all variety, to academics and average citizens had demonstrated a preoccupation with the subject since the time of Confederation; and while many modern nations had articulated their national character by means of great civic performances, Canadians seemed to have displayed their identity most often within the search for a coherent nationalism.[58] Unlike previous formulations that focused on ethnic purity (Anglo-Saxon) or duality (binationalism), discussions concerning both Canadian identity and nationalism during the period tended to concentrate on various facets of Canadian culture (in the hope of maintaining the country's distinctiveness from the United States) so that by the 1970s, the concept of "cultural nationalism" had become the dominant figure in expressions of Canadian identity.[59] Like previous nationalisms, this configuration lost currency toward the end of the twentieth century, and no other prevailing discourse replaced it. The underlying relationship between identity and nationalism, however, remains operative. David Taras's work on Canadian identity, for instance, has been quite excellent; but he has nonetheless assumed a nationalist model when speaking of issues relating to a lack of collective identity in Canada:

Canadians have a less certain and less coherent identity than do others. Canadians are still filling in the map of their identity, discovering who they are. Canada has never had the supreme moments of self-definition—bloody revolutions, ringing declarations of independence, or moments of catastrophic defeat—that have characterized the political histories of counties such as the United States, France, Israel, Ireland, or Japan. Lacking a great historical moment or a common language, and having few national institutions, heroes, or symbols that provide unity, Canadians have little of the "hardwiring" that can be found in other countries.[60]

"Hardwiring" may well be absent from the Canadian situation, but the principal issue obstructing the emergence of an effective nationalist discourse is that, in the Canadian context, identity undeniably revolves around the coexistence of virtually irreconcilably divergent elements. Most Canadians have not discovered a shared historical narrative—what Mill described as "community of recollections, collective pride and humiliation, pleasure and regret, connected with the same incidents in the past." As a consequence, Canada has never had the option of conceiving of itself as a culturally unified state. From the time of the Conquest in 1759—and in spite of English attempts to effect the assimilation of the French to British culture—minority forces have shaped Canadian life.[61] This is a primary fact of its history that Canadians cannot politically or emotionally outwit so long as they remain part of a confederated geopolitical body.

If we acquiesce to the possibility that an overarching national discourse is not possible in the Canadian situation, we are left then with the problem of identity as it relates to a community that cannot be defined as a nation, but is constituted by a form of statehood that sets it apart both geographically and politically from other states. The question, then, is whether such a collectivity can develop a common identity in spite of its obvious internal divergences. My answer is, not surprisingly perhaps, that this is distinctly possible. A lack of cultural unity rests at the basis of the state; it is, one might argue, a Confederation that is defined by a particular political and social fusion of disparate elements—by what I have chosen to call *métissage*. Certainly, many Métis have understood the practical and symbolic power of such a configuration, although their voices have been largely disregarded within discussions of Canadian identity. "The vast majority of Canadians," said Harry Daniels in 1978, "are still not willing to recognize that Canadian identity is inseparable from its aboriginal heritage"; and Yvon Dumont, in the mid-1990s, reiterated Daniel's conviction, claiming, "What we the Métis aim to do now . . . [is] to urge the reformulation of Canadian identity."[62]

In a striking manner, Riel the myth speaks to the possibility of *métissage* being a foundational factor in Canadian identity. In the mid-1960s, Carl Berger identified what he believed were the components of an authentic nationalism. What he was identifying, however, were much broader resources for the formulation of collective identity, of which nationalism is simply one form; and, if we substitute the word "identity" for "nationalism" in his formulation (as I have done below), it might well provide a lens through which Riel can be viewed in this respect:

> If Canadian [*identity*] is to be understood, its meaning must be sought and apprehended not simply in the sphere of political decisions, but also in myths, legends and symbols. . . . For by its very nature, [*identity*] must seize upon objective dissimilarities and tendencies and invest them in the language of religion, mission and destiny.[63]

In a number of respects, Riel constitutes a primary locus of such a "language of religion" in Canada. At a most basic level, he has not only been recognizably mythicized by various competing sectors within Canadian society but he has been consistently portrayed in religious terms since the time of his trial and execution. During the summer of 1885, in the midst of French Canadian accusations of unfairness in regard to Riel's trial, William McDougall (who Riel had infuriated by barring his entry to Red River in 1869) expressed the opinion that questions regarding the legitimacy of the court and process through which Riel was tried could potentially deflect attention from the fact of Riel's guilt and create national reverberations: "Canada cannot afford," he wrote, "to have her future content disturbed by any portion of her population believing that Riel died as a martyr." As noted earlier, Charles Bayer and E. Parage also placed the words of martyrdom in Riel's mouth in their play *Riel: Drame historique en quatre acts et un prologue* (1886). "If I am a victim of the dishonesty of my enemies," Riel was portrayed as saying, "if instead of a pardon, it is the scaffold that awaits me, my martyrdom will be useful to our cause."[64] The image of Riel as a martyr has remained to this day, appearing in literary works of all types.[65] He has also been called a prophet, a mystic (at times deluded), a savior, a saint, a "righteous rebel," a "mad messiah," a devil, "Canada's Joan of Arc," and a "wise m[a]n from the West."[66] We might note again here that there was a distinct shift in attitude toward Riel among Anglophones after the middle of the twentieth century, whereby he was recast as a cultural hero rather than a villain. Albert Braz suggested that this reinvention of Riel as a hero has amounted to a process of "deification."[67]

Alongside these descriptions of Riel in religious terms, there was also, during the last decades of the twentieth century, a reinterpretation of his religious visions and passions. In spite of the fact that Riel vigorously objected to the allegation of insanity at his trial, and the trial itself was concluded without formal recourse to the issue of his mental state, subsequent Canadian opinion generally resorted to the theory of insanity to explain both his actions and his sense of divine mission in 1884–85. In the latter part of the twentieth century, however, Riel's religion, which had previously been regarded as evidence of insanity, became valorized to some degree. J. M. Bumsted, for instance, believed that Riel's messianism bore a distinct resemblance to that of other North American "prophets" like Joseph Smith. The difference, according to Bumsted, was simply that Smith was able to avoid a comprehensive government-initiated military assault and, consequently, successfully established a community based on his vision; whereas Riel could not contend with the full force of the Canadian military, and was destroyed.[68] Similarly, the CBC's miniseries *Riel* (1979) did not avoid the issue of Riel's religion (as had been common in even sensitive portrayals of the man) but presented it as part of his patriotism, going so far as to "Canadianize" his religious awakening: his inaugural vision, which occurred in Washington, D.C., in 1875, was transferred to Montreal in the series, thus situating the source of his inspiration firmly within the Canadian context.[69]

Of the religious motifs that have been attached to Riel, one of the most common has been that of martyrdom—the notion that he was a man who died for the sake of something fundamental, willingly accepting death rather than renouncing his values. "We love and admire Louis Riel," wrote Rota Herzberg Lister, "for his courage, his devotion to a cause, his willingness to stake his all."[70] This language could point to a primordial configuration of sorts, an underlying cultural formation that signifies, at the same time, also a kind of "revolution." In this sense, Riel's Métis body might well be regarded as emblematic of the Canadian social and political body, where dichotomies run up against one another and seek some kind of viable resolution: as Harry Daniels said more broadly regarding the Métis in 1979, they are "a people who are the quintessence of what was, what is, and what will always be, Canadian."[71]

Taking another cue from Hannah Arendt, it could be constructive to reconsider the issue of revolution from this perspective. Arendt claimed that a violent protest against a regime can be called a revolution only if its violence is enacted under the aegis of a desire for fundamental change in the nature of a political body—an aspiration for a "new beginning."[72] The Great Revolutions of the modern period aspired to "new beginnings," but in some sense they may have lacked the kind of originary configuration that can be discerned in the mythicized figure of Riel. Although the revolutions incorporated imagined pasts into their visions of the future, these traditions also imagined the nation-state to be generated within its own time and space, and by its own volition. As Benedict Anderson has noted, the possibility of imagining a nation-state emerged only when three established premodern European beliefs were shaken: (1) that a particular written language contained universal truth; (2) that society was ordered in relation to a central individual who derived authority from some extra-human source; and (3) that time was ordered by an originary structure in which the world as it was known, and the human beings who inhabited it, had been created at virtually the same moment. These conceptions together had provided premodern Europeans with the necessary resources to orient themselves within their existence, since they allowed them to conceive of their political landscape as part of a structure rooted in the foundational nature of the world.

Economic shifts, social and scientific innovation, and improvements in systems of communication were the principal causes for the deterioration of these stabilizing conceptions of cosmic and political order; and their weakening hold on early modern societies opened the door to new modes of imagining the relationship between social organization, power, and temporality. Primarily, what this meant was that where God was presumed to signify a particular form of social order during the feudal period, the nation came to signify the social ordering of the modern era. To a notable degree, the French Revolution signaled this shift in European society's relationship to the source of sovereign power. Prior to the revolution, power was regarded as emanating from an external source, whereas the revolution vested sovereign power in the republic itself, supposedly desacralizing the state. However, as Stathis Gourgouris pointed out, this did not necessarily occur, since the sovereign condition of the state itself can be said to have assumed the metaphysical significance previously reserved for monarchs.[73] The issue that emerged, however, was whether generative power could satisfactorily emanate from the political entity that it created: in other words, could the nation-state create itself? The problem was solved by revolutionaries through an invocation of world history, unaffected by localized disparities; and Hegel, of course, would create the philosophical language concomitant with the revolutionary stylistic by conceiving of history as vehicle for the revelation of a "world spirit."[74]

When we turn to the Canadian situation, something rather different appears in terms of state creation. The mythic Riel is our entrée in this regard, since he appears to have repeatedly been placed in the position of raising questions concerning the origins of the state. He has never been portrayed as having died for the state; rather, he has always died in spite of it and for the sake of something prior to the state (and more resonant with Canadians) that is enmeshed in conflictual relations—those of French and English, Aboriginal and non-Aboriginal, western and central Canadian and, ultimately in the late twentieth century, even the English with their own imperialism. He has, generally, been cast as dying for the sake of communities that have been thrust unwillingly into contingent relationships that define their historical situation—for the possibility of order that transcends the disorder of their coexistence but that is inescapably rooted in the originary fact of their coming together. The mythic Riel might well direct our attention to the process of *métissage* as a primordial source for the Canadian state (and perhaps by association, other postcolonial states), since it refers to the creation of radically new individual and social bodies. In a sense, it might also constitute a revolutionary mode at the foundation of a state, although not according to the pattern of the Great Revolutions.

In her analysis, Arendt, as we noted, suggested that unlike other forms of organized political behavior, revolution is not simply an articulation of a desire for change but for an entirely new beginning. Prior to the American and French Revolutions the notion that human history could begin again in an entirely novel fashion was unknown in the West. The eighteenth-century revolutions were catalysts for an intellectual attempt to discover "absolute truth" within the changeable arena of human relations; thus revolutions were fueled by the belief that their actors were inaugurating a new form of human community that was significant for all human beings, regardless of location or nationality. It was in regard to their capacity to actually "begin again" that Arendt turned to a model for fundamental innovation set out by Augustine, and which might have some bearing on our discussion of Riel. According to Augustine, an entirely new beginning could occur only if normal time and space were ruptured by some form of transcendent force, and this had occurred but once in human history, with the appearance of Jesus Christ. From this theological perspective, then, nothing wholly new was possible in the human realm, in spite of the certainty of continual change. Augustine qualified this claim in one key respect: the only event, he said, that could approximate an absolutely new beginning was the birth of a human being.[75]

If the Métis might be regarded as "quintessential" Canadians, it is, finally, in this Augustinian frame that they must be so. In considering the origin of the Canadian state, we might likewise suggest that its political and social specificity—embedded in the predetermined tenuous, often bitter, interrelationships of its constituent ethnicities and regions—are innovations of the colonial period through which an absolutely new form of social body was created. *Métissage*, in Augustinian terms, is a phenomenon that can be regarded as among the most "revolutionary" acts possible in respect to the emergence not only of the individual body, but of a modern state. Riel is emblematic in this respect. The myth (and the martyr) has been repeatedly portrayed as the victim of unavoidable dichotomies, trapped within a New World source of human generation created in the colonial meeting of disparate peoples. This foundation for the emergence of Canada produced a new social and political configuration that is defined, unlike modern nation-states, by a distinct and self-conscious lack of cultural homogeneity; *métissage*, in this situation, was the mode by which this deficiency was resolved, whereby a new state could be conceived and configured on the basis of the foundational and preexisting fact of colonial contact and contestation. This originary structure transcends the Canadian Confederation, but has been persistently expressed within it. I would suggest that what is critical for our purposes here is that the mythicization of Riel and the rebellions, as well as the religious language attached to Riel, indicate that in the Canadian situation, dichotomies of ethnicity, language, and region that rest at the foundation of the postcolonial state are not merely historical problems but are matters of religious consequence.

Chapter 6

Riel and the Canadian State

Before proceeding further, I would like to invite Riel — as much as is possible — to speak to the issues that I have raised thus far. Although it is obviously impossible to know for certain how he would have reacted to this analysis, he was sufficiently prolific to have left a substantial body of personal writings that might provide some clues. Principally, I believe it can be argued that Riel would have agreed that (1) the creation of the Canadian state had religious implications; (2) dichotomies (particularly of ethnicity) were primary structures of the state, with the possibility of geopolitical order residing only within this primary configuration (and hence, the impossibility of Canada emerging as a nation-state); (3) the state could not will itself into being, but had to be a reflection of its originating structures; (4) violence, as a religious force, was implicated in the creation of the state; and (5) the Métis reflected the foundational meaning of New World states.

Riel believed deeply that he was situated at the cusp of the emergence of the Canadian state as a multiethnic, geopolitical entity, and that he had a critical role to play in its materialization. The process by which central Canada's national intentions for the rest of the country were to be undone and a different kind of state allowed to surface was, for Riel, a process that was religiously significant. Hence, before any other Canadian would refer to him as a martyr, he would use the same terminology in referring to himself. Under incarceration, and while awaiting the outcome of his appeal process, Riel wrote in his diary:

If the death sentence passed against me were carried out, I think that there would be no Conservative newspaper, not even the oldest or the most avowedly "blue," which would not be overcome with pain and chagrin. I can hear them declaiming about the martyr to arbitrary power. They would be speaking of me when they said in the name of Lower Canada: "Our beloved Louis Riel has been executed!"[1]

The fact that the recreation of the Canadian state had religious significance was a principal focus of Riel's diary throughout the 1885 uprising, while under arrest, and in the time during which he awaited execution. In the preface to the diary (written after the completion of the entire journal) he asked God to empower his public discourses, poetry, and prose: "Inspire my words and all my actions; and, through Jesus, Mary and Joseph, let all my words and actions which are in accord with Your holy Church produce extraordinary and wonderful results of salvation for myself, and for all of Christendom, and for all of Catholicism."[2] Salvation, for Riel, had a distinct political meaning relating directly to the cause for which the rebellion had occurred: recognition of the rights of Aboriginal—and all other marginalized—peoples within the Confederation. He prayed fervently throughout the summer and fall of 1885 for God's intervention in the realization of these rights:

My God! Through the divine grace and influence of Jesus Christ, let the people's interests and wishes persuade and compel the government to inquire into the reason for the troubles which have just occurred. . . . Enlighten them and support them so they give each man what belongs to him in justice and truth. . . . Justice is entirely on the side of the Métis and the Indians in the war which just took place; thus they should not be punished but indemnified.[3]

He was convinced throughout his trial and his appeal process that the hand of God could be discerned in all the events that had transpired in the North-West and that, further, political change in Canada would come about through the working out of God's plan for the country:

[T]he current state of opinion already allows one to surmise and predict, with a fair degree of certainty, that even the government newspapers are only a step or two from throwing aside all reserve.

It is becoming impossible for the Conservatives to maintain themselves in power. Fortunately for them, it seems to me that a way out has been prepared for them through the work of Providence.

I am confident that, if God sustains me through the divine grace and power of Jesus Christ, the Conservatives are going to march in the path of providential ideas, to make their policies conform to sounder notions of justice and to repair a good part of the public damage which they have caused in the last fifteen years. That, in my opinion, is the trend of politics in the eastern provinces as of today, August 21, 1885.[4]

Riel believed also that he would be blessed for having assumed a principal responsibility in the crusade to bring about God's intentions for the state, and he found a ready metaphor for his position in the figure of King David: "I, little David in the service of the great King, had the courage to go outside the camp of Israel for a moment, to try to hold off the giant who was marching against all of us with his redoubtable strength and reputation."[5] All this is to say that Riel was firmly convinced that the creation of the Canadian state was not only a political issue but, perhaps more critically, a religious one. Moreover, he believed that the New World had created a rupture in the course of human affairs, and it had become a site of transformation in both historical and religious terms: "If I understand the situation properly," he wrote in late August of 1885, "the political and religious wind which is blowing throughout the North is going to furnish the Catholic Church the two wings needed to take flight amidst the sublime destinies of the New World."[6]

Implicated in this destiny were primary structural diversities of ethnicity and geographical situation (center-peripheral relations) that were to be the essential elements of emerging postcolonial states. When Riel arrived at Prince Albert in the summer of 1884, he was immediately confronted with this dichotomous reality and the necessity of countering a dominant central Canadian initiative toward disregarding it. "I found the Indians suffering," he later said:

I found the half-breeds eating the rotten pork of the Hudson Bay Company and getting sick and weak every day. Although a half-breed, and having no pretension to help the whites, I also paid attention to them. I saw they were deprived of responsible government, I saw that they were deprived of their public liberties. I remembered that half-breed meant white and Indian . . . and I have directed my attention to help the Indians, to help the half-breeds and to help the whites to the best of my ability.[7]

From the time that Riel had been forced to contend with the Canada Firsters (who were prominent at Red River when he rose to prominence in 1869), he had repeatedly confronted central Canada's aspiration for a culturally uniform nation-state. By the time of the North-West Rebellion, he had fully formulated a notion of the state that took for granted European immigration but reacted vehemently against this culturally homogenous model, imagining instead a multicultural, indigenous body of regional partners in Confederation. During his trial, he claimed that the federal government had not upheld its responsibilities according to the agreement that had been negotiated in 1870, and that if Ottawa did not address this issue, the Métis would be forced to invite Italian, Irish, Polish, and Belgian immigrants from Europe or the United States to help the Métis regain one-seventh of the North-West, as they had been promised. In return each group would also be accorded one-seventh of the territory. To demonstrate that he had no bias against Protestants, he also planned to invite Danes, Swedes, and Norwegians who together would receive one-seventh, as well as Jews (so long as they converted) and Germans. These immigrant groups would create new postcolonial nations (e.g., "a new German-Indian world") that would be accommodated within the overarching structure of the Canadian state.[8]

The proposition of a multiethnic and multinational state was not intended to be a threat, although it might well have been perceived that way by the court. In fact, Riel would suggest later in the day that if he were treated fairly, acquitted, and permitted to assume a public career, he would still invite European immigrants to come to the North-West and assume a share of the land, while making certain that the English had also a "reasonable share." His chief concern with English Canadians was the fact that when the one-seventh agreement had been negotiated with the government in 1870, the Métis had not agreed to relinquish the remaining six-sevenths of the territory to Anglo-Canadians. His vision for the future of the North-West, however, did not in any way preclude the English, since he believed that there was substantial value in many aspects of British culture. The British constitution, for example, was a brilliant institution, "perfected for the nations of the world, and while I speak of having in future, if not during my lifetime after it, of having different nationalities in the North-West here, my hope that they will succeed is, that they will have it amongst them, the great Anglo-Saxon race."[9] In a letter written to the archbishop of St. Boniface, Alexandre-Antonin Taché, on July 24, 1885 (while the trial was underway), Riel reiterated his desire to see the Canadian state accommodate a community of various nations.[10] He believed that an acquittal would bring about a surge of public opinion in his favor, and he would thus be able to negotiate constitutionally for a land settlement through which the Métis would sell six-sevenths of the North-West to the government in exchange for the assurance that five-sevenths of the territory would be divided among people of different nations and religious faiths.[11] In the final analysis, Riel's vision of the Canadian state was one in which all Canadian nationalities would enjoy fair and equitable treatment, political representation, and cultural valuation. As he wrote in his poem "L'Ontario" (written while confined in an asylum at Beauport in 1876), the negotiations of 1870 had been concluded by the Métis on the basis of their belief that they had won this kind of cultural acknowledgment:

> Our government being only temporary
> Agreed to the union;
> But under the condition
> We were included in our history.[12]

For Riel the colonial period had created a culturally complex situation that was absolutely foundational, and geopolitical order was possible only in relation to this defining and preexistent ordering of human relations. The state, consequently, could not be justifiably created with the intention of achieving cultural—and national—homogeneity. This may have been possible in Europe where the dynamics of colonialism were not implicated directly in state creation, but not in the Americas. God, wrote Riel, "reveals more to the New World than He had judged appropriate to reveal to the Old."[13] Canada was to be a state containing various nations, beginning with Aboriginals, the French, and the English; and in a poem addressed to Macdonald, in which he berated the prime minister, he defined this foundation:

> You will be known for your lies.
> You are responsible for my banishment
> I did my time in exile: I am tormented
> And I am, even with all you did,
> Chief of my nation. . . .

> The children who were deported from New France
> Have known too much suffering under the English flag,
> For not hating the nation
> Who has governed them with so much hatred.[14]

Pointing to what would become a consistent Canadian theme, Riel's anger with the prime minister was rooted in a deeply held sense of the need for mutual respect among Canada's various regions and nationalities, something that he believed Ottawa had proven itself incapable of expressing. When, in the course of the Red River uprising, Riel permitted his provisional government to carry out the execution of Thomas Scott, his decision was made on the basis of his belief that the act would constitute an expression of sovereignty and would compel Ottawa to enter into sincere negotiations with the Métis. He was convinced that the federal government would take serious note only of those who were capable of violent action: "[W]e must make Canada respect us," he is reported to have said.[15] On the eve of hostilities in 1885, Riel would likewise write to his colleagues to suggest a united Métis–mixed-blood–settler action against the government, citing Ottawa's mismanagement of the grievances of all three groups. The people of the North-West were justified in taking up arms against the Dominion, he wrote, because "they respect no right."[16] The value he placed on expressions of respect was evident in the fact that in all his transactions with governing, administrative, and judicial bodies, he persistently stressed his own esteem for the institutions of the federal government. In a letter to Crozier dated March 21, 1885, for instance, he wrote: "Major, we respect you. Let the cause of humanity be a consolation to you for the reverses which the governmental misconduct has brought upon you"; and when the Métis defeated the police a week later at Duck Lake, he again wrote Crozier: "Major, we are Christians in war as in peace. We write in the name of God and of humanity to come and take away your dead, whom we respect. Come and take them to-morrow before noon."[17] Moreover, in the course of his trial, Riel repeatedly emphasized his regard for the institution and individuals confronting him. In reference to the Mounted Police, he said: "I have respected the policemen, and I do to-day, and I have respected the officers of the police; the paper that I sent to Major Crozier is a proof of it"; and to the court he affirmed:

> I respect you, although you are only half a jury, but your number
> of six does not prevent you from being just and conscientious. . . .

Your Honor, because you appointed these men, do not believe that I disrespect you. It is not by your own choice, you were authorized by those above you. . . . I do not disrespect this court. I do respect it, and what is called by my learned and good lawyers, the incompetency of the court must not be called in disrespect. I have all respect.[18]

In a broader sense, he expressed "the respect I have for the English population, the Anglo-Saxon race," and declared that he would work toward the establishment of new nations in the North-West only by the "constitutional means of the country," so long as "Canada is just with me, if Canada respects my life, my liberty and my reputation."[19]

Riel believed that Canada could not hope to establish itself as a unitary state with the kind of homogeneity that defines a nation-state. His vision of the state was one in which a number of nations could coexist so long as the ruling regime understood that these were indeed nations deserving of appropriate recognition, treatment, and status within the larger geopolitical configuration. Consequently, the attempt to constitute the state as a homogenous cultural entity would require an imaginative leap not commensurate with its predetermined human character. Riel raised a fundamental question concerning the source of the modern state: essentially, he asked whether a modern state can effectively constitute itself. So far as one can discern from his writings, his answer seems to have been negative: to exist in a coherent fashion, the state could ultimately come into being only as a reflection of its originary human profile, and by means of a transcendent force. To begin, we might note that the most significant mode of self-creation for states of the period was revolution, and Riel clearly assumed an antirevolutionary stance, apparently distrusting the possibility of state creation without recourse to an external generative power. He held, for instance, that the French Revolution (which he called a "monster") had undermined the papacy and was an affront toward God "who holds all the affairs of men in His hands."[20] In neither the uprising of 1869–70 nor that of 1885 did Riel have a desire to overthrow existing institutions of political or social power. The issues for him were of national recognition within established structures, and of constitutional reform, since he believed that both Canada's political–social arrangement and its constitutional framework had not been self-generated but were located in a much wider historical and cosmic arrangement. Thus he had no desire, for instance, to remove prominent public officials from office, so long as these individuals were brought into the new ordering of relations that he and the Métis were initiating. Dewdney, for example, was a man whom Riel believed to have been "favoured by Providence," with "excellent qualities of mind and heart."

> May God keep him then happy and prosperous, and may He deign to maintain him in the high position he occupies until he can supervise the beginning of the most beautiful emigration which the world has ever seen. Soon enough, in all probability, a constitution which suits that vast land will be drawn up. It will be good for the North-West that its civil liberties be inaugurated under the administration of a man who is not only eminent but also has in our eyes the advantage of being one of your friends.[21]

Time, for Riel, was not reordered at the inception of the state, as it was in revolutionary traditions. Rather, the state was part of a different arrangement founded in a preexisting temporal order. His "most precious interests," consequently, were "in time and eternity"; and the struggle in which he and the Métis were engaged was part of a plan for humanity that was not restricted to the Canadian period. They were striving for "the honour of religion, for the salvation of souls, for the welfare of society" in the New World.[22] Moreover, he believed that the way in which the jury at his trial would ultimately choose to deal with him would have implications well beyond the conventional notion of history: "What you will do in justice to me," he said, "in justice to my family, in justice to my friends, in justice to the North-West, will be rendered a hundred times to you in this world, and to use a sacred expression, life everlasting in the other."[23] The time and space of the Canadian Confederation was, consequently, defined by a prior structure of meaning and time located in this instance in both God and the altered temporal ordering that had occurred as a result of colonialism.

On December 8, 1874, while visiting a friend in Washington, D.C., Riel received his first vision, an experience that placed him in this transcendent temporal ordering:

> While I was seated on the top of a mountain near Washington . . . the same spirit who showed himself to Moses in the midst of the burning cloud appeared to me in the same manner. I was

stupefied. I was confused. He said to me, "Rise up, Louis David Riel, you have a mission to fulfil [sic]."

Stretching out my arms and bowing my head, I received this heavenly message.[24]

When Riel assumed leadership of the resistance in the North-West a decade later, he believed fully that the federal government's disregard for the rights of the local population was not simply unjust but was a moral transgression. Writing to both the Métis and English mixed-blood population at Lake Qu'Appelle, he claimed that, "For fifteen years they have made sport of our rights, and offended God by overwhelming us with acts of injustice of every kind."[25] In an earlier poem, he had likewise claimed that the government had shown nothing but "bad faith," and was consequently "lost."[26] In all his writing, both public and private, he consistently criticized English Canadians for failing to recognize the fact that the Anglo-Saxon heritage fueling their emerging nationalism was not their own creation but was the result of the intervention of God. In the context of addressing the issue of the legitimacy of Aboriginal claims to the land, for instance, he declared at his trial:

In England, in France, the French and the English have lands . . . they were the owners of the soil and they transmitted to generations. Now, by the soil they have had their start as a nation. Who starts the nations? The very one who creates them, God. . . . Now, here is a nation strong as it may be, it has its inheritance from God.

He would also claim at his trial that the "glory of the Anglo-Saxon race" was given to it by God along with its land.[27] And in his poem "You Resemble a Grain that we Discard," Riel pointedly assailed the Anglo-Saxon sense of cultural superiority, writing:

Grande Albion [England], you have made a mistake
The universe is stronger than you.[28]

Riel believed that nations could not be simply willed into existence, but that they required the intervention of a preexisting generative power—more specifically, God. The working out of this creative power, however, had been dramatically altered by the advent of the colonial era, a period that he believed had initiated a remarkable transformation of the Roman Catholic Church. At stake in Riel's antirevolutionary stance was a firm commitment to Catholicism; but his break with the clergy in 1885 (due to the clergy's refusal to support the Métis initiative against the Canadian government) left him no personal alternative but to respond to what he regarded as a divine commandment to reconsider the Church as having been partitioned into two distinct bodies. The universal structure of Catholicism had served him well in countering what appeared to be an equally universalizing tendency of Canadian expansion aimed at destroying Aboriginal peoples, and when the Church failed him at a dramatic moment in the contest for the definition of the new state, a mode of Catholicism emerged that contained the transcendent power of the original form while reflecting the extraordinary rupture in human history that had occurred as a result of European colonialism. As Dumont would later recall, Riel thus told his compatriots not to trust the clergy "because they did not follow the law of God."[29]

In 1875, Riel received a letter from Ignace Bourget in which the bishop informed him that "God, who has always led you and assisted you until the present hour, will not abandon you in the dark hours of your life, for He has given you a mission which you must fulfill in all respects." Despite Bourget's later assertion that he had never intended that the statement be interpreted in such a radical fashion, Riel was profoundly moved by the letter and kept it with him throughout his life, believing ultimately that it was a sign that he had been selected by God to be a New World prophet. Later in his life, when he came to believe that the Vatican's authority had collapsed, Riel felt certain that Bourget had been chosen as a vessel for the Holy Spirit and should be recognized as a new pope.[30] There were to be two Catholic Churches and two popes, he told Taché in July of 1885; "there is no longer a single Sovereign Pontiff here below. The only Sovereign Pontiff which the world had was crucified."[31] The reason for the division of the Church was twofold. First, and foremost, he claimed in court, it was because "while Rome did not pay attention to us, he [Bourget], as a bishop, paid attention to us."[32] Secondarily, Riel believed that Rome had been transformed into a mercantile city by revolutionary ideas and that a number of governments had contributed to the desecration of the papacy. He said that Rome was "the ravished spouse of Christ," having become the capital of an evil society led by a "Brigand King," and God could no longer remain in a city where there was "prostitution of impious ideas." As a consequence, the papacy could not fully rest with the bishop of Rome: "[E]ven if the Pope were personally a most holy man, the sole fact of his presence in the midst of the abomination of desolation seems naturally contrary to the desire of God."[33]

In the letter that he wrote to Taché, Riel was extremely deferential, preferring not to address what the bishop would have found to be some of the most disturbing aspects of his religious activities during the previous months—his ordination of his colleagues and his incarceration of the clergy during the rebellion. Still, his principal religious views were apparent in the letter. Primarily he stressed the fact that the papacy had been relocated to the Americas, that Bourget (who had died only a month earlier) had been chosen as the "Pontiff of the New World," and that he had been succeeded by Taché.[34]

> God wants to consider that holy Archbishop the first successor of Saint Peter, in spirit and in truth, in the New World. Divine Providence mercifully aided me to proclaim that in Saskatchewan with the métis. But since the death of the good Archbishop Bourget, see how God has cast his ineffably sweet eyes upon us. He wants to compensate you in the sight of the whole world and return to you a hundredfold the good works which you have sacrificed to Him during forty years of serving and pleasing Him. Through divine election, you are the true successor of Archbishop Bourget. And even as you rendered the last honours to the mortal remains of that great servant of God, you became yourself, to the good fortune of many and to the misfortune of none, the vicar of Jesus Christ on earth. God willed that I, captured in a terrible defensive war and in the midst of the greatest dangers, but aided by His loving help and by the firm faith of the métis, should proclaim the pontificat of Ignace Bourget.[35]

Riel added that the title of Pontifex Major Totius Novi Mundi (Greater Pontiff of the Entire New World) had been conferred upon Bourget, and he had been placed at the head of the "Holy Catholic, Apostolic and Living Church of the New World."[36] This conception of a New World Catholic Church pointed to a new locus for generative power made necessary by the radical change in human community that had occurred in the colonial period. "I wish to leave Rome aside," Riel announced during his trial.

If I have any influence in the new world it is to help in that way and even if it takes 200 years to become practical, then after my death . . . my children's children will shake hands with the Protestants of the new world in a friendly manner. I do not wish these evils that exist in Europe to be continued, as much as I can influence it, among the half-breeds. I do not wish that to be repeated in America.[37]

While Riel was clearly of the opinion that no state could come into being apart from the ultimate design of God as expressed in the changed world of the colonial period, he also believed that violence was a religious matter when it was employed for the creation of a state. Riel was a pacifist, and resisted violent conflict as much as possible, but when no other course of action seemed appropriate he embraced it as sincerely as did Macdonald:

[F]ifteen years of suffering, impoverishment and underhanded, malignant persecution have opened our eyes, and the sight of the abyss of demoralization into which the Dominion is daily plunging us deeper and deeper . . . has suddenly, by God's mercy as it were, stricken us with horror. And the half-breed people are more afraid of the hell into which the Mounted Police and their Government are openly seeking to drive us, than of their firearms, which, after all, can only kill our bodies.[38]

The rebellion was, from Riel's perspective, necessary for the sake of something more profound than simply the preservation of human life; it was required to bring about redemption in both a historical and metaphysical sense: "[M]ay God bless you," he wrote to his colleagues in the spring of 1884, "in all what is to be done for our common salvation. Justice commands to take up arms."[39]

In the context of the uprising, Riel persistently reminded those around him that their victories were purely the work of God. In the wake of the Métis success at Duck Lake, for instance, he wrote to the Métis and mixed-blood community at Qu'Appelle and Battleford saying, "Thanks to God, we have defeated them," and "Bless God with us for the success he has kindly granted us." And he reminded them: "All you do, do it for the love of God, and in the protection of Jesus Christ, the Blessed Virgin, St Joseph and St John the Baptist, and be certain that faith does wonders."[40] He also wrote to Crozier on March 27, informing him that:

A Calamity has fallen upon the country yesterday, you are responsible for it before God and man.

Your men cannot claim that their intentions were peaceable,
since they were bringing along cannons. And they fired many
shots first. God has been pleased to grant us the victory, and as our
movement is to save our lives, our victory is good, and we offer it
to the Almighty.[41]

For Riel, the violence of 1885 was profoundly religious, and the sign
under which it was enacted was of critical significance. He clearly believed
that the Canadian government was acting according to its own agency,
while the Métis were fighting according to the will of God—an economy
of power, so to speak, that transcended the colonial aspirations of central
Canada and that was destined to realize itself within the time and space of
the Canadian state. In this respect, he discerned within the experience of
the Métis a foundational meaning of not only Canada, but the entire postcolonial New World. He did not regard the problems confronting the Métis
of the North-West as localized, but considered them to be part of a history
of oppression that spanned the continent. In a poem dating from two years
before the rebellion, while he was living in Montana, he wrote,

> Is it not that from the Frontiers
> Of Mexico, to Sweet Grass Hills [Montana],
> Thousands of Halfbreeds live in tears,
> In the chasm of the same evils?[42]

Likewise, he believed that the necessity for redemption was a problem of hemi-
spheric proportion, and that the Métis were destined to assume a definitive role
in its realization. It may well have been for these reasons that he announced to
the courtroom in the summer of 1885 that "although the Province of Ontario
is great it is not as great as the North-West."[43] Nonetheless, while he was awaiting execution in a Regina jail cell, he experienced a number of relevant visions
that he recorded in his diary; and in what was undoubtedly the most poignant of these he saw his brother Charles who had died a decade earlier.[44] The
diary entry chronicled both Riel's initial elation in seeing his brother again
and a subsequent shift into metaphor as he discovered within the vision of
his twelve-year-old brother an image of the Métis in a future New World that
they, not colonial powers, defined. "O my brother," Riel began,

it is a long time since I have seen you! It is eleven years since I last embraced you. You were so little when I went away. But blessed be God who reunites us. I have taken flight on the wings of prayer. I am high in the sky. I come to you from far away. I arrive from the South and the countries of South America. You are all alone here in the North, O my brother! Nevertheless, it is good that the Spanish of the New World come to do their studies at Montreal and St. Boniface, and in return the Métis and the *Canadiens* go to study in the colleges of New Spain. Let us get acquainted in childhood. Later, when today's young people come of age, the two continents will follow each other's doings with interest. South America will hold the North in friendly admiration. And when Providence gives the glorious Spanish their turn to occupy the public stage, their beloved brothers in North America will make their cheers and prayers rise to heaven. They will jump with joy, blessing the religious zeal and gallantry of the Spanish nations.[45]

In this prospective world the Métis, as signified by Charles, were to be a defining reality of the social body—religiously, politically, intellectually, legally, and militarily:

My brother Charles is a man of the new faith.

My brother Charles is a man who will play a great role.

My brother Charles will exert much influence on the United Spanish States.

My brother Charles will make himself respected in the United States of Washington.

Name of Charles! How many times will you give luster to both North and South America?

My brother Charles is a scholar. His powerful mind investigates scientific questions and resolves them to the great astonishment of Catholicism.

My brother Charles is a famous doctor of Theology.

My brother Charles is a famous jurist. His books are recognized everywhere. He dies of old age. His hair is white, but of a whiteness kind and pure.

My brother Charles is a humble and inspired preacher. He converts society through the power of his sermons.

My brother Charles is a general whose victorious sword has promoted God's glory in the United States of Washington and in
the United States of Columbia.[46]

The necessity for historical and ontological redemption was undeniably
at the root of Riel's activities on behalf of his community. As a consequence,
he regarded state creation as a religious problem, and the formation of New
World states as a process fundamentally tied to preexisting orders of community as well as to modes of generative power located beyond the parameters of the state itself. In the Canadian situation this meant, primarily, that
the state's structure had to reflect its foundationally dichotomous ethnic
and regional character; and to generate such a state, he and his compatriots were willing to engage in violent actions under the aegis of a mode of
the sacred that was prior to the Confederation, but inextricably informed
by the time and space of post-Confederation Canada. Within this historical and religious contest over the structure of the Canadian state, Riel
resisted the central Canadian impulse toward nationhood and discerned a
meaning of the Métis—and the New World—that was deeply implicated
in the formation of not only Canada but all postcolonial states. Thus, in a
salient vision he experienced in the final weeks of his life, he learned that
his brother Charles was in paradise along with the Spanish American revolutionaries Simon Bolívar and Mariano Moreno, while Adam and Eve had
been in Purgatory until December 8, 1875 (the day Riel had his mystical
experience in Washington).[47]

Chapter 7

Heterogeneity and the Postcolonial State

As we noted earlier, Ernest Gellner argued that *"nationalist homogenization"* is an inherent property of modern nation-states, where "people can only live in units defined by a shared culture. . . . Genuine cultural pluralism ceases to be viable under current conditions." Gellner claimed that cultural homogeneity was fundamental to nationalism and that the modern period was the first in which dominant cultural configurations had come to assume a normative prerogative for entire societies. This, he maintained, was the foundation for the "age of nationalism," in which there has been a unification of culture and state; he argued further that modern nations would not survive if they attempted to maintain, simultaneously, cultural plurality and cultural inequality.[1] Gellner was not opposed to the idea of pluralistic cultural and national political organization, but he remained unconvinced that these were viable configurations of modern nationhood. Nationalism and wealth were for him simply the principal modes by which political bodies could legitimate themselves.[2]

There is obviously a good deal of evidence in support of such a theory in the modern period when genocide, ethnic removal, and compulsory assimilation have often been deeply implicated in constructions of nationhood. Yet it is also true that many nation-states have successfully employed political mechanisms that have provided alternatives to homogenization—devices that include federations, confederations, and multicultural and multinational political organizations. Some scholars have consequently raised the issue of whether the durability of these states and their political institutions are evidence that Gellner's formulation was somewhat inadequate.[3] Perhaps, however, the issue is not whether these kinds of states provide evidence of the limitation of Gellner's claim so much as whether such modern entities should be considered nation-states at all. To this end, the Canadian experience might provide an opportunity to consider geopolitical configurations such as confederations or federations in a different light.

In chapter 4 we noted that nationalism is an intellectual construct established in relation to the idea of the nation. It is unlike other approaches to the issue of identity insofar as it incorporates the notion of political sovereignty into its formulation of collective self-identification; and within the sovereign body, divergences of class, region, and ethnicity are imagined to be relatively inconsequential. The national body is thus regarded as being fundamentally unified. Canada has not conformed to this typical pattern of the nation and thus raises the question of whether it should truly be considered a nation-state. I suggest that perhaps it should not. Internal nationalisms in Canada (e.g., Québécois, Anglo-Saxon, First Nations, Métis) have certainly maintained this type of unity, but locating a similar kind of harmony across the larger body has proven to be impossible; the divisions, at a federal level, have been anything but superficial. Of course, this is something of which all Canadians have been aware since the late nineteenth century. In the midst of the turmoil that surrounded the trial of Riel, for instance, the *Orange Sentinel* declared:

> The French are as much French now as before Wolfe vanquished Montcalm upon the Heights of Abraham. The dividing line is sharply drawn, and although upon many previous occasions differences of race and religion have been made strongly apparent, never before was the demarcation as distinct as over the present Riel imbroglio. The signs of the times point to the fact that this artificial nationality cannot last much longer.[4]

A century later, Northrop Frye would claim that Canada was an idiosyncratic nation insofar as it appeared to him to have moved from a "pre-national" to a "post-national" posture without having conceived of itself as a nation. While postcolonial nations began to come into international view in Africa and Asia of the twentieth century, Canadian nationalism (such as it was) was hardly distinguishable.[5] Others have been even more tentative in defining the Canadian state. It has been suggested (as I have here) that in order to consider the issue of national discourse, one must first address the question of whether Canada exists as a bona fide nation, since the array of discrete and cohesive cultural factions within the country call an overarching sense of national identity into question. Stephen Clarkson, for instance, claimed in the mid-1960s that Canada did not conform to an alternate model of modern multinational states (like India or the Soviet Union). He was undoubtedly correct, insofar as Canada may well be characterized by a number of distinct nations, but its geopolitical order is also distinguished by a series of well-defined regionalisms that do not constitute nations (roughly represented geographically by provincial parameters and promoted politically by provincial legislatures). By the same token, Clarkson noted that it was impossible to ignore the fact that the country has been increasingly plagued by a "crisis of national identity" stemming from its peculiar cultural formation.[6] Perhaps Allan Smith was closest to the mark when he said, "Canada is a non-nation." But where, then, does this leave the country with respect to self-definition and a collective discourse?[7]

States are political bodies with authority to press their citizens into allegiance and legal compliance. Nations, on the other hand, are communities of individuals who regard themselves as being united by ties of culture, language, and a general consciousness of being a nation. Thus, in the case of the nation-state, the need to institute the nation as both socially and politically sovereign, as well as possessing a collective and cohesive self-identity, requires that ethnic groups be integrated into state configurations. In spite of their association with one another, the terms *nation* and *state* have distinct meanings, and it is not always appropriate to use them in the same context; this has been particularly true in the Canadian situation. At a fundamental level, Canada is simply not a nation; it is, nonetheless, a state. In some sense this might be a problematic stance to assume. After all, nationalism, and the nation-states it serves, has provided the validating political standard of modernity. Federations, for instance, have not generally achieved legitimacy unless they have been conceived of as "federations of nations."[8] Still, the difference in terminology is significant in the Canadian context.

The problem of Canadian nationhood has been addressed by a number of postmodern scholars in recent years. Bruce Powe, for instance, has suggested that unlike other nation-states that have formulated a clear goal for themselves, Canada is a "state in process" and the Canadian people are consequently without a stable national identity. Still, according to Powe, this is

not necessarily a deficiency since it allows Canadians a great deal of maneu-
verability in terms of formulating identity—the freedom to be, as one critic
of Powe has (disparagingly) suggested, "everything" and "anything." Linda
Hutcheon has made a similar claim that the propensity for bemoaning the
perennial Canadian quest for a common identity has limited Canadians'
capacity to recognize the virtue of their particular situation: "[I]nstead of
bewailing our fate in the name of some sort of collective cultural inferiority complex, what if we made a virtue of our fence-sitting?"⁹ Although
the desire on the part of postmodernists to shift Canadians' collective focus
away from the issue of national identity is appropriate, the notion that being
a "process" or "fence-sitting" population can be a virtue would not, I expect,
satisfy those Canadians who have some desire to articulate the basis of their
identification with their compatriots. Simply put, I doubt very much that we
can be "everything and anything." There is a political entity called Canada,
and a community of people called Canadians, both of which must be what
our historical circumstances have made of us.

The question remains, then, of how to speak of a coherent and viable
geopolitical body as a state in the modern period, while affirming that it
is definitively not a nation. To do so, it is perhaps necessary to revisit the
meaning of a confederation as more than simply a league of independent
states: in the case of Canada it has traditionally—and constitutionally—
referred to a union of three founding nations and a series of distinct communities that conceive of themselves as culturally and, to some degree,
politically autonomous. Canadians have not forged a sense of national
identity that mimics that of revolutionary modern states, but they have
managed to create a postcolonial state that is viable. The desire for a unitary
state (and the discourse concomitant with this desire) has been the product
of a will to conform to these other post-revolutionary models; and there
have been sound reasons for this tendency. Regardless of the relative benefits or limitations that have accrued of modern revolutions, it is clear that
they produced the political regimes of many of the world's dominant states.
Revolution has been a profound symbol of political and social creativity in
the modern era.¹⁰ The impossibility of creating a unitary state, and a discourse to match it, however, does not necessarily mean that there is not a
form of collective discourse appropriate to the Canadian situation that is
equally specific to modernity. In fact, I would suggest that there is, but it
may not be defined by the relative formlessness of postmodern discourse.
Rather, it may be located in the more explicit arena of the postcolonial.

To begin, we must seriously entertain the possibility that viable modern states need not be nation-states. In fact, in many cases, postcolonial states might well be better suited to confederated unions, given their cultural complexity. It is this issue of complexity with which postmodern cultural theory has been grappling but, ultimately, to the end that a coherent narrative (or formulation of identity) is difficult to achieve within this framework. According to many of these cultural theorists, an integrated collective identity is simply not appropriate to the world of the twenty-first century in which globalized communication and commerce has dissolved national boundaries. In this world, then, dichotomies of regions and metropoles, minorities and dominant sectors, are the norm: "In the postmodern world of counter-pointing influences, centres, and traditions, the claim that a single tradition can be central or orthodox has become meaningless."[11] Consequently, postmodern theorists suggest that a new form of the state is required to meet changed global circumstances, and they believe that Canada may be a model for this new political ordering. The journalist Richard Gwyn thus described Canada in 1995 as "the world's first postmodern state," the result of which has been that it has not developed a resounding sense of identity.[12] If Canada is indeed a postmodern state, this would undoubtedly be an accurate statement, since by its nature postmodern discourse defies the reified classification that national identity entails. If it is regarded as a postcolonial state, however, there may be latitude for a discourse about identity—specifically, confederated identity—that, while quite distinct from nationalist discourse, nonetheless speaks coherently about what it means to be Canadian.

By an idiosyncrasy of history, Canada was constitutionally defined as culturally and politically heterogeneous. In the first instance, this was related to the original situation of Canada as a colonial holding within the structure of a monarchical system. A monarchical political structure requires that its populace maintain nothing more than allegiance to the Crown; popular unanimity with respect to fundamental principles is not necessarily required in the way that it is in wholly democratic structures where citizens must rule over other citizens (the Quebec Act, for instance, was a prototypical articulation of this relationship).[13] More significantly, the existence—and collision—of multiple cultures is intrinsic to Canada. Prior to 1763, the British maintained a contested foothold in North America by means of a series of confrontations with both French and Native peoples; and the British military triumph in 1763 did not bring about an end to this conflict. Rather, the conquest of French Canada by England, and the overthrow of British colonial power by the United States in 1783 (that thrust a substantial population of French Canadians and American dissenters into a shared British colonial space, while rendering Native Canadians somewhat redundant in terms of British diplomacy) ensured that a fundamental incompatibility would define British North America.

Confined within the parameters of the British colonies, French, English, and First Nations peoples found themselves in an unavoidable contest for the preservation of their respective cultural, political, and judicial structures, alternately protecting and, in the case of the French and English, extending their spheres of influence. The British did not pursue a clear policy toward the province of Quebec in the decade following the Conquest. Working under the assumption that Anglo-Saxon immigrants would establish British political, religious, economic, and social structures in the colony, imperial policy remained vague until the 1770s, when revolutionary sentiment began to emerge in the Thirteen Colonies. In response to the situation, the British government drafted the Quebec Act, 1774, the first constitution created by parliamentary statute for a British colony.[14] French Catholics were guaranteed freedom of religion by the act, so long as they were willing to swear an oath of allegiance that had been stripped of any traditionally offensive references to Catholicism. Additionally, the Coutume de Paris was confirmed as legitimate with respect to property and civil issues alongside British criminal law; and the assets and properties of seigneurs (proprietors whose land was farmed by tenant farmers) were validated by the act.[15] Most significantly, the Quebec Act was the first British statute that conceded the presence of multiple ethnic groups in a colony. The colony was subsequently divided into two subcolonies, Upper Canada and Lower Canada in 1791, at the request of British colonists who were outnumbered in the region fifteen to one by Canadiens.[16]

Equally critical with respect to the inescapable reality of cultural plurality at the foundation of modern Canada was the Royal Proclamation, 1763, that legally recognized the principle of Aboriginal land ownership. The proclamation stipulated that no Aboriginal land could be infringed upon without the negotiation of a treaty and that such negotiations could be carried on only with the British government. Hoping to avoid abuses that had taken place in the British colonies along the American eastern seaboard, the British government confirmed at a fundamental level the legitimacy of Aboriginal title and, consequently, a distinct ethnic presence in the colonies:

[A]ny Lands whatever, which, not having been ceded to or purchased by Us as aforesaid, are reserved to the said Indians, or any of them.

And whereas, Great Frauds and Abuses have been committed in purchasing Lands of the Indians, to the Great Prejudice of Our Interests, and to the Great Dissatisfaction of the said Indians; in order, therefore, to prevent such Irregularities for the future, and to the End that the Indians may be convinced of Our Justice and determined Resolution, to remove all reasonable Cause of Discontent, We do, with the Advice of Our Privy Council, strictly enjoin and require, that no private Person do presume to make any purchase from the said Indians, of any Lands reserved to the said Indians, within those part of Our Colonies where We have thought proper to allow settlement; but that, if at any Time any of the said Indians should be inclined to dispose of the said Lands, the same shall be Purchased only for Us, in Our Name, at some public Meeting or Assembly of the said Indians, to be held for the Purpose by the Governor or Commander in Chief of our Colony respectively within which they shall lie.

Although "great frauds and abuses" were undoubtedly committed in the two centuries that followed, the proclamation legally recognized a third ethnic population in the colony. Sections of the text of the Indian Act, 1876, concerned with the disposal of reserve land would later replicate the text of the Royal Proclamation; and the proclamation would ultimately provide a legitimate mechanism for affirming Aboriginal land claims beginning in the late twentieth century.[17]

The following century saw a number of constitutional recognitions of the country's foundational ethnic plurality, culminating in the British North America Act, 1867. In its necessary adaptation to the presence of two powerful cultural entities, Confederation created a state in which subsequent calls for cultural conformity could not ultimately be sustained. As Cartier noted, "there could be no danger to the rights and privileges of either French Canadians, Scotchmen, Englishmen, or Irishmen . . . no one could apprehend that anything could be enacted which could harm or do injustice to persons of any nationality." A confederation was the most expedient way of forging a state from the British North American colonies. A legislative union, as Macdonald recognized, was not possible because it would irrevocably alienate French Canada and the Maritimes. Broadly based cultural compliance was not a possibility in a situation in which the best that could be hoped for was, as Cartier suggested, a compromise involving "kindred interests and sympathies." The compromise that resulted confirmed the monarchy and the British parliamentary system; but this form of government gained the support of all interested parties because, as Étienne-Paschal Taché noted, it was regarded as inherently capable of adapting to the needs of a culturally multifarious political body.[18]

The maintenance of a Francophone society in Quebec was a fundamental principle of Confederation and was consciously articulated within the British North America Act. The act provided for a standardization of civil law in all provinces except Quebec; it established that either the French or the English language could be used in the federal House of Commons and the Quebec Legislature, that the records of these legislative bodies would be written in both languages, that all acts passed by these legislatures would be published in both languages, and that either language could be used in federal and Quebec courts. In addition, Section 93 of the act was intended to prevent challenges to the rights of Catholic separate schools already established in the provinces, but it was only in Quebec that the Catholic population was sufficiently large to counter challenges to this issue of established possession that lay at the foundation of Section 93. These constitutional conditions did not provide French Canadians outside of Quebec with the kinds of cultural protection that would allow them to thrive; but by the same token, they became part of a political bargaining unit that they lacked prior to Confederation. Since issues of minority rights were a federal parliamentary responsibility, and the federal parliament was bound to contain Francophone members from Quebec, French minorities outside of Quebec were guaranteed of having advocates for their cause in Ottawa.[19]

The BNA Act undoubtedly ascribed primacy to French and English Canada, sanctioning a certain dualistic foundation for the nation; but the act also acknowledged a third group—Native peoples—who had a distinct relationship with the British Crown. This relationship laid the foundation for the recognition of Aboriginal Canadians' "special status" within the Confederation and, obviously, for further constitutionally recognized cultural heterogeneity. This status was partially the consequence of the fact that First Nations peoples could claim initial occupation of the continent, and partially the result of their unique relationship with the Crown that was transferred to the federal government at the time of Confederation without reference to provincial governments.[20] By the BNA Act, "Indians" were thus formally recognized as a founding ethnic community within Confederation. Subsequent federal governments, however, actively sought to divide this community through the creation of official categories such as registered, non-status, treaty, and non-treaty Indians, such that by the latter part of the twentieth century, two-thirds of Canada's Aboriginal population had no legal status, an issue that would begin to be dealt with in the talks that preceded patriation of the constitution in 1982.[21] Still, at the heart of the BNA Act was a presumption of cultural pluralism that lay at the foundation of the Canadian state, and its political structure was designed to accommodate that lack of cultural purity. The Manitoba Act, 1870, would accomplish the same end through its recognition of the Métis as a distinct cultural group, a recognition made by the federal government's acknowledgment of Métis land rights.

In a sense, Canada did not attain full autonomy as a state until the patriation of its constitution in 1982. It was also in this document that the principle of three charter groups was self-consciously and thoroughly articulated for the first time. In 1926, the Balfour Report had announced that Canada was an "autonomous community within the British Empire," instigating a move toward the establishment of Canadian embassies abroad; but amendment of the country's constitution was still the prerogative only of the British Parliament, and Canada's highest court of appeal remained the Privy Council.[22] True autonomy was not really achieved until the country was faced with the first systematic articulations of Quebec separatism and was forced to define itself as a fully independent state. In response to mounting threats of separation, Pierre Trudeau conceived of a means by which the Canadian Constitution could be renewed in order to wrest the power of amendment from the British Parliament (thus terminating Canada's colonial position) and to formulate a charter of rights that would ensure that French Canadians' rights within the country would be safeguarded through constitutional protections for bilingualism.

Despite resistance from the provinces, Trudeau managed to have the constitution patriated in 1982, thereby shifting the power of amendment from Britain to Canada and providing Canadians with their first Charter of Rights and Freedoms. At the outset of discussions, Aboriginal organizations, like the National Indian Brotherhood (which would later be renamed the Assembly of First Nations), the Inuit Committee on National Issues, and the Native Council of Canada (also later to be renamed the Congress of Aboriginal Peoples), recognized that the federal and provincial move toward constitutional talks provided a unique opportunity to press the government for the recognition of Aboriginal Canadians as founding people alongside the French and English. By the time the talks were taken up in earnest in the late 1970s, the term *Indian* had fallen out of favor and had been replaced with that of *First Nations*, a shift that reflected the approach that Aboriginal organizations were to assume with respect to constitutional change. Pressing for an official role in the talks, Aboriginal groups went so far as to petition the British government for recognition of the legitimacy of their claim to inclusion. At stake primarily was formal acknowledgment of certain Native rights, especially that of self-government. Harry Daniels, then president of the Native Council of Canada, and a consultant at the public hearings on the issue, outlined the principle Aboriginal demands:

> In short, we are saying that rights of indigenous peoples must be protected by the constitution. We are saying that any revision to the constitution must include native spokesmen as delegates on equal footing with provincial premiers, not just as witnesses at hearings like this. Métis rights, native rights, the rights of indigenous people have to be enshrined in the constitution of this country.[23]

Aboriginal peoples were not, however, included in the discussions in an official capacity; and when the federal and provincial governments (all except Quebec) presented their initial draft of the amended constitution, Aboriginal rights had been conspicuously omitted from the document. Rather than handling the issue of Aboriginal rights in the same fashion as it proposed for that of language rights—that is, as "fundamental objectives of the Canadian federation"—the government intended to include Aboriginals within the structure of the charter, thereby leaving unanswered the crucial question of whether non-status Indians could expect the same constitutional recognition and protection as status Indians. A joint lobby by Aboriginal and women's groups (the latter of which were incensed over the exclusion of rights concerning gender equality) was able to force the federal and provincial governments to retreat from their initial position and revisit the salient issues of Aboriginal and women's rights, a move that resulted in a redrafting of the constitution a year later, in the context of which certain rights were acknowledged with respect to both groups.[24]

Two important affirmations regarding the rights of Aboriginal peoples were made in the document, and these would have far-reaching implications. First, it confirmed that the Charter of Rights and Freedoms in no way superseded either Aboriginal or treaty rights (including those specified by the Royal Proclamation of 1763 and any land claims agreements that had been reached or would be reached in the future); and second, Section 35 identified what the term "Aboriginal" meant and what sorts of rights were being protected:

(1) The existing aboriginal and treaty rights of the aboriginal peoples of Canada are hereby recognized and affirmed.

(2) In this Act, "aboriginal peoples of Canada" includes the Indian, Inuit and Métis peoples of Canada.

(3) For greater certainty, in subsection (1) "treaty rights" includes rights that now exist by way of land claims agreements or may be so acquired.

(4) Notwithstanding any other provision of this Act, the aboriginal and treaty rights referred to in subsection (1) are guaranteed equally to male and female persons.[25]

A year later Section 35.1 was added specifying that any amendment to certain sections of the constitution (including Section 35) could be made only following a constitutional conference involving the prime minister and the provincial premiers, and in discussion with Aboriginal representatives.

The first stage of constitutional reform established a model that would characterize subsequent deliberations whereby Native Canadians, who were initially disregarded, emerged as key players. In the hope of persuading the Province of Quebec to enter into the country's new constitutional framework, Prime Minister Brian Mulroney met with the provincial first ministers at Meech Lake to draft an agreement that would address Quebec's concerns. Aboriginal leaders requested that the rights of First Nations be included in these deliberations, but they were unsuccessful; and the resulting Meech Lake Accord, ratified by all provincial premiers in 1987, was intended to confer upon Quebec the status of a "distinct society," while ignoring entirely Aboriginal appeals for recognition of a similar status. In the hope of having the accord endorsed by the federal and all provincial governments, Mulroney set a three-year deadline for provincial approval; but changes in provincial administrations proved detrimental to the agreement, and the legislatures of Newfoundland and Manitoba failed to lend their support as the 1990 limit approached. In the end, Manitoba proved to be a political wild card. The concerns of Aboriginal Canadians, ignored entirely in the process of drafting the accord, were taken up by Elijah Harper (with the support of the Assembly of Manitoba Chiefs and the Assembly of First Nations), who derailed the necessary unanimous consent of the provincial parliament by refusing ultimately to vote in favor of it. The failure of the accord provided separatist forces in Quebec with increased momentum.[26]

Constitutional discussions were effectively brought to a halt by the Charlottetown talks of 1992. Unlike earlier discussions, the Charlottetown deliberations included Aboriginal representatives (Native, Métis, and Inuit) and an arrangement was agreed upon in which the Aboriginal right to self-government was to be recognized constitutionally. The agreement was presented to the electorate for a vote in the fall of 1992, and it was overwhelmingly rejected by all groups implicated in it. The failure of the Charlottetown agreement signaled the termination of Aboriginal Canadian interest in pursuing constitutional recognition; and the subsequent recommendations of the Royal Commission on Aboriginal Peoples (1996), which included constitutionally bound commitments to the implementation of Native self-government, elicited virtually no concerted response from First Nations peoples.[27]

The Constitution Act, 1982, proved to be a turning point in the struggles of Aboriginal Canadians, since it affirmed existing Aboriginal and treaty rights and recognized First Nations, Inuit, and Métis as Aboriginal peoples. To be sure, much was left unspecified with respect to these "rights," but Aboriginal Canadians had achieved recognition within the text of the amended constitution and this significantly altered their legal situation in Canada. For the Métis, official recognition was long overdue. Riel had argued in court, after all, that the Manitoba Act constituted such recognition: "I said what belongs to us ought to be ours," he claimed. "Our right to the North-West is acknowledged, our co-proprietorship with the Indians is acknowledged." The constitution, in spite of its recognition of the Métis as Aboriginal, did little to clarify the issue of a land base for the Métis, who were never included even in the treaty negotiations through which Native Canadians were coerced onto reserves.[28] Additionally, the constitution did not fully legally define the term *Aboriginal*, and so there remained a further significant interpretive element to the document, given that the Indian Act had limited the recognition of Indian status to individuals who were members of either tribes or bands, or to their direct descendants. Due to their ethnic ambiguity, these collective Aboriginal rights stipulated in 1982 lacked the specificity reflected in the constitution's other principle articulation of liberties—the Charter of Rights and Freedoms; and it consequently became the responsibility of the courts to adjudicate their precise meaning.[29]

All this is to say that due to historical contingency, Canada is a state that has been constitutionally defined as culturally heterogeneous. By pure necessity, the Quebec Act and Royal Proclamation created the legal foundation for this structure. The maintenance of a distinct French society within a larger political body, as well as the presence of Aboriginal peoples with a particular relationship to the federal government, were conceded by the BNA Act; and recognition of the Métis as a distinct cultural group with land rights was contained within the Manitoba Act, through which the province came into existence. Finally, English, French, and Aboriginal Canadians were essentially recognized within the Constitution Act, 1982, as charter groups with distinct rights (although in the case of Aboriginals, the precise meaning of these rights has yet to be fully determined), thus establishing multiculturalism as a legal principle in a way that prior government initiatives could not.

The process of drafting a constitution forced Canadians to consciously consider and give form to their understanding of what defined their state. Constitutions are more than mechanisms for resolving public conflicts; they are legally binding documents that link a community with its past, express its shared principles, and address its aspirations for the future.[30] The patriation of the constitution compelled Canadians to consciously engage in this kind of self-definition as they had not done before; and in its aftermath, many Canadians began to address, with unprecedented vigor, familiar issues relating to cultural heterogeneity that had not been previously stated in a blatant and legally binding fashion. This has certainly been the case among Aboriginal peoples. More than this, however, the process of patriation induced many others to acknowledge the need to address issues relating to the rights of both Aboriginals and Québécois—a phenomenon that is indeed unusual among modern states. Setting aside the possibility of cultural chauvinism, it has been suggested that long-standing opposition to constitutional recognition of Quebec's distinct status betrayed the desire to regard the province as an equal partner within a joint venture of ten provinces. More recently, however, non-Québécois Canadians have begun to recognize the myopic nature of this attitude. Neil Bissoondath, for instance, has suggested that Quebec cannot be considered to be on an absolutely equal footing with the country's other provinces, since it has certain responsibilities that are unique within the Confederation pertaining to the protection of language and cultural formation. It is undeniable that exceptional responsibilities require equally exceptional political machinery to ensure their realization.[31]

There has also been an increasing realization among Canadians that recognition of Aboriginal peoples must be more than superficial. Joe Clark (prime minister from 1979 to 1980) wrote in 1994, for instance, that one way to demonstrate "respect" for the Métis would be to formally recognize "the unique and historic role of Louis Riel as a founder of Manitoba and his contribution in the development of Confederation"; and Governor General Adrienne Clarkson described Riel in 1999 as an advocate for "western rights and the rights of his people, [who] helped to lay the framework for minority rights—and as a result for cultural cooperation—in this country."[32] On March 9, 1992, while serving as minister of constitutional affairs, Joe Clark successfully gained unanimous parliamentary approval for a resolution stating:

> That this House take note that the Métis people of Rupert's Land and the North Western Territory through democratic structures and procedures took effective steps to maintain order and protect the lives, rights and property of the people of the Red River;

> That this House take note that, in 1870, under the leadership of Louis Riel, the Métis of the Red River adopted a List of Rights;

> That this House take note that, based on the List of Rights, Louis Riel negotiated the terms for admission of Rupert's Land and the North Western Territory into the Dominion of Canada;

> That this House take note that these terms for admission form part of the Manitoba Act;

> That this House take note that, after negotiating Manitoba's entry into Confederation, Louis Riel was thrice elected to the House of Commons;

That this House take note that, in 1885, Louis Riel paid with his life for his leadership in a movement which fought for the maintenance of the rights and freedoms of the Métis people;

That this House take note that the Constitution Act, 1982, recognizes and affirms the existing aboriginal and treaty rights of the Métis;

That this House take note that since the death of Louis Riel, the Métis people have honoured his memory and continued his purposes in their honorable striving for the implementation of those rights;

That this House recognize the unique and historic role of Louis Riel as a founder of Manitoba and his contribution in the development of Confederation; and

That this House support in its actions the true attainment, both in principle and practice, of the constitutional rights of the Métis people.[33]

Speaking at the unveiling of a Riel statue in front of the Manitoba Legislature on May 12, 1996, Lloyd Axworthy (minister of foreign affairs), likewise said: "For all Canadians, Riel was a Father of Confederation. Promises were made to the Métis that were not kept. As long as I am in a position of power, I will try to make sure that the Métis have full and equal participation in this country."[34] In addition, scholars have increasingly been claiming that First Nations have a historical right to assert special status within the Confederation.[35]

This is not to say that legal and social acknowledgment of Aboriginal rights has occurred at a pace commensurate with the recognition that change must occur, but only that for the first time in Canadian history, an authentic language of foundational cultural heterogeneity has begun to infuse public discourse in what must be regarded as a significant and potentially constructive fashion. Memory is the foundation of thought and action. It is, in the first instance, the mode by which the past is compressed into a language suitable for collective orientation, while also providing a practical template for action and subsequent thought. As Hannah Arendt put it:

Experiences and even the stories which grow out of what men do and endure, of happenings and events, sink back into the futility inherent in the living world and living deed unless they are talked about over and over again. What saves the affairs of mortal men from their inherent futility is nothing but this incessant talk about them, which in its turn remains futile unless certain concepts, certain guideposts for future remembrance, and even for sheer reference, arise out of it.[36]

An issue of collective memory—and its influence on human agency—rests in the balance as Canadians have begun to speak of unavoidable, and foundational, cultural heterogeneity; and this emerging "guidepost" can be discerned in a number of dramatic changes that have occurred in Canada's relationship to its Native population. J. R. Miller has noted that Aboriginal Canadians had become, by the turn of the twenty-first century, a constant presence within wider Canadian consciousness. In all sectors of the news media, and within public deliberations, First Nations issues were principal features, highlighting legal battles over land claims and treaty rights, social ills within Aboriginal communities, and initiatives aimed at bringing the federal government and Roman Catholic Church to account for the abuses perpetrated against Aboriginal peoples within the residential school system. In 1999, for instance, among the year's major news stories were the creation of the Aboriginal territory of Nunavut and the federal ratification of the Nisga'a treaty in British Columbia; while reports of legal contests over land and treaty rights were ongoing. The creation of Nunavut, in particular, was a striking moment in state development whereby the North-West Territories was divided into two distinct territories. The possibility had been discussed for decades, and on April 1, 1999, the central and eastern part of the Territories (a region constituting nearly one-fifth of Canada's land mass) was established as the Territory of Nunavut, marking the largest Aboriginal land claim settlement in Canadian history. The creation of Nunavut effectively gave the population (85 percent of which was Inuit) control over education, heath and social services, and management of natural resources.[37]

In light of this developing discourse (and the practice that reflects it), it seems clear that the idea of a nation-state is problematic in Canada. A confederation, rather than a nation-state, may be the best-suited geopolitical construction for dealing effectively with the nature of such a state, with its multiple founding nations and notable diversity of ethnicity, region, and language. It may be, however, that the attempt to formulate overarching national discourses and a collective commitment to regarding the country as a modern nation-state has undermined the initial idea of the Confederation, which reflected the historical experience—and recognized the existence—of three distinct cultural bodies (English, French, and Aboriginal). It has also undoubtedly threatened the viability of the structure, insofar as it has provided a catalyst for separatist movements. Given its foundational structure of constitutionally recognized diversity, Canada cannot be a nationally unified state. The *Sentinel & Orange and Protestant Advocate*, for instance, negatively recognized this fact as early as 1889: "As long as Canada has a dual nationality," the Anglophone newspaper claimed, "we cannot become a great and progressive country with common aspirations and an indivisible patriotism."[38]

In spite of the impossibility of national unity, however, Canada can be—and is—a state. It is, further, a state that rests on the acknowledgment of heterogeneity, and its existence depends upon the cultivation of a broad faith in the capacity of the state to serve the best interests of its constituent national parts. Clarkson was undoubtedly correct in noting that the country did not fit the classic model of the twentieth-century multinational state (e.g., India or the Soviet Union), but its political arrangement bears more of a resemblance to such states than to the modern nation-state, and argues for a conscious differentiation between confederations (and perhaps multinational states) and nation-states. Its distinct cultural composition, and the inherent challenges this composition presents to the state, mark it as a different kind of entity in which broad-based configurations of shared national identity are not desirable. Such states face a particular problem that their more unified counterparts do not: consensus cannot be achieved by means of a common cultural orientation; rather, the continuance of such states requires that all their constituent ethnicities, regionalisms, and nationalisms believe that their best interests are being served by their governments and that they are being dealt with fairly by all other nationalist, ethnic, and regional factions.[39] The 1977 Task Force on Canadian Unity adopted a definition of unity that reflects this clear difference between a confederation and a nation-state: "[I]t is the sum of conditions upon which the various communities and governments of Canada agree to support and sustain the Canadian state." From this vantage point, the notion of unity necessarily imparts upon each of the state's cultural components something more than it has in isolation from the collective body. It refers, in the words of the task force, to a harmonious and "just union of constituent elements."[40]

There is no doubt that an authentic confederation, devoid of aspirations toward nationhood, is in a sense a risky kind of union; it is inevitably, as David Taras has suggested in describing Canada, an inherently "fragile political coalition." Nonetheless, it is perhaps well-suited to collective political bodies of the postcolonial era. Taras argues that Canadian unity was threatened in the 1990s when many of the "certainties" of Canadian life (e.g., social welfare, an east-west economic arrangement that unified the nation, the support for the active role of government in Canadian life, and the tradition of political compromise) were thrown into question. He says that Canadians felt a sense of "unease" about the future of their geopolitical project. It may be, however, that there is nothing so very wrong with "uncertainties" and "unease," beyond the fact that they are perennially unsettling. Indeed, they may reside at the foundation of the Confederation project. As Taras himself pointed out later, Canadians seemed to have survived this crisis of the 1990s, experiencing "a new wave of optimism" at the turn of the twenty-first century.[41] There is a good possibility that doubts and apprehensions are foundational elements of this particular state configuration; and, further, that it may not be possible in a postcolonial state to have the kind of cultural or political certainty that is achievable within ethnically, regionally, or ideologically homogenous nation-states.

We noted earlier that there is a direct relationship between collective memory, collective identity, and nationalism, insofar as nations must recover and utilize placed memories so that a necessary form of shared identity can be forged. It is in collectively recalling historical episodes or heroes that a people can form a relationship with one another in spite of often divergent and conflicting aspirations. As Anthony Smith put it: "[N]o memory, no identity; no identity, no nation."[42] Given its inherently divisive potential, I believe that a successful confederation may well require some of the same elements of memory, but as a rule, Canadians have been uncertain about what to do with their past. It has often been said that Canadians lack a shared narrative and collective memory in spite of the fact that they appear to be perpetually consumed by the past. Northrop Frye wryly claimed that, "The past in Canada . . . is like the past of a psychiatric patient, something of a problem to be resolved: it is rather like what the past would be in the United States if it had started with the Civil War instead of the Revolutionary War."[43] The sense of disquietude about the past, and the inability to achieve collective resolution, was expressed also by Michael Ondaatje, who suggested that Canadians are "fixated by the preoccupying image of figures permanently travelling [sic] or portaging their past—we are all still arriving."[44] This sensation of eternally traveling has something to do with a broad inability to arrive at an understanding of the collective past that can nourish a shared sense of—and discourse about—political and cultural identity. Like nation-states, confederations must provide a context for the development of shared memories and identity in order to sustain the logic of even their sovereignty among their constituent communities; but it may be that, unlike a nation-state, the events and heroes of a confederation such as Canada must reflect the country's foundational *disunity*—rather than its unity—to be regarded as authentic representations of its sociopolitical character.

Daniel Francis has suggested that mythic heroes are recognized for their capacity to selflessly serve a society whose best ideals they somehow embody. He believes that such individuals have certainly surfaced in the Canadian context, but not in relation to the collective body. Rather, they have emerged from distinct regions, or within the context of the efforts of marginalized groups to resist oppression of various sorts. To have heroes, Francis has argued, a community must have a coherent and widely accepted historical narrative about itself; but this is something that has been consistently absent from the Canadian situation. For this reason, the mythic Riel is peculiar because his image has been used in the service of a variety of historical narratives that have often been formulated in opposition to one another. He has thus emerged as a "shape-shifter, someone whose story is complex enough to appeal to the kind of fragmented society Canada has become."[45] It has also been suggested that although Riel was propelled into action by a series of clearly defined geographical, cultural, political, and economic issues, he became emblematic of the entire country's unrelenting cultural and ethnic tensions.[46] There is something undeniably true in these claims; but from this perspective, Riel appears only as an incoherent myth, variously called upon to serve competing agendas. Moreover, his service to these divergent interests has elicited a fair amount of criticism. Some have claimed that in recreating Riel as a national symbol, Canadians have obscured his specificity as Métis—something that he himself would not have desired. This assimilation of Riel into a broader Canadian mythic framework has been criticized also for having exploited him in the interest of causes that he himself would never have espoused, especially "the creation of Canada."[47]

Of course, there is no arguing with the fact that Riel's Métis identity is of principal significance; however, the claim that he did not support the Confederation is not accurate. Riel led two uprisings fueled by the desire to enter into the Canadian Confederation on conditions established by the people of Red River and the North-West. He did not resist the Confederation project so much as the mode by which central Canada presumed to define the terms of the territories' entry into the union. Furthermore, during his trial he stressed repeatedly that although he wished to see dramatic changes occur in the North-West and British Columbia, he was concerned that these should occur by constitutional means. His sincere hope, expressed during his trial, was to become a leading political voice in Canada: "I will perhaps be one day acknowledged as more than a leader of the Halfbreeds, and if I am I will have an opportunity of being acknowledged as a leader of good in this great country."[48] Ultimately, Riel did not reject the idea of confederation; rather, he wanted to have a voice in the shape that the state would assume. While it is true that he hoped for a large trial in Central Canada with substantial publicity in order to garner support for his cause, his hope was also, ultimately, to assume a seat in the federal House of Commons (to which he was elected but denied entry on multiple occasions). So, while appreciating fully the fact that Riel was a Métis man caught in a particular historical situation, he was also a Canadian with a sincere desire to influence the profile of a state that he respected and to represent the needs of not only the Métis but every group of Canadians in the territories who were being oppressed by Ottawa. He had no personal vendetta against Canada; his issues were with the nationalist underpinnings of Canadian expansionist political forces. Riel might not have been surprised by the fact that many of the communities he hoped to represent subsequently turned to him as a hero of their particular causes; indeed, it might well have pleased him. In any case, his various mythic representations provide us with an entrée for thinking about Canadian identity differently, just as he himself did.

Our starting point, as was his, is the cultural diversity on which the Canadian state was founded; it is also with the variety of mythic Riels that have emerged from that context. It is precisely his mutable mythic character that points to a kind of coherence at the foundation of his various mythicizations—a set of collective values and a shared conception of the meaning of Canadian history that contain the resources for a discourse of Canadian identity. This is not a notion of identity based on a unified past, as is necessary in a nation-state, but one that concedes the meaning of fundamental disunity in defining the particularity of a confederated people. It is, presumably, because of this formative disunity that Riel has proven to be such a powerful historical and mythic resource. Like the mythic hero we discussed at the outset of this book—the individual who braves a journey (for example, to the underworld) to obtain something of value for a culture— Riel's rise to prominence, and his subsequent execution by the government that he wished to inform and serve, were in some sense a journey to the depths of the Canadian experience; and in the century following his hanging, a great many of his compatriots discovered a man who could provide a language about their experience of being Canadian. Like all heroes, Riel's concern was with those he served (in this case, God and the people being oppressed by the nationalist aspirations of a political regime), and not with himself, in spite of allegations to the contrary during his trial and appeals.

On December 12, 1884, for instance, he and Father André met for a discussion of the situation in the North-West, in the context of which Riel suggested that he had outstanding claims against Ottawa relating to land he had not received as set forth in the Manitoba Act, money owed to him for the period during which he had led the Manitoba government, and money or acknowledgment due to him both for his assistance in subduing a Fenian agitation, in 1871, and for having withdrawn his candidacy from the federal election of 1872 when the federal Conservatives wished to run Georges Cartier in his riding. Perceiving a possible mode of removing Riel from the center of the agitation brewing in the North-West, Father André asked Riel what he would do if his claims were met, and Riel replied that if he received adequate compensation, he would remove himself and return to the United States. The priest informed Riel that he would bring the matter before the federal government; and in the meantime, Riel related the exchange to the South Branch Métis council and, according to Napoleon Nault, gave no indication that he was prepared to return to the United States in the event of compensation. Rather, according to Nault, the group "talked at length about the figure to ask. Charles Nolin thought one hundred thousand dollars, but finally we agreed to settle for thirty-five thousand dollars, the sum which was thought necessary to purchase a printing press and all the equipment to start a newspaper."[49] Less than two weeks later (on December 23) Father André, accompanied by David Macdowell (a member of the North-West Council), returned to talk terms with Riel. In a letter to Dewdney, Macdowell subsequently indicated that he was certain that less than five thousand dollars would be sufficient to satisfy

Riel and effect his departure from the region.[50] Although it is clear that Riel was not interested in personal gain, and that he intended to use any money he obtained to support the cause of the Métis, the issue was central during both his trial and appeal process. In fact, in his comments on the appeal decision of the Court of Queen's Bench of Manitoba, Justice Taylor claimed that the evidence provided by Father André indicated that Riel's concern was not primarily with the Métis but with his own personal financial gain.

> He seems to have had in view, while professing to champion the interests of the Métis, the securing pecuniary advantage for himself. This is evident from, among other circumstances, the conversation detailed by the Rev. Mr. André. That gentleman, after he had spoken of the appellant claiming that he should receive from the Government $100,000, but would be willing to take at once $35,000 cash, was asked . . . [51]

Riel's disregard for his own best interests was obvious also when he faced the Regina court, knowing that a plea of insanity could save his life. He refused to accept the advice of his lawyers, however, believing that it would undermine the legitimacy of the Métis cause. Initial conversations with him convinced his lawyers that their most effective strategy was to have him proven demonstrably insane. The evidence was clear: he had spent two years in Quebec asylums, he entertained delusions of partitioning the Canadian west into a series of new creolized nations, he claimed to have received visions and dreams from God, and had turned his back on the Catholic Church, preferring to establish a new Catholicism based in the Americas. He was described by his lawyers as "a religious maniac," and "an idiot or a religious hypocrite—perhaps both."[52] There is a distinct possibility that if Riel had chosen to acquiesce to the pressure exerted by his lawyers in this respect, he may well have been acquitted. Even without his support, the jury made a plea to Richardson for mercy in sentencing Riel. Three of these jurors subsequently explained to a *Mail* correspondent that although Riel was "not absolutely insane in the ordinary accepted meaning of the word, he is a very decided crank."[53]

The insanity plea was unacceptable to Riel, although he admitted that given the situation, and the fact that he was defending himself in English, he might well be capable of making such a plea believable:

Your Honors, gentlemen of the jury: it would be easy for me to-day to play insanity, because the circumstances are such as to excite any man, and under the natural excitement of what is taking place to-day (I cannot speak English very well, but am trying to do so, because most of those here speak English), under the excitement which my trial causes me would justify me not to appear as usual, but with my mind out of its ordinary condition. I hope with the help of God I will maintain calmness and decorum as suits this honorable court, this honorable jury.[54]

The idea of pleading insanity was repugnant to him, and he fought his lawyers on this point: "Here I have to defend myself," he said at one point when he had reached a deadlock with his own defense team, "against the accusation of high treason, or I have to consent to the animal life of an asylum." When NWMP Superintendent R. B. Deane was questioned at the trial as to whether he had seen evidence of mental imbalance while Riel was in his charge, he replied that he had not. When asked whether he had seen evidence of a sound mind, he answered: "[H]e always gave me the impression of being very shrewd." According to Deane,

As I left the witness-box to return to my place in court, I had to pass the dock, and as I did so Riel said to me, "Thank you, Captain," and he meant it. He particularly resented the imputation of insanity, and did not seem to realize that it was the one hope of saving his life.[55]

Although he had no desire to die, he believed that a guilty verdict and execution would not only establish the fact of his sanity but authenticate his mission. Confinement in an insane asylum, on the other hand, would deny the validity of both.[56] In the end, Riel went to the gallows believing in the justice of his cause and with the certainty that God had sanctioned it. Yet he also died representing many of the experiences and values Canadians ultimately have come to recognize as integral to being Canadian: federal-regional (or federal-provincial) tension, the defining presence of the United States, transcontinental unity based on the experience of marginalization, the foundational meaning of Aboriginality, the multiethnic character of Canadian society, and the valuation of the Confederation.

At the most basic level, the federal-provincial tension Riel and the rebellions represented both at Red River and in the North-West has been a basic feature of Canadian political life since Confederation. Beginning with Macdonald, federal administrations have continually attempted to persuade Canadians generally that they are, in spite of their provincial affiliations, members first of a larger political body, administered by a federal government dedicated to treating all Canadians fairly, wherever they may live in Canada. Concomitantly, provincial politicians and advocates have continuously called Canadians to relate themselves principally to their more circumscribed provincial governments as bodies primarily obligated to representing their immediate interests.[57]

It has also been a defining fact that the United States has been a constant and significant presence in the Canadian psyche for most of the country's history. As we noted earlier, a common theme within discourses of national identity has been its relative nonexistence except with respect to a somewhat twisted sense of self-definition based on *not* being American. In addition, it has been argued often that a principal reason for a lack of constructive collective identity has been the result of the permeating influence of American culture and money, which Canadians have often willingly consumed while lamenting the fact that a coherent identity has not been possible under these circumstances.[58] Riel harbored the same ambivalent attitude toward the United States, recognizing that "[t]he door is wide open towards the south."[59] During the hostilities of 1885, he appears to have seriously entertained the possibility of uniting with the United States:

> [C]ommercially and politically the United States Government have done more for the North-West than ever England did. . . . Resolved, first, that our union is, and always will be most respectuous [*sic*] towards the American Government, their policy, their interest and towards the territorial Government of Montana as well. 2nd That our union will carefully avoid causing any difficulty whatever to the United States and will not conflict in any way with the constitution and laws of the Government. It is doubtful whether England really owns the North-West, because the first act of government that England ever accomplished over the North-West was to give it as a prey to the sordid monopoly of the Hudson Bay Company, two hundred years ago. Her second act of government of any importance over that country was to give It in 1870 as a prey to the Canadians. Our union is, and always will be most respectful towards the American annexation, against England and Rome.[60]

In addition, he spoke often about bringing immigrants from south of the forty-ninth parallel to populate the North-West, but during his trial he claimed that this was not his preferred option. If he was dealt with fairly, he informed the court, he would "go perhaps to the Dominion ministry, and there instead of calling the parties in the States, [I] will by means, constitutional means of the country, invite the same parties from Europe as emigration."[61] Ultimately, he admitted in his diary in the spring of 1885 that he distrusted the United States. Describing a vision he experienced, he wrote:

> I turned around to go back to where I came from. An area around me was clear and open; all the rest of the ground swarmed with snakes. There were more snakes than I could count. Oh, it is a dangerous step to ask the Americans for help. Beware of adventurers from the United States. For I assure you they are to be feared. They have neither morals, nor faith, nor heart. They are dirty dogs, foul jackals, ravishing wolves, raging tigers.
>
> O my God! Save me from the misfortune of getting involved with the United States. Let the United States protect us indirectly, spontaneously through an act of Your Holy Providence, but not through any commitment or agreement on our part. . . . The United States are hell for an honest man.[62]

One of the most striking ways in which Riel epitomized elemental aspects of the Canadian experience was in relation to the country's association with marginalized communities. Riel himself was a peripheral man, representing a marginalized community in a marginalized region; but he was also a man who believed deeply that Canada could accommodate the meaningful presence of French Canadians, Native peoples, and the Métis. It could also be the home of marginalized European Catholics: "The good Christians of France," for instance, "to whom the faith remains dear and who experience every day greater and greater difficulties in practicing their religion, would turn to Canada." If they were willing to convert to his new form of Catholicism, Riel also believed that it would "be delightful to see rising up on firm ground across from there a new Judea for Jews."[63]

Riel has been referred to as a symbol of the liminality that characterizes Canadian life; and it has even been suggested that he should be considered prototypically Canadian because the oppression of minority groups is a characteristic feature of Canadian life.[64] Although this may be going a little beyond the norm, Riel has nonetheless been regarded as a marginal figure, representing the interests of marginal people within a country of marginal communities. George Woodcock called Riel "the personification of a besieged minority," who is appealing because "most Canadians see themselves as members of besieged minorities." John Coulter wrote that in Riel he "saw the shape of a Canadian myth," a heroic individual driven by his conviction that God had chosen him to defend a peripheral community; and Margaret Atwood rather lightheartedly suggested that "Riel is the perfect all-Canadian failed hero—he's French, Indian, Catholic, revolutionary and possibly insane, and he was hanged by the Establishment."[65] What underlies all these descriptions is the fact that most Canadians (that is, Francophones, Aboriginals, peoples of color, and immigrants) have, in some way or another, felt the pressure of living on the periphery; and, of course, all Canadians have perennially felt the strain of maintaining an autonomous society and culture on the doorstep of the United States.

In addition, and although a relatively long time in coming, the late twentieth century saw the emergence of a distinct awareness on the part of nonnatives that Native Canadians represented a foundational meaning of the country. Native Canadians were essentially powerless with respect to Canada's political and judicial structures until the middle of the twentieth century. They were not permitted, for instance, to vote in federal elections until 1960; and between 1927 and 1951, they were not permitted to enter into legal contests over treaty rights with the government. During this period, lawyers were subject to prosecution and financial penalties if they chose to represent Aboriginal claims involving a government, or if they were involved in soliciting funds in support of such a claim.[66] The lack of rights and visibility that characterized the Native community for the first half of the twentieth century began to shift when it became obvious that many First Nations were living on land that was economically or militarily valuable. As J. R. Miller has pointed out, negotiations with First Nations were necessary for the construction of both the Alaska Highway by the U.S. Army Corps of Engineers and an oil pipeline into Yukon Territory during World War II. By the middle of the decade, an economic boom based on the exploitation of oil and gas, minerals, and hydroelectric power on Native land brought nonnative Canadians head to head with First Nations who had not, in many instances, entered into treaty for the lands they occupied. The confrontation that ensued resulted in the reentry of Native Canadians into the public psyche, a shift that was epitomized by a confrontation between Quebec and the James Bay Cree in the early 1970s. The James Bay hydroelectric project, backed by the Quebec government, was brought to a stop in 1972 when the Cree obtained a court injunction to halt construction. Despite the fact that the ruling was overturned, the message that Aboriginals could no longer be disregarded in the interest of economic expansion was unavoidable.

Although Native peoples began serious efforts to organize themselves at a national level in the early 1920s, it was not until the 1930s and 1940s that they were able to successfully create a number of organizations aimed at achieving recognition of their rights. Their efforts were provided with an impetus by the 1951 repeal of the Indian Act's ban on soliciting funds for land claims disputes, a change in law that made efforts aimed at organizing less complicated, and led to the establishment of the National Indian Council in 1961. In 1968, the organization was reconceived as the National Indian Brotherhood, and in 1982 it was again reorganized as the Assembly of First Nations. As noted previously, First Nations' organization and politicization would take a dramatic step forward as a result of the Trudeau government's ill-fated White Paper of 1969, a proposal for a new government policy concerning First Nations that was released formally by Indian Affairs minister Jean Chrétien in the summer of 1969. The white paper essentially outlined a plan by which First Nations could be legally eliminated through the repeal of their special status and their unique relationship with the government, the conclusion of treaties, and the turning over of responsibilities for Native education and health and welfare to provincial governments.

A broad protest was mounted by the National Indian Brotherhood, in the context of which Aboriginals from across Canada contended that the proposed legislation would negate their traditionally special relationship with the Crown while forcing them into an undesirable association with provincial governments that had rarely demonstrated sympathy toward their interests. The federal government's shelving of the plan was a definitive triumph for the National Indian Brotherhood and resulted in a significant improvement of its image among Aboriginal peoples across Canada. By the early 1970s, the organization had achieved another victory when the federal government agreed to allocate funds to the organization annually to support operational costs. The financial stability this provided allowed the Brotherhood to focus its attention on pursuing its political aims. The desire to revise the Canadian Constitution was a political focus of the 1970s, 1980s, and early 1990s, and it served to thrust Native peoples into the public sphere in a way that they had not been for over two hundred years.[67]

Aside from the obvious publicity that attended their demands for inclusion in the process of revision, the recognition of treaty and Aboriginal rights (based on prior occupation of continent) within the text of the new constitution dramatically altered First Nations' legal bargaining position, a turn of events that has continued to have repercussions into the twenty-first century. In essence, constitutional recognition confirmed what Riel had claimed nearly a century earlier while standing trial: "God is master of the universe," he said.

> [H]e gives a portion of his lands to that nation, to that tribe . . . that is his heritage, that is his share of the inheritance [*Aboriginal rights*].

> When [Anglophones] have crowded their country because they had no room To stay any more at home, it does not give them the right to come and take the share of all tribes besides them [*treaty rights*].

> [L]et it be well understood that as my right has been acknowledged as a co-proprietor of the soil with the Indians, I want to assert that right [*the Métis as Aboriginal peoples*].[68]

Moreover, he experienced a vision in the spring of 1885 in which he realized both "the extent of the rights which the Indian possesses to the land of the North-West," and the fact that "the extent of the Indian rights, the importance of the Indian cause are far above all other interests."[69]

By the beginning of the twenty-first century, the Canadian public had certainly not reached a point where it would wholeheartedly concur with Riel, but the fact remains that Aboriginal Canadians had become, by that time, a constant part of the wider Canadian consciousness. Constitutional (and subsequent judicial) recognition of treaty and Aboriginal rights was also recognition of an antecedent Native presence within the Canadian state, a foundational meaning that had been disregarded for a very long time. Although First Nations peoples were unsuccessful in enacting the kind of constitutional recognition they desired (primarily, the principle of self-government), the changes that were made to Canada's constitutional framework in 1982 enabled them to make use of the Canadian courts in advancing their interests in an unprecedented fashion; and in recent years, the courts have been noticeably critical of the Canadian government for failing to discharge its "trust responsibilities" as specified in the Indian Act. The Guerin Decision is a prime example in this regard. In 1956, the Shaughnessy Heights Golf Club wished to lease one hundred and sixty-two acres of land from the Musqueam Reserve, located on four hundred and sixteen acres of land in the city of Vancouver. The band requested that the Department of Indian Affairs represent its interests in negotiations with the country club, and within a few months an agreement had been reached between the club and the department. Members of the band were not satisfied with the terms of the draft agreement, which clearly favored the Shaughnessy Golf Club, and they provided Indian Affairs with a list of conditions they wanted met in the final lease; but the department utterly ignored this request and finalized the agreement. It subsequently managed to keep the band from obtaining a copy of the lease for twelve years. A copy was finally provided to the band in 1970, and in 1975 Chief Daniel Guerin, on behalf of his band, challenged the Department of Indian Affairs for having failed to adequately disclose details concerning the lease. In the subsequent lawsuit against the Canadian government, the court ruled in Guerin's favor, awarding ten million dollars in damages to the band.[70] The Canadian government appealed the court's decision in the appeal division of the federal court, and was successful in having the ruling overturned; but the band followed suit, appealing to the Supreme Court of Canada, which overturned the lower court ruling, saying, "In obtaining without consultation a much less valuable lease than that promised, the Crown breached the Fiduciary obligation it owed the Band. It must make good the loss suffered in consequence."[71]

There were other cases in the latter part of the twentieth century that made notable inroads toward recognition as well. During the 1950s and 1960s, nonnative development of natural resources created confrontations with First Nations, and the result was a sharp increase in arrests of Native people who continued to exercise traditional hunting and fishing rights. Clifford White and David Bob (two members of a Vancouver Island Nanaimo band), for instance, were charged with violating the terms of the Game Act (hunting without a license during the off-season) and the case was taken to the Supreme Court of British Columbia. On the basis of a series of nineteenth-century treaties, which stipulated that Aboriginals were "at liberty to hunt over the unoccupied lands, as formerly," the court ruled that the treaty agreements could not be abrogated by the provincial government; and since the two men had been apprehended with six deer in their possession, the ruling at least tacitly implied that Natives had the right to commercial harvest. *Bob and White* was a crucial decision that laid the foundation for subsequent land claims such as, for instance, *Calder, 1973*. Frank Calder, on behalf of the Nisga'a, demanded that, since no treaty had ever been negotiated with the Canadian government, the federal government acknowledge Nisga'a ownership of their traditional land base. The Supreme Court was split, and the deciding vote, based on a technicality, produced a ruling against the Nisga'a. In the immediate wake of the case, however, public support for the Nisga'a was sufficiently strident that Prime Minister Pierre Trudeau and his Indian Affairs minister Jean Chrétien initiated land claims negotiations with British Columbia and northern First Nations who had never entered into treaty agreements with the government. Twenty-seven years after the initial claim, the Nisga'a secured a treaty.[72]

Another landmark First Nations decision of the period was *Marshall, 1999*. In the mid-1990s, a Mi'kmaq man, Donald Marshall Jr., was found guilty in the Nova Scotia Court of Appeal of fishing eels out of season, fishing without a license, and fishing with an illegal net (by implication, for sale). A team of lawyers (four of whom were Mi'kmaq[73]) took the case to the Supreme Court of Canada, where the federal government argued that by treaties negotiated in 1760 and 1761, the Mi'kmaq had willingly made themselves subject to British—and then Canadian—law, and so were bound by subsequent provincial and federal laws. The court ultimately disagreed, and in September 1999 it upheld Marshall's right to catch and sell fish in accordance with the treaties.[74]

Cases involving the Métis also began emerging in the 1990s. A Saskatchewan case, that of *Morin and Daigneault, 1996*, established the Métis right to harvest in one particular situation, but was not necessarily applicable to the rest of the province; and *McPherson, 1992*, established the Métis right to harvest in the northern part of Manitoba.[75] An important case involving the Métis revolved around the arrest of Steve and Roddy Powley who, in 1993, killed a moose in contravention of Ontario hunting regulations. The two men argued that they had the right to hunt for food regardless of provincial laws by virtue of Section 35 of the Canadian Constitution, and in September 2003 the Supreme Court of Canada ruled in their favor, affirming that the Métis who lived in the area of Sault Ste. Marie had an Aboriginal right to hunt for food according to Section 35. This was the first decision made by the Supreme Court that upheld the right of the Métis to hunt on the basis of Aboriginal right as established by the Constitution Act, 1982.[76]

As the twentieth century drew to a close, Aboriginal Canadians had established a level of visibility they had not commanded since the earliest periods of colonial expansion. In a sense, their overt presence in the broader Canadian consciousness on the eve of the twenty-first century was not a new phenomenon, but reflected a relationship between Natives and Europeans that, as J. R. Miller has noted, had been established during their earliest interactions. First Nations peoples were essential to the survival of earliest colonial enterprise in Canada, and they remained a distinct presence within the consciousness of European immigrants until political or economic factors shifted the needs of colonial Canadians. This occurred at various times across the country, with Maritime Canada leading the way when the English wrested firm control of the region from the French in the 1760s and eliminated the need for Native allies in their contest for colonial domination. A similar need for Native allies ended in central Canada after the War of 1812; and in the west, the transition to a wheat-based economic structure enacted the same shift after mid-century. This was followed by the development of mining, first in British Columbia and finally in the north. These political and economic transitions effectively removed Native peoples from the interests and consciousness of nonnative Canadians. By the latter part of the twentieth century, however, having survived a period of imposed obscurity, Aboriginals reentered the public arena and had claimed a legitimate modern space within the sphere of Canadian self-consciousness; and, increasingly, Canadians were beginning to recognize that Aboriginal peoples constituted a third nation—alongside the French and English—with claims to sovereignty and self-government.[77] In fact, the Task Force on Canadian Unity (1979) went so far as to refer to Native peoples as "the country's real founders."[78]

Although it is unlikely that all Canadians would make the same statement at this point in time, most would agree with Riel in saying that Canada was a multiethnic state from the outset, constructed on the basis of at least three founding peoples. Canadians are generally aware of the fact that their state differs from most nation-states insofar as these other states do not cultivate the rights of cultural or linguistic minorities, and their governments attempt as much as possible to eliminate this kind of diversity in the interest of maintaining a unified state. In addition to the

presence of millions of people of disparate ethnicities, Canada is, fundamentally, a state composed of pronounced regionalisms and "distinct societies" with national consciousnesses; and these have managed to remain
within a unitary state framework. It has been argued that this is a multicultural phenomenon that is definitively Canadian: cultural and linguistic diversity, claimed Thomas Berger, have constituted the "essence of the
Canadian experience." Berger also claimed that ethnic diversity resides at
the center of Canadian public life, an assertion that certainly seems to have
been confirmed by Adrienne Clarkson on the occasion of her installation
as governor general.[79] The office of governor general was created by the
colonial British, and it was Jeffrey Amherst who held office first in Canada,
assuming the position in 1760. Yet, in her installation speech, Governor
General Clarkson claimed that the office had its foundation in New France:
"I take on the responsibility of becoming Canada's twenty-sixth governor
general since Confederation, fully conscious of the deep roots of this office,
stretching back to the governors of New France, and to the first of them,
Samuel de Champlain."[80] Clarkson's desire to locate the political foundations of the state in the French colonial enterprise betrayed a deep sensitivity to the need for the acknowledgment of the country's multiethnic
origins, even with respect to its firmly British political structure.

There is no doubt that Riel represented a number of collective experiences that reside at the core of the Canadian people; yet what is perhaps
most resonant is the fact that he deeply believed that a form of political
union could exist that would acknowledge the definitive meaning of the fundamental dichotomies of Canadian life revolving around federal-regional
and Canada-U.S. tensions, the shared experience of marginalization, and
the foundational meanings of Aboriginality and ethnic multiplicity. Riel
believed in a form of geopolitical order—that of a confederation—that could
accommodate these experiences. This belief was one that was also present
at the founding of the Canadian state, variously articulated throughout the
Confederation period and confirmed at the time of the formative North-
West Rebellion, in spite of competing discourses to the contrary. It has also
remained a unifying value of the Canadian people. The desire to create a
political structure that was unencumbered by the "excesses" inherent in
the U.S. Constitution was a concern that cut across party lines during the
Confederation debates, and it was generally articulated in terms of protections for minority groups within the national framework. Macdonald concerned himself with the rights of the wealthy: "The rights of the minority

must be protected, and the rich are always fewer in number than the poor." Richard Cartwright, a Liberal who shared Macdonald's concern with potential majority abuses of power, conceived of the issue perhaps a little more broadly: "Our chiefest care must be to train the majority to respect the rights of the minority to prevent the claims of the few from being trampled underfoot by the caprice or passion of the many." This latter formulation of the challenge left open the possibility of recognizing disempowered minorities—Francophones and Catholics outside Quebec, Anglophones and Protestants in Quebec, Native and Métis peoples, or immigrants—as groups requiring specific protections within the larger sociopolitical body.[81]

By the time of the North-West Rebellion in 1885, there is no doubt that Anglo-Saxon nationalism was beginning to flourish in Ontario; but it did not ultimately manage to override this deep-seated sense of the nature of a confederation as a structure designed to serve the best interests of all its cultural and regional constituents. In fact, the notion that the federal government had an obligation to respect the desires of the people of the North-West was a conviction that was notably present in the central Canadian press. Moreover, the belief that the Métis in particular had just cause for the grievances that led to the uprising was broadly held in the province, in spite of the firm contention that the insurrection had to be quelled and its leaders brought to justice: "[L]et us not forget the grievances which stirred these men to this dreadful extreme step," warned the *Ottawa Free Press*, while the *London Advertiser* added that their suffering "extenuates the offence of the rank and file at least."[82] The *Toronto Globe* was more critical in its condemnation of government policy:

> If the people of the North-West had been treated with due consideration, if due respect had been shown for their rights and for themselves, there would have been no Red River rebellion. . . . Sir John Macdonald's own inclinations led him to attempt the establishment of an arbitrary, irresponsible Government. . . . If he had given the people self-government, at first, as he did afterwards, and assured them that their right to the properties they held would be respected, rebellion or resistance would not have been thought of.
>
> The Halfbreeds some time ago adopted a series of resolutions in which their grievances were set forth, and their wishes were expressed. They have frequently held public meetings since. They

have employed all the usual constitutional means of gaining the attention of the Government, and obtaining redress of what they believe to be intolerable grievances. We are not prepared to say that everything they asked in those resolutions should be done, although it does seem that when lands were set apart for the Métis in Manitoba, the Métis in other parts of the North-West should have had as much done for them. . . . Sir John probably thought it a matter of little moment that those people were dissatisfied. Mr. Dewdney, who loves to play the role of arbitrary monarch, in all probability offended them and increased their discontent if he condescended to take any notice of them or of their proceedings.[83]

Editorials across the province made pronouncements such as "Sir John Macdonald is quite as much as his friend Riel responsible for all that have occurred within the last few weeks"; if the "[g]overnment had adopted a sound, sensible policy, and had selected intelligent, honest, earnest men to carry it out, there would have been no rebellion"; and "the present Ottawa government should be held directly responsible to the country for the late bloody and cruel rebellion, and indirectly responsible for the necessity of the execution of Louis Riel."[84]

In spite of widespread terror over the prospect of an Indian war, there were nonetheless voices in central Canada who likewise called the federal government to account for the Native hostilities occurring in the North-West. A report on a sermon preached by a prominent Toronto minister, Rev. C. B. Pitblado, in April 1885, for instance, quoted him as saying that Native peoples were starving to death and had remained patient longer than most nonnatives would have under the same circumstances. "Government exists in this country by the suffrages of and for the well-being of the commonwealth," he was reported to have said,

> and not for the benefit of the rulers or of the favoured few. . . . The wandering Indian of the Saskatchewan Valley is entitled under our constitutional government to the same legal rights and privileges so far as protection from wrong is concerned as the millionaire who treads the marble halls of his lordly mansion.[85]

In the aftermath of the uprising, the *Week* was noticeably critical of the verdict in Poundmaker's trial, claiming that the case against the man had been "very weak and inconclusive." Given that the Canadian forces had initiated hostilities against him and his band at Cut Knife, the newspaper suggested that the charges had been ill-advised and that he had been convicted solely on the grounds that he was Native: "[I]t is very doubtful whether there has not been a great injustice done to a man who was our friend throughout . . . and yet this man is condemned as a felon to imprisonment for three years, and because he is an Indian not a voice was raised to say one word for him."[86] In spite of the fact that central Canada wholeheartedly supported the suppression of the outbreak of violence in the North-West, it was to some degree the mode of dissent, not the grounds for it, which elicited this response. There were, consequently, many voices like these that called for an assumption of responsibility by the federal government for not having fulfilled its obligations to an ethnically and regionally marginalized population that they regarded as part of the Confederation.

For their part, the Métis were resolutely committed to the Confederation; they resisted impulses toward both national independence and amalgamation with the United States in 1869–70 and 1885, a stance they assumed because they believed that they could exist as a national body within the larger Canadian polity.[87] Even this fact was not entirely lost on central Canada. Considering the impending trial of Riel, for instance, the *Daily News* declared in mid-May 1885:

> Riel will certainly not be tried according to martial law, as it has not yet been officially declared in connection with the North-West troubles. Riel will probably be tried for high treason or for complicity in the murder of some of the killed. In his trial if Riel has fair play it will be a very difficult thing to make him out a rebel as he always claimed to be a loyal subject fighting not to sever his connections from the confederation, but to attach himself to it all the more, the principle clause of his programme being that the territories of the North-West should be formed into one province with representatives at Ottawa.[88]

This geopolitical vision of Canada, articulated at the state's formal inception and during the decisive period of the North-West Rebellion, was buttressed by the belief that a form of political union could exist that would acknowledge the definitive meaning of the fundamental dichotomies underlying the Confederation project. Subsequent nationalizing and politically centralizing tendencies failed ultimately to take root in any widespread and sustained fashion. Wilfrid Laurier, who had surfaced as a political contender in the immediate aftermath of—and on the basis of reaction to—Riel's execution, was a prime illustration of this underlying vision. Emerging from a context of Conservative Party and imperialist formulations of nationalism at the turn of the twentieth century, Laurier rose to prominence on the basis of a vision of the country as one in which "all the races, all the creeds and all the religions" would feel themselves unified by an overriding sense of "liberty." In an effort to protect the rights of minorities, he sought constitutional means of ensuring that provincial parliaments "be absolutely free of each other, and free from supervision." He regarded the relationship between federal and provincial legislatures as one in which "there is no superiority and inferiority; all are equal, with this exception that the Dominion Parliament is invested with larger powers, that is, powers of a more extended and more important character than the local legislature."[89]

Merle Curti suggested that John Locke was "America's philosopher," insofar as the nation's political consensus was created on the basis of Lockean ideals, and wherein the state was conceived of as the definitive articulation of a cultural or ideological orientation. Allan Smith suggested that, in the spirit of Curti, the British historian Lord Acton might be considered Canada's philosopher, since Canadians have generally assumed an Actonian viewpoint in relation to their state, requiring that it not be identified with any particular subculture or ideological position. Writing on the eve of the inception of the Canadian state, Lord Acton claimed that "the coexistence of several nations under the same state is the test as well as the best security of its freedom. . . . [W]e must conclude that those states are substantially the most perfect which . . . include various distinct nationalities without oppressing them."[90] Smith was overly confident in defining Canada fully in Actonian terms, but his point was well taken: to the extent that it has survived as a modern state, it has been because of this political expectation, while the forces that have threatened its continued viability have tended to emerge on the basis of nationalist formulations that run in opposition to this. In an Actonian state, a man like Riel can be a powerful symbol; regardless of the specificities of his portrayal, Riel has generally emerged on all accounts as (in the words of Adrienne Clarkson) a figure who "helped to lay the framework for minority rights—and as a result for cultural cooperation—in this country."[91]

The Canadian Confederation has weathered almost a century and a half, but its continued viability is not a certainty by any means. The particular experiences that underlie its logic—experiences of regional, ethnic, and national diversity—require ongoing formal acknowledgment if the political arrangement is to survive. There must be, as Riel said, "respect" at not only a cultural and social level, but at a structural level; and increasingly, it is becoming clear that many Canadians are losing faith in Canada's capacity to do this. The number of Québécois, for instance, who have expressed this kind of loss of faith in the state's capacity to protect their distinct identity within the Confederation and their position as one of the country's founding peoples has steadily increased since the 1960s. Concomitantly, the desire to reconstitute Quebec as a sovereign nation has also intensified, a situation made dramatically clear by the increased support for sovereignty-association (whereby Quebec would declare itself a sovereign state while sustaining a political and economic association with Canada) that was expressed in the referendum on the issue in October 1995, as opposed to that of May 1980. In 1980, 60 percent of Quebec voters rejected sovereignty-association, while in 1995 only 50.6 percent voted in favor of remaining within the Confederation. This was, obviously, no victory for Canada at all. The remaining 49.4 percent sent a clear message to the rest of the country that it did not regard the Confederation as a political arrangement that served the best interests of French Canadians in Quebec. The central issue for this segment of the population was the need for identifying Quebec as a distinct society representing an identifiable nationality within the Confederation.[92]

Quebec's sense of cultural distinctiveness lies at the foundation of its attitude toward the Confederation, a political arrangement that was made palatable in 1867 through the assurances of Francophone backers of the scheme that it would result in the establishment of a definitively French-dominated province with its own civil law and elected parliament. The Confederation was regarded as an "alliance" that would result in the constitutionalization of a French province within a broader state structure. The motivation to sustain a distinct Francophone society within the Confederation hinged on the ability of Quebec to establish itself as a recognized French society within the new political body. Silver has noted that contemporary Québécois do not necessarily aspire to a dismantling of Confederation but a realization of its original intention to create a state within which multiple societies could have their interests best served. This is, as Silver has said, an "old and legitimate" conception of what Canada was intended to be. Neither bilingualism nor multiculturalism at a state-wide level were the goals of the French in Quebec at the time of Confederation. In fact, they clearly identified their province as the locus of French culture within the broader alliance; and French federal members of Parliament were expected to place the interests of Quebec, rather than those of their individual constituents, at the center of their agendas. Section 133 of the BNA Act, which specified the use of French in federal institutions, was regarded as entirely consonant with this understanding of the Confederation as an "association" between a Francophone province and a group of Anglophone counterparts. It was, however, only a political "association" between multiple cultures, not a union that required cultural conformity. Consequently, the people of Quebec have long known that the Confederation is not an insoluble union, but one of expediency.[93]

The loss of faith in the capacity of the state to function in the best interests of its citizens was apparent at the end of the twentieth century not only in the undeniable stalemate between English Canada and Quebec, but in the efforts of Aboriginal peoples to gain recognition of their history and distinct status within the Canadian polity. Their increasing demands for self-government and separate systems of justice posed a critique of the Confederation that could not be ignored; and the traditional view of Aboriginals as a controllable minority became progressively untenable in the face of demands for recognition as a discrete community with whom the Canadian judicial system has dealt in bad faith.[94] As the century drew to a close, it was clear that there were serious chinks in the armor of the Canadian state, and these had to be overcome for the state to remain viable.

In a vision he recorded in April 1885, Riel foresaw the potential impact of Canada's inability to structurally accommodate its various ethnic and regional constituencies:

> I have seen the giant; he is coming, he is hideous. It is Goliath. He will not get to the place that he intends to occupy. I see him: he is losing his body, he is losing all his men. Nothing but his head remains. Because he will not humble himself, his head is cut off.[95]

For the Confederation to survive through the twenty-first century, it will require that Canadians continue to believe that the arrangement best serves their interests as a community of ethnicities, nations, and regions. Implicated in this is the necessity for a shared language about being Canadian that is situated outside the usual nationalist parameters of, for instance, language or ethnicity, as well as the nationalist tendency to regard differences of social and economic status, geographical situation, or ethnicity as comparatively superficial. In Canada these kinds of differences are deeply significant and, as I have tried to demonstrate, the various mythicizations of Riel point to this fact. Riel has proven to be a ready resource for the articulation of the fundamental dichotomies of Canadian life; but taken together, his various mythic modalities may well provide a foundation for a coherent discourse about what it means to be Canadian.

Conclusion

Within the shared imagination of a people, only those aspects of the past that impinge upon concerns of the present have the possibility of being reanimated and sustained. Perhaps more than most facets of collective memory, mythic heroes speak to this property of collective memory and present valuation; and in this respect, Riel is an exemplary case in point. In spite of his execution at the hands of the Canadian government, the ostensible failure of the Rebellion of 1885, and his disparagement in dominant historical narratives for a good part of the century following his death, Riel has remained alive in the collective imagination; as such, he provides a resource for determining what is of concern to the Canadian people. As the poet Marilyn Dumont put it: "Riel is dead/but he just keeps coming back."[1] Daniel Francis suggested that Riel's story has generally appealed to a society that has no agreed-upon historical narrative: "Riel is a model of what a uniquely Canadian hero has to be . . . someone whose story is complex enough to appeal to the kind of fragmented society Canada has become."[2] While this may be true, I believe that the mythic Riel in all his permutations may suggest a kind of basic ordering that lies beneath the surface of the cultural maze of Canadian society, and that, further, he may well provide a basis for a historical narrative that can coherently approximate the experience of Canada's people.

Canada is a society riddled with dichotomies that have given rise to cultural fragmentation, subnationalisms, ethnic oppression, separatist movements, and organized violent outbreaks ranging from the Conquest, the Rebellions of 1837, the Red River Uprising of 1869–70, and the North-West Rebellion of 1885 to the October Crisis of 1970 and the confrontation at Oka in 1990. It is also a society that has managed, thus far, to endure its intrinsic incompatibilities and remain a viable modern state. As Francis puts it, Canada is "decentralized, unstable, pluralistic, [and] truly democratic."[3] Amid the tumultuous—perhaps even chaotic—cultural and political history that has carried Canada into the twenty-first century, there has been a kind of order, epitomized perhaps by Riel. Looking back to our earlier reference to chaos theory, I would suggest at this point that insofar as Canada is a state system that has exhibited an internal tendency toward unusually complex forms of modern sociopolitical relations, Riel could be said to have become a "strange attractor" in relation to whom an ordered configuration might be discernable. This order revolves around what most Canadians would acknowledge as the central characteristic of their geo-political union: its humanly and culturally radical character, the result of a process of hybridization that I have chosen to call *métissage*. One might argue that this is the most revolutionary aspect of the entire postcolonial world in which Canada finds itself, but few Western states have been so thoroughly enmeshed in it at a structural level.

It has been a constant source of frustration to many Canadians that a collectively recognized historical narrative about the country has not emerged. Granatstein, in spite of his reactionary call for an imperialist narrative, has pointed this out in a particularly astute manner: "The nation is fragile indeed," he writes, "and one reason for this lamentable state of affairs might well be a lack of a history that binds Canadians together. It is not that we do not have such a history. It is simply that we have chosen not to remember it."[4] Daniel Francis has gone a step further, suggesting that the lack of a historical narrative has been related to the country's lack of a "myth of creation."[5] If we were to locate such a myth we would, presumably, find the repository of memories that Granatstein reminds us are out there somewhere, waiting to inform the shape of a collective historical narrative. It is no surprise, then, that at this point I should suggest that we look to the figure of Louis Riel, the man to whom, despite innumerable dissimilar portrayals, Canadians have quite consciously ascribed mythic and religious significance. Across the broad range of ostensibly contradictory Riels, we find a myth that bears a distinct resemblance to the man we have explored in the preceding chapters; and we may well discover that both the man and the myth provide an aperture through which we can discern the foundations for a collective narrative.

The form that this latent narrative might fully assume is obviously impossible to chart, but there are some basic elements that seem immediately obvious. First, Riel as myth leads us to a recognition of a foundational act of violence in the creation of modern Canada—a "myth of creation" perhaps. Canadians have tended to regard their country's lack of a revolutionary heritage as an indication that the state is fundamentally more peaceable than many other modern states. "The Canadian experience," wrote Allen Smith, "has had at its centre accommodation, compromise, and adjustment."[6] While there is undoubtedly much truth in the statement, one cannot disregard the significance of a broadly based memory of violence in the country preserved within the mythicization of Riel and the rebellions. In a curious reversal of a classic patterning of religious violence at the foundation of the state, Riel has undergone a dramatic religious augmentation of meaning since his execution. In his work on sacrifice in Mesoamerica, for instance, Davíd Carrasco noted that a central aspect of the sacred at the city of Tenochtitlán was human sacrifice in which victims were reconfigured as gods prior to their deaths.[7] Riel and the rebellions appear to have undergone this kind of religious valorization, not at the time they transpired but in the century following their defeat by the Canadian government. They have been, however, no less religiously significant. We might ask ourselves why it is that more has been written on Riel and the rebellions than on any other Canadian figure or event; and clearly in some measure our answer would have to be that there is a resonant—and hence foundational—mythic meaning of violence in modern Canada inextricably linked with both the Métis uprisings (especially that of 1885) and the execution of Riel.

Second, our historical narrative would undoubtedly revolve, at least to some degree, around the emergence of modern Canada as an alternative kind of state. This is a model of statehood not tied to the Great Revolutions, but equally legitimate in its capacity to produce an innovative political and social arrangement on the basis of both a seemingly failed instance of civil unrest and a radically altered form of human community created by the colonial enterprise. It is a model that contains multiple ethnicities, languages, regionalisms, and self-designated nations, all of which are formally integrated into the state structure; and so, it is one in which the concept of the nation-state (the most recognized benchmark of geopolitical legitimacy in the modern period) is inappropriate. To varying degrees, this confederated state has also provided an illustration of how a state can deal with the elemental human dichotomies of the postcolonial period. The violence enacted over the course of 1885 established and reified dichotomies of ethnicity, language, and region in a manner that would interminably impact on Canadian political and cultural life. In her discussion of the nature of revolution, Arendt suggests that one of the artifacts of revolution has been the creation of a dichotomous modern political vocabulary stemming from the contradictory aspirations of revolutionaries: (1) the desire for the creation of something absolutely new, and (2) the concern for establishing stability and constancy. She believed that the tendency of modern political language to function in binaries—right and left, conservative and liberal, "reactionary and progressive"—was a direct legacy of revolutions, and that these binaries continued to circumscribe the range of political ideologies possible well into the twentieth century. She argued, further, that the only way in which the full meaning of revolution could be apprehended was through an integration of these binaries into a single discursive framework.[8] Arendt was obviously dealing specifically with revolution, but she nonetheless identified a fundamental property of binary language: it can speak only to a part of reality. While it is true that no modern state has escaped the kind of political binaries of language to which she was speaking, we might add that no postcolonial state has avoided the internal dichotomies of ethnicity, language, location, and contested power relations that have formally characterized the Canadian state. To the extent that Canada has survived its own dichotomies, Canadians have known through experience the truth in Arendt's claim for the necessity of creating a single discourse in which all binary oppositions can be integrated.

From the mid-nineteenth century, for instance, a repeated feature in Canadian political life has been the success of political regimes that have provided the electorate with options that have brought together both English and French voters. It was Louis H. Lafontaine's and Robert Baldwin's Reform Party of the 1840s that won responsible government and managed to maintain power for a decade. Supporters of the largely French-supported Reform Party shifted their support to the Liberal-Conservative coalition of John A. Macdonald and George Etienne Cartier, which maintained political efficacy for nearly a generation until the traditionally English Liberal Party, under Wilfrid Laurier, garnered the support of Quebec voters and maintained it until 1957 through the exploitation of bi-ethnic alliances such as that of William Lyon Mackenzie King and Ernest Lapointe.[9] In a rather profound sense, the capacity to create a hybrid language (political or cultural) of compromise outside the parameters of various nationalist articulations in Canada—perhaps what Riel meant by "respect"—has been the mode by which subsequent Canadians have most often countered the divisive influence of the country's basic dichotomies. "The only possible basis for the solution of our national problems," said Henri Bourassa, in 1900, "is one of mutual respect for our racial characters and exclusive devotion to our common land."[10]

In spite of this recognition, Canadians have not been able to create a consistent and unified language about themselves that has proven capable of integrating the effects of the dichotomous character of their state. Hence, by the beginning of the twenty-first century, its continued viability was no certainty. There is no doubt that the creation of a coherent historical narrative is problematic for a state whose people cannot even agree on its primary defining events. The Conquest of Quebec cannot satisfy Anglophones' need for a foundational moment in their state, just as the Confederation of 1867 will never provide a focus for Québécois nationalists; and, obviously, neither event signals the beginning of modernity for Aboriginal peoples in Canada. This is only the tip of the iceberg. The province of Manitoba was not created by the BNA Act, nor were British Columbia, the Territories, Saskatchewan, Alberta, Prince Edward Island, or Newfoundland, each of which has, to varying degrees, regarded itself as a regional unit situated in an oppositional relation to central Canada. What is necessary, with respect to the creation of a historical and self-defining narrative is, in the first instance, a way of conceding that the state is a product of binary oppositions that are prior to, and explicitly expressed in, the Confederation. Secondarily, a moment of collective inception must be located in which the parameters of modern geopolitical association were established in some fundamental, and broadly acknowledged, fashion. As I have suggested in chapters 5 and 6, it may well be possible to argue that Canada, as a fully modern state, did not come into existence until 1885, that its dichotomous character (which would ultimately inform all aspects of its public life) was congealed at that time, and that it is for these reasons that the 1885 Rebellion and the man who led it have been afforded religious significance in the Canadian imagination.

Riel, however, was a revealer before he was a myth. Writing about the way in which dynamics of concealment might best be undermined, David Carrasco has suggested a prescription that could well have been penned with Riel in mind. It requires, he writes, a shift "away from comfortable dichotomies into an engagement with the nuances, spectrums, and shades of history, meanings, symbols, and power."[11] The man who found himself planted between dichotomies in life, has been a gun for hire in death, serving all of the dichotomies and by extension, none of them. In this sense, Riel has served something more. In him and the rebellions we have the possibility of a foundational myth, and so we have also an entrée to a collective narrative that can represent Canadians' image of their geopolitical association and the kind of identity that is possible within such an association. Myths, after all, make the creation of a common sense of identity possible; as the journalist Robert MacNeil said, "[I]f you're not a storied people, you have no identity really."[12] What this mythic moment, and a narrative constructed from it, would undoubtedly reveal is that in spite of the fact that the maintenance of a coherent modern state with contradictory ethnic and regional elements is not easy, this state of affairs does not undermine its legitimacy. It is simply the way things are. It is, after all, the defining framework of a country that was established before the state itself was conceived. The formal reification of this fundamental contradictory structure of the colonial period coincided with the creation of a modern state; and when Canadians have acknowledged and adapted to the defining property of this character, a sustaining measure of accord has been possible. The viability of the state has been jeopardized, however, when its foundational structures of diverse ethnicity, language, region, and so on have been made the objects of either centralizing political tendencies, attempts at aestheticization (e.g., official multiculturalism) or, conversely, efforts aimed at discounting the significance of the disparities existing among its constituent parts (e.g., the refusal to acknowledge that some communities within the larger order do indeed have "special status"). In other words, problems have emerged when Canadians have equated a confederated state with a nation-state. As a consequence, configurations of collective identity have floundered because they have generally been formulated according to the rules of national discourse in which underlying notions of prevailing ethnic (e.g., Anglo-Saxon) or ideological (e.g., technological) uniformity are definitive.

A conception of collective identity in this situation must take as its starting point the fundamental disunity that defines the Canadian state. Riel is, in this regard, a possible fulcrum on which to balance the need for a unified narrative and the reality of underlying, predetermined incongruity. A historical narrative that would buttress such a conception of identity would have the advantage of being capable of incorporating foundational experiences—experiences such as initial contact between indigenous peoples and Europeans, the European contest for sovereignty in the colonies, the Conquest, alienation of First Nations, Métis, and Inuit peoples from dominant structures of valuation, the Confederation of 1867, the emergence of distinct nationalisms, constitutional reform, and the creation of Nunavut—as well as the day-to-day reality of being or becoming Canadian in the twenty-first century. The creation of such a narrative is not simply a stylistic matter. Without a narrative, a firm understanding of shared identity is difficult to achieve, and in the absence of such structures of language and collective self-understanding, coherent nationalist discourses might ultimately win the day. If this should occur, a model for a potential alternative to the nation-state (which, when all is said and done, is a political configuration quite unsuited to the postcolonial period) will be lost.

Thomas Berger asked in 1981, "Isn't there a distinctive Canadian intellectual contribution to the legal and political order, a product of the encounter between the English and the French in North America, yet distinctive because it represents something essentially Canadian?"[13] In spite of his reduction of the Canadian situation to a primary binary of French-English, Berger was asking an appropriate question. In response, Ramsey Cook would undoubtedly have said: "[T]he value of the Canadian experience is, or at least could be, its explicitly nonnationalist, pluralistic character."[14] While this is true, it has not generally been the way in which discourses of identity have been formulated due, principally, to the fact that Canadians have not commonly ventured to conceive of their state as a "non-nation." Riel, of course, had grand visions of Canada's role as an international model, believing that the Manitoba Act could provide a foundation for the political structures of other modern states. In a letter to the prime minister, which he wrote while in custody, he said,

If my native land [Manitoba] will honour me one day by installing me as its first minister, I shall give you my views. . . . After having inaugurated [my ideas] in the young province, you will be able to examine how my ideas will work. If they are successful, you could generalize them through the nation. Then the Mother Land will be able to judge it. And soon you may have all the glory, and I the pleasure to see them applied to Ireland, by the High Authority of the English Parliament. The principles and the views that I have the honour to speak of, are taking seeds in the constitution, the Manitoba Act.[15]

The formulation of a sustaining historical narrative and notion of collective identity in Canada has been hampered to some degree by a desire to conform to the conventional, and definitive, model of the nation-state. This has undoubtedly obstructed the capacity to explore the potential value of a confederation as an alternate geopolitical arrangement in the postcolonial period. Can Canada provide a model for the state in a world that is still largely defined by the nation-state? It might, but only if it proves capable of remaining intact; and this is to some measure dependent upon the creation of a discursive and ideational framework about the country that affords primary value to its idiosyncratic formalization of colonial disparity. In this regard, as Canada faces the twenty-first century, it might be helpful to recall a moment of epiphany that Riel experienced on the road to Regina after his arrest. Perhaps Riel realized too late that the creation of a modern identity (what he would undoubtedly have regarded as historical redemption) could emerge only from the parameters of a world that was already created. He maintained to the end of his life that this kind of redemption was defined by the humanly radical nature of the postcolonial world, and God's "Providence"; but he also prayed unceasingly for divine intervention. In the end, however, God did not step in to alter the historical events that transpired in the North-West.

At the decisive Battle of Batoche, Riel did not carry a gun. Believing that a miracle would occur, he prayed feverishly and led the women around him in reciting the rosary. A comrade, Patrice Tourond, was said to have called out to Riel toward the end of the battle, "Work your miracle now, it's time." Arms lifted in the sign of the cross, Riel fell to his knees and directed those around him: "All together, let us say three times, very loudly, My God, have pity on us." The others knelt and did as he had instructed while Riel, arms held up by two Métis soldiers, cried out, "My God, stop those people, crush them."[16] Of course, God did not stop the Canadian forces, and the Métis were decisively defeated as they fought an unwinnable battle in which they were dramatically outnumbered, relying in the end on stones and nails for bullets. Under arrest following the rebellion, and traveling to Regina where he would be incarcerated to await trial, Riel realized that he had been mistaken. In the wake of the failed uprising, deliverance might still be possible, but divine intervention was no longer to be hoped for. Redemption, he realized, could occur only within the human parameters of the New World and the working out of an established historical trajectory (which he believed was God's preexisting providential plan for humanity).[17] "Oh my God," he wrote in his diary, "it is you who are waiting for me. And I was doing the opposite by waiting for You."[18]

Notes

Notes to Chapter 1

1. Bumsted, "The 'Mahdi' of Western Canada?" 47. See also D. Morton, *Queen v. Louis Riel*, xv.
2. Sprague, *Canada and the Métis*, 1.
3. According to the *Encyclopedia Canadiana*, 7:53, the term *Métis* derives of the same Latin root (*miscere*) as the Spanish word *mestizo*, meaning "to mix." Its original form was *matives*, and was altered to *métifs* before assuming its final form. Riel himself employed *métisse*.
4. L. H. Thomas, "Louis Riel"; J. Reid, "'Faire Place à une Race Métisse,'" 51.
5. My thanks to Kevin Christiano for clarifying the details pertaining to the death of Jean-Louis.
6. Adams, *Tortured People*, 32; Bumsted, *Louis Riel v. Canada*, 47, 320; Braz, *False Traitor*, 12–13. The Canada Council was the precursor to the Social Science and Humanities Research Council of Canada.
7. Braz, *False Traitor*, 193–97, provides an excellent discussion of the controversy involving these statues.
8. Clark, *A Nation too Good to Lose*, 80–81; cited in Braz, *False Traitor*, 13. See also *Canadian House of Commons*, Monday, October 21, 1996, at: www.parl.gc.ca/english/hansard/087_96-10-21/087PB1E.html (accessed June 2003): On March 9, 1992, the Minister of Constitutional Affairs, Joe Clark, successfully acquired unanimous approval for a resolution stating:

> That this House take note that the Métis people of Rupert's Land and the North Western Territory through democratic structures and procedures took effective steps to maintain order and protect the lives, rights and property of the people of the Red River;

> That this House take note that, in 1870, under the leadership of Louis Riel, the Métis of the Red River adopted a List of Rights;
> That this House take note that, based on the List of Rights, Louis Riel negotiated the terms for admission of Rupert's Land and the North Western Territory into the Dominion of Canada;

> That this House take note that these terms for admission form part of the Manitoba Act;

That this House take note that, after negotiating Manitoba's entry into Confederation, Louis Riel was thrice elected to the House of Commons;

That this House take note that, in 1885, Louis Riel paid with his life for his leadership in a movement which fought for the maintenance of the rights and freedoms of the Métis people.

9. Braz, *False Traitor*, 3, 10–11; Doyle, *From the Gallows*, 183.

10. William Yurko (Edmonton East, C) tabled Bill C-691 on September 23, 1983, an act to pardon Riel; then again on March 14, 1984, Bill C-257; and on December 13, 1984, Bill C-257. Les Benjamin (Regina-Lumsdon, NDP) tabled Bill C-257 and Bill C-217 on June 28, 1984, and December 13, 1984, both calling for the repeal of Riel's conviction. On November 28, 1985, in recognition of the centennial anniversary of Riel's execution, Sheila Copps (Hamilton East, L), who would later serve as deputy prime minister under Jean Chretien, requested a pardon for Riel. Nelson Riis (Kamloops, NDP) tabled Bill C-265 on September 16, 1987, calling for a posthumous pardon. Bill C-417 was put forward in 1998 by federal representatives of each political party with the express purposes of exonerating Riel and formally recognizing his contribution to Canada: "Louis Riel is hereby recognized as a Father of Confederation and the Founder of the Province of Manitoba." Bob Skelly (Comox-Alberni, NDP) tabled a motion on October 13, 1989, requesting that Riel be officially recognized as a Father of Confederation. On November 16, 1994, Suzanne Tremblay (Rimouski-Témiscouata, BQ) introduced Bill C-288 calling for the repeal of Riel's conviction. On February 22, 1996, Minister of Natural Resources (including Métis issues) Anne McLellan spoke in the House of Commons concerning the ways in which Riel had already been recognized as having influenced the development of the nation: stamps, statues (one of which graced the grounds of the provincial legislature and toward the commissioning of which the federal government had contributed $150,000), the arts, and a parliamentary resolution that was passed in 1982 confirming Riel as a founder of Manitoba. On October 21, 1996, Suzanne Tremblay moved a second reading of Bill C-297, intended to revoke Riel's conviction. *Canadian House of Commons*, Monday, October 21, 1996, at: www.parl.gc.ca/english/hansard/087_96-10-21/087PB1E.html (accessed June 2003). See Goulet, *Trial of Louis Riel*, 11.

11. Young, "Indian Problem," 467; Pocock, "The Lean Man," 97; Dickens, *Dickens of the Mounted*, 242.

12. Goulet, *Trial of Louis Riel*, 10.

13. D. B. Smith, "Right Dream, Wrong Time," *Globe and Mail*, December 15, 2001, F6; cited in Braz, *False Traitor*, 13.

14. G. F. G. Stanley, "Last Word on Louis Riel" (1988): 42, wrote that Riel was a personification of "the great themes of our human history." Friesen, *The Canadian Prairies*, 73, describes Riel as being "paramount" among "multicultural heroes"; Newman, "Rewriting History," 48, called him "one of our genuine frontier heroes." The above are cited in Goulet, *Trial of Louis Riel*, 13–14.

With respect to the mythic dimensions of Riel, see Johnson, "Riel in Canadian Drama," 196. Thomas Berger claimed that Riel is "a mythic figure in our history"; Bumsted writes of Riel as a figure of "mythological proportions," and "one of our few mythic heroes"; Mavor Moore has called him Canada's "most famous politico-mythological hero"; Stanley referred to him as a "Canadian legend"; Don Gutteridge regards him as a significant part of Canada's mythic history. See T. Berger, *Fragile Freedoms*, 26; Bumsted, *Louis Riel v. Canada*, 320; Bumsted, "The 'Mahdi' of Western Canada?" 47; Moore, "Haunted by Riel," 413; G. F. G. Stanley, "Last Word on Louis Riel" (1988): 42; Owram, "Myth of Louis Riel"; Gutteridge, "Riel: Historical Man?" 9.

15. Long, "Indigenous People," 169–70.

16. From the School Act, 1859, Section 19, cited in McLaren, "We Had No Desire to Be Set Apart," 38.

17. Arar was deported from the United States as he was returning to Canada from a family vacation through JFK Airport in New York City in October of 2002. He was released from the Syrian prison a year later. A subsequent inquiry revealed that the RCMP had supplied U.S. officials with inaccurate information in the early fall of 2002 and that Commissioner Guiliano Zaccardelli knew of the error almost immediately following the deportation, despite having earlier denied having this information. Zaccardelli resigned over the affair in December of 2006, and the federal government paid Arar $12.5 million in compensation. See CBC News, "In Depth: Maher Arar," at http://www.cbc.ca/news/background/arar/ (accessed March 2007).

18. Du Bois, *Souls of Black Folk*, 186.

19. Flanagan, *Louis "David" Riel*; Riel, *Diaries*; Mossman, "Charismatic Pattern"; Martel, *Le Messianisme de Louis Riel*; Martel, "L'idéologie messianique."

20. As Flanagan noted, the issue of Riel's sanity has too often eclipsed the more important issue of why he led the uprisings of 1869–70 and 1885. He added: "To focus on those questions requires moral judgment. . . . The issues remain the same today. Those who ask whether Riel was 'really crazy' are in effect looking for a way out of this moral dilemma" (Flanagan, "Louis Riel," 115). I would suggest that Riel's religion remains problematic in this perspective, given the focus on the way in which psychological processes (e.g., role playing and sublimation) led him to engage in clearly atypical religious behavior. By categorizing him with other millenarian figures of the modern period, he remains beyond the parameters of what is considered religiously normative and, perhaps more importantly, authentic. This form of messianism is regarded as a mode in which religious experience is entirely a product of social, political, or psychological forces, a self-stylization and imitation: "Riel slipped into the messianic role at times, as when he styled himself the redeemer of the Jews or when he speculated on his own resurrection. But whether as prophet or messiah, he was imitating models of biblical tradition and acting in a way typical of millenarian leaders" (Flanagan, *Louis "David" Riel*, 201). These more recent discussions of Riel's religion as an instance of a marginal and imitative enterprise that is reducible to social or psychological factors raise a significant issue relating to the study of religion in modernity: these arguments ensure that the religious content of his visions, poetry, and the movement that spiraled around him remains significant in an ultimate (rather than purely historical) sense for only a circumscribed group of nineteenth-century people. Hence, while the uprisings and Riel's final execution cannot be extricated from the

meaning—and study—of Canadian history, his visions, poetry, and the insurrections remain removed from the meaning—and study—of religion.

21. On May 2, 1670, Prince Rupert and seventeen aristocrat associates obtained a charter from Rupert's cousin Charles II, creating the Company of Adventurers of England Trading into Hudson's Bay—a mercantile venture that would subsequently come to be known as the Hudson's Bay Company. The charter pertained to a large area (roughly the size of western Europe) that was the watershed of Hudson Bay.

22. G. F. G. Stanley, *Birth of Western Canada*, 42.

23. The site of present-day Winnipeg, Manitoba.

24. The North-West Territory and Rupert's Land were in a distinctly discriminated position within the expanding Dominion. Section 146 of the British North America Act (through which the Confederation had been enacted) defined Newfoundland, Prince Edward Island, and British Columbia as "colonies or Provinces" that could join the Confederation through a combined action by their own and the federal parliaments. The western territories, specified as the North-West Territory and Rupert's Land in the Act, were designated as colonies, and their entry into the Confederation was made dependent solely upon an act of the federal parliament. Section 147 did not include a clause defining territorial representation in the Senate, as was done for the other colonies and provinces. As a consequence, the residents of the region had no voice in the negotiations that had brought about their territorial inclusion in the Confederation. See Bumsted, *Louis Riel v. Canada*, 16.

25. Boulton, *I Fought Riel*, 14–16. Riel's first task, once he had taken control of the *Nor'Wester* press, was to print a public announcement for a meeting, to include his council and twelve delegates chosen from the region's English parishes, to consider a course of action.

26. Arnold, "If Louis Riel Had Spoken in Parliament," 75; Flanagan, *Louis "David" Riel*, 33; Bumsted, "Crisis at Red River," 25; and Manitoba Culture, Heritage, and Recreation, *Ambroise-Didyme Lépine*, 6.

27. Cited in Makela, "Métis Justice Issues," 64.

28. Daniels, *We Are the New Nation*, 15; Makela, "Métis Justice Issues," 64; Beal and Macleod, *Prairie Fire*, 24.

29. Bumsted, *Louis Riel v. Canada*, 151, 182–83; Manitoba Culture, Heritage, and Recreation, *Ambroise-Didyme Lépine*, 6–8.

30. Cited in Bumsted, *Louis Riel v. Canada*, 212. See also Lettre à Ignace Bourget, May 1, 1876, in Riel, *The Collected Writings*, 2:44: "Tu es le David des temps chrétiens dont l'ancien David n'était que la figure."

31. Bumsted, *Louis Riel v. Canada*, 224.

32. D. Morton, *Queen v. Louis Riel*, 361.

33. Bumsted, *Louis Riel v. Canada*, 236–37; Walter, "Hundred Year Controversy of Louis Riel," 25.

34. Rens, *Invisible Empire*, 31; Payment, "Batoche after 1885," 173; Chartrand, "Aboriginal Rights," 472.

35. Bumsted, *Louis Riel v. Canada*, 241.

36. Devine, "The Killing of Joseph Cardinal," 39–42.

37. *Edmonton Bulletin*, February 3, 1883, Bobtail et al. to Macdonald, January 7, 1883. The letter was sent from Bear's Hill (Hobbema, Alberta). Beal and Macleod, *Prairie Fire*, 74–75.

38. Devine, "The Killing of Joseph Cardinal," 44–45; Macleod, *Reminiscences of a Bungle*, xix.

39. Macleod, *Reminiscences of a Bungle*, xxii; Bumsted, *Louis Riel v. Canada*, 242–44.

40. Macleod, *Reminiscences of a Bungle*, xxi–xxii.

41. Bumsted, *Louis Riel v. Canada*, 246–47; G. F. G. Stanley, *Birth of Western Canada*, 265.

42. G. F. G. Stanley, *Birth of Western Canada*, 317.

43. Riel, *Collected Writings*, "Notes for Speech in Prince Albert" (July 19, 1884), 3:10.

44. Riel, *Collected Writings*, "To His Excellency the Governor General, of Canada, in Council" (December 16, 1884), 3:26.

45. G. F. G. Stanley, *Louis Riel v. Canada*, 307.

46. *Daily British Whig*, March 24, 1885. Mika and Mika, *Riel Rebellion*, 4.

47. G. Dumont, *Gabriel Dumont Speaks*, 12.

48. D. Morton, *Queen v. Louis Riel*, 378. Exhibit 14 at Riel's trial: a letter written by Riel.

49. G. Dumont, *Gabriel Dumont Speaks*, 46, 12–13.

50. P. A. C. Dewdney Papers, Crozier to Dewdney, March 13, 1885, 1:348–51; cited in Beal and Macleod, *Prairie Fire*, 137. See also Boulton, *I Fought Riel*, 81–82.

51. Middleton was an Irishman who had a forty-year career of crushing dissident colonized peoples throughout the British Empire. He began his military career at the age of seventeen, serving in a variety of colonial uprisings including that of the Maori in New Zealand in 1846, and the Indian Mutiny of 1857–58, before being sent to Canada in 1861 as a major with the Twentieth Regiment during the Trent Affair. He was recalled to England ten years later, and then returned in 1884 as the commander of the Canadian militia, a post he would hold until 1890. Following the 1885 Rebellion, Middleton received twenty thousand dollars from the Canadian government in recognition of his efforts in the campaign, and he was made a knight commander of St. Michael and St. George. At the time of his death in 1898, he occupied the position of Keeper of the Crown Jewels in the Tower of London. See Middleton, *Suppression of the Rebellion*, xviii–xix; and Collins, *Voice from Afar*, 101.

52. It is fairly clear that Riel and Dumont did not know one another prior to 1884, but their relationship developed quickly during the period of the rebellion. Although they differed dramatically in terms of tactical matters, Dumont's unflagging support for Riel's ultimate goal of achieving recognition of the independent status of the Métis people compelled Riel to appoint Dumont his adjutant general during the military hostilities that ensued. See G. Dumont, *Gabriel Dumont Speaks*, 6–7.

53. G. Dumont, "Gabriel Dumont's Account," 251–53.

54. Collins, *Voice from Afar*, 106.

55. G. F. G. Stanley, "Campaign of 1885," 100; Rens, *Invisible Empire*, 31; Collins, *Voice from Afar*, 102.

56. Middleton, *Suppression of the Rebellion*, xi, xiii; Riel, *Collected Writings*, 5:318; G. F. G. Stanley, *Birth of Western Canada*, 363.

57. Although Middleton would ultimately receive official recognition for his conduct during the confrontation, many involved in the affair were intensely critical of him in the wake of hostilities. A surveyor involved in the confrontation by the name of A. O. Wheeler was critical of Middleton for having failed to take full advantage of the surveyors' skills and consequently delaying the end of the confrontation. Wheeler's colleague Louis Ord felt the same way, referring to the campaign as a "great bungle," and dedicating his book on the event in the following manner: "To the Everlasting Confusion of Red Tape, These Pages are Hopefully Inscribed." R. Burton Deane expressed similar criticism from the perspective of the NWMP, claiming that Middleton had more than sufficient troops to "eat the rebel Halfbreeds, moccasins and all," but was overly apprehensive about taking risks. The regiments under his command felt they were being forced to act foolishly. Waiser, "Surveyors at War," 51; Ord, *Reminiscences of a Bungle*, 23.

58. D. Morton, *Queen v. Louis Riel*, 381; Exhibit 19 at Riel's trial.

59. F. Anderson, "Gabriel Dumont," 5. Joseph Kinsey Howard claimed that the two men gave themselves up to the commanding officer at Fort Assiniboine, on the Montana border. Unsure about how to proceed, the officer telegraphed Washington and President Grover Cleveland responded personally, saying that the two men were to be considered legitimate political refugees and as such, had the right to asylum in the United States. The commissioner was ordered to release them from custody. Howard, *Strange Empire*, 555.

60. *Daily Intelligencer*, August 13, 1885; Mika and Mika, *Riel Rebellion*, 910. See also G. Dumont, *Gabriel Dumont Speaks*, 6–7.

61. Trial transcript, August 1, 1885, in D. Morton, *Queen v. Louis Riel*, 357.

62. F. Anderson, "Gabriel Dumont," 5.

63. Mercier was the founder of Quebec's Parti National, the province's first nationalist political party. He became premier of Quebec late in 1886.

64. G. Dumont, *Gabriel Dumont Speaks*, 7, my translation; F. Anderson, "Gabriel Dumon," 5–6; McLean, *Fifty Historical Vignettes*, 156.

65. D. Morton, *Queen v. Louis Riel*, xvi; D. Smith, "Rip Van Jaxon," 212; Cherwinski, "Honoré Joseph Jaxon," 124–33; Beal and Macleod, *Prairie Fire*, 339–40.

66. Stonechild and Waiser, *Loyal till Death*, 2–3.

67. Collins, *Voice from Afar*, 108–10; Dempsey, "Poundmaker"; Pannekoek, "Big Bear." At the outset of hostilities in the North-West, Big Bear was identified as the most problematic and potentially disruptive Native chief in the region, due to the fact that he was perceived, as Dewdney claimed, to be the most powerful. Big Bear had held out for better terms before taking treaty, and had spent a good deal of energy in the early to mid-1880s attempting to create a coalition among the region's various bands to press the federal government for increased assistance for an increasingly destitute population. Father Lestanc, who was cited in the *Saskatchewan Herald*, March 24, 1879, described

Riel as "the head and soul of all our Canadian Plains Indians." On Dewdney, see Dyck, *What Is the Indian "Problem"?* 66.

68. When the statute was enacted in England, the penalty accompanying a guilty verdict was death by hanging, disembowelment, decapitation, and dismemberment—a form of punishment that had become obsolete by the nineteenth century and had been replaced by simple execution. Goulet, *Trial of Louis Riel*, 47–50; Deane, *Mounted Police Life in Canada*, 191–92.

69. Beal and Macleod, *Prairie Fire*, 294.

70. Rambout, "Hudson Bay Half-Breeds," 155.

71. Beal and Macleod, *Prairie Fire*, 295. Although scholars have argued that the charges against Riel were entirely appropriate in respect to Riel's status as a British subject, the question of legitimacy is not as clear-cut in terms of geographical location. George Goulet, for instance, has argued that by the 1351 Statute of Treasons, an accusation of high treason required that the accused "levy War against our Lord the King in his Realm," a geographical restriction that definitely did not allow for the inclusion of North American territories. Goulet argues that by the Statute, the Crown's "Realm" was limited to England and Wales and the restricted "four seas" defined within the law, and as such could not be applied to the territory within which Riel was accused of having committed treason. In the context of the trial, the term "realm" was employed in reference to either the North-West or Canada or both, something that was simply not defensible.

D. H. Brown, "The Meaning of Treason in 1885," 71–72, has argued that Riel's U.S. citizenship was a moot point since legal precedent did not allow him to relinquish his obligations as a British subject in spite of citizenship. In the event that political factors contravened this precedent (e.g., the fact that his allegedly treasonous actions were perpetrated outside of Great Britain), the fact that he had resided in Canada prior to the rebellion meant that he remained legitimately subject to the charge of treason on the basis of the principle of "local allegiance," a point of law that was recognized in the United States as well as Canada. This is not to say that there is general agreement on this issue. Goulet, *Trial of Louis Riel*, 50–51, argues that British law had long recognized that a British subject was defined by birth and that subsequent naturalization within another nation did not affect this status. However, by Section 6 of the Naturalization Act, 1870, of the United Kingdom (which was adopted just days prior to the transfer of Rupert's Land to Canada) this long-standing tradition was changed such that one born within the dominions of the British Crown could no longer claim to be a subject once he or she had been naturalized elsewhere. Section 9 of the Naturalization Act, Canada, 1881, essentially articulated the same principle, although it is unclear whether either act was valid in 1885 in the North-West. Nonetheless, given that no attempt was made at Riel's trial to prove that he was indeed a British subject, this author believes that the three charges invoking natural allegiance were legally unsound. Goulet adds that to be judged guilty on the first three counts, Riel would have had to be proven to be a British subject at the times when he was accused of having committed treason. However, Richardson did not point this out to the jury, nor did he inform the six jurors that they were within the law to submit a separate verdict on each count. Unaware that the issue of whether Riel was indeed a British subject was relevant in terms of the first three counts, the jury was assured by Richardson "that any salient points that struck me as important . . . are brought to your attention" (p. 59).

72. Deane, *Mounted Police Life*, 186; D. Morton, *Queen v. Louis Riel*, xiv.

73. Christopher Robinson would later represent the interests of the federal government in the Bering Sea Arbitration, an 1893 dispute with the U.S. government over Canadian sealing rights in the Bering Strait.

74. D. Morton, *Queen v. Louis Riel*, xi–xiii; Deane, *Mounted Police Life*, 190–91.

75. The case of the settler (whose name was Conner of Kohner) had an impact on the claim made by Riel's lawyers that the court was not appropriate for trying this particular case. The man appealed his guilty verdict to the Manitoba Court of the Queen's Bench, challenging the legitimacy of the Regina Court, but the court rejected it. In so doing, it had already ruled on the issues of legality that Riel's lawyers attempted to raise. See D. Morton, *Queen v. Louis Riel*, xiv.

76. D. Morton, *Queen v. Louis Riel*, 371–72.

77. Report of Valade, November 8, 1885; cited in Wiebe and Beal, *War in the West*, 178.

78. *Detailed Report upon All Claims to Land and Rights to Participate in the North-West Halfbreed Grant by Settlers along the South Saskatchewan . . .* (Ottawa, 1886).

79. During the spring of 1990, the municipality of Oka, along with a local golf club, decided to enlarge a golf course on Mohawk land, on which was located a burial ground and a pine forest called "the Pines." The Mohawk occupied a section of the forest in mid-March and remained there for over six months, facing 2,500 Canadian troops that were placed in the area. See Grima, "Oka Crisis." See also Chartrand, "Aboriginal Rights," 472.

80. Devine, "Killing of Joseph Cardinal," 53–55.

Notes to Chapter 2

1. Bumsted, "The 'Mahdi' of Western Canada?" 47–48.

2. Braz, *False Traitor*, 78–79.

3. Lister, "A Distinctive Variant," 92–93.

4. Paquin, *Riel*; my translations from Johnson, "Riel in Canadian Drama," 179–80.

5. Bayer and Parage, *Riel*; my translation. See Lister, "A Distinctive Variant," 92. See also Johnson, "Riel in Canadian Drama," 179–80.

6. Dugast, *Histoire véridique*. See G. F. G. Stanley, "Last Word on Louis Riel," (1988): 8–9.

7. The work by de Trémaudan was a joint effort on the part of the author and the Union Nationale Métisse, and was published posthumously. See Maguet, introduction to Trémaudan, *Hold High Your Heads*; Bruchési, *Histoire du Canada*; Groulx, *Le Français au Canada*, and *Histoire du Canada Français*; Morice, *Critical History of the Red River Insurrection*; G. F. G. Stanley, "Last Word on Louis Riel," (1988): 8–9.

8. Maguet, introduction to *Hold High Your Heads*.

9. Johnson, "Riel in Canadian Drama," 187–90.

10. Johnson, "Riel in Canadian Drama," 196–97.

11. "Il est dommage que des jeunes spectateurs contemporains n'aient pas été members du jury lors des deliberations d'antan car aujourd'hi, Louis Riel n'est presque jamais condamné." Beddoes, "Tourisme scolaire," 29; my translation. Braz, *False Traitor*, 148–49.

12. "Un pardon pour Riel," *L'Express de Toronto*, October 1983; president of the Montreal St-Jean-Baptiste Society to the editor of *Franco*, published in Riel Project *Bulletin*, no. 9 (May 1983); Désilets, *Louis-Rodrigue Masson*, 133. Silver, "Ontario's Alleged Fanaticism," 21. My translations.

13. Stonechild and Waiser, *Loyal till Death*, 77; Braz, *False Traitor*, 3, 150.

14. "Speech on the Occasion of the National Celebration to Mark Louis Riel Day," Ottawa, November 16, 1999; see Braz, *False Traitor*, 13.

15. Enright, "Standing-in-Between," 45; Campbell, *Halfbreed*, 4–5; Culleton, *In Search of April Raintree*; Bouvier, *Une histoire de Métisses*; Braz, *False Traitor*, 201.

16. Adams, *Tortured People*, 108.

17. Borgerson, "Ile-à-le-Crosse," 49; Braz, *False Traitor*, 201–2.

18. Rock, *Missing Bell of Batoche*; Scofield, *Thunder through my Veins*, 200; Braz, *False Traitor*, 148.

19. Hathorn and Holland, introduction to *Images of Louis Riel*, 4–5.

20. Braz, *False Traitor*, 89.

21. Klassen, "Two Wise Men," 279. See also Braz, *False Traitor*, 149.

22. Goulet, *Trial of Louis Riel*, 10; Adrienne Clarkson, "Speech on the Occasion of the National Celebration to Mark Louis Riel Day," cited in Braz, *False Traitor*, 13. See also G. F. G. Stanley, "Making of a Historian," 14.

23. Klassen, "Two Wise Men," 283. Woodsworth was the first leader of the Cooperative Commonwealth Federation (CCF); Manning, who received a bible school education, served seven terms as premier of Alberta.

24. Goulet, *Trial of Louis Riel*, 10.

25. Moore and Languirand, *Louis Riel*; Braz, *False Traitor*, 134.

26. Braz, *False Traitor*, 150. See, for instance, Woodcock, *Gabriel Dumont*; Carefoot, *Gabriel Dumont at Batoche*; Mitchell, *The Plainsman*; Silver, *Lord of the Plains*; Zinovich, *Gabriel Dumont in Paris*.

27. Broughall, *The Ninetieth on Active Service*, 20–21. See also Lister, "A Distinctive Variant," 92; and Johnson, "Riel in Canadian Drama," 178–79.

28. Braz, *False Traitor*, 89, 192; Silver, "Ontario's Alleged Fanaticism," 21.

29. Robert Kroetsch, "On Being an Alberta Writer," 76, and "Canada is a Poem," 34. See Braz, *False Traitor*, 91–92.

30. D. Francis, *Imaginary Indian*, 90.

31. Niven, *The Flying Years*, 123.

32. Braz, *False Traitor*, 92; Dorothy Livesay, "Native People in our Canadian Literature," 22; Newlove, "The Pride," 106–7.

33. Wheeler, "The D. L. S. Intelligence Corps," 7; Waiser, "Surveyors at War," 52n67.

34. D. Morton, "Reflections on the Image of Louis Riel," 51.

35. A. S. Morton, *History of the Canadian West*; and G. F. G. Stanley, *Birth of Western Canada*. See Braz, *False Traitor*, 130; Maguet, introduction to *Hold High Your Heads*; Bumsted, "The 'Mahdi' of Western Canada?" 48; and Adams, *Tortured People*, 30.

36. W. L. Morton, "Red River Parish," 95, 49. See Sprague, *Canada and the Métis*, 4–5; McKillop, ed., *Contexts of Canada's Past*, 67.

37. Sprague has argued that the issue of Métis displacement is the most salient one to be considered, and that if the presumptions of government "good faith" and Métis primitivism are set aside, an obvious question presents itself relating to the nature of the situation of the Métis in Manitoba subsequent to the passage of the Manitoba Act.

   If, as Sprague suggests, the broad-based emigration from Red River was the product of untenable conditions in Manitoba, then arguments for a primitive Métis intransigence are unnecessary. Sprague goes on to criticize Thomas Flanagan for failing to question the accepted wisdom that the federal government was well within its rights to deal with Riel decisively. Although he admitted that the manipulation of psychiatric evidence by Macdonald and his government in the interest of assuring Riel's execution was an instance "not of delays or mistaken judgment, but of bad faith," ultimately Flanagan maintained that the prime minister and his government had not been engaged in "a calculated campaign to destroy the Métis or deprive them of their rights." Sprague, *Canada and the Métis*, 15–17; Flanagan, *Riel and the Rebellion*, 145.

38. G. F. G. Stanley, "Last Word on Louis Riel," (1986): 11; Braz, *False Traitor*, 130.

39. Howard, *Strange Empire*, 251; Braz, *False Traitor*, 132.

40. Coulter, *Riel*; Coulter, *In My Day*, 261; Moore, *Reinventing Myself*, 167; Braz, *False Traitor*, 95. This is not to say that Coulter's was the first work that consciously sought to cast Riel as a mythic or prophetic hero. Dorothy Livesay's poem, *Prophet of the New World* (first published in 1972, but written at least as early as 1945), for instance, was essentially a diatribe against the technological and dehumanizing character of the twentieth century, for which Riel is cast as a prophetic voice.

   > Call these things *sane*? And their existence,
   > *Bliss*?

   Cited in Holland, "Louis Riel and Modern Canadian Poetry," 215–17.

41. Johnson, "Riel in Canadian Drama," 184, 187.

42. Coulter, *Trial of Louis Riel*; Coulter, *Crime of Louis Riel*. On medieval passion plays, see Lister, "A Distinctive Variant," 96; on public perceptions, see Johnson, "Riel in Canadian Drama," 192–94. Lister notes that Coulter's presentation of an "artists' brief" to the Turgeon Parliamentary Committee in 1944 had been a decisive factor in the creation of the Canada Council.

43. Johnson, "Riel in Canadian Drama," 15, notes also that the introduction of fate in the play, as an active presence, is reminiscent of Roux's *Bois-Brûlés*. See also Goulet, *Trial of Louis Riel*, 10; Braz, *False Traitor*, 133.

44. Moore and Languirand, *Louis Riel*, 24–25; Lister, "A Distinctive Variant," 101; Braz, *False Traitor*, 133–34. On John Schultz, see Riel, *Collected Writings*, 5:342; on Charles Mair, see Riel, *Collected Writings*, 5302.

45. Gutteridge, *Poem for Voices*, 66–69. See also Holland, "Louis Riel and Modern Canadian Poetry," 217–18.

46. Braz, *False Traitor*, 142–43. The series boasted a notable cast that included Don Harron, Leslie Nielsen, Christopher Plummer, Jean-Louis Roux, and William Shatner.

47. Braz, *False Traitor*, 146–47. Braz points out that the tenth episode of *Canada: A People's History* (William Cobban's *Taking the West*) deals with the Rebellion of 1885 in a more balanced fashion, in spite of its virtual disregard for the implications of Canadian expansion on Aboriginals in the territory. Cobban displays a firm faith in the Confederation, notwithstanding the film's affirmation that many of the Métis' criticisms of the government were justifiable.

48. K. Roberts, "Riel," 182.

49. McLean, "1885," 79.

50. "Six Dry Cakes for the Hunted" was published as *Gabriel Dumont and the Northwest Rebellion* in 1976, and then again a year later with the original CBC title, along with the subtitle "A Canadian Myth." See Woodcock, *Gabriel Dumont and the Northwest Rebellion*; Woodcock, *Two Plays*; Lister, "A Distinctive Variant," 103; Johnson, "Riel in Canadian Drama," 199. See also Laroque, "Metis in English Canadian Literature," 90–91. Chris Johnson, "Riel in Canadian Drama," 197–98, points out that Rod Langley's *Tales from a Prairie Drifter*, staged first by the Twenty-Fifth Street Theatre in 1972, was an early instance of the elevation of Dumont rather than Riel. The play is critical of Riel, portraying him as a religious fanatic who obstructs the Métis rebellion being led by Gabriel Dumont—Langley's real hero in the piece. Driving the criticism home, Langley has a soldier reflect upon a devotional picture found at Batoche after the rebellion: "It started to rain while I was there and the cardboard picture became stained and limp as it got wet. It seemed significant. A cardboard shrine, in a cardboard capital of a new nation—led by a cardboard prophet."

Langley, an Australian by birth, appears to have called upon an Australian model for interpreting the events of 1885, and particularly the legendary figures of Ned Kelly and Joe Byrne. Kelly was a bushranger with revolutionary leanings whose companion, Byrne, has been remembered for being a "visionary poet." Johnson notes that while Canadians have tended (although not exclusively) to exalt Riel-the-prophet over Dumont-the-campaigner, Australians have traditionally chosen the opposite course, elevating Ned Kelly above his visionary companion.

51. Coutts-Smith, "CBC's 'Riel,'" 229. See also Holland, "Louis Riel and Modern Canadian Poetry," 232; Braz, *False Traitor*, 143–44.

52. D. Morton, *Queen v. Louis Riel*, xxviii.

53. Hawkins's *Louis Riel* is cited in Holland, "Louis Riel and Modern Canadian Poetry," and in Hathorn and Holland, *Images of Louis Riel*, 222. See also Gutteridge, *Poem for Voices*, 221–22.

54. Neff, *Ivanhoe Station*, 17.

55. Braz, *False Traitor*, 147–48, 202–3. George Fetherling, "George Woodcock Past and Present," 28, for instance, maintains that Riel is a paradigmatic link between Canadians of European descent and Native peoples and the nation itself. The problem has been mapped out in the following fashion by Terry Goldie: "The white Canadian looks at the Indian. The Indian is Other and therefore alien. But the Indian is indigenous and therefore cannot be alien. So the Canadian must be alien. But how can the Canadian be alien within Canada?" Goldie, *Fear and Temptation*, 12–13.

56. bpNichol, *Craft Dinner*. Howard Adams, as noted above, has expressed essentially the same criticism.

57. Long, *Alph*, 188–90.

58. Moore, "Haunted by Riel," 414.

59. William Klassen has made a similar argument for focusing on Riel in order to discern the relationship between religion and Canadian identity, but his focus on the notion of universal freedom and Riel's relationship with violence as the defender of such freedom takes him in a distinctly different direction than that which I am proposing here. See Klassen, *Two Wise Men*.

60. Dowbiggin, *Suspicious Minds*, 169. See also Braz, *False Traitor*, 203.

61. Bissoondath, *Selling Illusions*, 105.

62. Massey, *On Being Canadian*; W. L. Morton, *Canadian Identity*; Atwood, *Survival*; Frye, *Divisions on a Ground*. See also Bumsted, "Visions of Canada," 27–28, 30–31.

63. Kornberg and Stewart, "National Identification and Political Support," 74; D. Francis, *National Dreams*, 84–85; Bumsted, "Visions of Canada," 21.

64. G. Smith, *Canada and the Canadian Question*, 284; G. Smith, *Political Destiny of Canada*, 16–17. See also Preston, "Regionalism and National Identity"; Parkin, *Great Dominion*, 185; Bumsted, "Visions of Canada," 20. Parkin added that "no avowed annexationist could be elected to the Dominion Parliament."

65. Massey, *On Being Canadian*. On the shift in Canada's international position, see D. Francis, *National Dreams*, 84–85.

66. On bilingualism and multiculturalism see Wardhaugh, *Language and Nationhood*, 17; on the reaction to social welfare cuts, see Taras, *Passion for Identity*, 2. See also Bumsted, "Visions of Canada," 29–30.

67. On the west and the frontier, see Sullivan, "Summing Up," 144–58, 149, 155–56. On the meaning of violence, see Frye, *Divisions on a Ground*, 46–47. The early twentieth-century novelist Ralph Connor approached the issue in this fashion in his *Corporal Cameron of the North-West Mounted Police*, in which he asserted that there was no necessity in Canada for engaging in violent confrontations with Natives: "We don't keep them down," a Mountie informed an American who asked about the peaceable relations between the RCMP and the Native population, "We try to take care of them." See Connor, *Corporal Cameron*, 387. On the pattern of Canadian history, see W. L. Morton, *Canadian Identity*, 93. Morton argued that Canada's northern character gave the country a distinct intent that set it apart from the United States and made of the nation something more than simply a "second-rate United States, still less a United States that failed." See also D. Francis, *National Dreams*, 152.

For the failure of Canadian nationalism, see Allen Smith, "Metaphor and Nationality," 248; and on the lack of a Canadian identity see Taras, "Surviving the Wave," 185; Frye, *Divisions on a Ground*, 57.

68. Bissoondath, *Selling Illusions*, 105.

69. W. L. Morton, *Canadian Identity*, 4–5. See Harris, "Myth of the Land," 27–28.

70. In cultural terms, his argument might be validated by recalling the prominence that the "northern" and "wilderness" landscapes painted by the Group of Seven have assumed in the Canadian psyche as archetypical representations of Canada. Innis, *Fur Trade in Canada*. See Harris, "Myth of the Land," 28–29; Bumsted, "Visions of Canada," 25; Taras, "Surviving the Wave," 187; Allen Smith, "Metaphor and Nationality," 260.

71. Creighton, *Commercial Empire of the St. Lawrence*, 6–7. See Taras, "Surviving the Wave," 187; Allen Smith, "Metaphor and Nationality," 259–60; Bumsted, "Visions of Canada," 25–26.

72. W. L. Morton, "Clio in Canada."

73. W. L. Morton, *Canadian Identity*, 89, 111–12; Allen Smith, "Metaphor and Nationality," 261–62.

74. Allen Smith, "Metaphor and Nationality," 260.

75. See Allen Smith, "Metaphor and Nationality," 260; Bumsted, "Visions of Canada," 25–26. Cole Harris, "Myth of the Land," 29, leveled another criticism at the theory: in spite of the fact that the Canadian Shield was undoubtedly instrumental in the development of Canada, most Canadians have never seen it. In fact, far from being a "northern" people, the nation's population has been overwhelming concentrated in agriculturally productive territory between the forty-ninth parallel and the uncultivable north, with both French and English Canadians having developed their cultural personality in relation to the cultivation of this narrow band of terrain.

76. Kornberg and Stewart, "National Identification and Political Support," 75, argue that all forms of identity are adjudicated by "human interactions."

77. Laurence, "You Can Almost Hear the Skipping Rope Slapping"; Jeffrey, "Biblical Hermeneutic and Family History," 88. Both are cited in Sullivan, "Summing Up," 154.

78. W. L. Morton, "Comment on R. G. Trotter," 61. Cited in Dick, "Seven Oaks Incident," 1.

79. Cited in Granatstein, *Who Killed Canadian History?* 6.

80. Birney, *Collected Poems*, 138. See also Mandel, "Border League," 68.

81. D. Francis, *National Dreams*, 12.

82. D. Francis, *National Dreams*, 153–54.

83. Massey, *On Being Canadian*, 29–30. Cited in C. Berger, "True North," 22–23. See also p. 4.

84. W. L. Morton, *Canadian Identity*, 88–114. Cited in C. Berger, "True North," 23–24. Frye, *Divisions on a Ground*, 49.

85. *Toronto Star*, December 22, 1928, cited in D. Reid, *Group of Seven*, 202. See also D. Francis, *National Dreams*, 164, and Houser, *Canadian Art Movement*, 145.

86. D. Francis, *National Dreams*, 153–57, 171.

87. D. Francis, *National Dreams*, 15; Charland, "Technological Nationalism," 199, 200.

88. Macdonald, from House of Commons, *Debates*, January 17, 1881, p. 488, cited in Charland, "Technological Nationalism," 201; Berton, *National Dream*, 11.

89. Berton's series was produced in eight episodes, was broadcast in 1973–74, and repeated in 1982 and 1985. He was not alone in this judgment. W. Kaye Lamb, for instance, cast Macdonald as a consummate founder of a nation: "If he [Macdonald] had not found ways and means of constructing it when he did, Canada would almost certainly not extend today from sea to sea." Berton, *Great Railway*, 12; Lamb, *History of the Canadian Pacific Railway*, 436; D. Francis, *National Dreams*, 16–17.

90. MacBeth, *Romance of the Canadian Pacific Railway*, 172. See D. Francis, *National Dreams*, 17.

91. Kula, "Steam Movies," 247–57. Cited in D. Francis, *National Dreams*, 22–24.

92. D. Francis, *National Dreams*, 15, 26–28. Charland, "Technological Nationalism," 199, 202–3.

93. Sallot, *Nobody Said No*, 8; D. Francis, *National Dreams*, 29–30.

94. Colmer, introduction to Steele, *Forty Years in Canada*, vi–vii. See also Sallot, *Nobody Said No*, 13.

95. For other examples of Mountie memoirs see, for instance, Donkin, *Trooper and Redskin in the Far North-West*; Denny, *The Law Marches West*. Pierre Berton, *Hollywood's Canada*, 111, suggested that half the movies made about Canada during the period involved Mounties. See also D. Francis, *National Dreams*, 31–32.

96. Frye, *Divisions on a Ground*, 46–47.

97. Sallot, *Nobody Said No*, 38–39; D. Francis, *National Dreams*, 50. Cross, the British Trade Commissioner, was kidnapped on October 5, 1970; he was released in December. Laporte, a Quebec cabinet minister, was kidnapped on October 10 and murdered within a week. See "October Crisis" in the online edition of *The Canadian Encyclopedia*.

98. D. Francis, *National Dreams*, 50, notes in this respect Dave Broadfoot's character, Corporal Renfrew, who portrayed the Mountie as a buffoon, and the series *Due South*, which purposely ridiculed the force for a U.S. television audience. See also Sallot, *Nobody Said No*, 194.

99. D. Francis, *National Dreams*, 29.

100. C. G. D. Roberts, *History of Canada for High Schools and Academies*, 355. See D. Francis, *National Dreams*, 52–54.

101. Burpee and Doughty, eds., *Makers of Canada*. See D. Francis, *National Dreams*, 117–19.

102. C. G. D. Roberts, *History of Canada for High Schools and Academies*, 446; Dorland, *Our Canada*, 413. See also D. Francis, *National Dreams*, 54.

103. Hood, "Moral Imagination," 32. It was suggested in the 1960s, further, that this fundamental sense of collective inferiority resided at the root of an educational focus on anti-Americanism. S. Clarkson, "Programme for Binational Development," 34. See D. Francis, *National Dreams*, 84.

104. Hayward and Watson, *Romantic Canada*, 187. Cited in Allen Smith, "Metaphor and Nationality," 258–59; D. Francis, *National Dreams*, 80. O'Brien, introduction to Hayward and Watson, *Romantic Canada*, xiii. Cited in Allen Smith, "Metaphor and Nationality," 259.

105. K. Foster, *Our Canadian Mosaic*; D. Francis, *National Dreams*, 80. Gibbon, *Canadian Mosaic*; Allen Smith, "Metaphor and Nationality," 257.

106. Allen Smith, "Metaphor and Nationality," 249.

107. Gibbon, *Canadian Mosaic*, viii. Allen Smith, "Metaphor and Nationality," 257; D. Francis, *National Dreams*, 81–82. See also McKay, *Quest of the Folk*, 57–58.

108. See Allen Smith, "Metaphor and Nationality," 250, 251, 254; D. Francis, *National Dreams*, 83.

109. D. Francis, *National Dreams*, 21–22.

110. McKay, *Quest of the Folk*, 57; cited in D. Francis, *National Dreams*, 80–83. See also Hart, *Selling of Canada*.

111. D. Francis, *National Dreams*, 172.

112. D. Francis, *National Dreams*, 112–14. A history textbook was prohibited in British Columbia in 1920 because Bourassa was not portrayed as a traitor. Humphries, "Banning of a Book," 1–12.

113. On Mouré, see Holland, "Louis Riel and Modern Canadian Poetry," 224. See also the foreword to Hathorn and Holland, eds., *Images of Louis Riel*, v–vi; Bumsted, "Visions of Canada," 320–21; Vachon, "Riel Deal."

114. See "Chaos Theory." Edward Lorenz is credited with engaging in the first chaos experiment, in 1960, when he discovered that a system of predicting weather could be dramatically affected by the slightest of variations in the numerical data he entered at the outset of the experiment (the difference, in this case, between an initial input of .506 and .506127). The remarkable effect of this minor change became known as the "butterfly effect," described by Ian Stewart, *Does God Play Dice?* 141, in the following manner:

> The flapping of a single butterfly's wing today produces a tiny change in the state of the atmosphere. Over a period of time, what the atmosphere actually does diverges from what it would have done. So, in a month's time, a tornado that would have devastated the Indonesian coast doesn't happen. Or maybe one that wasn't going to happen does.

Also called "sensitive dependence on initial conditions," the butterfly effect refers to the fact that the most minor of changes in primary conditions can have far-reaching effects on a system's continued functioning.

115. Benítez-Rojo, *Repeating Island*, 2–3, 313, 296.

Notes to Chapter 3

1. Smith and Kornberg "Quebec Referendum," 353–54.

2. B. Anderson, *Imagined Communities*, 5–6. Melville Watkins, "Technology and Nationalism," 285, suggests that, fundamentally, nations consist of a group of people who simply regard themselves as a nation.

3. B. Anderson, *Imagined Communities*, 5–8.

4. Anthony Smith, "Memory and Modernity," 10. Gourgouris, *Dream Nation*, 15–16. See also Anthony Smith, *Ethnic Origins of Nations*, ix–x; Hobsbawm, *Nations and Nationalism*, 20; Tilly, "Afterward," 251–52. Tilly argues that emerging nations of the revolutionary period were not driven by later nineteenth-century contested notions of self-definition revolving around issues of ethnicity, language, religious affiliation, geographical area, or shared historical narrative. France and the United States may have emerged without these characteristics, but in the case of the United States, at least, skin color assumed this defining role.

5. Julian Huxley and A. C. Hadden, quoted in Shafer, *Nationalism, Myth, and Reality*, 6.

6. Gellner, *Nations and Nationalism*, 1.

7. Charles Tilly differentiates between "state-seeking nationalism" and "state-led nationalism." State-seeking nationalism generally involves the creation of a state from within a larger political body and as a rule involves assistance from outside forces. State-led nationalism tends to require the subsuming of sub-cultures by a dominant cultural group through a concerted policy of establishing official languages, educational systems, historical narratives, icons, public observances, and so on. The latter form of nationalism came into play in the creation of modern Germany, Russia, and Italy. See Tilly, "Afterward," 251–52. See also Emerson, *From Empire to Nation*, 102. See also Watkins, "Technology and Nationalism," 285; Seton-Watson, *Nations and States*, 6. Seton-Watson suggests that nationalism did indeed exist prior to the French Revolution, but that it was a comparatively rare occurrence related to imperial attempts to force a state religion on conquered people or to intensify control in regions that had traditionally been relatively autonomous.

8. Greenfield, *Nationalism*, 3–4. Daniel A. Segal, "Living Ancestors," 222–23, suggested that unlike European nationalisms, that of the United States does not regard national unity as related to a shared "primordial" past; rather, to begin again in America is to announce the end of time prior to immigration. The dominant nationalist formulation contains a temporal component that refigures the identity of immigrants at the moment they enter the country. Thus, regardless of the time of arrival, the act of entering is incorporated into a unifying nationalist narrative that confers upon each immigrant a "new beginning" within a shared history. The pre-American past of immigrants is consequently cast as a reservoir of elemental "disassociation" that is obsolete in the new American situation. Boyarin argued that the American example demonstrates that national unity is not dependant on a shared memory of prenational existence. In fact, prenational cultural disparity can be easily reconciled with national coherence, so long as the disparity is located within a conception of the past whose humanly constitutive meaning has been terminated.

9. See Chasteen, introduction to *Beyond Imagined Communities*, xx; Donghi, "Argentine Counterpoint," 15.

10. Haworth, *Canada's Printing Pioneers*, 7, 10.

11. Forty publications bore Mesplet's imprint, while an additional thirty have been cited in registers. Haworth, *Canada's Printing Pioneers*, 12, 17–20.

12. The Loyalist Robertson Press was responsible for creating the *Royal American Gazette* on Prince Edward Island, and Ryan introduced the *Royal St. John Gazette* in New Brunswick. See Haworth, *Canada's Printing Pioneers*, 23.

13. Haworth, *Canada's Printing Pioneers*, 25, 28–29.

14. Saskatchewan's first newspaper, the *Saskatchewan Herald*, was established in 1878 by Patrick Gammie Laurie; and Alberta's foray into print media began shortly afterward (1880), when Frank Oliver began publishing *The Bulletin*, at Edmonton, a paper he continued to publish until 1923. Haworth, *Canada's Printing Pioneers*, 36–38.

15. In the 1840s, no newspapers had what could be regarded as substantial readerships. In the middle to latter part of the decade, for example, *La Minerve* could claim a circulation of only about twelve hundred; and its competition, *L'Avenir*, had about fifteen hundred. See Rutherford, *Victorian Authority*, 36–37, 44.

16. Rutherford, *Victorian Authority*, 37–38.

17. Rutherford, *Victorian Authority*, 167, mentions in respect to the spread of Anglophone nationalism during he period, the *Ottawa Journal* and the *Winnipeg Tribune*.

18. Northrop Frye, *Divisions on a Ground*, 65–66, argued that nationalism requires a level of constructive and discursive self-expression at its foundation. The United States, he suggested, achieved its climax of such discourse with its founding fathers of the eighteenth century. What Washington, Jefferson, and Adams initiated with their discourse would ultimately become what is now the oldest nation-state in existence. Canada, on the other hand, possesses no such moment of discursive self-definition. The nation began with the extension of French mercantile interests in the seventeenth century and then found itself recreated by an incursion of Loyalists in the wake of the American Revolution. In this sense, he argued, it moved from the Baroque (early Enlightenment) to the Romantic (post-Enlightenment) period without ever having defined itself as a modern state.

19. Frye, *Divisions on a Ground*, 47–48.

20. Kroetsch, "Canada Is a Poem." See also Geddes, ed., *Divided We Stand*, 14; D. Francis, *National Dreams*, 18.

21. D. Francis, *National Dreams*, 18.

22. Hébert, "Quebec," 79.

23. Dufour, "A Little History"; and Bissoondath, *Selling Illusions*, 55.

24. The Mi'kmaq are the easternmost Algonkian-speaking peoples in the Atlantic provinces, as well as in Maine and Massachusetts.

25. My thanks to Elizabeth Marshall for her discussions of the Grand Council Seal.

26. B. Anderson, *Imagined Communities*, 191–92.

27. On the argument for nationalism in New France and the Conquest period see, for instance, Brunet, *La Priseni Anglais*; Wardhaugh, *Language and Nationhood*, 20–21. On its refutation see Ouellet, "Le nationalisme canadienne français"; Careless, "Metropolitanism and Nationalism," 275.

28. Chevier, "Canadian Federalism," 3. In 1791, there were ten thousand British colonists in the province, as opposed to one hundred and fifty thousand French.

29. Dubuc, "Decline of Confederation," 117.

30. Careless "Metropolitanism and Nationalism," 275–76.

31. Chevier, "Canadian Federalism," 3.

32. *La Gazette de Sorel*, June 23, 1864; Silver, *French Canadian Idea of Confederation*, 33.

33. *La Minerve*, September 9, 1864; Silver, *French Canadian Idea of Confederation*, 33.

34. *La Minerve*; Silver, *French Canadian Idea of Confederation*, 35.

35. Silver, "Impact on Eastern Canada," 46. See also Grant, *Church in the Canadian Era*, 82.

36. *Montreal Gazette*, November 17, 1885; Wiebe and Beal, *War in the West*, 183.

37. *Daily Intelligencer*, December 15, 1885.

38. Macdonald is cited in Sprague, *Canada and the Métis*, 180.

39. Silver, "Ontario's Alleged Fanaticism," 50.

40. *London Advertiser*, September 8, 1885; the *Week*, October 8, 1885; Silver, "Ontario's Alleged Fanaticism," 47n197. Also the *World*, September 21, 1885, and the *Mail*, November 28, 1885.

41. See Bumsted, *Louis Riel v. Canada*, 312; Daniels, *We Are the New Nation*, 5. Mercier organized the first post-Confederation conference of provincial premiers through which the federal government was forced to concede the principle of provincial autonomy in administrative and economic spheres. Mercier was also an architect of the Jesuit's Estate Act, whereby a dispute over Jesuit compensation for their substantial properties in Quebec that had been handed over to Lower Canada in 1831 was resolved. Pope Leo XIII had been asked by Mercier to arbitrate the dispute, and the Ontario Orange Order erupted in anger, a conflict that was carried into the House of Commons where the legality of papal intervention in Canadian politics was hotly debated in 1889. The act passed, but contributed to an increasing and enduring tension between French and English. See *The Canadian Encyclopedia* online: http://www.thecanadianencyclopedia.com (accessed September 6, 2004).

42. *La Patrie*, August 7, 1885; Silver, "Ontario's Alleged Fanaticism," 175.

43. The *Mail*, November 28, 1885; Silver, "Ontario's Alleged Fanaticism," 46.

44. Hébert, "Quebec," 79.

45. Known as the "Seven Oaks Massacre," the confrontation of 1816 resulted in the deaths of the settlement's governor, Robert Semple, and twenty-one settlers. See Bumsted, *Louis Riel v. Canada*, 10; Beal and Macleod, *Prairie Fire*, 14.

46. Chartrand, "Aboriginal Rights," 459–60; W. L. Morton, "Red River Parish," 48–49; Sprague, *Canada and the Métis*, 4–5; Braz, *False Traitor*, 22–23.

47. Daniels, *We Are the New Nation*, 5; Department of Culture and Youth, *Towards a New Past*, iii; Manitoba Métis Federation, *National Unity and Constitutional Reform*, 47.

48. Coates, *Marshall Decision*, 38–42, 80–81.

49. Shubenacadie was operated by the Sisters of Charity and the Roman Catholic Diocese of Halifax. In 1997, the Royal Commission on Aboriginal Peoples

found that "residential schools severely disrupted aboriginal families, cultures and identities." http://www.ptla.org/ptlasite/wabanaki/shubenacadie.htm (accessed July 11, 2003). This article "is based in part on articles appearing in the *Chronicle-Herald/Mail-Star* of Halifax, Nova Scotia."

50. Wardhaugh, *Language and Nationhood*, 229–30.

51. The Canadian government's White Paper of 1969, 6, is cited in Voyageur, "We Get Knocked Down," 147.

52. Wardhaugh, *Language and Nationhood*, 229–30; Voyageur, "We Get Knocked Down," 147; Chartrand, "Aboriginal Rights," 457.

53. Wardhaugh, *Language and Nationhood*, 20–21, says of English Canadian self-consciousness: "[T]here was nothing corresponding to the American Revolution. Instead, it evolved almost by accident and in a series of pragmatic, even defensive, moves. English life in Canada therefore lacks a unifying theme and a controlling set of values and symbols. The internal history of the English in Canada is a history of compromise and accommodation; moreover it is one shared by a mosaic of peoples and lacks any really central theme."

54. Careless, "Metropolitanism and Nationalism," 278.

55. PAC Macdonald Papers, Macdonald to T. C. Patterson, February 27, 1872. C. Brown, "Nationalism of the National Policy," 156.

56. C. Brown, "Nationalism of the National Policy," 161; Bumsted, "Visions of Canada," 20–21.

57. See Goulet, *Trial of Louis Riel*, 35. Sprague, *Canada and the Métis*, 2, raises the post-Confederation issue in relation to Stanley's *Birth of Western Canada*.

58. From W. A. Foster, "Canada First; or, Our New Nationality" (Toronto, 1871), and "Canada First: Address of the Canadian National Association to the People of Canada," both in W. A. Foster, *Canada First*, 49. On Canada First, see also Bumsted, "Visions of Canada," 19.

59. From "Canada First; or, Our New Nationality," in Foster, *Canada First*, 17.

60. Quoted in C. Berger, *Sense of Power*, 58–59.

61. From "Canada First; or, Our New Nationality," in Foster, *Canada First*, 43.

62. C. Berger, *Sense of Power*, 58–59.

63. C. Berger, "True North Strong and Free," 3–26; Allen Smith, "Metaphor and Nationality," 247–75.

64. *Brampton Conservator*, November 20, 1885. Also *Toronto Mail*, November 28, 1885; Silver, "Ontario's Alleged Fanaticism," 47n199.

65. *Winnipeg Tribune*, October 5, 1893; *Toronto Mail*, November 24, 1886; *Toronto News*, August 23, 1892; *Toronto Mail*, August 25, 1886; *Toronto Mail*, December 6, 1886; Rutherford, *Victorian Authority*, 168.

66. Bumsted, "Visions of Canada," 20–21.

67. Bumsted, "Visions of Canada," 26.

68. Wardhaugh, *Language and Nationhood*, 19.

69. Granatstein, *Who Killed Canadian History?* xvii.

70. Granatstein, *Who Killed Canadian History?*

71. Granatstein, *Who Killed Canadian History?* 101–2. See also T. J. Stanley, "Why I Killed Canadian History," 86–87.

72. Granatstein, *Who Killed Canadian History?* xiii, xvi; Goulet, *Trial of Louis Riel*, 13.

73. Granatstein, *Who Killed Canadian History?* xiv, 3–5, 139.

74. Granatstein, *Who Killed Canadian History?* 94.

75. McKillop, "Who Killed Canadian History?"; Stanley, "Why I Killed Canadian History," 87–88.

76. Stanley, "Why I Killed Canadian History," 88.

77. *Daily Intelligencer*, December 15, 1885; Mika and Mika, *Riel Rebellion*, 332–33.

78. O'Leary, "What States Can Do with Nations," 53–54.

79. From O'Leary's discussion of Gellner, *Nations and Nationalism*. See O'Leary, "What States Can Do with Nations," 55–56.

80. Craig, *Lord Durham's Report*, 33–34, 35; Dubuc, "Decline of Confederation," 117.

81. Cernetig, "Far Side of the Rockies," 415.

82. Dubuc, "Decline of Confederation," 117–18; D. Francis, *National Dreams*, 60.

83. *Hamilton Spectator*, February 24, 1890; Rutherford, *Victorian Authority*, 169.

84. Grant, *Church in the Canadian Era*, 83–84.

85. Crunican, "Manitoba Schools Question."

86. Alexander Morris, *Treaties of Canada*, 69; McNab, "Métis Participation," 65–66.

87. Alexander Morris to the Honourable Alexander Campbell, Minister of the Interior, October 14, 1873, in Morris, *Treaties of Canada*, 47–52; McNab, "Métis Participation," 65–66.

88. Sealey and Lussier, *Métis*.

89. Chartrand, "Aboriginal Rights," 474.

90. Coates, *Marshall Decision*, 81–82.

91. Coates, *Marshall Decision*, 82–83.

92. Teillet, *Métis Case Law*, 3.

93. D. N. Paul, *We Were Not the Savages*, 207. Native Canadians were given a limited right to vote in 1920, but only on the condition that they renounce their treaty rights and status as registered Indians. See "The Right to Vote in Canada: A Timeline," at http://citzine.ca/issue.php?lng=e&issue=vo2io2&art=tidbit.

94. See Charland, "Technological Nationalism," 197.

95. Hallman and Hindley, *Broadcasting in Canada*, 55. See also Babe, *Telecommunications in Canada*, 6–7. Babe suggests that infrastructure (highways, airlines, railways, the CBC) makes possible the expression of this diversity to the nation as a whole, and creates the collective experience of inhabiting such an enormous region as a national body.

96. See Rens, *Invisible Empire*, 28.

97. G. F. G. Stanley, *Birth of Western Canada*, 25.

98. Resolution of the Canadian Legislature, 1864, cited in G. F. G. Stanley, *Birth of Western Canada*, 26.

99. Charland, "Technological Nationalism," 199.

100. Irving, *Mass Media in Canada*, 3; Pike, "Kingston Adopts the Telephone," 33.

101. Pike, "Kingston Adopts the Telephone," 33; Pelletier is cited in Babe, *Telecommunications in Canada*, 5. Innis, *History of the Canadian Pacific Railway*, 287.

102. Harry J. Boyle, vice chairman of the CRTC, "The Canadian Broadcasting System," speech to the Canadian section of the Association for Professional Broadcasting, Education Seminar, Washington D.C., November 6, 1970; Babe, *Telecommunications in Canada*, 5. See also Charland, "Technological Nationalism," 202.

103. See Rens, *Invisible Empire*, xviii.

104. Babe, *Telecommunications in Canada*, 7.

105. House of Commons, Standing Committee of Broadcasting, Films and Assistance to the Arts, *Minutes of Proceedings and Evidence*, April 25, 1969; Babe, *Telecommunications in Canada*, 5–6.

106. Department of Communications, *Communications for the Twenty-First Century*, 5; Babe, *Telecommunications in Canada*, 6.

107. Charland, "Technological Nationalism," 196–97.

108. From the federal *White Paper on Broadcasting* in 1966; Babe, *Telecommunications in Canada*, 5.

109. Task Force on Canadian Unity, *A Future Together*, 9.

110. See Bumsted, "Visions of Canada," 17; and Heiman, "Nineteenth-Century Legacy," 337–38.

111. Kroker, *Technology and the Canadian Mind*; Babe, *Telecommunications in Canada*, 6.

112. Charland, "Technological Nationalism," 214–15, 198, provides an excellent discussion of this conundrum.

113. For a discussion of Innis with respect to this issue, see Carey and Quirk, "Mythos of the Electronic Evolution," 238. See also Charland, "Technological Nationalism," 198.

114. See Charland, "Technological Nationalism," 216; Babe, *Telecommunications in Canada*, 21; Martin, "*Hello, Central?*" 6.

115. Martin, "*Hello, Central?*" 8; Pike, "Kingston Adopts the Telephone," 35.

116. Babe, *Telecommunications in Canada*, 7–8, suggests that communication technologies have fostered continental assimilation more than national unity in the Canadian situation. The Canadian telegraph system, for instance, was allied with that of the United States from its inception. Most lines were created in order to link Canadian and American cities, and links with other Canadian towns generally took years to be constructed. By 1881, most of the telegraph industry in Canada had been acquired by U.S. companies, and Canadian-owned companies reemerged slowly (i.e., Canadian Pacific Telegraphs).

The telephone industry in Canada followed much the same route as that of the telegraph. It took only four years following the first successful telephone conversation for the patent and the original charter to be assumed by Americans; and Bell Canada, the country's largest company, did not acquire full control from U.S. interests until the 1970s.

117. Preston, "Regionalism and National Identity," 8.

118. Allen Smith, "Metaphor and Nationality," 269.

119. Although a nationalist discourse has arguably gained ascendancy in the United States, this has been achieved to a great degree also in spite of competing nationalisms. The key difference in the Canadian situation is that subnationalisms have maintained political and geographical ascendancy.

120. Cross and Kealey, eds., introduction to *Canada's Age of Industry*, 11.

121. C. Brown, "Nationalism of the National Policy," 161–62.

122. Holmes, "Nationalism in Canadian Foreign Policy," 204.

123. Dickens, *Dickens of the Mounted*, letter from Regina to Emily, November 20, 1885, 267–68.

124. As Harry Daniels pointed out, comprehensive federalism led to the Métis uprisings and the execution of Riel, which in turn nourished French Canadian nationalism. Likewise, the Parti Québécois' rise to power in Quebec was concomitant with a rise in Métis nationalism. While neither Riel's execution nor the Parti Québécois' mandate can be regarded as the source of French Canadian or Métis nationalist articulations, their concurrence points to the fact that a thorough federalism is not politically viable in Canada. See Daniels, *We Are the New Nation*, 5–6.

125. Taras, "Surviving the Wave," 185.

126. See Allen Smith, "Metaphor and Nationality," 248.

Notes to Chapter 4

1. Arendt, *On Revolution*, 2, 10–11.

2. Carrasco, *City of Sacrifice*, 3, 6.

3. See Dubuc, "Decline of Confederation," 117. Lister, "A Distinctive Variant," 93, lists only three plays based on the events of 1837: Robertson Davies's *At my Heart's Core*, Rick Salutin's *1837: The Farmer's Revolt*, and Louis-Honoré Fréchette's *Papineau*.

4. See Hildebrandt, "Official Images," 33–34; G. F. G. Stanley, *Birth of Western Canada*, 353.

5. *Toronto Mail*, August 27, 1884; Silver, "Ontario's Alleged Fanaticism," 38.

6. Telegraph of April 1, 1885, from Hartley Gisborne, district superintendent, to F. N. Gisborne, superintendent, Government Telegraph Service. Cited in Collins, *Voice from Afar*, 101.

7. Telegram of April 3, 1888, from Commander A. G. Irvine to Dewdney, in Middleton, *Suppression of the Rebellion*, 7, 15–16.

8. Letter from L. N. F. Crozier, May 29, 1885, to Commander A. G. Irvine, in Commissioners of the Royal North-West Mounted Police (NWMP), *Settlers and Rebels*, 43.

9. The *Toronto Globe*, March 31, 1885; Mika and Mika, *Riel Rebellion*, 33–34.

10. *Daily British Whig*, April 6, 1885; Mika and Mika, *Riel Rebellion*, 45–46.

11. The *Kingston Daily News*, April 10, 1885; Mika and Mika, *Riel Rebellion*, 52.

12. *Sarnia Observer*, April 17, 1885; *Acton Free Press*, April 16, 1885; *Ottawa Free Press*, April 10 and 11, 1885; *London Advertiser*, June 1885; *Ottawa Citizen*, April 24, 1885. Silver, "Ontario's Alleged Fanaticism," 38–39.

13. Collins, *Voice from Afar*, 102.

14. Commissioners of the Royal NWMP, *Settlers and Rebels*, 29.

15. *Suppression of the Northwest Insurrection*, 244.

16. Chapleau, *Riel Question*, 8.

17. *Daily Intelligencer*, December 15, 1885; Mika and Mika, *Riel Rebellion*, 332.

18. Chapleau, *Riel Question*, 8.

19. *London Free Press*, November 26, 1885, in Silver, "Ontario's Alleged Fanaticism," 38; *Daily Intelligencer*, December 15, 1885, in Mika and Mika, *Riel Rebellion*, 332–33; *Toronto Telegram*, November 20, 1885, in Silver, "Ontario's Alleged Fanaticism," 38–39.

20. *Toronto Mail*, November 16, 1885; *Toronto Week*, June 4, 1885; *Ottawa Free Press*, August 3, 1885; Silver, "Ontario's Alleged Fanaticism," 39.

21. Parkin, *Sir John A. Macdonald*, 244.

22. Trial proceedings, July 28, 1885, in D. Morton, *Queen v. Louis Riel*, 72, 74.

23. Trial proceedings, July 31–August 1, 1885, in D. Morton, *Queen v. Louis Riel*, 332, 341, 342.

24. Trial proceedings, August 1, 1885, in D. Morton, *Queen v. Louis Riel*, 371.

25. See Stonechild and Waiser, *Loyal till Death*, 3; D. Morton, "Cavalry or Police," 179; and Devine, "Killing of Joseph Cardinal," 45. Francis Dickens was astounded by the fact that the prisoners taken by Big Bear's band were treated well in spite of the fact that the Cree were frequently fired on in the days that followed. In fact, he wrote in a letter in the summer of 1885, the prisoners were fed when there was not enough food for the band, and the children were carried across brooks rather than being made to wade. They were eventually all freed. Dickens ultimately wondered how it was possible to hang Big Bear when he demonstrated a regard for the rules of war that would have surprised the teachers at the Royal Military College. Dickens, *Dickens of the Mounted*, 258. Letter from Battleford to Emily, August 12, 1885.

26. Stonechild and Waiser, *Loyal till Death*, 170–71.

27. See Devine, "Killing of Joseph Cardinal," 35–36; and Hildebrandt, "Official Images," 33–34.

28. Trial Proceedings, July 28, 1885, in D. Morton, *Queen v. Louis Riel*, 67–68.

29. G. F. G. Stanley, *Birth of Western Canada*, 363, 365.

30. *Daily Intelligencer*, May 30, 1885, in Mika and Mika, *Riel Rebellion*, 132.

31. See de Trémaudan, *Histoire de la National Métisse*, 414–15, 417; G. F. G. Stanley, *Birth of Western Canada*, 332–33.

32. D. Morton, "Cavalry or Police," 179.

33. Stonechild and Waiser, *Loyal till Death*, 1–2.

34. G. F. G. Stanley, *Birth of Western Canada*, 378. Stonechild and Waiser, *Loyal till Death*, 2, note by way of example, R. C. Brown, ed., *Illustrated History of Canada*, 356; Bumsted, *Peoples of Canada*, 26; Finkel, Conrad, Jaenen, and Strong-Boag, *History of the Canadian Peoples*, 49; Francis, Jones, and Smith, *Destinies*, 83–84.

35. Miller, *Skyscrapers Hide the Heavens*, 188; Stonechild and Waiser, *Loyal till Death*, 4.

36. Tobias, "Canada's Subjugation of the Plains Cree"; Beal and Macleod, *Prairie Fire*; and Carter, *Lost Harvests*, 128. In this respect, Stonechild and Waiser note also Dempsey, *Big Bear*; Friesen, *Canadian Prairies*; Stonechild, "Indian View of the 1885 Uprising"; and Miller, *Skyscrapers Hide the Heavens*.

37. Letter from Private Fred Harris, a telegraph operator and a member of the Queen's Own Rifles, April 24, 1885; reports by E. R. Johnston, city editor of the *St. Paul (Minnesota) Pioneer Press*, May 13, 1885 and April 28, 1885; Wiebe and Beal, *War in the West*, 84, 93–94, 106–7.

38. Deane, *Mounted Police Life in Canada*, 24; Roy, "Rifleman Forin," 100; Middleton, *Suppression of the Rebellion*, 38; and Deane, *Mounted Police Life in Canada*, 195, 200.

39. *Daily British Whig*, December 11, 1885, in Mika and Mika, *Riel Rebellion*, 328; *Story of Louis Riel the Rebel Chief*, 1, 176; and Ord, preface to *Reminiscences of a Bungle*.

40. Huntington, "Revolution and Political Order," 39; and Wolf, "Peasant Rebellion and Revolution," 179.

41. Huntington, "Revolution and Political Order," 39–40. A number of scholars have argued that the uprisings should be regarded as failed revolutions. Ron Bourgeault, for instance, suggests that the 1869 uprising was not a rebellion but a revolution because its primary aim was to bring down one political and economic system and replace it with another. The revolution failed primarily because it lacked a requisite foundational support from the middle class. When Riel recognized that complete sovereignty was unsustainable, he began negotiating the terms of a compromise by which the territory could enter into the Confederation on an equal footing with the other four provinces. Bourgeault, "Struggle Against British Colonialism," 30. I will argue in a later chapter that Riel had no intention of destroying the Canadian political system.

42. Stearns, *1848*, 1, 5–6. In terms of their divergences, Stearns notes that in France, for instance, 1848 marked a revolutionary attempt to consolidate the more radical stage of what had been enacted in 1789—the creation of a less guarded political system—in order to democratically ensure the extension of fundamental freedoms to all citizens and to achieve social reforms without damaging the nation's social structure. The 1848 revolution was, consequently, far less radical than that of 1789, since it did not seek to overthrow a firmly entrenched social order. In Germany, where the regime had already initiated a measure of reform, radicals lacked the level of passion that their French counterparts had displayed in 1789; and the changes they initiated, although significant in a number of ways, were consequently less disruptive to the social structure than those that had occurred in France. Italian revolutionaries of 1848 were fueled by nationalist ideologies that would reach their peak in the decades that followed. In Rome and in Sicily, revolutionaries pressed for social and political change; but apart from these instances, the Italian uprisings were focused on the imminent threat of Austrian domination already pronounced in northern Italy, rather than on exacting internal change. See Stearns, *1848*, 2–5.

43. In addition, it appears that the "failure" of the revolutions plummeted Europe's revolutionary factions into a state of political and social indifference. The 1850s

were marked by censorship, increased arrests of citizens on political grounds, and parliaments whose powers were dramatically reduced or eliminated. New coalitions with the Catholic Church allowed the Church to exercise power over education and expression, a situation that was exacerbated by Pius IX's reactionary stance towards modernization. Finally, opposition to these repressive conditions was noticeably restrained. See Stearns, *1848*, 237, 239.

44. Robertson, *Revolutions of 1848*, 412; and Stearns, *1848*, 240–41. The revolutions provided an impetus to the ideology of nationalism which, prior to the outbreaks of 1848, had been a relatively minor intellectual movement; and they contributed to the development of a distinctly modern class consciousness as the middle classes found themselves increasingly allied with elites (due to both newly acquired benefits and newly created apprehensions) and the peasant classes began to acquire a distinctly modern political self-awareness. See Stearns, *1848*, 8.

45. Beal and Macleod, *Prairie Fire*, 341–42.

46. Lewis H. Thomas, "Louis Riel's Petition of Rights," 18.

47. See D. Francis, *National Dreams*, 21–22; McLean, *Fifty Historical Vignettes*, 165; and editor G. H. Needler's introduction to Middleton, *Suppression of the Rebellion*, ix–x.

48. D. Francis, *National Dreams*, 21–22.

49. See Rens, *Invisible Empire*, xi, 31–32, 34 and Babe, *Telecommunications in Canada*, 55–56.

50. G. F.G. Stanley, *Birth of Western Canada*, 380–81.

51. Osler, *Louis Riel*, 308.

52. See Silver, "French Canadian Press," 9; and Silver, "Ontario's Alleged Fanaticism," 49. Honoré Mercier's Parti Nationale took the provincial election in 1886 by flaming the resentment aroused by the Riel affair. He is considered to have been the founder of Quebec nationalism. Mercier organized the first post-Confederation conference of provincial premiers through which the federal government was forced to concede the principle of provincial autonomy in administrative and economic spheres. Mercier was also an architect of the Jesuit's Estate Act, whereby a dispute over Jesuit compensation for their substantial properties in Quebec that had been handed over to Lower Canada in 1831 was resolved. Pope Leo XIII had been asked by Mercier to arbitrate the dispute, and the Ontario Orange Order erupted in anger, a conflict that was carried into the House of Commons where the legality of papal intervention in Canadian politics was hotly debated in 1889. The act passed, but contributed to an increasing and enduring tension between French and English. See "Honoré Mercier" in *The Canadian Encyclopedia* online: http://www.thecanadianencyclopedia.com (accessed September 6, 2004).

53. Silver, *French Canadian Idea of Confederation*, 76; *Le Canadien*, May 22, 1868; *La Minerve*, November 15, 1869; Silver, "French Canadian Press," 2, 11n5.

54. See, for instance, *Le Journal de Québec*, December 4 and 9, 1869; *La Gazette de Sorel*, November 24, 1869; *Le Courrier du Canada*, November 24, December 6 and 27; *Le Nouveau Monde*, November 27, 1869; *Le Courrier de St.-Hyacinthe*, April 28 and May 7, 1870; Silver, "French Canadian Press," 3, 11n7.

55. *Le Courrier de St.-Hyacinthe*, December 21, 1869, and May 7, 1870; *Montreal L'Ordre*, November 25, 1869; *Le Journal de Québec*, December 30, 1869; *L'Opinion Publique*, April 28, 1870; *Le Nouveau Monde*, April 14, 1870; Silver, "French Canadian Press," 3, 11n9.

56. McDougall, *Red River Rebellion*, 7, 46, 50; Silver, "French Canadian Press," 3, 11n10.

57. *La Gazette de Sorel*, February 9, 1870; *La Gazette de Sorel*, February 26, 1870; Silver, *French Canadian Idea of Confederation*, 79.

58. *Le Journal des Trois-Rivières*, April 18, 1870; *Le Journal de Québec*, April 11, 1870, and April 12, 1870; *Montreal L'Ordre*, December 31, 1869; Silver, *French Canadian Idea of Confederation*, 78–80.

59. Silver, "French Canadian Press," 4.

60. *La Presse*, March 31, 1885; Silver, "French Canadian Press," 4.

61. *La Revue Canadienne*, vol. 21, 1885, 447; Silver, "French Canadian Press," 4, 12n23. See also Silver, *French Canadian Idea of Confederation*, 156–57; Silver, "Ontario's Alleged Fanaticism," 29–30. Although it is generally accepted that French forces were not deployed against Riel, Desmond Morton argued that he had sufficient evidence to demonstrate that French troops had been deployed against the Métis. See *The Last War Drum*.

62. *Le Courrier de St.-Hyacinthe*, May 21, 1885; *La Patrie*, May 18, 1885; *La Presse*, July 31, 1885; Silver, *French Canadian Idea of Confederation*, 57.

63. Silver, "French Canadian Press," 5; and Rens, *Invisible Empire*, 33–34.

64. *Le Pionnier de Sherbrooke*, August 6, 1885; Silver, *French Canadian Idea of Confederation*, 159.

65. *Le Courrier de St.-Hyacinthe*, August 15, 1885; Silver, "French Canadian Press," 7. *La Minerve*, August 3, 5, and 6, 1885; *L'Union des Cantons de l'Est*, November 14, 1885; Silver, "Impact on Eastern Canada," 42.

66. Reprinted in the *Daily News*, Tuesday, August 4, 1885; Mika and Mika, *Riel Rebellion*, 243.

67. Petition from "French Canadians residing in Chicago in the State of Illinois, one of the United States" to Governor-General Charles Keith Petty Fitzmaurice, Marquis of Lansdowne.

68. PAC Macdonald Papers G 26, A, vol. 108, 1885, G. Amyot to Sir John A. Macdonald, Québec, November 12, 1885, correspondence relating to the execution of Riel, 1885; Silver, "French Canadian Press," 6. See also Silver, "Impact on Eastern Canada," 42; G. F. G. Stanley, *Birth of Western Canada*, 385–86; Silver, "Ontario's Alleged Fanaticism," 43n162.

69. Sprague, *Canada and the Métis*, 179.

70. *Weekly British Whig*, August 13, 1885, in Mika and Mika, *Riel Rebellion*, 249; *Weekly British Whig*, n.d., in Mika and Mika, *Riel Rebellion*, 260–61; the *Daily News*, August 19, 1885, in Mika and Mika, *Riel Rebellion*, 254.

71. *Le Courrier de St.-Hyacinthe*, August 15, 1885. See also *Le Nouveau Monde*, August 3, 1885; *La Presse*, August 3, 1885; Silver, *French Canadian Idea of Confederation*, 159–60. See also D. Morton, *Queen v. Louis Riel*, xvi; Lewis H. Thomas, "Louis Riel's Petition of Rights," 17; and Osler, *Louis Riel*, 295.

72. D. Morton, *Queen v. Louis Riel*, xvi.

73. *La Minerve*, November 17, 1885; Rens, *Invisible Empire*, 33. The article had been picked up from Regina the day before.

74. *Daily British Whig*, n.d., Mika and Mika, *Riel Rebellion*. My translation.

75. Silver, "French Canadian Press," 9. See also Rens, *Invisible Empire*, 33.

76. *Montreal Gazette*, November 17, 1885; report, Wiebe and Beal, *War in the West*, 183.

77. T. R. Berger, *Fragile Freedoms*, 51. See also Wiebe and Beal, *War in the West*, 191.

78. Wilfrid Laurier, prime minister, 1896–1911 in House of Commons, March 16, 1886, Wiebe and Beal, *War in the West*, 191.

79. Bingaman, "Trials of the 'White Rebels,'" 47.

80. Pamphlet, *La Mort de Riel et la voix du san*, n.p., n.d., 4; and *Le Courrier de St.-Hyacinthe*, November 17, 1885; both in Silver, "French Canadian Press," 9.

81. *Louis Riel, martyr du Nord-Ouest*. Montréal: La Presse, 1885, 77; Silver, *French Canadian Idea of Confederation*, 170.

82. *Le Courrier de St.-Hyacinthe*, July 23, 1885. See also July 30, 1885, and November 24, 1885. All are Silver, *French Canadian Idea of Confederation*, 170.

83. Silver, *French Canadian Idea of Confederation*, 170–272.

84. *La Minerve*, December 4, 1885; and *L'Électeur*, April 24, 1889; Rutherford, *Victorian Authority*, 168. My translation.

85. "Un pardon pour Riel," in *L'Express de Toronto*, October 18–25, 1983; president of the Montreal St-Jean-Baptiste Society to the editor of *Franco*, published in Riel Project *Bulletin*, no. 9 (May 1983) ; Désilets, *Louis-Rodrigue Masson*, 133. Silver, "Ontario's Alleged Fanaticism," 21, and Silver, "French Canadian Press," 10. My translation.

86. *Canadian House of Commons*, Monday, October 21, 1996, at: www.parl.gc.ca/english/hansard/087_96-10-21/087PB1E.html (accessed June 2003).

87. G. F. G. Stanley, "Last Word on Louis Riel," (1988):7. See also Silver, "French Canadian Press," 3.

88. *Toronto Telegram*, July 23, 1885; see Silver, "Ontario's Alleged Fanaticism," 25–26.

89. Silver, "Ontario's Alleged Fanaticism," 26, 29–33; The *Week*, June 25, 1885; Silver, "Ontario's Alleged Fanaticism," 27.

90. *London Free Press*, May 18, 1885; Silver, "Ontario's Alleged Fanaticism," 32–33.

91. From the *Montreal Herald*, *Toronto News*, and *News Herald*, all cited in "Will he Hang? Various Opinions on the Subject—What People say in Quebec," the *Daily News*, August 4, 1885. Mika and Mika, *Riel Rebellion*, 243.

92. G. F. G. Stanley, "Last Word on Louis Riel," (1986):8.

93. *Ottawa Free Press*, October 27, 1885. Also *London Advertiser*, August 13, 1885; and *Huron Expositor*, August 7, 1885; Silver, "Ontario's Alleged Fanaticism," 35. Charles Gordon was a British general who attempted to wrest control from Muhammad Ahmad al-Mahdi, the revolutionary Islamic leader in Sudan who was opposing Egyptian control in the region. Gordon lost and was killed by the rebels on January 26, 1885.

94. *Northern Advance*, November 5, 1885; Silver, "Ontario's Alleged Fanaticism," 36.

95. For Middleton, see Canada, *Debates of the House of Commons* (D. H. C.), May 13, 1885, p. 1823; cited in Bingaman, "Trials of the 'White Rebels,'" 43. *London Advertiser*, May 16, 1885; Silver, "Ontario's Alleged Fanaticism," 36.

96. *Canadian Statesman*, August 14, 1885; Silver, "Ontario's Alleged Fanaticism," 37.

97. *Toronto Globe, Hamilton Spectator, Toronto Telegram, Toronto Mail, World,* October 23, 1885; Silver, "Ontario's Alleged Fanaticism," 34.

98. Bumsted, "The 'Mahdi' of Western Canada?" 49.

99. Mika and Mika, *Riel Rebellion*, 258.

100. W. S. Porteous, Montreal, to Sir John Macdonald, November 4, 1885; "An Irish Canadian" to Macdonald, November 6, 1885. The same plea was made in an Anglican clergyman's letter to the *Mail*, November 10, 1885: "Regard the good of the country, its peace and harmony, as of far more consequence than the hanging of this wretched man, criminal though he may be, and justly deserving of death. Regard the feelings of thousands of our French fellow-countrymen." All are in Silver, "Ontario's Alleged Fanaticism," 34. See also Silver, "Ontario's Alleged Fanaticism," 22, 41.

101. *London Advertiser*, September 3, 1885; *Brampton Conservator*, November 13, 1885; *Evening Telegram*, September 9, 1885. All Silver, "Ontario's Alleged Fanaticism," 43–44, 84. See also Silver, "French Canadian Press," 8.

102. See Silver, "Ontario's Alleged Fanaticism," 45, 47–48; Rutherford, *Victorian Authority*, 60, 167. The *Ottawa Journal* and the *Winnipeg Tribune* quickly began to echo the *Mail*'s agenda.

103. See Rens, *Invisible Empire*, 33; and Beal and Macleod, *Prairie Fire*, 342.

104. G. F. G. Stanley, *Birth of Western Canada*, 381.

105. *La Vérité*, October 23, 1886; *La Patrie*, October 16, 1886, and in *L'Électeur*, July 2, 1886; Silver, *French Canadian Idea of Confederation*, 175.

106. Beal and Macleod, *Prairie Fire*, 342–43. *L'Électeur*, October 11, 1886; and *L'Électeur*, August 31, 1886; Silver, *French Canadian Idea of Confederation*, 175, and 175n160. See also Bumsted, *Louis Riel v. Canada*, 312.

107. Beal and Macleod, *Prairie Fire*, 343.

108. See Lewis G. Thomas, "Prairie Settlement," 61.

109. Lewis G. Thomas, "Prairie Settlement," 61–62.

110. See Makela, "Métis Justice Issues," 64; and Lewis G. Thomas, "Prairie Settlement," 61.

111. Cross and Kealey, eds., introduction to *Canada's Age of Industry*, 11. See also Chartrand, "Aboriginal Rights," 463–64.

112. Sprague, *Canada and the Métis*, 26.

113. Bumsted, *Louis Riel v. Canada*, 245.

114. Report by Amédée Forget, clerk of the North-West Council, to Lieutenant Governor Dewdney, September 18, 1884; Wiebe and Beal, *War in the West*, 16–17.

115. Miller, "First Nations," 37–54.

116. Hildebrandt, "Official Images," 33–38.

117. Trial transcript, July 31–August 1, 1885, in D. Morton, *Queen v. Louis Riel*, 289, 341, and 342.

118. *Story of Louis Riel the Rebel Chief*, 143–44.

119. *Story of Louis Riel the Rebel Chief*, 144–48.

120. Carter, "Exploitation and Narration," 31–32. Delaney and Gowanlock were the only white women living at Frog Lake at the time of the uprising. Delaney was the wife of the government farm instructor, John Delaney, and Gowanlock was married to Jon Gowanlock, an independent contractor who had been hired by the government to build a saw and grist mill. See Carter, "Exploitation and Narration," 36.

121. *Minneapolis Pioneer Press*, June 25, 1885; Carter, "Exploitation and Narration," 49.

122. The *Globe*, July 17, 1885; *Montreal Daily Star*, June 23, 1885; Carter, "Exploitation and Narration," 49–50.

123. Carter, "Exploitation and Narration," 35, 52–53, and 58.

124. Michael Barnholden, introduction to Dumont, *Gabriel Dumont Speaks*, 13–14. See also McLean, *Fifty Historical Vignettes*, 156. The first memoir was later published in an edited form as part of a larger volume: Adolphe Ouimet, *La verité sur la question Métisse au Nord-Ouest* (Montreal, 1889).

125. P. Vandale, "Going to War"; C. Vandale, "Money Making Deal"; Pilon, "Why Duck Lake Went to War"; and Ledoux, "And Muskeg Went to War"; in Department of Culture and Youth, *Towards a New Past*, 2, 4, 7, 9.

126. Leighton, "Profile of Native People," 16; and McNab, "Métis Participation," 63.

127. Chartrand, "Aboriginal Rights," 459, 467–69, and 471–72.

128. Cited in Sprague, *Canada and the Métis*, 181.

129. Chartrand, "Aboriginal Rights," 459.

130. See Bumsted, *Louis Riel v. Canada*, 24.

131. Fields, *Revival and Rebellion*, 6, 21, 274.

132. Fields, *Revival and Rebellion*, 274–76.

133. McFee and Sealey, eds., *Famous Manitoba Métis*, 24.

134. "J'ai toujours redouté l'entrée du Nord-Ouest dans la Confédération parceque j'ai toujours cru que l'élément franças catholique serait sacrifié. . . . Le nouveau systéme me semble de nature à amener la ruin de ce qui nus a coûté si cher." Letter of October 7, 1869, cited in G. F. G. Stanley, *Birth of Western Canada*, 60–61.

135. Sealey and Lussier, *Métis*, 86–87.

136. PAC Canada Sessional Papers, 1886, #52c, André to Dewdney, July 7, 1884, cited in Beal and Macleod, *Prairie Fire*, 109–10.

137. Report by Amédée Forget, clerk of the North-West Council, to Lieutenant Governor Dewdney, September 18, 1884, cited in Wiebe and Beal, *War in the West*, 16–17.

138. PAC Dewdney Papers, vol. 1, 338–40, Crozier to Dewdney, February 2, 1885; Dewdney Papers, vol. 1, 36–40, André to Dewdney, February 6, 1885; Beal and Macleod, *Prairie Fire*, 130.

Notes to Chapter 5

1. Glissant, *Le discours antillais*.

2. Lionnet, *Autobiographical Voices*, 6.

3. Laroque, "Native Identity and the Metis," 385, 396.

4. Indian and Northern Affairs Canada (INAC), "Royal Commission on Aboriginal Peoples," vol. 4, chapter 5, "Metis perspectives," 198–386; Laroque, "Native Identity and the Metis," 382.

5. See Bell, "Who are the Métis People in Section 35(2)?" 353; and INAC, "Royal Commission on Aboriginal Peoples," 219–20; Laroque, "Native Identity and the Metis," 398.

6. J. D. Harrison, *Metis*; Sawchuk, Sawchik, and Ferguson, *Metis Land Rights in Alberta*; and INAC "Royal Commission on Aboriginal Peoples," 199. All cited in Laroque, "Native Identity and the Metis," 381.

7. G. F. G. Stanley, *Birth of Western Canada*, 194.

8. Sealey and Laussier, *Métis*, are cited in Laroque, "Metis in English Canadian Literature," 87.

9. Connor, *The Foreigner*, 223. See also Laroque, "Metis in English Canadian Literature," 88–89.

10. Parker, *Pierre and His People*, 3, 5; Allen, *Blue Pete*, 108. Laroque, "Metis in English Canadian Literature," 88–89.

11. Wiebe, *Scorched-Wood People*; Wiebe, *Peace Shall Destroy Many*; George Woodcock, "Prairie Writers and the Metis," 1, 13. All discussed by Laroque, "Metis in English Canadian Literature," 89–90.

12. Laurence, *The Stone Angel*; *Jest of God*; *Fire-Dwellers*; *Bird in the House*; and *Diviners*. See Monkman, *Native Heritage*, 57; and Laroque, "Metis in English Canadian Literature," 91.

13. See Bumsted, "Visions of Canada," 22–23.

14. Massey, *On Being Canadian*, is discussed in respect to this formulation in Bumsted, "Visions of Canada," 27.

15. See Task Force on Canadian Unity, *Future Together*, 12; and Trudel and Jain, *Canadian History Textbooks*, 133; D. Francis, *National Dreams*, 107.

16. S. Clarkson, "Programme for Binational Development," 139–40.

17. See Daniels, *We Are the New Nation*, 5; Wardhaugh, *Language and Nationhood*, 22; and Bumsted, "Visions of Canada," 23.

18. My thanks to Kevin Christiano for pointing this out to me.

19. Wardhaugh, *Language and Nationhood*, 23.

20. See Miller, "First Nations," 45.

21. Daniels, *We Are the New Nation*, 3.

22. Task Force on Canadian Unity, *Future Together*, 22.

23. Birney, *One Muddy Hand*, 58.

24. The Act for the Preservation and Enhancement of Multiculturalism in Canada. See Bissoondath, *Selling Illusions*, 35–36.

25. McRoberts, "Dans l'oeil du castor," 41; Chevier, "Canadian Federalism," 10.

26. René Lévesque is quoted in Colombo, ed. *Dictionary of Canadian Quotations*; Dufour, *Le Défi québécois*, 77. The journalist Richard Gwyn retrospectively concluded that the policy had been a sham for a self-serving prime minister who "changed from doing what was right, rationally, to doing what was advantageous politically . . . he had been accused of sloughing off the ethnics; up sprang a trebled multiculturalism program that functioned as a slush

fund to buy ethnic votes." Gwyn, *Northern Magus*, 139. Bissoondath, *Selling Illusions*, 36–37.

27. See D. Francis, *National Dreams*, 83; and Bissoondath, *Selling Illusions*, 77. Trudeau is quoted by Francis.

28. Akenson, "Historiography of English-Speaking Canada," 391; D. Francis, *National Dreams*, 86.

29. Bissoondath, *Selling Illusions*, 39.

30. Bissoondath, *Selling Illusions*, 202–3.

31. "The Metis and Multiculturalism," brief presented by Harry W. Daniels, president of the Native Council of Canada to the Third Canadian Conference on Multiculturalism, Ottawa, October 27–29, 1978, in Daniels, *We Are the New Nation*, 51. Daniels noted also that Riel's subsequent leadership of the Saskatchewan Métis in 1885 was undertaken with a distinctly multicultural vision that aspired to a division of the western territory into distinct homelands for oppressed peoples including the Métis, Jews, Italians, and Irish, as well as Ukrainians.

32. Bissoondath, *Selling Illusions*, 114, 197–98.

33. "Canada First: Address of the Canadian National Association to the People of Canada" in W. A. Foster, *Canada First*, 48.

34. See D. Francis, *National Dreams*, 105–7; and A. B. Hodgetts, *What Culture? What Heritage?* 34. Patterson's comments appeared in the *Montreal Star*, June 26, 1893, in D. Francis, *National Dreams*, 106.

35. Task Force on Canadian Unity, *Future Together*, 3, 113, 5, 21, 6.

36. D. Francis, *National Dreams*, 105, 109; the Manitoba Métis Federation, *National Unity and Constitutional Reform*, 46.

37. Anthony D. Smith, *Ethnic Origins of Nations*, 225.

38. Waite, *Life and Times of Confederation*, 325–26.

39. D. Francis, *National Dreams*, 109–10.

40. See Landes, "Political Socialization of Political Support"; and Smith and Kornberg, "Quebec Referendum," 378–81.

41. *Toronto Globe*, July 1, 1867; *New Brunswick Reporter*, July 5, 1867; Waite, *Life and Times of Confederation*, 323.

42. *Toronto Globe*, August 21, 1886; *Manitoba Free Press*, August 6, 1892; Rutherford, *Victorian Authority*, 168.

43. Mill, *Utilitarianism*, 359–66; Hobsbawm, *Nations and Nationalism*, 18–19.

44. Galt was named minister of finance in Macdonald's government, and, in 1880, became Canada's first high commissioner to London.

45. See Dubuc, "Decline of Confederation," 114–15.

46. See Dubuc, "Decline of Confederation," 115–16.

47. My thanks to Kevin Christiano for pointing out to me the importance of the ship-building industry on Prince Edward Island. See also Waite, *Life and Times of Confederation*, 4–5, 323.

48. *Acadian Recorder*, July 1, 1867; *Halifax Morning Chronicle*, July 1, 1867; *Fredericton Head Quarters*, July 3, 1867; and *Charlottetown Examiner*, July 1, 1867. Waite, *Life and Times of Confederation*, 322–23.

49. Sprague, *Canada and the Métis*, 27–28.

50. The *Globe*, March 23, 1885; Mika and Mika, *Riel Rebellion*, 3.

51. Cited in Sprague, *Canada and the Métis*, 26.

52. See Heiman, *Nineteenth-Century Legacy*, 330; and Anthony D. Smith, "Memory and Modernity," 4–5, 10.

53. Greenfield, *Nationalism*, 3–4.

54. Frye, *Divisions on a Ground*, 48, 57. See also Taras, "Surviving the Wave," 185.

55. C. Brown, "Nationalism of the National Policy," 155; S. Clarkson, "Programme for Binational Development," 134; Allan Smith, "Metaphor and Nationality," 275; Cook, *Maple Leaf Forever*, 16; Trudeau, "La nouvelle trahison des clercs," 177.

56. Allan Smith, "Metaphor and Nationality," 273–74, suggested that nationalist discourses have been influenced to some degree by social scientists who have turned their attention to the defining character of a society's historical experience. This has also occurred because traditional foundations for conceiving of nationalism—racial, cultural, geographical unity—obviously became notably unfashionable in the wake of the Second World War, and Canadian nationalists were compelled to admit that Canada could not exist viably on the basis of such foundations.

57. Hartz, *Founding of New Societies*. See also Sullivan, "Summing Up," 148–49.

58. C. Brown, "Nationalism of the National Policy," 155.

59. See Bumsted, "Visions of Canada," 30.

60. Taras, "Surviving the Wave," 185. Taras similarly conflates the issues of identity and nationalism in his introduction to *A Passion for Identity*, when he discusses the work of J. M. Bumsted: "Although Jack Bumsted's masterful piece on 'Visions of Canada' appears in the 'Foundations' section at the beginning of the book, his article is a good starting point for understanding the vast forces of international change that have continually shaped and reshaped the Canadian identity. The first stirrings of Canadian nationalism occurred in response to British colonial and then Commonwealth policy. But they also emerged as a reaction to threats from the United States." See Taras, "Dilemmas of Canadian Identity," 4–5.

61. J. S. Mill is cited in C. Brown, "Nationalism of the National Policy," 155. See also T. R. Berger, *Fragile Freedoms*, xv.

62. "The Metis and Multiculturalism," brief presented by Harry W. Daniels, president of the Native Council of Canada to the Third Canadian Conference on Multiculturalism, Ottawa, October 27–29, 1978, in Daniels, *We Are the New Nation*, 52; Y. Dumont, "Métis Nationalism," 87.

63. C. Berger, "True North," 24.

64. McDougall was quoted in the *World*, August 8, 1885; Silver, "Ontario's Alleged Fanaticism," 33. Bayer and Parage's play is cited by Lister, "A Distinctive Variant," 93.

65. See, for instance, Braz, *False Traitor*, ix, 11; Goulet, *Trial of Louis Riel*, 9; Zinovich, *Gabriel Dumont in Paris*, 178.

66. For Riel as a "prophet," see T. Berger, *Fragile Freedoms*, 26; Beal and Macleod, *Prairie Fire*, 12; and Bumsted, "Visions of Canada," 321. For Riel as "mystic," see

Braz, *False Traitor*, ix; and T. Berger, *Fragile Freedoms*, 26. For Riel as "savior," see Bumsted, "Visions of Canada," 321. For Riel as "saint," see Moore, "Haunted by Riel," 413; Zinovich, *Gabriel Dumont in Paris*, 178; and Braz, *False Traitor*, 11. For Riel as "righteous rebel," see Beal and Macleod, *Prairie Fire*, 12. For Riel as "mad messiah," see Dickens, *Dickens of the Mounted*, 242; and Braz, *False Traitor*, 11. For Riel as "devil," see Moore, "Haunted by Riel," 413. For Riel as "Canada's Joan of Arc," see Lusty, *Louis Riel*, 5. And for Riel as a "wise m[a]n from the West," see Klassen, "Two Wise Men," 275.

67. Braz, *False Traitor*, 142.

68. Bumsted, "The 'Mahdi' of Western Canada?" 51.

69. Braz, *False Traitor*, 142–43. This is not to say that all quarters of Canadian society have abandoned the notion that Riel's religion was evidence of mental imbalance. The tenth episode of *Canada: A People's History* (2001), for instance, relied on an interpretation of Riel as unbalanced in terms of his religious sensibilities. The episode was William Cobban's *Taking the West*, in which the North-West Rebellion of 1885 figured. The episode was generally regarded as having provided a balanced appraisal of Riel and the Canadian government (in spite of its virtual disregard for the implications of Canadian expansion on Native peoples in the territory); however, much was made of Riel's mental imbalance and even William Jackson, Riel's secretary who converted to his new Catholicism, was portrayed as finding Riel's "increasingly bizarre" opinions disturbing. See Braz, *False Traitor*, 147.

70. Lister, "A Distinctive Variant," 106.

71. "The Metis and Multiculturalism," in Daniels, *We Are the New Nation*, 52.

72. Arendt, *On Revolution*, 28.

73. B. Anderson, *Imagined Communities*, 36; Singer, *Society, Theory, and the French Revolution*, 103–4; Gourgouris, *Dream Nation*, 24, 280.

74. Arendt, *On Revolution*, 46–47.

75. Arendt, *On Revolution*, 13, 20–21, 46–47.

Notes to Chapter 6

1. Riel, *Diaries*, 129–30, August 21, 1885.

2. Riel, *Diaries*, 100, preface.

3. Riel, *Diaries*, 95, preface.

4. Riel, *Diaries*, 130, August 21, 1885.

5. Riel, *Diaries*, 134, August 23, 1885.

6. Riel, *Diaries*, 134, August 23, 1885.

7. Trial transcript, July 31–August 1, 1885, in D. Morton, *Queen v. Louis Riel*, 312.

8. Trial transcript, August 1, 1885, in D. Morton, *Queen v. Louis Riel*, 355–56. Later that day, Riel would expand the number of proposed nations to ten. See also Flanagan, "Louis Riel's Religious Beliefs," 25–26.

9. Trial transcript, August 1, 1885, in D. Morton, *Queen v. Louis Riel*, 366–67.

10. Taché was among the first oblates to establish themselves in the western territories, arriving in 1845. At the age of twenty-seven, he was named coadjutor bishop of the North-West, and two years later, in 1853, he was appointed the second bishop of St. Boniface. During his tenure at Red River he succeeded in importing religious orders of teachers and in establishing settled parishes of Métis. See Grant, *Church in the Canadian Era*, 30.

11. Flanagan, "Louis Riel's Religious Beliefs," 25.

12. "L'Ontario," in Riel, *Collected Writings*, 4:118–19. My translation.

13. Flanagan, "Louis Riel's Religious Beliefs," 27. Riel made this statement in the context of his explanation to Taché as to why he believed that the Roman Catholic Church had been divided into two separate churches, one serving the Old World and one serving the New World.

14. Riel, *Collected Writings*, 4:238ff.

15. Flanagan, *Louis "David" Riel*, 33; Bumsted, "Crisis at Red River," 25.

16. Trial transcript, Exhibit 14, in D. Morton, *Queen v. Louis Riel*, 378.

17. Trial transcript, Exhibits 5 and 20, in D. Morton, *Queen v. Louis Riel*, 373, 382.

18. Trial transcript, July 31–August 1, 1885, in D. Morton, *Queen v. Louis Riel*, 317, 323.

19. Trial transcript, August 1, 1885, in D. Morton, *Queen v. Louis Riel*, 357, 366.

20. Flanagan, "Louis Riel's Religious Beliefs," 26–27.

21. Flanagan, "Louis Riel's Religious Beliefs," 25.

22. Riel, *Diaries*, 73, 137, April 26, 1885, and August 23, 1885.

23. Trial transcript, July 31–August 1, 1885, in D. Morton, *Queen v. Louis Riel*, 325.

24. Bumsted, *Louis Riel v. Canada*, 212, 224.

25. Trial transcript, Exhibit 10, in D. Morton, *Queen v. Louis Riel*, 376.

26. "Ottawa," in Riel, *Collected Writings*, 4:114. The poem was probably written in July of 1776 at Beauport. My translation.

27. Trial transcript, August 1, 1885, in D. Morton, *Queen v. Louis Riel*, 358, 366.

28. "Vous ressemblez au grain qu'on jette" in Riel, *Collected Writings*, 4:267ff. The poem was written while Riel was living in Montana, sometime in 1880 or 1881. My translation.

29. G. Dumont, *Gabriel Dumont Speaks*, 26.

30. G. F. G. Stanley, *Louis Riel*, 222; Beal and Macleod, *Prairie Fire*, 139.

31. Flanagan, "Louis Riel's Religious Beliefs," 24.

32. Trial transcript, July 31–August 1, 1885, in D. Morton, *Queen v. Louis Riel*, 322.

33. Flanagan, "Louis Riel's Religious Beliefs," 21–22.

34. Flanagan, "Louis Riel's Religious Beliefs," 16, 24.

35. Flanagan, "Louis Riel's Religious Beliefs," 22. Riel believed that Taché was uniquely situated to secure an acquittal in the trial: "My present position is a position which can be numbered among the most desperate which history mentions. To escape triumphantly is a blessing which can only come from God and His Church. I pray you and your clergy to come to my aid. And the proof which I offer of the will of Our Lord is that you will succeed miraculously. You are going to save me easily. My rescue will lead to the obvious conclusion that my difficult task is authorized by heaven and will mark with

a divine seal the sublime vocation which I announce to you with all the joy of proven knowledge." Flanagan, "Louis Riel's Religious Beliefs," 24.

36. Flanagan, "Louis Riel's Religious Beliefs," 24; Riel, *Diaries*, May 2, 1885, 80.
37. Trial transcript, July 31–August 1, 1885, in D. Morton, *Queen v. Louis Riel*, 319.
38. Trial transcript, Exhibit 8, in D. Morton, *Queen v. Louis Riel*, 375.
39. Trial transcript, Exhibit 13, in D. Morton, *Queen v. Louis Riel*, 377.
40. Trial transcript, Exhibit 7, in D. Morton, *Queen v. Louis Riel*, 374, 376.
41. Trial transcript, Exhibit 20, in D. Morton, *Queen v. Louis Riel*, 382.
42. "The Political Voice of Choteau!" in Riel, *Collected Writings*, 4:311. The poem was written at Fort Benton, likely sometime between the eleventh and the eighteenth of May 1883.
43. Trial transcript, July 31–August 1, 1885, in D. Morton, *Queen v. Louis Riel*, 321.
44. Charles Riel was twenty-one when he died.
45. "Voices of the Future," in Riel, *Diaries*, 150.
46. "Voices of the Future," in Riel, *Diaries*, 150–52.
47. Riel added that Henry IV was in hell for his immorality. "Vision," in Riel, *Diaries*, 166. Riel referred in his diary to Moreno, and was likely referring to Mariano Moreno (1778–1811), the child of a Spanish father and an Argentinean mother, who was a key figure in liberating Argentina from the Spanish, was editor of *La Gaceta*, and was secretary-general of the first military government. His reference to Henry IV was a pointed attack at his conflict with Pope Gregory VII over Henry's appointment of the archbishop of Milan. This led Henry to organize a synod of German bishops in 1076 that concluded that Gregory's claim to the papacy was bogus. Henry was excommunicated and deposed. He was forced ultimately to recant in the face of rebellion among the German nobility.

Notes to Chapter 7

1. Gellner, *Nations and Nationalism*, 55; Gellner, *Conditions of Liberty*, 105–8; cited also in O'Leary, "What States Can Do with Nations," 56.
2. Gellner, *Thought and Change*. See also O'Leary, "What States Can Do with Nations," 57.
3. O'Leary, "What States Can Do with Nations," 56.
4. *Orange Sentinel*, quoted in the *Montreal Star*, September 11, 1885; cited in G. F. G. Stanley, *Birth of Western Canada*, 389.
5. Frye, "Divisions on a Ground," 15–16.
6. S. Clarkson, "A Programme for Binational Development," 133.
7. Allen Smith, "Metaphor and Nationality," 275.
8. See Seton-Watson, *Nations and States*, 1; Anthony D. Smith, *Ethnic Origins of Nations*, 129, 221.
9. Powe, *Tremendous Canada of Light*, 101; Hutcheon, *Splitting Images*, vii. Both are discussed by D. Francis, *National Dreams*, 108–9. It is Francis who employs the phrase "everything" and "anything" in reference to Powe.
10. See Goldstone, *Revolutions*, 322.
11. Davey, *From There to Here*, 20. See also D. Francis, *National Dreams*, 108.

12. Gwyn, *Nationalism without Walls*, 243.

13. Allen Smith, "Metaphor and Nationality," 265.

14. G. F. G. Stanley, "Last Word on Louis Riel," (1986): 6–7; Lower, *Colony to Nation*, 71–72, 74–75.

15. Chevier, "Canadian Federalism," 3; Choquette, *Canada's Religions*, 155.

16. There were at that time 10,000 British colonists as opposed to 150,000 Francophones. See Chevier, "Canadian Federalism," 3.

17. D. N. Paul, *We Were Not the Savages*, 159, 161, 162.

18. *Parliamentary Debates on the Confederation of the British North American Provinces*, 6, 29. See Allen Smith, "Metaphor and Nationality," 254–55.

19. The Constitution Act, 1867 (called also the British North America Act, 1867, in the act's "Preliminary"), Section 9:133. See also Silver, *French Canadian Idea of Confederation*, 16.

20. Daniels, *We Are the New Nation*, 7. Section 6:91 specified that the Dominion's laws would be enacted through a joint effort of the Senate, the House of Commons, and the Queen, except in those cases where full provincial or federal jurisdiction has been identified. Included among these exceptions in Section 7:91:24 was "Indians and Lands reserved for the Indians."

21. Daniels, *We Are the New Nation*, 8–9. Native peoples were defined in much broader terms prior to Confederation. An Act for the Better Protection of the Lands and Property of the Indians in Lower Canada (1850), for instance, defined Native peoples with respect to their biological or adoptive ancestry or marriage, and their occupation of tribal land.

> First—All persons of Indian blood, reputed to belong to the particular Body or Tribe of Indians interested in such lands, and their descendants;

> Secondly—All persons intermarried with such Indians and residing amongst them, and the descendants of all such persons;

> Thirdly—All persons residing among such Indians, whose parents on either side were or are Indians of such Body or Tribe, or entitled to be considered as such; and

> Fourthly—All persons adopted in infancy by any such Indians; and residing in the Village or upon the Lands of such tribe or Body of Indians, and their descendants.

> Likewise, An Act to Encourage the Gradual Civilization of the Indian Tribes in this Province, and to Amend the Laws Respecting Indians, 1857, regarded as "Indian" those who had Native ancestry, or were married to a native person and whose residence was with a band occupying recognized aboriginal land: "The third section of the Act . . . shall apply only to Indians or persons of Indian blood or intermarried with Indians, who shall be acknowledged as members of Indian Tribes or Bands residing upon lands which have never been surrendered to the Crown." Both acts are cited in Daniels, *We Are the New Nation*, 14.

22. D. Francis, *National Dreams*, 17–18.

23. Daniels, *We Are the New Nation*, 6.

24. Miller, "First Nations at the Centre," 49; Coates, *Marshall Decision*, 77; "Towards Co-Equality: Integration vs. Assimilation," a brief presented by Harry W. Daniels, president of the Native Council of Canada, to the First Minister's Conference on the Constitution, Ottawa, October 30–November 1, 1978, in Daniels, *We Are the New Nation*, 47–49.

25. The Constitution Act, 1982.

26. Miller, "First Nations at the Centre," 49–50.

27. Miller, "First Nations at the Centre," 50.

28. Chartrand, "Aboriginal Rights," 457–59.

29. Trial transcript, August 1, 1885, in D. Morton, *Queen v. Louis Riel*, 355. See also Coates, *Marshall Decision*, 77–78; Chevier, "Canadian Federalism," 9.

30. See T. Berger, *Fragile Freedoms*, xiii–xiv.

31. Bissoondath, *Selling Illusions*, 202–3.

32. Clark, *A Nation too Good to Lose*, 80–81; and Adrienne Clarkson, "Speech on the Occasion of the National Celebration to Mark Louis Riel Day" (Ottawa, November 16, 1999). Both cited in Braz, *False Traitor*, 12–13.

33. *Canadian House of Commons*, Monday, October 21, 1996.

34. *Canadian House of Commons*, Monday, October 21, 1996.

35. See, for instance, T. Berger, *Fragile Freedoms*, xiv.

36. Arendt, *On Revolution*, 222.

37. Miller, "First Nations at the Centre," 37; White, "Government under the Northern Lights," 459.

38. *Sentinel & Orange and Protestant Advocate*, June 27, 1889; cited in Silver, "Impact on Eastern Canada," 4.

39. See Khazanov, "State without a Nation?" 103–4; and Allen Smith, "Metaphor and Nationality," 249. Smith discusses the issue in terms of the image of the mosaic.

40. Task Force on Canadian Unity, *Future Together*, 6.

41. Taras, "Dilemmas of Canadian Identity," 188; and Taras, "Surviving the Wave," 1–2.

42. Anthony D. Smith, "Memory and Modernity," 10.

43. Frye, "Divisions on a Ground," 48.

44. Ondaatje is quoted by A. Clarkson, "Installation Speech," 12.

45. D. Francis, *National Dreams*, 27, 113–14.

46. Sealey and Lussier, *Métis*, 88.

47. Braz, *False Traitor*, 15; Mattes, "Whose Hero?" 4, 77; cited in Braz, *False Traitor*, 139–40. See also Braz, *False Traitor*, 4–5.

48. Trial transcript, August 1, 1885, in D. Morton, *Queen v. Louis Riel*, 367. See also Goulet, *Trial of Louis Riel*, 14.

49. Nault was quoted by de Tremaudan, *Histoire de la Nation Métisse*, 418–19. See also Beal and Macleod, *Prairie Fire*, 125–26.

50. PAC, Dewdney Papers, 4:1329–34, Macdowell to Dewdney, December 24, 1884; cited in Beal and Macleod, *Prairie Fire*, 126.

51. *The Queen vs. Louis Riel: Accused and Convicted of the Crime of High Treason*, 189.

52. D. Morton, *Queen v. Louis Riel*, xiii–xiv. My translations.

53. *Toronto Mail*, August 3, 1885; cited in D. Morton, *Queen v. Louis Riel*, xxx.

54. Trial transcript, July 31–August 1, 1885, in D. Morton, *Queen v. Louis Riel*, 311.

55. Deane, *Mounted Police Life*, 208, 222–23.

56. See Flanagan, "Louis Riel's Religious Beliefs," 15.

57. See Kornberg and Stewart, "National Identification," 71.

58. See Kornberg and Stewart, "National Identification," 74.

59. Riel, *Diaries*, 152.

60. Trial transcript, Exhibit 15, in D. Morton, *Queen v. Louis Riel*, 379–80.

61. Trial transcript, August 1, 1885, in D. Morton, *Queen v. Louis Riel*, 357–58.

62. Riel, *Diaries*, April 29, 1885, 77–78.

63. Flanagan, "Louis Riel's Religious Beliefs," 25–26.

64. Braz, *False Traitor*, 15; Hood, "Moral Imagination," 32.

65. Woodcock, *Gabriel Dumont: The Métis Chief*, 14; Coulter, *In My Day*, 261; cited in Braz, *False Traitor*, 95; Atwood, *Survival*, 167.

66. Voyageur, "We Get Knocked Down," 11.

67. Miller, "First Nations at the Centre," 47–49.

68. Trial transcript, August 1, 1885, in D. Morton, *Queen v. Louis Riel*, 358.

69. Riel, *Diaries*, May 6, 1885, 83.

70. See D. N. Paul, *We Were Not the Savages*, 162, 214.

71. D. N. Paul, *We Were Not the Savages*, 215–16; Coates, 86.

72. Coates, *Marshall Decision*, 83–85.

73. The lawyers were Douglas Brown, Joe B. Marshall, Jim Michael, and Paul Prosper.

74. Wood, "Marshall Decision"; Indian and Northern Affairs Canada, "Long-Term Response to the *Marshall Decision*"; Coates, *Marshall Decision*, 92; and Wicken, *Mi'kmaq Treaties on Trial*, 3, 219–20.

75. Teillet, *Métis Case Law*, 19.

76. Indian and Northern Affairs Canada, "Supreme Court of Canada's Powley Decision."

77. Miller, "First Nations at the Centre," 37, 43–44, 52; Taras, "Surviving the Wave," 188.

78. Task Force on Canadian Unity, *Future Together*, 22.

79. T. Berger, *Fragile Freedoms*, xiii, 267–57.

80. A. Clarkson, "Installation Speech," 9.

81. Macdonald and Cartwright are cited by D. Morton, "Cavalry or Police," 169–70, 184n16. Macdonald's comment was made in the context of the Confederation Debates, in regard to the proposed Canadian Senate, April 6, 1865. See also Jennings, "Plains Indians and the Law," 51. Cartwright, a prominent businessman in the pre-Confederation period, would break with Macdonald and the Conservative Party in 1869 and join the Liberal Party. He held a number of Liberal Cabinet portfolios before being named to the Senate in 1909.

82. *Ottawa Free Press*, March 28, 1885; *London Advertiser*, June 9, 1885. Cited in Silver, "Ontario's Alleged Fanaticism," 27.

83. *Toronto Globe*, March 23, 1885; cited in Mika and Mika, *Riel Rebellion*, 3–4.

84. The *Globe*, April 15, 1885; May 18, 1885; *Daily British Whig*, December 11, 1885. Cited in Mika and Mika, *Riel Rebellion*, 65, 127, 328–29.

85. *Toronto Globe*, April 17, 1885; cited in Mika and Mika, *Riel Rebellion*, 67.

86. Lex, "Poundmaker's Trial," the *Week*, September 10, 1885, 645–46; cited in Stonechild and Waiser, *Loyal till Death*, 205.

87. See Daniels, *We Are the New Nation*, 6.

88. *Daily News*, May 16, 1885; cited in Mika and Mika, *Riel Rebellion*, 126.

89. Wilfrid Laurier, "Speech at Quebec City," January 4, 1894; "Speech in the House of Commons," March 3, 1896, *House of Commons Debates 1896*, 2740–43. Both are cited in Bumsted, *Louis Riel v. Canada*, 22.

90. Curti, "The Great Mr. Locke," 69–118; Acton, "Nationality," in *Essays on Freedom and Power*, 168. Cited in Allen Smith, "Metaphor and Nationality," 272–73.

91. Clarkson is cited by Braz, *False Traitor*, 12–13.

92. See Chevier, "Canadian Federalism," 2; Taras, "Dilemmas of Canadian Identity," 2; Silver, *French Canadian Idea of Confederation*, ix.

93. Silver, *French Canadian Idea of Confederation*, x–xi, 51; D. Francis, *National Dreams*, 110.

94. See D. Francis, *National Dreams*, 175–76.

95. Riel, *Diaries*, April 21, 1885, 68–69.

Notes to Conclusion

1. Marilyn Dumont, "Letter to Sir John A. Macdonald," in *A Really Good Brown Girl*, 52.

2. D. Francis, *National Dreams*, 127.

3. D. Francis, *National Dreams*, 109.

4. Granatstein, *Who Killed Canadian History?* xvii. See also C. Brown, "Nationalism of the National Policy," 155; Trudel and Jain, *Canadian History Textbooks*, 107; D. Francis, *National Dreams*, 105, 127; Bissoondath, *Selling Illusions*, 71.

5. D. Francis, *National Dreams*, 18.

6. Allen Smith, "Metaphor and Nationality," 273.

7. Carrasco, *City of Sacrifice*, 3.

8. Arendt, *On Revolution*, 225–26.

9. See Underhill, "French-English Relations in Canada," 109–10.

10. Quoted in Bumsted, "Visions of Canada," 23.

11. Carrasco, "America's Americas," 40.

12. Robert MacNeil, quoted in Granatstein, *Who Killed Canadian History?* 6.

13. T. Berger, *Fragile Freedoms*, 256.

14. Cook, *Maple Leaf Forever*, 16.

15. Riel to John A. Macdonald, in Deane, *Mounted Police Life*, 187–232. My translation.

16. Statement of Elie Dumont, cited in Flanagan, *Louis "David" Riel*, 157, 204.

17. Riel maintained this notion of "Providence" throughout his period of leadership, in spite of his devotion to prayer. He said to Richardson in the context of his trial, "I trust the Providence of God will bring out good of what you have done conscientiously"; and speaking of his mission in a letter to Taché, he said, "God was leading me through His Providence to a difficulty greater than any of my earlier ones," and "he wanted to lead me to an extraordinary result, according to the intention of His Providence." Trial transcript, July 31–August 1, 1885, in D. Morton, *Queen v. Louis Riel*, 324; Flanagan, "Louis Riel's Religious Beliefs," 21.

18. Riel, *Diaries*, May 16, 1885, 90.

Bibliography

Acton, John. *Essays on Freedom and Power.* London: Meridian, 1956.

Adams, Howard. *Tortured People: The Politics of Colonization.* 2nd ed. Penticton, BC: Theyts Books, 1999.

Akenson, Donald Harman. "The Historiography of English-Speaking Canada and the Concept of Diaspora: A Skeptical Appreciation." *Canadian Historical Review* 76, no. 3 (September 1995).

Allen, Luke. *Blue Pete: Rebel.* London: Herbert Jenkins, 1940.

Anderson, Benedict. *Imagined Communities: Reflections on the Origin and Spread of Nationalism.* Rev. ed. London and New York: Verso, 1991.

Anderson, Frank. "Gabriel Dumont." *Alberta Historical Review* 7, no. 9 (1959): 1–6.

Arendt, Hannah. *On Revolution.* Westport, CT: Greenwood Publishers, 1963.

Arnold, Abraham. "If Louis Riel Had Spoken in Parliament or, Louis Riel's Vision." *Prairie Fire* (Autumn/Winter 1985): 75–83.

Atwood, Margaret. *Survival: A Thematic Guide to Canadian Literature.* Toronto: Anansi Press, 1972.

Babe, Robert E. *Telecommunications in Canada: Technology, Industry, and Government.* Toronto: University of Toronto Press, 1990.

Barron, F. Laurie, and James B. Waldram, eds. *1885 and After: Native Society in Transition.* Regina: University of Regina Press, 1986.

Bayer, Charles, and E. Parage. *Riel: Drame historique en quatre actes et un prologue.* Saint Boniface: Editions des Plaines, 1984. First published 1886 by Imprimerie de l'Etendard.

Beal, Bob, and Rod Macleod. *Prairie Fire: The 1885 North-West Rebellion.* Edmonton: Hurtig Publishers, 1984.

Beddoes, Joël. "Tourisme scolaire: Louis Riel suscite encore la controverse." *Liaison* 82 (1995): 28–29.

Bell, Catherine. "Who are the Métis People in Section 35(2)?" *Alberta Law Review* 29, no 2 (1991): 351–81.

Benítez-Rojo, Antonio. *The Repeating Island: The Caribbean and the Postmodern Perspective.* Translated by James E. Maraniss. Durham: Duke University Press, 1996.

Berger, Carl. *The Sense of Power: Studies in the Ideas of Canadian Imperialism 1867–1914.* Toronto: University of Toronto Press, 1970.

———. "The True North Strong and Free." In *Nationalism in Canada*, edited by Peter Russell, 3–26. Toronto: McGraw-Hill, 1966.

Berger, Thomas, R. *Fragile Freedoms: Human Rights and Dissent in Canada.* Toronto: Clarke, Irwin and Company, 1981.

Berry, Reginald, and James Acheson, eds. *Regionalism and National Identity: Multi-Disciplinary Essays on Canada, Australia, and New Zealand.* Christchurch, New Zealand: Association for Canadian Studies in Australia and New Zealand, 1985.

Berton, Pierre. *Hollywood's Canada.* Toronto: McClelland and Stewart, 1975.

———. *The Great Railway, 1871–1881.* Toronto: McClelland and Stewart, 1972.

———. *The National Dream.* Toronto: McClelland and Stewart, 1970.

Bingaman, Sandra Elizabeth. "The Trials of the 'White Rebels,' 1885." *Saskatchewan History* 25 (1972): 41–54.

Birney, Earle. *One Muddy Hand: Selected Poems.* Edited by Sam Solecki. Madeira Park, BC: Harbour, 2006.

———. *The Collected Poems of Earle Birney.* Vol. 1. Toronto: McClelland and Stewart, 1975.

Bissoondath, Neil. *Selling Illusions: The Cult of Multiculturalism in Canada.* Rev. ed. Toronto: Penguin, 2002.

Borgerson, Lon. "Ile-à-le-Crosse: Upisasik Theatres in Our Schools." *Canadian Theatre Review* 65 (1990): 48–51.

Boulton, Charles A. *I Fought Riel: A Military Memoir.* Edited by Heather Robertson. Toronto: James Lorimer and Company, 1985. First published 1886 by Davis & Henderson.

Bourgeault, Ron. "The Struggle Against British Colonialism and Imperialism." *New Breed* 15, no. 10 (October 1984): 30–33.

Bouvier, Laure. *Une histoire de Métisses.* Montreal: Leméac, 1995.

Bowsfield, Hartwell, ed. *Louis Riel: Selected Readings.* Mississauga, Ontario: Copp Clark Pitman, 1988.

Boyarin, Jonathan, ed. *Remapping Memory: The Politics of TimeSpace.* Minneapolis: University of Minnesota Press, 1994.

Braz, Albert. *The False Traitor: Louis Riel in Canadian Culture.* Toronto: University of Toronto Press, 2003.

Broughall, George. *The Ninetieth on Active Service: Campaigning in the North West.* Winnipeg: George Bishop, 1885.

Brown, Craig. "The Nationalism of the National Policy." In *Nationalism in Canada*, edited by Peter Russell, 155–63. Toronto: McGraw-Hill, 1966.

Brown, D. H. "The Meaning of Treason in 1885." *Saskatchewan History* 28, no. 2 (1975): 65–80.

Brown, R. C., ed. *The Illustrated History of Canada.* Toronto: Key Porter Books, 1991.

Bruchési, Jean. *Histoire du Canada pour tous.* 2 vols. Montreal: Editions Beauchemin, 1940.

Brunet, Michel. *La presence Anglaise et les Canadiens.* Montreal: Beauchemin, 1958.

Bumsted, J. M. "Crisis at Red River." *The Beaver* 75, no. 3 (June–July 1995): 23–34.

———. *Louis Riel v. Canada: The Making of a Rebel.* Winnipeg, Manitoba: Great Plains Publications, 2001a.

———. "The 'Mahdi' of Western Canada?: Louis Riel and His Papers." *The Beaver* (August–September 1987): 47–54.

———. *The Peoples of Canada: A Post-Confederation History.* Toronto: Oxford University Press, 1992.

———. "Visions of Canada: A Brief History of Writing in the Canadian Character and the Canadian Identity." In *A Passion for Identity: Canadian Studies for the 21st Century*, edited by David Taras and Beverly Rasporich, 17–36. Scarborough, Ontario: Nelson, 2001b.

Burpee, Lawrence T., and Arthur G. Doughty, eds. *Makers of Canada*. Toronto: Morang, 1911.

Campbell, Maria. *Halfbreed*. Halifax: Goodread Biographies, 1983.

Canadian House of Commons, Monday, October 21, 1996. http://www.parl.gc.ca/english/hansard/087_96-10-21/087PB1E.html (accessed June 2003).

Carefoot, E. H. *Gabriel Dumont at Batoche*. Saskatoon, 1973.

Careless, Maurice. "Metropolitanism and Nationalism." In *Nationalism in Canada*, edited by Peter Russell, 271–83. Toronto: McGraw-Hill, 1966.

Carey, James W., and John J. Quirk. "The Mythos of the Electronic Evolution." *American Scholar* 39, no. 1 (1970): 219–51.

Carrasco, Davíd. "America's Americas: The Brown Millennium, Three Archés, and the Ecumenopolis." *Nanzan Bulletin* 24 (2000): 38–47.

———. *City of Sacrifice: The Aztec Empire and the Role of Violence in Civilization*. Boston: Beacon Press, 1999.

Carter, Sarah A. "The Exploitation and Narration of the Captivity of Theresa Delaney and Theresa Gowanlock, 1885." In *Making Western Canada: Essays on European Colonization and Settlement*, edited by Catherine Cavanaugh and Jeremy Mouat, 31–61. Toronto: Garamond, 1996.

———. *Lost Harvests: Prairie Indian Reserve Farmers and Government Policy*. Montreal: McGill–Queen's University Press, 1990.

Castro-Klarén, Sara, and John Charles Chasteen, eds. *Beyond Imagined Communities: Reading and Writing the Nation in Nineteenth-Century Latin America*. Baltimore and London: Johns Hopkins University Press, 2003.

Cavanaugh, Catherine, and Jeremy Mouat, eds. *Making Western Canada: Essays on European Colonization and Settlement*. Toronto: Garamond, 1996.

CBC News. "In Depth: Maher Arar." http://www.cbc.ca/news/background/arar/ (accessed March 2007).

Cernetig, Miro. "The Far Side of the Rockies: Politics and Identity in British Columbia." In *A Passion for Identity: Canadian Studies for the 21st Century*, edited by David Taras and Beverly Rasporich, 413–28. Scarborough, Ontario: Nelson, 2001.

"Chaos Theory." http://en.wikipedia.org/wiki/Chaos_theory (accessed September 2004).

Chapleau, J. A. *The Riel Question*. Ottawa, November 28, 1885.

Charland, Maurice. "Technological Nationalism." *Canadian Journal of Political and Social Theory* 10, nos. 1 and 2 (1986): 196–220.

Chartrand, Paul L. A. H. "Aboriginal Rights: The Dispossession of the Métis." *Osgoode Hall Law Journal* 29 (1991): 457–82.

Chasteen, John Charles. "Introduction: Beyond Imagined Communities." In *Beyond Imagined Communities: Reading and Writing the Nation in Nineteenth-Century Latin America*, edited by Sara Castro Klarén and John Charles Chasteen, ix–xxv. Baltimore and London: Johns Hopkins University Press, 2003.

Cherwinski, W. J. C. "Honoré Joseph Jaxon, Agitator, Disturber, producer of plans to make me think, and Chronic Objector . . ." *Canadian Historical Review* 46, no. 2 (June 1965): 122–33.

Chevier, Marc. "Canadian Federalism and the Autonomy of Quebec: A Historical Viewpoint." 1996. http://www.mri.gouv.qc.ca/la_bibliotheque/federalisme/fede_canadien_an.html, 3 (accessed November 2003).

Choquette, Robert. *Canada's Religions: An Historical Introduction.* Ottawa: University of Ottawa Press, 2004.

Clark, Joe. *A Nation too Good to Lose: Renewing the Purpose of Canada.* Toronto: Key Porter, 1994.

Clarkson, Adrienne. "Installation Speech." In *A Passion for Identity: Canadian Studies for the 21st Century,* edited by David Taras and Beverly Rasporich, 9–16. Scarborough, Ontario: Nelson, 2001.

Clarkson, Stephen. "A Programme for Binational Development." In *Nationalism in Canada,* edited by Peter Russell, 133–54. Toronto: McGraw-Hill, 1966.

Coates, Ken S. *The Marshall Decision and Native Rights.* Montreal and Kingston: McGill–Queen's University Press, 2000.

Collins, Robert. *A Voice from Afar: The History of Telecommunications in Canada.* Toronto: McGraw-Hill Ryerson, 1977.

Colmer, J. G. "Introduction." S. B. Steele. *Forty Years in Canada: Reminiscences of the Great North-West with Some Account of his Service in South Africa.* Toronto: McClelland, Goodchild, Stewart, 1918.

Colombo, John Robert, ed. *The Dictionary of Canadian Quotations.* Toronto: Stoddart, 1991.

Commissioners of the Royal North-West Mounted Police. *Settlers and Rebels, Being the Official Reports to Parliament of the Activities of the Royal North-West Mounted Police from 1882–1885.* Toronto: Coles Publishing Company, 1973. First published 1886 by Maclean, Roger.

Communications Canada. *Communications for the Twenty-First Century: Media and Messages in the Information Age.* Ottawa: Supply and Services, 1987.

Connor, Ralph. *Corporal Cameron of the North-West Mounted Police.* Toronto: The Westminster Company, 1912.

———. *The Foreigner: A Tale of Saskatchewan.* Toronto: The Westminster Company, 1909.

Cook, Ramsey. *The Maple Leaf Forever: Essays on Nationalism and Politics in Canada.* Toronto: Macmillan, 1977.

Coulter, John. *The Crime of Louis Riel.* Toronto: Playwrights Co-op, 1976.

———. *In My Day.* Toronto: Hounslow, 1980.

———. *Riel.* Hamilton: Cromlech Press, 1972.

———. *The Trial of Louis Riel.* Ottawa: Oberon Press, 1968.

Coutts, Robert and Richard Stuart, eds. *The Forks and the Battle of Seven Oaks in Manitoba History.* Winnipeg: Manitoba Historical Society, 1994.

Coutts-Smith, Kenneth. "CBC's 'Riel.'" *Centerfold* 3, no. 5 (1979): 228–36.

Craig, Gerald. *Lord Durham's Report.* Toronto: McClelland and Stewart, 1963.

Creighton, Donald. *The Commercial Empire of the St. Lawrence, 1760–1850*. Toronto: The Ryerson Press, 1937. (Reprinted as *The Empire of the St. Lawrence: A Study in Commerce and Politics*. Toronto: University of Toronto Press, 2002.)

Cross, Michael, S., and Gregory S. Kealey, eds. *Canada's Age of Industry, 1849–1896*. Toronto: McClelland and Stewart, 1982.

Crunican, Paul E. "Manitoba Schools Question." *The Canadian Encyclopedia Online*. http:www.thecanadianencyclopedia.com (accessed May 7, 2005).

Culleton, Beatrice. *In Search of April Raintree*. Winnipeg: Peguis, 1992. First published 1983.

Curti, Merle. "The Great Mr. Locke, America's Philosopher, 1783–1862." In *Probing Our Past*, 69–118. New York: Harper, 1955.

Daniels, Harry W. *We Are the New Nation: The Métis and National Native Policy*. Ottawa: Native Council of Canada, 1979.

Davey, Frank. *From There to Here*. Erin, Ontario: Press Porcépic, 1974.

Davies, Robertson. *At my Heart's Core*. Toronto: Clark Irwin, 1966.

Deane, R. Burton. *Mounted Police Life in Canada: A Record of Thirty-one Years' Service*. London and New York: Cassell and Company, 1916.

Dempsey, H. A. *Big Bear: The End of Freedom*. Vancouver: Douglas and McIntyre, 1984.

Dempsey, Hugh, ed. *The CPR West The Iron Road and the Making of a Nation*. Vancouver: Douglas and McIntyre, 1984.

Dempsey, Hugh. "Poundmaker." *The Canadian Encyclopedia Online*. http://www.thecanadianencyclopedia.com/index (accessed April 12, 2005).

Denny, Cecil. *The Law Marches West* (1939). Toronto: Dent, 1972.

Department of Culture and Youth. *Towards a New Past: Found Poems of the Métis People*. Vol. 2. Saskatchewan: Government of Saskatchewan, 1975.

Désilets, Andrée. *Louis-Rodrigue Masson: Un seigneur sans titres*. Montreal: Boréal Express, 1985.

Devine, Heather. "The Killing of Joseph Cardinal: The Northwest Rebellion, Ethnic Identities, and Treaty Six Bands in Northern Alberta." In *Selected Papers of Rupert's Land Colloquium 2000*, 35–58. Winnipeg, Manitoba: The Centre for Rupert's Land Studies, 2000.

Dick, Lyle. "The Seven Oaks Incident and the Construction of a Historical Tradition, 1816 to 1970." In *Making Western Canada: Essays on European Colonization and Settlement*, edited by Catherine Cavanaugh and Jeremy Mouat, 1–30. Toronto: Garamond, 1996.

Dickens, Francis. *Dickens of the Mounted: The Astonishing Long-Lost Letters of Inspector F. Dickens NWMP, 1874–1886*. Edited by Eric Nicol. Toronto: McClelland and Stewart, 1989.

Dodge, William, ed. *Boundaries of Identity*. Toronto: Lester Publishing, 1992.

Donghi, Tulio Halperín. "Argentine Counterpoint: Rise of the Nation, Rise of the State." In *Beyond Imagined Communities: Reading and Writing the Nation in Nineteenth-Century Latin America*, edited by Sara Castro-Klarén and John Charles Chasteen, 33–53. Baltimore and London: The Johns Hopkins University Press, 2003.

Donkin, John. *Trooper and Redskin in the Far North-West: Recollections of Life in the North West Mounted Police, Canada, 1884–1888*. Toronto: Coles, 1973. First published 1889 by S. Low, Marston, Searle, and Rivington.

Dorland, Arthur. *Our Canada*. Toronto: Copp Clark, 1949.

Dowbiggin, Ian. *Suspicious Minds: The Triumph of Paranoia in Everyday Life*. Toronto: Macfarlane, Walter, and Ross, 1999.

Doyle, David G. *From the Gallows: The Lost Testimony of Louis Riel*. Summerland, BC: Ethnic Enterprises, 2000.

Du Bois, W. E. B. *The Souls of Black Folk*. New York: Bantam Books, 1989.

Dubuc, Alfred. "The Decline of Confederation and the New Nationalism." In *Nationalism in Canada*, edited by Peter Russell, 112–32. Toronto: McGraw-Hill, 1966.

Dufour, Christian. "A Little History." In *Boundaries of Identity*, edited by William Didge. Toronto: Lester Publishing, 1992.

———. *Le Défi québécois*. Montreal: l'Hexagone, 1989.

Dugast, George. *Histoire véridique*. Montreal, 1905.

Dumont, Gabriel. "Gabriel Dumont's Account of the North West Rebellion, 1885." Introduction and translation by George F. G. Stanley. *The Canadian Historical Review* 30, no. 3 (September 1949): 249–69.

———. *Gabriel Dumont Speaks*. Translated by Michael Barnholden. Vancouver: Talonbooks, 1993.

Dumont, Marilyn. *A Really Good Brown Girl*. London, Ontario: Brick, 1996.

Dumont, Yvon. "Métis Nationalism: Then and Now." In *The Forks and the Battle of Seven Oaks in Manitoba History*, edited by Robert Coutts and Richard Stuart, 82–89. Winnipeg: Manitoba Historical Society, 1994.

Dyck, Noel. *What Is the Indian "Problem"?: Tutelage and Resistance in Canadian Indian Administration*. St. John's, Newfoundland: Institute of Social and Economic Research, Memorial University of Newfoundland, 1991.

Emerson, Rupert. *From Empire to Nation: The Rise to Self-Assertion of Asian and African Peoples*. Boston: Beacon Press, 1962.

Encyclopedia Canadiana. Vol. 7, s.v. "Métis." Toronto: Grolier, 1968.

Enright, Robert. "Standing-in-Between: A Conversation with Métis Writer Emma LaRocque." *Arts Manitoba* 4, no. 3 (1983): 45–46.

Fetherling, George. "George Woodcock Past and Present." In *The Blue Notebook: Reports on Canadian Culture*, 21–32. Oakville, Ontario: Mosaic, 1985.

Fields, Karen E. *Revival and Rebellion in Colonial Africa*. Princeton: Princeton University Press, 1985.

Finkel, A., Margaret Conrad, Cornelius J. Jaenen, and Veronica Strong-Boag. *1867 to the Present*. Vol. 1 of *History of the Canadian Peoples*. Toronto: Copp Clark Pitman, 1993.

Flanagan, Thomas. *Louis "David" Riel: "Prophet of the New World."* Rev. ed. Toronto: University of Toronto Press, 1996.

———. "Louis Riel's Religious Beliefs: A Letter to Bishop Taché." *Saskatchewan History* 27, no. 1 (1974): 15–28.

———. "Louis Riel: Was He Really Crazy?" In *1885 and After: Native Society in Transition*, edited by Laurie Barron and James B. Waldram. Regina, Saskatchewan: University of Regina, 1986.

———. *Riel and the Rebellion: 1885 Reconsidered*. Toronto: University of Toronto Press, 2000.

Foster, Kate. *Our Canadian Mosaic*. Toronto: Dominion Council, YWCA, 1926.

Foster, William A. *Canada First: A Memorial*. With introduction by Goldwin Smith. Toronto: Hunter, Rose, 1890.

Francis, Daniel. *The Imaginary Indian: The Image of the Indian in Canadian Culture*. Vancouver: Arsenal Pulp Press, 1992.

———. *National Dreams: Myth, Memory, and Canadian History*. Vancouver: Arsenal Pulp Press, 1997.

Francis, R. D., Richard Jones, and Donald B. Smith. *Destinies: Canadian History Since Confederation*. Toronto: Harcourt, 1992.

Fréchette, Louis-Honoré. *Papineau*. Montreal: Chapleau and Lavigne, 1880.

Friesen, Gerald. *The Canadian Prairies: A History*. Toronto: University of Toronto Press, 1987.

Frye, Northrop. *Divisions on a Ground: Essays on Canadian Culture*. Toronto: Anansi, 1982.

Geddes, Gary, ed. *Divided We Stand*. Toronto: Peter Martin Associates, 1977.

Gellner, Ernest. *Conditions of Liberty: Civil Society and its Rivals*. London: Hamish Hamilton, 1994.

———. *Nations and Nationalism*. Ithaca, NY: Cornell University Press, 1983.

———. *Thought and Change*. London: Weidenfeld and Nicolson, 1964.

Gibbon, J. Murray. *Canadian Mosaic*. Toronto: McClelland and Stewart, 1938.

Giraud, Marcel. *Le Métis Canadien: Son role dans l'histoire des provinces de l'Ouest*. Paris: Institut d'ethnologie, 1945.

Glissant, Edouard. *Le discours antillais*. Paris: Seuil, 1981.

Goldie, Terry. *Fear and Temptation: The Image of the Indigene in Canadian, Australian, and New Zealand Literatures*. Kingston and Montreal: McGill–Queen's University Press, 1989.

Goldstone, Jack A., ed. *Revolutions: Theoretical, Comparative, and Historical Studies*. New York: Harcourt Brace Jovanovich, 1986.

Gosse, Richard, James Youngblood Henderson, and Roger Carter, compilers. *Continuing Poundmaker and Riel's Quest: Presentations Made at a Conference on Aboriginal Peoples and Justice*. Saskatchewan: Purich Publishing, 1994.

Goulet, George R. D. *The Trial of Louis Riel: Justice and Mercy Denied*. Calgary, Alberta: Tellell Publishing, 1999.

Gourgouris, Stathis. *Dream Nation: Enlightenment, Colonization, and the Institution of Modern Greece*. Stanford: Stanford University Press, 1996.

Granatstein, J. L. *Who Killed Canadian History?* Toronto: Harper Collins, 1998.

Grant, John Webster. *The Church in the Canadian Era*. Rev. ed. Burlington: Welch Publishing, 1988.

Greenfield, Liah. *Nationalism: Five Roads to Modernity*. Cambridge, MA: Harvard University Press, 1992.

Grima, Adrian. "The Oka Crisis." http://www.geocities.com/adriangrima/oka.htm (accessed April 12, 2005).

Groulx, Lionel. *Histoire du Canada Français*. Montreal: Fides, 1962.

———. *Le Farnçais au Canada*. Paris: Delagrave, 1932.

Gutteridge, Don. *Riel: A Poem for Voices*. Toronto: Van Nostrand Reinhold, 1972. First published 1968 by Fiddlehead Books.

———. "Riel: Historical Man or Literary Symbol?" *Humanities Association Bulletin* 21, no. 3 (1970): 3–15.

Gwyn, Richard. *Nationalism without Walls: The Unbearable Lightness of Being Canadian*. Toronto: McClelland and Stewart, 1995.

———. *The Northern Magus*. Toronto: McClelland and Stewart, 1980.

Hallman, E. S., and H. Hindley. *Broadcasting in Canada*. Don Mills: General Publishing, 1977.

Harris, Cole. "The Myth of the Land in Canadian Nationalism." In *Nationalism in Canada*, edited by Peter Russell, 27–43. Toronto: McGraw-Hill, 1966.

Harrison, Dick, ed. *Best Mounted Police Stories*. Edmonton: University of Alberta Press, 1978.

———. *Crossing Frontiers: Papers in American and Canadian Western Literature*. Edmonton: University of Alberta Press, 1979.

Harrison, Julia D. *Metis: People between Two Worlds*. Vancouver: Douglas and McIntyre, 1985.

Hart, E. J. *The Selling of Canada*. Banff: Altitude Books, 1983.

Hartz, Louis. *The Founding of New Societies: Studies in the History of the United States, Latin America, South Africa, Canada, Australia*. New York: Harcourt, Brace and World, 1964.

Hathorn, Ramon, and Patrick Holland, eds. *Images of Louis Riel in Canadian Culture*. Lewiston, NY: Edwin Mellen Press, 1992.

Haworth, Eric. *Canada's Printing Pioneers: Provincial's Paper Volume 31, No. 2, 1966*. Toronto: Provincial Paper, 1966.

Hayward, Victoria, and Edith S. Watson. *Romantic Canada*. Toronto: Macmillan, 1922.

Hébert, Anne. "Quebec: The Core of First Time." In *A Passion for Identity: Canadian Studies for the 21st Century*, edited by David Taras and Beverly Rasporich, 79–82. Scarborough, Ontario: Nelson, 2001.

Heiman, George. "The Nineteenth-Century Legacy: Nationalism or Patriotism?" In *Nationalism in Canada*, edited by Peter Russell, 323–40. Toronto: McGraw-Hill, 1966.

Hildebrandt, Walter. "Official Images of 1885." *Prairie Fire* 6, no. 4 (1985): 31–38.

Hobsbawm, E. J. *Nations and Nationalism since 1780: Programme, Myth, Reality*. Cambridge: Cambridge University Press, 1992.

Hodgetts, A. B. *What Culture? What Heritage? A Study of Civic Education in Canada*. Toronto: Ontario Institute for Studies in Education, 1968.

Holland, Patrick. "Louis Riel and Modern Canadian Poetry." In *Images of Louis Riel in Canadian Culture*, edited by Ramon Hathorn and Patrick Holland, 211–33. Lewiston, NY: Edwin Mellen Press, 1992.

Holmes, John. "Nationalism in Canadian Foreign Policy." In *Nationalism in Canada*, edited by Peter Russell, 203–20. Toronto: McGraw-Hill, 1966.

Hood, Hugh. "Moral Imagination: Canadian Thing." In *A Guide to the Peaceable Kingdom*, edited by William Kilbourn, 29–35. Toronto: Macmillan, 1970.

Houser, F. B. *A Canadian Art Movement: The Story of the Group of Seven*. Toronto: Macmillan, 1926.

Howard, Joseph Kinsey. *Strange Empire: A Narrative of the Northwest*. New York: William Morrow, 1952.

———. *Strange Empire: Louis Riel and the Métis People*. Toronto: James Lewis and Samuel, 1974.

Humphries, Charles W. "The Banning of a Book in British Columbia." *BC Studies* 1 (Winter 1968–69): 1–12.

Huntington, Samuel P. "Revolution and Political Order." In *Revolutions: Theoretical, Comparative, and Historical Studies*, edited by Jack A. Goldstone, 39–46. New York: Harcourt Brace Jovanovich, 1986.

Hutcheon, Linda. *Splitting Images: Contemporary Canadian Ironies*. Toronto: Oxford University Press, 1991.

Indian and Northern Affairs Canada. "Long-Term Response to the *Marshall Decision*." http://www.ainc-inac.gc.ca/pr/info/ltr_e.html (accessed June 2005).

———. "Report of the Royal Commission on Aboriginal Peoples." http://www.ainc-inac .gc.ca/ch/rcap/sg/sjm5_e.html.

———. "The Supreme Court of Canada's Powley Decision." http://www.ainc-inac .gc.ca/interloc/pow_e.html (accessed June 2005).

Innis, Harold. *A History of the Canadian Pacific Railway*. Toronto: University of Toronto Press, 1971. First published 1923.

———. *The Fur Trade in Canada*. New Haven: Yale University Press, 1930.

Irving, J. A. *Mass Media in Canada*. Toronto: Ryerson Press, 1962.

Jeffrey, David L. "Biblical Hermeneutic and Family History in Contemporary Canadian Fiction: Webe and Lawrence." *Mosaic* 11, no. 3 (Spring 1978).

Jennings, John. "The Plains Indians and the Law." In *Men in Scarlet*, edited by Hugh A. Dempsey. Calgary: McClelland and Stewart West, 1974.

Johnson, Chris. "Riel in Canadian Drama, 1885–1985." In *Images of Louis Riel in Canadian Culture*, edited by Ramon Hathorn and Patrick Holland, 175–210. Lewiston, NY: Edwin Mellen Press, 1992.

Khazanov, Anatoly M. "A State without a Nation? Russia after Empire." In *The Nation-State in Question*, edited by T. V. Paul, G. John Ikenberry, and John A. Hall, 79–105. Princeton: Princeton University Press, 2003.

Kilbourn, William, ed. *A Guide to the Peaceable Kingdom*. Toronto: Macmillan, 1970.

Klassen, William. "Two Wise Men from the West." In *Religion and Culture in Canada (Religion et culture au Canada)*, edited by Peter Slater, 271–88. Canadian Society for the Study of Religion (Corporation Canadienne des Sciences Religieuses), 1977.

Kornberg, Allen, and Harold D. Clarke, eds. *Political Support in Canada: The Crisis Years*. Durham, NC: Duke University Press, 1983.

Kornberg, Allen, and Marianne C. Stewart. "National Identification and Political Support." In *Political Support in Canada: The Crisis Years*, edited by Allen

Kornberg and Harold D. Clarke, 73–102. Durham, NC: Duke University Press, 1983.

Kroetsch, Robert. "Canada is a Poem." *Open Letter*, 5th series, no. 4 (1983a): 33–35.

———. "On Being an Alberta Writer." *Open Letter*, 5th series, no. 4 (1983b): 69–80.

Kroker, Arthur. *Technology and the Canadian Mind: Innis, McLuhan, Grant*. Montreal: New World Perspectives, 1984.

Kula, Sam. "Steam Movies." In *The CPR West: The Iron Road and the Making of a Nation*, edited by Hugh Dempsey, 247–57. Vancouver: Douglas and McIntyre, 1984.

Lamb, W. Kaye. *History of the Canadian Pacific Railway*. New York: Macmillan, 1977.

Landes, Ronald G. "The Political Socialization of Political Support." In *Political Support in Canada: The Crisis Years*, edited by Allen Kornberg and Harold D. Clarke, 103–23. Durham, NC: Duke University Press, 1983.

Laroque, Emma. "Native Identity and the Metis: Otehpayimsuak Peoples." In *A Passion for Identity: Canadian Studies for the 21st Century*, edited by David Taras and Beverly Rasporich, 381–400. Scarborough, Ontario: Nelson, 2001.

———. "The Metis in English Canadian Literature." *Canadian Journal of Native Studies* 3, no. 1 (1983): 85–94.

Laurence, Margaret. *A Bird in the House*. Toronto: McClelland and Stewart, 1970.

———. *A Jest of God*. Toronto: McClelland and Stewart, 1966.

———. *The Diviners*. Toronto: McClelland and Stewart, 1974.

———. *The Fire-Dwellers*. Toronto: McClelland and Stewart, 1969.

———. *The Stone Angel*. Toronto: McClelland and Stewart, 1964.

———. "You Can Almost Hear the Skipping Rope Slapping," review of Dennis Lee's *Alligator Pie*. *Toronto Globe and Mail*, October 5, 1974.

Ledoux, Isadore. "And Muskeg Went to War." In *Towards a New Past: Found Poems of the Métis People*, edited by the Department of Youth and Culture, 2:9. Saskatchewan: Government of Saskatchewan, 1975.

Leighton, Douglas. "A Profile of Native People in Ontario." Ontario Ministry of Citizenship and Culture, January 1983.

Lionnet, Françoise. *Autobiographical Voices: Race, Gender, Self-Portraiture*. Ithaca: Cornell University Press, 1989.

Lister, Rota Herzberg. "A Distinctive Variant: 1885 in Canadian Drama." In *Swords and Ploughshares: War and Agriculture in Western Canada*, edited by R. C. Macleod, 91–107. Edmonton: University of Alberta Press, 1993.

Livesay, Dorothy. "The Native People in our Canadian Literature." *English Quarterly* 4, no. 1 (1971): 21–32.

Lodge, R. C., ed. *Manitoba Essays*. Toronto: Macmillan, 1937.

Long, Charles H. *Alpha: The Myths of Creation*. Atlanta: Scholars Press, 1963.

———. "Indigenous People, Materialities, and Religion: Outline for a New Orientation to Religious Meaning." In *Religion and Global Culture: New Terrain in the Study of Religion and the Work of Charles H. Long*, edited by Jennifer I. M. Reid, 167–80. Lanham, MD: Lexington Press, 2003.

Louis Riel, martyr du Nord-Ouest. Montreal: La Presse, 1885.

Lower, Arthur R. M. *Colony to Nation*. Toronto: McClelland and Stewart, 1977. First published 1946 by Longmans, Green.

Lusty, Terrence. *Louis Riel: Humanitarian*. Calgary: Northwest Printing, 1973.

MacBeth, R. G. *The Romance of the Canadian Pacific Railway*. Toronto: Ryerson Press, 1924.

Macleod, R. C. *Reminiscences of a Bungle by One of the Bunglers; and Two Other Northwest Rebellion Diaries*. Edmonton: University of Alberta Press, 1983.

———, ed. *Swords and Ploughshares: War and Agriculture in Western Canada*. Edmonton: University of Alberta Press, 1993.

Maguet, Elizabeth. Introduction to *Hold High Your Heads: History of the Métis Nation in Western Canada*, by A. H. de Trémaudan. Translated by Elizabeth Maguet. Winnipeg, Manitoba: Pemmican Publications, 1982.

Makela, Kathleen. "Métis Justice Issues." In *Continuing Poundmaker and Riel's Quest: Presentations Made at a Conference on Aboriginal Peoples and Justice*, compiled by Richard Gosse, James Youngblood Henderson, and Roger Carter. Saskatchewan: Purich Publishing, 1994.

Mandel, Eli, ed. *Contexts of Canadian Criticism*. Chicago: University of Chicago Press, 1971.

———. "'The Border League: American 'West' and Canadian 'Region.'" In *Crossing Frontiers: Papers in American and Canadian Western Literature*, edited by Dick Harrison, 67–71. University of Alberta Press, 1979.

Manitoba Culture, Heritage, and Recreation. *Ambroise-Didyme Lépine*. 1985.

Manitoba Métis Federation. *National Unity and Constitutional Reform: The Report of the Manitoba Métis Senate Commission*. Native Women's Association of Canada: Constitutional Document 8, 1991.

Martel, Gilles. "L'idéologie messianique de Louis Riel et ses determinants sociaux." *Transactions of the Royal Society of Canada* 5, no. 1 (1986): 229–38.

———. *Le Messianisme de Louis Riel*. Waterloo, Ontario: Wilfrid Laurier University Press, 1984.

Martin, Michèle. *"Hello, Central?": Gender, Technology, and Culture in the Formation of Telephone Systems*. Montreal and Kingston: McGill–Queen's University Press, 1991.

Massey, Vincent. *On Being Canadian*. London and Toronto: J. M. Dent, 1948.

Mattes, Catherine. "Whose Hero? Images of Louis Riel in Contemporary Art and Métis Nationhood." Master's thesis, Concordia University, 1998.

McDougall, William. *The Red River Rebellion*. Toronto: Hunter, Rose, 1870.

McFee, Janice, and Bruce Sealey, eds. *Famous Manitoba Métis*. Winnipeg: Manitoba Métis Federation Press, 1974.

McKay, Ian. *The Quest of the Folk: Antimodernism and Cultural Selection in Twentieth-Century Nova Scotia*. Montreal: McGill-Queen's University Press, 1994.

McKenzie, N. M. W. J. *The Men of the Hudson's Bay Company*. Fort William, Ontario: 1921.

McKillop, A. B., ed. *Contexts of Canada's Past: Selected Essays of W. L. Morton*. Toronto: Macmillan, 1980.

———. "Who Killed Canadian History? A View from the Trenches." *Canadian Historical Review* 80, no. 2 (June 1999): 269–99.

McLaren, Kristin. "We Had No Desire to Be Set Apart: Forced Segregation of Black Students in Canada West Public Schools and Myths of British Egalitarianism." *Histoire Sociale (Social History)* 37, no. 73 (May 2004): 27–50.

McLean, Don. *Fifty Historical Vignettes*. Regina: Gabriel Dumont Institute of Native Studies and Applied Research, 1987.

———. "1885: Métis Rebellion or Government Conspiracy?" In *1885 and After: Native Society in Transition*, edited by F. Laurie Barron and James B. Waldram, 79–104. Regina: University of Regina Press, 1986.

McNab, David T. "Métis Participation in the Treaty-Making Process in Ontario." *Native Studies Review* 1, no. 2 (1985): 57–79.

McRoberts, Kenneth. "Dans l'oeil du castor." *Possibles* 16 (1992): 35–48.

Middleton, Fred. *Suppression of the Rebellion in the North West Territories of Canada, 1885*. Edited by G. H. Needler. Toronto: University of Toronto, 1948.

Mika, Nick, and Helma Mika, compilers. *The Riel Rebellion, 1885*. Belleville, Ontario: Mika Screening, 1972.

Mill, J. S. *Utilitarianism, Liberty and Representative Government*. London: Everyman Edition, 1910.

Miller, J. R. "First Nations at the Centre of Canadian Memory." In *A Passion for Identity: Canadian Studies for the 21st Century*, edited by David Taras and Beverly Rasporich, 37–54. Scarborough, Ontario: Nelson, 2001.

———. *Skyscrapers Hide the Heavens: A History of Indian-White Relations in Canada*. Toronto: University of Toronto Press, 1989.

Mitchell, Ken. *The Plainsman*. Regina: Coteau, 1992.

Monkman, Leslie. *A Native Heritage: Images of the Indian in English Canadian Literature*. Toronto: University of Toronto Press, 1981.

Moore, Mavor. "Haunted by Riel." In *Images of Louis Riel in Canadian Culture*, edited by Ramon Hathorn and Patrick Holland, 411–16. Lewiston, NY: Edwin Mellen Press, 1992.

———. *Reinventing Myself*. Toronto: Stoddart, 1994.

Moore, Mavor, and Jacques Languirand. *Louis Riel*. Composed by Harry Somers. Toronto: Canadian Opera Company, 1967.

Morice, A. G. *A Critical History of the Red River Insurrection after Official Documents and Non-Catholic Sources*. Winnipeg: Canadian Publishers, 1935.

Morris, Alexander. *The Treaties of Canada with the Indians*. Toronto: Coles Canadiana Reprint, 1971.

Morton, A. S. *A History of the Canadian West to 1870–71*. Toronto: University of Toronto Press, 1973. First published 1939 by T. Nelson & Sons.

Morton, Desmond. "Cavalry or Police: Keeping the Peace on Two Adjacent Frontiers, 1870 1900." In *Canada's Age of Industry, 1849–1896*, edited by Michael S. Cross and Gregory S. Kealey, 168–87. Toronto: McClelland and Stewart, 1982.

———. "Reflections on the Image of Louis Riel a Century Later." In *Images of Louis Riel in Canadian Culture*, edited by Ramon Hathorn and Patrick Holland, 47–62. Lewiston, NY: Edwin Mellen, 1992.

———. *The Last War Drum*. Toronto: Hakkert, 1972.

———. *The Queen v. Louis Riel*. Toronto: University of Toronto Press, 1974.

Morton, W. L. "Clio in Canada: The Interpretation of Canadian History." *University of Toronto Quarterly* 15, no. 3 (April 1946): 227–34.

———. "Comment on R. G. Trotter, 'Aims in the Study and Teaching of History in Canadian Universities Today.'" *Canadian Historical Association Annual Report*, 1943.

———. *The Canadian Identity*. Toronto: University of Toronto Press, 1962.

———. "The Red River Parish." In *Manitoba Essays Written in Commemoration of the Sixtieth Anniversary of the University of Manitoba by Members of the Teaching Staffs of the University and Its Affiliated Colleges*, edited by R C. Lodge, 83–105. Toronto: Macmillan, 1937.

Mossman, Manfred. "The Charismatic Pattern: Canada's Riel Rebellion of 1885 as a Millenarian Protest Movement." *Prairie Forum* 10 (1985): 307–25.

Naylor, R. T. *Canada in the European Age, 1453–1919*. Vancouver: New Star Books, 1987.

Neff, Lyle. *Ivanhoe Station*. Vancouver: Anvil, 1997.

Newlove, John. "The Pride." In *Black Night Window*. Toronto: McClelland and Stewart, 1968: 105–11.

Newman, Peter C. "Rewriting History: Louis Riel as a Hero?" *Maclean's Magazine*, April 12, 1999.

bpNichol. *Craft Dinner: Stories and Texts 1966–1976*. Toronto: Aya, 1978.

Niven, Frederick. *The Flying Years*. Toronto: McClelland and Stewart, 1974. First published 1935 by Collins.

O'Brien, Edward J. Introduction to *Romantic Canada*, by Victoria Hayward and Edith S. Watson. Toronto: Macmillan, 1922.

"October Crisis." *The Canadian Encyclopedia Online*. http://www.thecanadian-encyclopedia.com (accessed April 25, 2005).

O'Leary, Brendan. "What States Can Do with Nations: An Iron Law of Nationalism and Federation?" In *The Nation-State in Question*, edited by T. V. Paul, G. John Ikenberry, and John A. Hall, 51–78. Princeton: Princeton University Press, 2003.

Ord, Lewis Redman. *Reminiscences of a Bungle by One of the Bunglers*. In *Reminiscences of a Bungle by One of the Bunglers; and Two Other Northwest Rebellion Diaries*, edited by R. C. Macleod, 1–98. Edmonton: University of Alberta Press, 1983. First published anonymously 1886 in Toronto.

Osler, E. B. *Louis Riel: The Man Who Had to Hang*. Toronto: Longmans, Green, 1961.

Ouellet, Fernand. "Le nationalisme canadienne français: De ces origins à l'insurrection de 1837." *Canadian Historical Review* 45 (1964).

Ouimet, Adolphe. *La veritésu la question Métisse au Nord-Ouest*. Montreal, 1889.

Owram, Douglas. "The Myth of Louis Riel." *Canadian Historical Review* 63, no. 3 (1982): 315–36.

———. *Promise of Eden: The Canadian Expansionist Movement and the Idea of the West 1856–1900*. Toronto: University of Toronto Press, 1980.

Pannekoek, Fritz. "Big Bear." *The Canadian Encyclopedia Online*. http://www.thecanadianencyclopedia.com/index (accessed April 12, 2005).

Paquin, Elizéar. *Riel: Tragédie en quatre actes*. Montreal: C. O. Beauchemin, 1886.

Parker, Gilbert. *Pierre and His People: Tales of the Far North*. Chicago: Stone and Kimball, 1894.

Parkin, George. *Makers of Canada: Sir John A. Macdonald*. Toronto: Morang, 1908.

———. *The Great Dominion: Studies of Canada*. London: Macmillan, 1894.

Parliamentary Debates on the Confederation of the British North American Provinces. Ottawa: The Queen's Printer, 1865.

Paul, Daniel N. *We Were Not the Savages: A Micmac Perspective on the Collision of European and Aboriginal Civilization*. Halifax: Nimbus, 1993.

Paul, T. V., G. John Ikenberry, and John A. Hall, eds. *The Nation-State in Question*. Princeton: Princeton University Press, 2003.

Payment, Diane. "Batoche after 1885: A Society in Transition." In *1885 and After: Native Society in Transition*, edited by F. Laurie Barron and James B. Waldram, 173–87. Regina: University of Regina Press, 1986.

Pearce, William. *Detailed Report upon All Claims to Land and Rights to Participate in the North-West Half-Breed Grant by Settlers along the South Saskatchewan . . .* Ottawa, 1886.

Pike, Robert M. "Kingston Adopts the Telephone: The Social Diffusion and Use of the Telephone in Urban Central Canada, 1876 to 1914." *Urban History Review* 18, no. 1 (June 1989): 32–47.

Pilon, Charles. "Why Duck Lake Went to War." In *Towards a New Past: Found Poems of the Métis People*, compiled by the Department of Culture and Youth, 7. Vol. 2. Saskatchewan: Government of Saskatchewan, 1975.

Pocock, Roger. "The Lean Man." In *Best Mounted Police Stories*, edited by Dick Harrison, 94–107. Edmonton: University of Alberta Press, 1978. First published 1887 in *Toronto World*.

Powe, B. W. *A Tremendous Canada of Light*. Toronto: Coach House Press, 1993.

Preston, Richard. "Regionalism and National Identity: Canada." In *Regionalism and National Identity: Multi-Disciplinary Essays on Canada, Australia, and New Zealand*, edited by Reginald Berry and James Acheson, 3–12. Christchurch, New Zealand: Association for Canadian Studies in Australia and New Zealand, 1985.

The Queen vs. Louis Riel: Accused and Convicted of the Crime of High Treason. Report of Trial at Regina—Appeal to the Court of Queen's Bench, Manitoba—Appeal to the Privy Council, England—Petition for Medical Examination of the Convict—List of Petitions for Commutation of Sentence. Ottawa: The Queen's Printer, 1886.

Rambout, Thomas D. "The Hudson Bay Half-Breeds and Louis Riel." *Political Science Quarterly* 2 (1887): 135–67.

Reid, Dennis. *The Group of Seven*. Ottawa: Catalogue for Exhibition at the National Gallery of Canada, June 19–September 8, 1970.

Reid, Jennifer I. "Faire Place à une Race Métisse: Colonial Crisis and the Vision of Louis Riel." In *Religion and Global Culture: New Terrain in the Study of Religion and the Work of Charles H. Long*, edited by Jennifer Reid, 51–66. Lanham, MD: Lexington Press, 2003.

———. *Religion and Global Culture: New Terrain in the Study of Religion and the Work of Charles H. Long*. Lanham, MD: Lexington Press, 2003.

Rens, Jean-Guy. *The Invisible Empire: A History of the Telecommunications Industry in Canada, 1846–1956*. Translated by Käthe Roth. Montreal and Kingston: McGill–Queen's University Press, 2001.

Riel, Louis. "Louis Riel's Account of the Capture of Fort Gary, 1870." Trans. Auguste Henri de Tremaudan. *The Canadian Historical Review*, 5, no. 2 (June 1924): 146–59.

———. *The Collected Writings of Louis Riel (Les ecrits complets de Louis Riel)*. 5 vols. Edited by George F. G. Stanley, Raymond Huel, Gilles Martel, Thomas Flanagan, Glen Campbell, and Claude Rocan. Edmonton: University of Alberta Press, 1985.

———. *The Diaries of Louis Riel*. Edited by Thomas Flanagan. Edmonton: Hurtig Publishers, 1976.

Roberts, Charles G. D. *A History of Canada for High Schools and Academies*. Toronto: Morang Educational Co., 1897.

Roberts, Kevin. "Riel." In *No Feather, No Ink*, edited by George Amabile and Kim Dales. Saskatoon: Thistledown, 1985.

Robertson, Priscilla. *Revolutions of 1848: A Social History*. New York: Harper and Row, 1952.

Rock, Bob. *The Missing Bell of Batoche*. Prince Albert: Bob Rock, 1994.

Ross, Alexander. *The Fur Hunters of the Far West: A Narrative of Adventures in the Oregon and Rocky Mountains*. Vol. 1. London: Smith, Elder, 1885.

Roy, R. H. "Rifleman Forin in the Riel Rebellion." *Saskatchewan History* 21 (1968): 100–111.

Rusden, Harold Penryn. *Notes on the Suppression of the Northwest Insurrection*. In *Reminiscences of a Bungle by One of the Bunglers; and Two Other Northwest Rebellion Diaries*, edited by R. C. Macleod, 241–312. Edmonton: University of Alberta Press, 1983.

Russell, Peter, ed. *Nationalism in Canada*. Toronto: McGraw-Hill, 1966.

Rutherford, Paul. *A Victorian Authority: The Daily Press in Late-Nineteenth-Century Canada*. Toronto: University of Toronto Press, 1982.

Sallot, Jeff. *Nobody Said No: The Real Story About How the Mounties Always Get their Man*. Toronto: James Lorimer, 1979.

Salutin, Rick. *1837: The Farmer's Revolt*. Toronto: James Lorimer, 1976.

Sawchuk, Joe, Patricia Sawchik, and Terry Ferguson. *Metis Land Rights in Alberta: A Political History*. Edmonton: Métis Association of Alberta, 1981.

Scofield, Gregory A. *Thunder through My Veins: Memories of a Métis Childhood*. Toronto: Harper Flamingo Canada, 1999.

Sealey, D. Bruce, and Antoine S. Lussier. *The Métis: Canada's Forgotten People*. Winnipeg: Pemmican Publications, 1983. First published 1975 by Manitoba Metis Federation Press.

Segal, Daniel A. "Living Ancestors: Nationalism and the Past in Postcolonial Trinidad and Tobago." In *Remapping Memory: The Politics of TimeSpace*, edited by Jonathan Boyarin, 221–39. Minneapolis: University of Minnesota Press, 1994.

Selected Papers of Rupert's Land Colloquium 2000. Winnipeg, Manitoba: The Centre for Rupert's Land Studies, 2000.

Seton-Watson, Hugh. *Nations and States: An Enquiry into the Origins of Nations and the Politics of Nationalism*. Boulder, CO: Westview Press, 1977.

Shafer, B. C. *Nationalism: Myth, and Reality*. New York: Harcourt Brace, 1955.

Shimp, Mitsuru. "Native Religion in Sociocultural Change: The Cree and Saulteaux in Southern Saskatchewan, 1830–1900." In *Religion and Culture in Canada (Religion et culture au Canada)*, edited by Peter Slater, 128–40. Canadian Society for the Study of Religion (Corporation Canadienne des Sciences Religieuses), 1977.

Siggins, Maggie. *Riel: A Life of Revolution*. Toronto: Harper-Collins, 1994.

Silver, A. I. "Ontario's Alleged Fanaticism in the Riel Affair." *Canadian Historical Review* 69, no. 1 (1988): 21–50.

———. *The French Canadian Idea of Confederation*. 2nd ed. Toronto: University of Toronto Press, 1997.

———. "The French Canadian Press and 1885." *Native Studies Review* 1 (1984): 2–15.

———. "The Impact on Eastern Canada of Events in Saskatchewan in 1885." In *1885 and After: Native Society in Transition*, edited by F. Laurie Barron and James B. Waldram, 39–51. Regina: University of Regina Press, 1986.

———. *The Lord of the Plains*. 2nd ed. New York: Ballantine, 1992.

Singer, Brian C. J. *Society, Theory, and the French Revolution: Studies in the Revolutionary Imaginary*. London: Macmillan, 1986.

Slater, Peter, ed. *Religion and Culture in Canada (Religion et culture au Canada)*. Canadian Society for the Study of Religion (Corporation Canadienne des Sciences Religieuses), 1977.

Smith, Allen. "Metaphor and Nationality in North America." *Canadian Historical Review* 51, no. 3 (September 1970): 247–75.

Smith, Anthony D. "Memory and Modernity: Reflection on Ernest Gellner's Theory of Nationalism." The Ernest Gellner Memorial Lecture. London School of Economics. http://members.tripod.com/GellnerPage/SmithLec.html (accessed April 2004).

———. *The Ethnic Origins of Nations*. New York: Basil Blackwell, 1986.

Smith, Donald B. "Rip Van Jaxon: The Return of Riel's Secretary in 1884–1885 to the Canadian West, 1907–1909." In *1885 and After: Native Society in Transition*, edited by F. Laurie Barron and James B. Waldram, 211–23. Regina: University of Regina Press, 1986.

Smith, Goldwyn. *Canada and the Canadian Question*. London: Macmillan, 1891.

———. *The Political Destiny of Canada*. Toronto: Willing and Williamson, 1878.

Smith, Joel, and Allan Kornberg. "The Quebec Referendum: National or Provincial Event?" In *Political Support in Canada: The Crisis Years*, edited by Allen Kornberg and Harold D. Clarke, 353–79. Durham, NC: Duke University Press, 1983.

Sprague, D. N. *Canada and the Métis, 1869–1885*. Waterloo, Ontario: Wilfrid Laurier Press, 1988.

———. *Post-Confederation History: The Structure of Canadian History Since Confederation*. Scarborough: Prentice-Hall Canada, 1990.

Stanley, George F. G. *Louis Riel*. Toronto: Ryerson, 1963.

——. *The Birth of Western Canada: A History of the Riel Rebellions*. Toronto: University of Toronto Press, 1978. First published 1936 by Longmans, Green.

——. "The Campaign of 1885: A Contemporary Account." *Saskatchewan History* 13, no. 3 (1960): 100–107.

——. "The Last Word on Louis Riel: The Man of Several Faces." In *1885 and After: Native Society in Transition*, edited by F. Laurie Barron and James B. Waldram, 3–22. Regina: Canadian Plains Research Center, 1986.

——. "The Last Word on Louis Riel: The Man of Several Faces." In *Louis Riel: Selected Readings*, edited by Hartwell Bowsfield, 42–60. Mississauga, Ontario: Copp Clark Pitman, 1988.

——. "The Making of an Historian: An Autobiographical Essay." In *Swords and Ploughshares: War and Agriculture in Western Canada*, edited by R. C. Macleod, 3–19. Edmonton: University of Alberta Press, 1993.

Stanley, Timothy J. "Why I Killed Canadian History." *Histoire sociale (Social History)* 33, no. 65 (May 2000): 79–103.

Stearns, Peter N. *1848: The Revolutionary Tide in Europe*. New York: W. W. Norton, 1974.

Steele, S. B. *Forty Years in Canada: Reminiscences of the Great North-West with Some Account of his Service in South Africa*. Toronto: McClelland, Goodchild, Stewart, 1918.

Stewart, Ian. *Does God Play Dice? The Mathematics of Chaos*. New York: Blackwell, 1989.

Stonechild, Blair. "The Indian View of the 1885 Uprising." In *1885 and After: Native Society in Transition*, edited by F. L. Barron and J. B. Waldram. Regina: Canadian Plains Research Centre, 1986.

Stonechild, Blair, and Bill Waiser. *Loyal till Death: Indians and the North-West Rebellion*. Calgary, Alberta: Fifth House, 1997.

The Story of Louis Riel the Rebel Chief. Facsimile ed. Toronto: Coles Publishing, 1970. First published 1885 by J. S. Robertson and Brothers.

Sullivan, Rosemary. "Summing Up." In *Crossing Frontiers: Papers in American and Canadian Western Literature*, edited by Dick Harrison, 144–58. Edmonton: University of Alberta Press, 1979.

Taras, David. "Introduction: The Dilemmas of Canadian Identity." In *A Passion for Identity: Canadian Studies for the 21st Century*, edited by David Taras and Beverly Rasporich, 1–7. Scarborough, Ontario: Nelson, 2001a.

——. "Surviving the Wave: Canadian Identity in the Era of Digital Globalization." In *A Passion for Identity: Canadian Studies for the 21st Century*, edited by David Taras and Beverly Rasporich, 185–200. Scarborough, Ontario: Nelson, 2001b.

Taras, David, and Beverly Rasporich, eds. *A Passion for Identity: Canadian Studies for the 21st Century*. Scarborough, Ontario: Nelson, 2001.

Task Force on Canadian Unity. *A Future Together: Observations and Recommendations*. Ottawa: Minister of Supply and Services, 1979.

Teillet, Jean. *Métis Case Law: Summary and Analysis*. http://www.metisnation.ca/ LINKS/pdf_downloads/Sum-Metis_Cases-Update_2000.PDF (accessed May 4, 2004).

Thomas, Lewis Herbert. "Louis Riel." *Dictionary of Canadian Biography Online.* Library and Archives Canada. http://www.biographi.ca/EN/ShowBio.asp?Biold=39918&query= (accessed March 2007).

———. "Louis Riel's Petition of Rights, 1884." *Saskatchewan History* 23, no. 1 (1970): 16–26.

Thomas, Lewis G. "Prairie Settlement: Western Responses in History and Fiction; Social Structures in a Canadian Hinterland." In *Crossing Frontiers: Papers in American and Canadian Western Literature*, edited by Dick Harrison, 59–66. Edmonton: University of Alberta Press, 1979.

Tilly, Charles. "Afterward: Political Memories in Space and Time." In *Remapping Memory: The Politics of TimeSpace*, edited by Jonathan Boyarin, 241–56. Minneapolis: University of Minnesota Press, 1994.

Tobias, J. L. "Canada's Subjugation of the Plains Cree, 1879–1885." *Canadian Historical Review* 64, no. 4 (1983): 519–48.

de Trémaudan, Auguste-Henri. *Histoire de la Nation Métisse dans Ouest Canadien.* Saint Boniface, Manitoba: Editions des Plaines, 1984. First published 1936 by Editions Albert Levesque.

Trudeau, Pierre Elliott. *Federalism and the French Canadians.* Toronto: Macmillan, 1968.

———. "La nouvelle trahison des clercs." *Cité Libre* (April 1962).

Trudel, Marcel, and Genevieve Jain. *Canadian History Textbooks: A Comparative Study.* Studies of the Royal Commission on Bilingualism and Biculturalism no. 5. Ottawa: The Queen's Printer, 1970.

Underhill, F. H. "French-English Relations in Canada." In *Contexts of Canadian Criticism*, edited by Eli Mandel, 71–92. Chicago: University of Chicago Press, 1971.

Vachon, V. H. "The Riel Deal: A Parliamentary Pardon for Canada's Che Guevara." *Windspeaker* (September 1999).

Vandale, Caroline. "A Money Making Deal." In *Towards a New Past: Found Poems of the Métis People*, compiled by the Department of Culture and Youth. Vol. 2. Saskatchewan: Government of Saskatchewan, 1975.

Vandale, Pierre. "Going to War." In *Towards a New Past: Found Poems of the Métis People*, compiled by the Department of Culture and Youth. Vol. 2. Saskatchewan: Government of Saskatchewan, 1975.

Voyageur, Cora J. "We Get Knocked Down, but We Get Up Again: Surviving and Adapting as First Nations in Canada." In *A Passion for Identity: Canadian Studies for the 21st Century*, edited by David Taras and Beverly Rasporich, 139–60. Scarborough, Ontario: Nelson, 2001.

Waiser, W. A. "Surveyors at War: A. O. Wheeler's Diary of the North-West Rebellion." *Saskatchewan History* 38, no. 2 (1985): 41–52.

Waite, P. B. *The Life and Times of Confederation, 1864–1867: Politics, Newspapers, and the Union of British North America.* Toronto: University of Toronto Press, 1962.

Walter, Dave. "The Hundred Year Controversy of Louis Riel." *Montana Magazine* 68 (November–December 1984): 22–26.

Wardhaugh, Ronald. *Language and Nationhood: The Canadian Experience.* Vancouver: New Star Books, 1983.

Watkins, Melville. "Technology and Nationalism." In *Nationalism in Canada,* edited by Peter Russell, 284–302. Toronto: McGraw-Hill, 1966.

Wheeler, A. O. "The D. L. S. Intelligence Corps and the Riel Rebellion, 1885." *The Canadian Surveyor* (April 1934): 3–8.

White, Graham. "Government under the Northern Lights: Treaties, Land Claims, and Political Change in Nunavut and the Northwest Territories." In *A Passion for Identity: Canadian Studies for the 21st Century,* edited by David Taras and Beverly Rasporich, 457–76. Scarborough, Ontario: Nelson, 2001.

Wicken, William C. *Mi'kmaq Treaties on Trial: History, Land, and Donald Marshall Junior.* Toronto: University of Toronto Press, 2002.

Wiebe, Rudy. *Peace Shall Destroy Many.* Toronto: McClelland and Stewart, 1962.

———. *The Scorched-Wood People.* Toronto: McClelland and Stewart, 1977.

Wiebe, Rudy, and Bob Beal. *War in the West: Voices of the 1885 Rebellion.* Toronto: McClelland and Stewart, 1985.

Williams, W. H. "Poundmaker: Personal Characteristics of the North Cree Chief." *Toronto Globe,* Saturday, May 30, 1885.

Wolf, Eric R. "Peasant Rebellion and Revolution." In *Revolutions: Theoretical, Comparative, and Historical Studies,* edited by Jack A. Goldstone, 173–81. New York: Harcourt Brace Jovanovich, 1986.

Wood, Owen. "The Marshall Decision." *CBC News Online,* August 2000. http://www.cbc.ca/news/indepth/fishing/marshall.html (accessed July 11, 2003).

Woodcock, George. *Gabriel Dumont and the Northwest Rebellion.* Toronto: Playwrights Co-op, 1976.

———. *Gabriel Dumont: The Métis Chief and his Lost World.* Edmonton: Hurtig, 1975.

———. "Prairie Writers and the Metis: Rudy Wiebe and Margaret Laurence." *Canadian Ethnic Studies* 14, no. 1 (1982): 9–22.

———. *Two Plays.* Vancouver: Talonbooks, 1977.

Young, Egerton Ryerson. "The Indian Problem." *Canadian Methodist Magazine* 21 (1885): 465–69.

Zinovich, Jordan. *Gabriel Dumont in Paris: A Novel History.* Edmonton: University of Alberta Press, 1999.

Newspapers

Acadian Recorder. July 1, 1867.

Acton Free Press. April 16, 1885.

Brampton Conservator. November 13, 1885; November 20, 1885.

Charlottetown Examiner. July 1, 1867.

Daily British Whig. April 6, 1885; December 11, 1885.

Daily Intelligencer. May 30, 1885; August 13, 1885; October 23, 1885; December 15, 1885.

Edmonton Bulletin. February 3, 1883; July 7, 1883; August 4, 1883; June 14, 1884; August 9, 1884; March 28, 1885.

Fredericton Head Quarters. July 3, 1867.

Halifax Morning Chronicle. July 1, 1867.

Hamilton Spectator. October 23, 1885; February 24, 1890.

Huron Expositor. August 7, 1885.

Kingston Daily News. April 10, 1885; May 16, 1885; August 4, 1885; August 19, 1885.

L'Électeur. July 2, 1886; August 31, 1886; October 11, 1886; April 24, 1889.

L'Express de Toronto. October 18–25, 1983.

L'Opinion Publique. April 28, 1870.

L'Ordre (Montreal). November 25, 1869; December 31, 1869.

L'Union des Cantons de l'Est. November 14, 1885.

La Gazette de Sorel. June 23, 1864; November 24, 1869; February 9, 1870; February 26, 1870.

La Minerve (Montreal). September 9, 1864; November 15, 1869; April 8, 1870; November 17, 1885; December 4, 1885.

La Patrie. May 8, 1885; August 7, 1885; October 16, 1886.

La Presse (Montreal). March 31, 1885; July 31, 1885; August 3, 1885.

La Revue Canadienne. Vol. 21, 1885.

La Vérité. October 23, 1886.

Le Canadien (Quebec). May 22, 1868.

Le Courrier de St.-Hyacinthe. December 21, 1869; April 28, 1870; May 7, 1870; May 21, 1885; July 23, 1885; July 30, 1885; August 15, 1885; November 17, 1885; November 24, 1885.

Le Courrier du Canada. November 24, 1869; December 6, 1869; December 27, 1869.

Le Journal de Québec. December 4, 1869; December 9, 1869; December 30, 1869; April 11, 1870; April 12, 1870.

Le Journal des Trois-Rivières. April 18, 1870.

Le Manitoba. July 24, 1884.

Le Nouveau Monde (Montreal). November 27, 1869; April 14, 1870; August 3, 1885.

Le Pionnier de Sherbrooke. August 6, 1885.

London Advertiser. June 9, 1885; August 13, 1885; September 3, 1885; September 8, 1885.

London Free Press. November 26, 1885.

Manitoba Free Press. May 16, 1884; August 6, 1892.

Minneapolis Pioneer Press. June 25, 1885.

Montreal Daily Star. June 23, 1885.

Montreal Gazette. November 17, 1885.

Montreal Star. September 11, 1885.

New Brunswick Reporter (Fredericton). July 1, 1867.

Northern Advance (Barrie). November 5, 1885.

Ottawa Citizen. April 24, 1885.

Ottawa Free Press. March 28, 1885; April 10, 1885; April 11, 1885; August 3, 1885; October 27, 1885.

Ottawa Times. December 4, 1867.

Prince Albert Times. July 25, 1884.

Sarnia Observer. April 17, 1885.

Saskatchewan Herald. March 24, 1879; July 5, 1880; May 31, 1884.

Sentinel & Orange and Protestant Advocate. June 27, 1889.

Toronto Globe. July 1, 1867; December 4, 1867; March 23, 1885; March 31, 1885; April 15, 1885; April 17, 1885; May 18, 1885; May 30, 1885; July 17, 1885; October 23, 1885; August 21, 1886.

Toronto Globe and Mail. October 5, 1974.

Toronto Mail. August 3, 1885; October 23, 1885; November 16, 1885; November 28, 1885; August 25, 1886; November 24, 1886; December 6, 1886.

Toronto News. August 23, 1892.

Toronto Star. December 22, 1928.

Toronto Telegram. July 23, 1885; October 23, 1885; November 20, 1885.

Toronto Week. June 4, 1885; June 25, 1885; September 10, 1885; October 8, 1885.

Weekly British Whig. August 13, 1885.

Winnipeg Tribune. October 5, 1893.

World. August 8, 1885; September 21, 1885; October 23, 1885.

Index